contents

3 Designer Spotlight:
   Mark Englund

4 Kitchen Planner
   A guide to the busiest room in your home

6 A Splash of Color!
   A palette of our best-selling designs

8 Joining a Homeowners' Association
   Is a community with rules right for you?

Smooth stucco juxtaposed against rough stone gives the facade of our cover home its rich texture. A touch of copper atop a bay window provides added appeal. See Plan KLF-9710 on page 51.

Design by T.A.S.K. Designs, Inc.
Photography by Mark Englund/HomeStyles

12 Let LifeStyle HomeDesign
    customize your home plan

15 Blueprint Order Form

16 Meet Our Exclusive Designers
    The men and women behind the facades

65 Homes with Luxurious Appointments

129 First Look! 64 Stunning New Designs

193 More Well-Appointed Homes

Classic design elements like a Palladian window and a high hip roof receive a fresh interpretation in this gorgeous executive-style home. You'll find the interior spaces equally pleasing. See Plan DD-3639 on page 63.

Design by Danze & Davis Architects, Inc.
Photography by Mark Englund/HomeStyles

letter from the editor

As a kid, I drew pictures to entertain myself. When I grew older, I sketched floor plans of the home I wanted to live in someday. Actually, I designed several homes. One version was a mountain retreat with floor-to-ceiling windows that faced west to frame the sun setting over the Rockies. Another version was a stuccoed, tile-roofed affair with a stepped terrace in the backyard that led down to a pool. I never gave much thought to practical issues like load-bearing walls or plumbing lines or how much storage space I'd need. Maybe that's why we call them dream homes.

Chances are, if you've picked up this issue of home plans, you've given far more consideration to your future home than I ever did. Maybe you already have an idea of the style you want and the general layout of the floor plan. This issue showcases a host of interior features you may not have considered yet. They're the amenities that will make life in your new home more comfortable—from built-in entertainment units to butler's pantries, from walk-in closets to window seats. We call these designs luxury homes, not because of their grand scale—though some will certainly take your breath away—but because of the thoughtful attention that has been paid to what life will be like after the roofers have moved on and the paint is dry.

Within these pages you'll also find helpful articles on how to design the perfect kitchen (page 4) and whether a neighborhood with a community association is right for you (page 8). Hopefully you'll also find the home you've been dreaming about, or maybe even sketched out on paper. Our designers have done the hard part. But keep your pencil handy. You'll need to figure out where all the furniture will go.

Kirk A. Baruth

Kirk A. Baruth
Editor

E-mail: kbaruth@homestyles.com

EDITOR
Kirk Baruth

DESIGNER
Leon Thompson

EDITORIAL
Brian Boese, Steve Gramins, Laura Lentz, Jason Miller, Pamela Robertson

NEW TECHNOLOGY
Lee Buescher

MARKETING
Kris Donnelly, Shelley Junker, Brian Medenwaldt

TELERELATIONS
Heather Anderson, Jennifer Banks, Heidi Bjorlo, Bill Breen, Erika Brewer, Carol Green, Erin Liebl, Debra Matei, Jessica Miller, Caryn Muellerleile, Julie Schaetzel, Mikeya Strowder, Laura Voetberg, Rebecca Wadsworth, Narkeetha Warren

INFORMATION SYSTEMS
Kevin Gellerman, Brad Olson, Eric Rautio

ACCOUNTING
Barbara Marquardt, Kellie Pierce, Robert Schultz

ADMINISTRATION
Tamiko Trott, Kristy Walsh

HUMAN RESOURCES
Rick Erdmann

COMPANY LEADERS
Jeffrey B. Heegaard, Roger W. Heegaard

STRATEGIC LEADERS
Craig Bryan–Marketing
Diana Jasan–Publishing
Wayne Ramaker–Telerelations
Jeff Schachtman–New Business Development
Dennis Weaver–Finance/Organizational Development

OPERATIONAL LEADERS
Eric Englund–Editorial/Designer Relations
Dorothy Jordan–Joint-Venture Marketing
Bruce Krause–Production
Jeanne Marquardt–Accounting
Michael Romain–Telerelations

PUBLISHED BY HOMESTYLES
P.O. Box 75488
St. Paul, MN 55175-0488
Tel.: (612) 602-5000 Fax: (612) 602-5001
International: (612) 602-5003

FOR INFORMATION ON ADVERTISING,
CONTACT KEVIN MILLER at (888) 311-7756

INTERNET ADDRESS:
www.homestyles.com

Copyright 1998, HomeStyles Publishing and Marketing Inc. All rights reserved. Printed in U.S.A.

The trademark HomeStyles is registered in the U.S. Patent and Trademark Office by Gruner and Jahr, Inc., and is used under license therefrom.

designer spotlight

Mark Englund
LifeStyle HomeDesign

Mark Englund is managing partner of LifeStyle HomeDesign of St. Paul, Minn., and Des Moines, Iowa. In this role, he consistently strives to improve the quality of home plans available to both builders and consumers. He promotes a variety of styles, as well as floor plans with personal flair. "Like snowflakes," Englund says, "no two home plans are exactly alike."

This philosophy has paid tremendous dividends for the company. Since 1994, LifeStyle has been one of the nation's leading design and modification companies for builders and consumers.

LifeStyle formed as a merger of HomeStyles Plan Service, founded in 1946, and Bloodgood Sharp Buster Plan Service, founded by Jack Bloodgood in 1966. Englund has acted previously as editor and associate publisher at HomeStyles and as national marketing director for Bloodgood Sharp Buster, Architects.

Englund currently serves the housing industry as a design-awards judge, a speaker on housing trends and a guest expert on national and local TV and radio programs, commenting on home design in America. He has also written several articles on building and home design.

To study the homes by LifeStyle HomeDesign that are featured in this issue, look for plan numbers that begin with the prefixes "AGH," "B," "H" or "LS." For more information on Plan B-86159 (right), see page 101.

> He promotes a variety of styles, as well as floor plans with personal flair. "Like snowflakes," Englund says, "no two home plans are exactly alike."

Photos by Mark Englund/HomeStyles

Kitchen Planner

A Guide to the Busiest Room in Your Home

For most of us, one of the most eagerly anticipated rooms in a new home is the kitchen. Regardless of our current kitchens' amenities, we all want more counter space, extra storage for utensils or better lighting in key work areas.

That makes sense. After all, the kitchen serves as the hub of family activities—day in and day out. Besides cooking here, we eat, pay bills, work on crafts, plan the week's menus, visit with friends and catch up after a day at work or school.

Building a new home gives you the opportunity to get exactly what you need and want out of this important area, with none of the limitations of remodeling an existing kitchen.

So what do you do with this blank slate? First, you ask yourself a lot of questions. Take a look at your current kitchen and the way your family uses it.

- Do one or more people cook at one time?
- How many join in cleanup?
- Do you have enough counter space?
- Are the countertops too high or too low?
- Is the work triangle—made up of the sink, stove and refrigerator—outside the flow of traffic?
- Do you need more storage space?
- Do you use the kitchen for other activities?
- Do you need an informal eating area?
- How many small appliances do you use daily?
- How do you handle recycling?

In addition to considering the nuts and bolts of a kitchen, look around for as many ideas as possible.

Don't Forget the Details! 10 Tips for a Better Kitchen

1. Look for a kitchen that opens to adjacent living areas, letting the cook visit with the family.
2. Make sure there are plenty of electrical outlets for appliances.

Do you have kids? If so . . .

3. Choose countertops with rounded corners.
4. Get a cooktop with the controls on top.
5. Install a hot-water limiter on the faucet.
6. Put childproof locks on drawers with cleaning supplies and knives.

7. Install counters at varied heights—one for chopping, one for kneading, etc.
8. Create a sit-down workspace for planning menus, taking messages, etc.
9. Get skid-proof flooring.
10. Storage! Storage! Storage!

Leaf through shelter magazines and product literature, visit showrooms and check out friends' kitchens. Keep a file of all the good ideas you find.

Don't pass by anything at this point because of cost. Right now you want ideas and inspiration. Later on, take those ideas and adapt them to your specific needs and budget.

Also, when looking at kitchen layouts in home plans, don't rule out a design you otherwise like just because the kitchen needs tweaking. Maybe you want a vegetable sink in the island, or storage for dishes and flatware closer to the dishwasher. With the help of a professional designer, you can probably incorporate these details into the design.

Before you make your kitchen a reality, settle on a budget. Most often, the price tag for the kitchen runs higher than any other room in the home, so careful attention to the bottom line is crucial.

When most of us undertake an expensive project like building a home, we start with a dream and then scale back to meet a realistic budget.

To do this, make lists of what you need and what you want out of a kitchen, and prioritize them. Use those lists to decide what you will go without or what you will add later on down the road.

When choosing appliances and products, weigh bargains against quality. High-quality appliances save money on maintenance and utility bills, so a cheap price tag up front could end up costing more money in the long run. If you find a bargain, make sure you are getting a product that will stand the tests of time and family use—or abuse.

Once you have a framework for your kitchen in mind, go out and make it happen. Remember that your family will probably be spending a significant amount of time in this space. Take the time now to make sure you end up with a kitchen that reflects and meets your family's lifestyle. ■

—Jessica Tolliver

Clip-n-save

Expense Calculator

Cabinetry *(including a planning desk and interior storage units)*	$
Countertops and backsplashes	$
Dishwasher	$
Flooring	$
Garbage disposal	$
Indoor grill	$
Lighting	$
Microwave	$
Pantry organizer	$
Plumbing	$
Range (or cooktop and ovens)	$
Range hood	$
Refrigerator/freezer	$
Sink(s) and faucet(s)	$
Telephone/intercom	$
Trash compactor	$
TV/VCR	$
Ventilation	$
Warming oven	$
Water (hot or cold) dispenser	$
Water purifier	$
Wine cooler	$
Total	$

Cyber Kitchen

For those who like to cook *and* embrace the information age, a new World Wide Web site provides a mountain of kitchen-related information at the click of the mouse.
Located at http://www.kitchen-bath.com, the site, called Kitchen.net, includes articles on do-it-yourself topics, a product guide and a buyer's guide. Also, browsers can ask questions of Dr. Kitchen, a real-life Certified Kitchen Designer.

A SPLASH OF COLOR!

Photo by Mark Englund

Fantastic Floor Plan!

- This is the famous house shown on the PBS "Hometime" television series.
- Impressive floor plan includes a deluxe master suite with a private courtyard, magnificent bath and large closet.
- The large island kitchen/nook combination includes a corner pantry and easy access to a rear deck.
- The spacious family room includes a fireplace and vaulted ceiling.
- The two upstairs bedrooms share a bath with double sinks.
- Note the convenient laundry room in the garage entry area.

Plan B-88015

Bedrooms: 3	Baths: 2½

Space:
Upper floor: 534 sq. ft.
Main floor: 1,689 sq. ft.

Total living area: 2,223 sq. ft.
Basement: approx. 1,689 sq. ft.
Garage: 455 sq. ft.

Exterior Wall Framing: 2x4

Foundation options:
Standard basement only.
(Foundation & framing conversion diagram available — see order form.)

Blueprint Price Code: C

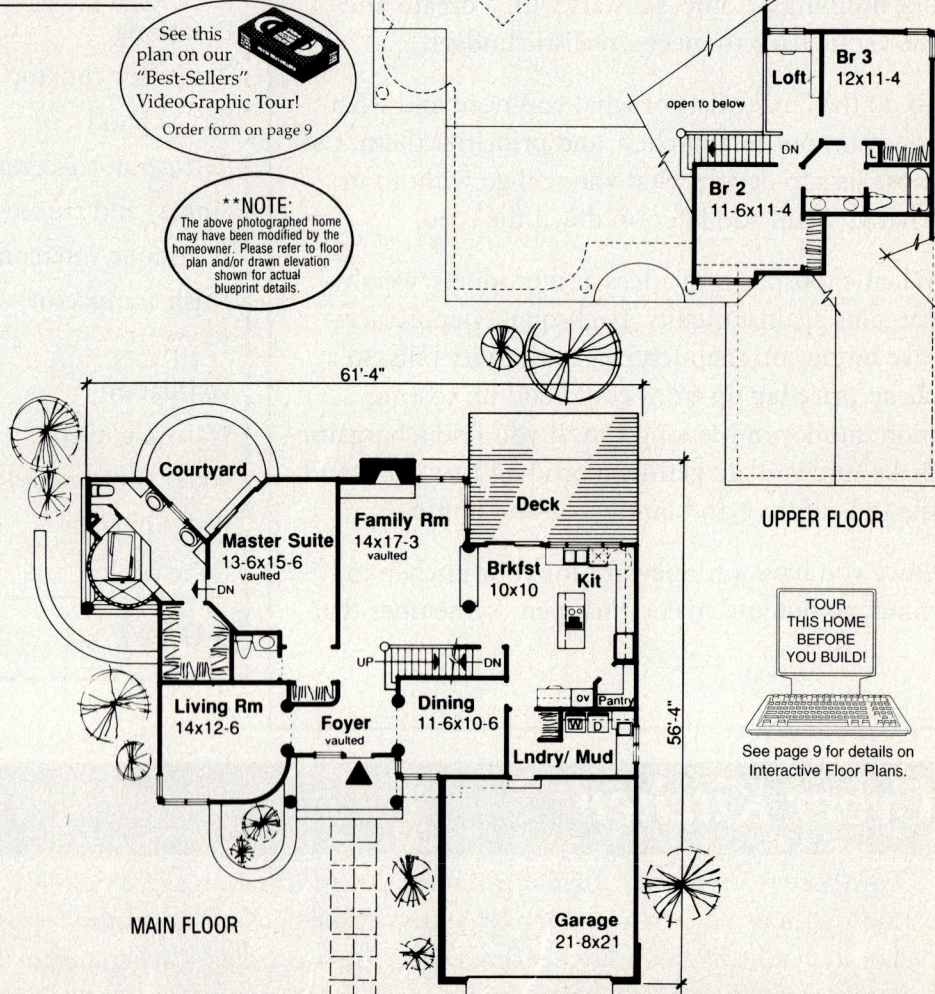

See this plan on our "Best-Sellers" VideoGraphic Tour!
Order form on page 9

NOTE: The above photographed home may have been modified by the homeowner. Please refer to floor plan and/or drawn elevation shown for actual blueprint details.

TOUR THIS HOME BEFORE YOU BUILD!

See page 9 for details on Interactive Floor Plans.

ORDER BLUEPRINTS ANYTIME!
CALL TOLL-FREE 1-888-626-2026

Plan B-88015

PRICES AND DETAILS ON PAGES 12-15

6

"There oughta be a law...." If you find yourself repeating that sentiment daily as you wander through the neighborhood and behold the neighbors' backyard jungles and collections of beater cars, a community with a homeowners' association could be just the place for you. After all, a homeowners' association that prohibits lawn ornaments and inoperative cars outside of garages would soothe your assaulted sensibilities.

Joining a HOMEOWNERS' Association

If, on the other hand, Spot needs a kennel of his own, the kids like to camp out in the yard on summer nights and you have a large collection of pink flamingos and ceramic jockeys to display out front, you had better think twice about living in a community with a homeowners' association. A 50- or 60-page document filled with regulations would probably offend your sense of freedom.

Whichever way you lean, if you're building a home today, chances are you will encounter these planned communities, and need to decide if you want to locate your new home in one.

According to the Community Associations Institute (CAI), based in Virginia, over 32 million people in the United States in 1992 lived in communities governed by a homeowners' association. In large metropolitan areas, 50 percent of new-home buyers live in communities with homeowners' associations.

These associations go by a number of names, including homeowners' associations, planned unit developments, owners' associations, community associations and property owners' associations.

Some associations own the common property in a community, while the residents own their homes and properties. In other associations, the residents hold the titles to their homes and jointly own the common properties, like a clubhouse.

Community associations feature three common qualities:
1. All homeowners in the community are automatically members of the association.
2. The association's governing documents bind the owners to the association and its rules.
3. The association levies mandatory fees against the owners for its operation.

Many community associations also offer amenities that individuals could not afford otherwise, like a swimming pool or tennis courts. The community association maintains these spaces, along with other common areas like a playground, park or boulevard.

Another priority for community associations is to ensure the general upkeep of all the homes and lots in the neighborhood so property values stay consistent.

Tour our most popular homes on your TV!

HomeStyles' 3-D computer-animated **VideoGraphic Home Tours**™ take you on a personal tour of the interior and exterior highlights of our most popular homes. These Home Tours help you get a feel for the size and shape of your dream home! Each video shows you 25 home plans for only $9.95! Or order all four videos and get a complete library of 100 popular plans for only $29.95.

Visit our Web site at **www.homestyles.com**

Order now! Call toll-free 1-888-626-2026 (U.S. & Canada). International orders, please call 612-602-5003.

❏ Check enclosed (payable to HomeStyles Plan Service)
or charge my: ❏ MasterCard ❏ VISA ❏ AmEx ❏ Discover
Acct.# _____ Exp. Date _____
Signature _____
Name _____
Address _____
City/Prov. _____ State _____ Country _____
ZIP _____ Day Phone _____

Please send me:
❏ **HSV10** "Best-Sellers" - $9.95
❏ **HSV11** "One-Story" - $9.95
❏ **HSV12** "Two-Story" - $9.95
❏ **HSV13** "Country & Traditional" - $9.95
❏ **HSV14** "4-Video Library" - $29.95

Mail to: HomeStyles
P.O. Box 75488
St. Paul, MN 55175-0488
or fax: (612) 602-5002

Subtotal $ _____
Minnesota residents
add 6.5% sales tax $ _____
Add Shipping $ _____
Grand Total $ _____

Source Code: HD28

Video Shipping Chart

	per video	per library
United States	$5.00	$8.75
Canada/Mexico	$10.00	$15.00
International	$15.00	$20.00

TOUR YOUR DREAM HOME BEFORE YOU BUILD WITH INTERACTIVE FLOOR PLANS™!

Using photo-realistic, color images on computer diskettes you can see a variety of furnished interior views and exterior perspectives of your favorite dream home plan. Tour the home from room to room on your home computer! Interactive Floor Plans™ let you see what the home will look like—before it's built.

Each interactive tour costs **only** $29.95, plus $5.00 for shipping

Interactive Floor Plan™ diskettes are available for home plans that carry this logo. Look for it in this book! Some plans may be featured.

System Requirements: • 4MB RAM • 386SX (486DX/33 recommended) • Microsoft® Windows 3.1
• 256 color display on SVGA monitior • 7MB free on hard disk

Interactive Home Plans™ are now available for the following plans:
- AX-91312 (IFP#100)
- B-88015 (IFP#101)
- C-8920 (IFP#102)
- DD-1696 (IFP#103)
- E-3000 (IFP#104)
- H-1427-3A, 3B (IFP#106)
- HDS-99-177 (IFP#107)
- J-86155 (IFP#108)
- L-023-HD (IFP#200)
- L-105-VC (IFP#201)
- L-2176-MC (IFP#202)
- L-222-VSB (IFP#203)
- L-2360-MC (IFP#204)
- L-262-HC (IFP#205)
- L-270-SA (IFP#206)
- L-2908-FC (IFP#207)
- L-3163 (IFP#208)
- L-483-HB (IFP #209)
- L-720-CSB (IFP#210)
- L-841-VSC (IFP#211)
- L-934-VSB (IFP#212)
- P-6580-3A.3D (IFP#109)
- S-4789 (IFP#110)

ORDER YOUR INTERACTIVE FLOOR PLAN™ TODAY!
CALL TOLL-FREE 1-888-626-2026
OR SEND YOUR NAME, ADDRESS, INTERACTIVE FLOOR PLAN™ (IFP) NUMBER, AND PAYMENT TO:
HOMESTYLES™ IFP, P.O. BOX 75488, ST. PAUL, MN 55175-0488

Source Code   HD28

TIPS FOR A HAPPY ASSOCIATION

1. Read all the documents regarding the association before you agree to buy a lot or build.
2. Read them again when you move in.
3. Pay your assessments on time.
4. Attend the annual meeting.
5. Read the newsletters and meeting minutes.
6. Follow the rules.
7. Volunteer to serve on a committee.
8. Volunteer to serve on the board.
9. Take care of your property.

Courtesy of Community Associations Institute

The bylaws of a community association in a St. Paul, Minn. suburb states that the group's goal is to "provide for the preservation of the values and amenities in the community and for the maintenance of the private open spaces . . . ."

To ensure that communities maintain their values, homeowners' associations regulate everything from the number and types of pets in your home, to the color of your home and whether you can keep the grill on the back porch.

Once you buy a home or property in a community association, membership is automatic and mandatory.

Membership includes adherence to the community's regulations and the annual payment of an assessment to the organization.

The organization board uses these assessments to carry out the group's regular business and responsibilities. Some associations charge residents a flat fee, while others base their fees on the size and value of each home and property.

According to the CAI, the median monthly assessment for a community association totals $123.

Sometimes community associations also vote to assess additional fees to residents for unplanned or large projects on common property.

If you violate a community regulation, you are required to remedy the situation at your own expense when notified by the community group. If you fail to fix the problem within the allotted time period, the community association can arrange to do so themselves and charge you for the work. You are legally bound to pay these fees.

Because you will automatically be held accountable to the rules of your community's homeowners' organization, you need to decide—before you make any written or verbal agreements to build there—if those regulations suit your own lifestyle.

You can save yourself frustration if you find out beforehand that a community prohibits home businesses or pet monkeys.

Get a copy of the community association's documents and read them over carefully. No matter how long and unintelligible they are, you need to get a good understanding of the rules.

If the legal-speak gets too confusing, hire a lawyer to go over the documents with you. The investment now could save you time and money later, fixing a situation that resulted from a misunderstanding.

Talk to your potential neighbors to get their ideas about the community association. They can tell you plenty about the group's logistics, as well as their opinions about how well the association carries out its goals and manages the community.

Finally, if you decide to live in a neighborhood governed by a community association, make a commitment to that group.

At the very least, pay your assessments on time and read the newsletters. Attend the annual meetings, where you vote on amendments to the guidelines and elect members to the board.

If you want to play a bigger role in the community, join a committee, serve on the board or volunteer to help out with a project.

Most importantly, remember the bottom line. You agreed to abide by the rules when you joined the community. Follow them.

If you must paint your house purple or build a multi-level treehouse in the backyard, follow the established paths to get permission.

— Jessica Tolliver

Community Association: A residential development in which each owner is bound to a real-estate organization by governing documents that require adherence to a set of rules, and the payment of assessments.

—Courtesy of Community Associations Institute

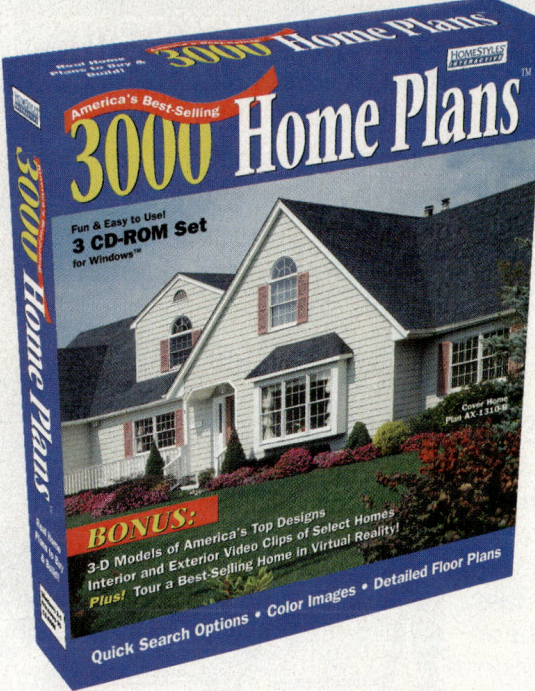

Find a New Plan, Stan

3-DISK CD-ROM SET PRICED UNDER $15

You can find the home of your dreams with *America's Best-Selling 3000 Home Plans*™, a new CD-ROM by HomeStyles®, the home plans people. This fun and easy software package places 3,000 hot home plans at your fingertips, and it offers the latest interactive functions to customize the browsing process. Search for your home plan by selecting the style, size, and number of bedrooms and bathrooms that are right for you. The program will bring up the plans that match your criteria. This powerful package also includes a Virtual Reality Home Tour and VideoGraphic Home Tours™ video clips. Priced under $15, you can't afford to pass this up!

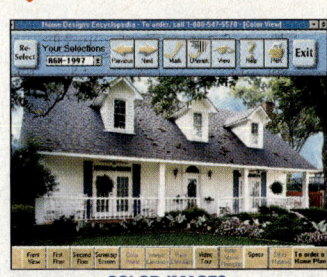
COLOR IMAGES

VIRTUAL HOME TOUR

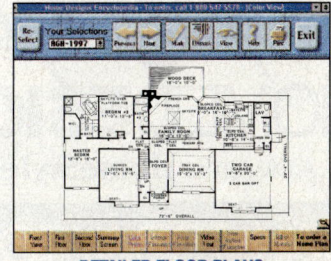
DETAILED FLOOR PLANS

FIVE DOLLAR REBATE OFFER

Receive a $5 rebate when you purchase *America's Best-Selling 3000 Home Plans*™ at your nearest WAL-MART®. Simply mail a copy of your store receipt along with this coupon to the address below. You will receive a $5 check directly from HomeStyles®.   **PRODUCT CODE CD2-1WAL**

Name _____

Address _____

City _____

State _____ ZIP _____

Mail to: HomeStyles • P.O. Box 75488 • St. Paul, MN 55175-0488   **SOURCE CODE HD28**

This product is available *exclusively* at WAL★MART®

NEED TO MAKE PLAN CHANGES? IT'S EASY AS A-B-C!

HomeStyles offers modification services through its affiliate company, **LifeStyle HomeDesign**. Every year, **LifeStyle** helps hundreds of HomeStyles plan customers make their dreams a built reality by modifying plans to better suit their lifestyle needs and preferences. With their modification experience, extensive knowledge of the HomeStyles inventory, and easy accessibility to the electronic files of most designers, **LifeStyle** can make your changes faster, more convenient, and more cost-effective than they would be at a local design company.

A ORDER YOUR PLANS
It's easy to work with the staff of **LifeStyle HomeDesign** to make changes to your favorite home plans. Simply order a reproducible set from HomeStyles and ask the operator to transfer you to the **LifeStyle** modification advisor. You can also call **1-888-2MODIFY**.

B TELL US WHAT YOU WANT TO CHANGE
LifeStyle can pull a copy of your plan from the HomeStyles files, answer your questions and prepare an estimate for the cost and turn-around time of customizing your plan. Your detailed estimate will be ready within 24 hours.

C WE'LL GO TO WORK
Once you have confirmed your desired changes, our expert computer drafters will go to work. Most modifications are completed within ONE WEEK. Remember, faster modifications mean cost savings for you, and you can start sooner to make your dream home a reality.

ABOVE: Love the floor plan but think the exterior is too contemporary? **BELOW:** We can modify the plans to create a traditional country farmhouse look, complete with a front porch and dormers!

A Division of HomeStyles®

213 East 4th Street
St. Paul, Minnesota 55101
Visit us on the Web at: www.lifestylehomedesign.com
E-mail to: plan?@lifestylehomedesign.com

CALL TODAY TO MAKE YOUR DREAM HOME A REALITY!
1-888-2MODIFY

OUR BLUEPRINTS INCLUDE

HomeStyles construction blueprints are detailed, clear and concise. All blueprints are designed by licensed architects or members of the American Institute of Building Design (AIBD), and each plan is designed to meet one of the nationally recognized building codes (the Uniform Building Code, Standard Building Code or Basic Building Code) at the time and place they were drawn.

The blueprints for most home designs include the following elements, but the presentation of these elements may vary depending on the size and complexity of the home and the style of the individual designer:

1. **EXTERIOR ELEVATIONS** show the front, rear and sides of the house, including exterior materials, details and measurements.

2. **FOUNDATION PLANS** include drawings for a standard, daylight or partial basement, crawlspace, pole, pier, or slab foundation. All necessary notations and dimensions are included. (Foundation options will vary for each plan. If the home you want does not have the type of foundation you desire, a generic foundation conversion diagram is available from HomeStyles.)

3. **INTERIOR ELEVATIONS** show the specific details of cabinets (kitchen, bathroom, and utility room), fireplaces, built-in units, and other special interior features, depending on the nature and complexity of the item. *NOTE: To save money and to accommodate your own style and taste, we suggest contacting local cabinet and fireplace distributors for sizes and styles.*

4. **ROOF DETAILS** show slope, pitch and location of dormers, gables and other roof elements, including clerestory windows and skylights. These details may be shown on the elevation sheet or on a separate diagram. *NOTE: If trusses are used, we suggest using a local truss manufacturer to design your trusses to comply with your local codes and regulations.*

5. **SCHEMATIC ELECTRICAL LAYOUTS** show the suggested locations for switches, fixtures and outlets. These details may be shown on the floor plan or on a separate diagram.

6. **DETAILED FLOOR PLANS** show the placement of interior walls and the dimensions for rooms, doors, windows, stairways, etc., of each level of the house.

7. **CROSS SECTIONS** show details of the house as though it were cut in slices from the roof to the foundation. The cross sections specify the home's construction, insulation, flooring and roofing details.

8. **GENERAL SPECIFICATIONS** provide general instructions and information regarding structure, excavating and grading, masonry and concrete work, carpentry and wood, thermal and moisture protection, and specifications about drywall, tile, flooring, glazing, caulking and sealants.

OTHER HELPFUL BUILDING ITEMS

Every set of plans that you order will contain the details your builder needs. However, HomeStyles provides additional guides and information that you may order, as follows:

1. **REPRODUCIBLE SET** is useful if you plan to make changes to the stock home plan you've chosen. This set consists of line drawings produced on erasable, reproducible paper for the purpose of modification. When alterations are complete, working copies can be made. See chart on next page for availability.
   Bonus: Includes free working set!

2. **MIRROR-REVERSED PLANS** (available on all plans) are used when building the home in reverse of the illustrated floor plan. Reversed plans are available for an additional one-time surcharge. Since the lettering and dimensions will read backwards, we recommend that you order only one or two reversed sets in addition to the regular-reading sets.

3. **ITEMIZED LIST OF MATERIALS** details the quantity, type and size of basic materials needed to build your home. This list is helpful in acquiring an accurate construction estimate. See chart on next page for availability.

4. **DESCRIPTION OF MATERIALS** describes the type and quality of materials suggested for the home. This form may be required for obtaining FHA or VA financing. See chart on next page for availability.

5. **GENERIC "HOW-TO" DIAGRAMS**—Plumbing, Wiring, Solar Heating, and Framing and Foundation Conversion Diagrams. Each of these diagrams details the basic tools and techniques needed to plumb; wire; install a solar heating system; convert plans with 2x4 exterior walls to 2x6 (or vice versa); or adapt a plan for a basement, crawlspace or slab foundation.
NOTE: These diagrams are generic and not specific to any one plan.

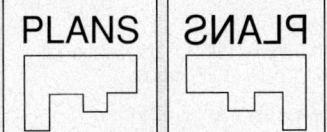

NOTE: Due to regional variations, local availability of materials, local codes, methods of installation, and individual preferences, it is impossible to include much detail on heating, plumbing, and electrical work on your plans. The duct work, venting, and other details will vary depending on the type of heating and cooling system (forced air, hot water, electric, solar) and the type of energy (gas, oil, electricity, solar) that you use. These details and specifications are easily obtained from your builder, contractor, and/or local suppliers.

BEFORE YOU ORDER, PLEASE READ

BLUEPRINT PRICES
Our pricing schedule is based on "Total heated living space." Garages, porches, decks and unfinished basements are not included.

EXCHANGE INFORMATION
We want you to be happy with your blueprint purchase. If, for some reason, the blueprints that you ordered cannot be used, we will be pleased to exchange them within 30 days of the purchase date. Please note that a handling fee will be assessed for all exchanges. For more information, call us toll-free.
NOTE: Reproducible sets cannot be exchanged for any reason.

LICENSE AGREEMENT, COPY RESTRICTIONS AND COPYRIGHT INFORMATION
When you purchase a HomeStyles blueprint or reproducible set, we, as Licensor, grant you, as Licensee, the right to use these documents **to construct a single unit.** All of the plans in the publication are protected under the Federal Copyright Act, Title XVII of the United States Code and Chapter 37 of the Code of Federal Regulations. Each HomeStyles designer retains title and ownership of the original documents. The blueprints licensed to you cannot be resold or used by any other person, copied, or reproduced by any means. When you purchase a reproducible set, you reserve the right to modify and reproduce the plan. Reproducible sets cannot be resold or used by any other person.

ESTIMATING BUILDING COSTS
Building costs vary widely depending on style, size, type of finishing materials you select, and the local rates for labor and building materials. A local average cost per square foot of construction can give you a rough estimate. To get the average cost per square foot in your area, you can call a local contractor, your state or local builders association, the National Association of Home Builders (NAHB), or the American Institute of Building Design (AIBD). A more accurate estimate will require a professional review of the working blueprints and the types of materials you will be using.

FOUNDATION OPTIONS & EXTERIOR CONSTRUCTION
Depending on your location and climate, your home will normally be built with a slab, crawlspace or basement foundation; the exterior walls will usually be of 2x4 or 2x6 framing. Most professional contractors and builders can easily adapt a home to meet the foundation and exterior wall requirements that you desire.

If the home that you select does not offer the foundation or exterior wall requirements that you prefer, HomeStyles offers a typical foundation and framing conversion diagram. (See order form.)

Every state, county and municipality has its own codes, zoning requirements, ordinances, and building regulations. **Modifications may be necessary to comply with your specific requirements—snow loads, energy codes, seismic zones, etc.**

REVISIONS, MODIFICATIONS AND CUSTOMIZING
The tremendous variety of designs available from HomeStyles allows you to choose the home that best suits your lifestyle, budget and building site. Through your choice of siding, roof, trim, decorating, color, etc., your home can be customized easily.

Minor changes and material substitutions can be made by any professional builder without the need for expensive blueprint revisions. However, if you will be making major changes, we strongly recommend that you order a reproducible set and seek the services of an architect or professional designer.

COMPLIANCE WITH CODES
Depending on where you live, you may need to modify your plans to comply with local building requirements—snow loads, energy codes, seismic zones, etc. All HomeStyles plans are designed to meet the specifications of seismic zones I or II. HomeStyles authorizes the use of our blueprints expressly conditioned upon your obligation and agreement to strictly comply with all local building codes, ordinances, regulations, and requirements—including permits and inspections at the time of construction.

ARCHITECTURAL AND ENGINEERING SEALS
The increased concern over energy costs and safety has prompted many cities and states to require an architect or engineer to review and "seal" a blueprint prior to construction. There may be a fee for this service. Please contact your local lumber yard, municipal building department, builders association, or local chapter of the American Institute of Building Design (AIBD) or the American Institute of Architects (AIA).

NOTE: (Plans for homes to be built in Nevada may have to be re-drawn and sealed by a Nevada-licensed design professional.)

HOW MANY SETS TO ORDER?
BLUEPRINT CHECKLIST
- Owner (**1 SET**)
- Lending Institution (usually **1 SET** for conventional mortgage; **3 SETS** for FHA or VA loans)
- Builder (usually requires at least **3 SETS**)
- Building Permit Department (at least **1 SET**)

*Call for availability

AVAILABILITY

Plan Prefix	Reproducible Set	Itemized List of Materials	Description of Materials	Next Day Delivery
A	•			
AG	•			
AGH	•			•
AHP	•	•	•	
AM				
APS	•	*		
AX	•	*		•
B	•	*		
BOD	•	*		
BRF	•			•
C	•	•	•	
CAR	•	•		
CC	•	•		•
CDG	*	*		
CH	•			
CPS	•			
DBI	•			
DCL	•			
DD	•	*		•
DP	•			•
DW	•	•	•	
E	•	•	•	
EOF	•			
FB	•			
G	•	•		
GA	•			•
GL	•			
H	•	•	•	•
HDS	•			
HFL	•			
HOM	•	•		•
I		*		
IDG	•			
J	•	•		•
JWA	•			
JWB	•			•
K	•			
KD	•			•
KLF	•			•
KY				
L	•	*		•
LMB		*		
LRD	•	•		•
LS	•			•
NBV	•			
NW	•	*		
OH	•			
P	•	•	•	
PH	•	•		•
PI	•			
Q				
R	•	•		
RD	•			•
S	•	•	•	
SAN				•
SD				
SDG	•			
SG	•	*		
SUL	•		•	
SUN	•	•		
THD	•			•
TS	•			•
U	•	•	•	•
UD	•			
UDA	•	•		
UDG	•	•		
V	•			
VL	•		•	
WH	•	•		
YS		•	•	

Blueprint Order Form
CALL ANYTIME!

BLUEPRINTS
(PRICES SUBJECT TO CHANGE)

Price Code	1 Set	4 Sets	8 Sets	Reproducible Set*
AAA	$265	$310	$350	$435
AA	$305	$350	$390	$475
A	$385	$430	$470	$555
B	$425	$470	$510	$595
C	$465	$510	$550	$635
D	$505	$550	$590	$675
E	$545	$590	$630	$715
F	$585	$630	$670	$755
G	$625	$670	$710	$795
H	$665	$710	$750	$835
I	$705	$750	$790	$875

SHIPPING & HANDLING

	1-3 sets	4-7 sets	8 sets or more	Reproducible Set
U.S. Next Day* (order before Noon Central) (See availability chart on opposite page)	$45.00	$47.50	$50.00	$45.00
U.S. Express (2-3 business days)	$30.00	$32.50	$35.00	$30.00
U.S. Regular (5-7 business days)	$15.00	$17.50	$20.00	$15.00
Canada Regular (5-7 business days)	$35.00	$40.00	$45.00	$35.00
Canada Express (2-4 business days)	$50.00	$55.00	$60.00	$50.00
International (7-10 business days)	$60.00	$70.00	$80.00	$60.00

HomeStyles
THE HOME PLANS PEOPLE

Visit our Web site at: www.homestyles.com

ADDITIONAL ITEMS

MIRROR-REVERSED PLANS: A **$50 surcharge.** From the total number of sets you order, choose the number of these that you want to be reversed. Pay only $50.
NOTE: All writing on mirror-reversed plans is backward. We recommend ordering only one or two reversed sets in addition to the regular-reading sets.

***ITEMIZED LIST OF MATERIALS:** Available for $50; each additional set is $15.
Details the quantity, type and size of basic materials needed to build your home.

***DESCRIPTION OF MATERIALS:** Sold only in set of two for $50.
(For use in obtaining FHA or VA financing.)

*Refer to availability chart on opposite page or call for further information.

Plan Number
HD28

PRICE CODE _____
FOUNDATION _____
Carefully review the foundation option(s) available for your plan—basement, crawlspace, pole, pier, or slab. If several options are offered, *choose only one.*

NO. OF SETS (See Blueprint Chart below)
☐ **ONE SET** (STAMPED "NOT FOR CONSTRUCTION")
  •RECOMMENDED FOR REVIEW/STUDY
☐ **FOUR SETS**   ☐ **EIGHT SETS** $_____
  •RECOMMENDED FOR BIDDING   •RECOMMENDED FOR CONSTRUCTION
☐ **REPRODUCIBLE SET** (See availability chart on opposite page.)
  •RECOMMENDED FOR CONSTRUCTION/MODIFICATION

ADDITIONAL SETS ($50 each) _____ $_____
(Available on all plans; with minimum 4-set order only)

MIRROR-REVERSED SETS ($50 one-time surcharge) _____ $_____
(See availability chart on opposite page.)

ITEMIZED LIST OF MATERIALS ($50; $15 for each additional) _____ $_____
(See availability chart on opposite page.)

DESCRIPTION OF MATERIALS ($50 for two sets) $_____

GENERIC HOW-TO DIAGRAMS $_____
☐ PLUMBING   ☐ WIRING   ☐ SOLAR HEATING   ☐ FRAMING & FOUNDATION CONVERSION
(One set $20. Two sets $30. Three sets $40. All four only $45.)

SUBTOTAL $_____

Minnesota Residents Only: Add 6.5% Sales Tax $_____

(See chart at left) **SHIPPING/HANDLING** $_____

TOTAL $_____

Make checks payable to: **HomeStyles**
☐ Check/Money Order enclosed (in U.S. funds)
☐ VISA   ☐ MasterCard   ☐ AmEx   ☐ Discover

CREDIT CARD NUMBER _____ EXPIRATION DATE _____
NAME _____
ADDRESS _____ CITY _____
STATE _____ COUNTRY _____ ZIP _____
DAYTIME PHONE NUMBER _____ FAX NUMBER _____
•For international orders, please indicate fax number.

☐ I am a builder.
☐ I do not wish to receive any future mailings.

MAIL TO:
HomeStyles
P.O. Box 75488
St. Paul, MN 55175-0488

OR FAX TO:
1-612-602-5002

ORDER BLUEPRINTS ANYTIME! CALL TOLL-FREE:

1-888-626-2026
Source Code HD28

International Phone Number 612-602-5003

Meet Our Exclusive Designers!

The following designers and architects have shown exceptional commitment to the HomeStyles Designers' Network. Their quality home designs in this publication are available exclusively through HomeStyles. To find home plans by a particular designer, check the letters in parentheses and look for plan numbers with that prefix.

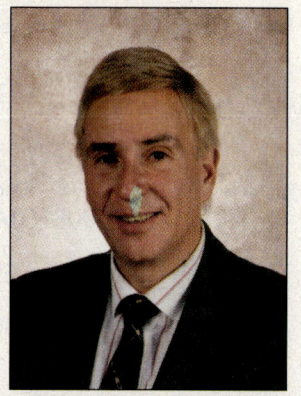

Jerold Axelrod
Jerold Axelrod & Associates, P.C., Commack, N.Y. (AX)

Edsel Breland
Breland & Farmer Designers, Inc., Ridgeland, Miss. (E, HOM, THD)

Louie Carini
Carini Engineering Designs, P.C., Fairport, N.Y. (A)

Donovan Davis
Danze & Davis Architects, Inc., Austin, Tex. (DD)

Ken Dick
Ken Dick & Associates, Inc., Fort Worth, Tex. (KD)

Mark Englund
LifeStyle HomeDesign, St. Paul, Minn., and Urbandale, Iowa (AGH, B, H, HOM, LS)

Larry Garnett
Larry W. Garnett & Associates, Inc.,
Pasadena, Tex. (L)

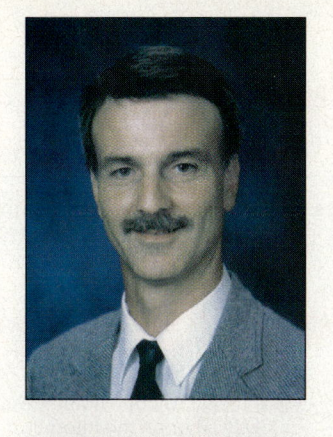

Larry James
Larry James & Associates, Inc.,
Monroe, La. (J)

Gene Laneri
Greater Living Architecture, P.C.,
Rochester, N.Y. (GL)

Jim Mei
Suntel Design Associates, Inc.,
Tigard, Ore. (S)

Barbara Morris
Corley Plan Service, Inc.,
East Point, Ga. (C)

Bill Sutton,
Caddhomes,
Vienna, Va. (CH)

Miguel Weinstein,
American Home Plans,
Bellmore, N.Y. (AHP)

Jim Zirkel
Home Design Services, Inc.,
Altamonte Springs, Fla. (HDS)

Not Pictured:

Ken Dahlin, *Genesis Architecture and Planning, Franksville, Wis.* (GA)
Ronald Dick, *Ronald K. Dick, Designer, Fort Worth, Tex.* (RD)
Don Evans, *Encore of Florida, Orlando, Fla.* (EOF)
Kirby Fleming, *T.A.S.K. Designs, Inc., Houston, Tex.* (KLF)
Jim French, *Home Designs by Santiago, Ruidoso, N.M.* (SAN)

Jim Gola, *Lewis River Design, Woodland, Wash.* (LRD)
Roger Kennedy, *Stephen's Design Group, Norman, Okla.* (SDG)
Michael Nelson, *The Nelson Group, Inc., Springdale, Ark.* (NBV)
Debra Purvis, *DesignHouse, Wiggins, Miss.* (DP)
Tim Stockton, *Building Designs by Stockton, Tigard, Ore.* (TS)
Chris Vaughn, *Sullivan & Associates, Germantown, Tenn.* (SUL)

IMPORTANT COPYRIGHT NOTICE

The following statement is provided by HomeStyles and the Council of Publishing Home Designers, an affiliation of the American Institute of Building Design.

1. HOME PLANS ARE COPYRIGHTED

Just like books, movies and songs, federal copyright laws protect the intellectual property of architects and home designers. These legal protections exist to protect all parties. Copyright laws respect and support the intellectual property of the original architect or designer, and prevent anyone from using the design without written permission.

2. DON'T USE PLANS TO BUILD MORE THAN ONE HOUSE

All home plans include a copyright release and a license to use the documents to construct a single home. When you purchase construction documents, we, as licensor, are granting to you, as licensee, the right to use the documents to construct a single unit. This is an exclusive license, which may not be resold, duplicated, published or distributed without written permission of the designer, architect or publisher.

3. REPRODUCING BLUEPRINTS

Construction blueprints may not be reproduced without prior written consent of the designer or publisher. If additional sets are required for estimating or construction, please contact us for additional sets at a nominal cost. Copy shops and blueprinters are prohibited from making copies of these copyrighted documents.

4. REPRODUCIBLE HOME PLANS (MYLARS, VELLUMS, SEPIAS)

With the purchase of a reproducible set (mylars, vellums or sepias), a license and copyright release are also provided. In this case, as licensee, you are allowed to make up to 12 copies of the design, but such copies may only be used for the construction of a single home. For the construction of more than one unit, it is necessary to obtain an additional release or multiple licenses from the publisher, architect or designer.

5. MAKING DESIGN MODIFICATIONS

As a plan licensee, you may customize the design to fit your personal preferences, but you must understand that the modification of the plan is performed at your own risk and should be reviewed by a professional architect, home designer or engineer prior to the start of construction. Modified plans are considered "derivative works" of the original, and it is critical that you understand that these "derivative works," as well as the original work, still retain copyright protection. Any "derivative work" or revised design, even if completely redrawn, may not be sold, duplicated, distributed or used to construct any units without the purchase of a license from the publisher, architect or designer.

6. DON'T COPY DESIGNS/FLOOR PLANS FROM THIS MAGAZINE OR ANY OTHER PUBLICATION, ELECTRONIC MEDIUM OR EXISTING HOME

It is illegal to copy home designs found in any plan book, on a CD-ROM or on the Internet. It is a common misunderstanding that it is permissible to copy, adapt or change a floor plan or a design found in this book. It is not! It is also illegal to copy any existing home that may have been built, that is protected by copyright, even if you have never seen the plans for the home. If a particular home plan or existing home is desired, a set of plans must be purchased from an authorized source.

7. USING THE HOME PLANS

As a plan licensee, you may lend the home plans to third parties (builders, contractors, sub-contractors, inspectors, governmental agencies, etc.) as necessary to assist in the construction of the dwelling involved. All such lent plans must be retrieved and destroyed, except for the owner's reference sets, and those sets required by governmental agencies, after such assistance has been completed.

8. WHO IS RESPONSIBLE FOR COPYRIGHT INFRINGEMENT?

All parties, including the purchasers, designers, drafters, home owners, builders, contractors, sub-contractors, copy shops and blueprinters may be responsible if a copyright is violated. It does not matter whether an individual knows that a violation is being committed. You've heard it before: ignorance of the law is not a valid defense! To avoid legal complications and damages, it is critical that you be certain of the original plan source, and refuse to be a party to any illicit copying or borrowing of designs, derivative works, prints and design features.

9. PLEASE RESPECT HOME DESIGN COPYRIGHTS

In the event of any suspected violation of a copyright, or if there is any uncertainty about the plans purchased, the publisher, architect or designer should be contacted before proceeding. If a violation of a home designer's copyright is suspected, HomeStyles, the designer or architect, and the Council of Publishing Home Designers should be contacted. Awards are sometimes offered for information about home design copyright infringement.

10. PENALTIES FOR INFRINGEMENT

Penalties for violating a copyright may be very severe. The responsible parties are required to pay the designer or architect's actual damages (which may be substantial), plus any profits made. The copyright law also allows the designer or architect to recover statutory damages, which may be as high as $100,000. Finally, the infringer may be required to pay the architect or designer's reasonable legal fees, which often exceed the damages.

Formally French

- This sprawling French Provincial design offers an attractive, efficient balance of living and sleeping areas.
- The central family room is a pleasant gathering place, with its handsome fireplace and adjoining screened porch.
- The formal spaces flow together to the right of the entry.
- A U-shaped kitchen is open to a bayed breakfast area with outdoor views.
- The master bedroom offers ample closet space and a skylighted spa bath. Two more bedrooms share another full bath.

Photo by Mark Englund/HomeStyles

NOTE: The above photographed home may have been modified by the homeowner. Please refer to floor plan and/or drawn elevation shown for actual blueprint details.

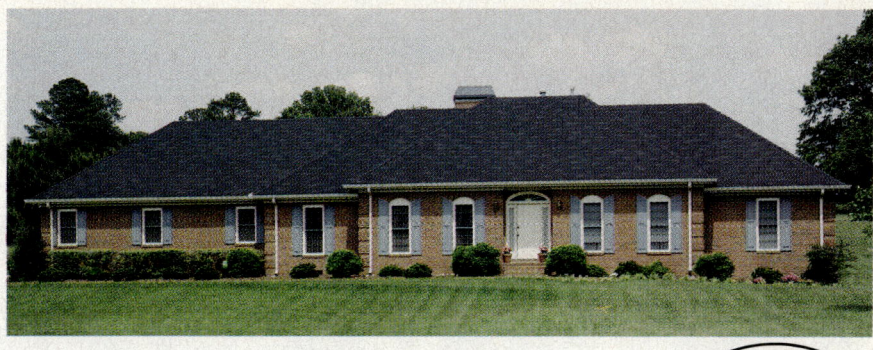

Plan C-8363	
Bedrooms: 3	**Baths:** 2½
Living Area:	
Main floor	2,400 sq. ft.
Total Living Area:	**2,400 sq. ft.**
Daylight basement	2,400 sq. ft.
Garage	546 sq. ft.
Exterior Wall Framing:	2x4
Foundation Options:	
Daylight basement	
Crawlspace	
Slab	

(All plans can be built with your choice of foundation and framing. A generic conversion diagram is available. See order form.)

BLUEPRINT PRICE CODE:	**C**

MAIN FLOOR

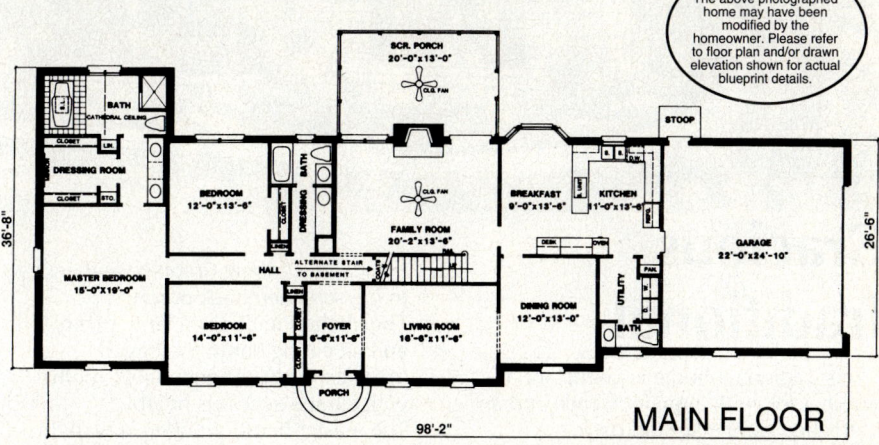

ORDER BLUEPRINTS ANYTIME!
CALL TOLL-FREE 1-888-626-2026

PRICES AND DETAILS ON PAGES 12-15

LWG LARRY W. GARNETT & ASSOCIATES RESIDENTIAL DESIGNERS

Home Plans

Call Toll-Free: 1-800-721-7209

- ❑ *Americana (12 Victorian-style plans) - $15.00*
- ❑ *Heritage Collection (22 plans) - $15.00*
- ❑ *European Traditions (25 plans) - $12.00*
- ❑ *French Collection (32 plans) - $12.00*
- ❑ *Classical Collection (40 plans) - $15.00*
- *Victorian and Farmhouse Collections*
  - ❑ *Volume 1 (29 plans) - $12.00*
  - ❑ *Volume 2 (24 plans) - $12.00*
- ❑ *Village Series (33 plans) - $10.00*
- ❑ *Cottage Retreats (12 plans) - $7.95*
- ❑ *Garages and Guest Quarters (14 plans) - $7.95*
- ❑ *Interactive Computer Home Tour Demonstration Disk and Plan Portfolio - $7.95*
- ❑ *Executive Collection of One-Story Designs (50 plans) - $15.95*
- ❑ *Country Collection (25 plans) Portfolio and CD-ROM - $29.95*

Sales Tax (MN add 6.5%)

NAME ____________________

ADDRESS ____________________

CITY ____________________

STATE ____________ ZIP ____________

*Please allow 7-10 business days for delivery

credit card orders:
❑ VISA ❑ MasterCard ❑ American Express ❑ Discover
Signature ____________________
Exp. Date ____________________
Card Number ____________________

Source Code LHD28

HOMESTYLES®
P.O. Box 75488
St. Paul, MN 55175-0488

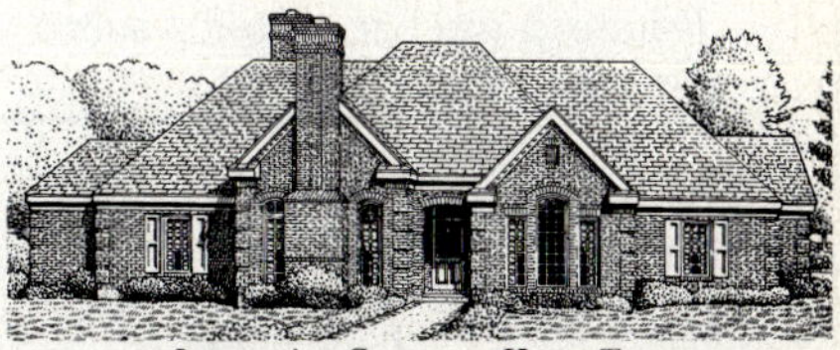

Interactive Computer Home Tour Demonstration Disk and Plan Portfolio

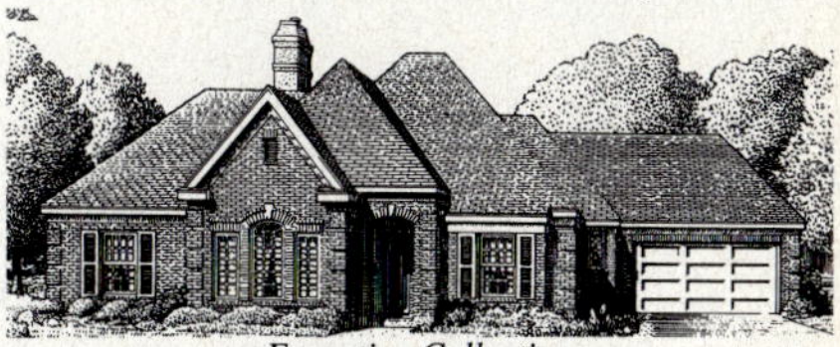

Executive Collection One-Story Designs from 1650 to 2900 sq. ft.

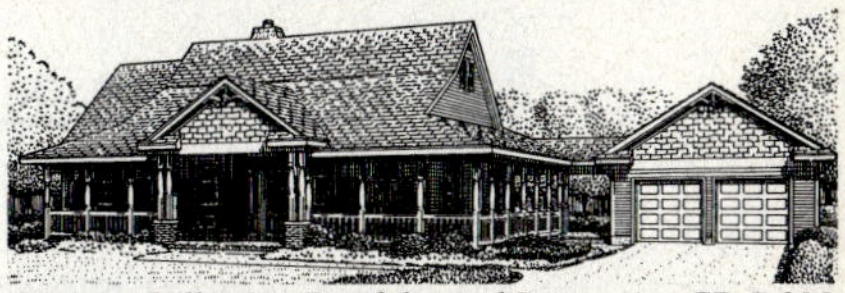

Country Collection Portfolio and Interactive CD-ROM 1600 to 3300 sq. ft. country and farmhouse designs "Tour" 5 of the homes on your computer (Requires 486/DX Windows and CD-ROM)

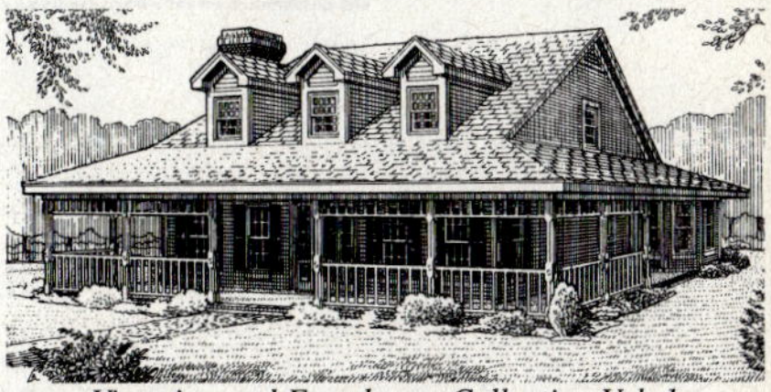

Victorian and Farmhouse Collection Vol. 1 1000 to 2000 sq. ft.

Gracious Traditional

- This traditional home is perfect for a corner lot, with a quaint facade and an attached garage around back.
- Tall windows, elegant dormers and a covered front porch welcome guests to the front entry and into the foyer.
- Just off the foyer, the formal dining room boasts a built-in hutch and views to the front porch.
- The expansive, skylighted Great Room features a wet bar, a 16-ft. vaulted ceiling, a stunning fireplace and access to the screened back porch.
- The kitchen includes a large pantry and an eating bar to the bayed breakfast nook. A large utility room with garage access is nearby.
- The master bedroom offers a walk-in closet and a bath with a large corner tub and his-and-hers vanities.
- Two additional bedrooms have big walk-in closets, built-in desks and easy access to another full bath.
- Upstairs, a loft overlooks the Great Room and is perfect as an extra bedroom or a recreation area.

Plan C-8920

Bedrooms: 3+	Baths: 3

Living Area:
Upper floor — 305 sq. ft.
Main floor — 1,996 sq. ft.
Total Living Area: 2,301 sq. ft.
Daylight basement — 1,996 sq. ft.
Garage — 469 sq. ft.
Exterior Wall Framing: 2x4
Foundation Options:
Daylight basement
Crawlspace
(All plans can be built with your choice of foundation and framing. A generic conversion diagram is available. See order form.)

BLUEPRINT PRICE CODE: C

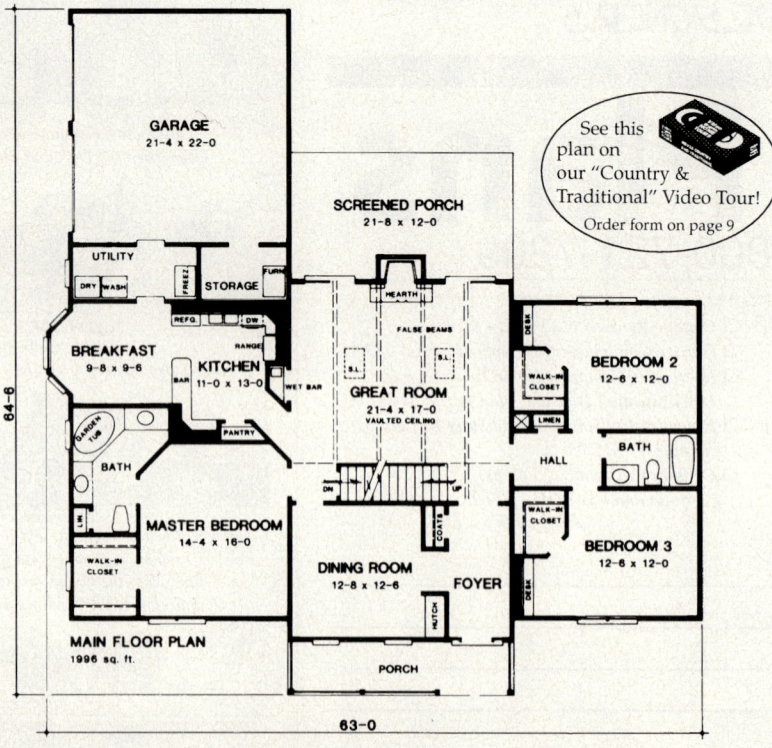

MAIN FLOOR

See this plan on our "Country & Traditional" Video Tour! Order form on page 9

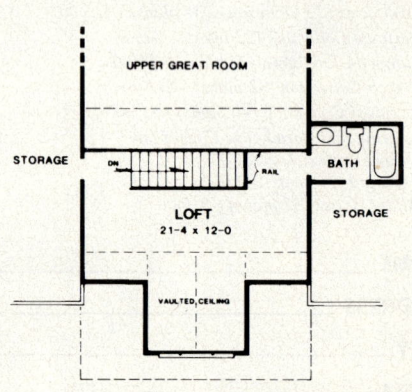

TOUR THIS HOME BEFORE YOU BUILD!
See page 9 for details on Interactive Floor Plans.

UPPER FLOOR

Plan C-8920

ORDER BLUEPRINTS ANYTIME! CALL TOLL-FREE 1-888-626-2026

PRICES AND DETAILS ON PAGES 12-15

Affordable Living

Best-Sellers

Brick Exteriors

Contemporary Living

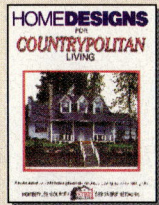
Countrypolitan Living

Country Style Living

Energy-Efficient Living

Family & Great Rooms

Indoor-Outdoor Living

Luxury Living

Master Suites & Baths

Move-Up Families

Find Your Dream Home & Save $45.00

Choose any 10 home plan books for only $39.95 and get a *Free CD-ROM & Free Delivery!*

Narrow Lots

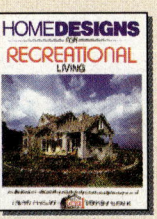
One-Story Living

Recreational Living

Sloping Lots

Sunbelt Living

Two-Story Living

Call now and get a *Free CD-ROM* with 500 interactive floor plans.

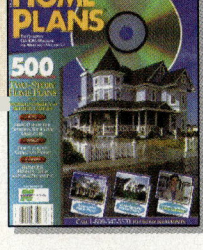

☐ FAMILY ROOMS & GREAT ROOMS • PGW30
☐ INDOOR-OUTDOOR LIVING • PGW21
☐ LUXURY LIVING • PGW28
☐ MASTER SUITES & BATHS • PGW31
☐ MOVE-UP FAMILIES • PGW11
☐ NARROW LOTS • PGW35
☐ ONE-STORY LIVING • PGW29
☐ RECREATIONAL LIVING • PGW33
☐ SLOPING LOTS • PGW32
☐ SUNBELT LIVING • PGW37
☐ TWO-STORY LIVING • PGW34

☐ AFFORDABLE LIVING • PGW36
☐ BEST-SELLERS • PGW22
☐ BRICK EXTERIORS • PGW24
☐ CONTEMPORARY LIVING • PGW27
☐ COUNTRYPOLITAN LIVING • PGW20
☐ COUNTRY STYLE LIVING • PGW8
☐ ENERGY-EFFICIENT LIVING • PGW9

*Book substitutions may be made depending on availability.

☐ Check enclosed or charge my: ☐ MasterCard ☐ Am. Ex. ☐ Visa ☐ Discover

Acct# _____ Exp. Date _____

Name _____

Address _____

City _____ State _____ Zip _____

Day Phone (____) _____

Mail To: HomeStyles Plan Service
P.O. Box 75488   St. Paul, MN 55175-0488

Fax Number 1-612-602-5002
International Phone Number 1-612-602-5003

product code HSF500
source code HD28-2

ORDER TOLL-FREE FOR FASTER SERVICE: 1-800-547-5570

Free Delivery with your 10-book order (U.S. and Canada only)

Contemporary Elegance

- This striking contemporary design combines vertical siding with elegant traditional overtones.
- Inside, an expansive activity area is created with the joining of the vaulted living room, the family/dining room and the kitchen. The openness of the rooms creates a spacious, dramatic feeling, which extends to an exciting two-story sun space and a patio beyond.
- A convenient utility/service area near the garage includes a clothes-sorting counter, a deep sink and ironing space.
- Two main-floor bedrooms share a bright bath.
- The master suite includes a sumptuous skylighted bath with two entrances. The tub is uniquely positioned on an angled wall, while the shower and toilet are secluded behind a pocket door. An optional overlook provides views down into the sun space, which is accessed by a spiral staircase.
- A versatile loft area and a bonus room complete this design.

Plan LRD-1971

Bedrooms: 3+	Baths: 2

Living Area:
Upper floor	723 sq. ft.
Main floor	1,248 sq. ft.
Sun space	116 sq. ft.
Bonus room	225 sq. ft.
Total Living Area:	**2,312 sq. ft.**
Standard basement	1,248 sq. ft.
Garage	483 sq. ft.

Exterior Wall Framing:	2x6

Foundation Options:
Standard basement
Crawlspace
(All plans can be built with your choice of foundation and framing. A generic conversion diagram is available. See order form.)

BLUEPRINT PRICE CODE: C

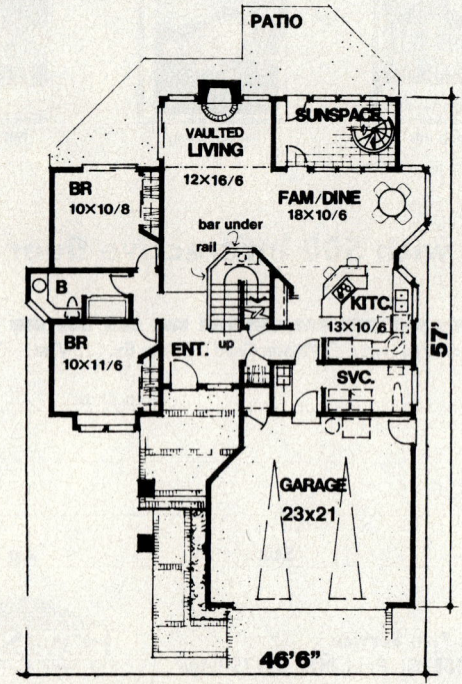

MAIN FLOOR

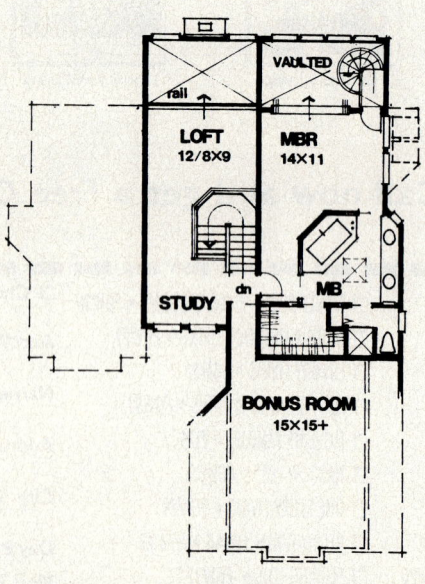

UPPER FLOOR

ORDER BLUEPRINTS ANYTIME! CALL TOLL-FREE 1-888-626-2026 — Plan LRD-1971 — PRICES AND DETAILS ON PAGES 12-15

Having Trouble Finding the Perfect Home Plan? Let Our Design Professionals Help You!

To aid in your search for the perfect home, our designers have access to:
Thousands of designs on interactive CD-ROM.
Books and magazines featuring the latest home design plans.
Videographic tours of many of our plans.
Interactive Floor Plans™.

There's a designer near you! Call today!

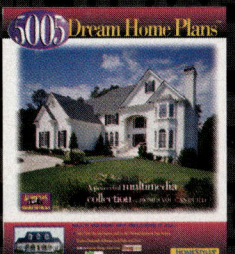

Before You Settle on Your Dream Home, Get Professional Advice from One of the Nation's Top Home Designers at a Location Near You!

Breland and Farmer Designers, Inc.
119 Sawbridge Drive
Ridgeland, MS 39157
(601) 898-1030

Danze and Davis, Architects
8240 Mopac N-Suite 215
Austin, TX 78759
(512) 343-0714

Home Design Services
580 Cape Cod Ln., Ste. #9
Altamonte Springs, FL 32714
(407) 862-5444

Interactive Home Center
12817-C Gulf Freeway
Houston, TX 77034
(713) 484-5050

Larry James and Associates
2208 Justice Street
Monroe, LA 71201
(318) 322-4627

LifeStyle HomeDesign
213 East Fourth Street
St. Paul, MN 55101
(612) 602-5050

Perfect Home Plans
66 Harned Rd.
Commack, NY 11725
(516) 864-4411

Suntel Design Associates
7165 SW Fir Loop Suite 104
Tigard, OR 97223
(503) 624-0555

800 HOME PLANS interactive on CD-ROM
SPECIAL EDITION

featuring an exclusive virtual reality home tour of the
CountryHome® Magazine Showhouse for MALL OF AMERICA!

HomeStyles® proudly presents the latest installment of Interactive Home Plans™, the first quarterly home plans magazine on CD-ROM. This special edition features 800 of our best-selling home plans with a highlight on country and traditional homes. You'll see architects' renderings, color photos and detailed floor plans. Multimedia functions help you find your dream home and hot new home products, too! We have added a special bonus plan and virtual reality tour for the CountryHome® Magazine Showhouse for Mall of America! Come tour the home and hear from its designer, Larry Garnett!

SUBSCRIBE TODAY!
MAIL THIS COMPLETED COUPON OR CALL
U.S./Canada 1-888-626-2026 / International 612-602-5003

SEND ME:

☐ One-year subscription: $29.95
4 issues, 500 plans per issue
(product code CDSUB)

☐ Country & Traditional Homes $9.95
(product code CDF97)

Subtotal _____
Minnesota residents add 6.5% sales tax _____
Grand Total _____

☐ Check enclosed or charge my:
☐ AmEx ☐ Discover ☐ MasterCard ☐ VISA

Acct. # _____ Exp. Date _____
Name _____
Address _____
City _____
State _____ ZIP _____

Mail to:
HomeStyles Plan Service
P.O. Box 75488
St. Paul, MN 55175-0488

Source Code: HD28

Call Our 24-Hour Service Center Toll-Free **1-888-626-2026**
Complete construction blueprints available for all 800 home designs.

Ask for HomeStyles® Interactive Home Plans™ on CD-ROM at fine bookstores and software stores near you!

Visit our Web site at www.homestyles.com
CD-ROM for Windows™ and Macintosh®

You Asked for It!

- Our most popular plan in recent years, E-3000, has now been downsized for affordability, without sacrificing character or excitement.
- Exterior appeal is created with a covered front porch with decorative columns, triple dormers and rail-topped bay windows.
- The floor plan has combined the separate living and family rooms available in E-3000 into one spacious family room with corner fireplace, which flows into the dining room through a columned gallery.
- The kitchen serves the breakfast room over an angled snack bar, and features a huge pantry.
- The stunning main-floor master suite offers a private sitting area, a walk-in closet and a dramatic, angled bath.
- There are two large bedrooms upstairs accessible via a curved staircase with bridge balcony.

Plan E-2307	
Bedrooms: 3	Baths: 2½
Living Area:	
Upper floor	595 sq. ft.
Main floor	1,765 sq. ft.
Total Living Area:	**2,360 sq. ft.**
Standard basement	1,765 sq. ft.
Garage	484 sq. ft.
Storage	44 sq. ft.
Exterior Wall Framing:	2x6

Foundation Options:
Standard basement
Crawlspace
Slab
(All plans can be built with your choice of foundation and framing. A generic conversion diagram is available. See order form.)

BLUEPRINT PRICE CODE: C

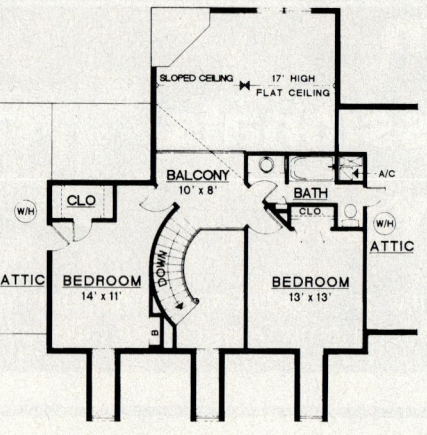
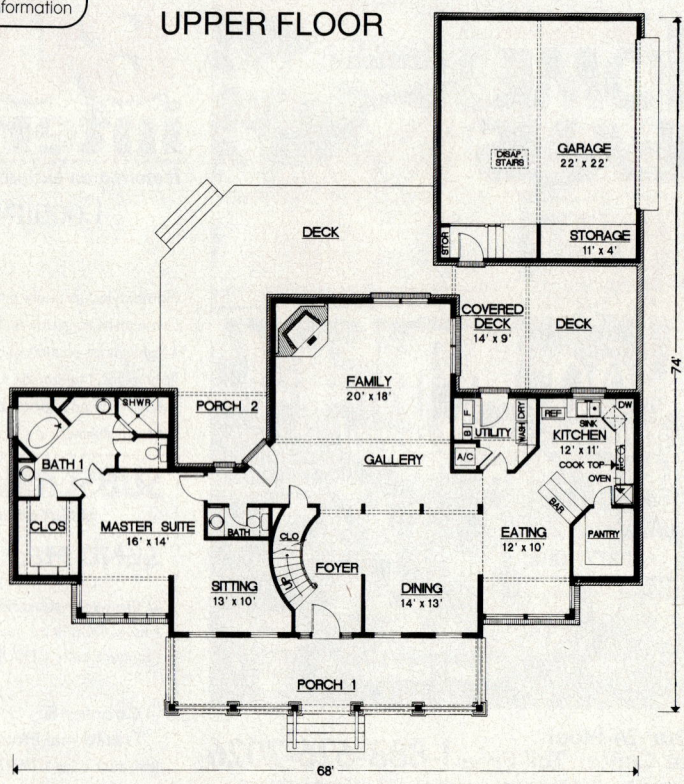

ORDER BLUEPRINTS ANYTIME!
CALL TOLL-FREE 1-888-626-2026

Plan E-2307

PRICES AND DETAILS ON PAGES 12-15

Traditional Neighborhood Design

TIRED OF THE STATUS QUO?

The Problem:
Conventional, "cookie-cutter" houses that are poorly proportioned, lack true privacy and, with their dominant garages, seem more intent on welcoming cars home than people.

The Solution:
Traditional Neighborhood Design Volume I®, a presentation-quality portfolio filled with 150 home plans that revisit the days when community was more important than cars. Some of the nation's most prominent architects and designers are represented, bringing you homes that deliver classic exteriors with updated interiors! This exciting volume includes diagrams for each home's recommended lot width, plus a handy index for locating plans according to your lifestyle, lot size and building size.

HOMES LIKE THESE ARE A PHONE CALL AWAY!

timeless, well-proportioned designs   porches   modern interiors   private spaces   innovative parking solutions

PRAISE FROM THE EXPERTS:

"It's a fabulous effort, much better than anything that has been done before."
Andres Duany, Duany Plater-Zyberk, Architects and Town Planners, Miami, Fla.

"There has never been a resource like this."
James Constantine, Community Planning & Research, Inc., Princeton, New Jersey

"Update timeless styles to live for today . . . You cannot create greater value than that."
J. Carson Looney, Looney Ricks Kiss Architects, Memphis, Tenn.

You can own this plan book for only $30
Call TOLL-FREE 1-888-505-1001

source code HD28

Brought to you by **HOMESTYLES®** and **Town Planning Collaborative**

Traditional Neighborhood Design (TND) is a new town-planning effort that brings our culture back to what it once was: Integrated neighborhoods that foster a safe, vibrant sense of community.

High Luxury in One Story

- Beautiful arched windows lend a luxurious feeling to the exterior of this one-story home.
- Twelve-foot-high ceilings add volume to both the wide entry area and the central living room, which boasts a large fireplace and access to a covered porch and the patio beyond.
- Double doors separate the formal dining room from the corridor-style kitchen. Features of the kitchen include a pantry, a trash compactor, garage access and an angled eating bar with double sinks and a dishwasher. The sunny, bayed eating area is perfect for casual family meals.
- The plush master suite has amazing amenities: patio access, a walk-in closet, a skylighted, angled whirlpool tub, a separate shower, and private access to the laundry/utility room.
- Three bedrooms and a full bath are situated on the opposite side of the home.

Plan E-2302

Bedrooms: 4	Baths: 2
Living Area:	
Main floor	2,396 sq. ft.
Total Living Area:	**2,396 sq. ft.**
Standard basement	2,396 sq. ft.
Garage	484 sq. ft.
Exterior Wall Framing:	2x6

Foundation Options:
Standard basement
Crawlspace
Slab
(Typical foundation & framing conversion diagram available—see order form.)

BLUEPRINT PRICE CODE: C

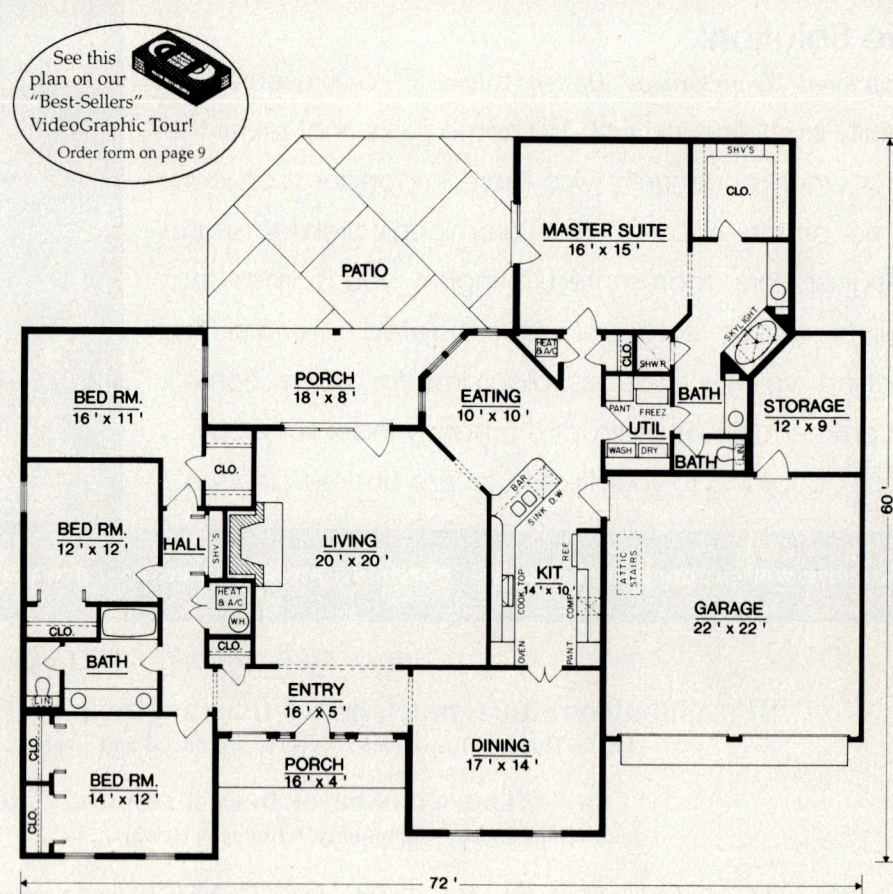

MAIN FLOOR

LANDSCAPE PLAN AVAILABLE
Call 1-888-626-2026 for more information

ORDER BLUEPRINTS ANYTIME!
CALL TOLL-FREE 1-888-626-2026

Plan E-2302

PRICES AND DETAILS ON PAGES 12-15

MORE HOME PLANS ON CD-ROM THAN ANYWHERE ELSE IN THE GALAXY
(AS FAR AS WE KNOW...)

MORE SELECTION

HomeStyles has packed more home plans than ever before into the 5005 Dream Home Plans™ CD-ROM. There's a home for every dream and every budget! This power-packed CD-ROM set makes it fun to find your dream home with easy-to-use tools for selecting bedrooms, baths, style, size and many other custom features. The latest home viewing options like vectorized floor plans and virtual reality home tours let you review your selections in detail!

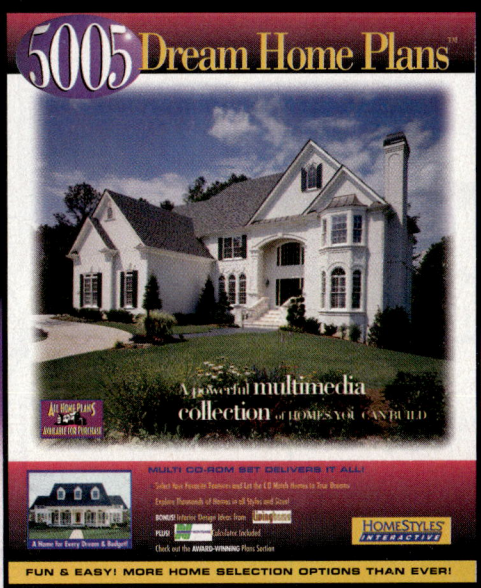

VIRTUAL REALITY
Walk yourself through the featured homes in the virtual reality library!

- Interior Design Tips From livinghome

- Handy Mortgage Calculator From NORWEST MORTGAGE

- Internet Access Offer From AT&T WorldNet™ Service
  (Including Netscape Navigator™ Software)

Call 1-888-626-2026 to order your 5005 Dream Home Plans for $39.95 plus shipping, or just $34.95 after the $5.00 mail-in rebate when you purchase the CD's at your local retailer.

HoMeStyles THE HOME PLANS PEOPLE
Product Code CDW3-O

Please send my $5.00 Rebate! I have enclosed a copy of my retail receipt.

Name _____
Address _____
City _____ State ___ ZIP ____

Mail To: HomeStyles
P.O. Box 75488
St. Paul, MN 55175-0488

SOURCE CODE HD28

Available At Your Local Software Retailer

COMPUSA THE COMPUTER SUPERSTORE

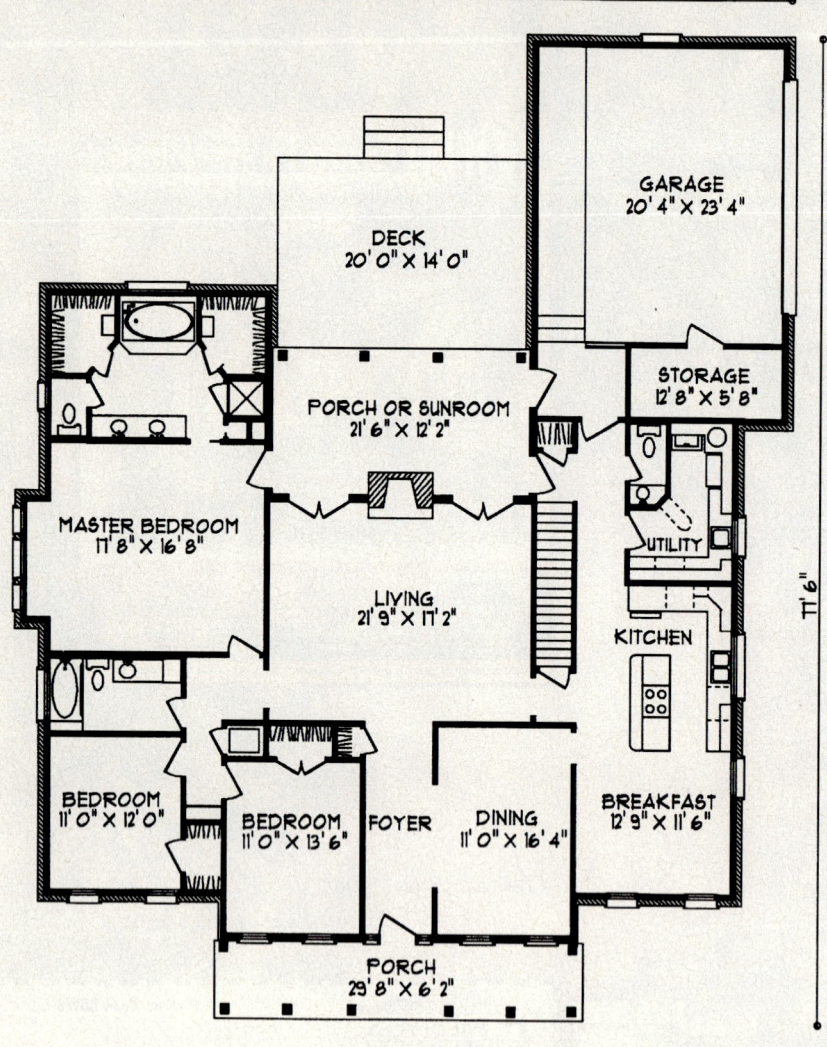

MAIN FLOOR

Wonderful Detailing

- The wonderfully detailed front porch, with its graceful arches, columns and railings, gives this home a character all its own. Dormer windows and arched transoms further accentuate the porch.
- The floor plan features a central living room with a 10-ft.-high ceiling and a fireplace framed by French doors. These doors open to a covered porch or a sun room, which in turn overlooks a sheltered deck.
- The eat-in island kitchen and the breakfast area are just off the living room, providing a spacious place for family or for guests. The nearby formal dining room has arched transom windows and a 10-ft. ceiling, as does the bedroom off the foyer. All of the remaining rooms have 9-ft. ceilings.
- The unusual master suite includes a window alcove, access to the porch and a fantastic bath with a garden tub.
- An oversized utility room, a storage area off the garage and a 1,000-sq.-ft. attic expansion space are other bonuses of this unique design.

Plan J-90019	
Bedrooms: 3	Baths: 2½
Living Area:	
Main floor	2,410 sq. ft.
Total Living Area:	**2,410 sq. ft.**
Standard basement	2,410 sq. ft.
Garage	512 sq. ft.
Storage	86 sq. ft.
Exterior Wall Framing:	2x6
Foundation Options:	
Standard basement	
Crawlspace	
Slab	
(Typical foundation & framing conversion diagram available—see order form.)	
BLUEPRINT PRICE CODE:	C

Plan J-90019

Timeless Style

- The dramatic two-story entry porch and stately pillars add a timeless style and presence to this exciting two-story.
- The interior is pleasantly updated with features designed for the '90s. Open living areas extend from the unique raised entry, which offers direct access to each. The formal spaces sit on either side, while a spacious two-story family room with a fireplace and a built-in media center is showcased ahead.
- A handy snack counter extends from the adjoining kitchen, which also features a bayed breakfast nook, a pantry and sliding glass doors to the deck.
- A quiet den or extra bedroom is tucked away near the main floor's half-bath.
- The upper-floor balcony overlooks the family room and foyer, and connects two secondary bedrooms to a large master suite. The master bedroom boasts a tray ceiling and corner windows. The master bath has an oval tub and a separate shower.
- The skylighted bonus room above the garage could be finished as a playroom, hobby room or extra bedroom.

Plan B-92016

Bedrooms: 3+	Baths: 2½
Living Area:	
Upper floor	1,000 sq. ft.
Main floor	1,416 sq. ft.
Total Living Area:	**2,416 sq. ft.**
Bonus room	259 sq. ft.
Standard basement	1,416 sq. ft.
Garage	692 sq. ft.
Exterior Wall Framing:	2x6
Foundation Options:	
Standard basement	

(All plans can be built with your choice of foundation and framing. A generic conversion diagram is available. See order form.)

BLUEPRINT PRICE CODE: C

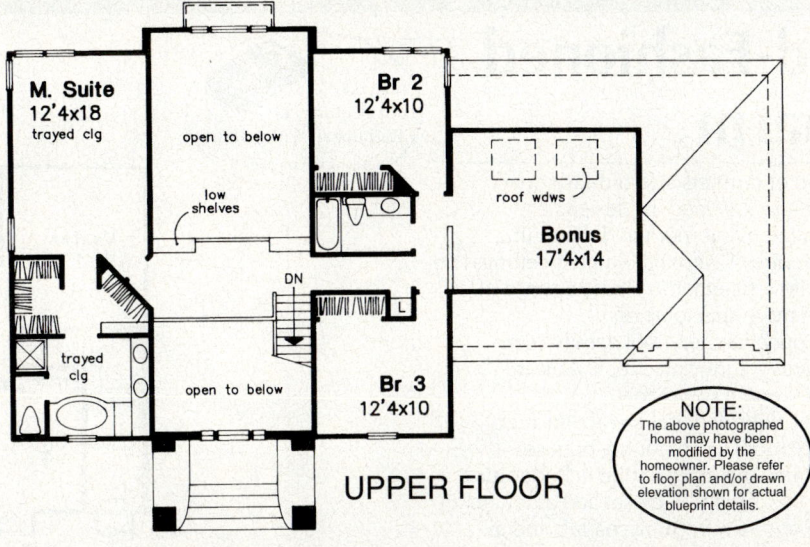

UPPER FLOOR

NOTE: The above photographed home may have been modified by the homeowner. Please refer to floor plan and/or drawn elevation shown for actual blueprint details.

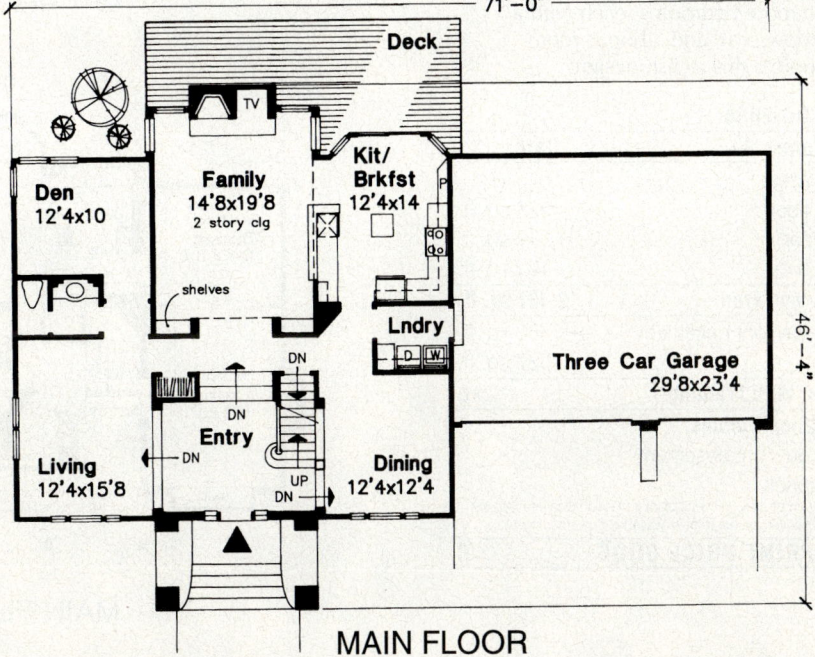

MAIN FLOOR

ORDER BLUEPRINTS ANYTIME!
CALL TOLL-FREE 1-888-626-2026

Plan B-92016

PRICES AND DETAILS ON PAGES 12-15

29

Old-Fashioned Charm

- A trio of dormers add old-fashioned charm to this modern design.
- Both the living room and the dining room offer 12-ft.-high vaulted ceilings and flow together to create a sense of even more spaciousness.
- The open kitchen/nook/family room features a sunny alcove, a walk-in pantry and a woodstove.
- A first-floor den and a walk-through utility room are other big bonuses.
- Upstairs, the master suite includes an enormous walk-in closet and a deluxe bath with a refreshing spa tub and a separate shower and water closet.
- Two more bedrooms, each with a window seat, and a bonus room complete this stylish design.

Plan CDG-2004

Bedrooms: 3+	Baths: 2½
Living Area:	
Upper floor	928 sq. ft.
Main floor	1,317 sq. ft.
Bonus area	192 sq. ft.
Total Living Area:	**2,437 sq. ft.**
Partial daylight basement	780 sq. ft.
Garage	537 sq. ft.
Exterior Wall Framing:	2x6

Foundation Options:
Partial daylight basement
Crawlspace
(All plans can be built with your choice of foundation and framing. A generic conversion diagram is available. See order form.)

BLUEPRINT PRICE CODE: C

See this plan on our "Country & Traditional" Video Tour! Order form on page 9

NOTE: The above photographed home may have been modified by the homeowner. Please refer to floor plan and/or drawn elevation shown for actual blueprint details.

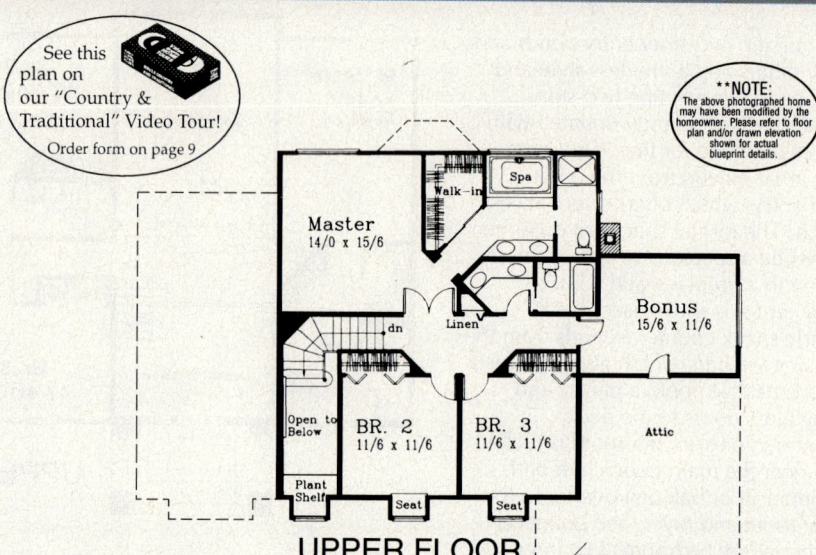

UPPER FLOOR

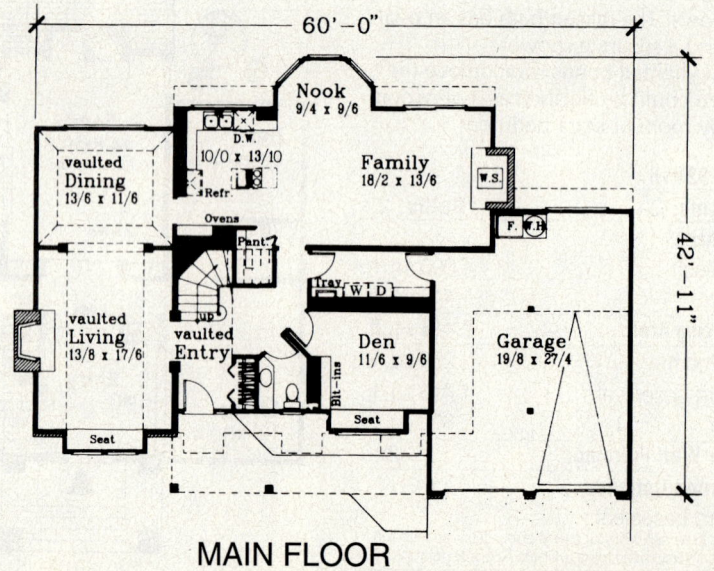

MAIN FLOOR

ORDER BLUEPRINTS ANYTIME! CALL TOLL-FREE 1-888-626-2026

Plan CDG-2004

PRICES AND DETAILS ON PAGES 12-15

Dramatic Interior Spaces

- This home's design utilizes unique shapes and angles to create a dramatic and dynamic interior.
- Skylights brighten the impressive two-story entry from high above, as it flows to the formal living areas.
- The sunken Great Room features a massive stone-hearthed fireplace with flanking windows, plus a 19-ft. vaulted ceiling. Sliding glass doors open the formal dining room to a backyard patio.
- The spacious kitchen features an oversized island, plenty of counter space and a sunny breakfast nook.
- A den or third bedroom shares a full bath with another secondary bedroom to complete the main floor.
- An incredible bayed master suite takes up the entire upper floor of the home. The skylighted master bath features a bright walk-in closet, a dual-sink vanity, a sunken tub and a separate shower.

Plans P-6580-3A & -3D

Bedrooms: 2+	Baths: 2
Living Area:	
Upper floor	705 sq. ft.
Main floor	1,738 sq. ft.
Total Living Area:	**2,443 sq. ft.**
Daylight basement	1,738 sq. ft.
Garage	512 sq. ft.
Exterior Wall Framing:	2x4
Foundation Options:	Plan #
Daylight basement	P-6580-3D
Crawlspace	P-6580-3A

(All plans can be built with your choice of foundation and framing. A generic conversion diagram is available. See order form.)

BLUEPRINT PRICE CODE: C

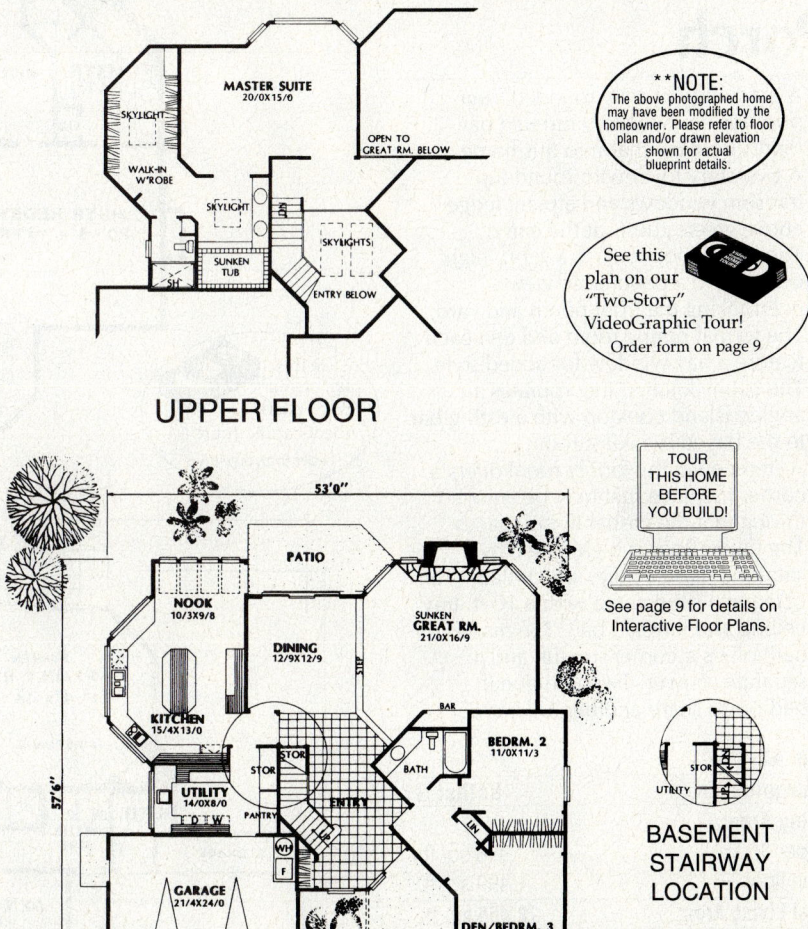

Plans P-6580-3A & -3D

Panoramic Porch

- A gracious, ornately rounded front porch and a two-story turreted bay lend Victorian charm to this home.
- A two-story foyer with round-top transom windows and a plant ledge above greets guests at the entry.
- The living room enjoys a 13-ft.-high ceiling and a panoramic view overlooking the front porch and yard.
- The formal dining room and den each feature a bay window for added style.
- The sunny kitchen incorporates an angled island cooktop with a eating bar to the bayed breakfast room.
- A step down, the family room offers a corner fireplace that may be enjoyed throughout the casual living spaces.
- The upper floor is highlighted by a stunning master suite, which flaunts an octagonal sitting area with a 10-ft. tray ceiling and turreted bay. The master bath offers a corner spa tub and a separate shower. Two additional bedrooms share another full bath.

Plan AX-90307

Bedrooms: 3+	Baths: 3
Living Area:	
Upper floor	956 sq. ft.
Main floor	1,499 sq. ft.
Total Living Area:	**2,455 sq. ft.**
Standard basement	1,499 sq. ft.
Garage	410 sq. ft.
Exterior Wall Framing:	2x4

Foundation Options:
Standard basement
Slab
(All plans can be built with your choice of foundation and framing. A generic conversion diagram is available. See order form.)

BLUEPRINT PRICE CODE: C

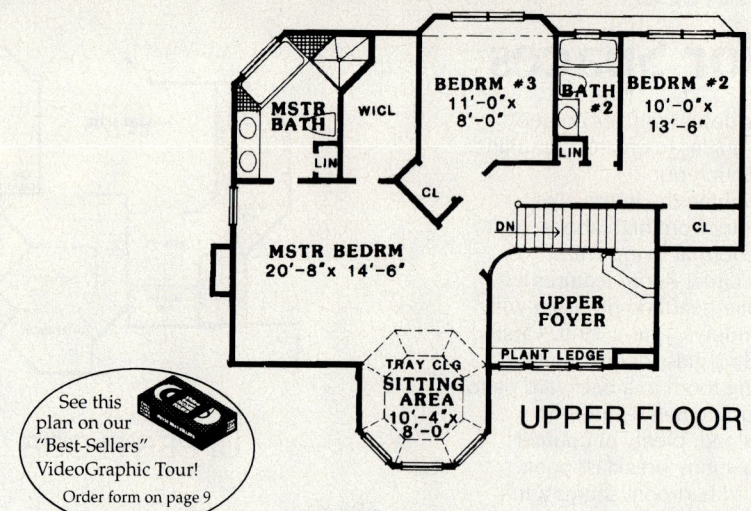

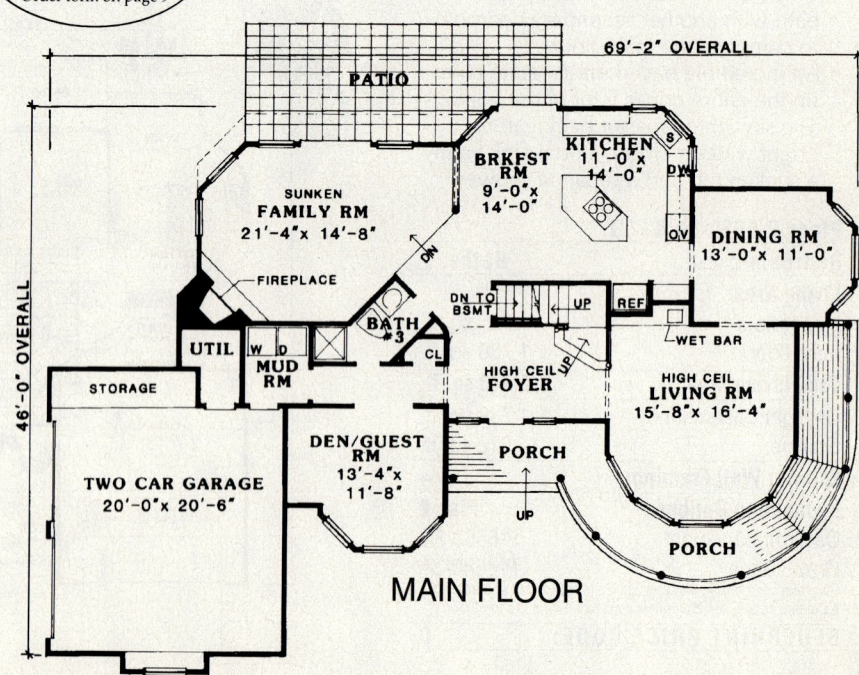

ORDER BLUEPRINTS ANYTIME!
CALL TOLL-FREE 1-888-626-2026

Plan AX-90307

PRICES AND DETAILS ON PAGES 12-15

All-American Country Home

- Romantic, old-fashioned and spacious living areas combine to create this modern home.
- Off the entryway is the generous living room with fireplace and French doors which open onto the traditional rear porch.
- Country kitchen features an island table for informal occasions, while the adjoining family room is ideal for family gatherings.
- Practically placed, a laundry/mud room lies off the garage for immediate disposal of soiled garments.
- This plan is available with garage (H-3711-1) or without garage (H-3711-2) and with or without basement.

NOTE: The above photographed home may have been modified by the homeowner. Please refer to floor plan and/or drawn elevation shown for actual blueprint details.

PLANS H-3711-1 & H-3711-1A (WITH GARAGE)

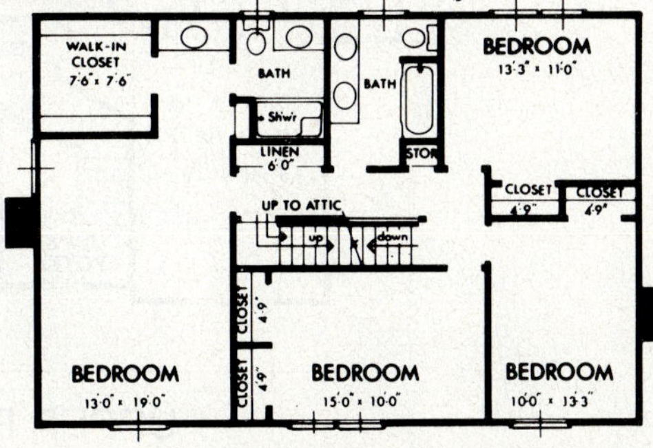

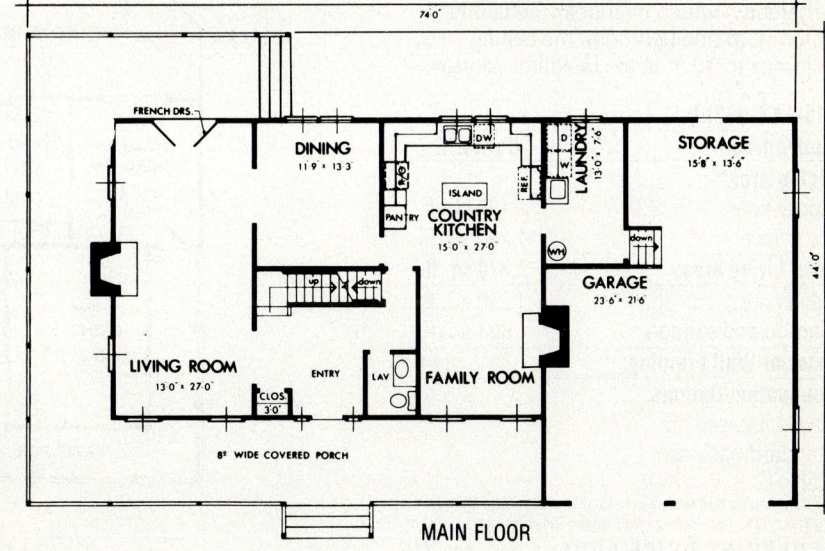

Plans H-3711-1/1A & -2/2A	
Bedrooms: 4	**Baths:** 2½

Space:
Upper floor: 1,176 sq. ft.
Main floor: 1,288 sq. ft.
Total living area: 2,464 sq. ft.
Basement: approx. 1,176 sq. ft.
Garage: 505 sq. ft.

Exterior Wall Framing: 2x6

Foundation options:
Standard basement (Plans H-3711-1 & -2).
Crawlspace (Plans H-3711-1A & -2A).
(Foundation & framing conversion diagram available — see order form.)

Blueprint Price Code: C

See this plan on our "Best-Sellers" VideoGraphic Tour! Order form on page 9

LANDSCAPE PLAN AVAILABLE
Call 1-888-626-2026 for more information

ORDER BLUEPRINTS ANYTIME! CALL TOLL-FREE 1-888-626-2026

Plans H-3711-1/1A & -2/2A

PRICES AND DETAILS ON PAGES 12-15

Large-Scale Living

- Eye-catching windows and an appealing wraparound porch highlight the exterior of this outstanding home.
- Inside, high ceilings and large-scale living spaces prevail, beginning with the foyer, which has an 18-ft. ceiling.
- The spacious living room flows into the formal dining room, which opens to the porch and to an optional rear deck.
- The island kitchen extends to a bright breakfast room with deck access. The family room offers an 18-ft. vaulted ceiling and a corner fireplace.
- Unless otherwise noted, every main-floor room boasts a 9-ft. ceiling.
- Upstairs, the lushs master bedroom boasts an 11-ft. vaulted ceiling and two walk-in closets. The skylighted master bath features a spa tub, a separate shower and a dual-sink vanity.
- Three more bedrooms are reached by a balcony, which overlooks the family room. In one bedroom, the ceiling jumps to 10 ft. at the beautiful window.

Plan AX-93309

Bedrooms: 4	Baths: 2½
Living Area:	
Upper floor	1,180 sq. ft.
Main floor	1,290 sq. ft.
Total Living Area:	**2,470 sq. ft.**
Basement	1,290 sq. ft.
Garage and storage	421 sq. ft.
Exterior Wall Framing:	2x4
Foundation Options:	
Daylight basement	
Standard basement	
Slab	
(All plans can be built with your choice of foundation and framing. A generic conversion diagram is available. See order form.)	
BLUEPRINT PRICE CODE:	**C**

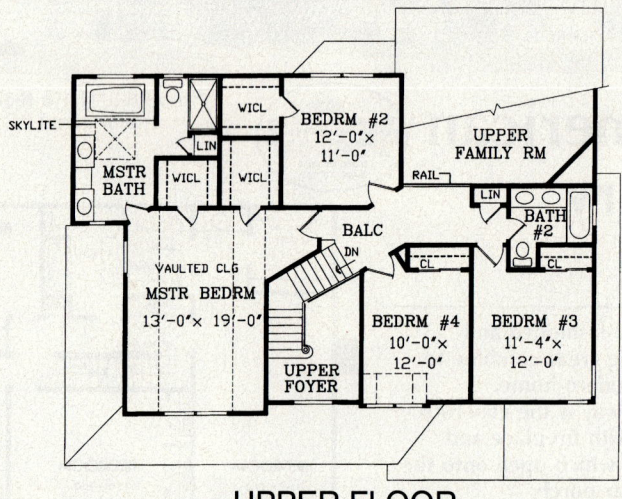

UPPER FLOOR

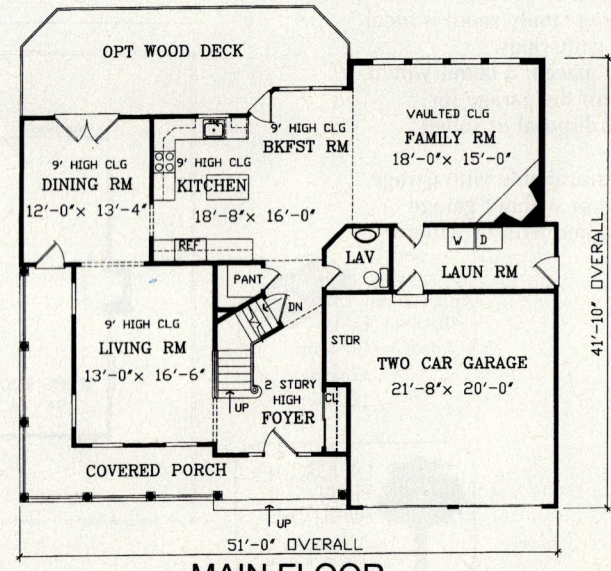

MAIN FLOOR

ORDER BLUEPRINTS ANYTIME!
CALL TOLL-FREE 1-888-626-2026

Plan AX-93309

PRICES AND DETAILS ON PAGES 12-15

REAR VIEW

Fantastic Facade, Stunning Spaces

- Matching dormers and a generous covered front porch give this home its fantastic facade. Inside, the open living spaces are just as stunning.
- A two-story foyer bisects the formal living areas. The living room offers three bright windows, an inviting fireplace and sliding French doors to the Great Room. The formal dining room overlooks the front porch and has easy access to the kitchen.
- The Great Room is truly grand, featuring a fireplace and a TV center flanked by French doors that lead to a large deck.
- A circular dinette connects the Great Room to the kitchen, which is handy to a mudroom and a powder room.
- The main-floor master suite boasts a 14-ft. cathedral ceiling, a walk-in closet and a private bath with a whirlpool tub.
- Upstairs, four large bedrooms share another whirlpool bath. One bedroom offers a 12-ft. sloped ceiling.

Plan AHP-9397

Bedrooms: 5	Baths: 2½
Living Area:	
Upper floor	928 sq. ft.
Main floor	1,545 sq. ft.
Total Living Area:	**2,473 sq. ft.**
Standard basement	1,545 sq. ft.
Garage and storage	432 sq. ft.
Exterior Wall Framing:	2x4 or 2x6
Foundation Options:	
Standard basement	
Crawlspace	
Slab	
(All plans can be built with your choice of foundation and framing. A generic conversion diagram is available. See order form.)	
BLUEPRINT PRICE CODE:	**C**

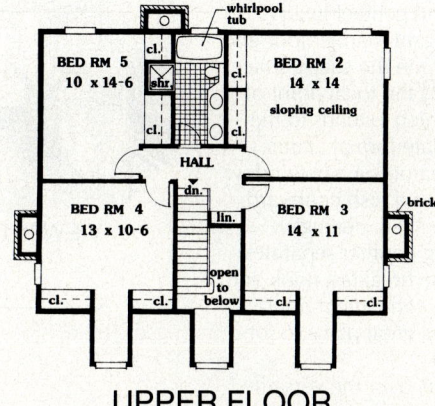
UPPER FLOOR

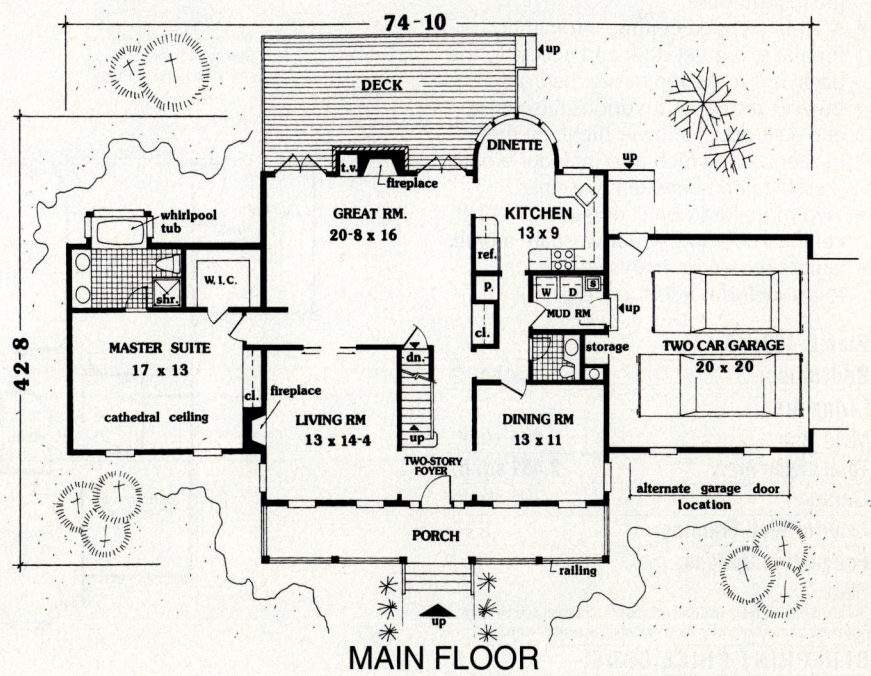
MAIN FLOOR

ORDER BLUEPRINTS ANYTIME!
CALL TOLL-FREE 1-888-626-2026

Plan AHP-9397

PRICES AND DETAILS
ON PAGES 12-15

35

Genteel Luxury

- This extraordinary home offers countless details and genteel luxury.
- In the foyer, an elegant marble floor and an 11-ft. ceiling define the sunny space.
- A fireplace serves as the focal point of the living room, which extends to the dining room to isolate formal affairs. The dining room features a bay window and a French door to a lush courtyard. Both rooms feature 11-ft. ceilings.
- A columned serving counter separates the kitchen from the breakfast nook and the family room. A convenient built-in desk to the right is a great place to jot down a grocery list.
- A 14-ft. ceiling soars over the versatile family room, where a corner fireplace and a French door to the backyard are great additions.
- A 10-ft. stepped ceiling, a romantic fireplace, a quiet desk and access to the backyard make the master bedroom an inviting retreat. A luxurious raised tub and a sit-down shower highlight the master bath, which also includes a neat dressing table between two sinks.
- Two more bedrooms, one with an 11-ft. ceiling and a bay window, share a bath.
- Unless otherwise mentioned, each room includes a 9-ft. ceiling.

Plan L-483-HB	
Bedrooms: 3	Baths: 2
Living Area:	
Main floor	2,481 sq. ft.
Total Living Area:	**2,481 sq. ft.**
Garage	706 sq. ft.
Exterior Wall Framing:	2x4
Foundation Options:	
Slab	
(All plans can be built with your choice of foundation and framing. A generic conversion diagram is available. See order form.)	
BLUEPRINT PRICE CODE:	**C**

VIEW INTO KITCHEN

REAR VIEW

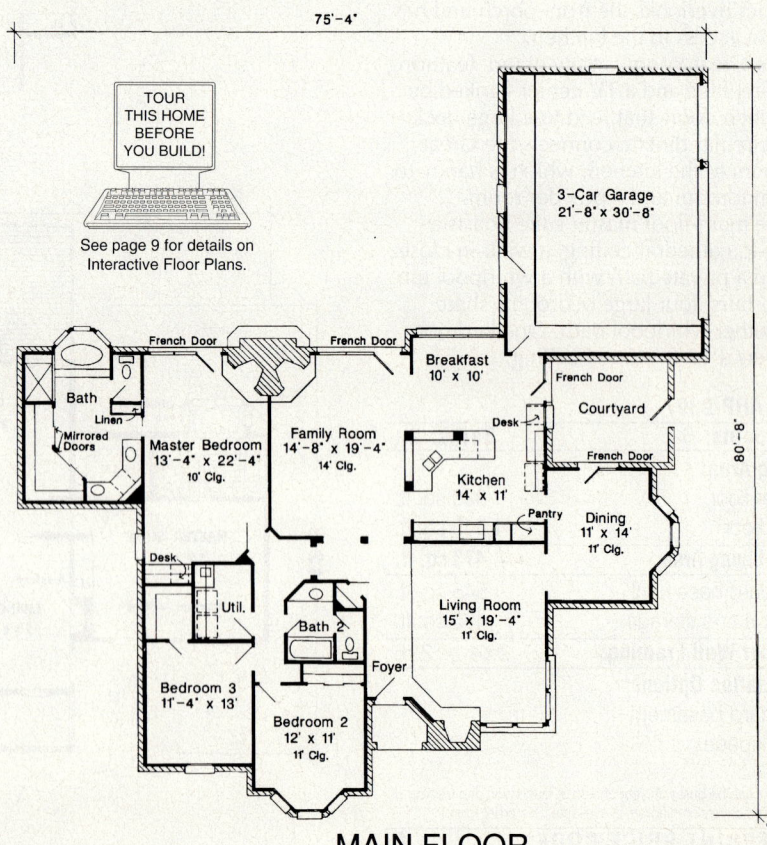

MAIN FLOOR

36   **ORDER BLUEPRINTS ANYTIME!** CALL TOLL-FREE 1-888-626-2026   Plan L-483-HB   **PRICES AND DETAILS ON PAGES 12-15**

Full of Surprises

- While dignified and reserved on the outside, this plan presents intriguing angles, vaulted ceilings and surprising spaces throughout the interior.
- The elegant, vaulted living room flows from the expansive foyer and includes a striking fireplace and a beautiful bay.
- The spacious island kitchen offers wide corner windows above the sink and easy service to both the vaulted dining room and the skylighted nook.
- The adjoining vaulted family room features a warm corner woodstove and sliding doors to the backyard patio.
- The superb master suite includes a vaulted sleeping area and an exquisite private bath with a skylighted dressing area, a large walk-in closet, a step-up spa tub and a separate shower.
- Three secondary bedrooms are located near another full bath and a large laundry room with garage access.

Plans P-7711-3A & -3D

Bedrooms: 4	Baths: 2
Living Area:	
Main floor (crawlspace version)	2,510 sq. ft.
Main floor (basement version)	2,580 sq. ft.
Total Living Area:	**2,510/2,580 sq. ft.**
Daylight basement	2,635 sq. ft.
Garage	806 sq. ft.
Exterior Wall Framing:	2x6
Foundation Options:	**Plan #**
Daylight basement	P-7711-3D
Crawlspace	P-7711-3A

(All plans can be built with your choice of foundation and framing. A generic conversion diagram is available. See order form.)

BLUEPRINT PRICE CODE: D

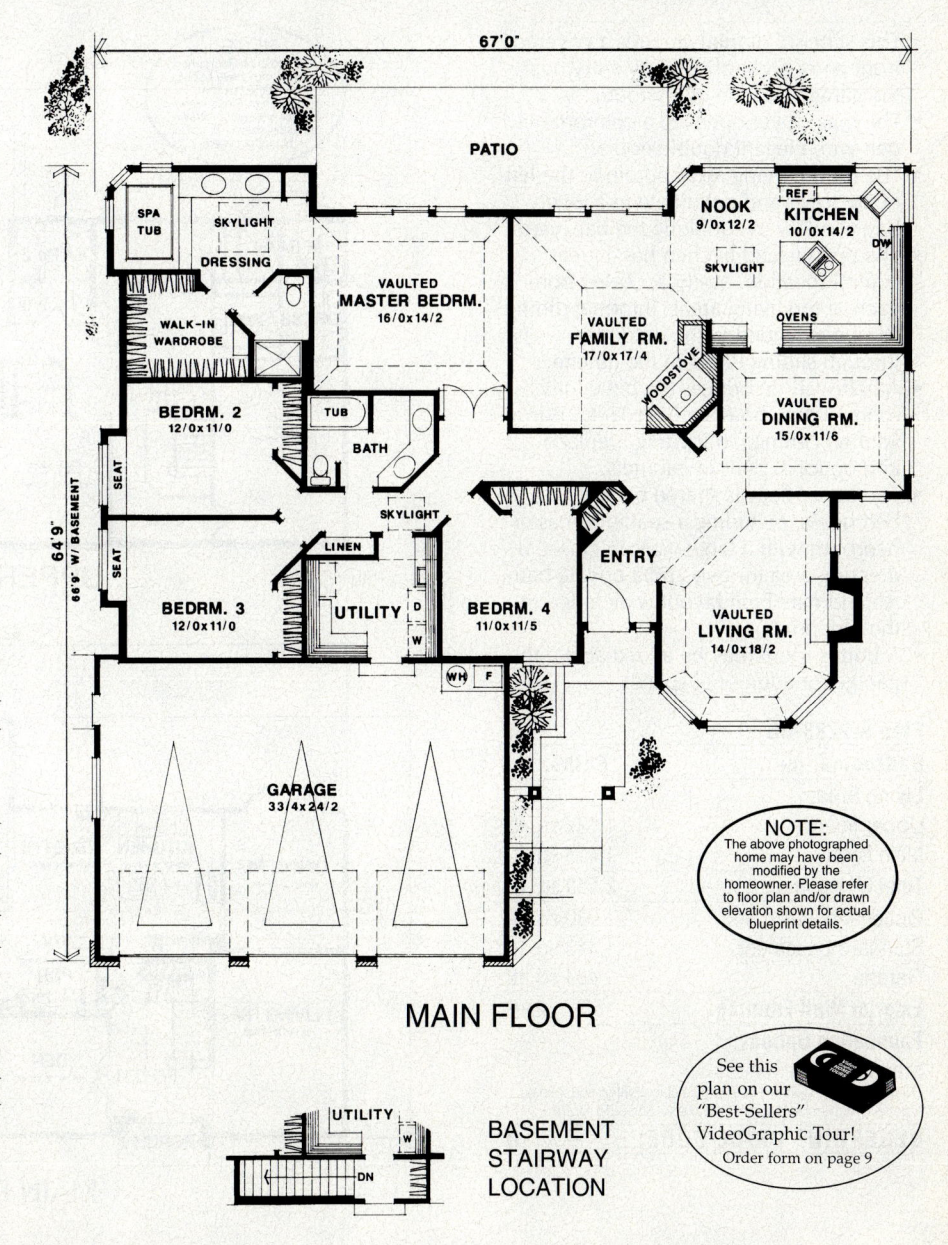

MAIN FLOOR

BASEMENT STAIRWAY LOCATION

NOTE: The above photographed home may have been modified by the homeowner. Please refer to floor plan and/or drawn elevation shown for actual blueprint details.

See this plan on our "Best-Sellers" VideoGraphic Tour! Order form on page 9

ORDER BLUEPRINTS ANYTIME!
CALL TOLL-FREE 1-888-626-2026

Plans P-7711-3A & -3D

PRICES AND DETAILS ON PAGES 12-15

37

Stately Colonial

- This stately Colonial features a covered front entry and a secondary entry near the garage and the utility room.
- The main foyer opens to a comfortable den with elegant double doors.
- The formal living areas adjoin to the left of the foyer and culminate in a lovely bay window overlooking the backyard.
- The open island kitchen has a great central location, easily accessed from each of the living areas. Informal dining can be extended to the outdoors through sliding doors in the dinette.
- A half-wall introduces the big family room, which boasts a high 16-ft., 9-in. vaulted ceiling, an inviting fireplace and optional built-in cabinets.
- The upper floor is shared by four bedrooms, including a spacious master bedroom with a large walk-in closet, a dressing area for two and a private bath. An alternate bath layout is included in the blueprints.
- A bonus room may be added above the garage for additional space.

Plan A-2283-DS

Bedrooms: 4+	Baths: 2½
Living Area:	
Upper floor	1,137 sq. ft.
Main floor	1,413 sq. ft.
Total Living Area:	**2,550 sq. ft.**
Optional bonus room	280 sq. ft.
Standard basement	1,413 sq. ft.
Garage	484 sq. ft.
Exterior Wall Framing:	2x6
Foundation Options:	
Standard basement	
(All plans can be built with your choice of foundation and framing. A generic conversion diagram is available. See order form.)	
BLUEPRINT PRICE CODE:	**D**

NOTE: The above photographed home may have been modified by the homeowner. Please refer to floor plan and/or drawn elevation shown for actual blueprint details.

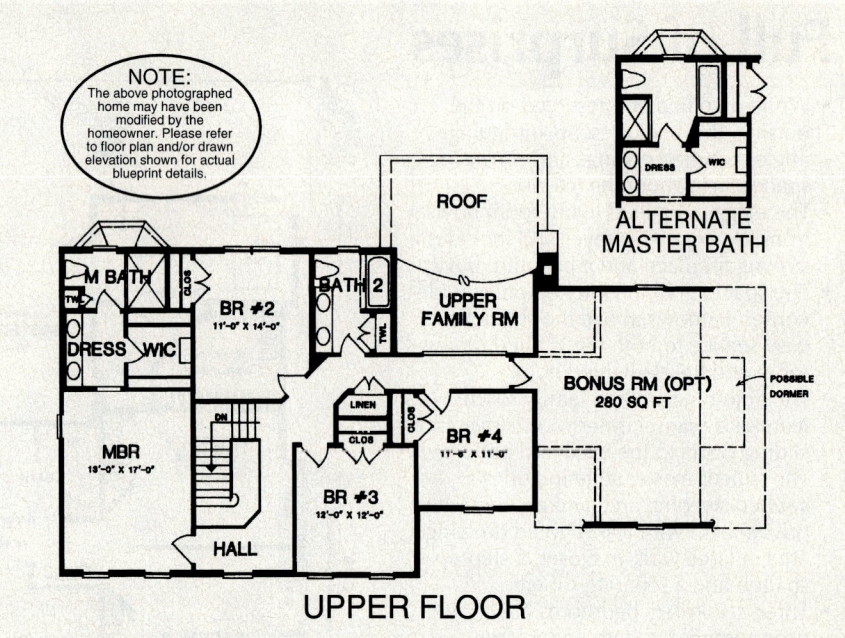

UPPER FLOOR

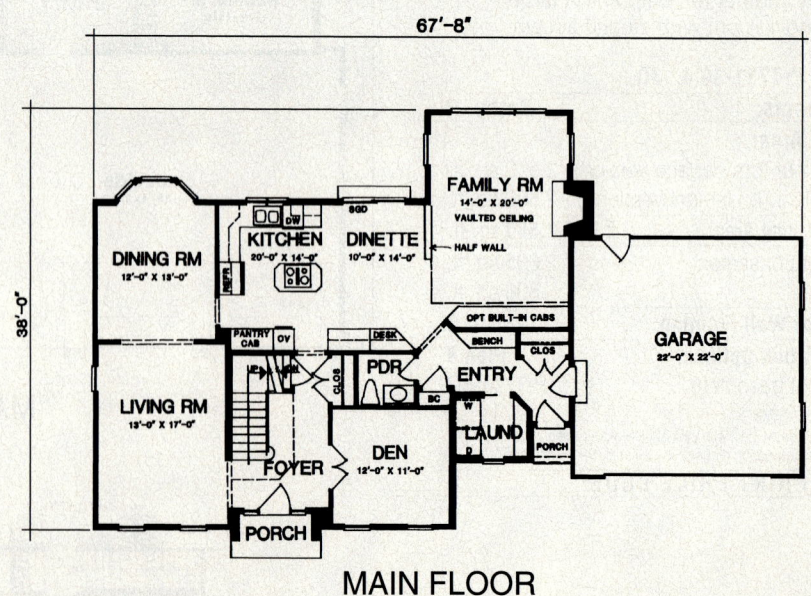

ALTERNATE MASTER BATH

MAIN FLOOR

ORDER BLUEPRINTS ANYTIME! CALL TOLL-FREE 1-888-626-2026

Plan A-2283-DS

PRICES AND DETAILS ON PAGES 12-15

38

Dynamic Design

- Angled walls, vaulted ceilings and lots of glass set the tempo for this dynamic home.
- The covered front entry opens to a raised foyer and a beautiful staircase with a bayed landing.
- One step down, a spectacular see-through fireplace with a raised hearth and built-in wood storage is visible from both the bayed dining room and the stunning Great Room.
- The Great Room also showcases an 18-ft.-high vaulted ceiling, wraparound windows and access to a deck or patio.
- The adjoining nook has a door to the deck and is served by the kitchen's snack bar. The kitchen is enhanced by a 9-ft. ceiling, corner windows and a pass-through to the dining room.
- Upstairs, the master suite offers a 10-ft.-high coved ceiling, a splendid bath, a large walk-in closet and a private deck.

Plan S-41587

Bedrooms: 3+	Baths: 3

Living Area:

Upper floor	1,001 sq. ft.
Main floor	1,550 sq. ft.
Total Living Area:	**2,551 sq. ft.**
Basement	1,550 sq. ft.
Garage (three-car)	773 sq. ft.
Exterior Wall Framing:	2x6

Foundation Options:
Daylight basement
Standard basement
Crawlspace
Slab
(All plans can be built with your choice of foundation and framing. A generic conversion diagram is available. See order form.)

BLUEPRINT PRICE CODE: D

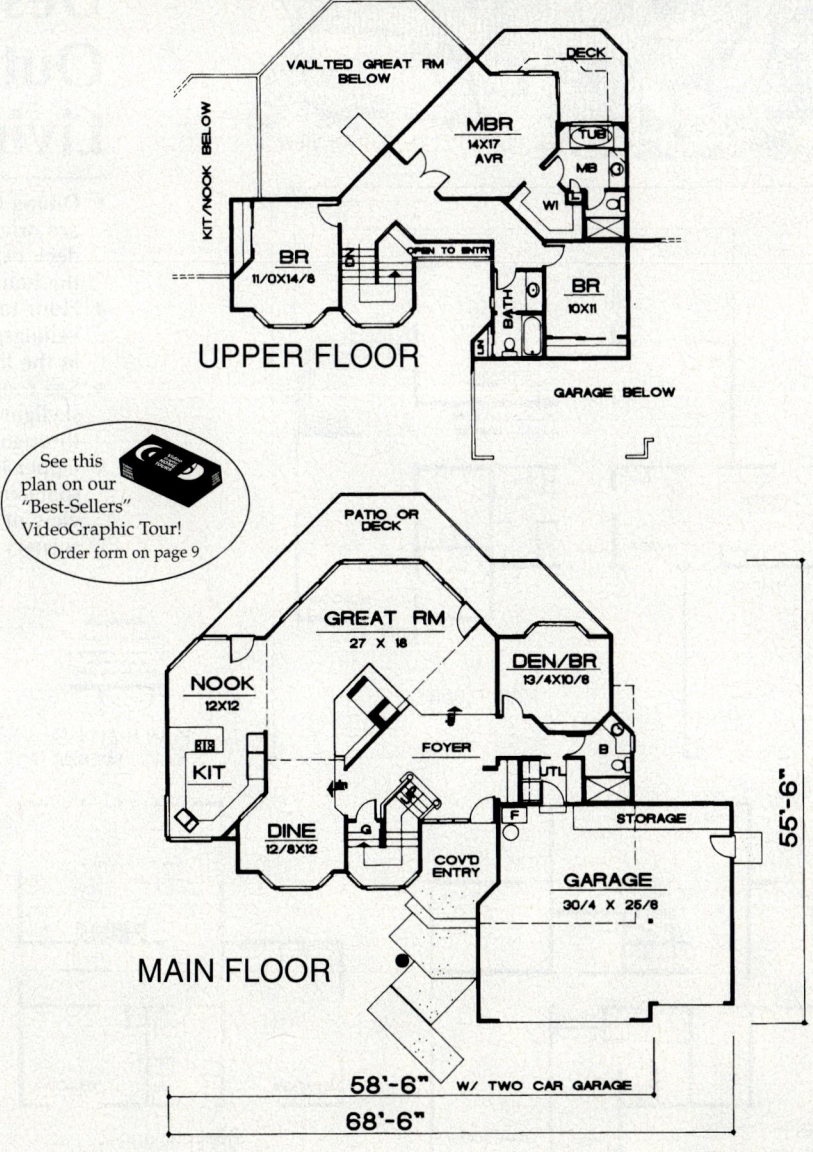

See this plan on our "Best-Sellers" VideoGraphic Tour! Order form on page 9

ORDER BLUEPRINTS ANYTIME!
CALL TOLL-FREE 1-888-626-2026

Plan S-41587

PRICES AND DETAILS ON PAGES 12-15

Designed for Outdoor Living

See this plan on our "Two-Story" VideoGraphic Tour! Order form on page 9

- Dining room, living room, and spa are oriented toward the full-width deck extending across the rear of the home.
- Floor-to-ceiling windows, vaulted ceilings, and a fireplace are featured in the living room.
- Spa room has tile floor, operable skylights, and private access through connecting master suite.
- Upper level offers two bedrooms, spacious bathroom, and a balcony view of the living room and scenery beyond.

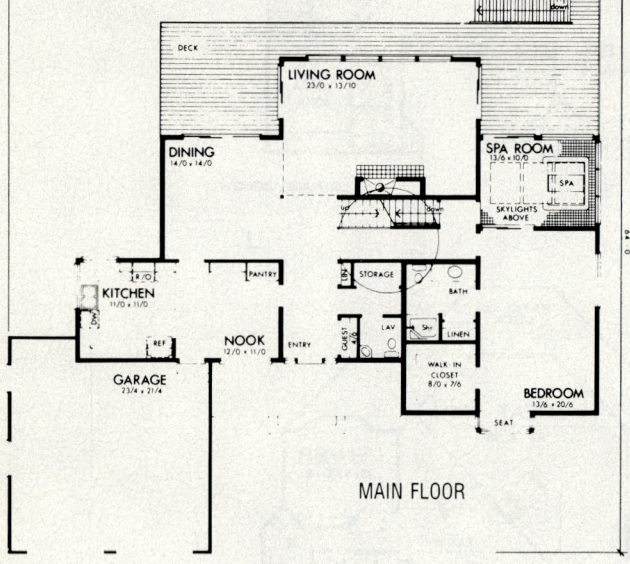

PLAN H-2114-1B REAR VIEW

MAIN FLOOR

PLAN H-2114-1A WITHOUT BASEMENT

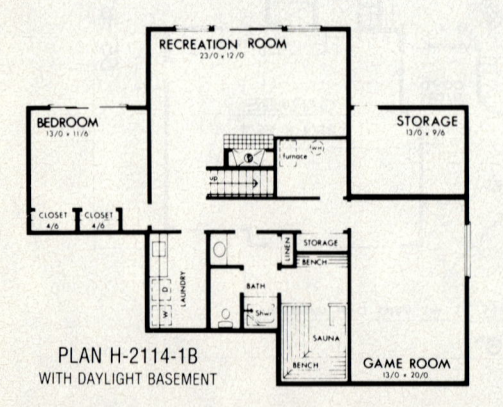

PLAN H-2114-1B WITH DAYLIGHT BASEMENT

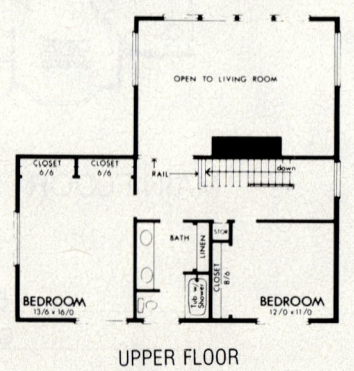

UPPER FLOOR

Plans H-2114-1A & -1B

Bedrooms: 3-4	Baths: 2½-3½

Space:
Upper floor:	732 sq. ft.
Main floor:	1,682 sq. ft.
Spa room:	147 sq. ft.
Total living area:	**2,561 sq. ft.**
Basement:	approx. 1,386 sq. ft.
Garage:	547 sq. ft.

Exterior Wall Framing: 2x6

Foundation options:
Daylight basement (Plan H-2114-1B).
Crawlspace (Plan H-2114-1A).
(Foundation & framing conversion diagram available — see order form.)

Blueprint Price Code:
Without basement: D
With basement: F

ORDER BLUEPRINTS ANYTIME! CALL TOLL-FREE 1-888-626-2026

Plans H-2114-1A & -1B

PRICES AND DETAILS ON PAGES 12-15

Elegant Interior

- An inviting covered porch welcomes guests into the elegant interior of this spectacular country home.
- Just past the entrance, the formal dining room boasts a stepped ceiling and a nearby server with a sink.
- The adjoining island kitchen has an eating bar that serves the breakfast room, which is enhanced by a 12-ft. cathedral ceiling and a bayed area of 8- and 9-ft.-high windows. Sliding glass doors lead to a covered side porch.
- Brightened by a row of 8-ft.-high windows and a glass door to the backyard, the spacious Great Room features a stepped ceiling, a built-in media center and a corner fireplace.
- The master bedroom has a tray ceiling and a cozy sitting area. The skylighted master bath boasts a whirlpool tub, a separate shower and a walk-in closet.
- A second main-floor bedroom, or optional study, offers private access to a compartmentalized bath. Two more bedrooms share a third bath on the upper floor. Generous storage space is also included.

Plan AX-3305-B

Bedrooms: 3+	Baths: 3
Living Area:	
Upper floor	550 sq. ft.
Main floor	2,017 sq. ft.
Total Living Area:	**2,567 sq. ft.**
Upper-floor storage	377 sq. ft.
Standard basement	2,017 sq. ft.
Garage	415 sq. ft.
Exterior Wall Framing	2x4
Foundation Options:	
Standard basement	
Crawlspace	
Slab	
(All plans can be built with your choice of foundation and framing. A generic conversion diagram is available. See order form.)	
BLUEPRINT PRICE CODE:	**D**

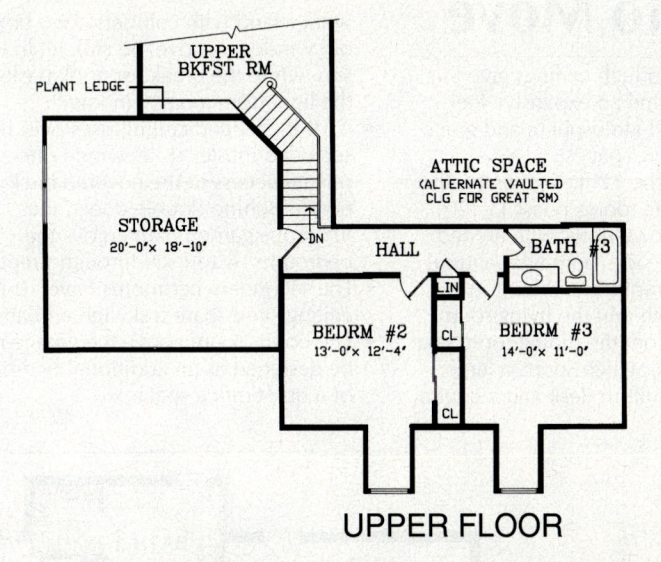

ORDER BLUEPRINTS ANYTIME!
CALL TOLL-FREE 1-888-626-2026

Plan AX-3305-B

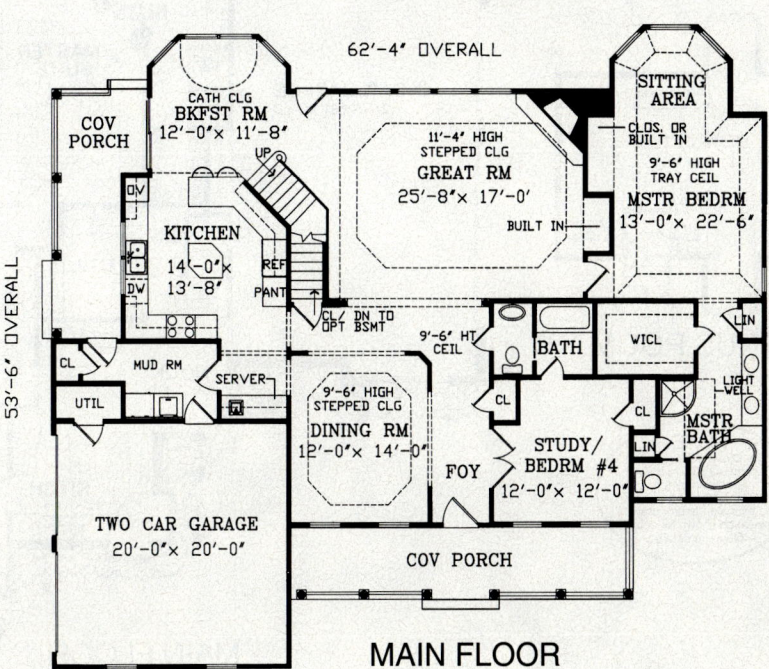

PRICES AND DETAILS ON PAGES 12-15

Room to Move

- Large rooms and high ceilings give this French-style home an expansive feel; ceiling fans lend atmosphere and grace to the main living spaces.
- Accessed from the 12-ft.-high entry, the dining and living rooms boast 11-ft. ceilings. Lovely windows with arched transoms flood each room with natural light, while a fireplace and built-in bookshelves highlight the living room.
- Double doors from the dining room lead into the kitchen, which sports a large serving bar, a built-in desk and a central work island with cabinets. Two boxed-out windows above the sink let in the sun, while the breakfast nook basks in the light from a bay window.
- A 10-ft. stepped ceiling rises over the secluded master suite, which offers private access to the covered backyard porch. Behind double doors, the luxurious garden bath enjoys the bedrooms' warm see-through fireplace.
- The secondary bedrooms have 10-ft. ceilings and share a skylighted bath.
- The bonus room above the garage may be designed as an additional bedroom or a quiet office space.

Plan RD-2240

Bedrooms: 4+	Baths: 2½
Living Area:	
Main floor	2,240 sq. ft.
Bonus room	349 sq. ft.
Total Living Area:	**2,589 sq. ft.**
Garage	737 sq. ft.
Exterior Wall Framing:	2x4

Foundation Options:
Crawlspace
Slab
(All plans can be built with your choice of foundation and framing. A generic conversion diagram is available. See order form.)

BLUEPRINT PRICE CODE: D

NOTE: The above photographed home may have been modified by the homeowner. Please refer to floor plan and/or drawn elevation shown for actual blueprint details.

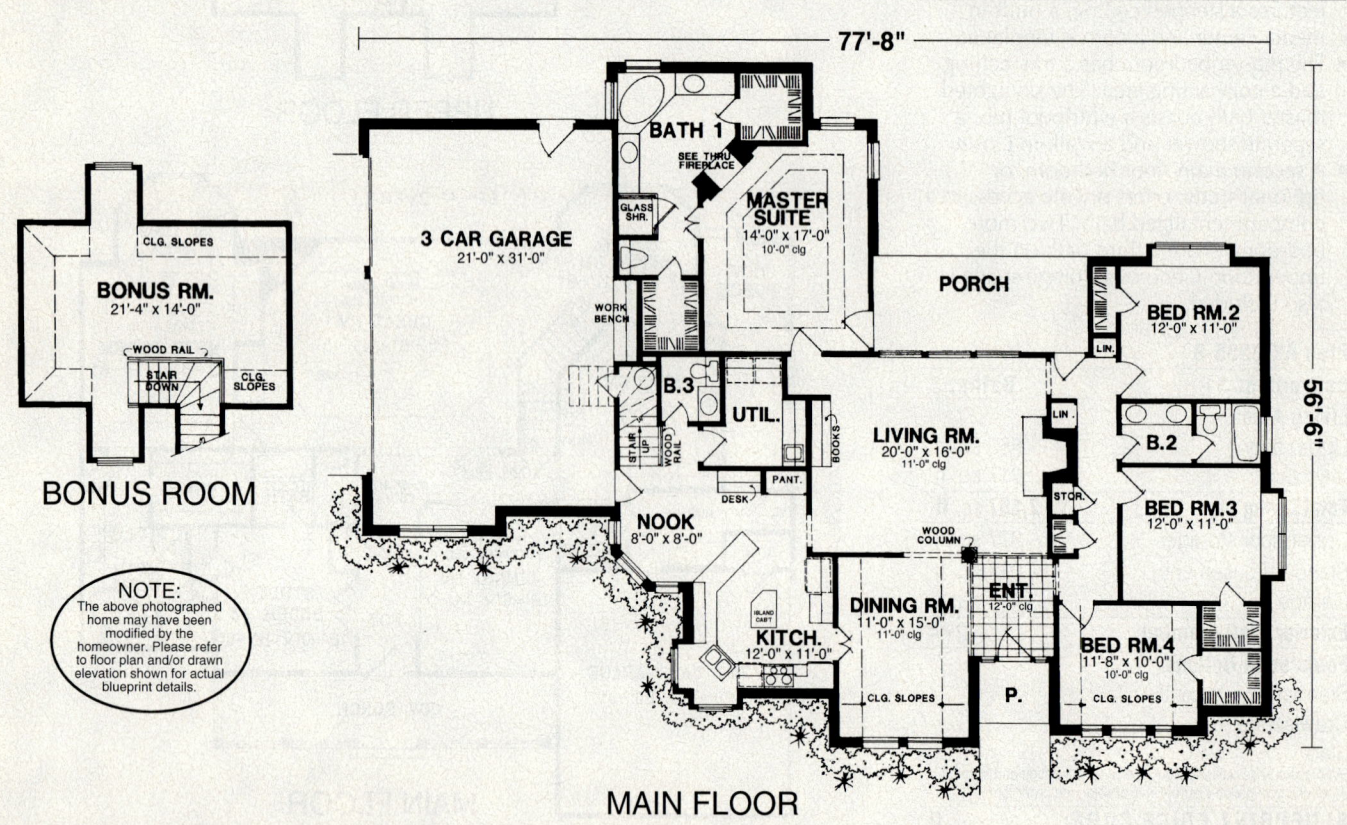

ORDER BLUEPRINTS ANYTIME!
CALL TOLL-FREE 1-888-626-2026

Plan RD-2240

PRICES AND DETAILS ON PAGES 12-15

Extraordinary Estate Living

- Extraordinary estate living is at its best in this palatial beauty.
- The double-doored entry opens to a large central living room that overlooks a covered patio with a vaulted ceiling. High 14-ft. ceilings are found in the living room, in the formal dining room and in the den or study, which may serve as a fourth bedroom.
- The gourmet chef will enjoy the spacious kitchen, which flaunts a cooktop island, a walk-in pantry and a peninsula snack counter shared with the breakfast room and family room.
- This trio of informal living spaces also shares a panorama of glass and a corner fireplace centered between TV and media niches.
- Isolated at the opposite end of the home is the spacious master suite, which offers private patio access. Dual walk-in closets define the entrance to the adjoining master bath, complete with a garden Jacuzzi, a designer shower and separate dressing areas.
- The hall bath also opens to the outdoors for use as a pool bath.

Plan HDS-99-177

Bedrooms: 3+	**Baths:** 3
Living Area:	
Main floor	2,597 sq. ft.
Total Living Area:	**2,597 sq. ft.**
Garage	785 sq. ft.
Exterior Wall Framing:	2x4

Foundation Options:
Slab
(All plans can be built with your choice of foundation and framing. A generic conversion diagram is available. See order form.)

BLUEPRINT PRICE CODE: D

NOTE: The above photographed home may have been modified by the homeowner. Please refer to floor plan and/or drawn elevation shown for actual blueprint details.

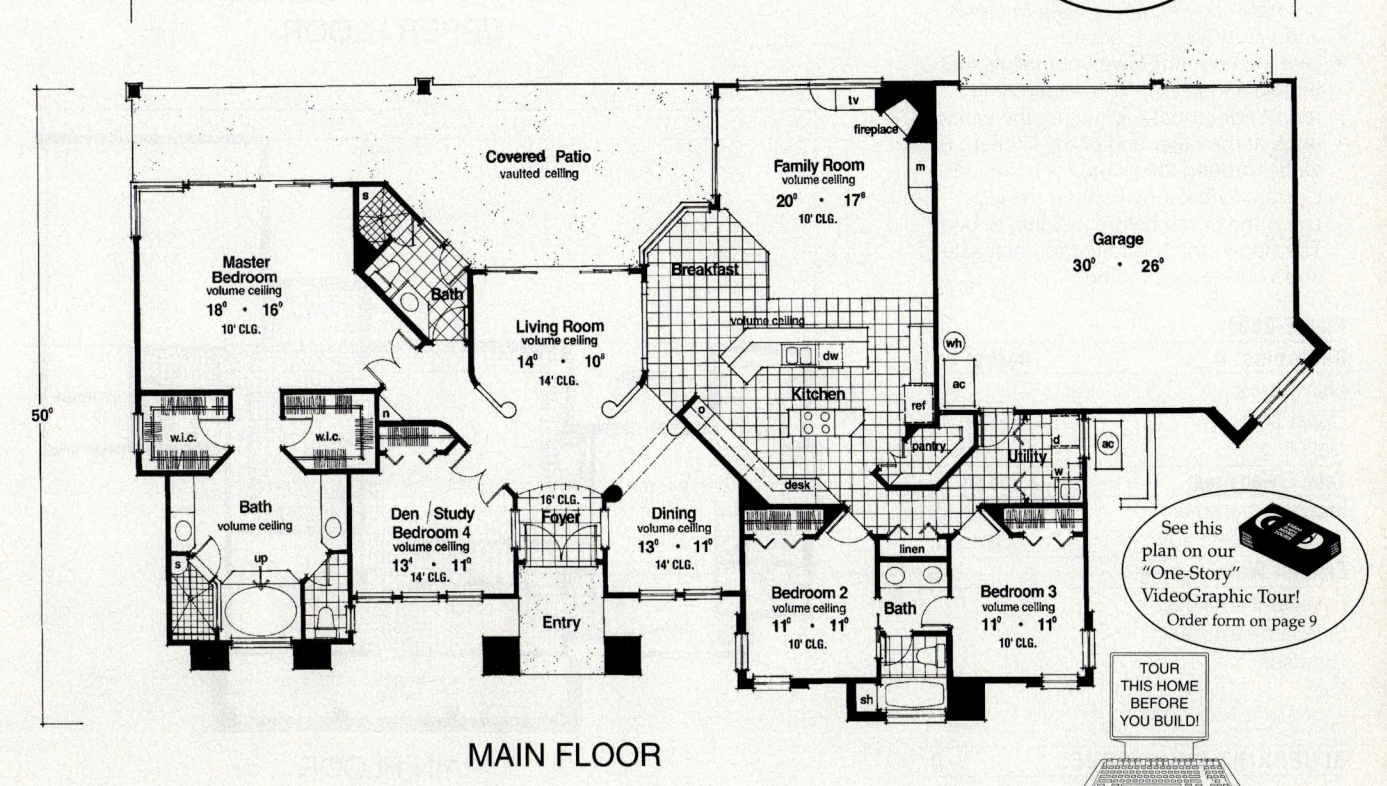

MAIN FLOOR

See this plan on our "One-Story" VideoGraphic Tour! Order form on page 9

TOUR THIS HOME BEFORE YOU BUILD!

See page 9 for details on Interactive Floor Plans.

ORDER BLUEPRINTS ANYTIME!
CALL TOLL-FREE 1-888-626-2026

Plan HDS-99-177

PRICES AND DETAILS ON PAGES 12-15

Shaded Kiss

- Columned porches give this brick and stucco home a shaded kiss of Old World charm and grace. Dormer windows and a soaring roofline complete the facade.
- The magic continues inside, with a massive living room that boasts a cozy fireplace to satisfy your passion for romance. French doors grant passage to a secluded porch.
- Privacy reigns in the isolated master suite, which offers a sitting area and a built-in desk. Double doors introduce the luxurious bath with style. There, you'll find a marvelous oval tub, a separate shower, and a walk-in closet and vanity for each of you.
- Like to entertain? Give your meals that personal touch in the formal dining room! For casual cuisine, try the eating nook at the other end of the kitchen, or gather around the island for munchies.
- Upstairs, a balcony hall lets the kids enjoy the porch before heading to bed. The upper porch is railed for their safety and your peace of mind.

Plan E-2604	
Bedrooms: 4	**Baths:** 2½
Living Area:	
Upper floor	855 sq. ft.
Main floor	1,750 sq. ft.
Total Living Area:	**2,605 sq. ft.**
Standard basement	1,655 sq. ft.
Garage and storage	569 sq. ft.
Exterior Wall Framing:	2x6
Foundation Options:	
Standard basement	
Crawlspace	
Slab	
(All plans can be built with your choice of foundation and framing. A generic conversion diagram is available. See order form.)	
BLUEPRINT PRICE CODE:	**D**

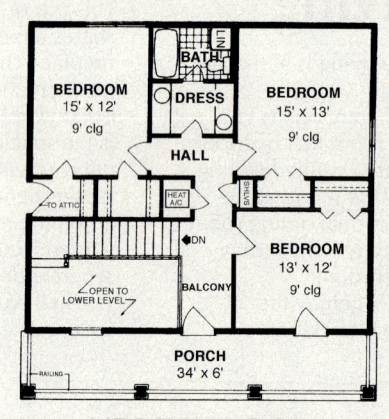

ORDER BLUEPRINTS ANYTIME!
CALL TOLL-FREE 1-888-626-2026

Plan E-2604

PRICES AND DETAILS ON PAGES 12-15

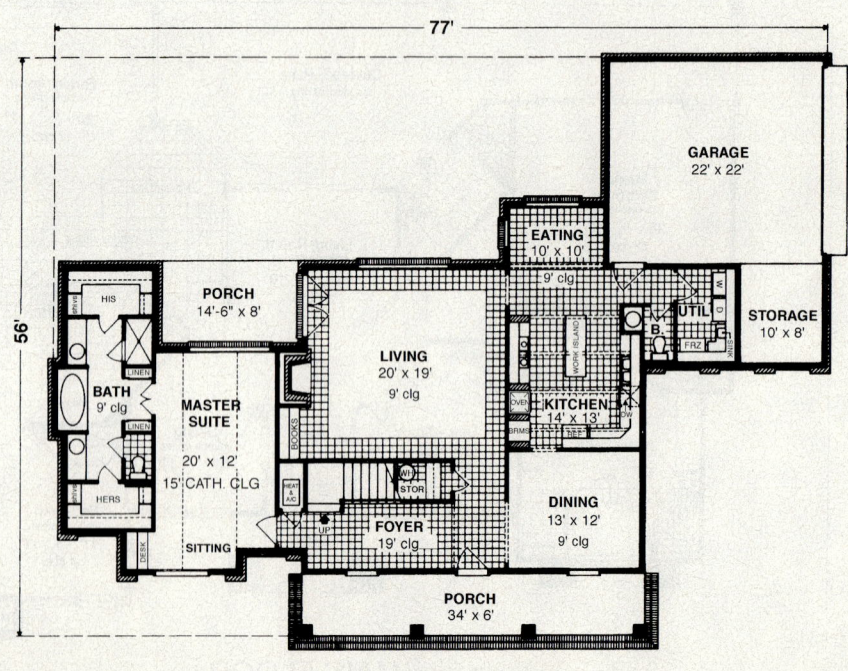

Alluring Arches

- Massive columns, high, dramatic arches and expansive glass attract passersby to this alluring one-story home.
- Inside, coffered ceilings are found in the living and dining rooms and the foyer. A bank of windows in the living room provides a great view of the covered patio, creating a bright, open effect that is carried throughout the home.
- The informal, family activity areas are oriented to the back of the home as well. Spectacular window walls in the breakfast room and family room offer tremendous views. The family room's inviting corner fireplace is positioned to be enjoyed from the breakfast area and the spacious island kitchen.
- Separated from the secondary bedrooms, the superb master suite is entered through double doors and features a sitting room and a garden bath. Another full bath is across the hall from the den, which would also make a great guest room or nursery.

Plan HDS-99-179

Bedrooms: 3+	**Baths:** 3

Living Area:

Main floor	2,660 sq. ft.
Total Living Area:	**2,660 sq. ft.**
Garage	527 sq. ft.
Exterior Wall Framing:	2x4

Foundation Options:

Slab
(All plans can be built with your choice of foundation and framing. A generic conversion diagram is available. See order form.)

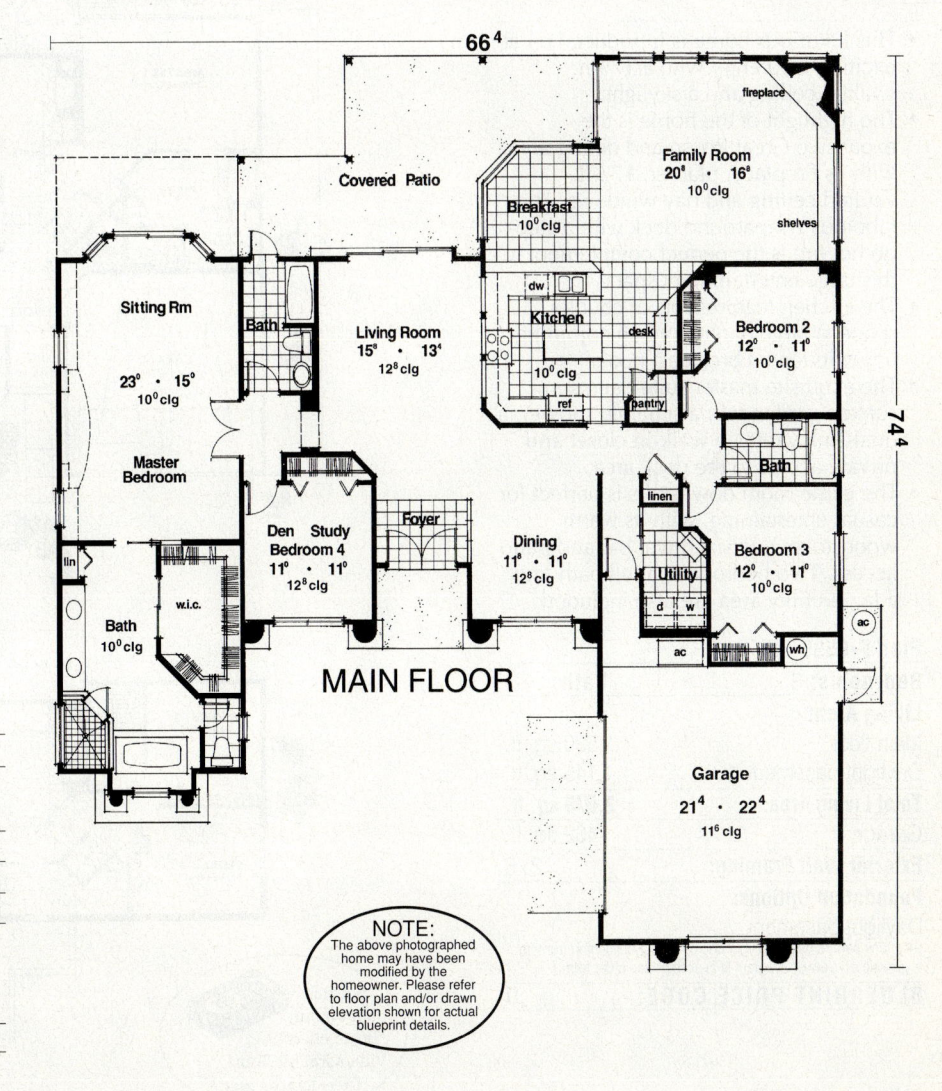

BLUEPRINT PRICE CODE: D

NOTE: The above photographed home may have been modified by the homeowner. Please refer to floor plan and/or drawn elevation shown for actual blueprint details.

ORDER BLUEPRINTS ANYTIME!
CALL TOLL-FREE 1-888-626-2026

Plan HDS-99-179

PRICES AND DETAILS ON PAGES 12-15

45

Luxurious Interior

- This luxurious home is introduced by an exciting tiled entry with a 17½-ft. vaulted ceiling and a skylight.
- The highlight of the home is the expansive Great Room and dining area, with its fireplace, planter, 17½-ft. vaulted ceiling and bay windows. The fabulous wraparound deck with a step-up hot tub is the perfect complement to this large entertainment space.
- The kitchen features lots of counter space, a large pantry and an adjoining bay-windowed breakfast nook.
- The exquisite master suite flaunts a sunken garden tub, a separate shower, a dual-sink vanity, a walk-in closet and private access to the deck area.
- The game room downstairs is perfect for casual entertaining, with its warm woodstove, oversized wet bar and patio access. Two bedrooms, a full bath and a large utility area are also included.

Plan P-6595-3D

Bedrooms: 3	Baths: 2½
Living Area:	
Main floor	1,530 sq. ft.
Daylight basement	1,145 sq. ft.
Total Living Area:	**2,675 sq. ft.**
Garage	462 sq. ft.
Exterior Wall Framing:	2x6

Foundation Options:
Daylight basement
(All plans can be built with your choice of foundation and framing. A generic conversion diagram is available. See order form.)

BLUEPRINT PRICE CODE: D

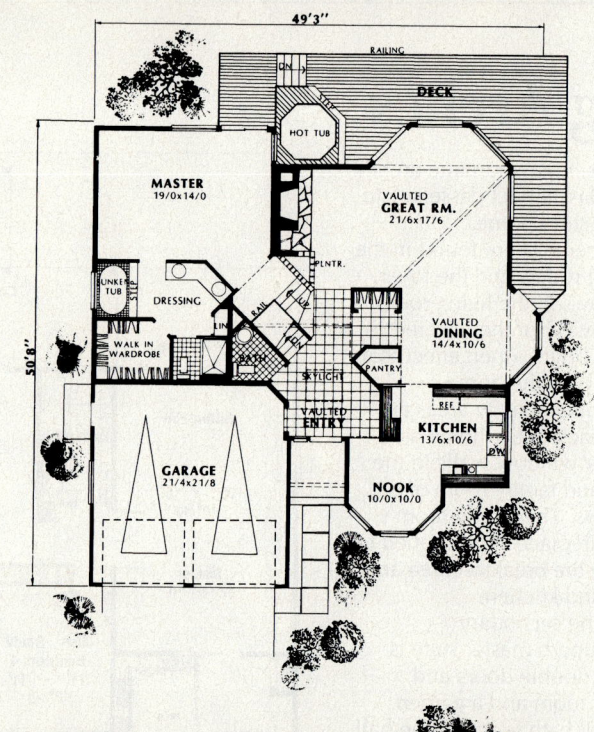

MAIN FLOOR

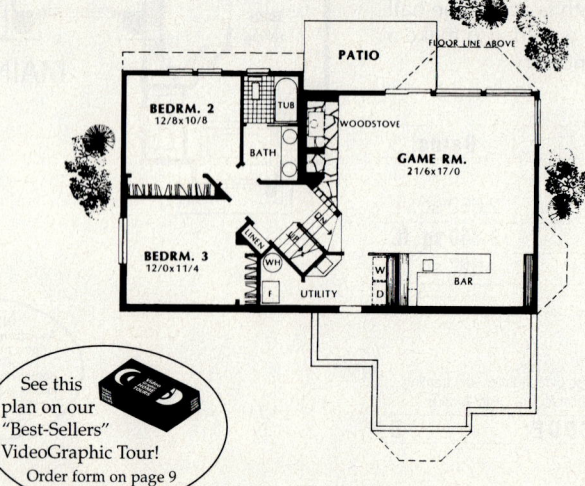

DAYLIGHT BASEMENT

See this plan on our "Best-Sellers" VideoGraphic Tour! Order form on page 9

ORDER BLUEPRINTS ANYTIME!
CALL TOLL-FREE 1-888-626-2026

Plan P-6595-3D

PRICES AND DETAILS ON PAGES 12-15

Award Winner!

- A successful combination of a traditional exterior and modern interior spaces makes this home a winner.
- A winning entry in a recent national design competition, this design has a facade that is filled with character and free of overbearing garage doors. The focus instead goes to the front entry, with decorative columns supporting a covered porch highlighted by a curved shed roof.
- A two-story foyer greets guests. Graceful arched openings and pillars separate the foyer from the formal dining room and the Great Room, which boasts a fireplace and views of a backyard patio.
- The gourmet kitchen features an island cooktop, a walk-in pantry and a snack bar to the sunny breakfast room.
- The main-floor master suite offers a private porch and a spacious personal bath with a garden tub, a separate shower and a large walk-in closet.
- Another bedroom and a full bath round out the main floor. Two more bedrooms are located upstairs, with a third full bath and a loft reading area under a dormer. A central game room features access to a sunny corner deck.

Plan BOD-26-8A	
Bedrooms: 4	**Baths:** 3
Living Area:	
Upper floor	792 sq. ft.
Main floor	1,904 sq. ft.
Total Living Area:	**2,696 sq. ft.**
Garage	528 sq. ft.
Exterior Wall Framing:	2x4

Foundation Options:
Crawlspace
Slab
(All plans can be built with your choice of foundation and framing. A generic conversion diagram is available. See order form.)

BLUEPRINT PRICE CODE: D

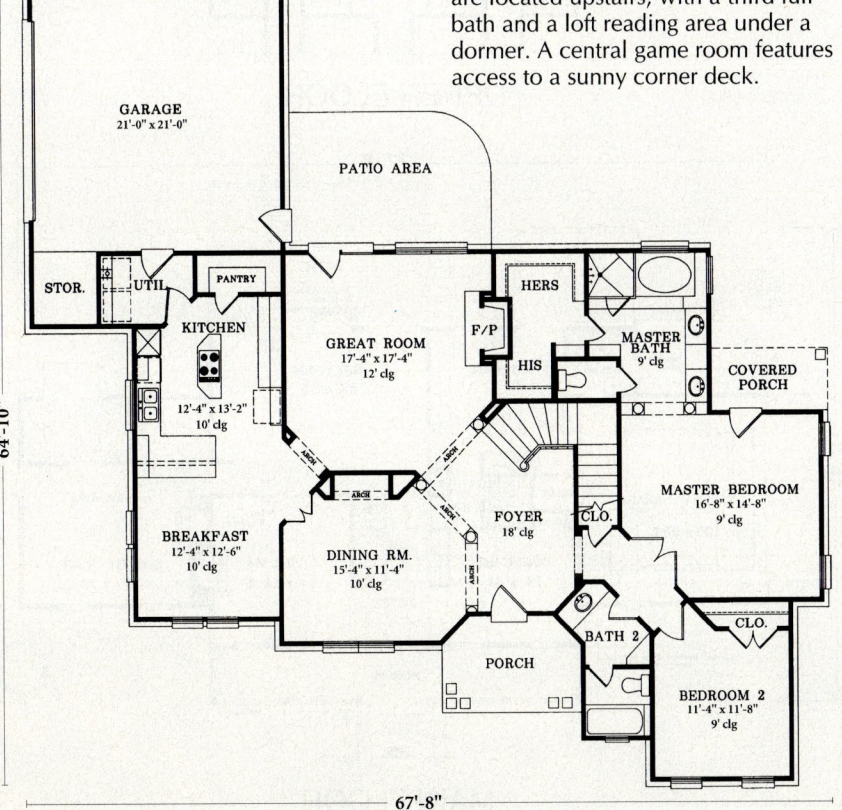

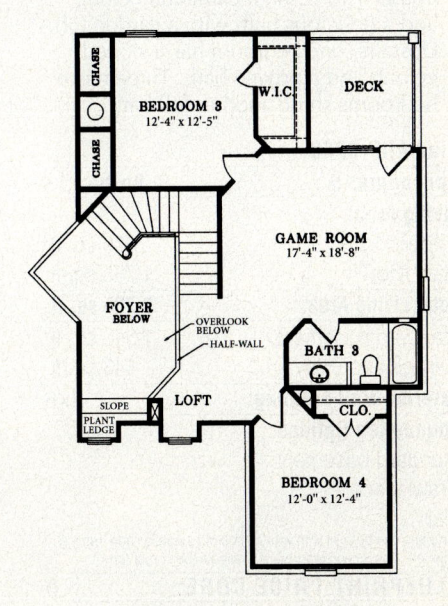

MAIN FLOOR

UPPER FLOOR

ORDER BLUEPRINTS ANYTIME!
CALL TOLL-FREE 1-888-626-2026

Plan BOD-26-8A

PRICES AND DETAILS ON PAGES 12-15

47

Innovative Floor Plan

- The wide, covered front porch, arched windows and symmetrical lines of this traditional home conceal the modern, innovative floor plan found within.
- A two-story-high foyer guides guests to the front-oriented formal areas, which have views to the front porch.
- The hotspot of the home is the Great Room, with one of the home's three fireplaces and a media wall. Flanking doors open to a large backyard deck.
- The island kitchen and glassed-in eating nook overlook the deck and access a handy mudroom. High 9-ft. ceilings add to the aura of warmth and hospitality found on the main floor of this home.
- Another of the fireplaces is offered in the master suite. This private oasis also boasts a 13-ft.-high cathedral ceiling and a delicious bath with a garden tub.
- Upstairs, one bedroom has a sloped ceiling and a private bath. Three more bedrooms share another full bath.

Plan AHP-9360

Bedrooms: 5	Baths: 3½
Living Area:	
Upper floor	970 sq. ft.
Main floor	1,735 sq. ft.
Total Living Area:	**2,705 sq. ft.**
Standard basement	1,550 sq. ft.
Garage and utility area	443 sq. ft.
Exterior Wall Framing:	2x6

Foundation Options:
Standard basement
Crawlspace
Slab
(All plans can be built with your choice of foundation and framing. A generic conversion diagram is available. See order form.)

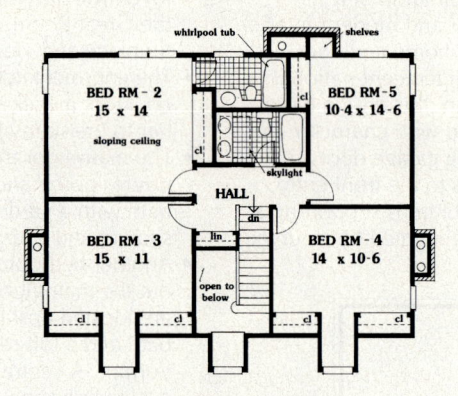

BLUEPRINT PRICE CODE: D

See this plan on our "Country & Traditional" Video Tour! Order form on page 9

UPPER FLOOR

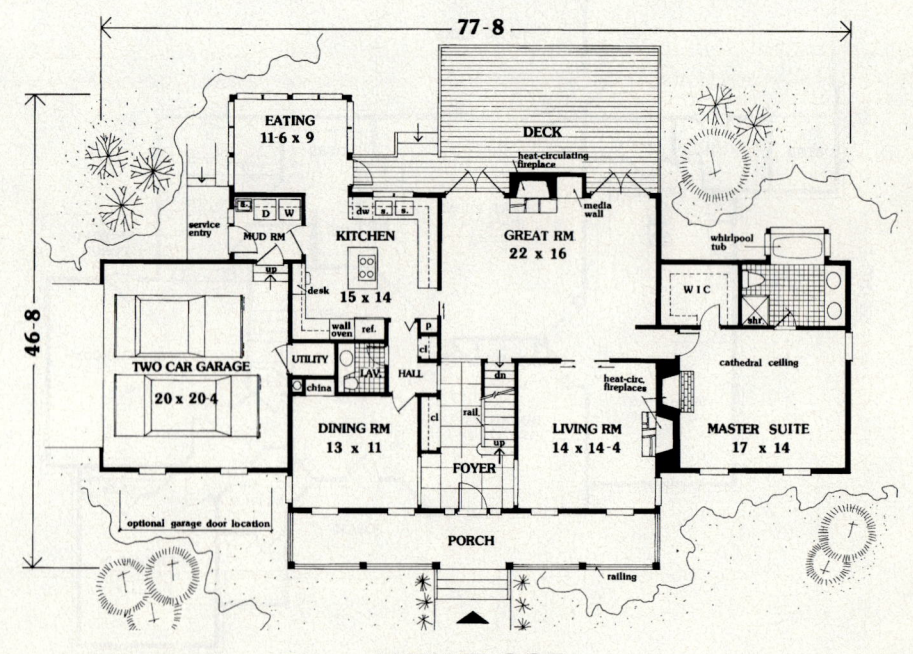

MAIN FLOOR

Plan AHP-9360

ORDER BLUEPRINTS ANYTIME!
CALL TOLL-FREE 1-888-626-2026

PRICES AND DETAILS ON PAGES 12-15

Easy-Living Atmosphere

- Clean lines and a functional, well-designed floor plan create a relaxed, easy-living atmosphere for this sprawling ranch-style home.
- An inviting front porch with attractive columns and planter boxes opens to an airy entry, which flows into the living room and the family room.
- The huge central family room features a 14-ft. vaulted, exposed-beam ceiling and a handsome fireplace with a built-in wood box. A nice desk and plenty of bookshelves give the room a distinguished feel. A French door opens to a versatile covered rear porch.
- The large gourmet kitchen is highlighted by an arched brick pass-through to the family room. Double doors open to the intimate formal dining room, which hosts a built-in china hutch. The sunny informal eating area features lovely porch views on either side.
- The isolated sleeping wing includes four bedrooms. The enormous master bedroom has a giant walk-in closet and a private bath. A compartmentalized bath with two vanities serves the remaining bedrooms.

Plan E-2700
Bedrooms: 4 **Baths:** 2½
Living Area:
Main floor 2,719 sq. ft.
Total Living Area: **2,719 sq. ft.**
Garage 533 sq. ft.
Storage 50 sq. ft.
Exterior Wall Framing: 2x6
Foundation Options:
Crawlspace
Slab
(All plans can be built with your choice of foundation and framing. A generic conversion diagram is available. See order form.)
BLUEPRINT PRICE CODE: D

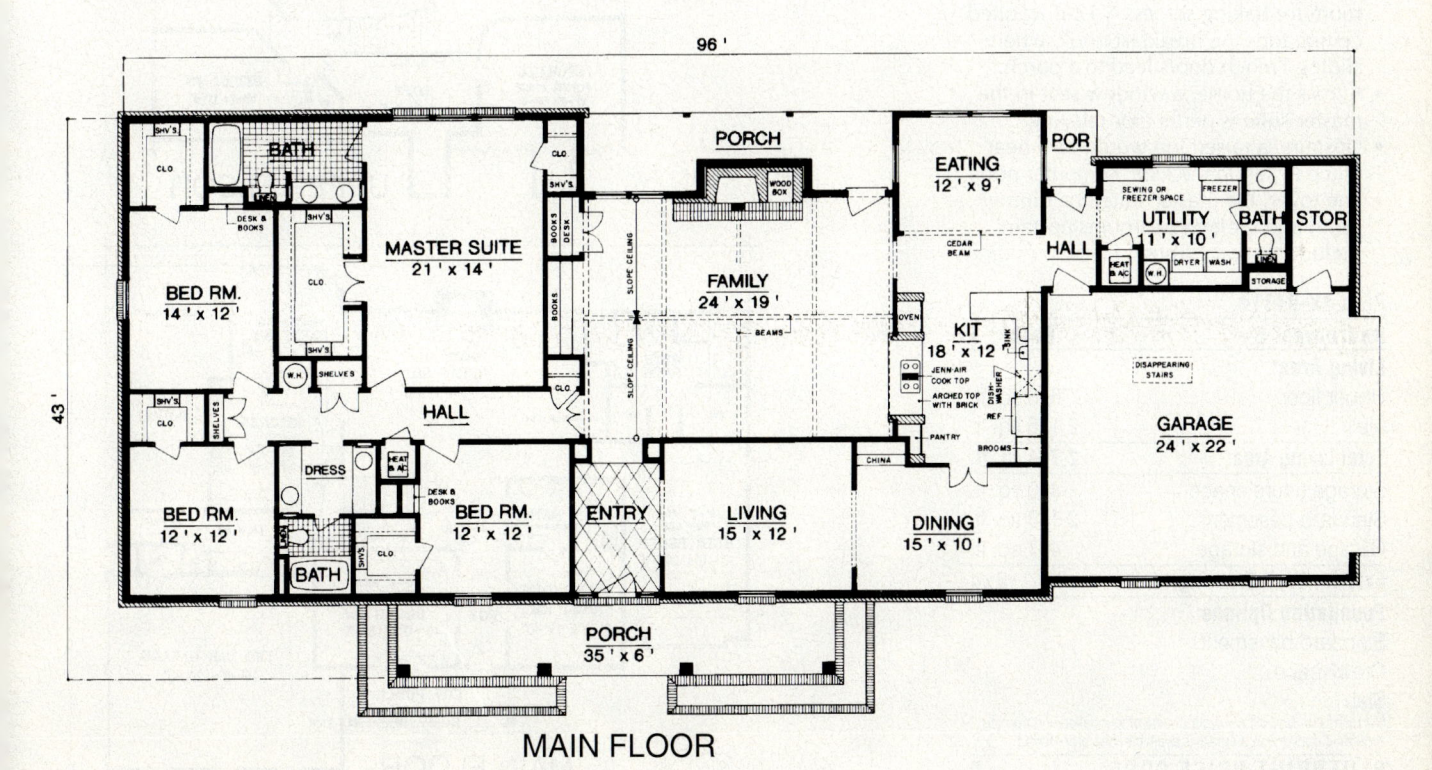

Plan E-2700

ORDER BLUEPRINTS ANYTIME!
CALL TOLL-FREE 1-888-626-2026

PRICES AND DETAILS ON PAGES 12-15

Country Charm

- While the facade of this home features country details, the interior includes many up-to-date amenities.
- Inside, a stepped ceiling crowns the dining room, where French doors allow guests to enjoy the sounds of raindrops. A wet bar makes serving easy.
- With a closet and private access to a split bath, the office near the entry would also serve well as a bedroom. A 9-ft. ceiling here adds a spacious feel.
- An 18-ft., 5-in. vaulted ceiling soars over the Great Room, which will be the setting for many family meetings.
- In the kitchen, an island counter makes room for baking sprees. A 12-ft. vaulted ceiling tops the breakfast nook, where sliding French doors lead to a porch.
- Across the home, a window seat in the master suite is perfect for relaxing.
- Upstairs, a raised loft would be a neat place to set up the kids' computer nook.
- The foyer, the master suite, the dining room and the two bedrooms upstairs include 9½-ft. ceilings.

Plan AX-94314

Bedrooms: 3+	Baths: 3

Living Area:
Upper floor	646 sq. ft.
Main floor	2,118 sq. ft.
Total Living Area:	**2,764 sq. ft.**
Storage/future space	400 sq. ft.
Standard basement	2,118 sq. ft.
Garage and storage	497 sq. ft.

Exterior Wall Framing: 2x4

Foundation Options:
Standard basement
Crawlspace
Slab
(All plans can be built with your choice of foundation and framing. A generic conversion diagram is available. See order form.)

BLUEPRINT PRICE CODE: D

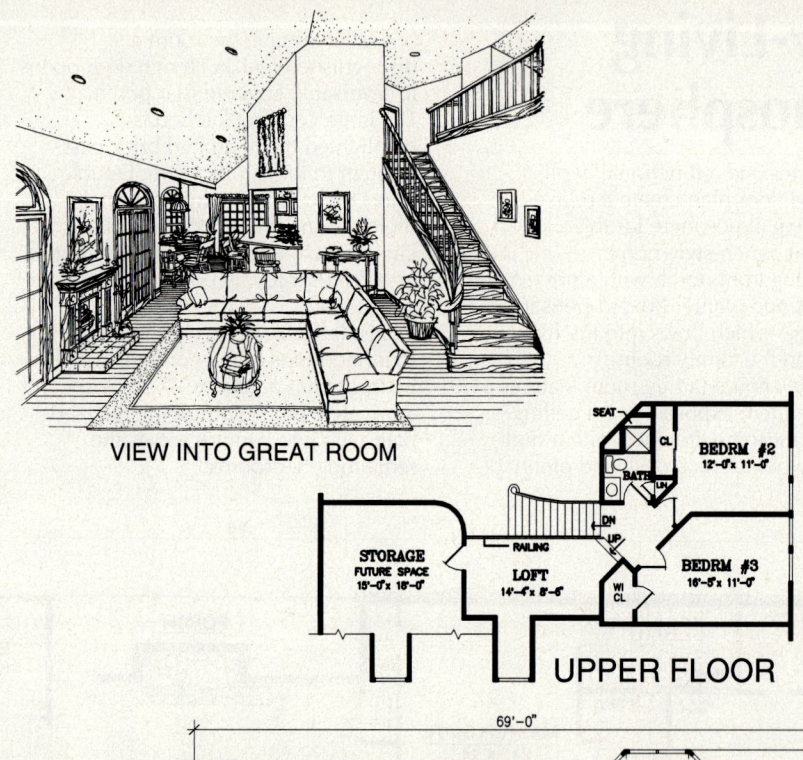

VIEW INTO GREAT ROOM

UPPER FLOOR

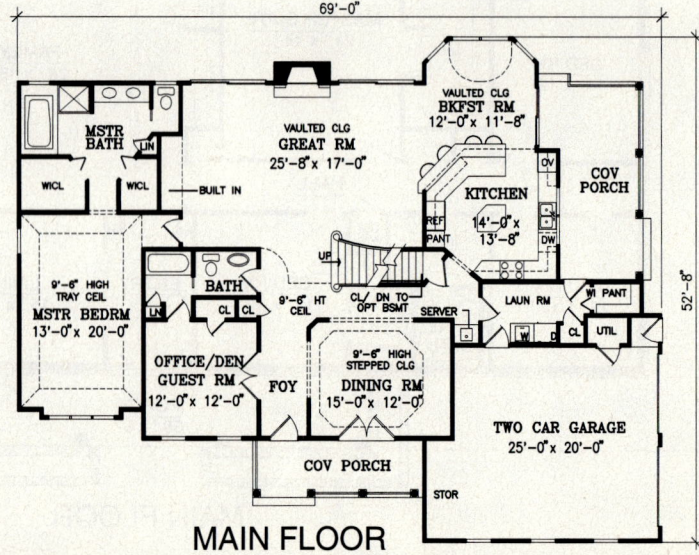

MAIN FLOOR

ORDER BLUEPRINTS ANYTIME!
CALL TOLL-FREE 1-888-626-2026

Plan AX-94314

PRICES AND DETAILS ON PAGES 12-15

Innovative Use of Space

- Strategic angles, built-in shelving and multi-access rooms exemplify the innovative use of space in this exciting stucco and stone home.
- Elaborate ceilings and windows further enhance the volume of the living areas.
- Adjacent to the airy foyer, the living room's built-in cabinets, shelves and plant niches add function to its beautiful fireplace wall.
- More shelves display your personal library in the double-doored study.
- Wraparound counter space frames the octagonal kitchen, which can be accessed from the foyer and formal dining room, as well as from the casual spaces on the other side.
- A luxurious garden bath and a winding walk-in closet adjoin the spacious master bedroom; a compartmentalized bath serves the secondary bedrooms.
- The unfinished bonus room upstairs is available for future use as an extra bedroom, game room or hobby area.

Plan KLF-9710	
Bedrooms: 3+	Baths: 2½
Living Area:	
Main floor	2,747 sq. ft.
Total Living Area:	**2,747 sq. ft.**
Unfinished bonus room	391 sq. ft.
Garage and storage	504 sq. ft.
Exterior Wall Framing:	2x4
Foundation Options:	
Slab	

(All plans can be built with your choice of foundation and framing. A generic conversion diagram is available. See order form.)

BLUEPRINT PRICE CODE: D

NOTE: The above photographed home may have been modified by the homeowner. Please refer to floor plan and/or drawn elevation shown for actual blueprint details.

MAIN FLOOR

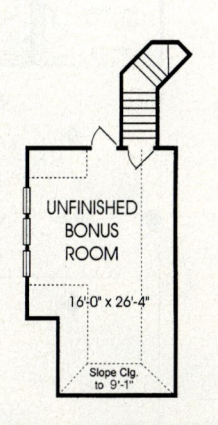

BONUS ROOM

ORDER BLUEPRINTS ANYTIME!
CALL TOLL-FREE 1-888-626-2026

Plan KLF-9710

PRICES AND DETAILS
ON PAGES 12-15

51

Photo by Mark Englund/HomeStyles

Take the Plunge!

- From the elegant portico to the striking rooflines, this home's facade is magnificent. But the rear area is equally fine, with its spa, waterfall and pool.
- Double doors lead from the entry into the open foyer, where a 12-ft. ceiling extends into the central living room beyond. A sunken wet bar juts into the pool area, allowing guests to swim up to the bar for refreshments.
- The dining room boasts window walls and a tiered pedestal ceiling that steps up from 10 ft. at the center to 12 ft. at the outside edges. The island kitchen easily services both the formal and the informal areas of the home.
- A big breakfast room flows into a family room with a fireplace and sliding glass doors to the patio and pool.
- The master suite offers an opulent bath, patio access and views of the pool through a curved window wall. A 12-ft. ceiling tops both the master suite and the nearby den or study.
- A railed staircase leads to the upper floor, where there are two bedrooms, a continental bath and a shared balcony deck overlooking the pool area.
- The observatory features high windows to accommodate an amateur stargazer's telescope. This room could also be used as a nice activity area for hobbies or games.

Plan HDS-99-154	
Bedrooms: 3+	**Baths:** 3
Living Area:	
Upper floor	675 sq. ft.
Main floor	2,212 sq. ft.
Total Living Area:	**2,887 sq. ft.**
Garage	479 sq. ft.
Exterior Wall Framing:	2x4
Foundation Options:	
Slab	

(All plans can be built with your choice of foundation and framing. A generic conversion diagram is available. See order form.)

BLUEPRINT PRICE CODE: D

**NOTE: The above photographed home may have been modified by the homeowner. Please refer to floor plan and/or drawn elevation shown for actual blueprint details.

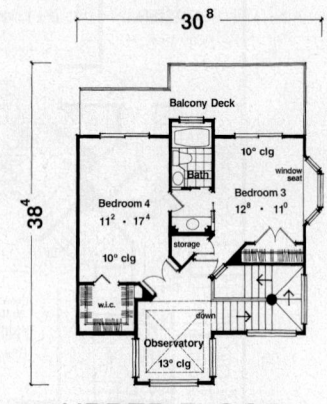

MAIN FLOOR

UPPER FLOOR

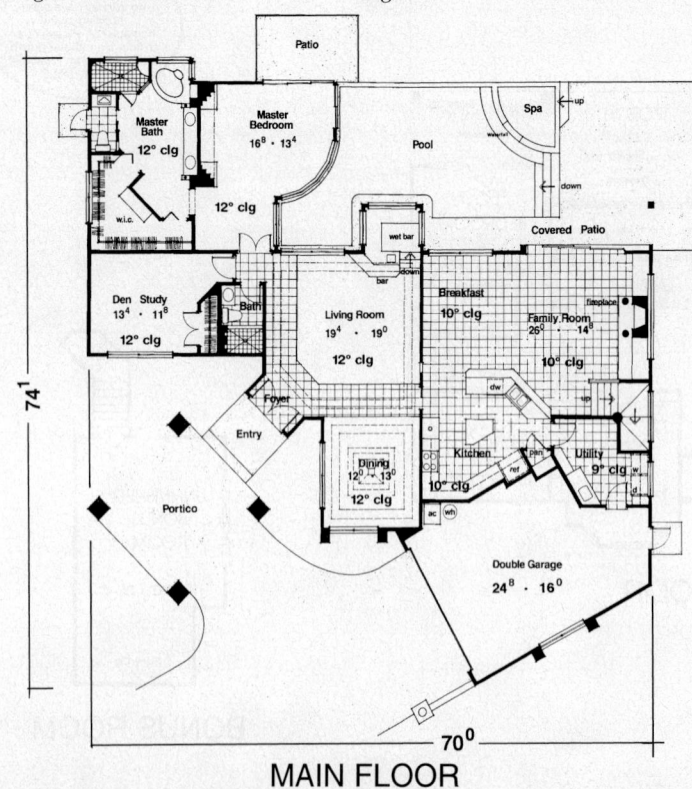

See this plan on our "Best-Sellers" VideoGraphic Tour! Order form on page 9

52   ORDER BLUEPRINTS ANYTIME! CALL TOLL-FREE 1-888-626-2026   Plan HDS-99-154   PRICES AND DETAILS ON PAGES 12-15

Dramatic Rear Views

- Columned front and rear porches offer country styling to this elegant two-story.
- The formal dining room and living room flank the two-story-high foyer.
- A dramatic array of windows stretches along the informal, rear-oriented living areas, where the central family room features a 17-ft.-high vaulted ceiling and a striking fireplace.
- The modern kitchen features an angled snack counter, a walk-in pantry and a work island, in addition to the bayed morning room.
- The exciting and secluded master suite has a sunny bayed sitting area with its own fireplace. Large walk-in closets lead to a luxurious private bath with angled dual vanities, a garden spa tub and a separate shower.
- The centrally located stairway leads to three extra bedrooms and two full baths on the upper floor.

Plan DD-2912

Bedrooms: 4	Baths: 3½
Living Area:	
Upper floor	916 sq. ft.
Main floor	2,046 sq. ft.
Total Living Area:	**2,962 sq. ft.**
Standard basement	1,811 sq. ft.
Garage	513 sq. ft.
Exterior Wall Framing:	2x4

Foundation Options:
Standard basement
Crawlspace
Slab
(All plans can be built with your choice of foundation and framing. A generic conversion diagram is available. See order form.)

BLUEPRINT PRICE CODE: D

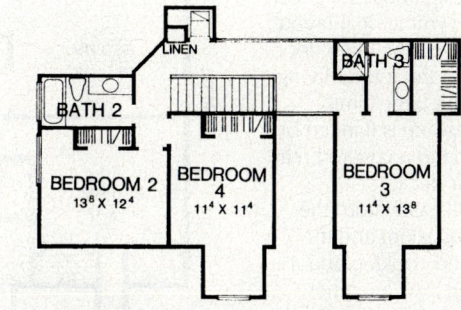

UPPER FLOOR

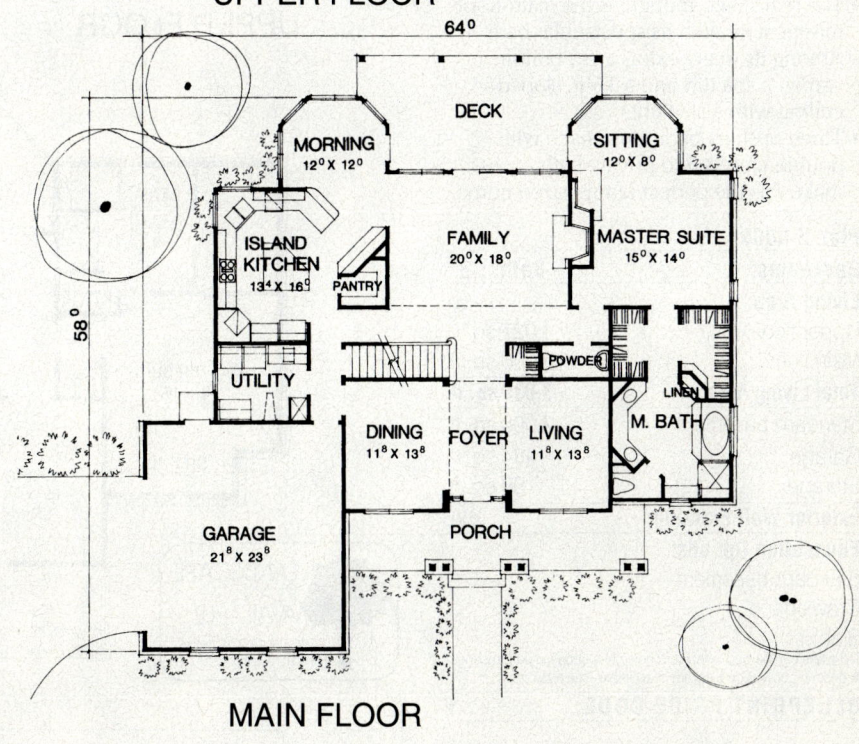

MAIN FLOOR

ORDER BLUEPRINTS ANYTIME!
CALL TOLL-FREE 1-888-626-2026

Plan DD-2912

PRICES AND DETAILS
ON PAGES 12-15

53

Spacious and Stately

- This popular home design boasts a classic Creole exterior and a symmetrical layout, with 9-ft.-high ceilings on the main floor.
- French doors lead from the formal living and dining rooms to the large family room. The central fireplace is flanked by French doors that open to a covered rear porch and an open-air deck.
- The kitchen is reached easily from the family room, the dining room and the rear entrance. An island cooktop and a window-framed eating area are other features found here.
- The real seller, though, is the main-floor master suite with its spectacular bath. Among its many extras are a built-in vanity, a spa tub and a 16-ft. sloped ceiling with a skylight.
- Three upstairs bedrooms, each with double closets and private bath access, make this the perfect family-sized home.

Plan E-3000

Bedrooms: 4	Baths: 3½
Living Area:	
Upper floor	1,027 sq. ft.
Main floor	2,008 sq. ft.
Total Living Area:	**3,035 sq. ft.**
Standard basement	2,008 sq. ft.
Garage	484 sq. ft.
Storage	96 sq. ft.
Exterior Wall Framing:	2x6

Foundation Options:
Standard basement
Crawlspace
Slab
(All plans can be built with your choice of foundation and framing. A generic conversion diagram is available. See order form.)

BLUEPRINT PRICE CODE: E

Photo by Gil Ford

See this plan on our "Best-Sellers" VideoGraphic Tour! Order form on page 9

NOTE: The above photographed home may have been modified by the homeowner. Please refer to floor plan and/or drawn elevation shown for actual blueprint details.

TOUR THIS HOME BEFORE YOU BUILD!
See page 9 for details on Interactive Floor Plans.

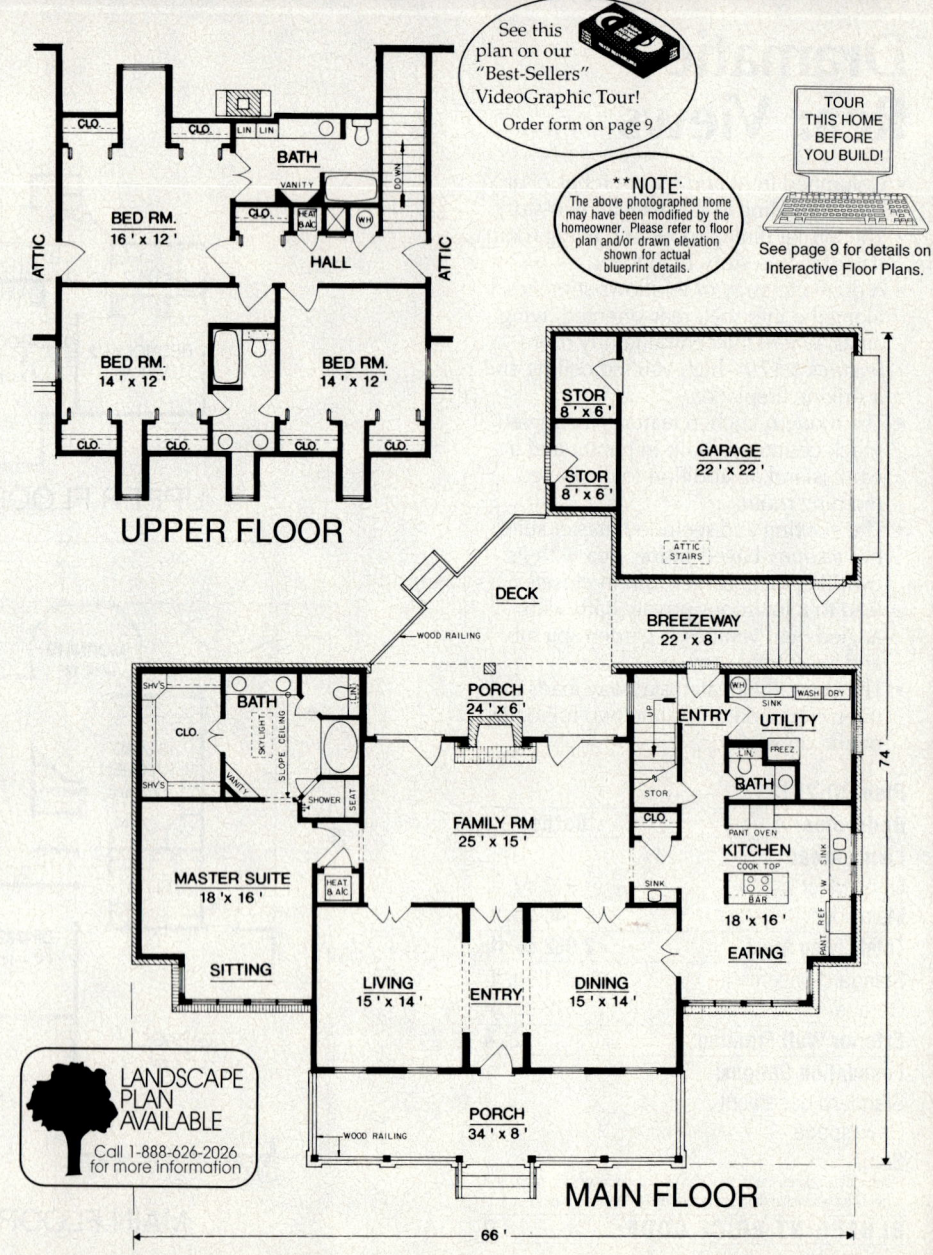

UPPER FLOOR

MAIN FLOOR

LANDSCAPE PLAN AVAILABLE
Call 1-888-626-2026 for more information

---

54 | **ORDER BLUEPRINTS ANYTIME!** CALL TOLL-FREE 1-888-626-2026 | Plan E-3000 | PRICES AND DETAILS ON PAGES 12-15

Victorian Farmhouse

- Fish-scale shingles and horizontal siding team up with the detailed front porch to create a look of yesterday. Brickwork enriches the sides and rear of the home.
- The main level features 10-ft.-high ceilings throughout the central living space. The front-oriented formal areas merge with the family room via three sets of French doors.
- The island kitchen and skylighted eating area have 16-ft. sloped ceilings.
- A breezeway off the deck connects the house to a roomy workshop. A two-car garage is located under the workshop and a large utility room is just inside the rear entrance.
- The main-floor master suite offers an opulent skylighted bath with a garden vanity, a spa tub, a separate shower and an 18-ft.-high sloped ceiling.
- The upper floor offers three more bedrooms, two full baths and a balcony that looks to the backyard.

Plan E-3103
Bedrooms: 4   **Baths:** 3½

Living Area:
Upper floor	1,113 sq. ft.
Main floor	2,040 sq. ft.
Total Living Area:	**3,153 sq. ft.**
Daylight basement	2,040 sq. ft.
Tuck-under garage and storage	580 sq. ft.
Workshop and storage	580 sq. ft.

Exterior Wall Framing: 2x6

Foundation Options:
Daylight basement
Crawlspace
Slab

(All plans can be built with your choice of foundation and framing. A generic conversion diagram is available. See order form.)

BLUEPRINT PRICE CODE: E

See this plan on our "Country & Traditional" Video Tour! Order form on page 9

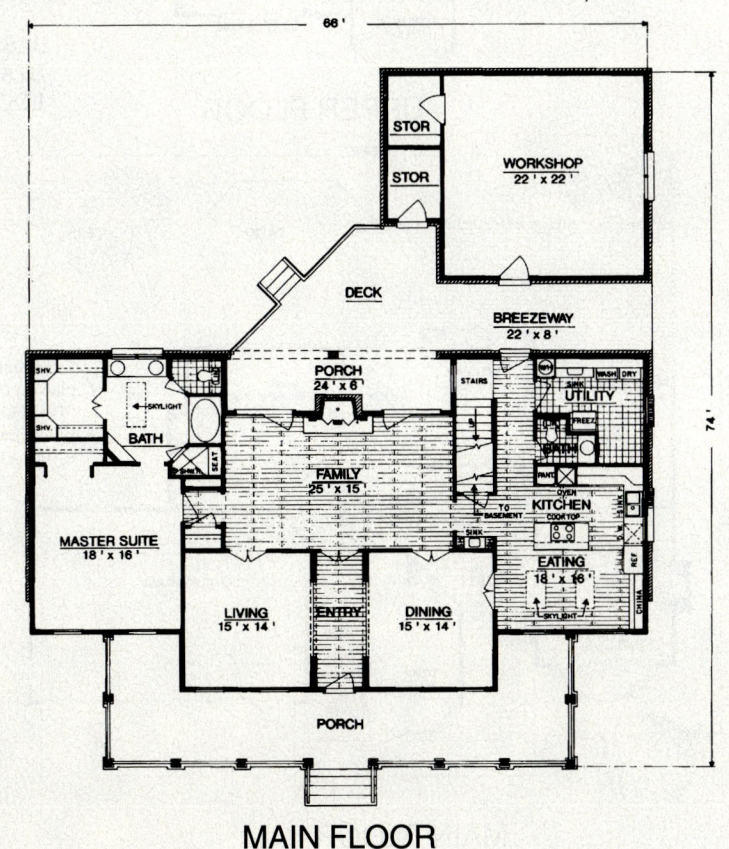

MAIN FLOOR

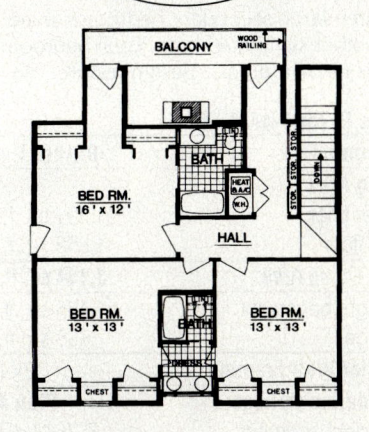

UPPER FLOOR

ORDER BLUEPRINTS ANYTIME!
CALL TOLL-FREE 1-888-626-2026

Plan E-3103

PRICES AND DETAILS ON PAGES 12-15

Creative Spaces

- This expansive home uses vaulted ceilings and multiple levels to create a functional, airy floor plan.
- The broad, vaulted entry foyer leads to the bayed living room, which is warmed by a striking fireplace. A few steps down, the dining room opens to a wide backyard deck.
- The island kitchen features a sunny sink area and a breakfast nook with deck access. A laundry room, a half-bath and a den or extra bedroom are also found on this level.
- Adjacent to the nook, the sunken family room boasts a wet bar, a second fireplace and a bright window wall with sliding glass doors to a lovely patio.
- Upstairs, the master suite includes a sunken bedroom with a private deck. The lavish master bath offers a sunken garden tub, a dual-sink vanity and a skylight near the private shower.
- Three large secondary bedrooms share another skylighted bath. Each bedroom has its own unique design feature.

Plans P-7664-4A & -4D

Bedrooms: 4+	Baths: 2½
Living Area:	
Upper floor	1,301 sq. ft.
Main floor	1,853 sq. ft.
Total Living Area:	**3,154 sq. ft.**
Daylight basement	1,486 sq. ft.
Garage	668 sq. ft.
Exterior Wall Framing:	2x4
Foundation Options:	Plan #
Daylight basement	P-7664-4D
Crawlspace	P-7664-4A

(All plans can be built with your choice of foundation and framing. A generic conversion diagram is available. See order form.)

BLUEPRINT PRICE CODE: E

NOTE: The above photographed home may have been modified by the homeowner. Please refer to floor plan and/or drawn elevation shown for actual blueprint details.

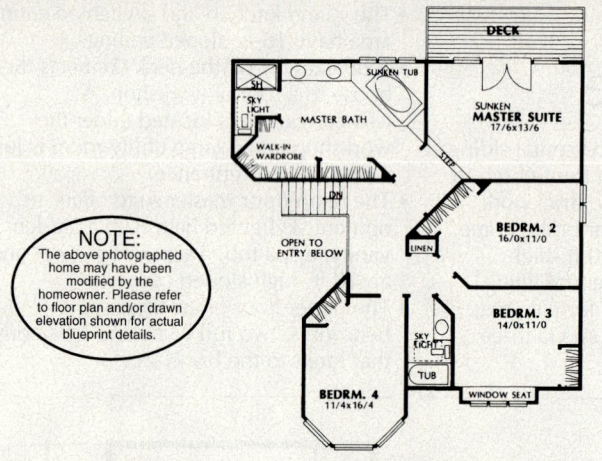

UPPER FLOOR

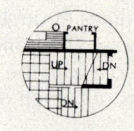

BASEMENT STAIRWAY LOCATION

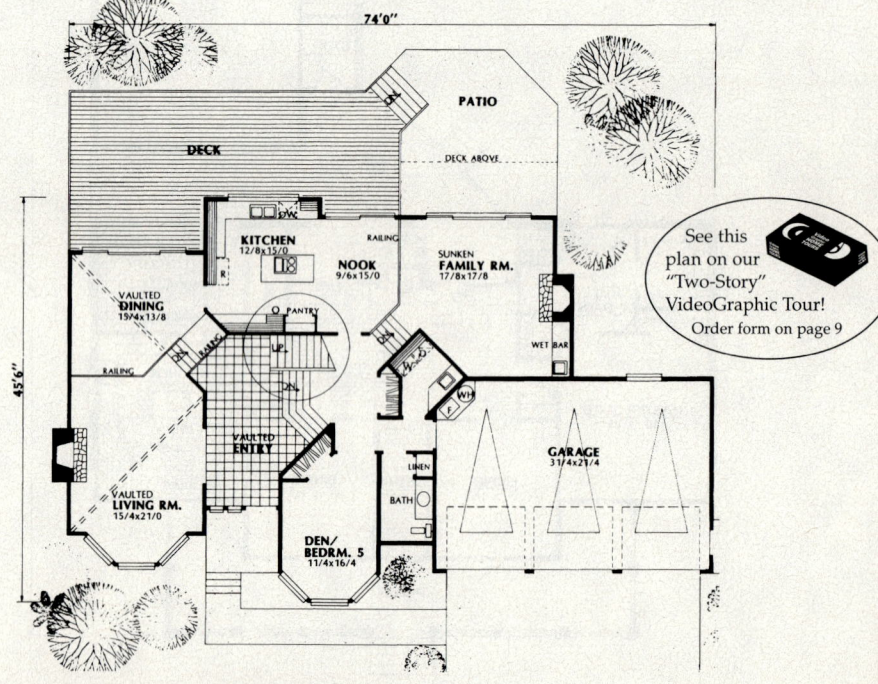

MAIN FLOOR

See this plan on our "Two-Story" VideoGraphic Tour! Order form on page 9

Photo by Mark Englund/HomeStyles

ORDER BLUEPRINTS ANYTIME! CALL TOLL-FREE 1-888-626-2026

Plans P-7664-4A & -4D

PRICES AND DETAILS ON PAGES 12-15

REAR VIEW

Photos courtesy of Larry Garnett and Associates

Vivacious Victorian

- The facade of this classic Victorian home is enhanced by a covered veranda bordering three sides.
- Inside, the modern interior begins with an airy two-story foyer that flows directly into a cozy bayed parlor.
- Past a bright window wall and a door to the side yard, the bay-windowed formal dining room boasts a wonderful built-in china hutch.
- Behind bifold doors, the island kitchen sports a nifty built-in desk and a cheery bayed morning room with speedy access to the veranda.
- Beautiful views are also offered from the family room, which flaunts a handsome fireplace, a wet bar and a wine rack.
- French doors access a bayed study that may be used as an extra bedroom.
- An angled staircase leads up to three secondary bedrooms, one of which has a 13-ft. ceiling. A compartmentalized bath and a laundry room are nearby.
- At the end of the hall, the master bedroom features a long, private deck. The gorgeous master bath offers a stunning, bay-windowed bathing area.
- Unless otherwise noted, each room has a 9-ft. ceiling.

Plan L-3163	
Bedrooms: 4+	**Baths:** 2½
Living Area:	
Upper floor	1,598 sq. ft.
Main floor	1,565 sq. ft.
Total Living Area:	**3,163 sq. ft.**
Garage (detached)	576 sq. ft.
Exterior Wall Framing:	2x4
Foundation Options:	
Slab	

(All plans can be built with your choice of foundation and framing. A generic conversion diagram is available. See order form.)

BLUEPRINT PRICE CODE: E

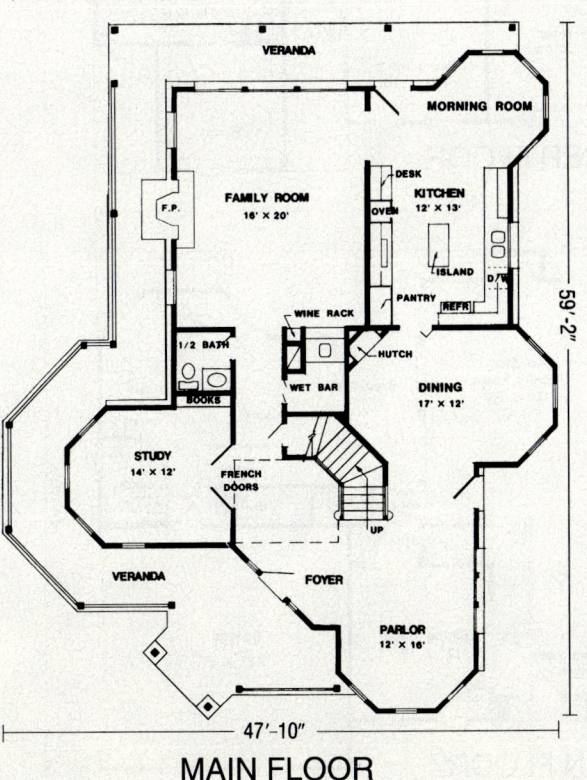

MAIN FLOOR

UPPER FLOOR

NOTE: The above photographed home may have been modified by the homeowner. Please refer to floor plan and/or drawn elevation shown for actual blueprint details.

TOUR THIS HOME BEFORE YOU BUILD!
See page 9 for details on Interactive Floor Plans.

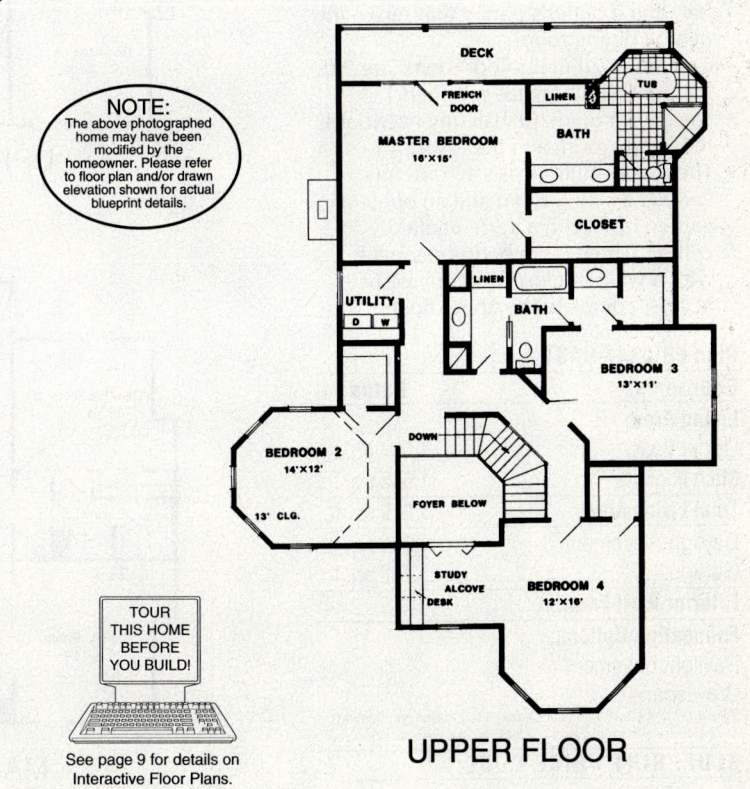

ORDER BLUEPRINTS ANYTIME!
CALL TOLL-FREE 1-888-626-2026

Plan L-3163

PRICES AND DETAILS ON PAGES 12-15

57

Ornate Design

- This exciting home is distinguished by an ornate facade with symmetrical windows and a columned entry.
- A beautiful arched window highlights the two-story-high foyer, with its open-railed stairway and high plant shelf. The foyer separates the two formal rooms and flows back to the family room.
- With an 18-ft. ceiling, the family room is brightened by corner windows and warmed by a central fireplace.
- Columns introduce the sunny breakfast area and the gourmet kitchen, which features an angled island and serving bar, and a butler's pantry that serves the nearby dining room.
- Ceilings in all main-floor rooms are 9 ft. high unless otherwise specified.
- Upstairs, a dramatic balcony overlooks the family room and the foyer.
- The master suite boasts a 10-ft. tray ceiling, a sitting room and an opulent garden bath with a 12-ft. vaulted ceiling. Three more bedrooms, each with a walk-in closet and private bath access, complete the upper floor.

NOTE: The above photographed home may have been modified by the homeowner. Please refer to floor plan and/or drawn elevation shown for actual blueprint details.

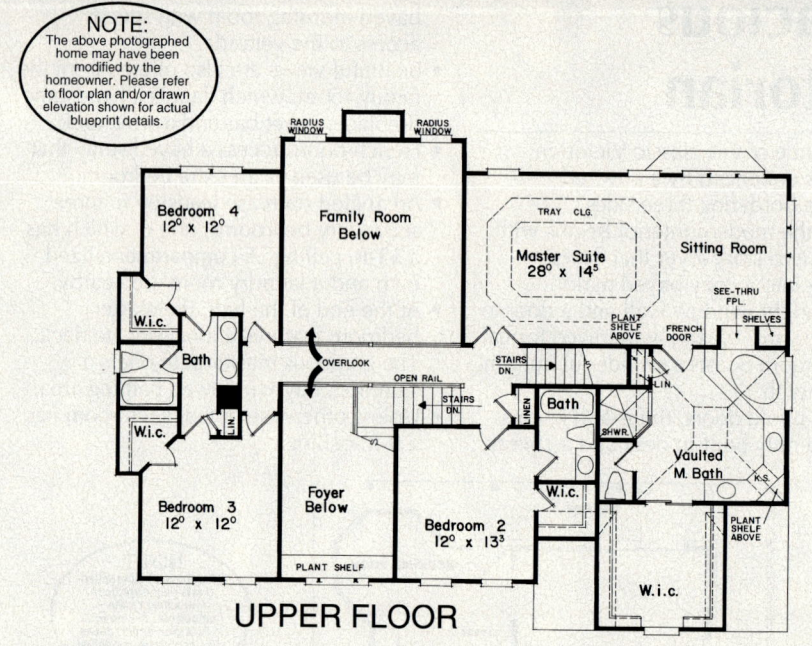

Plan FB-5347-HAST	
Bedrooms: 4+	**Baths:** 4
Living Area:	
Upper floor	1,554 sq. ft.
Main floor	1,665 sq. ft.
Total Living Area:	**3,219 sq. ft.**
Daylight basement	1,665 sq. ft.
Garage	462 sq. ft.
Exterior Wall Framing:	2x4
Foundation Options:	
Daylight basement	
Crawlspace	
(All plans can be built with your choice of foundation and framing. A generic conversion diagram is available. See order form.)	
BLUEPRINT PRICE CODE:	**E**

UPPER FLOOR

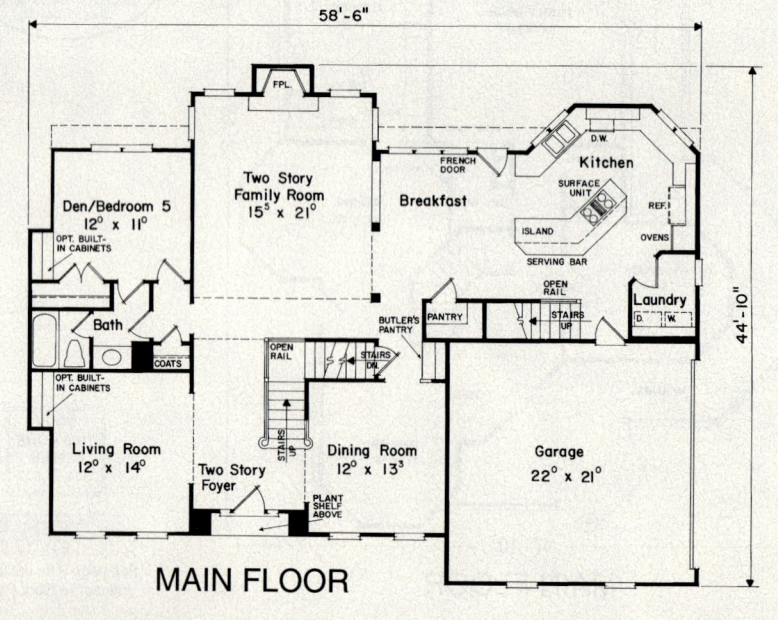

MAIN FLOOR

ORDER BLUEPRINTS ANYTIME!
CALL TOLL-FREE 1-888-626-2026

Plan FB-5347-HAST

PRICES AND DETAILS ON PAGES 12-15

Designed with Elegance in Mind

- This expansive home boasts 3,220 sq. ft. of living space designed with elegance in mind.
- The front of the home is finished in stucco, with the rest in lap siding for economy.
- The vaulted foyer leads directly into an impressive sunken and vaulted living room, guarded by columns that echo the exterior treatment.
- The formal dining room is visually joined to the living room to make an impressive space for entertaining.
- An unusually fine kitchen opens to a large family room, which boasts a vaulted ceiling, a corner fireplace and access to a sizable rear deck.
- In the front, the extra-wide staircase is a primary attraction, with its dramatic feature window.
- A terrific master suite includes a splendid master bath with double sinks and a huge walk-through closet.
- A second upstairs bedroom also includes a private bath.

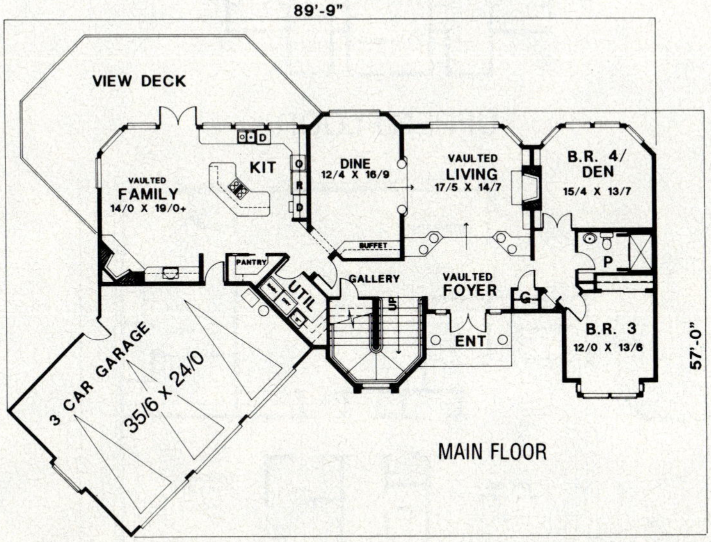

NOTE: The above photographed home may have been modified by the homeowner. Please refer to floor plan and/or drawn elevation shown for actual blueprint details.

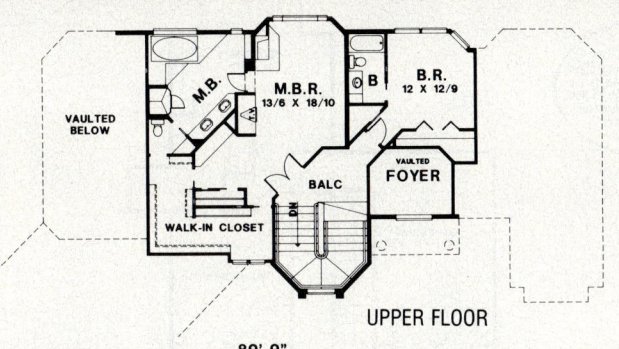

Photo by Mark Englund/HomeStyles

Plan LRD-11388

Bedrooms: 3-4	Baths: 3

Living Area:
Upper floor:	1,095 sq. ft.
Main floor:	2,125 sq. ft.
Total Living Area	**3,220 sq. ft.**
Standard basement	2,125 sq. ft.
Garage	802 sq. ft.

Exterior Wall Framing: 2x6
Foundation Options:
Standard basement
Crawlspace
Slab
(Typical foundation & framing conversion diagram available—see order form.)
BLUEPRINT PRICE CODE: E

ORDER BLUEPRINTS ANYTIME!
CALL TOLL-FREE 1-888-626-2026

Plan LRD-11388

PRICES AND DETAILS ON PAGES 12-15

59

Country Masterpiece!

- A handsome railed veranda punctuated by colonial columns bids a warm welcome to this French Country home.
- Historic hardwood floors in the foyer and dining room coupled with an abundance of windows, glass doors and 9-ft. ceilings give the interior the style and character of a masterpiece!
- Pocket doors isolate the study or guest room from the noise of incoming traffic.
- At the core of the informal spaces is an airy kitchen that interacts with the family room and the breakfast area over a 42-in.-high snack counter.
- The sprawling master suite basks in the comfort of a garden bath and a sunny sitting area that opens to the backyard.
- A window seat is centered between built-in bookshelves in the second main-floor bedroom.
- The upper-floor bedrooms share the use of a full bath and a huge game room.
- A detached three-car garage is included with the blueprints.

Plan L-308-FC

Bedrooms: 4+	**Baths:** 3
Living Area:	
Upper floor	787 sq. ft.
Main floor	2,519 sq. ft.
Total Living Area:	**3,306 sq. ft.**
Detached three-car garage	942 sq. ft.
Exterior Wall Framing:	2x4
Foundation Options:	
Slab	

(All plans can be built with your choice of foundation and framing. A generic conversion diagram is available. See order form.)

BLUEPRINT PRICE CODE: E

NOTE: The above photographed home may have been modified by the homeowner. Please refer to floor plan and/or drawn elevation shown for actual blueprint details.

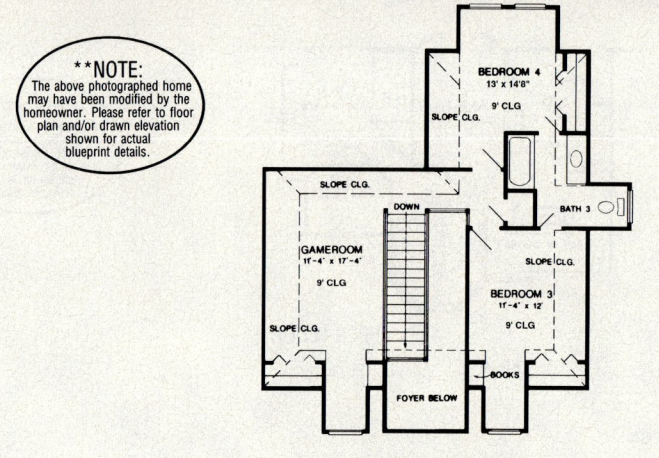

UPPER FLOOR

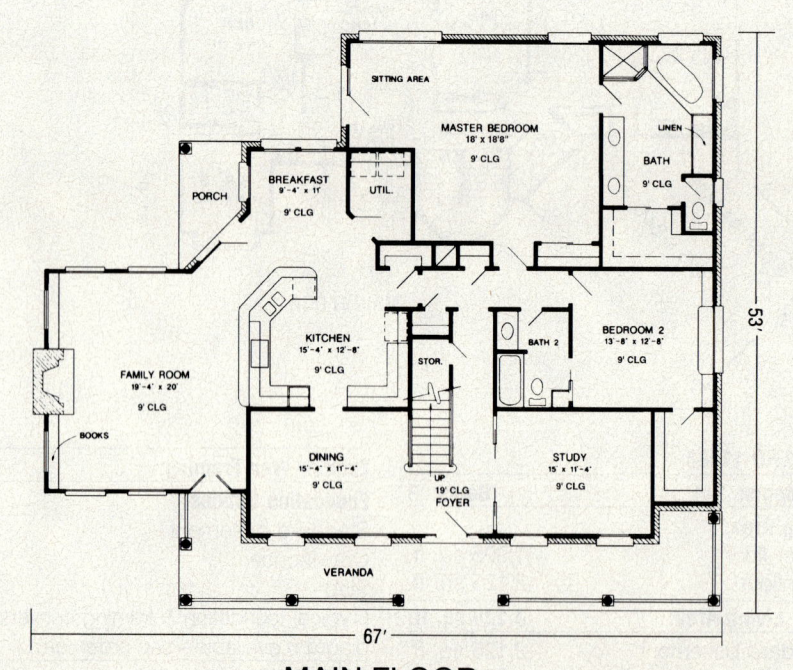

MAIN FLOOR

Plan L-308-FC

ORDER BLUEPRINTS ANYTIME! CALL TOLL-FREE 1-888-626-2026

PRICES AND DETAILS ON PAGES 12-15

Deluxe Master Suite

- This traditional home has an enticing style all its own, with a deluxe main-floor master suite.
- In from the covered porch, the front entry flows into the main living areas.
- Straight ahead, the family room features a handsome fireplace flanked by doors to a screened back porch.
- The kitchen easily services the formal dining room and offers a snack bar to the bayed breakfast nook. A nice utility room with a pantry and a half-bath is just off the nook and the garage entry.
- The secluded master suite boasts a 9-ft. tray ceiling and a luxurious bath with a garden tub, a separate shower and two vanities, one with knee space.
- Upstairs, each of the two additional bedrooms has a walk-in closet and a private bath. The optional bonus room can be finished as a large game room, a bedroom or an office.

Plan C-8915

Bedrooms: 3+ **Baths:** 3 full, 2 half

Living Area:
Upper floor	832 sq. ft.
Main floor	1,927 sq. ft.
Bonus room	624 sq. ft.
Total Living Area:	**3,383 sq. ft.**
Daylight basement	1,674 sq. ft.
Garage	484 sq. ft.

Exterior Wall Framing: 2x4

Foundation Options:
Daylight basement
Crawlspace
(All plans can be built with your choice of foundation and framing. A generic conversion diagram is available. See order form.)

BLUEPRINT PRICE CODE: E

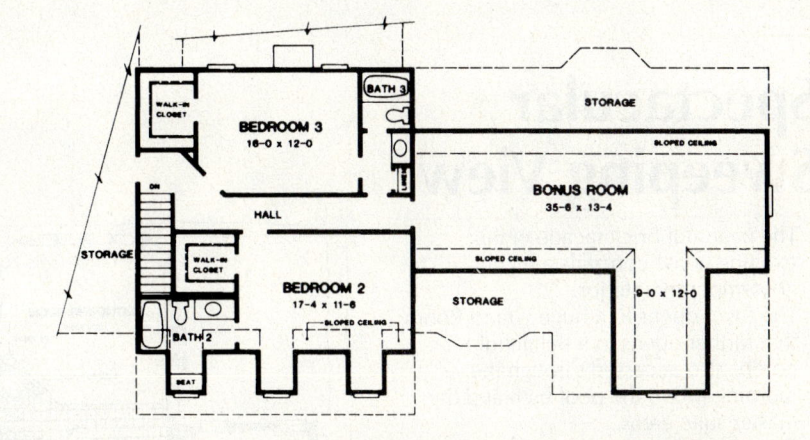

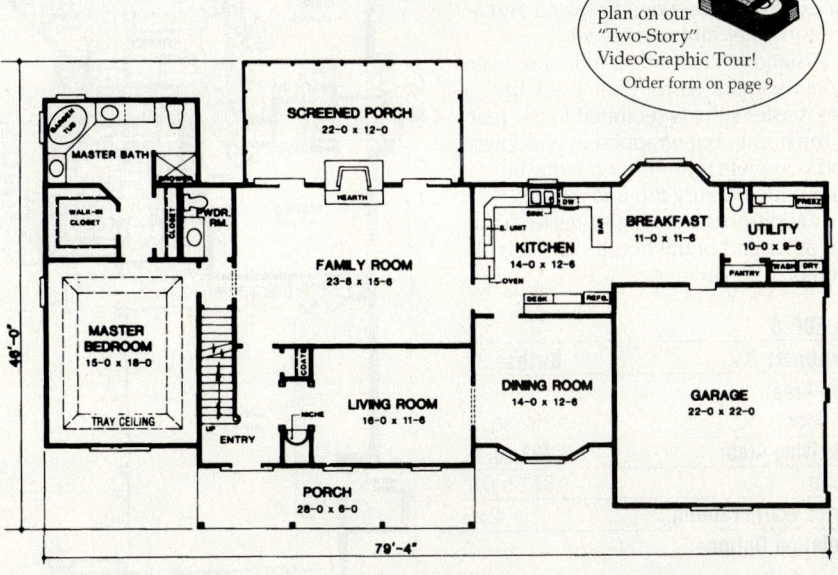

UPPER FLOOR

MAIN FLOOR

See this plan on our "Two-Story" VideoGraphic Tour! Order form on page 9

ORDER BLUEPRINTS ANYTIME!
CALL TOLL-FREE 1-888-626-2026

Plan C-8915

PRICES AND DETAILS ON PAGES 12-15

Spectacular Sweeping View

- The beautiful brick facade of this exciting home conceals a highly contemporary interior.
- The foyer opens to a huge Grand Room that further opens to a delightful rear porch, also accessed through the morning room, the pool bath and the master suite areas.
- Completely surrounded in windows is a spacious gathering room, also featuring an exciting three-sided fireplace and a built-in entertainment center.
- The island kitchen offers a double oven, a pantry and a convenient snack bar.
- The master suite is secluded to the rear of the home, but wrapped in windows and complete with its own fantastic bath with a luxury tub and a bidet.
- Two additional sleeping suites found at the other end of the home share a bath with private vanities.

Plan EOF-8	
Bedrooms: 3+	Baths: 3½
Living Area:	
Main floor	3,392 sq. ft.
Total Living Area:	**3,392 sq. ft.**
Garage	871 sq. ft.
Exterior Wall Framing:	2x6
Foundation Options: Slab (All plans can be built with your choice of foundation and framing. A generic conversion diagram is available. See order form.)	
BLUEPRINT PRICE CODE:	**E**

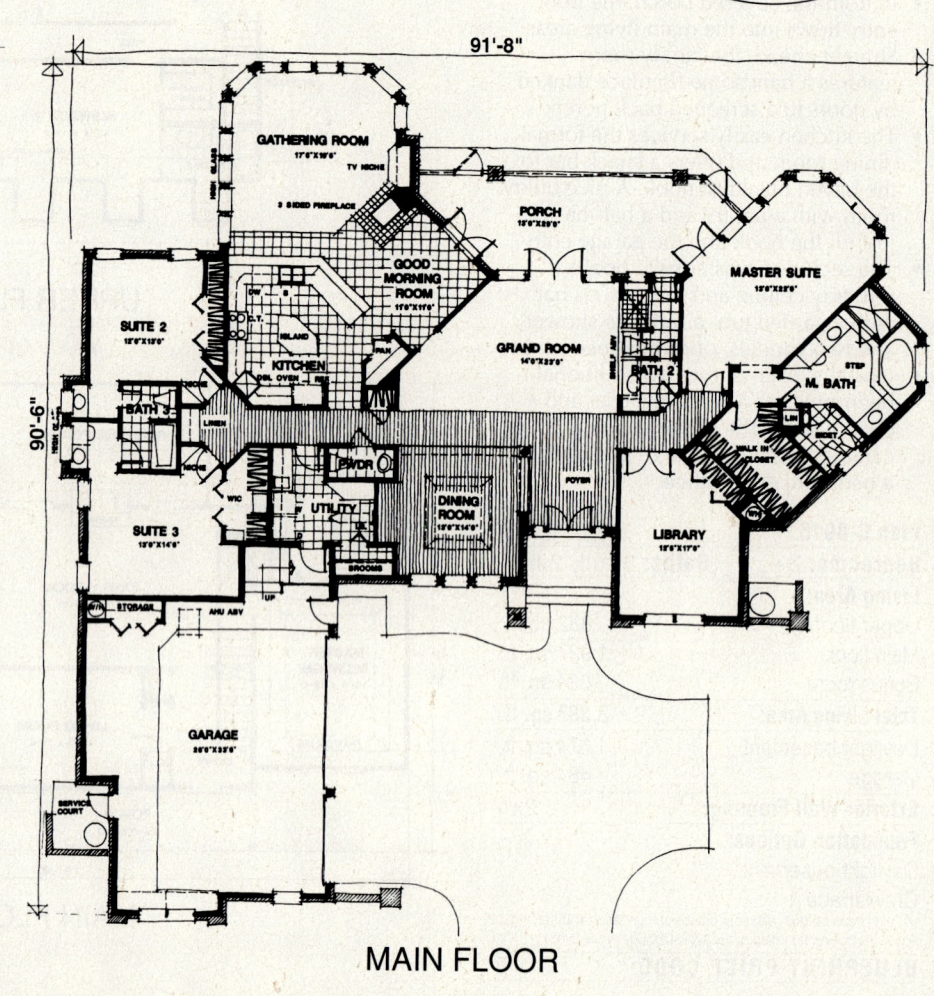

See this plan on our "One-Story" VideoGraphic Tour! Order form on page 9

MAIN FLOOR

ORDER BLUEPRINTS ANYTIME!
CALL TOLL-FREE 1-888-626-2026

Plan EOF-8

PRICES AND DETAILS
ON PAGES 12-15

Elegant Arches

- Gracious arched windows and an entry portico create rhythm and style for this home's brick-clad exterior.
- An elegant curved staircase lends interest to the raised, 17-ft. high foyer.
- Two steps down to the left of the foyer lies the living room, with its dramatic 14-ft. cathedral ceiling. Lovely columns define the adjoining dining room. A cozy fireplace warms the entire area.
- The island kitchen overlooks the bayed breakfast room and offers a handy pass-through to the adjoining family room.
- The family room boasts an 18-ft. ceiling, a second fireplace and a wall of windows topped by large transoms.
- The quiet master bedroom features a bay window and an 11-ft. sloped ceiling. The master bath shows off a garden tub and a separate shower.
- A sizable deck is accessible from both the breakfast room and the master suite.
- Three more bedrooms and two baths share the upper floor. A balcony bridge overlooks the foyer and the family room.

Plan DD-3639	
Bedrooms: 4+	**Baths:** 3½
Living Area:	
Upper floor	868 sq. ft.
Main floor	2,771 sq. ft.
Total Living Area:	**3,639 sq. ft.**
Standard basement	2,771 sq. ft.
Garage	790 sq. ft.
Exterior Wall Framing:	2x6
Foundation Options:	
Standard basement	
Crawlspace	
Slab	
(All plans can be built with your choice of foundation and framing. A generic conversion diagram is available. See order form.)	
BLUEPRINT PRICE CODE:	F

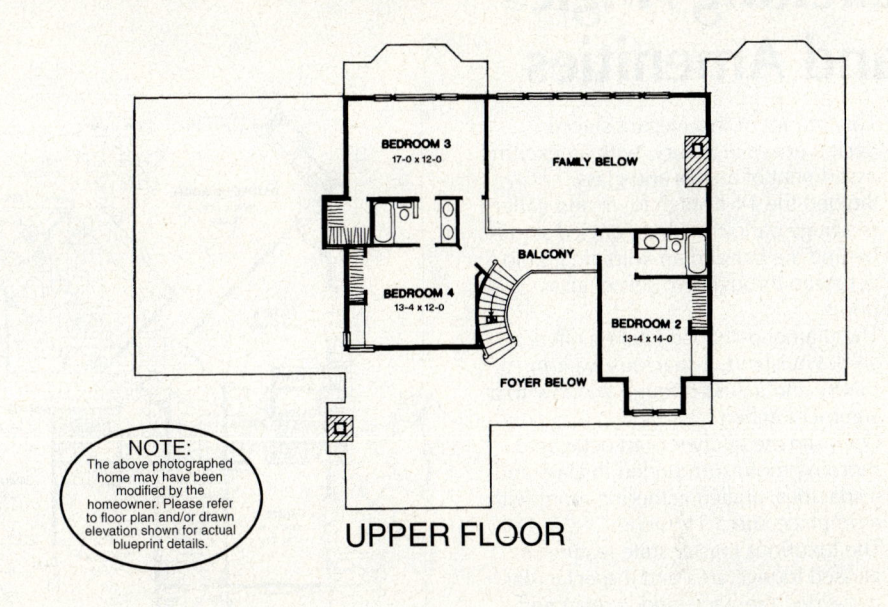

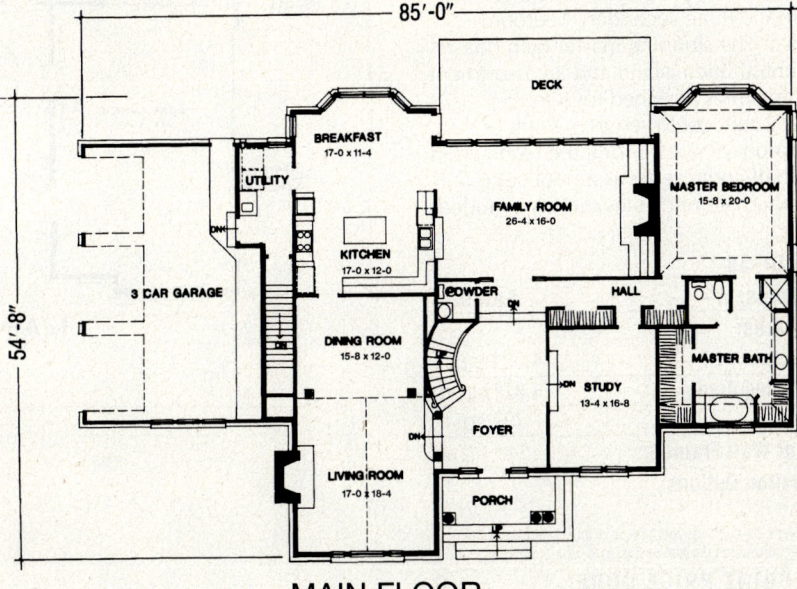

ORDER BLUEPRINTS ANYTIME!
CALL TOLL-FREE 1-888-626-2026

Plan DD-3639

PRICES AND DETAILS
ON PAGES 12-15

Exciting Angles and Amenities

- The interior of this elegant stucco design oozes in luxury, with an exciting assortment of angles and glass.
- Beyond the 14-ft.-high foyer and gallery is a huge parlour with an angled stand-behind ale bar and an adjoining patio accessed through two sets of glass doors.
- The diamond-shaped kitchen offers a sit-down island, a spacious walk-in pantry and a pass-through window to a summer kitchen.
- Opposite the kitchen is an octagonal morning room surrounded in glass and a spacious, angled gathering room with a fireplace and a TV niche.
- The luxurious master suite features a glassed lounge area and a spectacular two-sided fireplace, and is separated from the three secondary bedroom suites. The stunning master bath boasts a central linen island and an assortment of amenities designed for two.
- The library could serve as a fifth bedroom or guest room; the bath across the hall could serve as a pool bath.
- An alternate brick elevation is included

Plan EOF-59

Bedrooms: 4+	**Baths:** 4
Living Area:	
Main floor	4,021 sq. ft.
Total Living Area:	**4,021 sq. ft.**
Garage	737 sq. ft.
Exterior Wall Framing:	2x6

Foundation Options:
Slab
(All plans can be built with your choice of foundation and framing. A generic conversion diagram is available. See order form.)

BLUEPRINT PRICE CODE: G

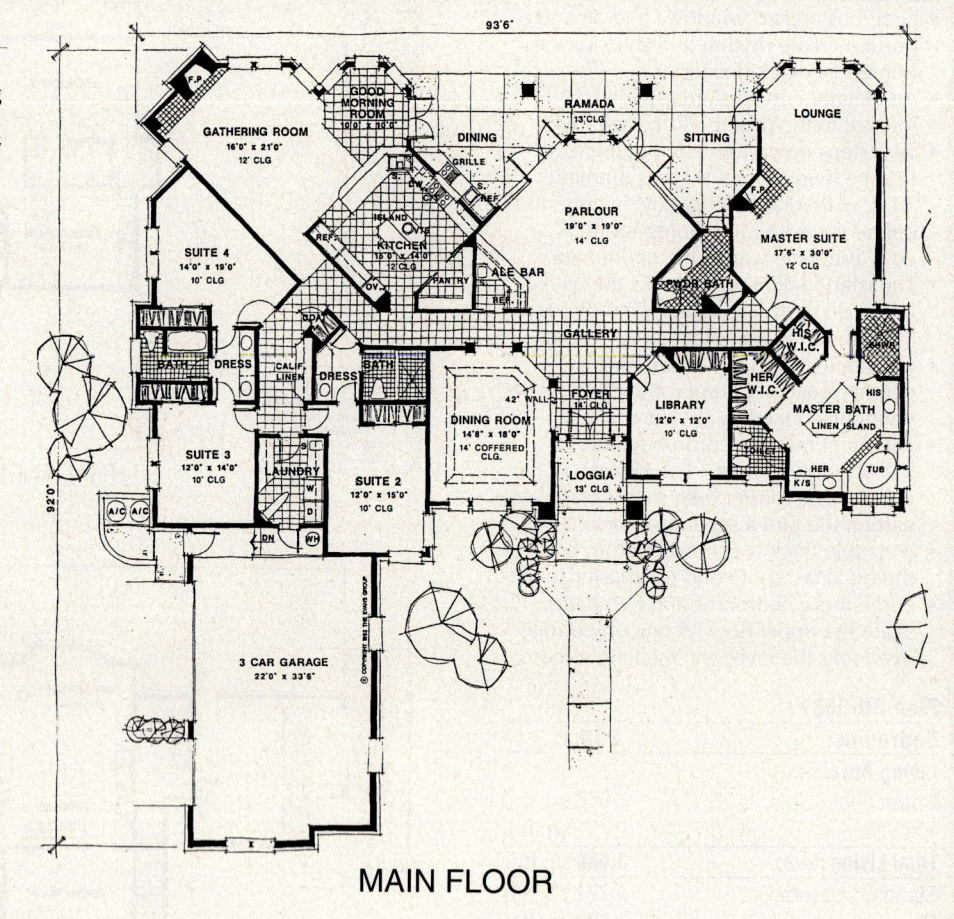

MAIN FLOOR

64   ORDER BLUEPRINTS ANYTIME! CALL TOLL-FREE 1-888-626-2026   Plan EOF-59   PRICES AND DETAILS ON PAGES 12-15

HOMES WITH LUXURIOUS APPOINTMENTS

Classic Styling

- This handsome one-story traditional would look great in town or in the country. The shuttered and paned windows, narrow lap siding and brick accents make it a classic.
- The sprawling design begins with the spacious, central living room, featuring a beamed ceiling that slopes up to 14 feet. A window wall overlooks the covered backyard porch, and an inviting fireplace includes an extra-wide hearth and built-in bookshelves.
- The galley-style kitchen features a snack bar to the sunny eating area and a raised-panel door to the dining room.
- The isolated master suite is a quiet haven offering a large walk-in closet, a dressing room and a spacious bath.
- Three more bedrooms, two with walk-in closets, and a compartmentalized bath are located at the opposite side of the home.

Plan E-2206

Bedrooms: 4	Baths: 2
Living Area:	
Main floor	2,200 sq. ft.
Total Living Area:	**2,200 sq. ft.**
Standard basement	2,200 sq. ft.
Garage and storage	624 sq. ft.
Exterior Wall Framing:	2x6

Foundation Options:
Standard basement
Crawlspace
Slab
(All plans can be built with your choice of foundation and framing. A generic conversion diagram is available. See order form.)

BLUEPRINT PRICE CODE: C

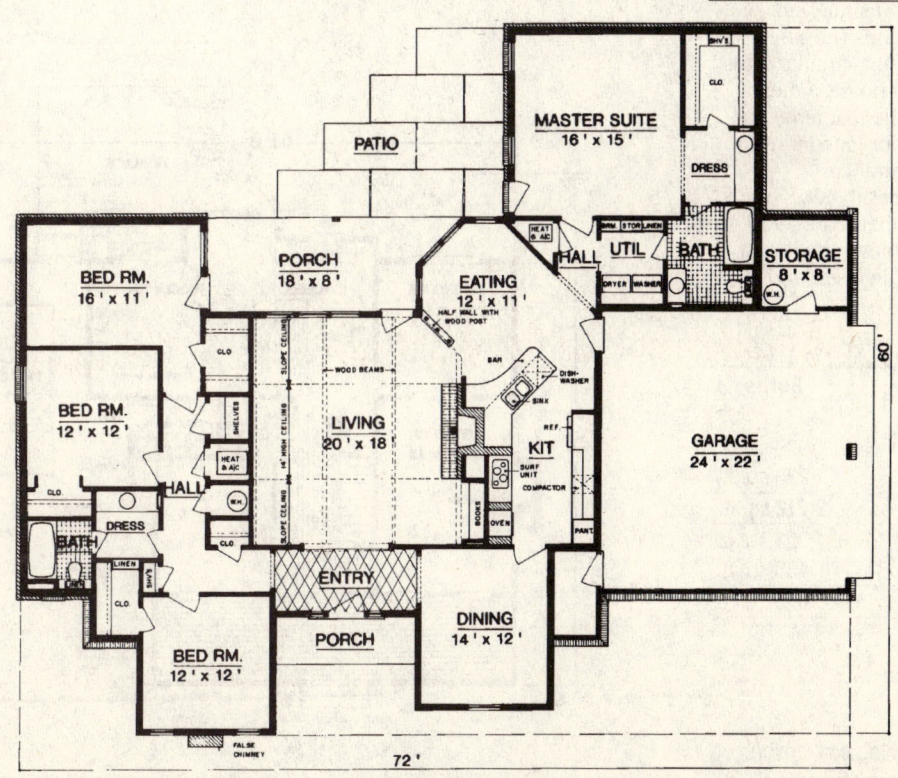

MAIN FLOOR

ORDER BLUEPRINTS ANYTIME! CALL TOLL-FREE 1-888-626-2026

Plan E-2206

PRICES AND DETAILS ON PAGES 12-15

Tradition Recreated

- Classic traditional styling is recreated in this home with its covered porch, triple dormers and half-round windows.
- A central hall stems from the two-story-high foyer and accesses each of the main living areas.
- A large formal space is created with the merging of the living room and the dining room. The living room boasts a fireplace and a view of the front porch.
- The informal spaces merge at the rear of the home. The kitchen features an oversized cooktop island. The sunny dinette is enclosed with a circular glass wall. The family room boasts a media center and access to the rear terrace.
- A convenient main-floor laundry room sits near the garage entrance.
- The upper floor includes three secondary bedrooms that share a full bath, and a spacious master bedroom that offers dual walk-in closets and a large private bath.

Plan AHP-9393

Bedrooms: 4+	Baths: 3
Living Area:	
Upper floor	989 sq. ft.
Main floor	1,223 sq. ft.
Total Living Area:	**2,212 sq. ft.**
Standard basement	1,223 sq. ft.
Garage and storage	488 sq. ft.
Exterior Wall Framing:	2x4 or 2x6

Foundation Options:
Standard basement
Crawlspace
Slab
(Typical foundation & framing conversion diagram available—see order form.)

BLUEPRINT PRICE CODE: C

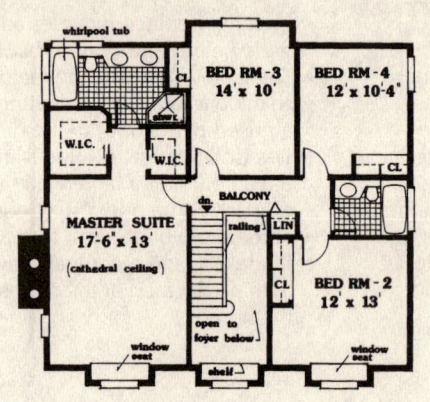

UPPER FLOOR

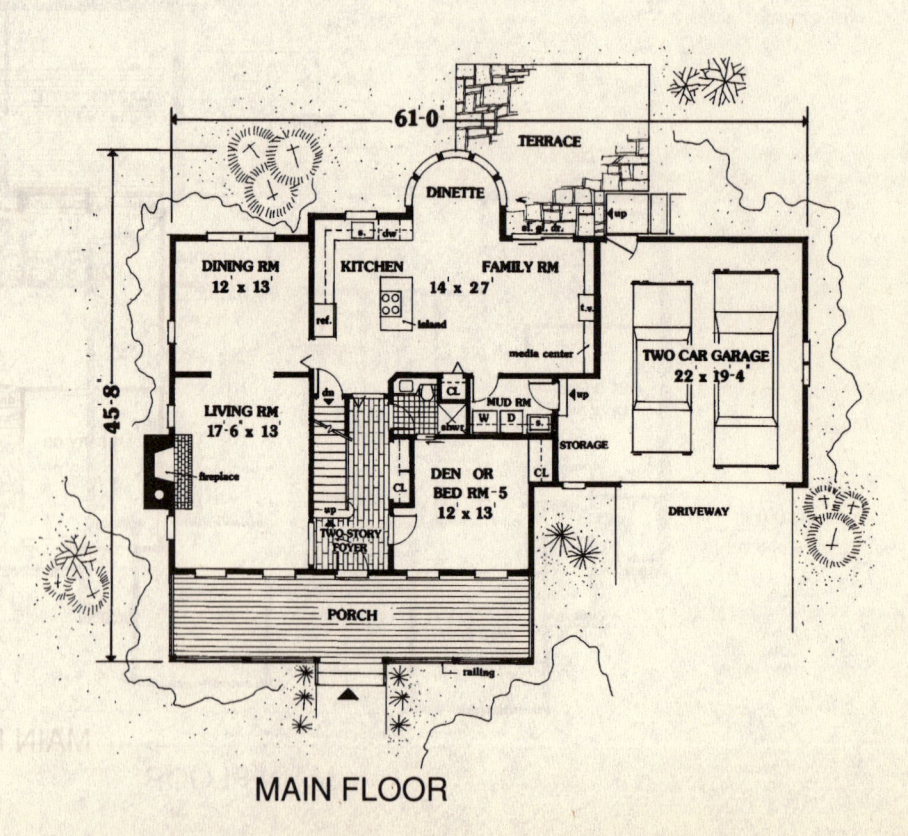

MAIN FLOOR

Plan AHP-9393

Graceful Facade

- Elegant half-round transoms spruce up the wood-shuttered facade of this charming traditional two-story.
- The wide front porch opens to a two-story foyer that flows between the formal dining room and a two-story-high library or guest room. Sliding French doors close off the library from the Great Room.
- Perfect for entertaining, the spacious Great Room shows off a handsome fireplace and a TV center. Beautiful French doors on either side extend the room to a large backyard deck.
- The adjoining dinette has its own view of the backyard through a stunning semi-circular glass wall, which sheds light on the nice-sized attached kitchen.
- A pantry and a laundry room are neatly housed near the two-car garage. The adjacent full bath could be downsized to a half-bath with storage space.
- The master suite and its private whirlpool bath are isolated from the three upper-floor bedrooms and features a 14-ft.-high cathedral ceiling.
- Unless otherwise specified, all main-floor ceilings are 9 ft. high.

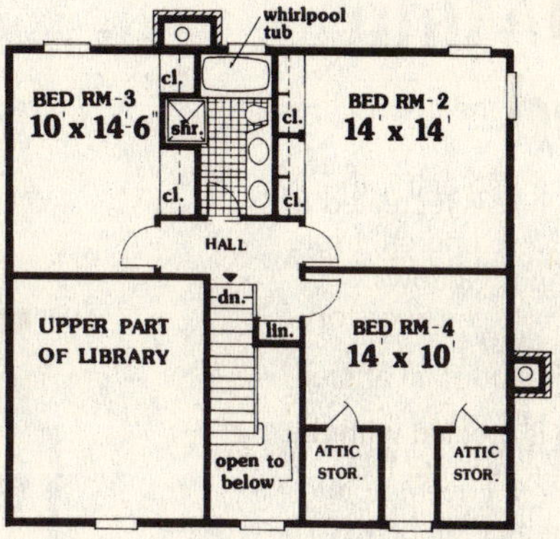

Plan AHP-9490

Bedrooms: 4+	Baths: 2½-3
Living Area:	
Upper floor	722 sq. ft.
Main floor	1,497 sq. ft.
Total Living Area:	**2,219 sq. ft.**
Standard basement	1,165 sq. ft.
Garage	420 sq. ft.
Exterior Wall Framing:	2x4 or 2x6

Foundation Options:
Standard basement
Crawlspace
Slab
(All plans can be built with your choice of foundation and framing. A generic conversion diagram is available. See order form.)

BLUEPRINT PRICE CODE: C

UPPER FLOOR

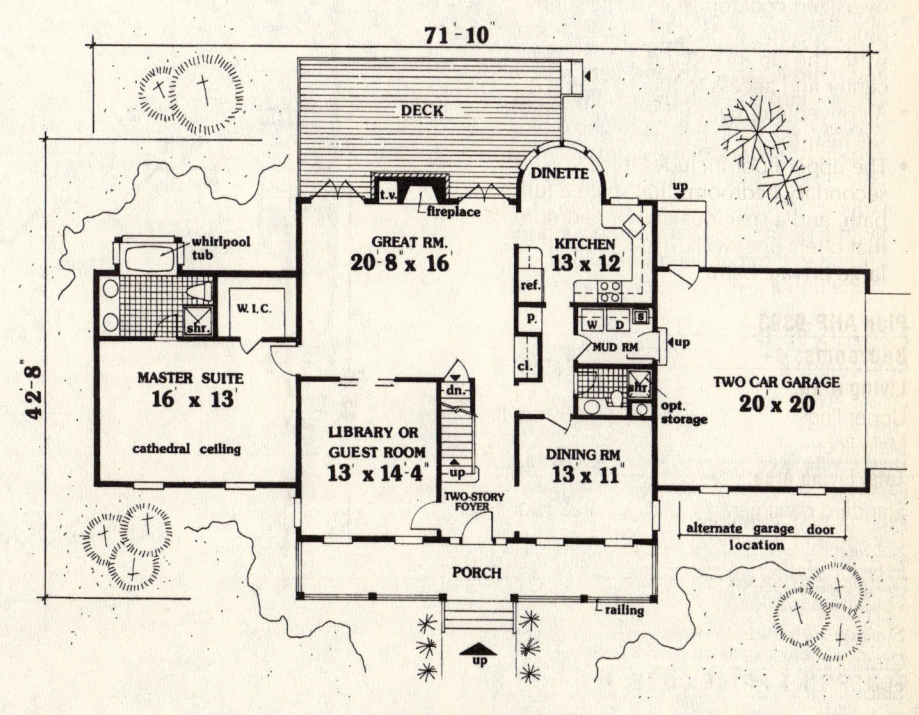

MAIN FLOOR

ORDER BLUEPRINTS ANYTIME!
CALL TOLL-FREE 1-888-626-2026

Plan AHP-9490

PRICES AND DETAILS ON PAGES 12-15

Peace of Mind

- Peace and privacy were the inspiration for this tranquil home.
- Past the inviting columned entry, the bright foyer flows into the spacious 13½-ft.-high vaulted living room, which includes a wet bar.
- The gourmet kitchen enjoys a 14-ft. vaulted ceiling and includes an angled snack counter and a large pantry. Sliding glass doors in the adjoining breakfast nook lead to a covered patio with a functional summer kitchen.
- The adjacent family room boasts a 15-ft. vaulted ceiling and a handsome window-flanked fireplace.
- The master suite offers an 11½-ft. vaulted ceiling, a windowed sitting area and patio access. His-and-hers walk-in closets flank the entrance to the plush master bath, which is highlighted by a garden tub overlooking a privacy yard.
- Three more bedrooms have vaulted ceilings that are at least 11½ ft. high. With a nearby full bath and back door entrance, the rear bedroom could be made into a great guest or in-law suite.

Plan HDS-99-157

Bedrooms: 4	Baths: 3

Living Area:
Main floor	2,224 sq. ft.
Total Living Area:	**2,224 sq. ft.**
Garage	507 sq. ft.

Exterior Wall Framing:
2x4 and concrete block

Foundation Options:
Slab
(All plans can be built with your choice of foundation and framing. A generic conversion diagram is available. See order form.)

BLUEPRINT PRICE CODE: C

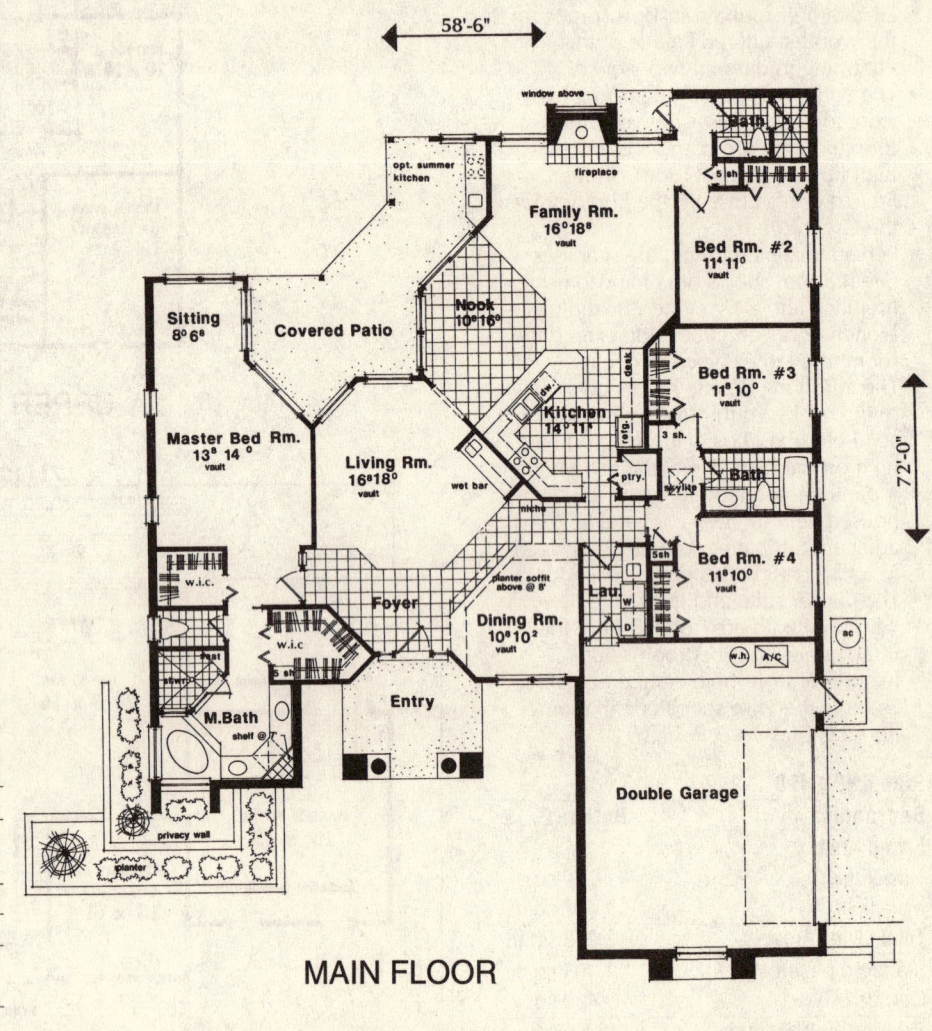

MAIN FLOOR

Charming Chateau

- A two-story arched entry introduces this charming French chateau.
- To the left of the tiled foyer, the elegant formal dining room will impress friends when you entertain.
- In the kitchen, a handy island worktop and a step-in pantry take advantage of the unique space. The cheery breakfast nook is a great spot for family meals.
- A neat see-through fireplace and built-in bookshelves define the formal living room and the casual family room. Lovely French doors open to a quiet covered porch in back.
- The secluded master suite on the main floor boasts two enormous walk-in closets and a lush private bath with an inviting marble tub, a separate shower and his-and-hers vanities.
- The kitchen and the nook have 9- and 8-ft. ceilings, respectively. All other main-floor rooms are enhanced by soaring 10-ft. ceilings.
- On the upper floor, two bedrooms share a unique bath. The front bedroom offers a 10-ft. ceiling. A bonus room can be adapted to fit your future needs.

Plan RD-2225	
Bedrooms: 3	**Baths:** 2½
Living Area:	
Upper floor	547 sq. ft.
Main floor	1,678 sq. ft.
Total Living Area:	**2,225 sq. ft.**
Bonus room (unfinished)	136 sq. ft.
Garage and storage	519 sq. ft.
Exterior Wall Framing:	2x4

Foundation Options:
Crawlspace
Slab
(All plans can be built with your choice of foundation and framing. A generic conversion diagram is available. See order form.)

BLUEPRINT PRICE CODE: C

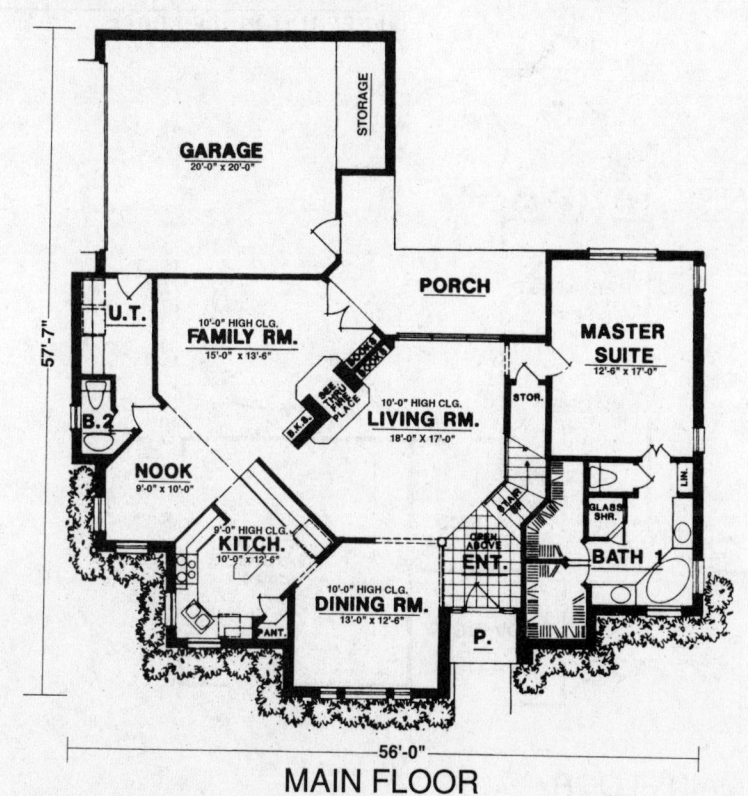

MAIN FLOOR

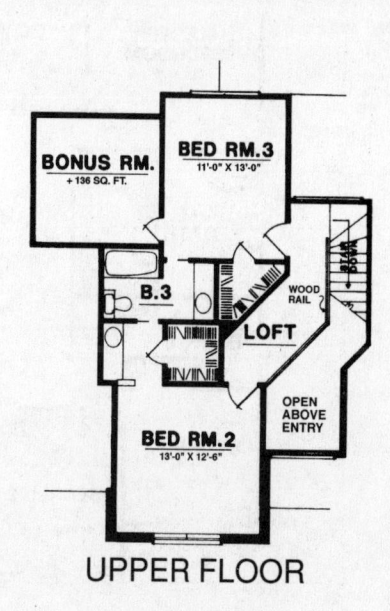

UPPER FLOOR

ORDER BLUEPRINTS ANYTIME! CALL TOLL-FREE 1-888-626-2026

Plan RD-2225

PRICES AND DETAILS ON PAGES 12-15

Nicely Done!

- An inviting window-covered exterior, coupled with an interior designed to give a sunny, open feel, will have you saying, "Nicely done!"
- Two eye-catching dormers, front-facing gables and two stately columns on the covered porch add a balanced sense of high style.
- The gallery, with its 13-ft. ceiling, presents guests with a dramatic entrance, and offers a gorgeous view into the huge Great Room through three elegantly inviting openings.
- The island kitchen will lure any gourmet. Nestled between the formal dining room and the breakfast room, it stands ready for all types of meals. Just steps away, the mudroom lets you keep an eye on the laundry while you cook.
- The lovely master bedroom greets you with an abundance of charms: an enormous walk-in closet, a private bath with a dual-sink vanity and a garden tub, plus convenient access to the large covered patio in back.
- That patio, you'll find, is the stuff of dreams—allowing you to enjoy outdoor meals come rain or shine!

Plan DD-2228

Bedrooms: 3	Baths: 2

Living Area:
Main floor	2,228 sq. ft.
Total Living Area:	**2,228 sq. ft.**
Standard basement	2,228 sq. ft.
Garage	431 sq. ft.

Exterior Wall Framing:	2x4

Foundation Options:
Standard basement
Crawlspace
Slab
(All plans can be built with your choice of foundation and framing. A generic conversion diagram is available. See order form.)

BLUEPRINT PRICE CODE: C

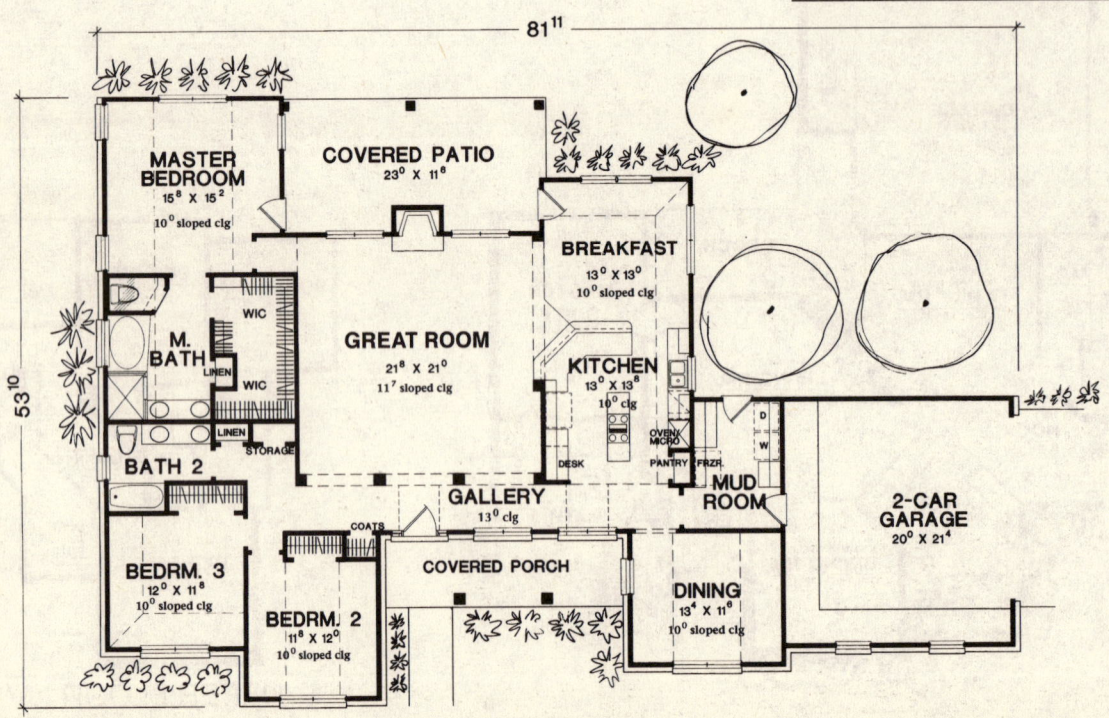

MAIN FLOOR

Plan DD-2228

Appealing and Well-Appointed

- A feature-filled interior and a warm, appealing exterior are the keynotes of this spacious two-story home.
- Beyond the charming front porch, the foyer is brightened by sidelights and an octagonal window. To the right, a cased opening leads into the open living room and dining room. Plenty of windows, including a beautiful boxed-out window, bathe the formal area in light.
- The casual area consists of an extra-large island kitchen, a sizable breakfast area and a spectacular family room with a corner fireplace and a skylighted cathedral ceiling that slopes from 11 ft. to 17 ft. high.
- The upper floor hosts a superb master suite, featuring a skylighted bath with an 11-ft. sloped ceiling, a platform spa tub and a separate shower.
- A balcony hall leads to two more bedrooms, a full bath and an optional bonus room that would make a great loft, study or extra bedroom.

Plan AX-8923-A

Bedrooms: 3+	Baths: 2½
Living Area:	
Upper floor	853 sq. ft.
Main floor	1,199 sq. ft.
Optional loft/bedroom	180 sq. ft.
Total Living Area:	**2,232 sq. ft.**
Standard basement	1,184 sq. ft.
Garage	420 sq. ft.
Exterior Wall Framing:	2x4

Foundation Options:
Standard basement
Slab
(All plans can be built with your choice of foundation and framing. A generic conversion diagram is available. See order form.)

BLUEPRINT PRICE CODE: C

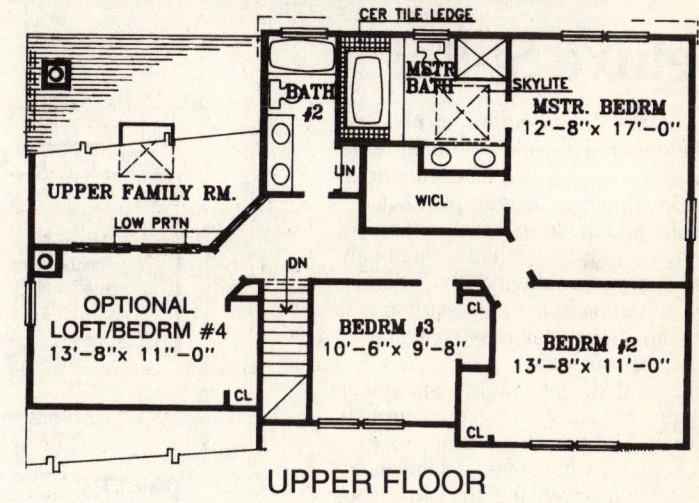

UPPER FLOOR

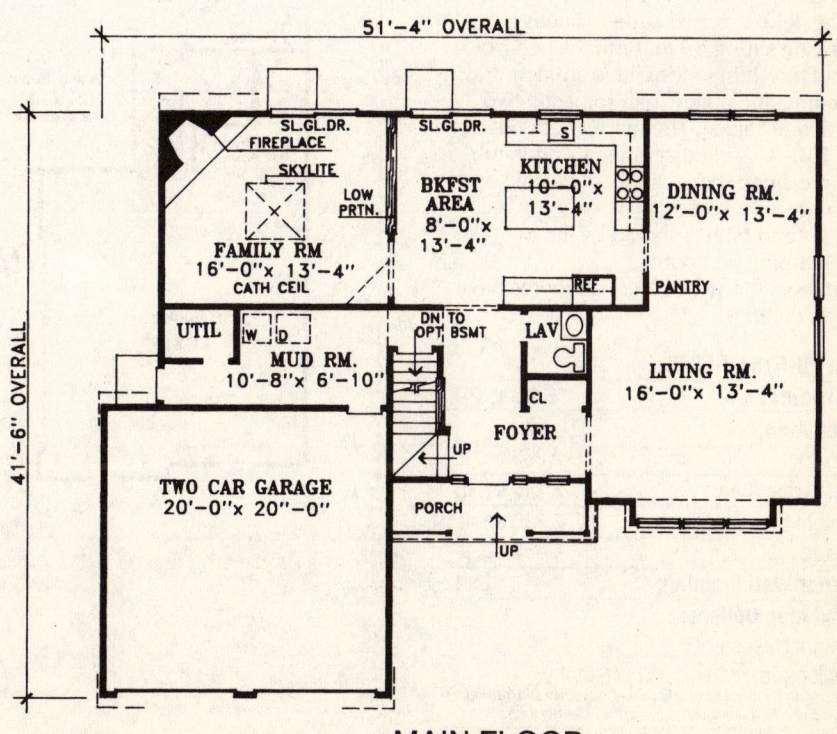

MAIN FLOOR

ORDER BLUEPRINTS ANYTIME!
CALL TOLL-FREE 1-888-626-2026

Plan AX-8923-A

PRICES AND DETAILS
ON PAGES 12-15

Deluxe Suite!

- Decorative corner quoins, arched windows and a sleek hip roofline give this charming home a European look.
- The inviting foyer extends its 12-ft. ceiling into the formal spaces. The airy living room is brightened by high half- and quarter-round windows.
- The adjoining formal dining room is set off with elegant columned openings and high plant shelves.
- The island kitchen features a pantry and a sunny breakfast bay. A pass-through over the sink serves the family room.
- Boasting a 17-ft. vaulted ceiling and a glass-flanked fireplace, the family room also enjoys backyard access.
- The deluxe master suite includes a private sitting room. Both the bedroom and the sitting room have an 11-ft. tray ceiling and a view of a romantic two-sided fireplace. The master bath boasts a 13½-ft. vaulted ceiling, a garden tub, a three-sided mirror and a dual-sink vanity with knee space.
- A second bath is shared by the two remaining bedrooms.
- Unless otherwise noted, all rooms have 9-ft. ceilings.

Plan FB-5154-GEOR

| Bedrooms: 3 | Baths: 2½ |
|---|---|//
Living Area:	
Main floor	2,236 sq. ft.
Total Living Area:	**2,236 sq. ft.**
Daylight basement	2,236 sq. ft.
Garage	483 sq. ft.
Exterior Wall Framing:	2x4

Foundation Options:
Daylight basement
Crawlspace
(All plans can be built with your choice of foundation and framing. A generic conversion diagram is available. See order form.)

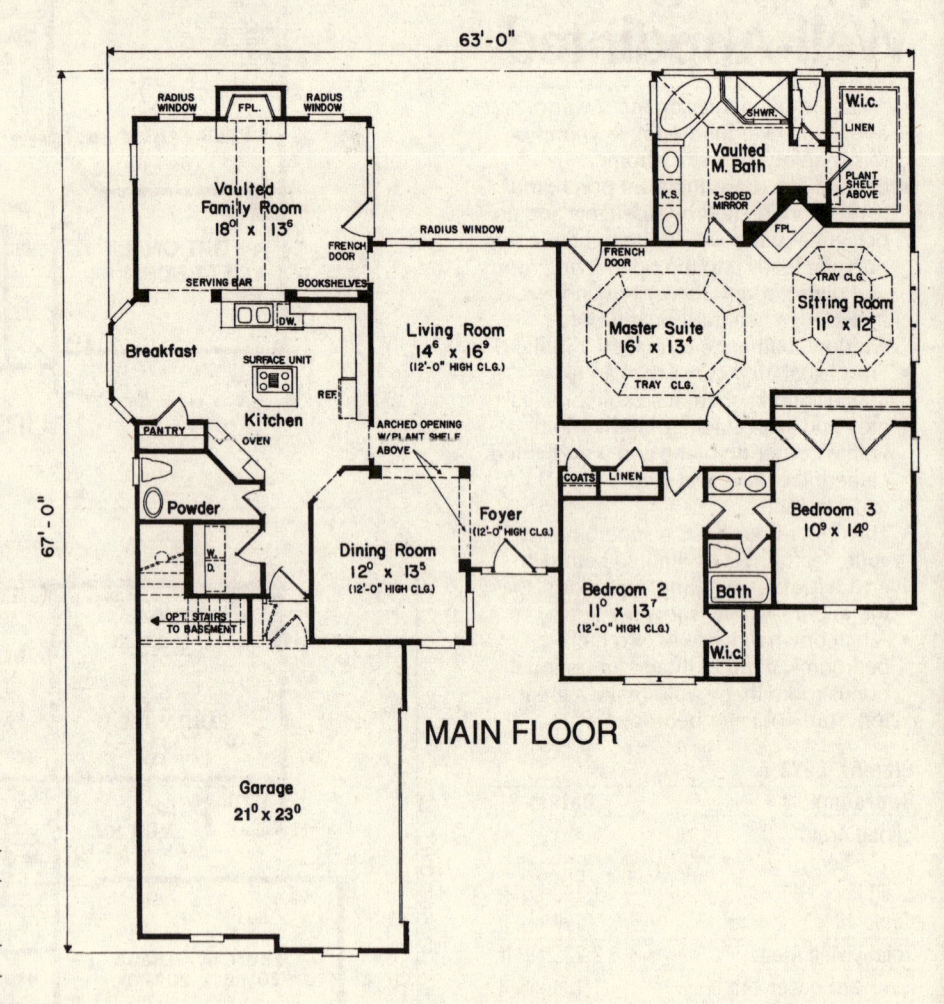

BLUEPRINT PRICE CODE: C

MAIN FLOOR

ORDER BLUEPRINTS ANYTIME! CALL TOLL-FREE 1-888-626-2026

Plan FB-5154-GEOR

PRICES AND DETAILS ON PAGES 12-15

Sunny Charmer

- A huge wraparound porch highlights this bright and airy country charmer.
- Inside, the two-story vaulted foyer is bathed in sunlight from the expansive arched window above. The formal dining room and a cozy parlor complete the front area.
- Straight ahead is the spectacular family room, featuring a 17-ft. vaulted ceiling, a unique three-sided fireplace and double French doors leading to a large back porch and deck.
- A breakfast bar divides the U-shaped kitchen from the sunny breakfast nook, which overlooks the backyard.
- The expansive master bedroom features a large walk-in closet and private access to the front porch. The master bath includes dual vanities, a garden tub, a private toilet and a tray ceiling.
- Ceilings in all main-floor rooms are at least 9 ft. high for added spaciousness.
- Upstairs, the two remaining bedrooms share a second full bath.
- A two-car detached garage with an optional studio and bath above is included in the blueprints.

Plan APS-2218

Bedrooms: 3	Baths: 2½
Living Area:	
Upper floor	607 sq. ft.
Main floor	1,632 sq. ft.
Total Living Area:	**2,239 sq. ft.**
Detached garage	624 sq. ft.
Exterior Wall	2x4

Foundation Options:
Crawlspace
(All plans can be built with your choice of foundation and framing. A generic conversion diagram is available. See order form.)

BLUEPRINT PRICE CODE: C

UPPER FLOOR

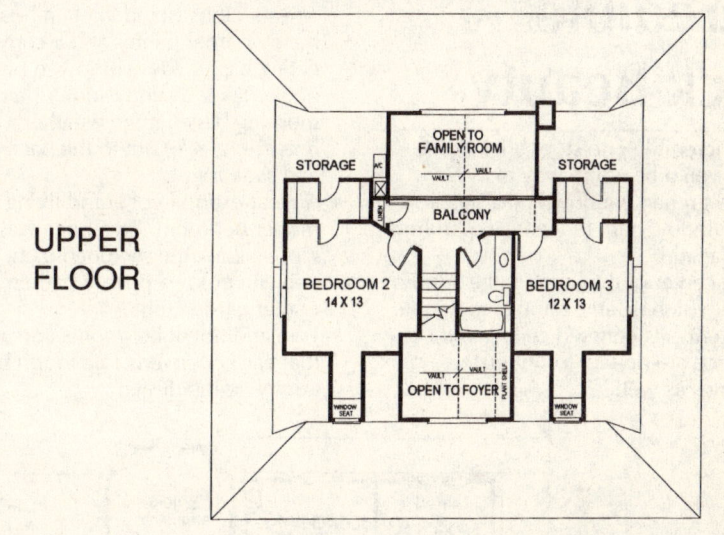

MAIN FLOOR

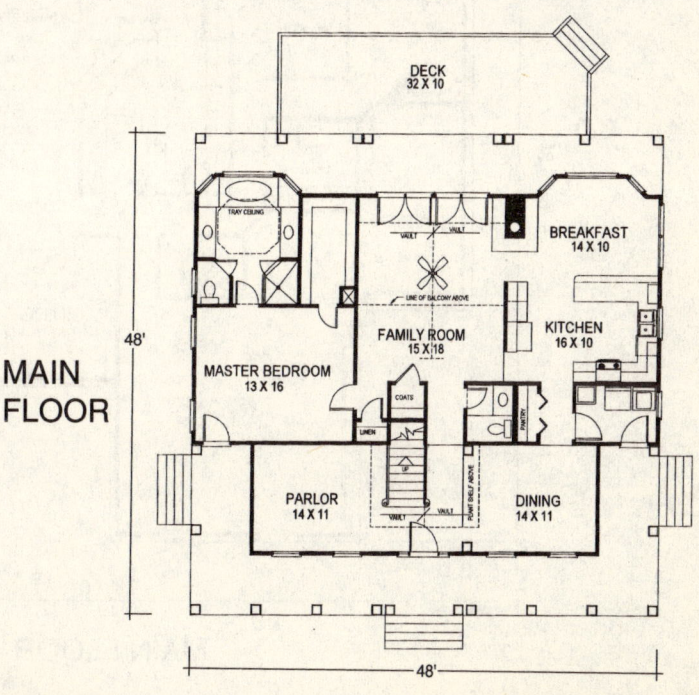

Plan APS-2218

Incredible Brick Beauty

- This incredible one-story brick home offers you a beautiful way to live.
- A bold arched window and a stylish, oval window help to create a sparkling front facade.
- At the center of the home is the family room, which is large enough to handle big events. Its coffered ceiling and cozy fireplace are perfect for intimate evenings as well.
- The spacious island kitchen boasts a handy corner pantry and a convenient eating bar. A bay-windowed breakfast nook makes a sunny spot for a quick morning bagel; if the weather's irresistible, step out to the back porch and soak it up!
- A great example of grand living is the master bedroom. Two huge walk-in closets flank the secluded bath, where you can enjoy a private bath in the corner garden tub.
- Two additional bedrooms and a study that easily converts to a fourth bedroom complete the design.

Plan KLF-973

Bedrooms: 3+	Baths: 2

Living Area:
Main floor — 2,244 sq. ft.
Total Living Area: — **2,244 sq. ft.**
Garage — 791 sq. ft.
Exterior Wall Framing: — 2x4
Foundation Options:
Slab
(All plans can be built with your choice of foundation and framing. A generic conversion diagram is available. See order form.)
BLUEPRINT PRICE CODE: C

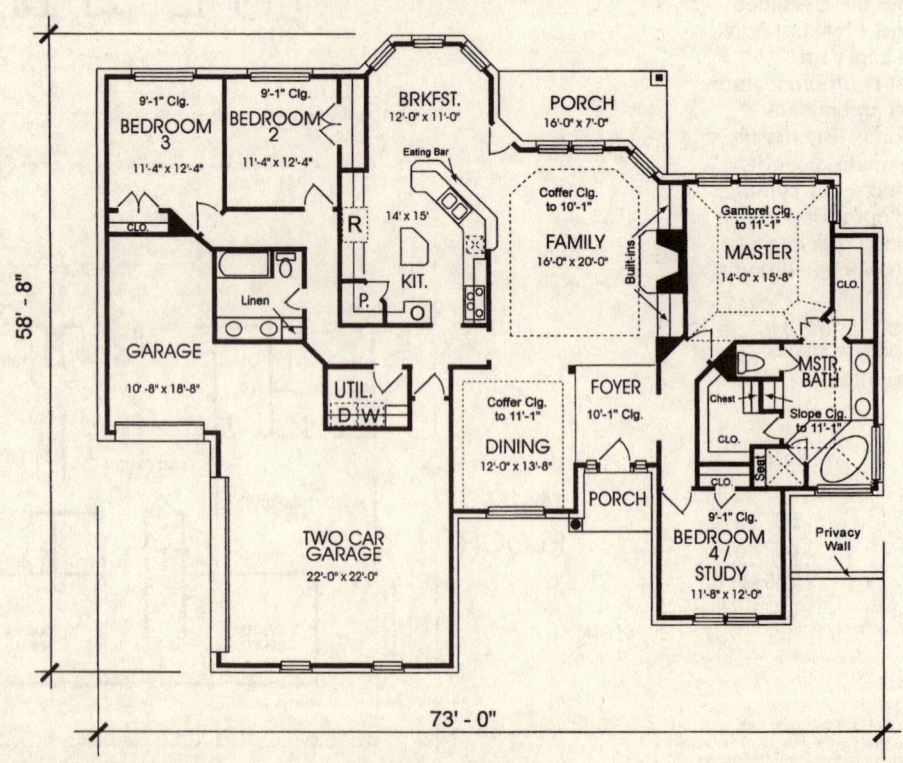

MAIN FLOOR

Plan KLF-973

ORDER BLUEPRINTS ANYTIME! CALL TOLL-FREE 1-888-626-2026

PRICES AND DETAILS ON PAGES 12-15

Sunny Comfort

- A covered wraparound porch and lovely arched windows give this home a comfortable country style.
- Inside, an elegant columned archway introduces the formal dining room.
- The huge Great Room features an 18-ft. vaulted ceiling, a dramatic wall of windows and two built-in wall units on either side of the fireplace.
- Ample counter space and a convenient work island allow maximum use of the roomy kitchen.
- The sunny breakfast nook opens to a porch through sliding glass doors.
- On the other side of the home, a dramatic bay window and a 10-ft. ceiling highlight the master bedroom. The enormous master bath features a luxurious whirlpool tub.
- Unless otherwise noted, all main-floor rooms have 9-ft. ceilings.
- Open stairs lead up to a balcony with a magnificent view of the Great Room. Two upstairs bedrooms, one with an 11-ft. vaulted ceiling, share a bath.

Plan AX-94317

Bedrooms: 3	Baths: 2½
Living Area:	
Upper floor	525 sq. ft.
Main floor	1,720 sq. ft.
Total Living Area:	**2,245 sq. ft.**
Standard basement	1,720 sq. ft.
Garage	502 sq. ft.
Storage/utility	51 sq. ft.
Exterior Wall Framing:	2x4

Foundation Options:
Standard basement
Crawlspace
Slab
(All plans can be built with your choice of foundation and framing. A generic conversion diagram is available. See order form.)

BLUEPRINT PRICE CODE: C

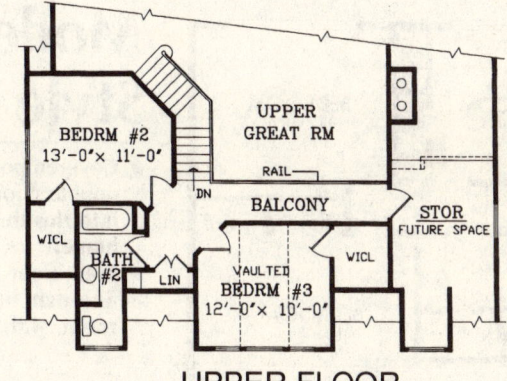

ORDER BLUEPRINTS ANYTIME!
CALL TOLL-FREE 1-888-626-2026

Plan AX-94317

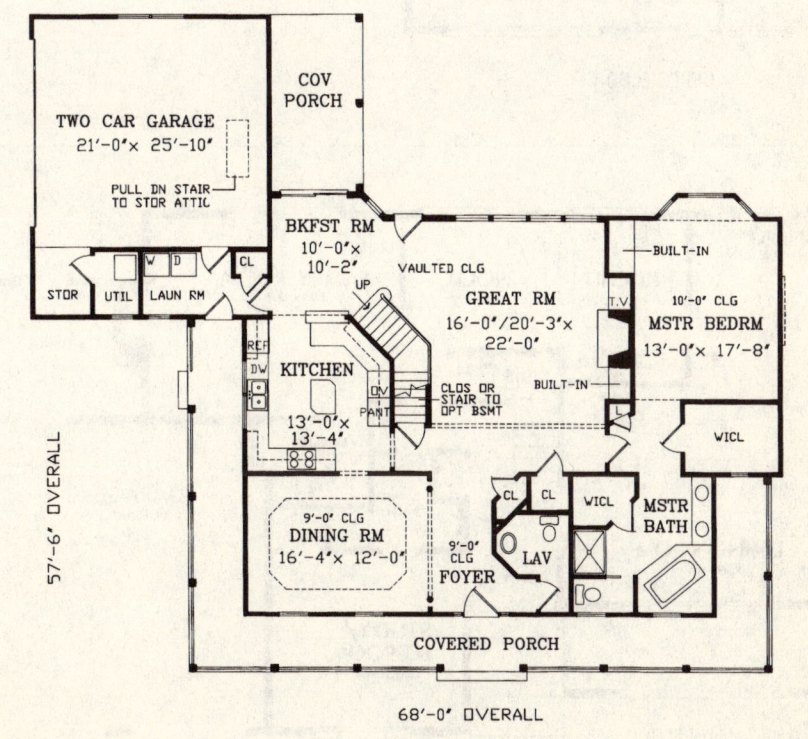

PRICES AND DETAILS ON PAGES 12-15

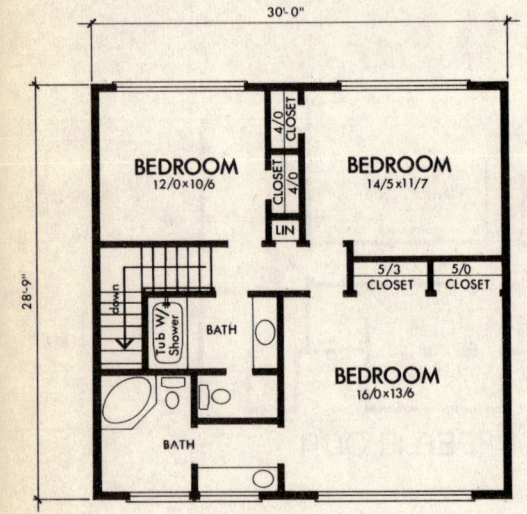

Modern Traditional-Style Home

- Covered porch and decorative double doors offer an invitation into this three or four bedroom home.
- Main floor bedroom may be used as a den, home office, or guest room, with convenient bath facilities.
- Adjoining dining room makes living room seem even more spacious; breakfast nook enlarges the look of the attached kitchen.
- Brick-size concrete block veneer and masonry tile roof give the exterior a look of durability.

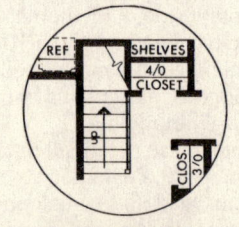

PLAN H-1351-M1A
WITHOUT BASEMENT
(CRAWLSPACE FOUNDATION)

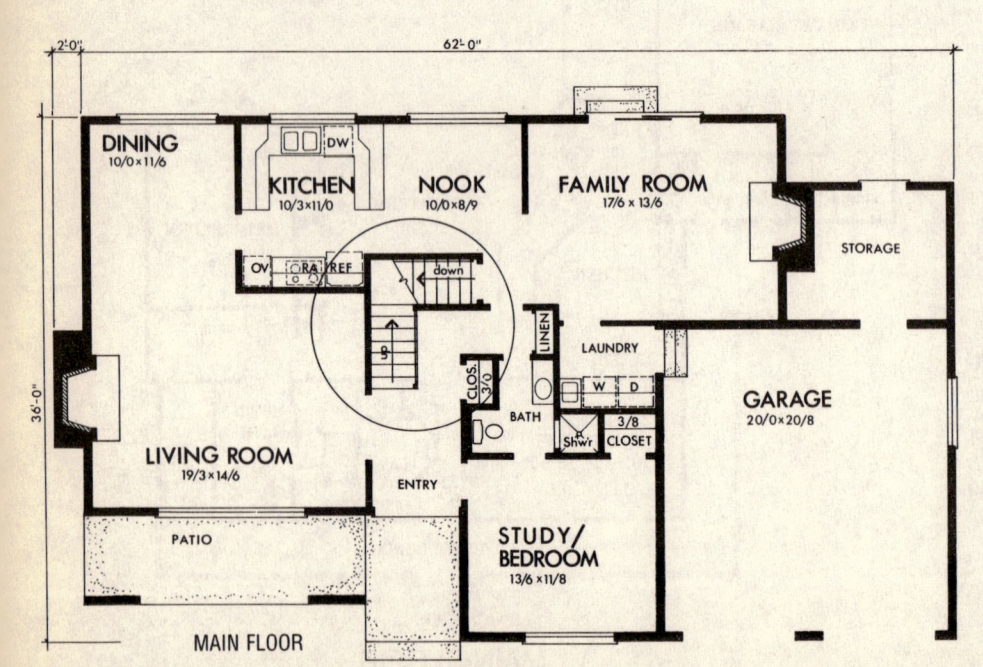

Plans H-1351-M1 & -M1A

Bedrooms: 3-4	Baths: 3

Space:
Upper floor:	862 sq. ft.
Main floor:	1,383 sq. ft.
Total living area:	2,245 sq. ft.
Basement:	1,383 sq. ft.
Garage:	413 sq. ft.

Exterior Wall Framing: 2x6

Foundation options:
Standard basement (Plan H-1351-M1).
Crawlspace (Plan H-1351-M1A).
(Foundation & framing conversion diagram available — see order form.)

Blueprint Price Code: C

ORDER BLUEPRINTS ANYTIME! CALL TOLL-FREE 1-888-626-2026

Plans H-1351-M1 & -M1A

PRICES AND DETAILS ON PAGES 12-15

Luxurious Living on One Level

- The elegant exterior of this spacious one-story presents a classic air of quality and distinction.
- Three French doors brighten the inviting entry, which flows into the spacious living room. Boasting a 13-ft. ceiling, the living room enjoys a fireplace with a wide hearth and adjoining built-in bookshelves. A wall of glass, including a French door, provides views of the sheltered backyard porch.
- A stylish angled counter joins the spacious kitchen to the sunny bay-windowed eating nook.
- Secluded for privacy, the master suite features a nice dressing area, a large walk-in closet and private backyard access. A convenient laundry/utility room is adjacent to the master bath.
- At the opposite end of the home, double doors lead to three more bedrooms, a compartmentalized bath and lots of closet space.

Plan E-2208

Bedrooms: 4	**Baths:** 2

Living Area:
Main floor — 2,252 sq. ft.
Total Living Area: — **2,252 sq. ft.**
Standard basement — 2,252 sq. ft.
Garage and storage — 592 sq. ft.
Exterior Wall Framing: 2x6
Foundation Options:
Standard basement
Crawlspace
Slab
(All plans can be built with your choice of foundation and framing. A generic conversion diagram is available. See order form.)

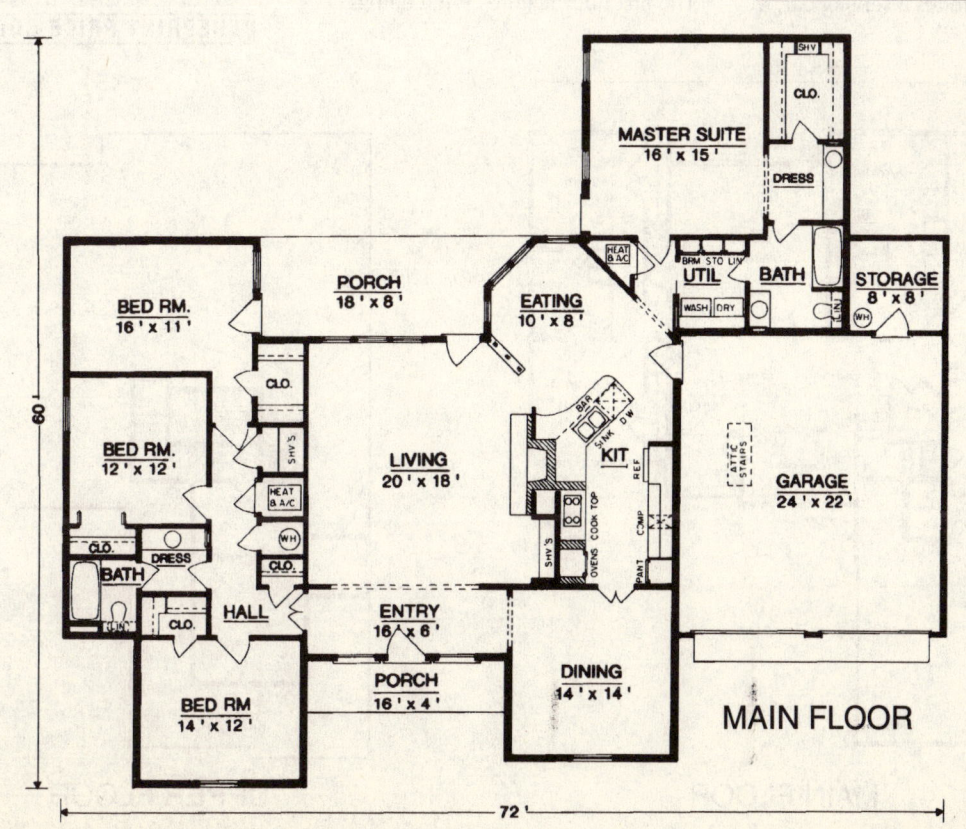

BLUEPRINT PRICE CODE: C

ORDER BLUEPRINTS ANYTIME!
CALL TOLL-FREE 1-888-626-2026

Plan E-2208

PRICES AND DETAILS ON PAGES 12-15

Vaulted Living

- The covered porch leads into the grand foyer of this home, where vaulted ceilings and spectacular views leave you breathless.
- Entertain friends in the vaulted living room while a fire roars in the fireplace. A beautiful radius window provides picturesque views of backyard wildlife.
- A boxed column helps to define the formal dining area, creating the ideal setting for an elegant meal.
- Informal dining is a snap in the large kitchen, which includes a serving bar, a separate pantry and a sunny breakfast nook with a built-in desk.
- A unique master bath with a whirlpool tub, a dual-sink vanity and a huge walk-in closet invites you to retreat to the master suite, which is crowned by a magnificent tray ceiling.
- A full bath with a dual-sink vanity may be accessed from the remaining two bedrooms, which boast spacious closets and plenty of natural light.
- The bonus room above the garage, with a full bath and a walk-in closet, is the perfect space for a fourth bedroom.
- The first floor features 9-ft. ceilings.

Plan FB-5500-BAGW	
Bedrooms: 3+	Baths: 3½
Living Area:	
Upper floor	409 sq. ft.
Main floor	1,845 sq. ft.
Total Living Area:	**2,254 sq. ft.**
Daylight basement	1,845 sq. ft.
Garage	529 sq. ft.
Exterior Wall Framing:	2x4
Foundation Options:	
Daylight basement	
Crawlspace	

(All plans can be built with your choice of foundation and framing. A generic conversion diagram is available. See order form.)

BLUEPRINT PRICE CODE: C

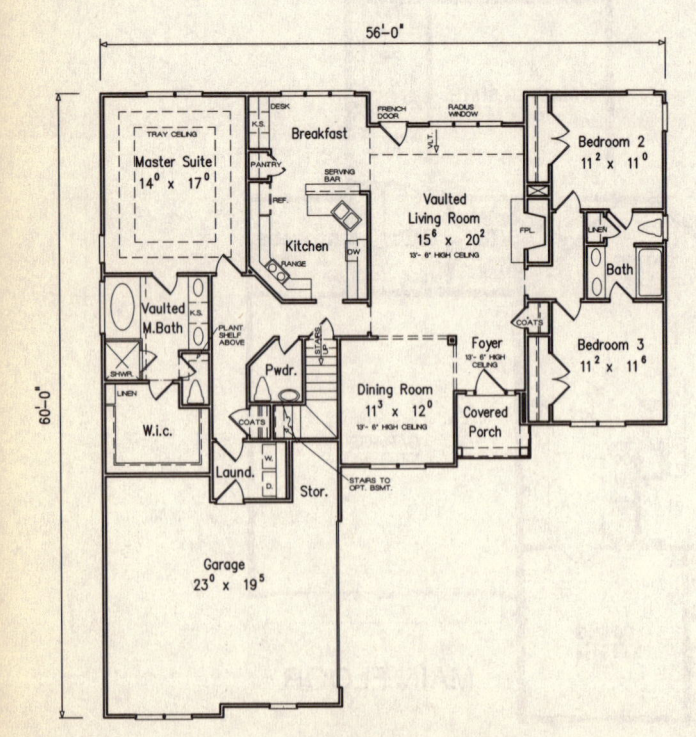

MAIN FLOOR

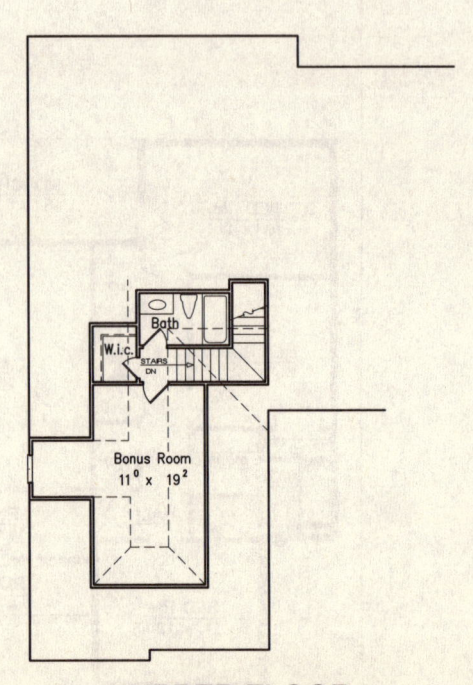

UPPER FLOOR

ORDER BLUEPRINTS ANYTIME! CALL TOLL-FREE 1-888-626-2026

Plan FB-5500-BAGW

PRICES AND DETAILS ON PAGES 12-15

Family-Style Traditional

- An inviting covered porch, shuttered windows and a beautiful bay welcome guests to this elegant traditional home.
- Formal living spaces flank the 17-ft.-high vaulted foyer, while the informal areas are oriented to the rear of the home. Direct access to the family room is possible with a pair of optional doors in the living room.
- The spacious family room is the highlight of the home's activity center, with its fireplace, built-in entertainment center and patio access.
- An angled serving bar sets off the bright and roomy kitchen, complete with a vaulted, bayed breakfast nook.
- Three bedrooms, two full baths and an optional bonus room are located upstairs. The bonus room offers extra storage areas with limited clearance.
- The master suite boasts built-in cabinets, a walk-in closet and a sumptuous private bath with a garden tub, a separate shower, a dual-sink vanity and a compartmentalized toilet.

Plan S-12293

Bedrooms: 3+	Baths: 2½

Living Area:
Upper floor	868 sq. ft.
Main floor	1,066 sq. ft.
Bonus room	320 sq. ft.
Total Living Area:	**2,254 sq. ft.**
Standard basement	1,025 sq. ft.
Garage	515 sq. ft.
Exterior Wall Framing:	2x6

Foundation Options:
Standard basement
Crawlspace
Slab
(All plans can be built with your choice of foundation and framing. A generic conversion diagram is available. See order form.)

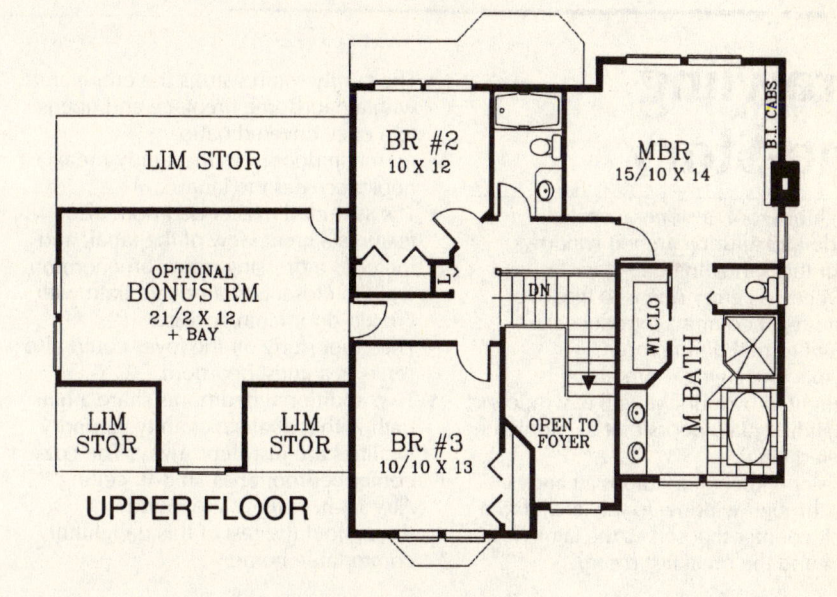

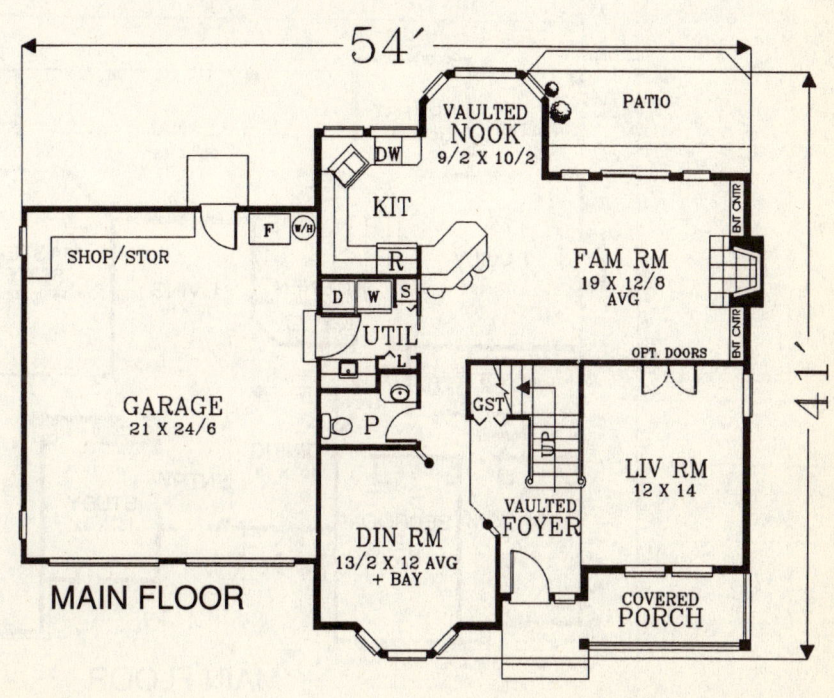

BLUEPRINT PRICE CODE: C

ORDER BLUEPRINTS ANYTIME!
CALL TOLL-FREE 1-888-626-2026

Plan S-12293

PRICES AND DETAILS ON PAGES 12-15

Sprawling One-Story

- A high hip roof, a stone-accented facade and alluring arched windows adorn this sprawling one-story.
- The recessed entry opens to the foyer, where regal columns introduce the elegant formal dining room.
- The spacious living room ahead is highlighted by a bright wall of windows and sliding glass doors that overlook the covered lanai.
- The island kitchen includes a handy pass-through window to the lanai and a snack counter that serves the family room and the breakfast room.
- The family room warms the entire area with a handsome fireplace and opens to a cozy covered patio.
- A French door from the sunny breakfast nook accesses the lanai.
- The secluded master bedroom also features a great view of the lanai, and includes a dressing room, an enormous walk-in closet and a private bath with French-door lanai access.
- The quiet study off the foyer could also serve as a guest bedroom.
- Two additional bedrooms share a hall bath with a dual-sink vanity. Laundry facilities are just steps away. The cozy corner bedroom has an 8-ft. ceiling. Airy 10-ft. ceilings are found throughout the rest of this delightfully comfortable home.

Plan DD-2241-1

Bedrooms: 3+	Baths: 2

Living Area:
Main floor — 2,256 sq. ft.
Total Living Area: **2,256 sq. ft.**
Standard basement — 2,256 sq. ft.
Garage — 469 sq. ft.

Exterior Wall Framing: 2x4

Foundation Options:
Standard basement
Crawlspace
Slab
(All plans can be built with your choice of foundation and framing. A generic conversion diagram is available. See order form.)

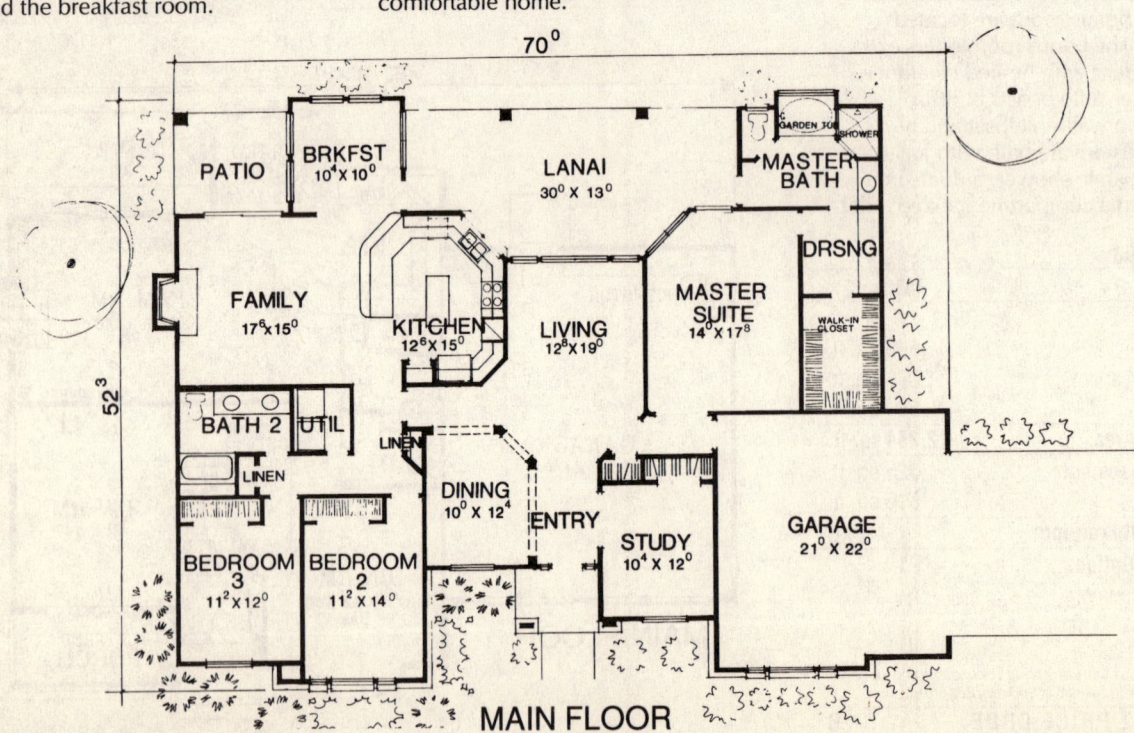

BLUEPRINT PRICE CODE: C

Plan DD-2241-1

Soulful Enclosure

- This home's warm country accents and delightful interior appointments combine to bring peace to your soul and comfort to your days.
- The high entry introduces the bayed dining room to the left; straight ahead, the expansive living room beckons. Here, radiant windows bathe the space in natural light. A French door leads to a backyard porch. For romantic weekend nights, the fireplace is perfect.
- A boxed-out window brightens the breakfast nook. A raised bar smoothly joins the nook to the walk-through kitchen. There is plenty of room for two cooks here, plus a young apprentice!
- Sublime quietude reigns in the secluded master suite. A cute window seat provides a sweet spot for reading or needlepoint. The private bath spoils you with two big walk-in closets and a stunning oval tub.
- The upper floor is no less tempting. It offers two additional bedrooms with a shared bath, and a vast bonus room that could become a media room or a suite for your boomerang child.

Plan RD-2000

Bedrooms: 3+	Baths: 2½
Living Area:	
Upper floor	560 sq. ft.
Main floor	1,440 sq. ft.
Bonus room	267 sq. ft.
Total Living Area:	**2,267 sq. ft.**
Standard basement	1,430 sq. ft.
Garage	424 sq. ft.
Exterior Wall Framing:	**2x4**

Foundation Options:
Standard basement
Crawlspace
Slab
(All plans can be built with your choice of foundation and framing. A generic conversion diagram is available. See order form.)

BLUEPRINT PRICE CODE: C

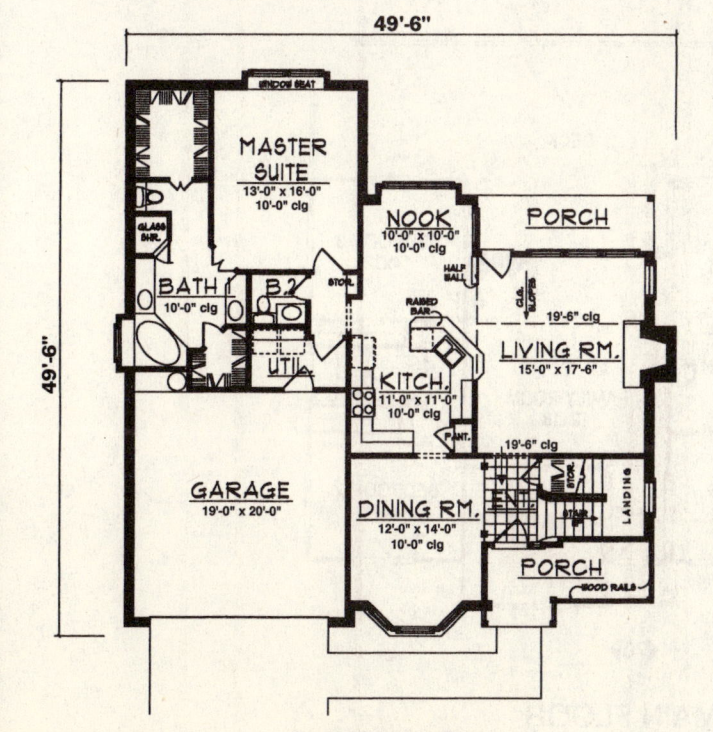

MAIN FLOOR

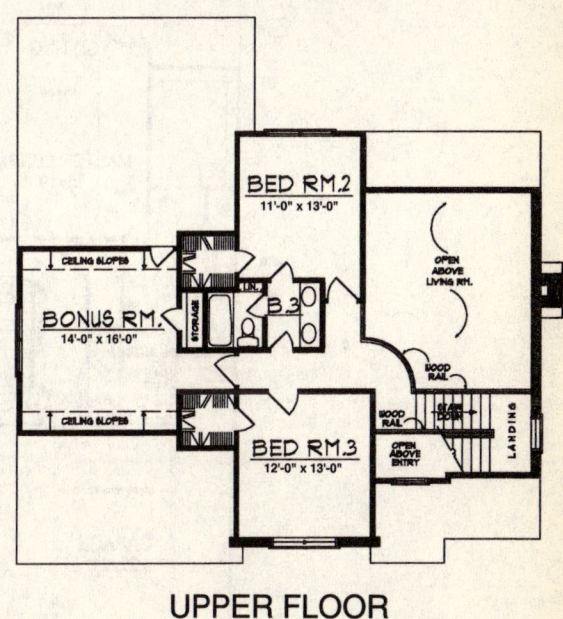

UPPER FLOOR

ORDER BLUEPRINTS ANYTIME! CALL TOLL-FREE 1-888-626-2026

Plan RD-2000

PRICES AND DETAILS ON PAGES 12-15

Family Ties

- This home's wonderful design, both inside and out, will enhance the ties that bind your family together.
- Decorative columns frame the entry of the living room, where a soaring 14-ft. vaulted ceiling crowns the space.
- Special occasions call for special meals in the formal dining room.
- Topped by a 14-ft. ceiling, the family room begs you to relax beside a glowing fire. Step out to the backyard deck through a sliding glass door to enjoy a bright summer day.
- The roomy kitchen easily accesses both the formal dining room and the sunny breakfast nook. All three spaces boast 11-ft. ceilings.
- Retreat to the stunning master suite, where a 14-ft. vaulted ceiling brightens the space. A bayed sitting area unfolds beyond a private deck access, and the luxurious bath offers a relaxing spa tub.
- Create another bedroom or a rec room in the bonus area above the garage.
- Unless specified otherwise, this home features 9-ft ceilings.

Plan APS-2219

Bedrooms: 3	**Baths:** 2½
Living Area:	
Main floor	2,290 sq. ft.
Total Living Area:	**2,290 sq. ft.**
Bonus room	234 sq. ft.
Daylight basement	2,290 sq. ft.
Garage	504 sq. ft.
Exterior Wall Framing:	2x4

Foundation Options:
Daylight basement
(All plans can be built with your choice of foundation and framing. A generic conversion diagram is available. See order form.)

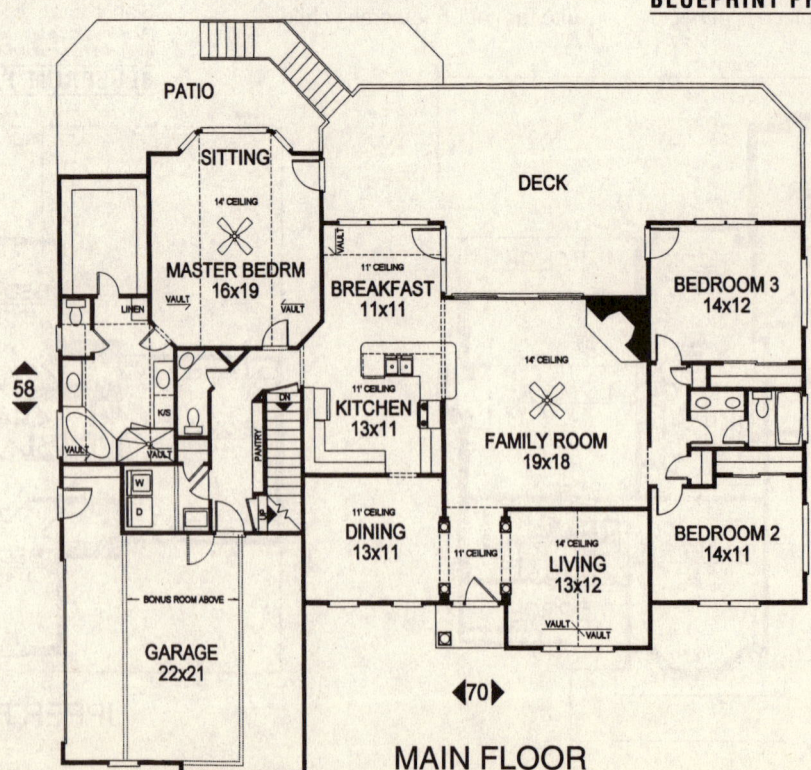

BLUEPRINT PRICE CODE: C

MAIN FLOOR

Plan APS-2219

ORDER BLUEPRINTS ANYTIME!
CALL TOLL-FREE 1-888-626-2026

PRICES AND DETAILS ON PAGES 12-15

Distinctive Two-Story

- The playful and distinctive exterior of this two-story encloses a functional, contemporary interior.
- The living areas unfold from the skylighted foyer, which is open to the upper-floor balcony. The formal sunken living room features a soaring 17-ft. cathedral ceiling. The adjoining step-down family room offers a fireplace and sliding glass doors to a wonderful deck.
- A low partition allows a view of the family room's fireplace from the breakfast area and the island kitchen.
- A luxurious master suite with a 13-ft. cathedral ceiling and room for three additional bedrooms are found on the upper floor, in addition to a dramatic view of the foyer below.

Plan AX-8922-A

Bedrooms: 4	Baths: 2½
Living Area:	
Upper floor	1,080 sq. ft.
Main floor	1,213 sq. ft.
Total Living Area:	**2,293 sq. ft.**
Standard basement	1,138 sq. ft.
Garage	470 sq. ft.
Exterior Wall Framing:	2x4

Foundation Options:
Standard basement
Slab
(All plans can be built with your choice of foundation and framing. A generic conversion diagram is available. See order form.)

BLUEPRINT PRICE CODE: C

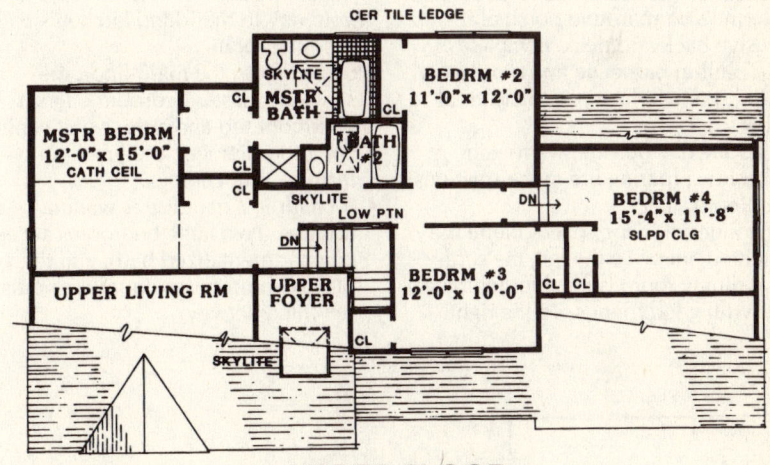

UPPER FLOOR

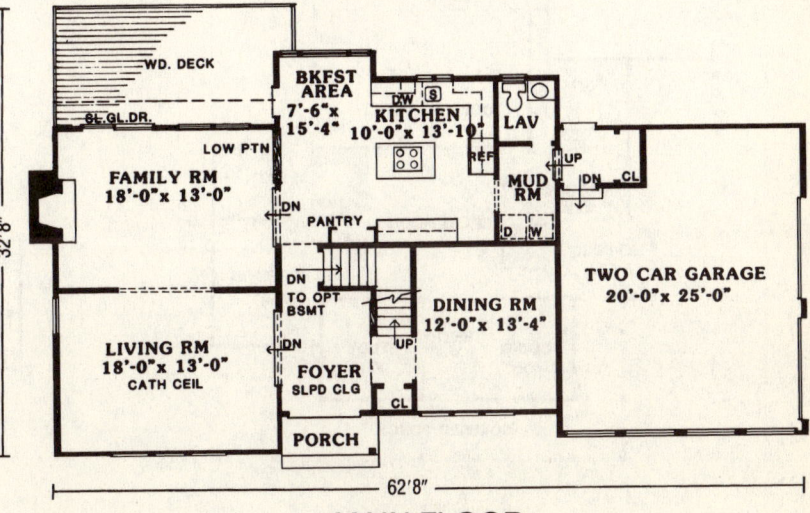

MAIN FLOOR

ORDER BLUEPRINTS ANYTIME!
CALL TOLL-FREE 1-888-626-2026

Plan AX-8922-A

PRICES AND DETAILS
ON PAGES 12-15

The Great Outdoors

- This home's wraparound porch and expansive backyard deck, complete with a built-in barbecue and room for a relaxing spa, will lure you to the great outdoors.
- After a long day outside, warm your toes beside a roaring fire in the spacious Great Room.
- Two wonderful living spaces frame the sidelighted entry. To the left, the sunny, formal dining room is ideal for intimate meals with good friends. To the right, the large study provides a quiet place to finish that novel you've been putting off for years.
- A steaming cup of coffee and a beautiful sunrise are great ways to start your day in the island kitchen's bayed morning room.
- Secluded on the main floor, the spacious master bedroom offers a whirlpool tub and a dual-sink vanity.
- For a roomier feel, the first floor features 9-ft. ceilings.
- A children's paradise is waiting upstairs. Two large bedrooms access a compartmentalized bath, and the playroom promises countless hours of fun-filled activity.

Plan DD-2298-1	
Bedrooms: 3+	**Baths:** 2½
Living Area:	
Upper floor	782 sq. ft.
Main floor	1,517 sq. ft.
Total Living Area:	**2,299 sq. ft.**
Upper floor storage	112 sq. ft.
Standard basement	1,517 sq. ft.
Garage and storage	456 sq. ft.
Exterior Wall Framing:	2x4

Foundation Options:
Standard basement
Crawlspace
Slab
(All plans can be built with your choice of foundation and framing. A generic conversion diagram is available. See order form.)

BLUEPRINT PRICE CODE: C

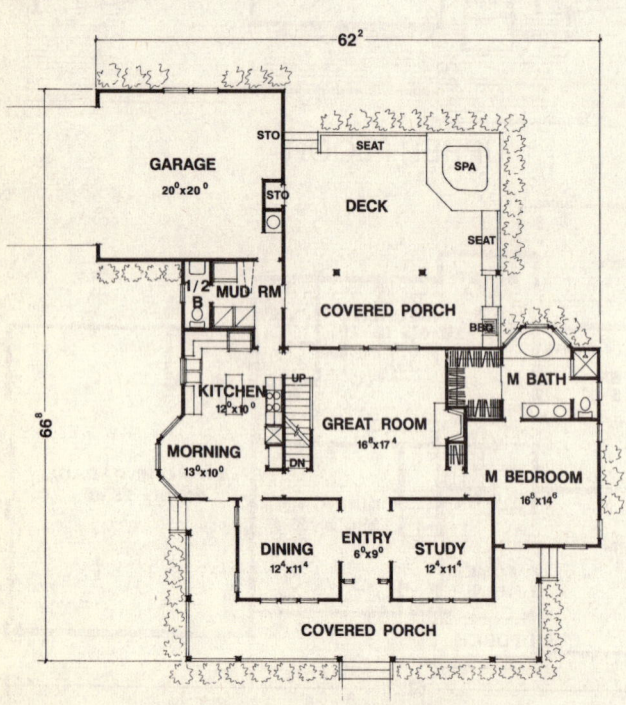

REAR VIEW

MAIN FLOOR

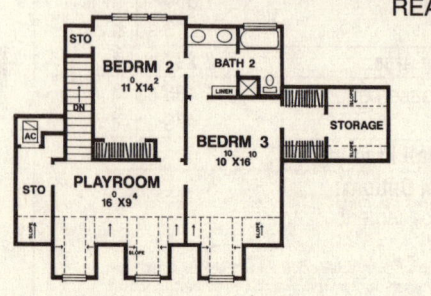

UPPER FLOOR

Plan DD-2298-1

Grand Colonial Home

- This grand Colonial home boasts a porch entry framed by bay windows and gable towers.
- The two-story foyer flows to the dining room on the left and adjoins the bayed living room on the right, with its warm fireplace and flanking windows.
- At the rear, the family room features a 17-ft. ceiling, a media wall, a bar and terrace access through French doors.
- Connected to the family room is a high-tech kitchen with an island work area, a pantry, a work desk and a circular dinette.
- A private terrace, a romantic fireplace, a huge walk-in closet and a lavish bath with a whirlpool tub are featured in the main-floor master suite.
- Three bedrooms and two full baths share the upper floor.

Plan AHP-9120

Bedrooms: 4	Baths: 3½
Living Area:	
Upper floor	776 sq. ft.
Main floor	1,551 sq. ft.
Total Living Area:	**2,327 sq. ft.**
Standard basement	1,580 sq. ft.
Garage	440 sq. ft.
Exterior Wall Framing:	2x4 or 2x6

Foundation Options:
Standard basement
Crawlspace
Slab
(All plans can be built with your choice of foundation and framing. A generic conversion diagram is available. See order form.)

BLUEPRINT PRICE CODE: C

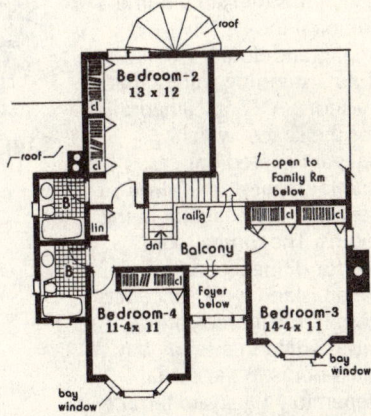

UPPER FLOOR

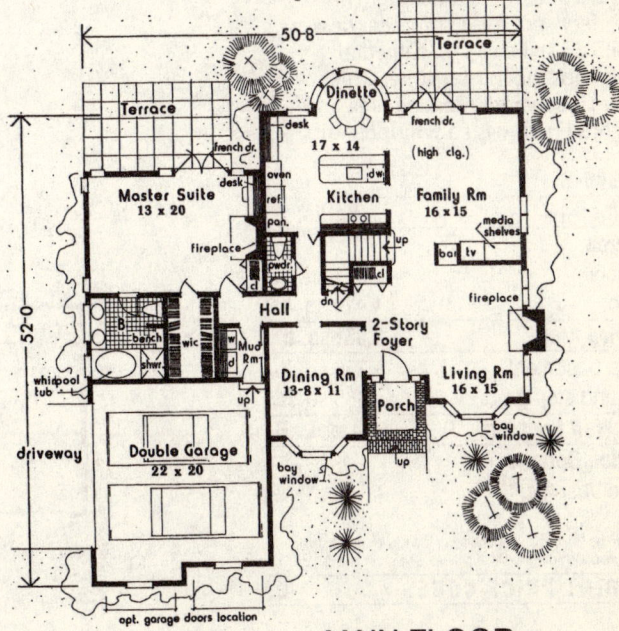

MAIN FLOOR

ORDER BLUEPRINTS ANYTIME!
CALL TOLL-FREE 1-888-626-2026

Plan AHP-9120

PRICES AND DETAILS
ON PAGES 12-15

85

A Peaceful Look

- Three dormers and a railed porch with five columns give this two-story home a peaceful, traditional look.
- From the porch, grand double doors swing open into a stunning gallery that will impress visitors. A 17-ft. cathedral ceiling crowns the space, which includes an elegant curved staircase.
- When you entertain, guests will stroll from the gallery into the beautiful living and dining rooms. The dining room includes space for dinners of any size.
- In the kitchen, an island work space lets extra hands join in meal preparation. The dinette sits cradled in a sunny bay, and sliding glass doors in the casual family room open to a backyard terrace.
- At the front of the home, the guest room includes a sunny boxed-out window under a 10-ft. vaulted ceiling. This is the perfect spot for a computer desk.
- Upstairs, a stylish 11-ft. cathedral ceiling tops the master suite, which features a separate dressing area and a skylighted bath with a whirlpool tub.

Plan K-806-R

Bedrooms: 4+	**Baths:** 3
Living Area:	
Upper floor	921 sq. ft.
Main floor	1,410 sq. ft.
Total Living Area:	**2,331 sq. ft.**
Standard basement	1,336 sq. ft.
Garage and storage	465 sq. ft.
Exterior Wall Framing:	2x4 or 2x6

Foundation Options:
Standard basement
Slab
(All plans can be built with your choice of foundation and framing. A generic conversion diagram is available. See order form.)

BLUEPRINT PRICE CODE: C

VIEW INTO FAMILY ROOM

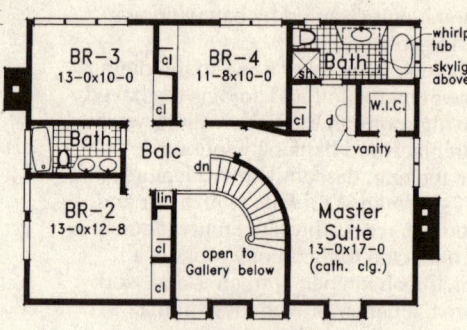

UPPER FLOOR

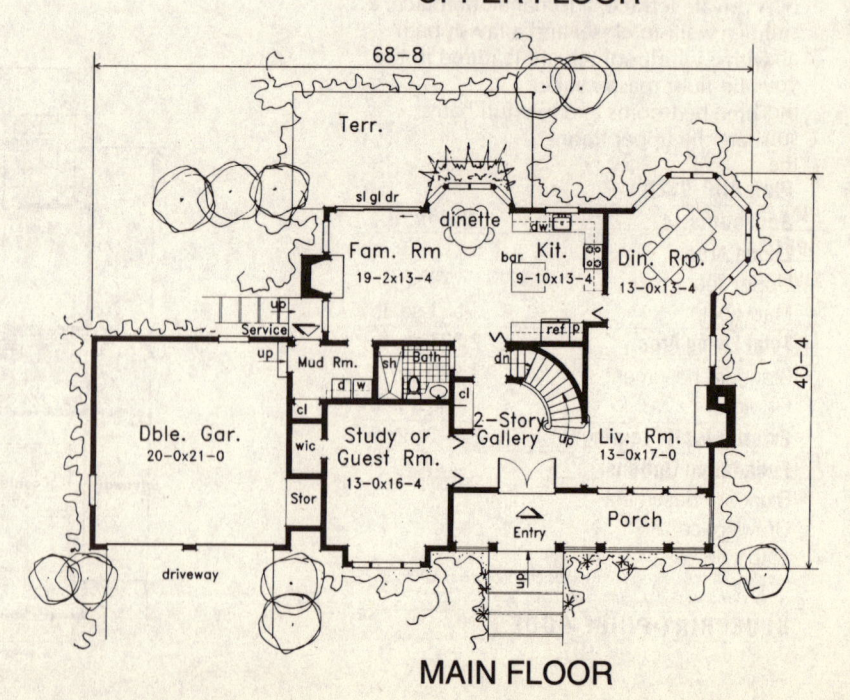

MAIN FLOOR

Plan K-806-R

ORDER BLUEPRINTS ANYTIME!
CALL TOLL-FREE 1-888-626-2026

PRICES AND DETAILS ON PAGES 12-15

Better by Design

- For the family that values an easygoing lifestyle, but also wants to impress friends with a beautiful home, this Southern-style design fits the bill.
- Hanging baskets dripping with vibrant flowers will dress up the front porch.
- Inside, handsome columns lend a look of distinction to the formal dining room, the ideal spot for classy meals. After dinner, guests can drift into the living room to continue their conversation. Plant shelves above display lush florals and greenery for all to admire.
- Casual meals have a place of their own in the kitchen and breakfast nook. While Mom and Dad prepare dinner in the kitchen, they can chat with the kids doing homework in the nook.
- Across the home, the master suite's sitting room provides an oasis of peace and quiet. The handy wet bar there puts you steps closer to that first cup of morning coffee, while a skylight lets sunshine pour in. Two more skylights in the bath brighten this space as well.

Plan J-9320	
Bedrooms: 3+	**Baths:** 2½
Living Area:	
Main floor	2,348 sq. ft.
Total Living Area:	**2,348 sq. ft.**
Future upper floor	860 sq. ft.
Standard basement	2,348 sq. ft.
Garage	579 sq. ft.
Exterior Wall Framing:	2x4
Foundation Options:	
Standard basement	
Crawlspace	
Slab	
(All plans can be built with your choice of foundation and framing. A generic conversion diagram is available. See order form.)	
BLUEPRINT PRICE CODE:	**C**

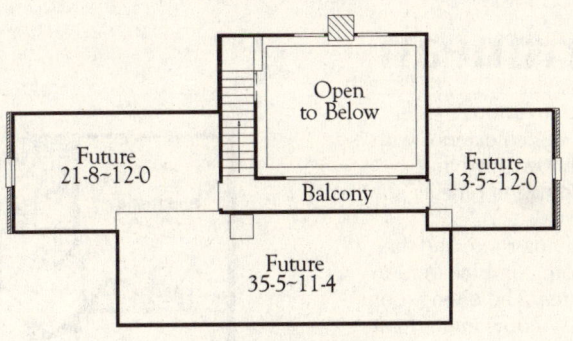

UPPER FLOOR

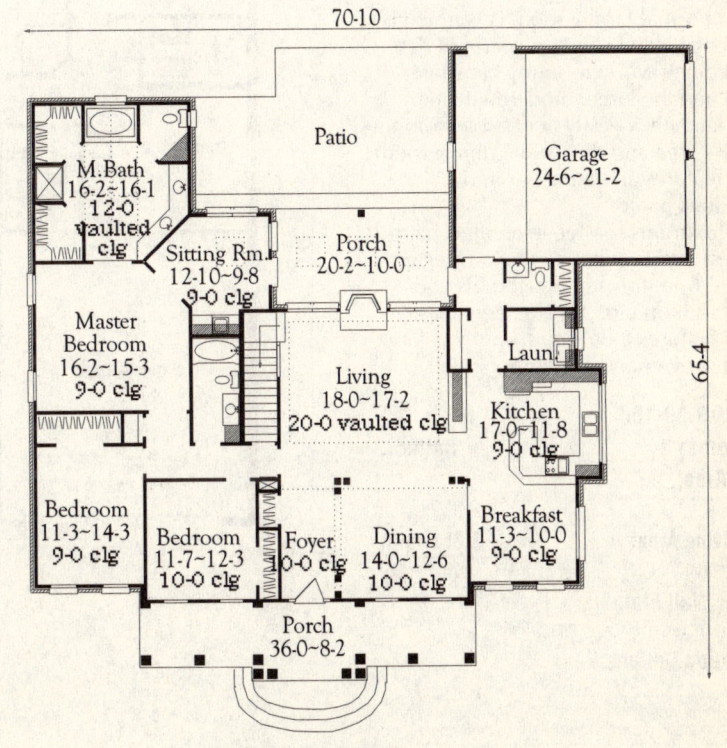

MAIN FLOOR

ORDER BLUEPRINTS ANYTIME!
CALL TOLL-FREE 1-888-626-2026

Plan J-9320

PRICES AND DETAILS ON PAGES 12-15

Ultra-Modern Mediterranean

- Soaring ceilings, a luxurious master suite and a clean stucco exterior with stylish arched windows give this nouveau-Mediterranean home its unique appeal.
- The magnificent living room and the elegant dining room combine to form one large, open area. The dining room has a tall, arched window and a 12-ft. coffered ceiling. The living room boasts a flat ceiling that is over 12 ft. high, a convenient wet bar and sliding glass doors to the covered patio.
- The informal family room is warmed by a fireplace and shares a soaring 12-ft. flat ceiling with the sunny breakfast area and the large, modern kitchen.
- The kitchen is easily accessible from the family area and the formal dining room, and features an eating bar and a spacious pantry.
- The luxurious master suite offers patio access and is enhanced by an elegant 11-ft., 6-in. tray ceiling and his-and-hers walk-in closets. The huge master bath features a dual-sink vanity, a large tiled shower and a whirlpool tub.

Plan HDS-99-158

Bedrooms: 4	Baths: 3

Living Area:
Main floor	2,352 sq. ft.
Total Living Area:	**2,352 sq. ft.**
Garage	440 sq. ft.

Exterior Wall Framing:
8-in. concrete block and 2x4

Foundation Options:
Slab

(All plans can be built with your choice of foundation and framing. A generic conversion diagram is available. See order form.)

BLUEPRINT PRICE CODE: C

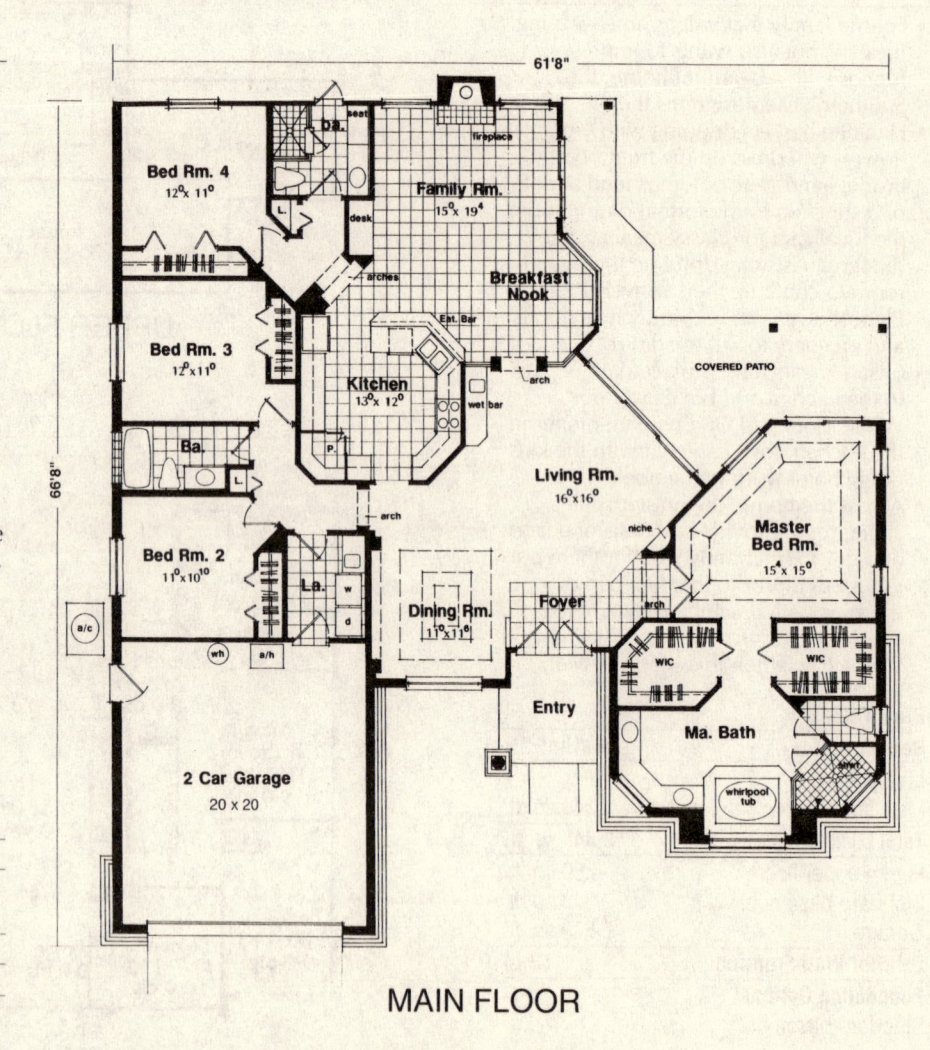

MAIN FLOOR

ORDER BLUEPRINTS ANYTIME! CALL TOLL-FREE 1-888-626-2026

Plan HDS-99-158

PRICES AND DETAILS ON PAGES 12-15

88

Abundant Space for Entertaining

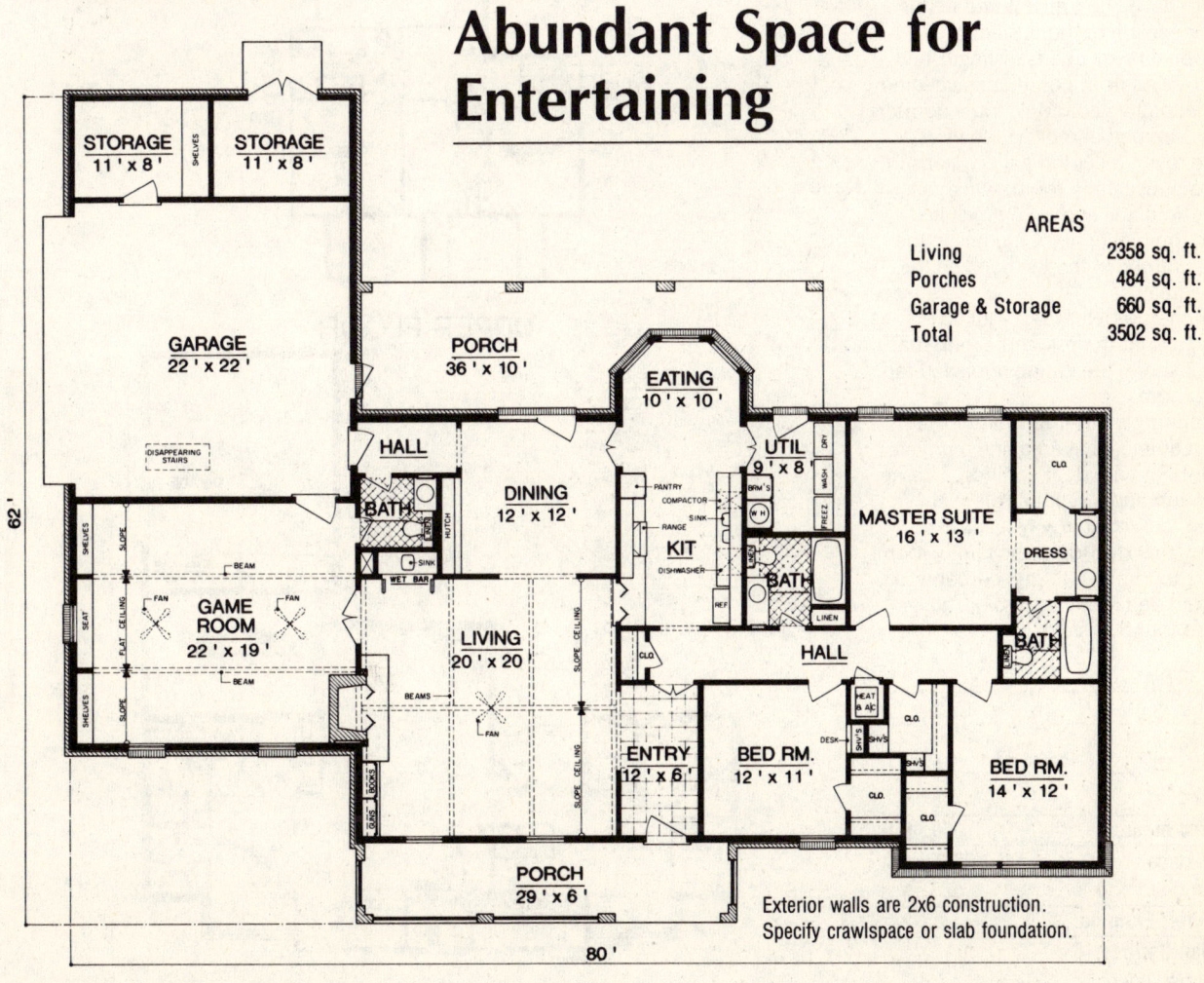

AREAS
Living 2358 sq. ft.
Porches 484 sq. ft.
Garage & Storage 660 sq. ft.
Total 3502 sq. ft.

Exterior walls are 2x6 construction.
Specify crawlspace or slab foundation.

BLUEPRINT PRICE CODE C
Plan E-2304

ORDER BLUEPRINTS ANYTIME!
CALL TOLL-FREE 1-888-626-2026

PRICES AND DETAILS
ON PAGES 12-15

One More Time!

- The character and excitement of our most popular plan in recent years, E-3000, have been recaptured in this smaller version of the design.
- The appealing facade is distinguished by a covered front porch and accented with decorative columns, triple dormers and rail-topped corner windows.
- Off the foyer, a central gallery leads to the spacious family room, where a corner fireplace and a 17-ft. vaulted ceiling are highlights. Columns in the gallery introduce the kitchen and the dining areas.
- The kitchen showcases a walk-in pantry, a built-in desk and a long snack bar that serves the eating nook and the dining room.
- The stunning main-floor master suite offers a quiet sitting area and a private angled bath with dual vanities, a corner garden tub and a separate shower.
- A lovely curved stairway leads to a balcony that overlooks the family room and the foyer. Two large bedrooms, a split bath and easily accessible attics are also found upstairs.

Plan E-2307-A

Bedrooms: 3	Baths: 2½
Living Area:	
Upper floor	595 sq. ft.
Main floor	1,765 sq. ft.
Total Living Area:	**2,360 sq. ft.**
Standard basement	1,765 sq. ft.
Garage and storage	528 sq. ft.
Exterior Wall Framing:	2x6

Foundation Options:
Standard basement
Crawlspace
Slab
(All plans can be built with your choice of foundation and framing. A generic conversion diagram is available. See order form.)

BLUEPRINT PRICE CODE: C

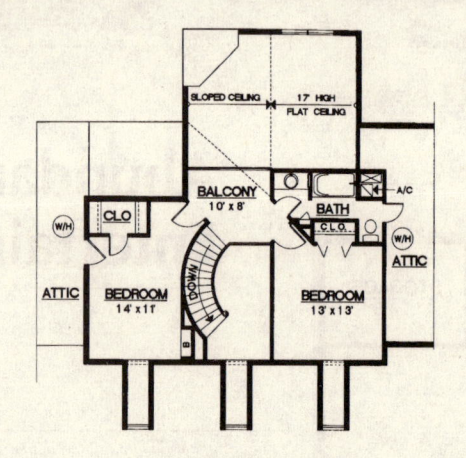

UPPER FLOOR

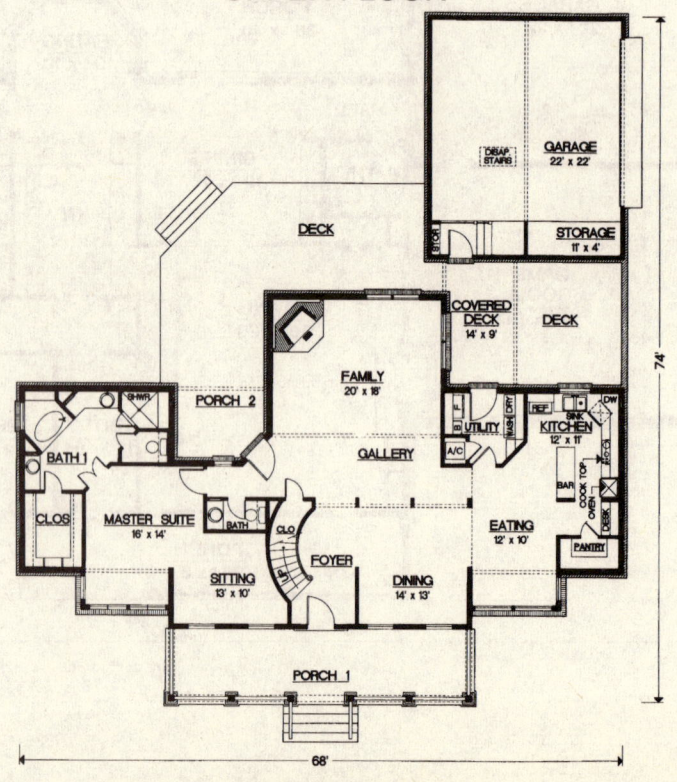

MAIN FLOOR

Plan E-2307-A

Great Features, Great Design

- A covered front porch that is roomy enough for your rocking chair fronts this delightful country home.
- To the right of the foyer, double doors swing wide to grant passage to a quiet study. If you wish, this room could easily serve as an extra bedroom.
- The joined living and dining rooms spread out beneath a breathtaking cathedral ceiling. A crackling fireplace and bright windows paint the scene with vibrant light.
- At the back of the home, a big family room offers perfection in both design and function. A second fireplace and a TV nook make this room the obvious choice for weekend fun.
- On hot summer days, the pleasant terrace is a great spot to unwind.
- The secluded master suite boasts a skylighted bath and a private terrace!

Plan AHP-9616	
Bedrooms: 5+	**Baths:** 3½
Living Area:	
Upper floor	798 sq. ft.
Main floor	1,570 sq. ft.
Total Living Area:	**2,368 sq. ft.**
Standard basement	1,570 sq. ft.
Garage and storage	502 sq. ft.
Exterior Wall Framing:	2x4 or 2x6

Foundation Options:
Standard basement
Crawlspace
Slab
(All plans can be built with your choice of foundation and framing. A generic conversion diagram is available. See order form.)

BLUEPRINT PRICE CODE: C

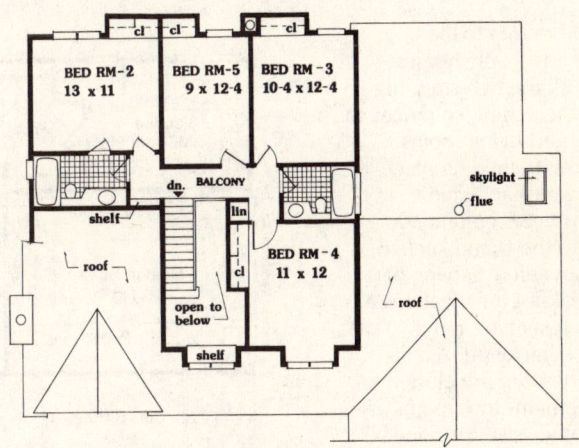

UPPER FLOOR

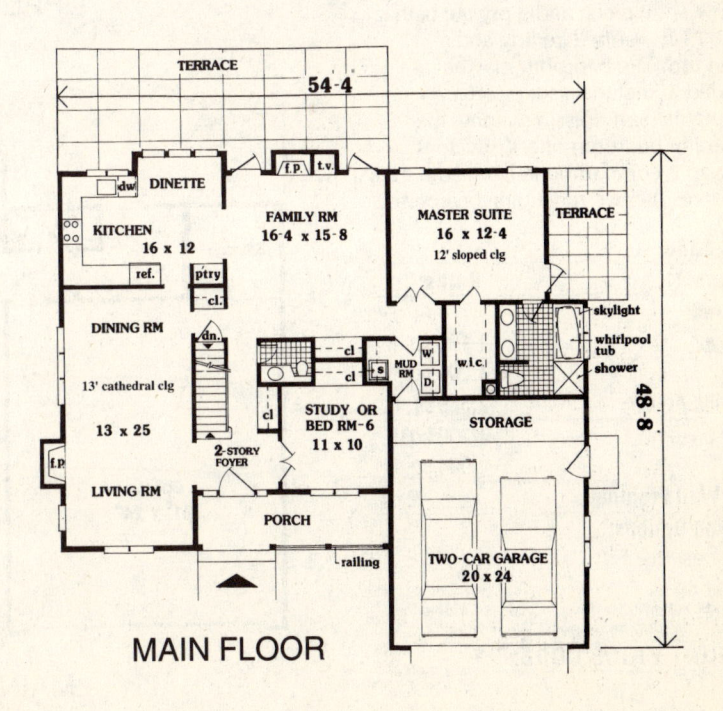

MAIN FLOOR

ORDER BLUEPRINTS ANYTIME!
CALL TOLL-FREE 1-888-626-2026

Plan AHP-9616

PRICES AND DETAILS ON PAGES 12-15

Arched Accents

- Elegant arches add drama to the covered porch of this lovely home.
- Interior arches flank the two-story-high foyer, offering eye-catching entrances to the formal dining and living rooms.
- A dramatic window-framed fireplace and a 17-ft. ceiling enhance the spacious family room. A columned archway leads into the island kitchen, which offers a convenient serving bar.
- The adjoining breakfast area features a pantry closet, open shelves and a French door to the backyard. A half-bath and a laundry room are close by.
- The ceilings in all main-floor rooms are 9 ft. high unless otherwise specified.
- Upstairs, a balcony overlooks the family room and the foyer. The master suite flaunts a 10-ft. tray ceiling, a beautiful window showpiece and a private bath with a 13-ft. vaulted ceiling and a garden tub. The bedroom may be extended to include a sitting area.
- Boasting its own dressing vanity, the rear-facing bedroom offers private access to a compartmentalized bath that also serves the two remaining bedrooms.

Plan FB-2368

Bedrooms: 4	Baths: 2½
Living Area:	
Upper floor	1,168 sq. ft.
Main floor	1,200 sq. ft.
Total Living Area:	**2,368 sq. ft.**
Daylight basement	1,200 sq. ft.
Garage	504 sq. ft.
Exterior Wall Framing:	2x4

Foundation Options:
Daylight basement
Slab
(All plans can be built with your choice of foundation and framing. A generic conversion diagram is available. See order form.)

BLUEPRINT PRICE CODE: C

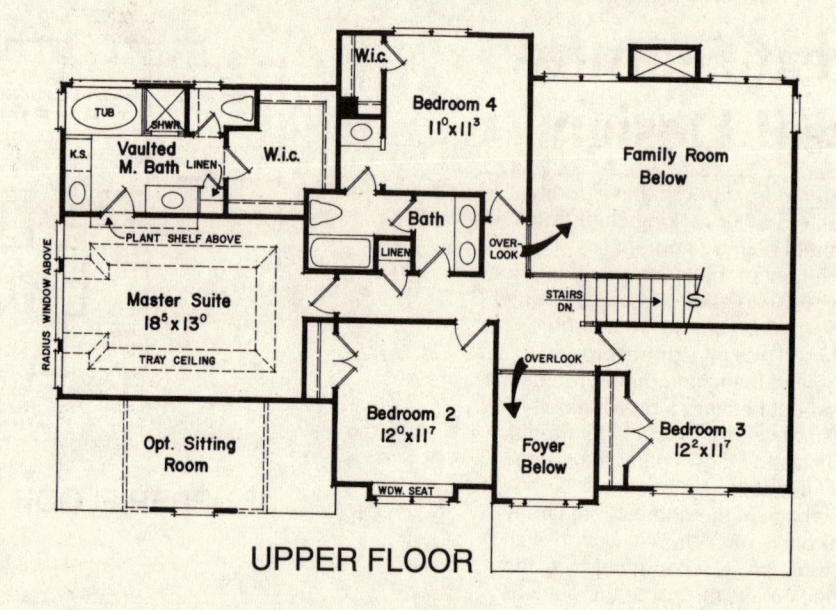

UPPER FLOOR

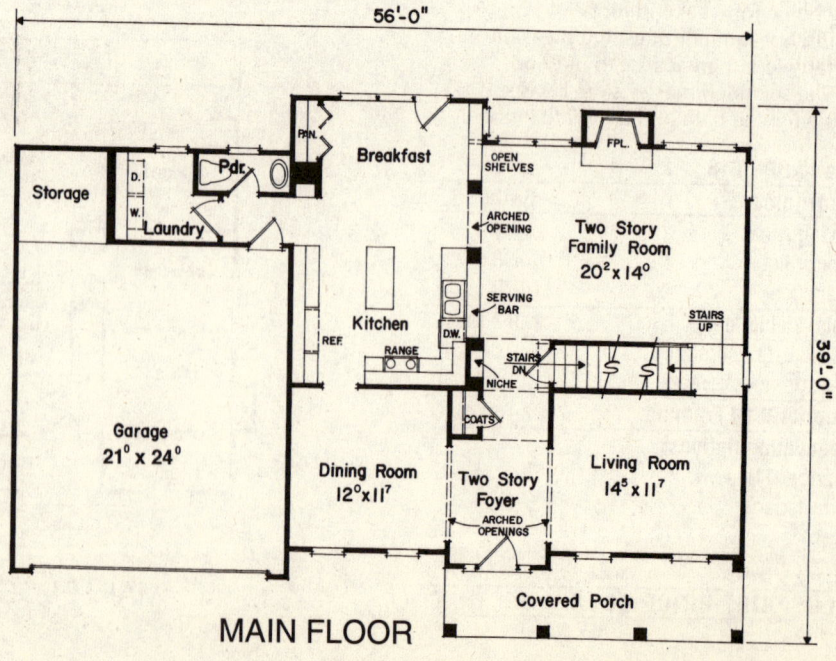

MAIN FLOOR

Plan FB-2368

ORDER BLUEPRINTS ANYTIME! CALL TOLL-FREE 1-888-626-2026

PRICES AND DETAILS ON PAGES 12-15

Rich Victorian Comes to Life

- With a veranda wrapped around an octagonal turret, decorative shingle siding and double posts atop brick pedestals, this design brings to life the rich Victorian-style home.
- The covered entry provides a pretty place to greet arriving guests.
- A bay window, a built-in bookcase and a handsome fireplace are three of the features found in the huge family room.
- French doors lead from the family room to a playful game room, which can quickly be turned into a spare bedroom for overnight visitors.
- The efficient kitchen is ready to serve the formal dining room and the casual breakfast nook with equal ease.
- Three upper-floor bedrooms are highlighted by the master suite, where you'll find a walk-in closet, a skylighted private bath and a nice sitting area.
- Each secondary bedroom boasts a walk-in closet and a built-in bookcase.
- Plans for a two-car detached garage are included with the blueprints.

Plan L-2368

Bedrooms: 3+	Baths: 3
Living Area:	
Upper floor	1,069 sq. ft.
Main floor	1,299 sq. ft.
Total Living Area:	**2,368 sq. ft.**
Detached garage	576 sq. ft.
Exterior Wall Framing:	2x4

Foundation Options:
Slab
(All plans can be built with your choice of foundation and framing. A generic conversion diagram is available. See order form.)

BLUEPRINT PRICE CODE: C

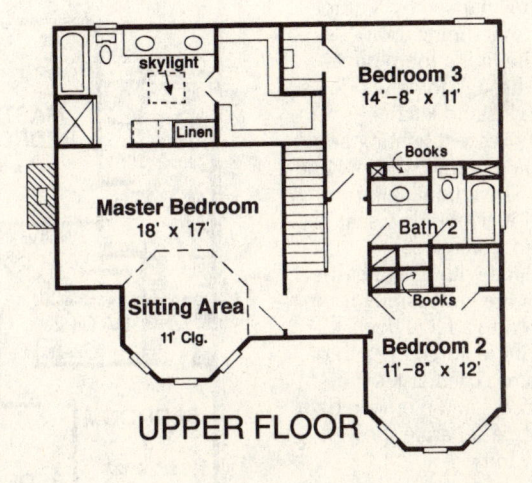

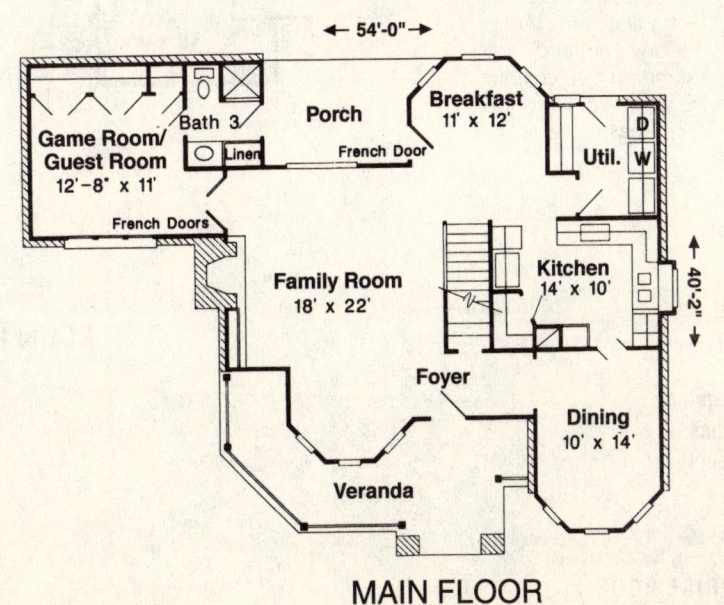

ORDER BLUEPRINTS ANYTIME!
CALL TOLL-FREE 1-888-626-2026

Plan L-2368

PRICES AND DETAILS
ON PAGES 12-15

Light and Bright

- This outstanding home features a light, inviting facade with arched windows, unique transoms and twin dormers.
- The sheltered front porch opens to an airy entry, which is flanked by a quiet study and the formal dining room. Straight ahead, the living room offers backyard views through three windows.
- The well-designed island kitchen is brightened by fluorescent lighting and enhanced by a nice corner window and a step-in pantry. The adjoining morning room features a lovely window seat, a built-in hutch and a snack bar.
- An inviting fireplace with a tile hearth is the focal point of the cozy family room. French doors open to a large deck.
- Walk-in closets are featured in each of the three bedrooms. The master suite includes deck access and a private bath with a garden tub, a separate shower and a dual-sink vanity.
- In the second bedroom, the ceiling slopes up to 11½ ft., accenting the elegant front window. The third bedroom has a standard 8-ft. ceiling.
- Unless otherwise specified, all rooms have high 10-ft. ceilings.

Plan DD-2372

Bedrooms: 3+	Baths: 2½
Living Area:	
Main floor	2,376 sq. ft.
Total Living Area:	**2,376 sq. ft.**
Standard basement	2,376 sq. ft.
Garage	473 sq. ft.
Exterior Wall Framing:	2x4 |//
Foundation Options:	

Standard basement
Crawlspace
Slab
(All plans can be built with your choice of foundation and framing. A generic conversion diagram is available. See order form.)

| **BLUEPRINT PRICE CODE:** | C |

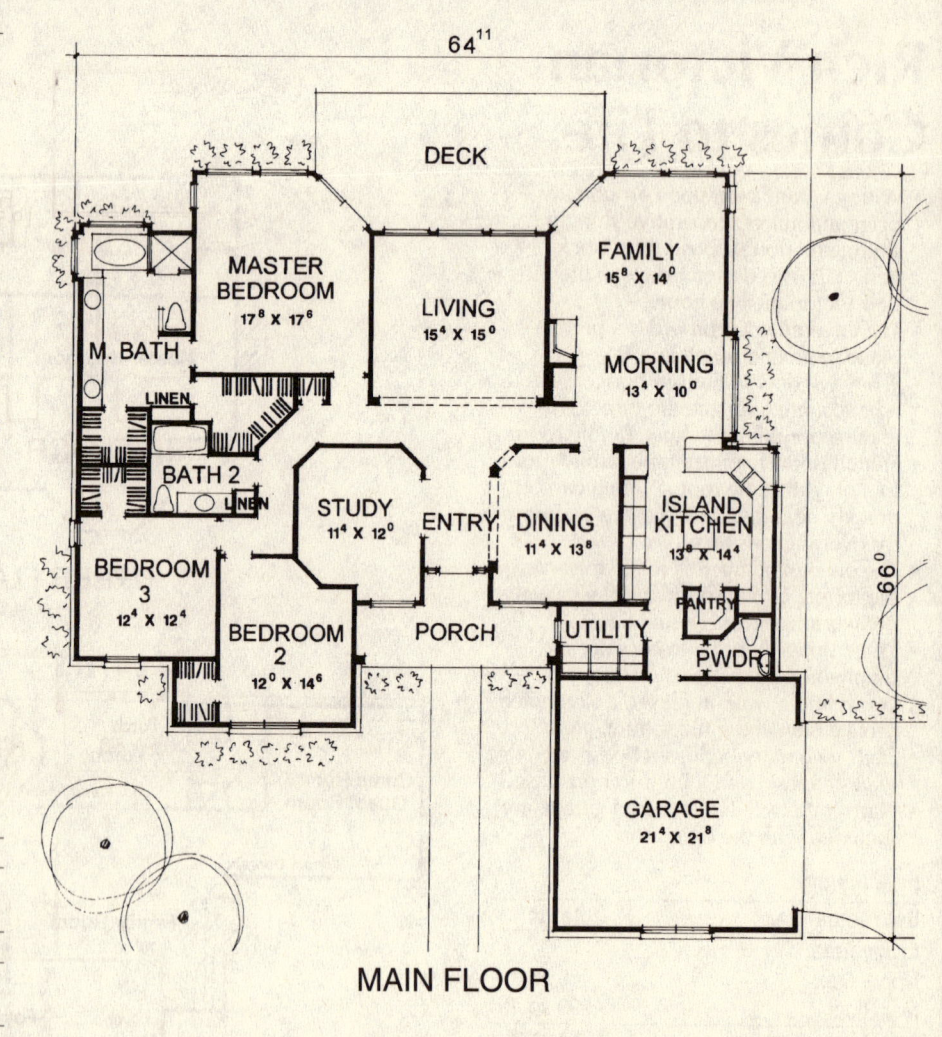

MAIN FLOOR

Plan DD-2372

The Big Easy

- The simple ease of a country home blends with understated elegance to make this home an ideal choice.
- You will yearn for the days when you can retreat to the breezy porch with a cold lemonade and a good novel.
- During the frosty months, guests will love to gather in front of the living room's mood-setting fireplace. Nearby, regal columns introduce the dining room, where you will enjoy years of holiday feasts and birthday dinners.
- In the den, a great media center frames a gorgeous picture window. The center includes room to store your books and games, plus shelves to display family photos. A computer desk nearby is great for catching up on family business.
- The family cook will love the huge kitchen, which features a large pantry, tons of counterspace and a snack bar where kids can grab a quick lunch.
- The master suite's highlight is the private bath, where a window over the tub adds splendor to this ritual.

Plan J-9303

Bedrooms: 3+	Baths: 2½

Living Area:	
Upper floor (balcony)	65 sq. ft.
Main floor	2,335 sq. ft.
Total Living Area:	**2,400 sq. ft.**
Future areas	1,096 sq. ft.
Standard basement	2,335 sq. ft.
Garage and storage	593 sq. ft.
Exterior Wall Framing:	2x4

Foundation Options:
Standard basement
Crawlspace
Slab
(All plans can be built with your choice of foundation and framing. A generic conversion diagram is available. See order form.)

BLUEPRINT PRICE CODE: C

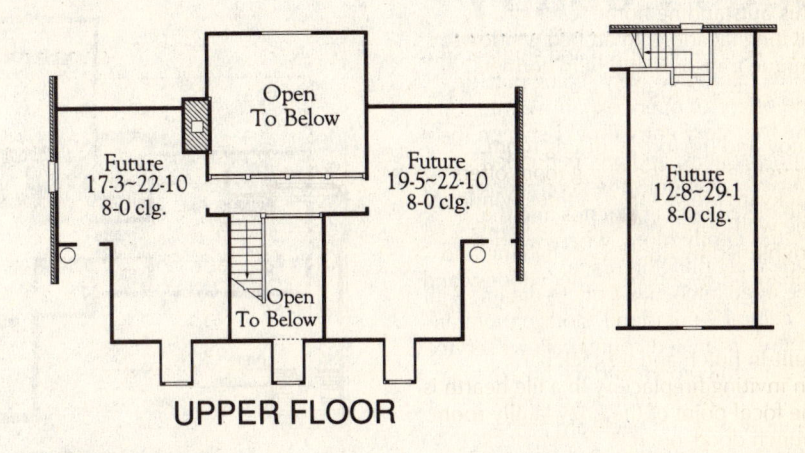

UPPER FLOOR

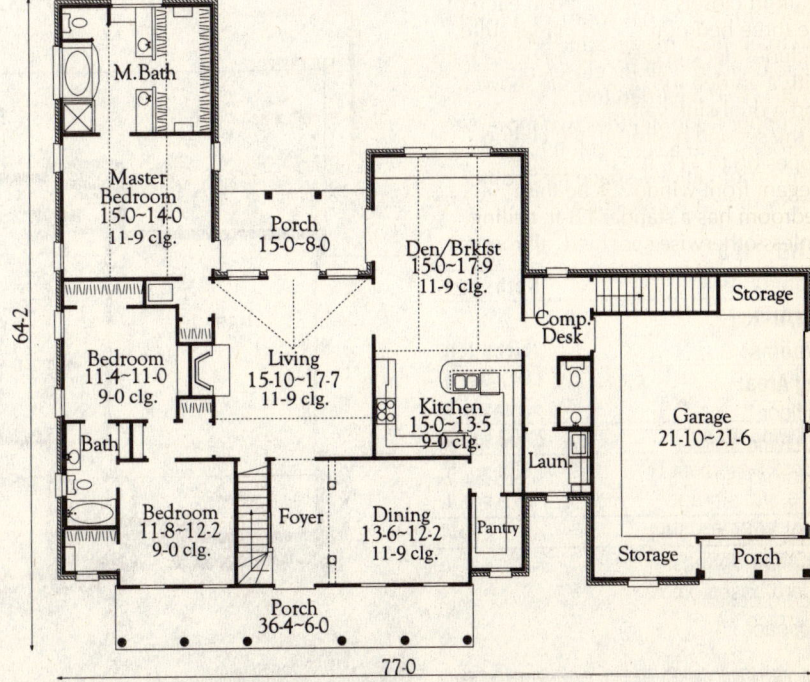

MAIN FLOOR

ORDER BLUEPRINTS ANYTIME!
CALL TOLL-FREE 1-888-626-2026

Plan J-9303

PRICES AND DETAILS ON PAGES 12-15

Open Country

- With its covered porch and shutters, this home exudes country styling outside and offers an open, expansive interior.
- The two-story entry flows between the formal spaces, and an open-railed stairway overlooks the family room.
- The raised ceiling extends into the central family room, where windows flank a soothing fireplace.
- The open kitchen is a chef's dream, with its central work island, storage room and pantry. Its angled counter allows service to the family room and the breakfast nook. The nook includes a corner window seat and backyard access.
- Nearby, a door opens from the garage, and a utility area has room for a freezer.
- The main-floor master suite boasts a huge, divided walk-in closet, dual vanities and a garden tub.
- The upper floor includes two more bedrooms and a second full bath. A bonus room allows space for another bedroom or a home studio.

Plan RD-2168

Bedrooms: 3+	**Baths:** 2½
Living Area:	
Upper floor	521 sq. ft.
Main floor	1,647 sq. ft.
Bonus room	240 sq. ft.
Total Living Area:	**2,408 sq. ft.**
Standard basement	1,639 sq. ft.
Garage and storage	576 sq. ft.
Exterior Wall Framing:	2x4
Foundation Options:	
Standard basement	
Crawlspace	
Slab	

(All plans can be built with your choice of foundation and framing. A generic conversion diagram is available. See order form.)

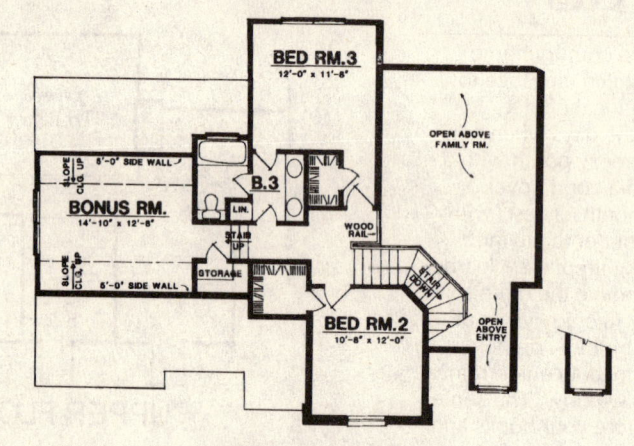

BLUEPRINT PRICE CODE: C

UPPER FLOOR

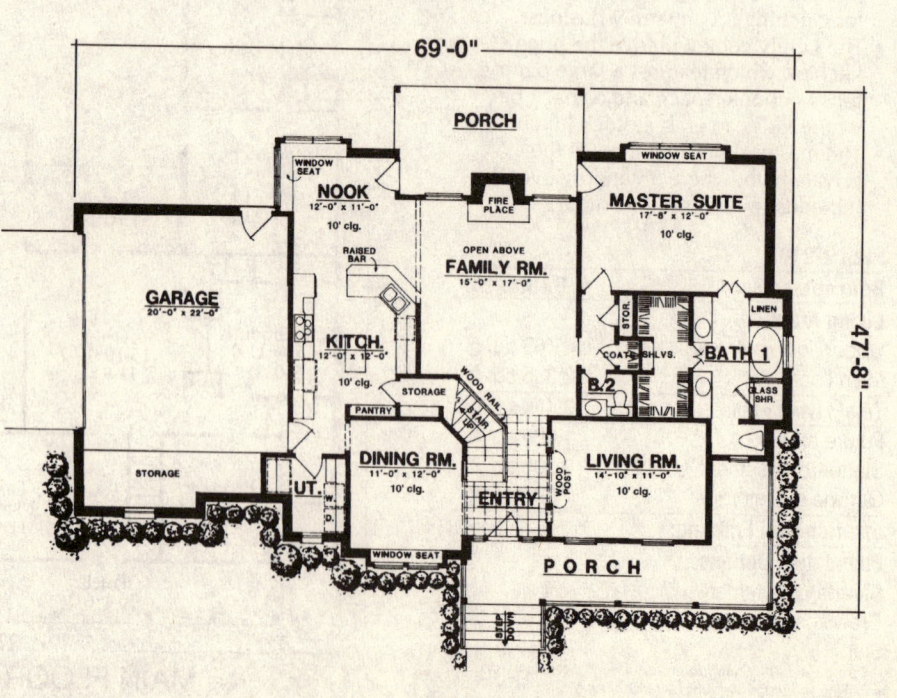

MAIN FLOOR

ORDER BLUEPRINTS ANYTIME! CALL TOLL-FREE 1-888-626-2026

Plan RD-2168

PRICES AND DETAILS ON PAGES 12-15

Play to Win

- You'll stack the deck of life in your favor by choosing this beautiful classy Colonial as your "home base."
- Your guests will feel secure as they stride up to the warmly lit entry and are ushered into the foyer and past arches into the living and dining rooms.
- An island cooktop in the kitchen helps you prepare culinary delights that would turn a master chef green with envy!
- After a delicious meal, you may choose to escort everyone to the family room, where a fireplace will spark invigorating conversation. Sliding glass doors open to a wide deck, if the weather allows.
- After the company has left, you may retire to the master bedroom, which boasts twin walk-in closets flanking the walk to your private bath.
- Three more bedrooms should handle all the kids or even overnight visitors.
- If you wish, a vast bonus room may be added. Imagine the possibilities here: a game or hobby room, a home office, even an artist's loft!

Plan B-95014

Bedrooms: 3+	Baths: 2½

Living Area:	
Upper floor	1,034 sq. ft.
Main floor	1,375 sq. ft.
Total Living Area:	**2,409 sq. ft.**
Bonus room (unfinished)	265 sq. ft.
Standard basement	1,375 sq. ft.
Garage and storage	534 sq. ft.
Exterior Wall Framing:	2x6

Foundation Options:
Standard basement
(All plans can be built with your choice of foundation and framing. A generic conversion diagram is available. See order form.)

BLUEPRINT PRICE CODE: C

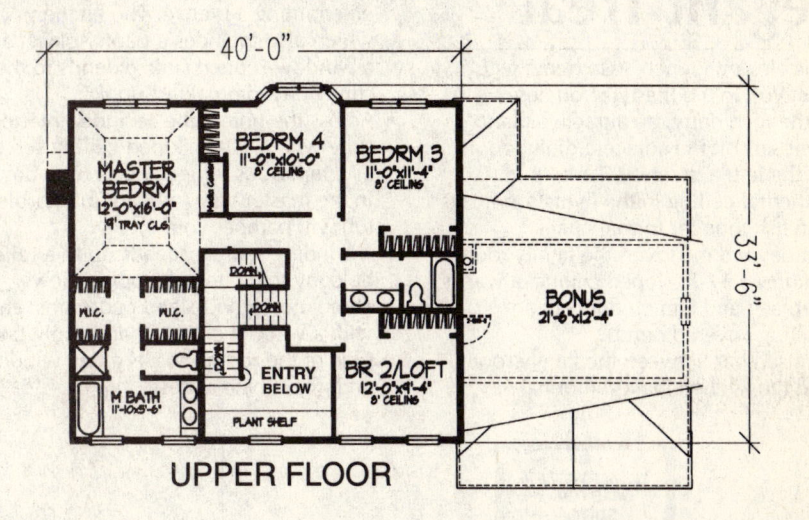

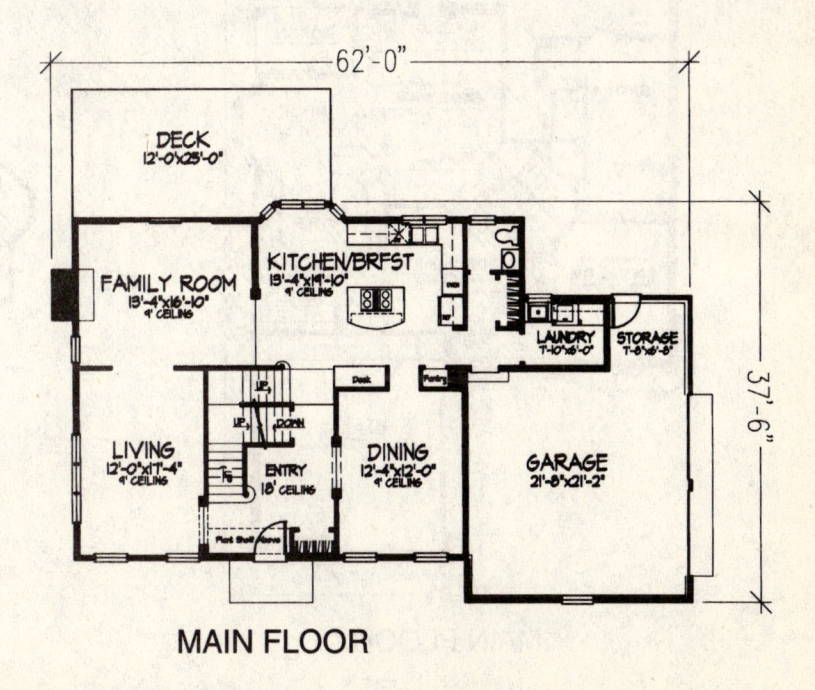

ORDER BLUEPRINTS ANYTIME!
CALL TOLL-FREE 1-888-626-2026

Plan B-95014

PRICES AND DETAILS
ON PAGES 12-15

Elegant Treat

- This elegant French-style home will treat you to the lifestyle you deserve.
- In the tiled entry, an attractive plant shelf sets off the adjacent dining room. To the left, a dramatic 12-ft., 8-in. cathedral ceiling in the living room sets a stylish tone for formal affairs.
- Just beyond the foyer, the family room features a 17-ft. sloped ceiling, a warm fireplace and French doors to an inviting covered porch.
- A raised bar between the family room and the kitchen makes informal entertaining a breeze. The kitchen, which also includes a pantry closet and a window-topped sink, extends to the sunny bayed breakfast nook.
- Across the home, the secluded master suite with a 10-ft. sloped ceiling serves as a luxurious refuge after a busy day. In the master bath, a beautiful marble tub will pamper you.
- A winding staircase leads up to a railed balcony that offers sweeping views.
- Three more good-sized bedrooms, each with a walk-in closet, share a split bath. One of the rooms boasts a bay window and direct bath access.

Plan RD-2440	
Bedrooms: 4	Baths: 2½
Living Area:	
Upper floor	630 sq. ft.
Main floor	1,780 sq. ft.
Total Living Area:	2,410 sq. ft.
Garage and storage	509 sq. ft.
Exterior Wall Framing:	2x4
Foundation Options:	
Crawlspace	
Slab	

(All plans can be built with your choice of foundation and framing. A generic conversion diagram is available. See order form.)

BLUEPRINT PRICE CODE: C

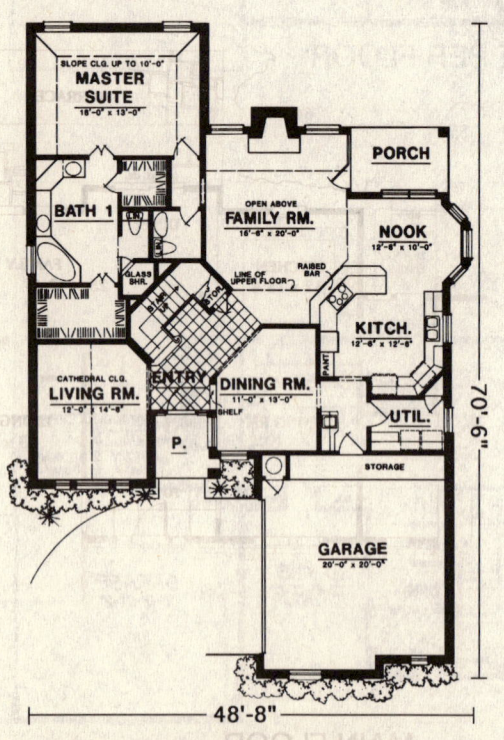

MAIN FLOOR

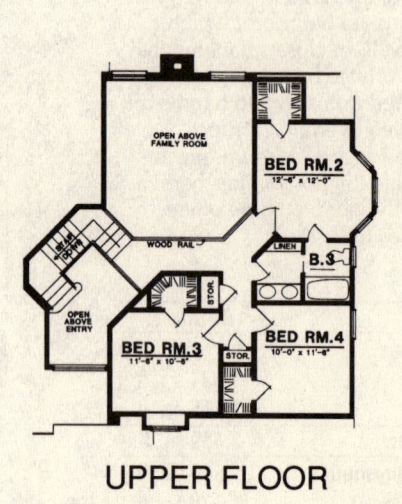

UPPER FLOOR

Plan RD-2440

Five-Bedroom Traditional

- This sophisticated traditional home makes a striking statement both inside and out.
- The dramatic two-story foyer is flanked by the formal living spaces. The private dining room overlooks the front porch, while the spacious living room has outdoor views on two sides.
- A U-shaped kitchen with a snack bar, a sunny dinette area and a large family room flow together at the back of the home. The family room's fireplace warms the open, informal expanse, while sliding glass doors in the dinette access the backyard terrace.
- The second floor has five roomy bedrooms and two skylighted bathrooms. The luxurious master suite has a high ceiling with a beautiful arched window, a dressing area and a huge walk-in closet. The private bath offers dual sinks, a whirlpool tub and a separate shower.
- Attic space is located above the garage.

Plan AHP-9392

Bedrooms: 5	Baths: 2½
Living Area:	
Upper floor	1,223 sq. ft.
Main floor	1,193 sq. ft.
Total Living Area:	**2,416 sq. ft.**
Standard basement	1,130 sq. ft.
Garage	509 sq. ft.
Storage	65 sq. ft.
Exterior Wall Framing:	2x4 or 2x6

Foundation Options:
Standard basement
Crawlspace
Slab
(Typical foundation & framing conversion diagram available—see order form.)

BLUEPRINT PRICE CODE: C

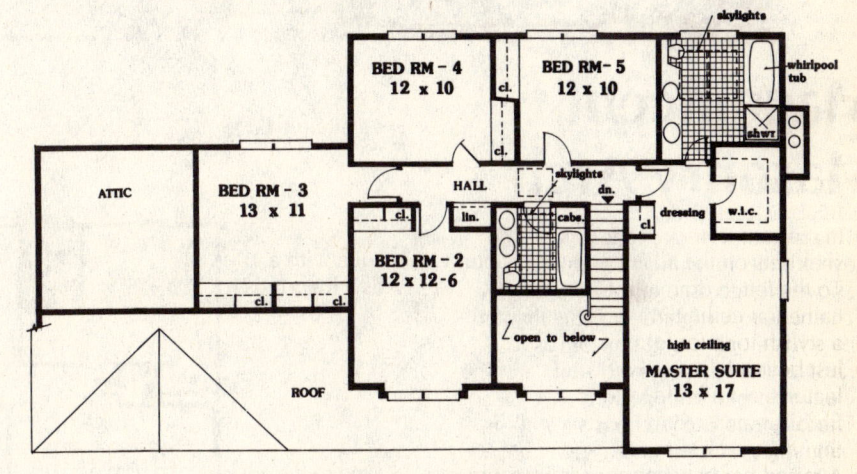

ORDER BLUEPRINTS ANYTIME!
CALL TOLL-FREE 1-888-626-2026

Plan AHP-9392

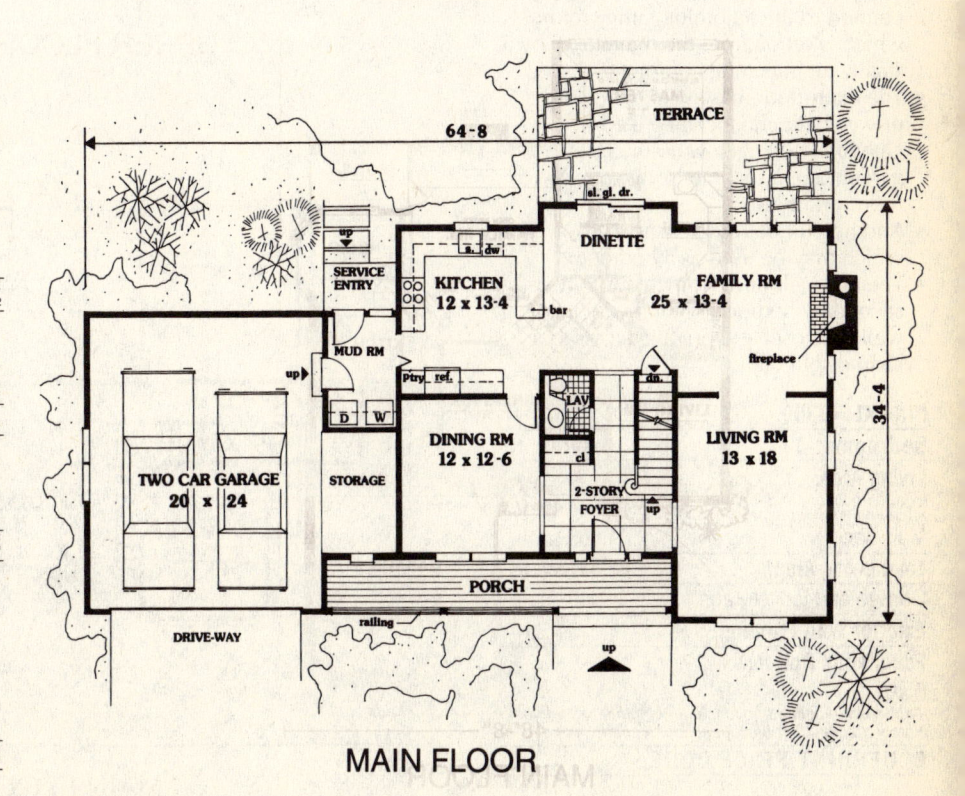

PRICES AND DETAILS ON PAGES 12-15

Magnificent Masonry Arch

- This beautiful brick home attracts the eye with its magnificent arch high above the recessed entry.
- The two-story-high foyer is highlighted by a huge half-round transom as it radiates between a bayed study and the elegant formal dining room.
- The fabulous kitchen boasts a walk-in pantry, a snack bar and a sunny bayed breakfast nook with backyard access.
- A fireplace flanked by windows brings comfort to the adjoining family room, which is set off from the main foyer by a stately architectural column.
- The main-floor master suite includes a private bath enhanced by a 13-ft. cathedral ceiling, a walk-in closet, a garden tub, a separate shower and two roomy vanities.
- Another full bath serves the study, which may be used as a bedroom.
- The upper-floor balcony leads to two secondary bedrooms, each with a tidy walk-in closet and private access to a shared split bath.

Plan KLF-9309

Bedrooms: 3+	Baths: 3
Living Area:	
Upper floor	574 sq. ft.
Main floor	1,863 sq. ft.
Total Living Area:	**2,437 sq. ft.**
Garage and tool storage	519 sq. ft.
Exterior Wall Framing:	2x4
Foundation Options:	
Slab	
(All plans can be built with your choice of foundation and framing. A generic conversion diagram is available. See order form.)	
BLUEPRINT PRICE CODE:	**C**

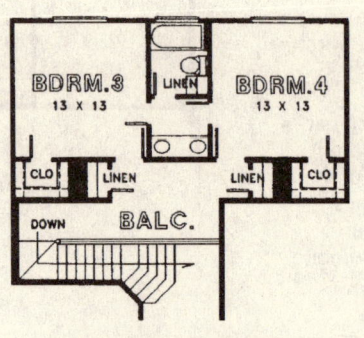

UPPER FLOOR

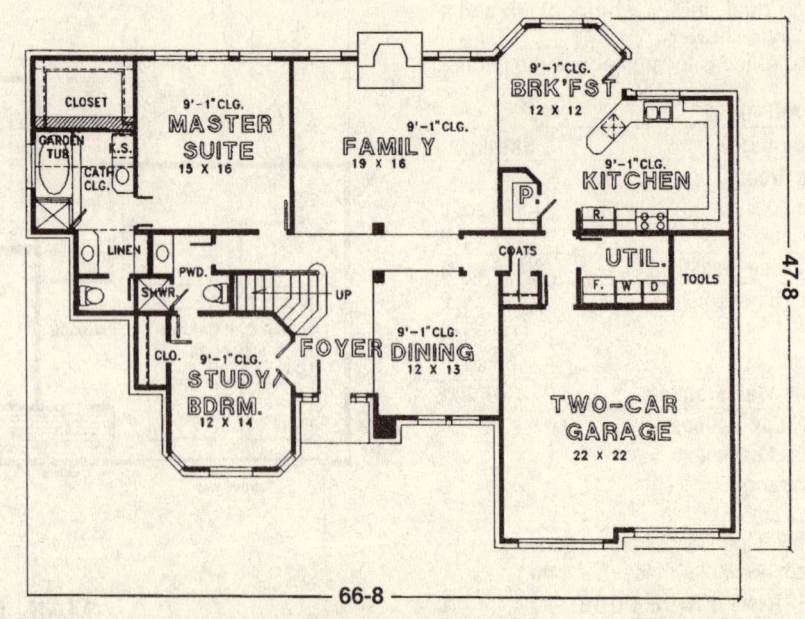

MAIN FLOOR

Plan KLF-9309

Two-Story for Today

- The charm and character of yesterday are re-created in this two-story design for today. The quaint exterior is highlighted by half-round windows, decorative planter boxes and a covered front porch.
- The dramatic skylighted entry preludes a formal, sunken living room with a stunning corner fireplace and an adjoining formal dining room with a built-in hutch. Both rooms are also enhanced by vaulted ceilings.
- A large kitchen with a built-in desk and a pantry opens to a sunny breakfast room and a large, sunken family room at the rear of the home. The family room features an exciting fireplace wall with windows, plus French doors that open to a backyard deck.
- The upstairs loft leads to a luxurious master bedroom with a vaulted ceiling, an angled walk-in closet and a private bath. Two to three additional bedrooms and a second bath are also included.

Plan B-86159

Bedrooms: 3+	Baths: 2½

Living Area:

Upper floor	1,155 sq. ft.
Main floor	1,290 sq. ft.
Total Living Area:	**2,445 sq. ft.**
Standard basement	1,290 sq. ft.
Garage	683 sq. ft.
Exterior Wall Framing:	2x4

Foundation Options:
Standard basement
(All plans can be built with your choice of foundation and framing. A generic conversion diagram is available. See order form.)

BLUEPRINT PRICE CODE: C

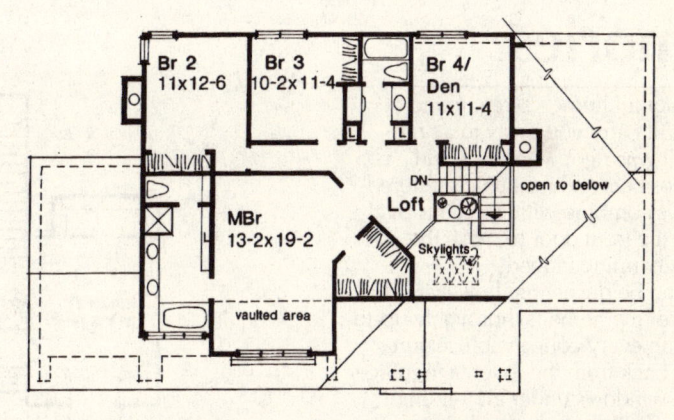

UPPER FLOOR

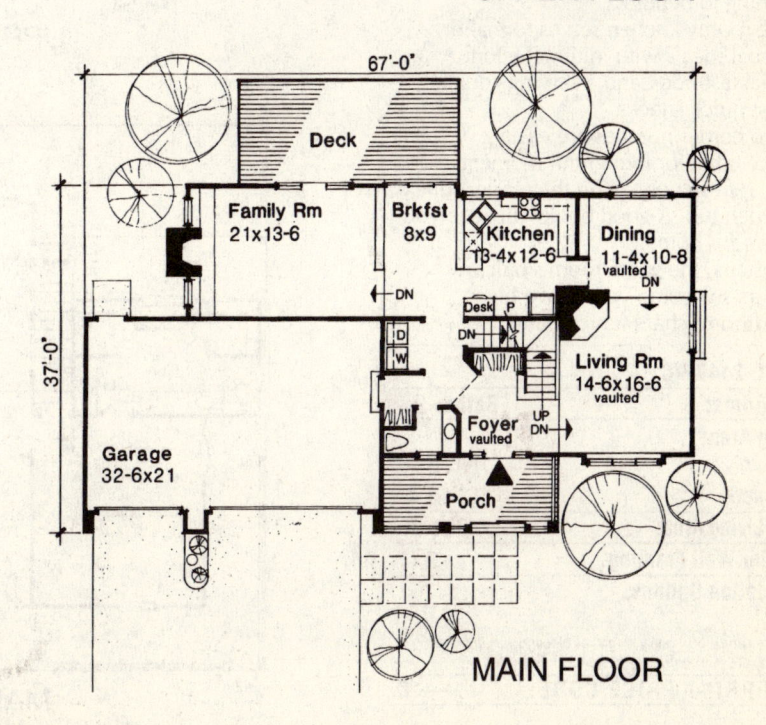

MAIN FLOOR

ORDER BLUEPRINTS ANYTIME!
CALL TOLL-FREE 1-888-626-2026

Plan B-86159

PRICES AND DETAILS ON PAGES 12-15

Rapt in Country Memories

- This beautiful home's wraparound porch will carry you away to a time when all was right with the world.
- Triple dormers and nostalgic shuttered windows combine with gorgeous oval glass in the front door to make the facade charming indeed!
- Looks can be deceiving, however. The interior of the home is thoroughly up-to-date, with every conceivable feature.
- Straight back from the foyer, a fireplace and tall windows under a 19-ft.-high cathedral ceiling make the living room a thing to behold.
- The roomy kitchen serves formal or casual meals with minimal effort. A breakfast nook and a serving counter host quick snacks.
- Two corner porches are easily accessible for thoughtful moments.
- Or, refresh yourself in the master suite's garden tub. A good book will keep you there for hours.
- Upstairs, the game room's balcony offers sweeping views; two big bedrooms share a nice bath.

Plan L-2449-VC

Bedrooms: 3	Baths: 2½
Living Area:	
Upper floor	780 sq. ft.
Main floor	1,669 sq. ft.
Total Living Area:	**2,449 sq. ft.**
Exterior Wall Framing:	2x4
Foundation Options:	
Slab	
(All plans can be built with your choice of foundation and framing. A generic conversion diagram is available. See order form.)	
BLUEPRINT PRICE CODE:	**C**

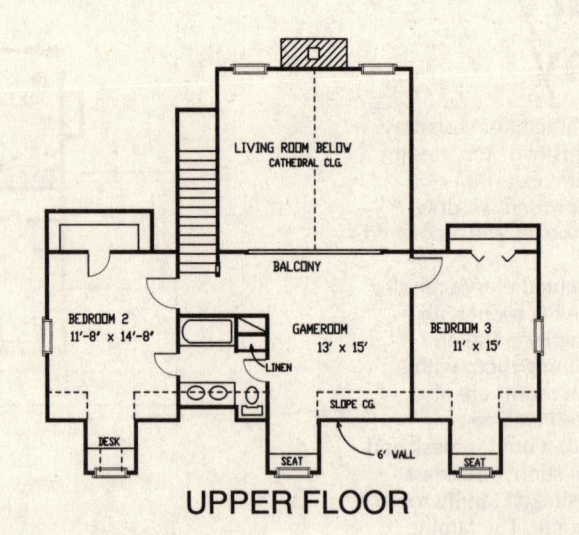

UPPER FLOOR
- Living Room Below — Cathedral Clg.
- Balcony
- Bedroom 2 — 11'-8" x 14'-8"
- Gameroom — 13' x 15'
- Bedroom 3 — 11' x 15'
- Linen, Desk, Seat, Seat, 6' Wall, Slope Clg.

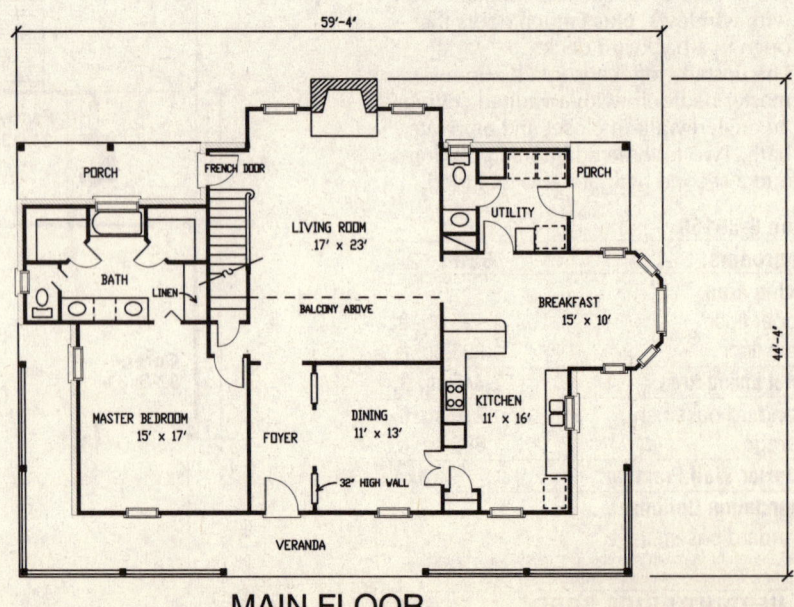

MAIN FLOOR (59'-4" x 44'-4")
- Porch, French Door, Utility, Porch
- Bath, Linen
- Living Room — 17' x 23'
- Balcony Above
- Breakfast — 15' x 10'
- Master Bedroom — 15' x 17'
- Foyer
- Dining — 11' x 13'
- Kitchen — 11' x 16'
- 32" High Wall
- Veranda

ORDER BLUEPRINTS ANYTIME! CALL TOLL-FREE 1-888-626-2026

Plan L-2449-VC

PRICES AND DETAILS ON PAGES 12-15

Tasteful Style

- Traditional lines and a contemporary floor plan combine to make this home a perfect choice for the '90s.
- The two-story-high entry introduces the formal living room, which is warmed by a fireplace and brightened by a round-top window arrangement. The living room's ceiling rises to 13 ft., 9 inches.
- A handy pocket door separates the formal dining room from the kitchen for special occasions. The U-shaped kitchen features an eating bar, a work desk and a bayed nook with access to an outdoor patio.
- The spacious family room includes a second fireplace and outdoor views.
- Ceilings in all main-floor rooms are at least 9 ft. high for added spaciousness.
- Upstairs, the master suite features a 12-ft. vaulted ceiling, two walk-in closets and a compartmentalized bath with a luxurious tub in a window bay.
- Two additional bedrooms share a split bath. A versatile bonus room could serve as an extra bedroom or as a sunny area for hobbies or paperwork.

Plan S-8389

Bedrooms: 3+	Baths: 2½

Living Area:

Upper floor	932 sq. ft.
Main floor	1,290 sq. ft.
Bonus room	228 sq. ft.
Total Living Area:	**2,450 sq. ft.**
Standard basement	1,290 sq. ft.
Garage	429 sq. ft.

Exterior Wall Framing: 2x6

Foundation Options:
Standard basement
Crawlspace
Slab
(All plans can be built with your choice of foundation and framing. A generic conversion diagram is available. See order form.)

BLUEPRINT PRICE CODE: C

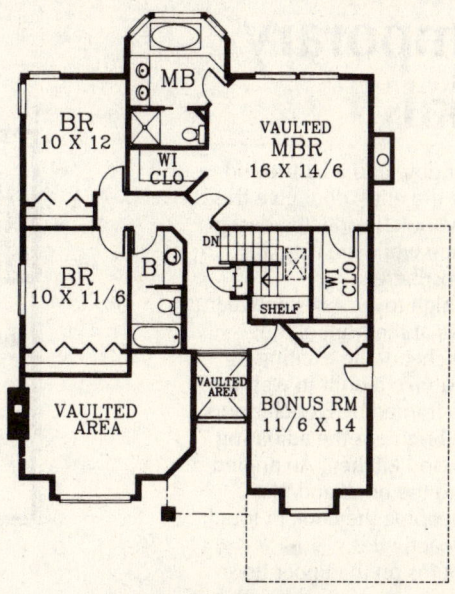

UPPER FLOOR

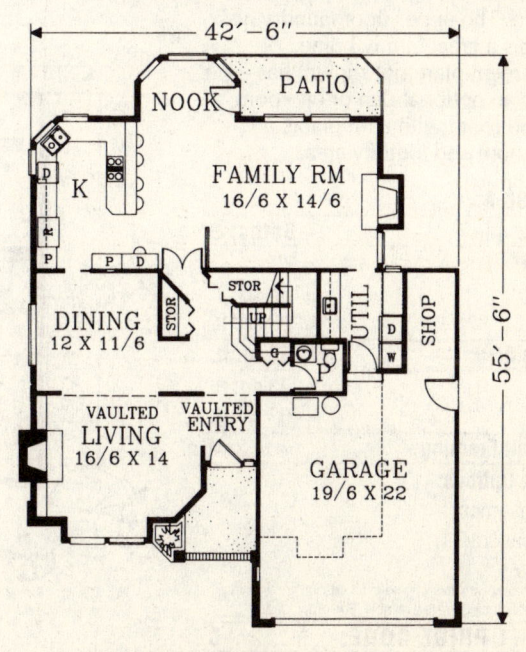

MAIN FLOOR

ORDER BLUEPRINTS ANYTIME!
CALL TOLL-FREE 1-888-626-2026

Plan S-8389

PRICES AND DETAILS ON PAGES 12-15

Contemporary Colonial

- A Palladian window and a half-round window above the entry door give this Colonial a new look. Inside, the design maximizes space while creating an open, airy atmosphere.
- The two-story-high foyer flows between the formal areas at the front of the home. Straight ahead, the exciting family room features a built-in wet bar and a fireplace framed by French doors.
- A bay window brightens the adjoining breakfast nook and kitchen. An angled counter looks to the nook and the family room, keeping the cook in touch with the family activities.
- The four bedrooms on the upper floor include a luxurious master suite with an 11-ft. vaulted ceiling and a skylighted bathroom. The upper-floor laundry also makes this a great family home.
- The basement plan (not shown) has room for an optional den or bedroom, a recreation room with a fireplace, a storage room and a utility area.

Plan CH-320-A

Bedrooms: 4+	Baths: 3
Living Area:	
Upper floor	1,164 sq. ft.
Main floor	1,293 sq. ft.
Total Living Area:	**2,457 sq. ft.**
Basement	1,293 sq. ft.
Garage	462 sq. ft.
Exterior Wall Framing:	2x4

Foundation Options:
Daylight basement
Standard basement
Crawlspace
(All plans can be built with your choice of foundation and framing. A generic conversion diagram is available. See order form.)

BLUEPRINT PRICE CODE: C

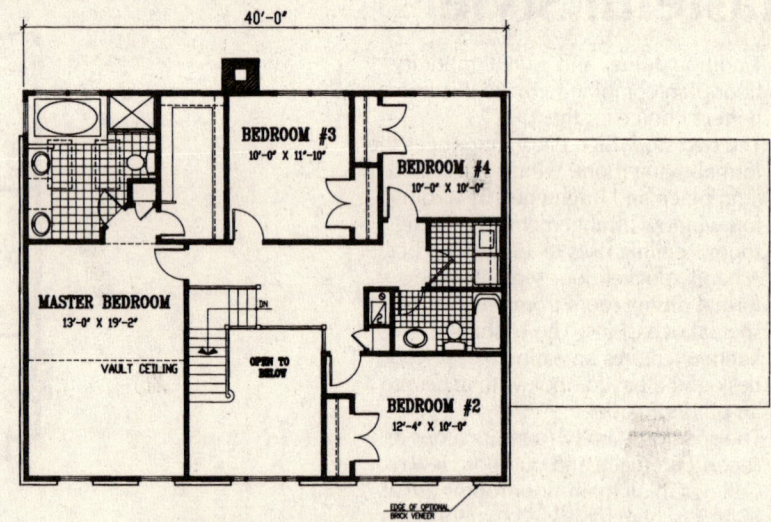

UPPER FLOOR

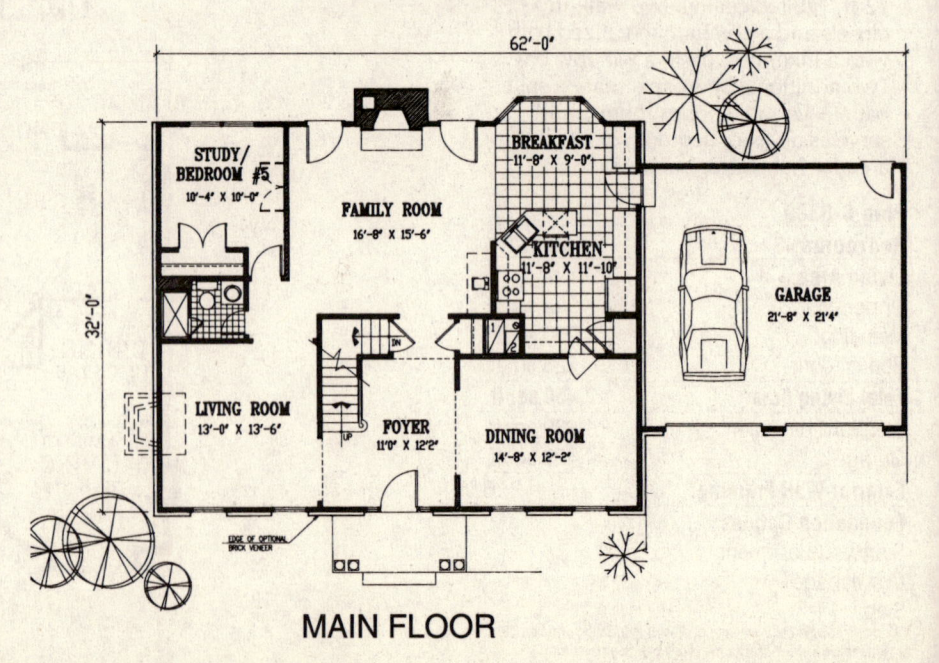

MAIN FLOOR

Plan CH-320-A

Sophisticated One-Story

- Beautiful windows accentuated by elegant keystones highlight the exterior of this sophisticated one-story design.
- An open floor plan is the hallmark of the interior, beginning with the foyer that provides instant views of the study as well as the dining and living rooms.
- The spacious living room boasts a fireplace with built-in bookshelves and a rear window wall that stretches into the morning room.
- The sunny morning room has a snack bar to the kitchen. The island kitchen includes a walk-in pantry, a built-in desk and easy access to the utility room and the convenient half-bath.
- The master suite features private access to a nice covered patio, plus an enormous walk-in closet and a posh bath with a spa tub and glass-block shower.
- A hall bath serves the two secondary bedrooms. These three rooms, plus the utility area, have standard 8-ft. ceilings. Other ceilings are 10 ft. high.

Plan DD-2455

Bedrooms: 3+	Baths: 2½

Living Area:
Main floor	2,457 sq. ft.
Total Living Area:	**2,457 sq. ft.**
Standard basement	2,457 sq. ft.
Garage	585 sq. ft.
Exterior Wall Framing:	2x4

Foundation Options:
Standard basement
Crawlspace
Slab
(All plans can be built with your choice of foundation and framing. A generic conversion diagram is available. See order form.)

BLUEPRINT PRICE CODE: C

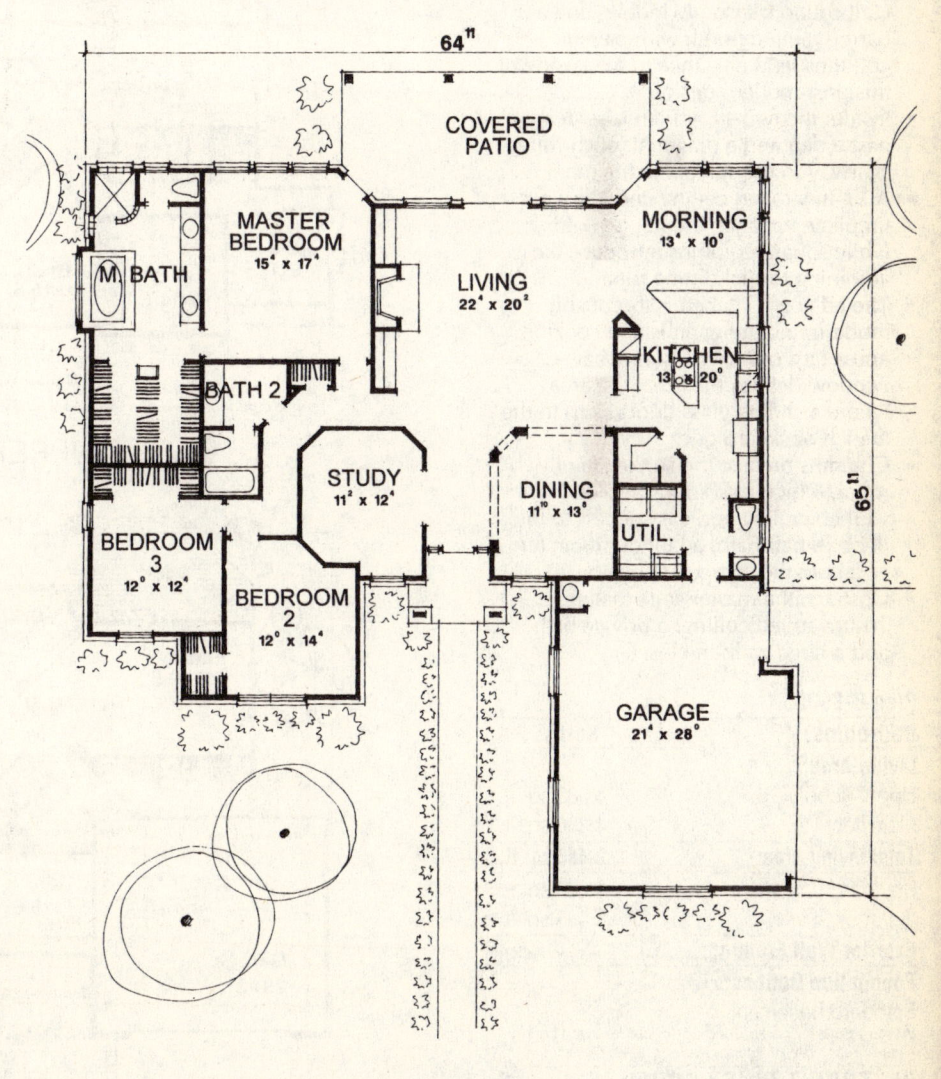

ORDER BLUEPRINTS ANYTIME!
CALL TOLL-FREE 1-888-626-2026

Plan DD-2455

PRICES AND DETAILS ON PAGES 12-15

MAIN FLOOR

Modern Elegance

- Half-round transom windows and a barrel-vaulted porch with paired columns lend elegance to the facade of this post-modern design.
- Inside, the two-story-high foyer leads past a den and a diagonal, open-railed stairway to the sunken living room.
- A 17-ft. vaulted ceiling and a striking fireplace enhance the living room, while square columns introduce the adjoining formal dining room.
- The adjacent kitchen is thoroughly modern, including an island cooktop and a large pantry. A sunny bay window defines the breakfast area, where a sliding glass door opens to the angled backyard deck.
- Columns preface the sunken family room, which also sports a 17-ft.-high vaulted ceiling and easy access to the deck. A half-bath, a laundry room and access to the garage are nearby.
- Upstairs, the master suite features a 10-ft. vaulted ceiling, a private bath and a large walk-in closet.

Plan B-89005	
Bedrooms: 4	Baths: 2½
Living Area:	
Upper floor	1,083 sq. ft.
Main floor	1,380 sq. ft.
Total Living Area:	**2,463 sq. ft.**
Standard basement	1,380 sq. ft.
Garage	483 sq. ft.
Exterior Wall Framing:	2x4
Foundation Options:	
Standard basement	
(All plans can be built with your choice of foundation and framing. A generic conversion diagram is available. See order form.)	
BLUEPRINT PRICE CODE:	**C**

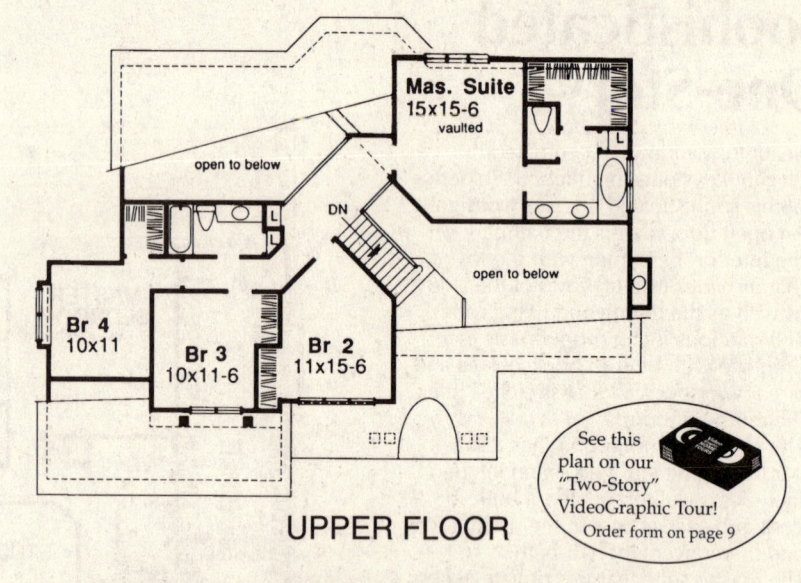

UPPER FLOOR

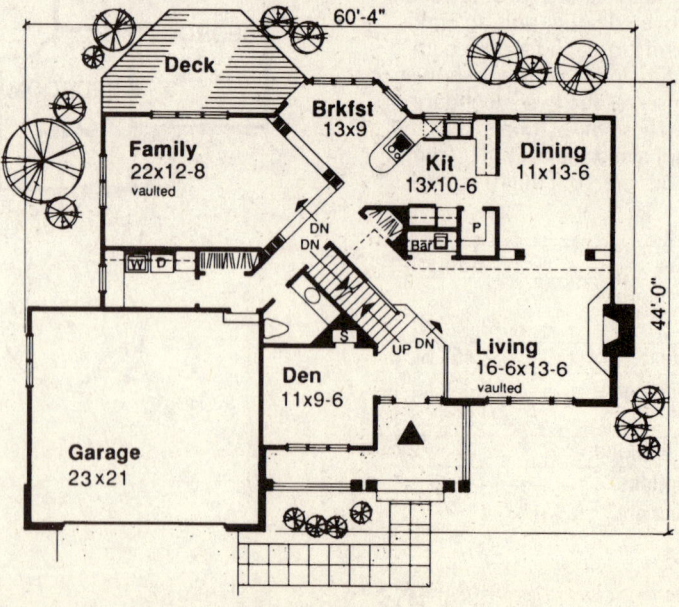

MAIN FLOOR

Plan B-89005

Comfortable Contemporary

- This home's contemporary facade and roofline give way to an impressive Great Room for ultimate comfort.
- The sidelighted two-story foyer unfolds directly to the spectacular sunken Great Room, which is highlighted by a 10-ft., open-beam ceiling. A wood-burning stove, a pair of ceiling fans and two French doors that open to a rear wraparound deck are also showcased.
- Sharing the Great Room's 10-ft. ceiling, the open kitchen boasts an eating bar and a pass-through to the dining area.
- The secluded master bedroom features a TV wall with his-and-hers dressers. A French door provides access to a covered deck. The master bath flaunts a relaxing whirlpool tub and two vanities.
- Where not otherwise noted, the main-floor rooms have 9-ft. ceilings.
- A long balcony on the second level overlooks the foyer. Two good-sized bedrooms offer nice views of the backyard and share a full bath.

Plan LRD-22994

Bedrooms: 3	Baths: 2½
Living Area:	
Upper floor	692 sq. ft.
Main floor	1,777 sq. ft.
Total Living Area:	**2,469 sq. ft.**
Standard basement	1,655 sq. ft.
Garage	550 sq. ft.
Exterior Wall Framing:	2x6

Foundation Options:
Standard basement
Crawlspace
Slab
(All plans can be built with your choice of foundation and framing. A generic conversion diagram is available. See order form.)

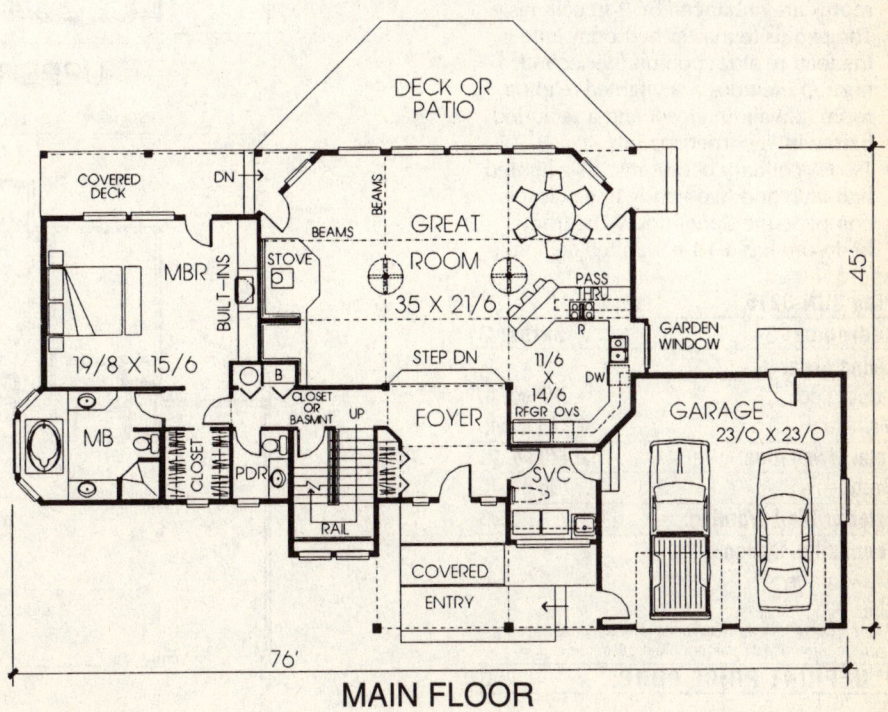

BLUEPRINT PRICE CODE: C

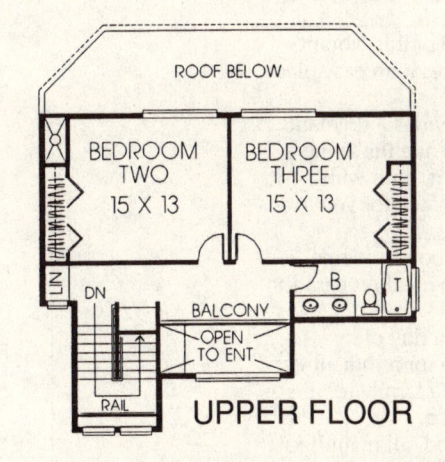

ORDER BLUEPRINTS ANYTIME!
CALL TOLL-FREE 1-888-626-2026

Plan LRD-22994

PRICES AND DETAILS ON PAGES 12-15

Quiet Vibrance

- The distinctive charm of this vibrant two-story design makes it an easy place to come home to.
- A two-story foyer provides a dramatic entrance for guests, while the living room and dining room, both with 14-ft. vaults, make a great place for you to entertain them.
- The gourmet kitchen boasts a large center island to make meal preparation easy and fun.
- Defrost the kids after a day of tobogganing, or retire for a romantic evening, in front of the family room's heartwarming fireplace.
- Unless otherwise noted, all main-floor rooms are enhanced by 9-ft. ceilings.
- The exquisite master bedroom suite is the feature attraction on the second floor. It includes a skylighted reading room, a walk-in closet and a secluded bath with a corner spa tub.
- Two secondary bedrooms, a skylighted hall bath and two handy linen closets complete the upper floor. The front bedroom has a 14-ft. vaulted ceiling.

Plan SUN-3215	
Bedrooms: 3+	**Baths:** 3
Living Area:	
Upper floor	1,097 sq. ft.
Main floor	1,373 sq. ft.
Total Living Area:	**2,470 sq. ft.**
Garage	706 sq. ft.
Exterior Wall Framing:	2x6
Foundation Options:	
Crawlspace	
Slab	

(All plans can be built with your choice of foundation and framing. A generic conversion diagram is available. See order form.)

BLUEPRINT PRICE CODE: C

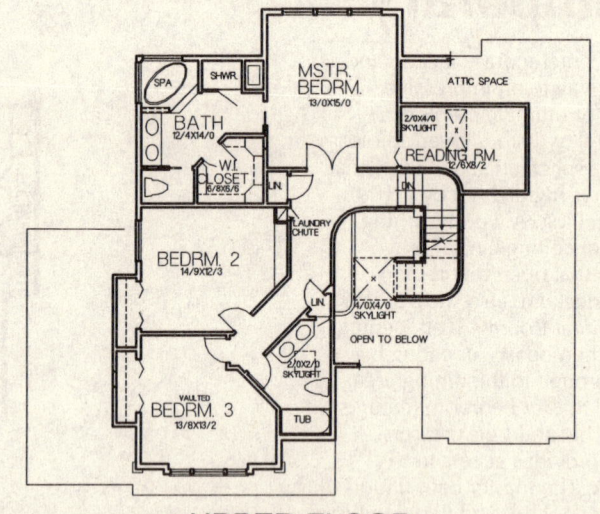

UPPER FLOOR

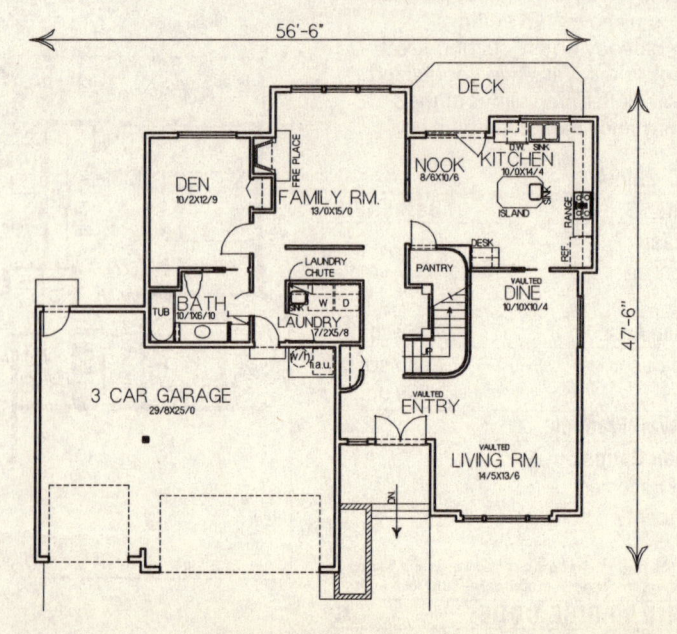

MAIN FLOOR

Plan SUN-3215

Exquisite Farmhouse

- This exquisite home is characterized by a nostalgic facade that disguises a uniquely modern floor plan.
- The covered front porch leads guests to the bright, sidelighted foyer. The foyer is flanked by the formal dining room and a quiet study as it flows to the living room.
- The spacious living room boasts an 11-ft. stepped ceiling and a handsome corner fireplace. French doors open to a covered back porch.
- The walk-through kitchen features a sunny bayed breakfast nook, a nifty work desk and an angled sink and snack counter.
- A half-bath, a laundry room and access to the two-car garage are all close by.
- The isolated master suite boasts two walk-in closets and a lavish private bath with a bayed garden tub, a separate shower and a dual-sink vanity.
- At the opposite end of the home, three additional bedrooms are serviced by two full baths.

Plan VL-2483

Bedrooms: 4	Baths: 3½
Living Area:	
Main floor	2,483 sq. ft.
Total Living Area:	**2,483 sq. ft.**
Garage	504 sq. ft.
Exterior Wall Framing:	2x4

Foundation Options:

Crawlspace
Slab

(All plans can be built with your choice of foundation and framing. A generic conversion diagram is available. See order form.)

BLUEPRINT PRICE CODE: C

Plan VL-2483

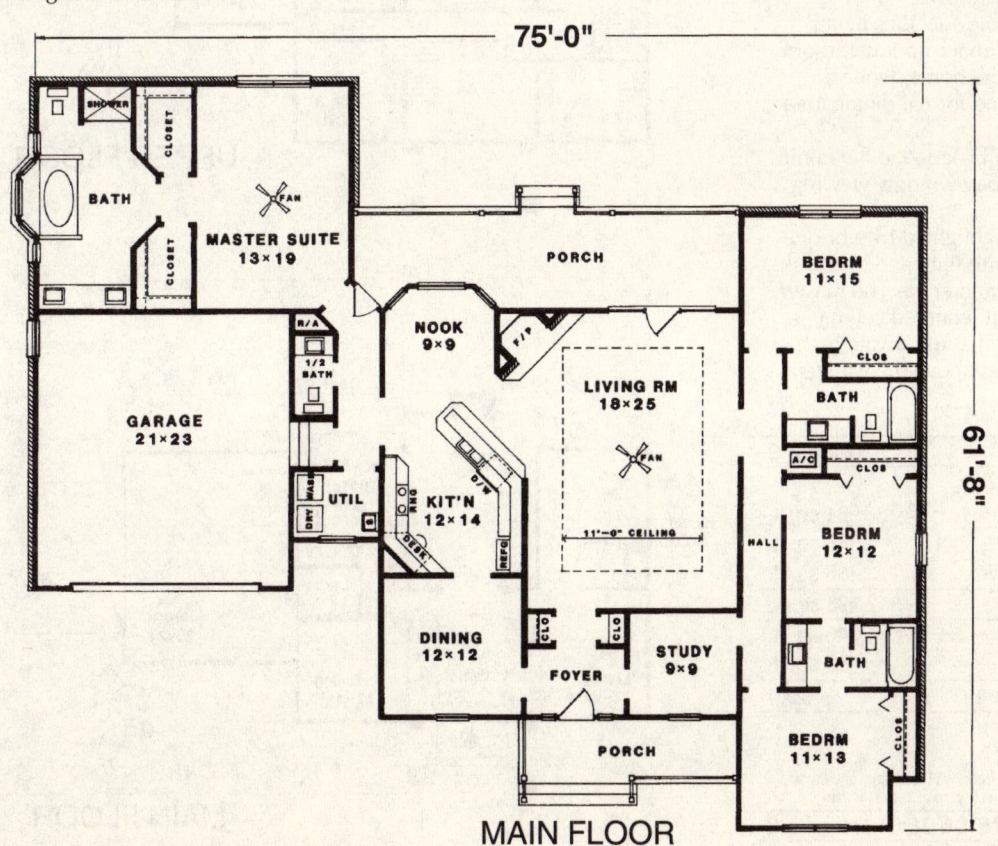

Formal Yet Friendly

- The formal yet friendly atmosphere of this elegant two-story home draws immediate attention from casual passers-by and welcome guests.
- The two-story entry extends a warm greeting, with its columned court, gabled roof and exciting windows. Inside, the raised, 20-ft. vaulted entry focuses on the 20-ft. soaring family room, with its fireplace and surrounding two-story-high windows.
- A cozy den and the spacious living room flank a full main-floor bathroom on one wing of the home, while a roomy kitchen and formal dining area fill out the other.
- The eat-in kitchen is open to the family room and has a bay window viewing out to the deck.
- The upstairs is highlighted by a bridge that is flooded with light and overlooks the family room and entry. The master suite enjoys a 9-ft. coffered ceiling, a walk-in closet and a full private bath.
- A bonus room lies above the garage.

Plan B-91011

Bedrooms: 3+	Baths: 3
Living Area:	
Upper floor	961 sq. ft.
Main floor	1,346 sq. ft.
Bonus room	186 sq. ft.
Total Living Area:	**2,493 sq. ft.**
Standard basement	1,346 sq. ft.
Garage	480 sq. ft.
Exterior Wall Framing:	2x4

Foundation Options:
Standard basement
(All plans can be built with your choice of foundation and framing. A generic conversion diagram is available. See order form.)

BLUEPRINT PRICE CODE: C

REAR VIEW

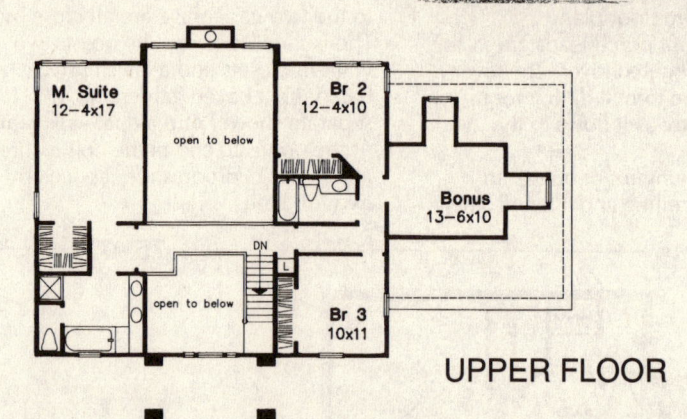

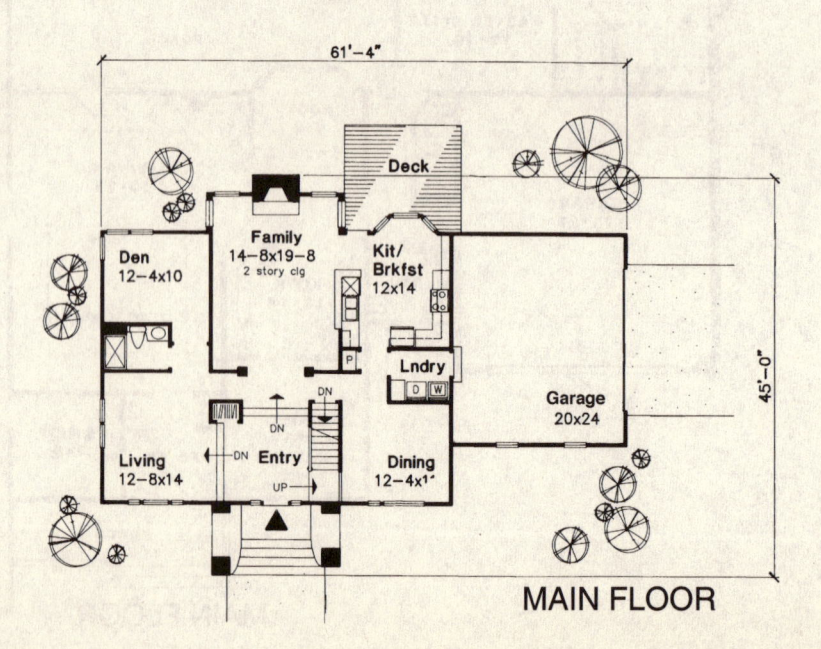

UPPER FLOOR

MAIN FLOOR

ORDER BLUEPRINTS ANYTIME!
CALL TOLL-FREE 1-888-626-2026

Plan B-91011

PRICES AND DETAILS ON PAGES 12-15

Elegant Effects

- Repeating arches accent the covered entry of this elegant one-story home.
- The volume entry opens to the formal spaces. The dining room features an 11-ft. ceiling and a built-in hutch. The living room shows off a dramatic boxed window topped with high glass.
- The gourmet kitchen unfolds to a gazebo dinette and a spacious family room with a fireplace and flanking bookshelves. A handy snack bar is incorporated into the kitchen's central island cooktop.
- A nice-sized laundry room sits near the entrance to the garage and offers room for an extra freezer.
- The sleeping wing consists of three bedrooms, two baths and a versatile den that could serve as a fourth bedroom. With the addition of double doors, bedroom no. 3 easily converts to a sitting area for the master suite.
- The luxurious master bath offers a huge walk-in closet and his-and-hers vanities. An exciting oval whirlpool tub is set into a bay window.
- A full basement offers expansion possibilities when the time arrives.

Plan DBI-2206

Bedrooms: 3+	**Baths:** 2½
Living Area:	
Main floor	2,498 sq. ft.
Total Living Area:	**2,498 sq. ft.**
Standard basement	2,498 sq. ft.
Garage	710 sq. ft.
Exterior Wall Framing:	2x4

Foundation Options:
Standard basement
(All plans can be built with your choice of foundation and framing. A generic conversion diagram is available. See order form.)

BLUEPRINT PRICE CODE: C

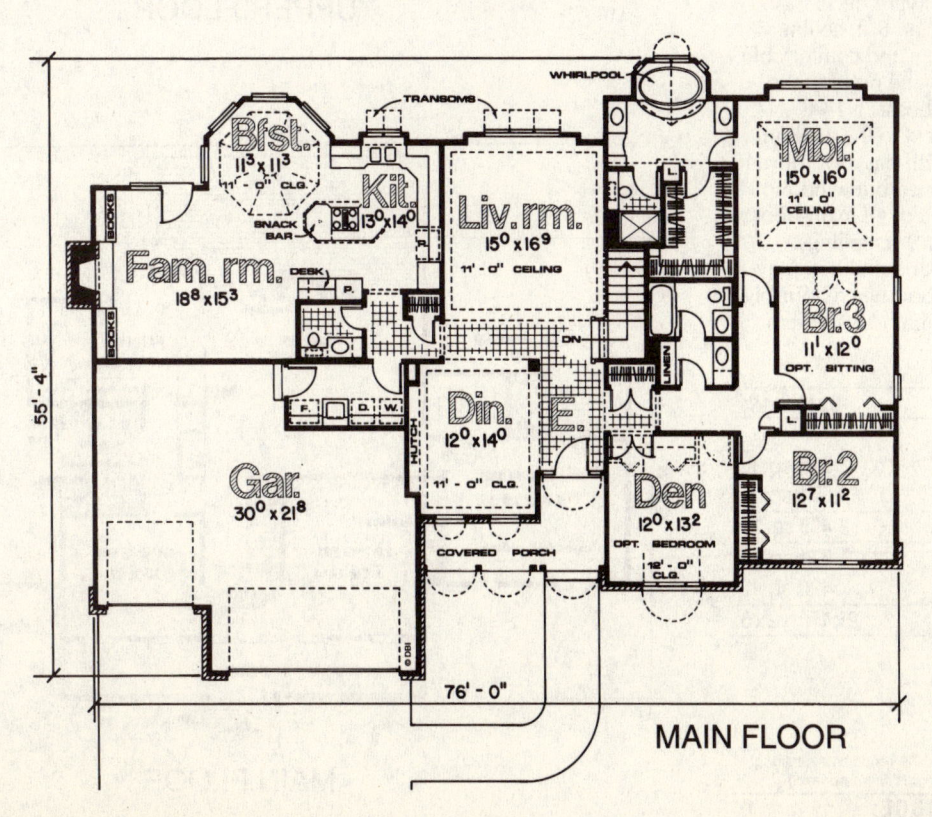

MAIN FLOOR

Plan DBI-2206

ORDER BLUEPRINTS ANYTIME!
CALL TOLL-FREE 1-888-626-2026

PRICES AND DETAILS ON PAGES 12-15

111

Picture-Perfect

- Those tall, cold glasses of summertime lemonade will taste even better when enjoyed on the shady front porch of this picture-perfect home.
- Inside, the two-story, sidelighted foyer unfolds to the formal living areas and the Great Room beyond.
- Fireplaces grace the living room and the Great Room, which are separated by French pocket doors. A TV nook borders the fireplace in the Great Room, letting the kids catch their favorite show while Mom and Dad fix dinner in the kitchen. Two sets of French doors swing wide to reveal a backyard deck.
- A glassy dinette with an 8-ft. ceiling makes breakfasts cozy and comfortable.
- Restful nights will be the norm in the master suite, which boasts a 14-ft. cathedral ceiling. Next to the walk-in closet, the private bath has a whirlpool tub in a fabulous boxed-out window.
- Unless otherwise noted, all main-floor rooms are topped by 9-ft. ceilings.
- At day's end, guests and children may retire to the upper floor, where four big bedrooms and a full bath await them.

Plan AHP-9512

Bedrooms: 5	Baths: 2½
Living Area:	
Upper floor	928 sq. ft.
Main floor	1,571 sq. ft.
Total Living Area:	**2,499 sq. ft.**
Standard basement	1,571 sq. ft.
Garage and storage	420 sq. ft.
Exterior Wall Framing:	2x4 or 2x6

Foundation Options:
Standard basement
Crawlspace
Slab
(All plans can be built with your choice of foundation and framing. A generic conversion diagram is available. See order form.)

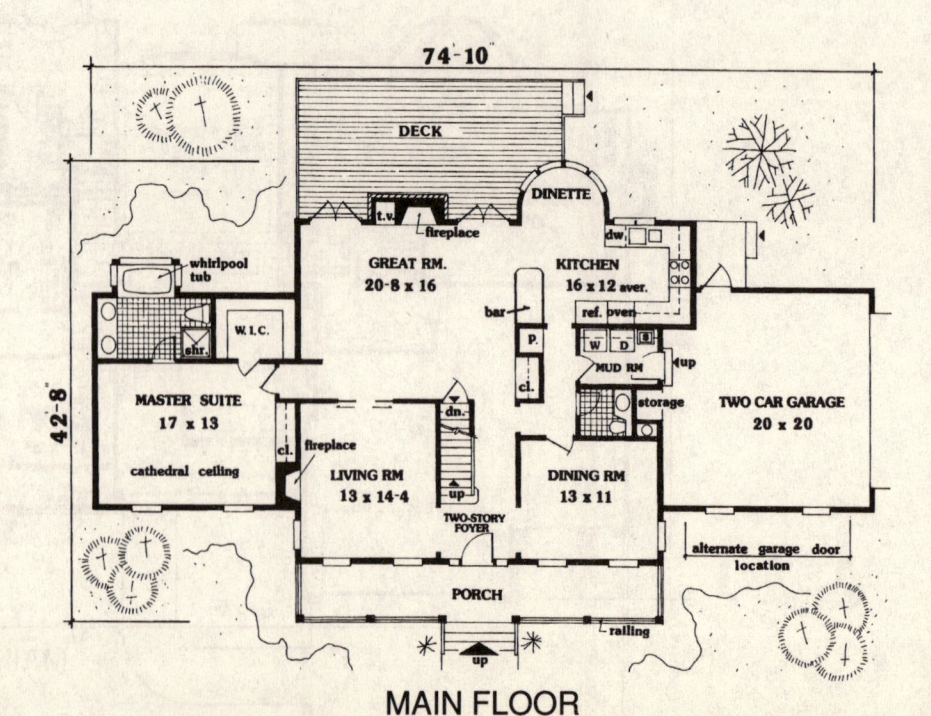

BLUEPRINT PRICE CODE: C

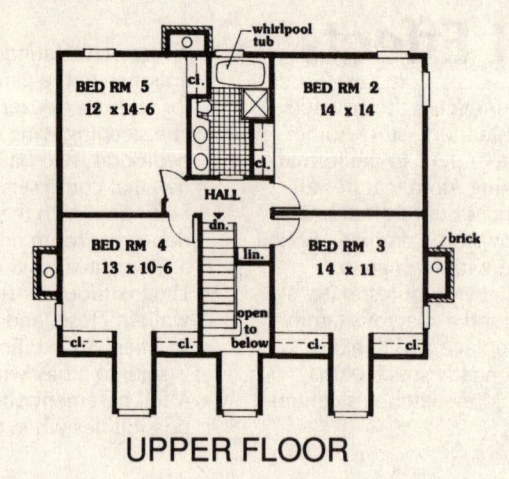

ORDER BLUEPRINTS ANYTIME!
CALL TOLL-FREE 1-888-626-2026

Plan AHP-9512

PRICES AND DETAILS ON PAGES 12-15

Enjoyable Porch

- This stylish home offers an exciting four-season porch and a large deck. Transom windows adorn the exterior and allow extra light into the interior.
- The airy 17-ft., 4-in.-high foyer provides views into all of the living areas.
- The sunken Great Room boasts a see-through fireplace, a Palladian window and a 13-ft., 4-in. cathedral ceiling.
- An island cooktop highlights the corner kitchen, which is open to both the formal dining room and the casual dinette. Double doors access the porch, with its 12-ft. vaulted ceiling and French door to the inviting deck.
- The master bedroom is enhanced by a 10-ft., 3-in. tray ceiling and the see-through fireplace. The master bath has a whirlpool tub and a separate shower, each with striking glass-block walls.
- The front bedroom boasts an arched window under an 11-ft., 9-in. ceiling.
- The den off the foyer may be used to accommodate overnight guests.
- Unless otherwise noted, all rooms have 9-ft. ceilings.

Plan PI-92-535	
Bedrooms: 2+	**Baths:** 2½
Living Area:	
Main floor	2,302 sq. ft.
Four-season porch	208 sq. ft.
Total Living Area:	**2,510 sq. ft.**
Daylight basement	2,302 sq. ft.
Garage	912 sq. ft.
Exterior Wall Framing:	2x6
Foundation Options:	
Daylight basement	

(All plans can be built with your choice of foundation and framing. A generic conversion diagram is available. See order form.)

BLUEPRINT PRICE CODE: D

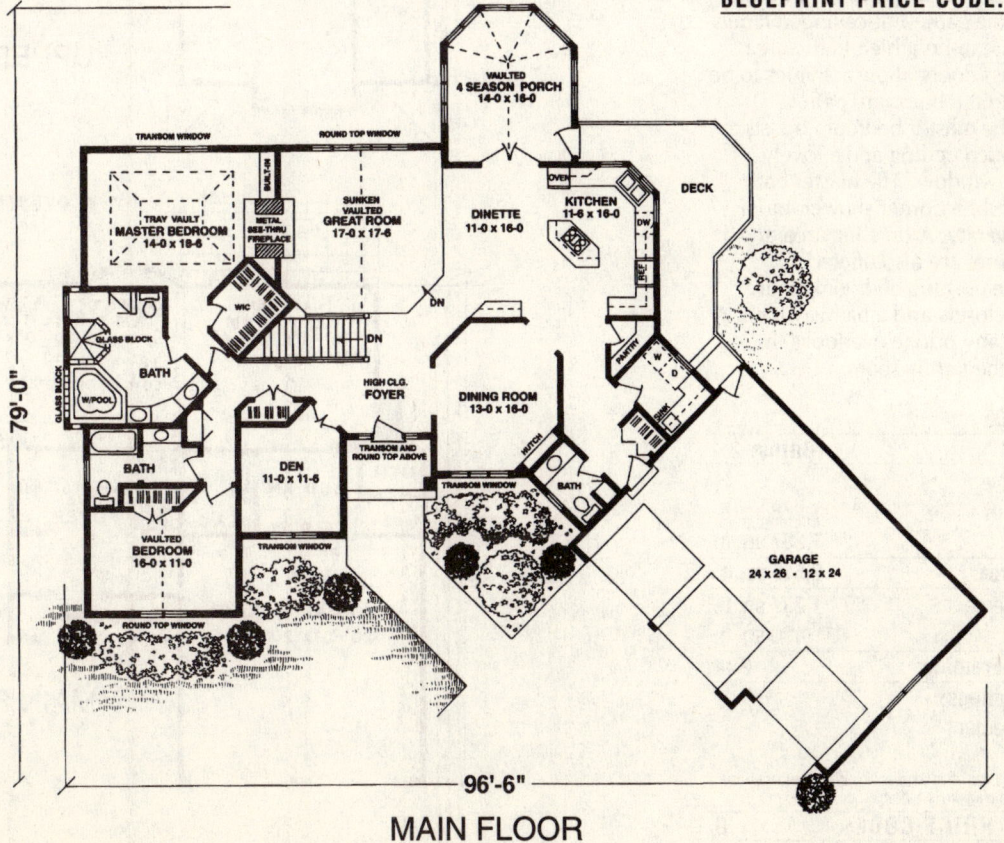

MAIN FLOOR

ORDER BLUEPRINTS ANYTIME!
CALL TOLL-FREE 1-888-626-2026

Plan PI-92-535

Nostalgic Exterior Appeal

- A covered front porch, large half-round windows and Victorian gable details give this nostalgic home classic appeal.
- A stunning two-story foyer awaits guests at the entry, which is flooded with light from the half-round window above.
- The central island kitchen is brightened by the bay-windowed breakfast room, which looks into the family room over a low partition.
- Highlighted by a skylight and a corner fireplace, the cathedral-ceilinged family room is sure to be a high-traffic area. Sliding glass doors allow activities to be extended to the backyard patio.
- Upstairs, the master bedroom boasts a unique sloped ceiling and a lovely boxed-out window. The master bath has a spa tub, a corner shower and a dual-sink vanity. A dressing area and a walk-in closet are also offered.
- Three more upstairs bedrooms share two linen closets and a hallway bath. A railed balcony bridge overlooks the foyer and the family room.

Plan AX-90305

Bedrooms: 4	Baths: 2½
Living Area:	
Upper floor	1,278 sq. ft.
Main floor	1,237 sq. ft.
Total Living Area:	**2,515 sq. ft.**
Standard basement	1,237 sq. ft.
Garage	400 sq. ft.
Exterior Wall Framing:	2x4
Foundation Options:	
Standard basement	
Slab	
(All plans can be built with your choice of foundation and framing. A generic conversion diagram is available. See order form.)	
BLUEPRINT PRICE CODE:	**D**

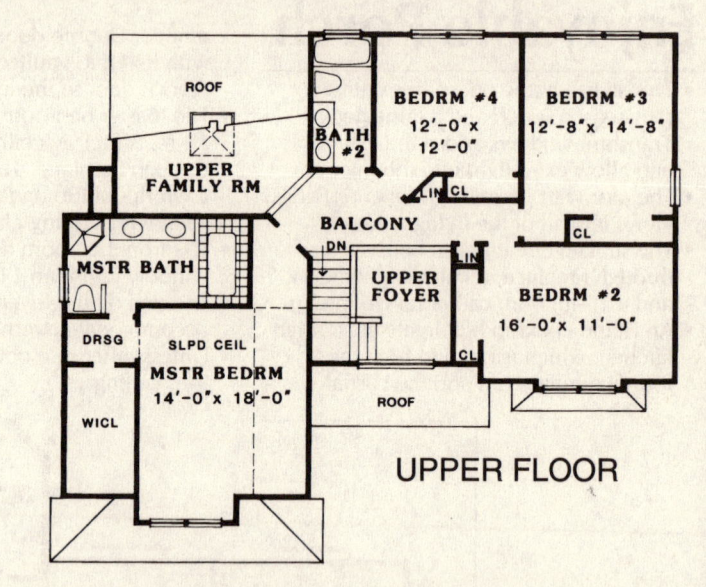

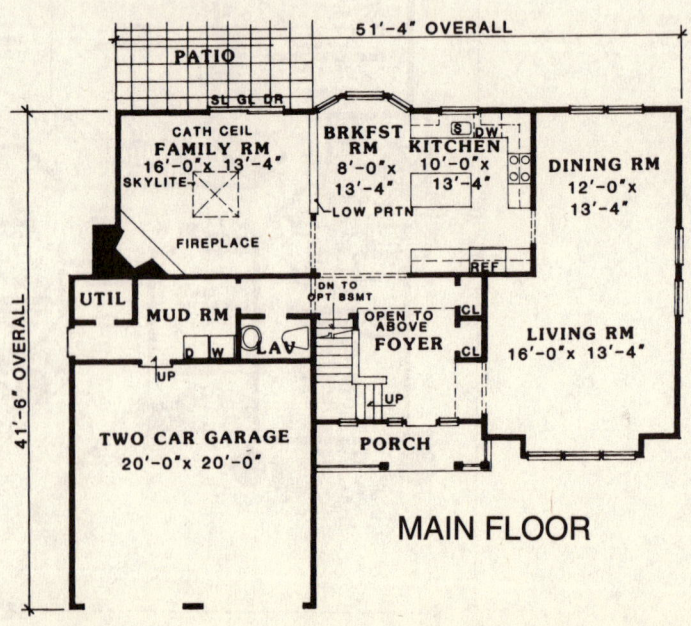

ORDER BLUEPRINTS ANYTIME!
CALL TOLL-FREE 1-888-626-2026

Plan AX-90305

PRICES AND DETAILS ON PAGES 12-15

Thoroughly Country

- The pleasing warmth that shines through this Early American farmhouse will assure you that it's thoroughly country in both appearance and charm.
- Enjoy a sunny Saturday on your railed front porch, which also protects visitors from inclement weather.
- The spacious living room will handle any occasion, large or small. It features a corner fireplace, a raised ceiling and access to the rear porch—the ideal spot to gather neighbors and show off your barbecuing prowess.
- Quietly secluded in a back corner, the master bedroom suite provides a nice retreat after a long day. Dual walk-in closets and a private whirlpool bath add extra comfort.
- On the opposite side of the home are three good-sized bedrooms; each boasts ample closet space. Two full-sized baths easily serve all three.
- All rooms, unless otherwise noted, gain a nice feeling of added space with expanded 9-ft. ceilings.

Plan VL-2519	
Bedrooms: 4+	**Baths:** 3½
Living Area:	
Main floor	2,519 sq. ft.
Total Living Area:	**2,519 sq. ft.**
Garage	504 sq. ft.
Exterior Wall Framing:	2x4

Foundation Options:
Crawlspace
Slab
(All plans can be built with your choice of foundation and framing. A generic conversion diagram is available. See order form.)

BLUEPRINT PRICE CODE: D

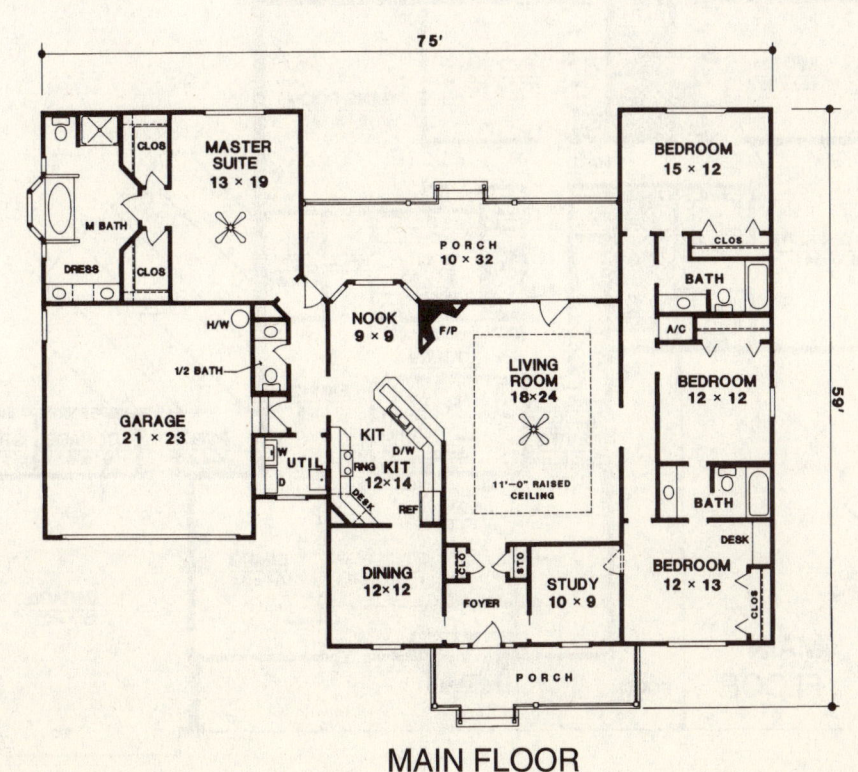

MAIN FLOOR

Plan VL-2519

Wonderful Ranch-Style

- This wonderful ranch-style home offers an L-shaped porch with ornate post detail, an interesting roofline and a classic cupola atop the garage.
- The open floor plan is ultra-modern, beginning with the huge living and dining area. The living room is highlighted by a raised ceiling with rustic beams. The dining room, one step up, is outlined by a railing.
- The super U-shaped kitchen has tons of counter and storage space, including an island cabinet, a desk, a pantry closet and two lazy Susans. The adjoining eating area offers views to the patio and access to the side porch.
- An oversized utility room, a sewing room and a game room are extra features, as are the two storage areas at the rear of the garage.
- The big master suite hosts plenty of closet space, plus a deluxe bath behind double doors. The two smaller bedrooms, each with double closets, share a compartmentalized bath.

Plan E-2502

Bedrooms: 3+	Baths: 2½
Living Area:	
Main floor	2,522 sq. ft.
Total Living Area:	**2,522 sq. ft.**
Garage	484 sq. ft.
Storage	90 sq. ft.
Exterior Wall Framing:	2x6

Foundation Options:
Crawlspace
Slab
(All plans can be built with your choice of foundation and framing. A generic conversion diagram is available. See order form.)

BLUEPRINT PRICE CODE: D

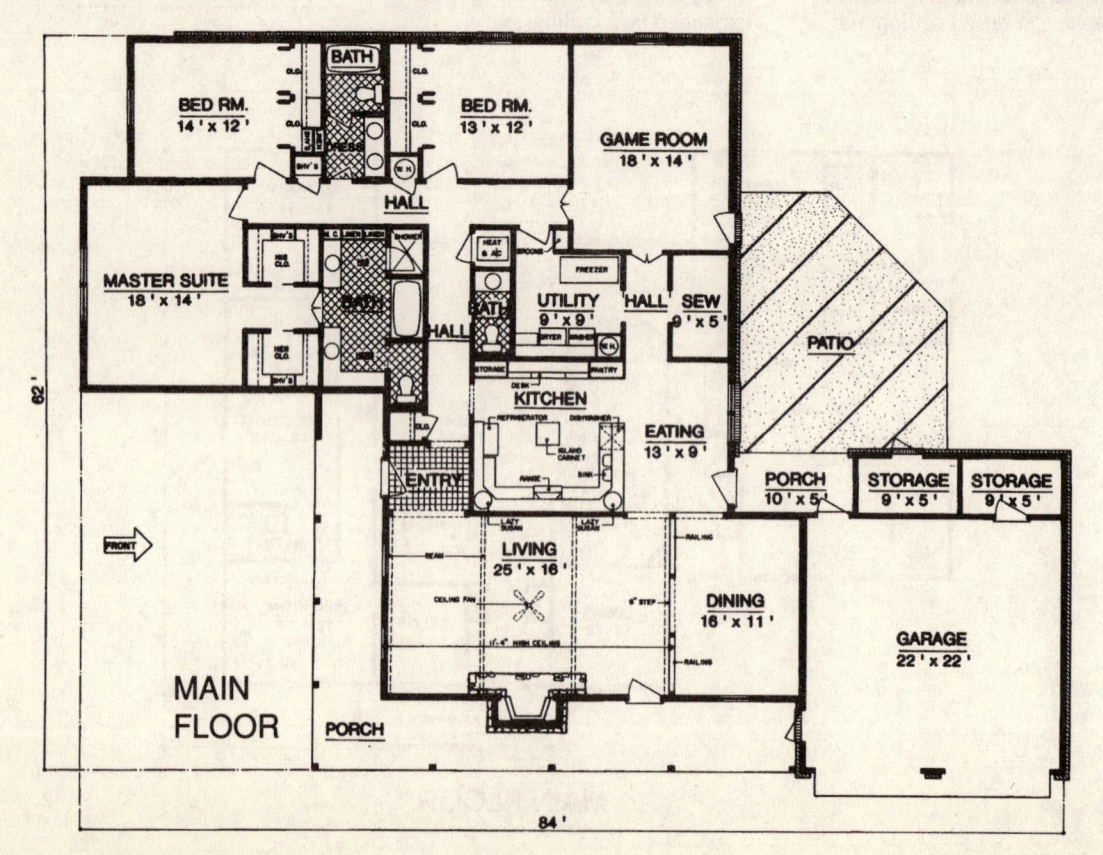

Plan E-2502

Striking Facade

- Flattering windows and a striking roofline grace the facade of this comfortable and appealing home.
- Down the short hallway to the right of the two-story foyer, the living room offers a cozy atmosphere. The adjoining den, with attractive window seats, may be converted into a bedroom, if desired.
- Directly ahead of the foyer, the large family room sports a 16-ft., 8-in. tray ceiling and a crackling fireplace.
- Around the corner, the island kitchen flows into a dinette with a built-in desk and sliding doors to the backyard. The nearby garage entrance has a cute changing bench.
- All main-floor rooms have 9-ft. ceilings.
- Beautiful balcony views highlight the upstairs sleeping area.
- The master bedroom is enhanced by a 10-ft. tray ceiling and a large walk-in closet. The master bath boasts a platform tub, a separate shower and a private toilet.
- Three secondary bedrooms and an optional bonus room round out the upper floor.

Plan A-2353-DS

Bedrooms: 4+	Baths: 2½
Living Area:	
Upper floor	1,135 sq. ft.
Main floor	1,411 sq. ft.
Total Living Area:	**2,546 sq. ft.**
Bonus room (unfinished)	312 sq. ft.
Standard basement	1,411 sq. ft.
Garage	549 sq. ft.
Exterior Wall Framing:	2x6

Foundation Options:
Standard basement
(All plans can be built with your choice of foundation and framing. A generic conversion diagram is available. See order form.)

BLUEPRINT PRICE CODE: D

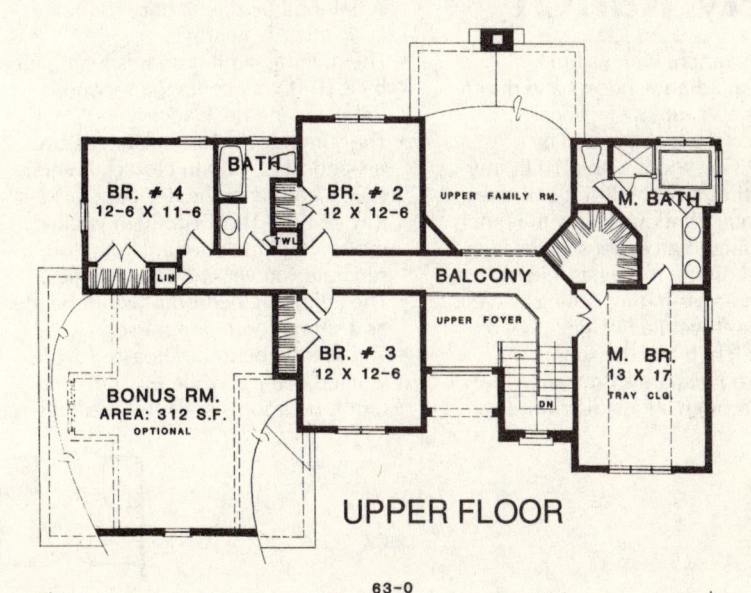

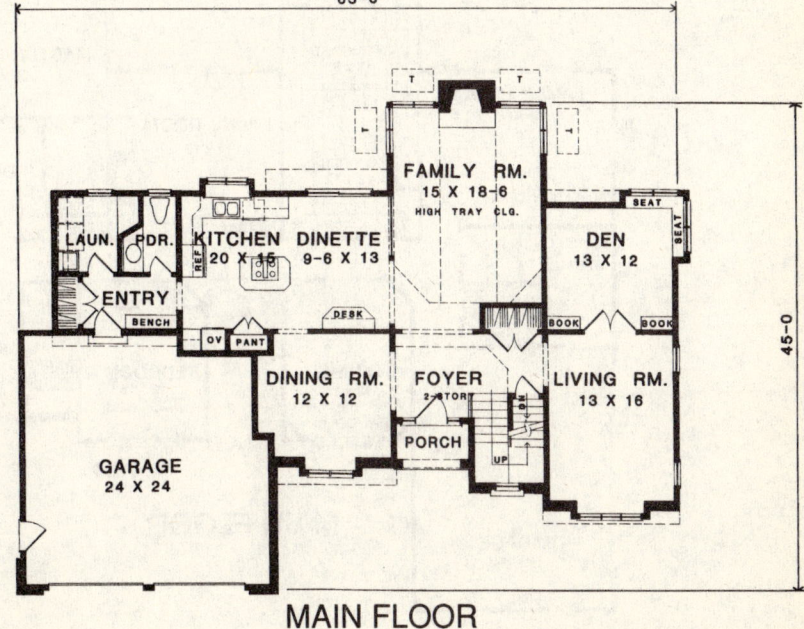

ORDER BLUEPRINTS ANYTIME!
CALL TOLL-FREE 1-888-626-2026

Plan A-2353-DS

PRICES AND DETAILS ON PAGES 12-15

Stately Ranch

- This stately ranch, with its brick exterior, Palladian windows and quoin accents, is a vision of elegance.
- Inside, guests will be greeted by a dramatic living room with a 10-ft. tray ceiling, a fireplace, built-in bookcases and a unique window wall with French doors leading to an expansive deck.
- The formal dining room has mitered corners and a 10-ft. tray ceiling as well.
- Under a 14-ft. vaulted ceiling, the gourmet kitchen and the sunny breakfast room share a dramatic view of the deck through a Palladian window.

A half-bath and a laundry room are conveniently nearby.
- The inviting family room is highlighted by a 10-ft. tray ceiling, a second fireplace and deck access.
- The sumptuous master suite features his-and-hers walk-in closets, French doors leading to the deck and a 10-ft. tray ceiling. The 14-ft.-high vaulted master bath includes a garden tub, a separate shower and twin vanities.
- The adjoining bedroom would be ideal as a sitting room or a nursery.
- The second bedroom boasts a 14-ft. vaulted ceiling, while the third and fourth bedrooms have 9-ft. ceilings.

Plan APS-2410

Bedrooms: 4	**Baths:** 2½-3½

Living Area:
Main floor .... 2,559 sq. ft.
Total Living Area: .... **2,559 sq. ft.**
Standard basement ...... 2,559 sq. ft.
Garage .... 456 sq. ft.
Exterior Wall Framing: 2x4
Foundation Options:
Standard basement
Crawlspace
Slab
(All plans can be built with your choice of foundation and framing. A generic conversion diagram is available. See order form.)

BLUEPRINT PRICE CODE: D

MAIN FLOOR

OPTIONAL EXTRA BATH

Plan APS-2410

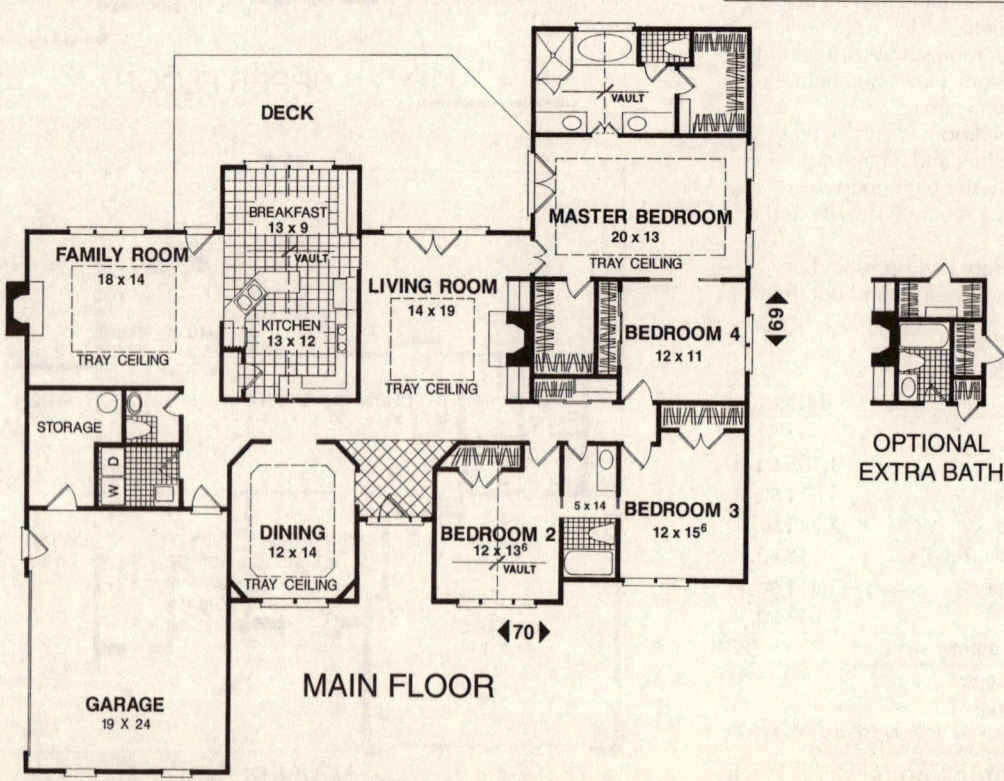

Classic Country-Style

- Almost completely surrounded by an expansive porch, this classic plan exudes warmth and grace.
- The foyer is liberal in size and leads guests to a formal dining room to the left or the large living room to the right.
- The open country kitchen includes a sunny, bay-windowed breakfast nook. A utility area, a full bath and garage access are nearby.
- Upstairs, the master suite is impressive, with its large sleeping area, walk-in closet and magnificent garden bath.
- Three secondary bedrooms share a full bath with a dual-sink vanity.
- Also note the stairs leading up to an attic, which is useful for storage space.

See this plan on our "Country & Traditional" Video Tour! Order form on page 9

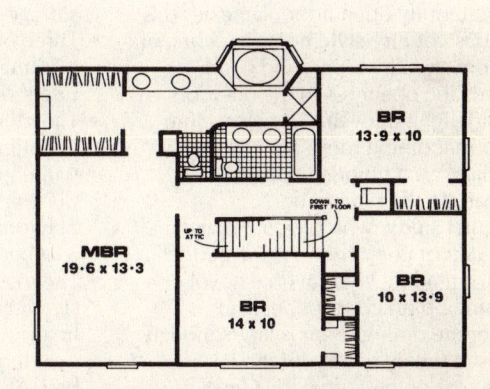

Plan J-86134

Bedrooms: 4	Baths: 3
Living Area:	
Upper floor	1,195 sq. ft.
Main floor	1,370 sq. ft.
Total Living Area:	**2,565 sq. ft.**
Standard basement	1,370 sq. ft.
Garage	576 sq. ft.
Exterior Wall Framing:	2x4

Foundation Options:
Standard basement
Crawlspace
Slab
(All plans can be built with your choice of foundation and framing. A generic conversion diagram is available. See order form.)

BLUEPRINT PRICE CODE: D

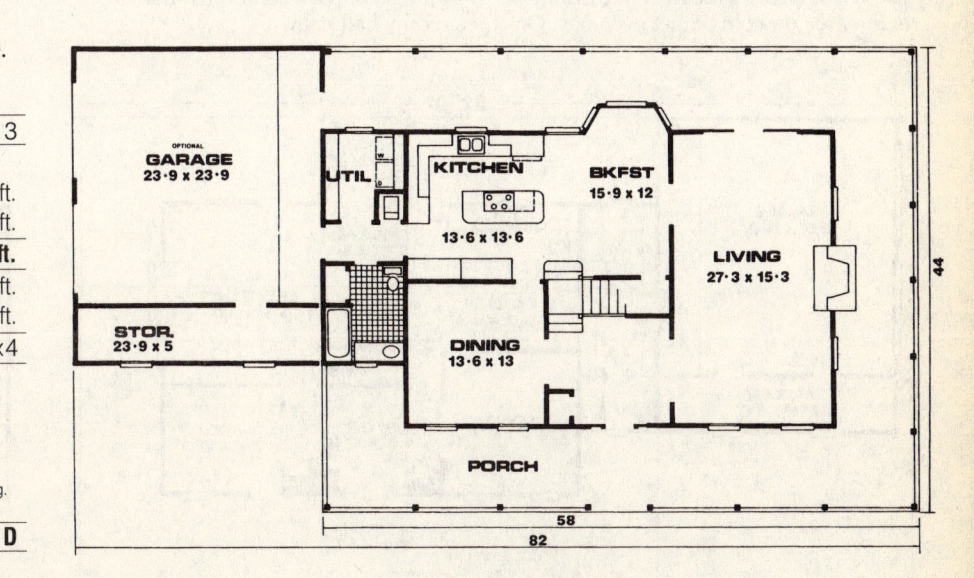

UPPER FLOOR
- BR 13·9 x 10
- MBR 19·6 x 13·3
- BR 14 x 10
- BR 10 x 13·9

MAIN FLOOR
- OPTIONAL GARAGE 23·9 x 23·9
- UTIL
- KITCHEN 13·6 x 13·6
- BKFST 15·9 x 12
- LIVING 27·3 x 15·3
- STOR. 23·9 x 5
- DINING 13·6 x 13
- PORCH
- 58
- 82
- 44

ORDER BLUEPRINTS ANYTIME!
CALL TOLL-FREE 1-888-626-2026

Plan J-86134

PRICES AND DETAILS ON PAGES 12-15

Gracious, Open Living

- A wonderfully open floor plan gives this gracious country-style home a feeling of freedom. A full wraparound porch extends the openness to the outdoors.
- The sidelighted foyer offers views into the formal dining room and the study, and displays a unique two-way staircase to the upper floor.
- The quiet study, which would make a great den or guest room, is the perfect spot for reading your favorite novel or catching up on correspondence.
- The serene dining room is large enough to host a turkey dinner for the relatives.
- At the rear of the home, the Great Room, breakfast nook and island kitchen combine for an informal setting.
- The Great Room's fireplace warms the entire area on cold winter evenings. On either side of the bayed breakfast nook, French doors open to the porch.
- A laundry/utility room and a full bath flank the hallway to the two-car, side-entry garage, which includes a wide storage room.
- Three bedrooms, two baths and an exciting playroom are located on the upper floor.
- The railed playroom is brightened by a beautiful Palladian window. The kids will enjoy this room for hours on end, playing cards or video games. The playroom is large enough to be finished as a bedroom if needed.
- The master bedroom boasts a huge sleeping area and a walk-in closet. The luxurious private bath features a nice oval tub housed in a beautiful window bay. A separate shower, a dual-sink vanity and a private toilet are other notable amenities.
- Two secondary bedrooms share a roomy hall bath.

Plan J-9289	
Bedrooms: 3+	Baths: 3
Living Area:	
Upper floor	1,212 sq. ft.
Main floor	1,370 sq. ft.
Total Living Area:	**2,582 sq. ft.**
Standard basement	1,370 sq. ft.
Garage and storage	720 sq. ft.
Exterior Wall Framing:	2x4

Foundation Options:
Standard basement
Crawlspace
Slab

(All plans can be built with your choice of foundation and framing. A generic conversion diagram is available. See order form.)

BLUEPRINT PRICE CODE: D

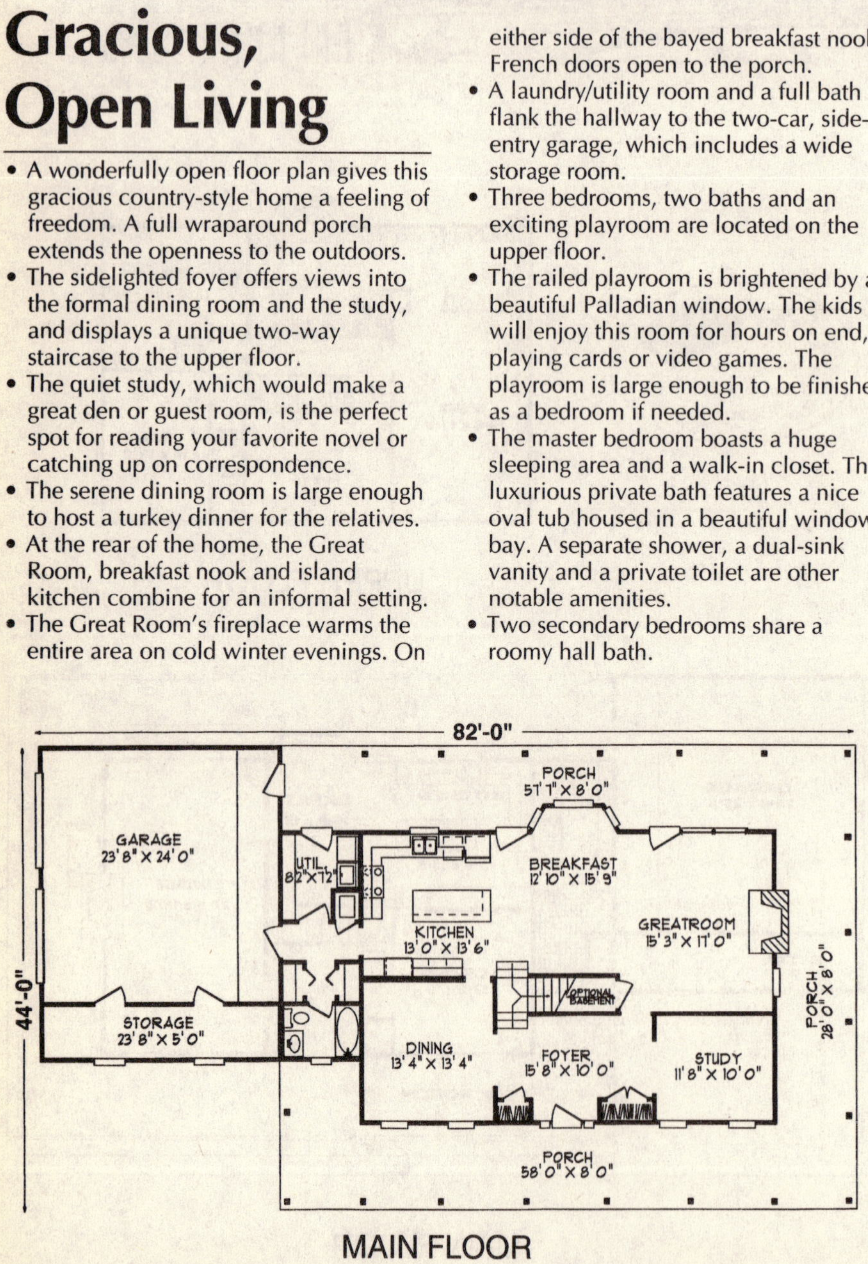

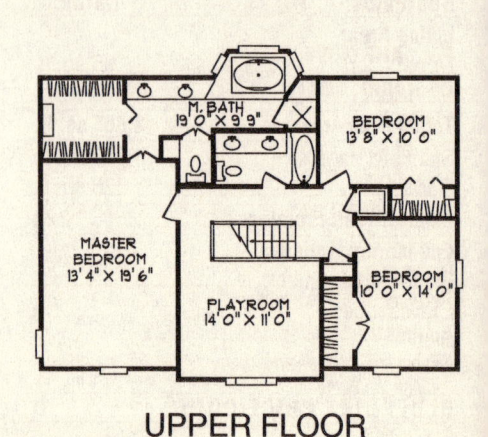

Plan J-9289

Sheer Genius!

- With five bedrooms, a home office and plenty of special touches, this two-story design combines the thoughtful use of space with a sheer pleasure in details.
- An inviting porch and paned windows with half-round transoms grace the home's exterior.
- Inside, the 21-ft.-high foyer greets guests and provides immediate access to the formal dining room and the living room.
- Straight ahead, the informal areas create a haven of casual family togetherness. The warm family room boasts a roaring fireplace and a nice spread of windows overlooking the rear terrace.
- The sunny dinette includes sliding glass doors to the terrace, and it shares a snack bar with the U-shaped kitchen.
- Upstairs, the master suite enjoys the luxury of a 10½-ft. ceiling, an arched window arrangement, a walk-in closet and a private, skylighted spa bath.
- The office features its own entry and staircase; it can be reached from the backyard or the mudroom.

Plan AHP-9624

Bedrooms: 5+	Baths: 2½
Living Area:	
Upper floor	1,395 sq. ft.
Main floor	1,190 sq. ft.
Total Living Area:	**2,585 sq. ft.**
Standard basement	1,128 sq. ft.
Garage and storage	566 sq. ft.
Exterior Wall Framing:	2x4 or 2x6

Foundation Options:
Standard basement
Crawlspace
Slab
(All plans can be built with your choice of foundation and framing. A generic conversion diagram is available. See order form.)

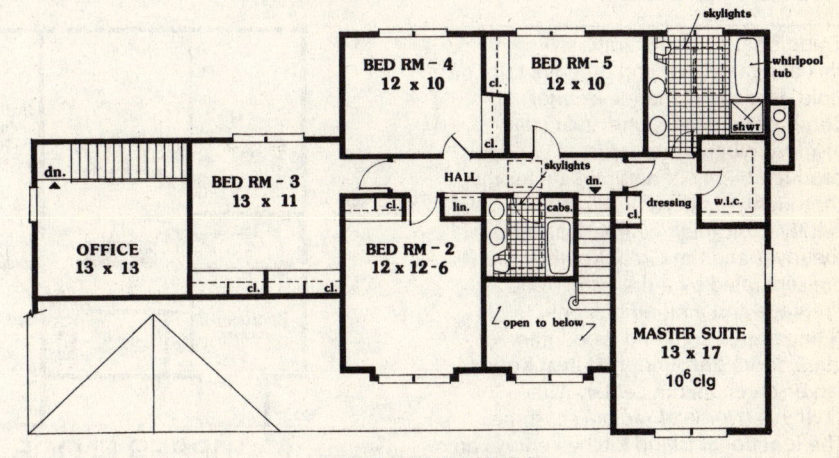

BLUEPRINT PRICE CODE: D

UPPER FLOOR

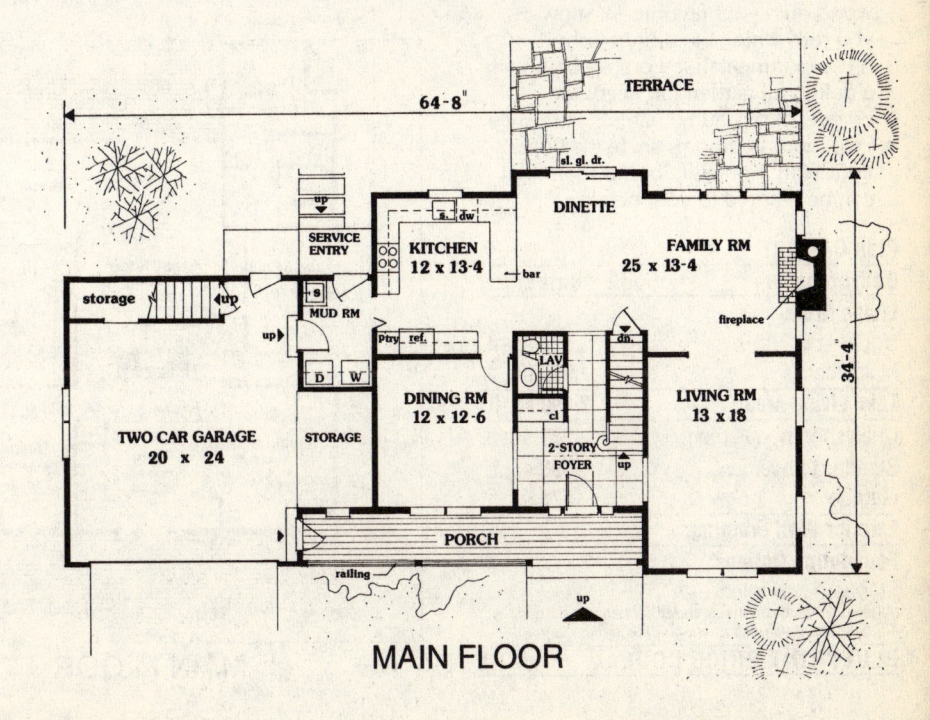

MAIN FLOOR

ORDER BLUEPRINTS ANYTIME!
CALL TOLL-FREE 1-888-626-2026

Plan AHP-9624

PRICES AND DETAILS
ON PAGES 12-15

True Grit

- Traditional Arts and Crafts styling gives this bungalow grit and durability. Its bold, low-maintenance exterior combines natural stone and cedar.
- Inside, skylights and transom windows produce plenty of natural light for the thoroughly modern floor plan.
- A lofty 20-ft.-high ceiling soars above the foyer and the Great Room, which are separated by a dramatic stone fireplace and a railed balcony.
- A decorative arch and wood-framed glass doors surround the Great Room's large-screen media center, while skylights overhead radiate sunshine.
- The functional island kitchen enjoys an ideal location near the busy living spaces and the laundry room. You won't miss your favorite TV show as you're washing the dinner dishes!
- A compartmentalized private bath with a delightful garden tub keeps the owners of this home pampered in style.
- Two more bedrooms share the upper floor with a versatile bonus room that can be tailored to your needs.

Plan GA-9601

Bedrooms: 3+	Baths: 2½

Living Area:

Upper floor	594 sq. ft.
Main floor	1,996 sq. ft.
Total Living Area:	**2,590 sq. ft.**
Unfinished bonus room	233 sq. ft.
Standard basement	1,996 sq. ft.
Garage	576 sq. ft.
Exterior Wall Framing:	2x6

Foundation Options:
Standard basement
(All plans can be built with your choice of foundation and framing. A generic conversion diagram is available. See order form.)

BLUEPRINT PRICE CODE: D

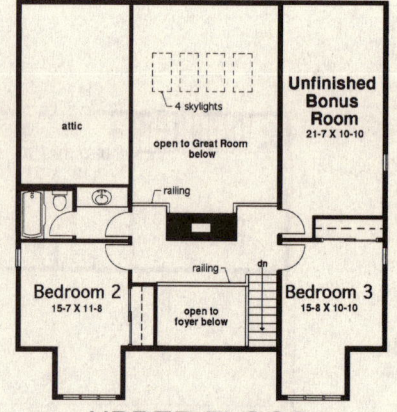

UPPER FLOOR

VIEW INTO GREAT ROOM

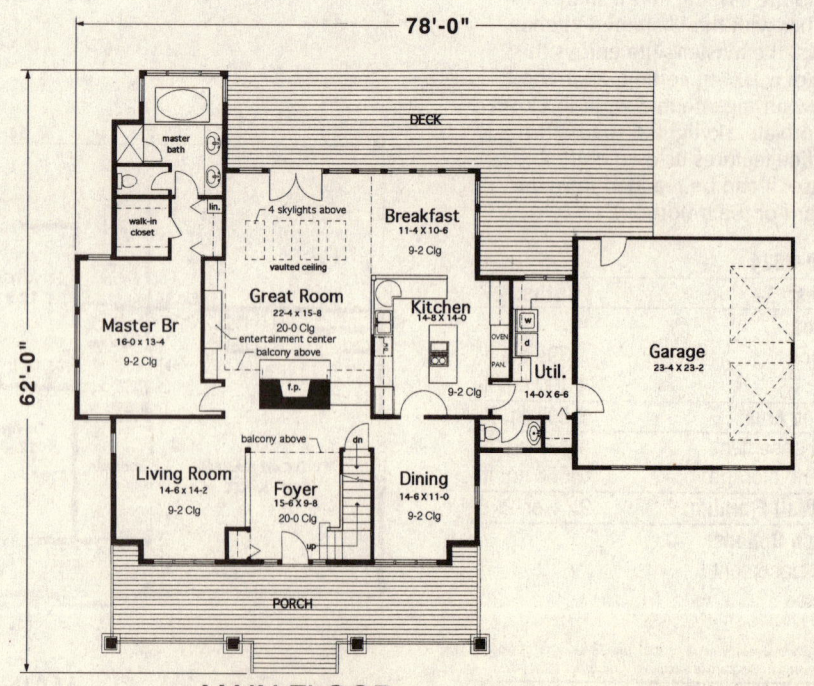

MAIN FLOOR

ORDER BLUEPRINTS ANYTIME!
CALL TOLL-FREE 1-888-626-2026

Plan GA-9601

PRICES AND DETAILS ON PAGES 12-15

Double the Impact!

- An elaborate curb presence and breathtaking backyard views give the front and rear elevations of this one-story home high impact!
- A deep, angled foyer, columned arches and a succession of lofty ceilings create entry drama.
- Enjoy the beautiful scenery of your lake or golf course property through expansive glass in the Great Room, family/sun room and breakfast room.
- Between the Great Room and the family room, a stunning see-through fireplace stimulates your senses further. A unique domed ceiling above the breakfast table adds a splash of style to the bright sun of the bay window.
- In the kitchen, an island cooktop, a walk-in pantry and a serving bar put the fun back into cooking!
- Behind double doors, a private whirlpool bath adjoins the master bedroom. Another full bath serves the secondary bedrooms; the fourth bedroom converts to a study.

Plan BOD-26-9A

Bedrooms: 3+	Baths: 2½
Living Area:	
Main floor	2,598 sq. ft.
Total Living Area:	**2,598 sq. ft.**
Garage and storage	511 sq. ft.
Exterior Wall Framing:	2x4

Foundation Options:
Crawlspace
Slab
(All plans can be built with your choice of foundation and framing. A generic conversion diagram is available. See order form.)

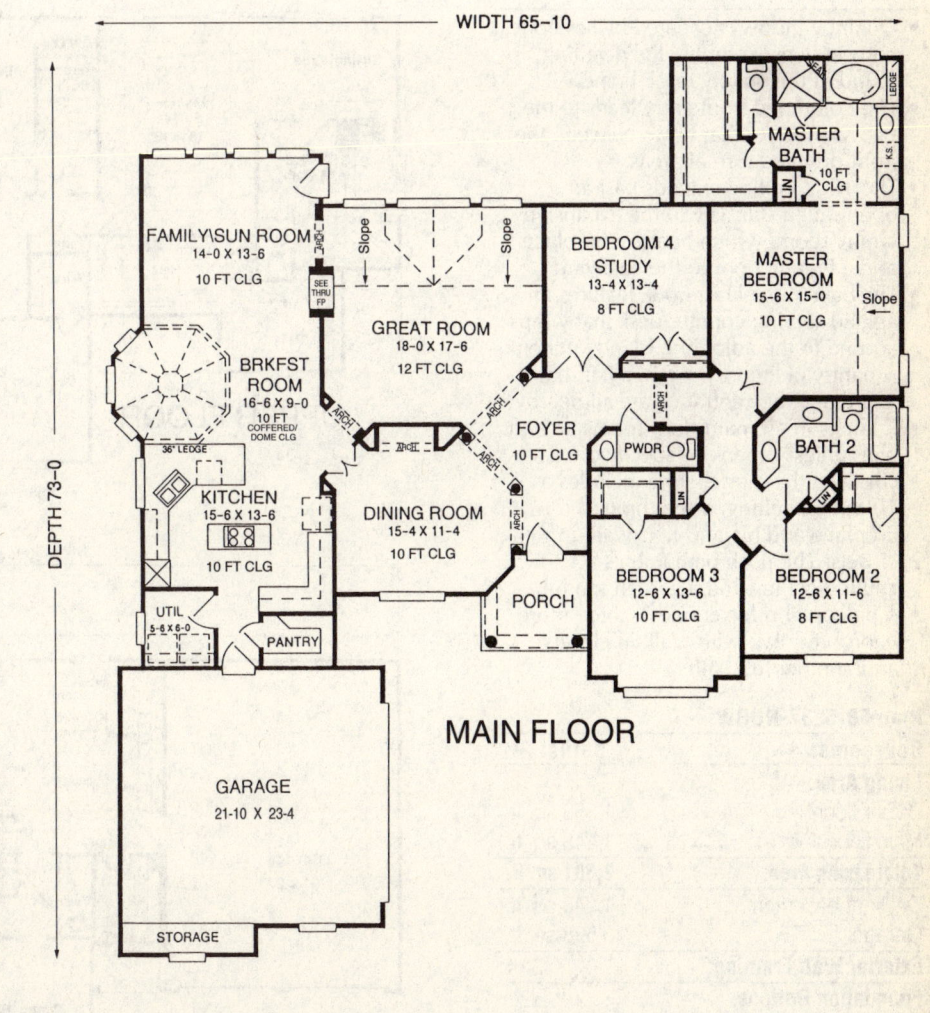

BLUEPRINT PRICE CODE: D

ORDER BLUEPRINTS ANYTIME!
CALL TOLL-FREE 1-888-626-2026

Plan BOD-26-9A

PRICES AND DETAILS ON PAGES 12-15

Quaint Detailing

- Quaint windows accented by keystones and shutters exemplify the detailing found in this stately brick home.
- The columned front entry leads to the two-story foyer that flows between the front-oriented formal areas.
- The 18-ft. ceiling extends past an open-railed stairway to the expansive family room, which boasts a fireplace and a French door to the backyard.
- The bayed breakfast nook features an angled serving counter/desk that wraps around to the adjoining island kitchen. A pantry, a laundry room, a half-bath and the garage entrance are all nearby.
- Ceilings in all main-floor rooms are 9 ft. high unless otherwise specified.
- Upstairs, the master suite includes a 10-ft. tray ceiling, a see-through fireplace and his-and-hers walk-in closets. The posh bath flaunts a 12-ft. vaulted ceiling and a garden spa tub.
- A balcony bridge connects three more bedrooms, two with walk-in closets, and another full bath.

Plan FB-5237-NORW

Bedrooms: 4	Baths: 2½
Living Area:	
Upper floor	1,353 sq. ft.
Main floor	1,248 sq. ft.
Total Living Area:	**2,601 sq. ft.**
Daylight basement	1,248 sq. ft.
Garage	528 sq. ft.
Exterior Wall Framing:	2x4

Foundation Options:
Daylight basement
(All plans can be built with your choice of foundation and framing. A generic conversion diagram is available. See order form.)

BLUEPRINT PRICE CODE: D

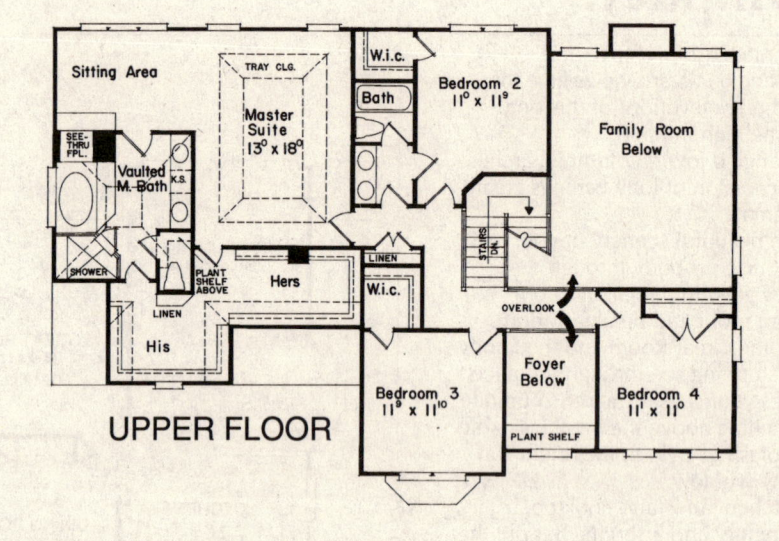

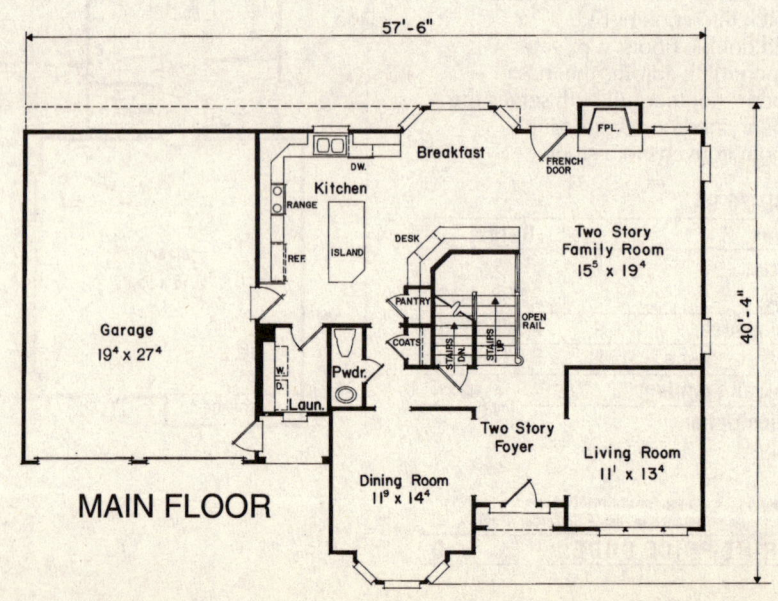

ORDER BLUEPRINTS ANYTIME!
CALL TOLL-FREE 1-888-626-2026

Plan FB-5237-NORW

PRICES AND DETAILS ON PAGES 12-15

Splendid Glass

- Splendid half-round-topped windows add a taste of high class to the facade of this inviting European-style home.
- Adjacent to the sidelighted foyer, double doors introduce a study that can also be used to sleep overnight guests.
- An 11-ft. tray ceiling crowns the bright, formal dining room.
- The living room's windows offer great views of a covered patio and the backyard beyond.
- Private patio access enhances the posh master suite. The master bath is entered through double doors, and hosts a spa tub and his-and-hers walk-in closets under an 8-ft. ceiling.
- A 14-ft.-long serving bar connects the island kitchen to the breakfast nook, where a French door opens to the patio. The fireplace in the adjoining family room creates a cozy atmosphere.
- Three secondary bedrooms with standard 8-ft. ceilings share two full baths, one of which offers access to the backyard or a future pool!
- Unless otherwise noted, all rooms flaunt 10-ft. ceilings.

Plan DD-2607

Bedrooms: 4+	Baths: 3½
Living Area:	
Main floor	2,602 sq. ft.
Total Living Area:	**2,602 sq. ft.**
Standard basement	2,602 sq. ft.
Garage and storage	487 sq. ft.
Exterior Wall Framing:	2x4

Foundation Options:

Standard basement
Crawlspace
Slab

(All plans can be built with your choice of foundation and framing. A generic conversion diagram is available. See order form.)

BLUEPRINT PRICE CODE: D

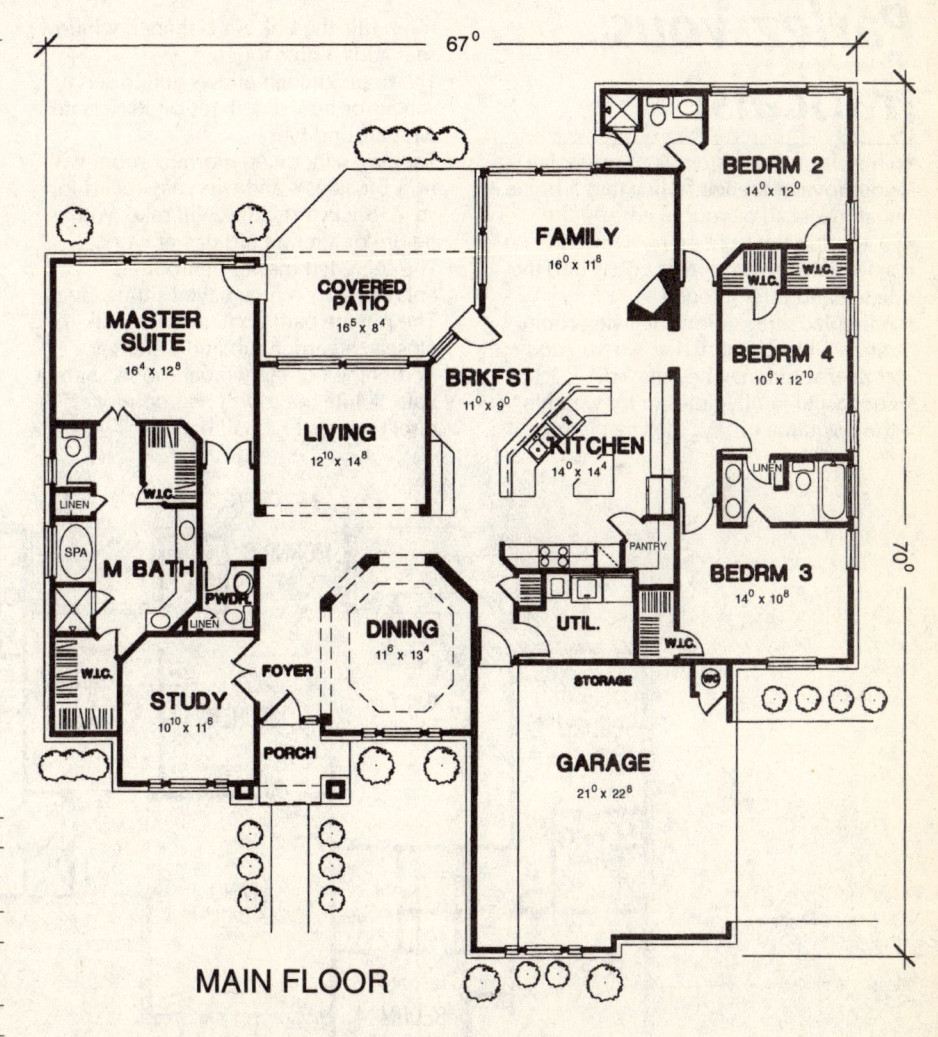

ORDER BLUEPRINTS ANYTIME!
CALL TOLL-FREE 1-888-626-2026

Plan DD-2607

PRICES AND DETAILS ON PAGES 12-15

Parlez-vous français?

- This elegant one-story lets you parlay your love of French styling into a home that meets all of your needs.
- Just inside the front entry, a raised, sidelighted foyer directs guests into the living and dining rooms.
- A fireplace transforms the living room into a welcoming parlor, where good conversation may be enjoyed.
- For casual family times or for watching the big game on TV, the large family room fills the bill. An L-shaped window seat adds a nice touch.
- The open kitchen allows you to serve snacks or hors d'oeuvres on its versatile wraparound bar.
- The bay-windowed morning room will host breakfasts and everyday meals in style. Backyard views will relax you before or after a hard day at work.
- The secluded master bedroom is enhanced by a nice bayed sitting area. The private bath contains two walk-in closets, a garden tub and a shower.
- Across the home, two bedrooms share a bath, while the fourth bedroom offers direct access to a hall bath.

Plan L-2602-C

Bedrooms: 4	Baths: 3

Living Area:
Main floor — 2,602 sq. ft.
Total Living Area: 2,602 sq. ft.
Exterior Wall Framing: 2x4
Foundation Options:
Slab
(All plans can be built with your choice of foundation and framing. A generic conversion diagram is available. See order form.)

BLUEPRINT PRICE CODE: D

(Plans for a detached two-car garage included with blueprints.)

MAIN FLOOR

Plan L-2602-C

Large Deck Wraps Home

- A full deck and an abundance of windows surround this exciting two-level contemporary.
- The brilliant living room boasts a huge fireplace and a 14-ft.-high cathedral ceiling, plus a stunning prow-shaped window wall.
- Skywalls brighten the island kitchen and the dining room. A pantry closet and laundry facilities are nearby.
- The master bedroom offers private access to the deck. The master bath includes a dual-sink vanity, a large tub and a separate shower. A roomy hall bath serves a second bedroom.
- A generous-sized family room, another full bath and two additional bedrooms share the lower level with a two-car garage and a shop area.

Plan NW-579

Bedrooms: 4	Baths: 3

Living Area:
Main floor	1,707 sq. ft.
Daylight basement	901 sq. ft.
Total Living Area:	**2,608 sq. ft.**
Tuck-under garage	588 sq. ft.
Shop	162 sq. ft.

Exterior Wall Framing: 2x6

Foundation Options:
Daylight basement
(All plans can be built with your choice of foundation and framing. A generic conversion diagram is available. See order form.)

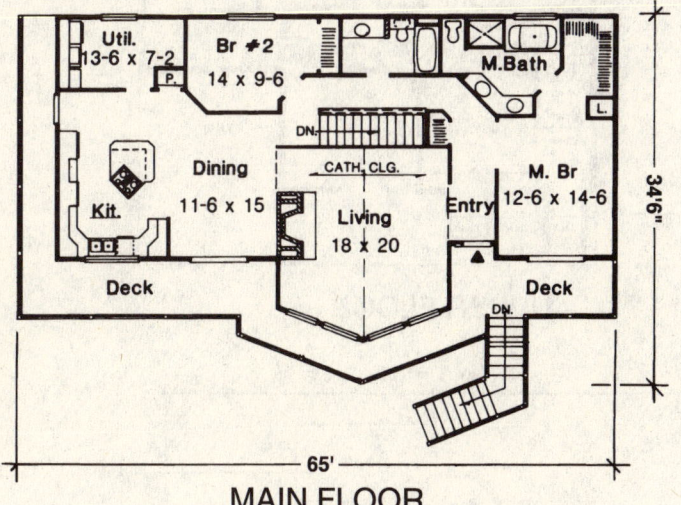

BLUEPRINT PRICE CODE: D

MAIN FLOOR

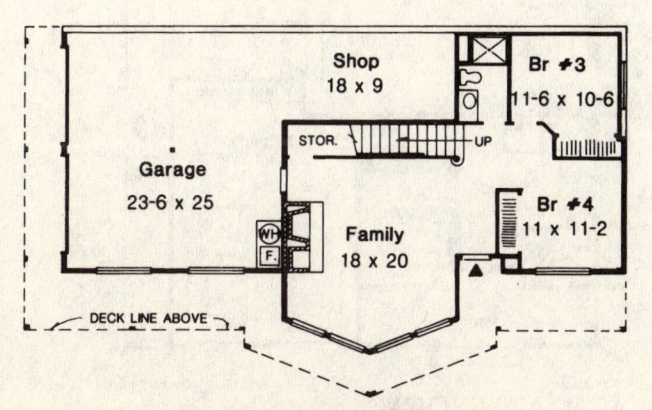

DAYLIGHT BASEMENT

VIEW INTO LIVING ROOM

ORDER BLUEPRINTS ANYTIME!
CALL TOLL-FREE 1-888-626-2026

Plan NW-579

PRICES AND DETAILS
ON PAGES 12-15

House of Gables

- This country home boasts a columned front porch protected by three upstairs gables and flanked by a fourth.
- Inside, a 17-ft. foyer introduces your visitors to this efficient floor plan.
- Use the cozy den off the foyer for a private office or a play area for the kids.
- Impress your visitors with the formal living room, which offers a vaulted ceiling, a fireplace and a window seat.
- Serve your guests with pride in the vaulted dining room.
- The kitchen has an island cooktop and a breakfast nook overlooking the patio.
- The large family room allows Dad plenty of space to romp with the kids in front of a second fireplace.
- Upstairs, a luxurious bath is featured off the master suite, with a walk-in closet and dual-sink vanities. At the end of a long day, hop in your spa and relax!

Plan CDG-2087	
Bedrooms: 3+	**Baths:** 2½
Living Area:	
Upper floor	1,063 sq. ft.
Main floor	1,377 sq. ft.
Bonus room	178 sq. ft.
Total Living Area:	**2,618 sq. ft.**
Standard basement	1,377 sq. ft.
Garage	540 sq. ft.
Exterior Wall Framing:	2x6
Foundation Options:	
Standard basement	
Crawlspace	
(All plans can be built with your choice of foundation and framing. A generic conversion diagram is available. See order form.)	
BLUEPRINT PRICE CODE:	**D**

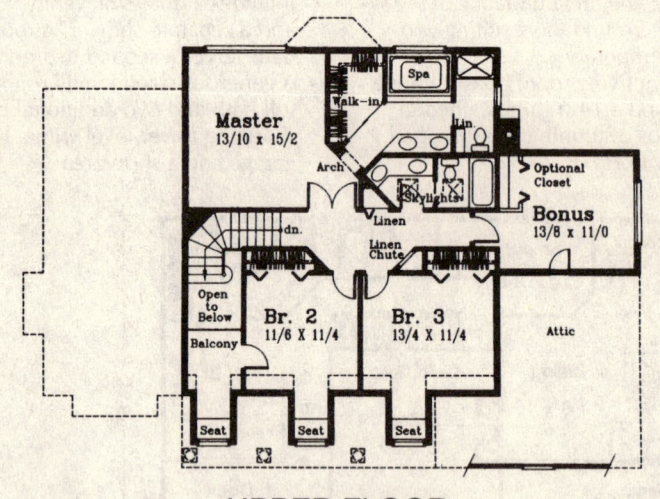

UPPER FLOOR

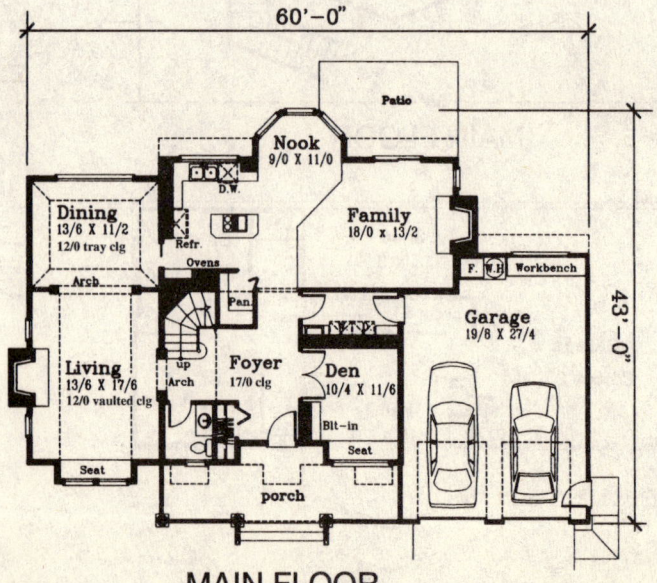

MAIN FLOOR

ORDER BLUEPRINTS ANYTIME!
CALL TOLL-FREE 1-888-626-2026

Plan CDG-2087

PRICES AND DETAILS ON PAGES 12-15

FIRST LOOK! 64 STUNNING NEW DESIGNS

Victoriana

- A wraparound veranda, an oval-windowed front door, fishscale shingles and an octagonal turret give this home a sense of nineteenth-century craftsmanship.
- The foyer is defined by a sweeping staircase leading upstairs.
- Fireplaces abound; they warm the parlor, the family room and the master bedroom.
- A formal dining room features built-in corner cabinets, and adjoins both the kitchen and the parlor.
- A bay window in the dinette and sliding glass doors in the family room overlook a rear terrace.
- In addition to the fireplace, the master suite enjoys a whirlpool tub surrounded by windows on three sides.
- There are three more bedrooms upstairs, sharing a compartmentalized bath with two sinks and a laundry chute to the mudroom on the main floor.
- The blueprints for this home allow for a one- or two-car garage.

Plan AS-5190

Bedrooms: 4	Baths: 2½

Living Area:

Upper floor	1,071 sq. ft.
Main floor	1,134 sq. ft.
Total Living Area:	**2,205 sq. ft.**
Standard basement	1,134 sq. ft.
One-car garage	256 sq. ft.
Optional two-car garage	462 sq. ft.
Exterior Wall Framing:	2x4

Foundation Options:
Standard basement
(All plans can be built with your choice of foundation and framing. A generic conversion diagram is available. See order form.)

BLUEPRINT PRICE CODE: C

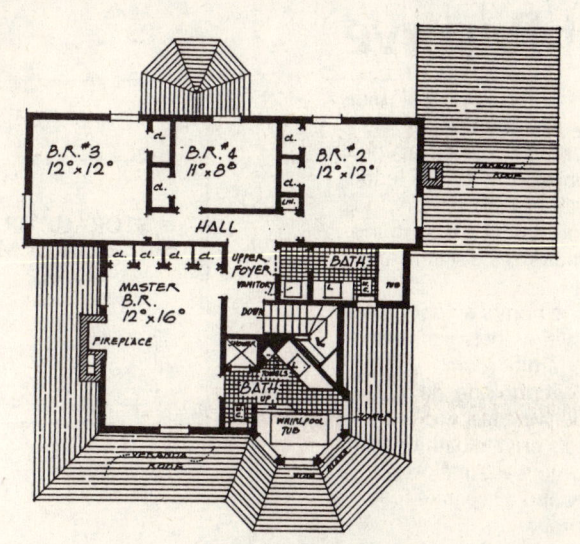

UPPER FLOOR

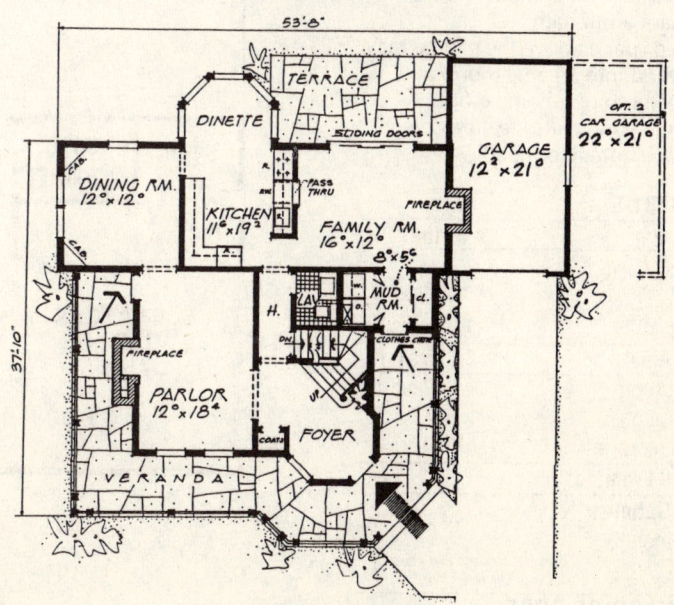

MAIN FLOOR

ORDER BLUEPRINTS ANYTIME!
CALL TOLL-FREE 1-888-626-2026

Plan AS-5190

PRICES AND DETAILS
ON PAGES 12-15

FIRST LOOK! 64 STUNNING NEW DESIGNS

Federal Reserve

- The classic lines of this Federal design pay tribute to our nation's rich architectural heritage. A brick facade, shutters, keystones and dormers lend the home its distinct 18th-century look.
- Formal living and dining rooms in the front of the home provide stately areas for entertaining.
- At the back of the home, an open floor plan allows easy flow between the kitchen and the family room.
- A bay window overlooking the rear patio defines the breakfast nook.
- The master suite's private bath boasts a garden tub, a large walk-in closet, a dual-sink vanity and a separate toilet and shower room.
- A balcony overlooking the two-story foyer leads to two additional bedrooms, which share a full bath.
- Unfinished space above the garage may be converted into a game room, a fourth bedroom or a home office.
- The two-car garage also features plenty of space for storage or hobbies.

Plan JWA-7601-E

Bedrooms: 3+	Baths: 2½
Living Area:	
Upper floor	999 sq. ft.
Main floor	1,226 sq. ft.
Total Living Area:	**2,225 sq. ft.**
Optional bedroom	349 sq. ft.
Partial basement	884 sq. ft.
Garage and storage	510 sq. ft.
Exterior Wall Framing:	2x4
Foundation Options:	

Partial basement
(All plans can be built with your choice of foundation and framing. A generic conversion diagram is available. See order form.)

BLUEPRINT PRICE CODE: C

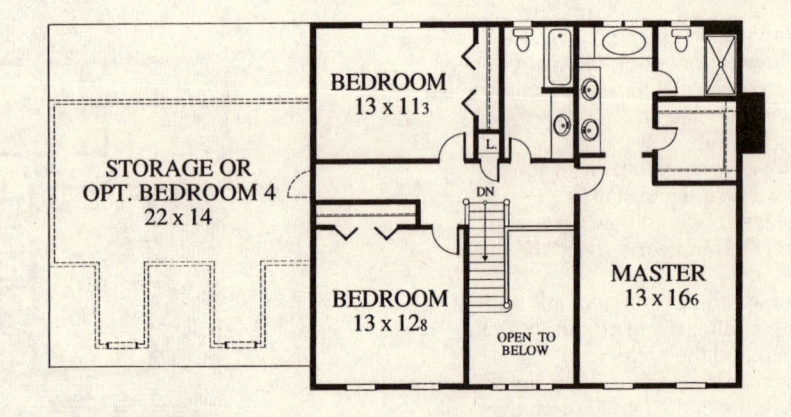

UPPER FLOOR

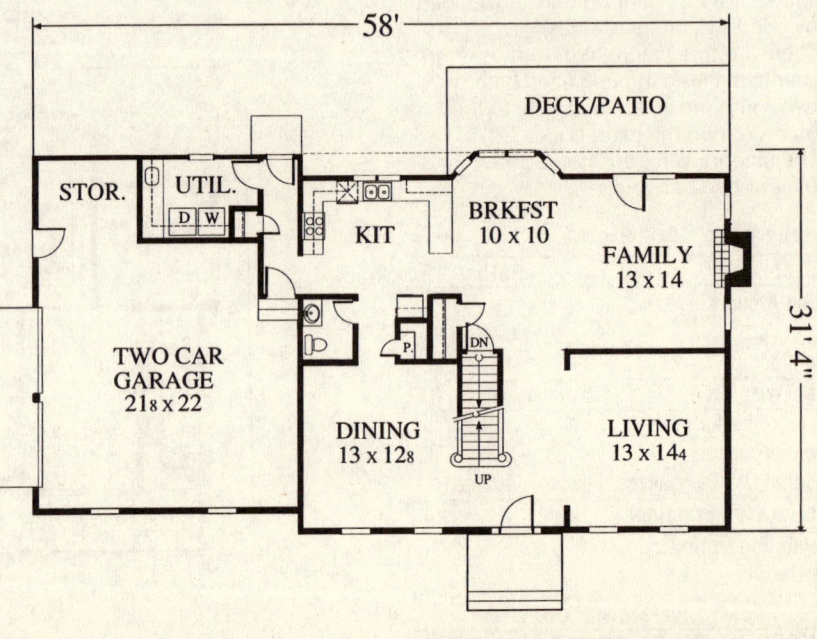

MAIN FLOOR

ORDER BLUEPRINTS ANYTIME!
CALL TOLL-FREE 1-888-626-2026

Plan JWA-7601-E

PRICES AND DETAILS
ON PAGES 12-15

FIRST LOOK! 64 STUNNING NEW DESIGNS

Single-Floor Splendor

- The facade of this splendid one-story design is accented by decorative quoins and keystones, a columned front porch and three graceful arches.
- Formal entertaining has a place in the living room and the dining room, which flank the entry. Tall windows in both rooms provide plenty of natural light.
- A raised snack bar in the kitchen accommodates on-the-go meals and also services the nearby family room. A cozy nook provides space for a leisurely lunch or doing homework.
- Anchoring the family room is a corner fireplace that beckons you on chilly autumn nights. A French door opens onto a covered porch that extends the family space during warmer seasons.
- The master suite pampers the owners of the home with two walk-in closets and a bright bay window. The suite's private bath contains an opulent marble tub, an oversized shower and twin vanities.
- Two additional bedrooms share a full bath just down the hall.

Plan RD-2238

Bedrooms: 3	Baths: 2
Living Area:	
Main floor	2,238 sq. ft.
Total Living Area:	2,238 sq. ft.
Garage and storage	560 sq. ft.
Exterior Wall Framing:	2x4
Foundation Options:	
Crawlspace	
Slab	

All plans can be built with your choice of foundation and framing. A generic conversion diagram is available. See order form.

BLUEPRINT PRICE CODE: C

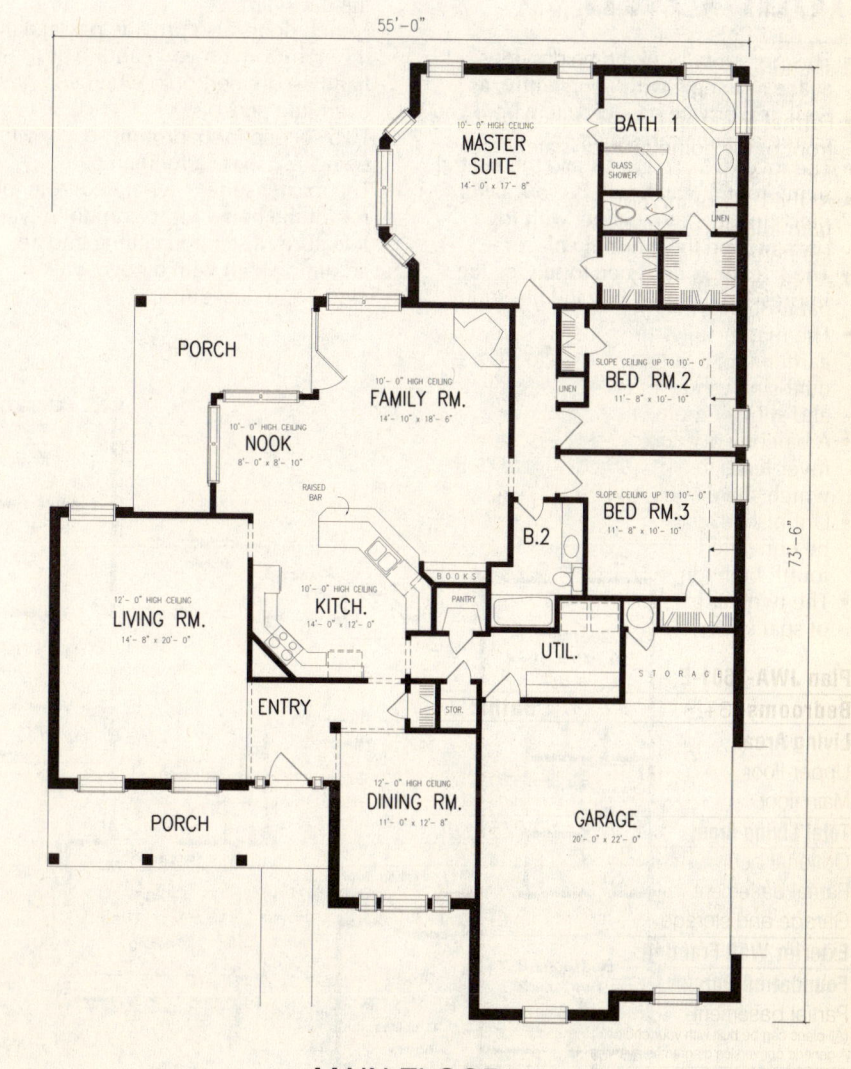

MAIN FLOOR

ORDER BLUEPRINTS ANYTIME!
CALL TOLL-FREE 1-888-626-2026

Plan RD-2238

PRICES AND DETAILS
ON PAGES 12-15

131

FIRST LOOK! 64 STUNNING NEW DESIGNS

A Suite of Your Own

- This one-story brick home provides space to mingle with your family, as well as a private master suite where you can relax your cares away.
- The foyer sweeps guests into the central living room, which will be your favorite place to entertain. Gather with loved ones around the warm fireplace.
- The kitchen is designed to service the impressive dining room and the sunny breakfast room. The breakfast room, brightened by light from three windows, also boasts a French door to the backyard.
- French doors also provide passage into the study, which you can use as a handy spare bedroom when you have overnight guests.
- Two secondary bedrooms, each with its own sink, share a full hall bath.
- The master suite is separated from the rest of the home for maximum privacy. It features a stepped ceiling and an adjoining bath with a huge walk-in closet and dual sinks.

Plan L-274-FB

Bedrooms: 3+	**Baths:** 2

Living Area:
Main floor ..... 2,260 sq. ft.
Total Living Area: ..... **2,260 sq. ft.**
Garage and utility room ..... 543 sq. ft.
Exterior Wall Framing: 2x6
Foundation Options:
Slab
(All plans can be built with your choice of foundation and framing. A generic conversion diagram is available. See order form.)
BLUEPRINT PRICE CODE: C

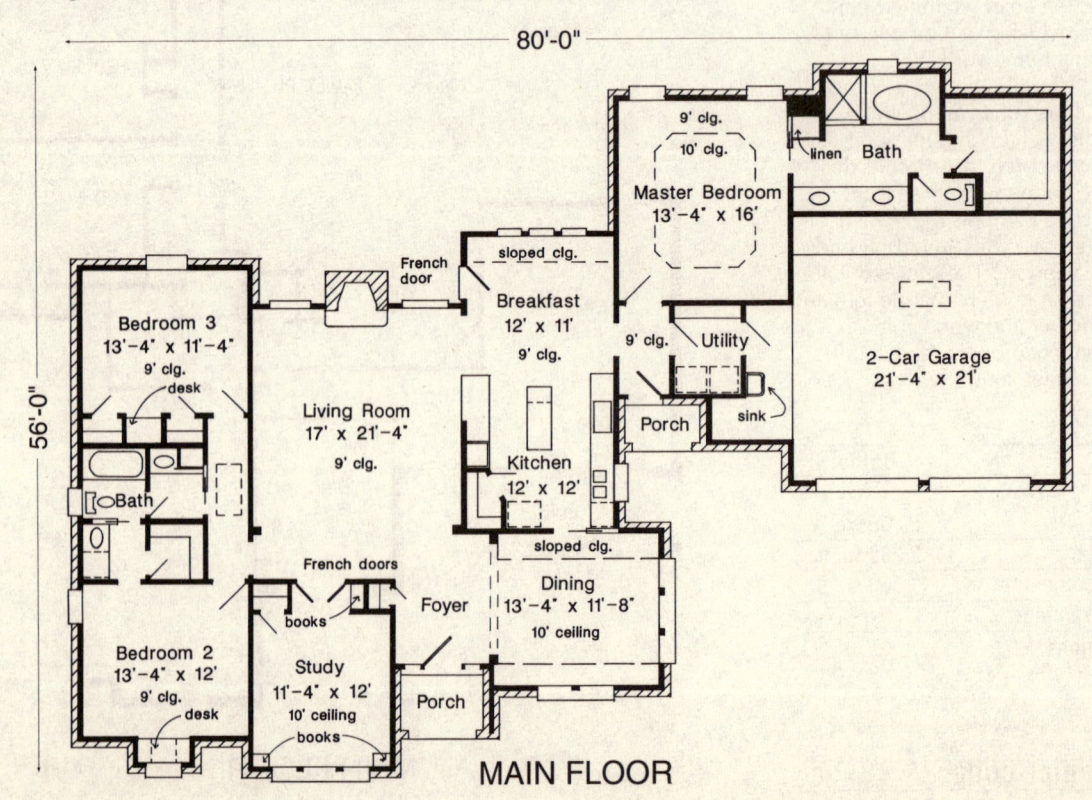

MAIN FLOOR

ORDER BLUEPRINTS ANYTIME!
CALL TOLL-FREE 1-888-626-2026

Plan L-274-FB

PRICES AND DETAILS
ON PAGES 12-15

132

FIRST LOOK! 64 STUNNING NEW DESIGNS

Meaningful Living

- Let the elegant columns, subtle arches and plentiful windows on the exterior of this home give meaning to your days, while the luxury of the interior brings comfort to your nights.
- After welcoming guests in the grandeur of a foyer whose ceiling soars to 18 ft., delight them in the formal living and dining rooms—spaces clearly designed for entertaining.

The family room's fireplace and proximity to the kitchen and breakfast nook make it the natural site for intimate gatherings. Throughout the main floor, 9-ft. ceilings add volume. The opulence of the master suite, with its 9-ft., 8-in. tray ceiling, 12-ft. vaulted bath and walk-in closet, will draw you happily to bed. The whirlpool tub, flooded with light from a radius window, will beckon you on lazy weekend mornings.

Plan FB-5579-BLAN

Bedrooms: 3+	Baths: 3

Living Area:
Upper floor	917 sq. ft.
Main floor	1,135 sq. ft.
Bonus room	216 sq. ft.
Total Living Area:	**2,268 sq. ft.**
Daylight basement	1,135 sq. ft.
Garage	452 sq. ft.
Exterior Wall Framing	2x4

Foundation Options:
Daylight basement

All plans can be built with your choice of foundation and framing. A generic conversion diagram is available. See order form.

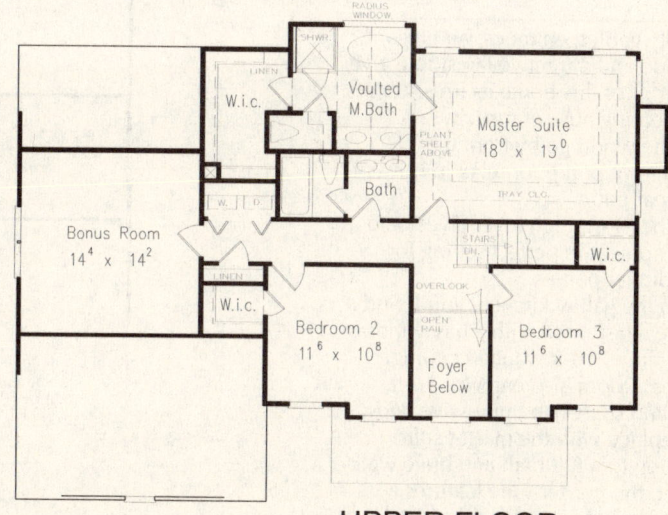

BLUEPRINT PRICE CODE: C

UPPER FLOOR

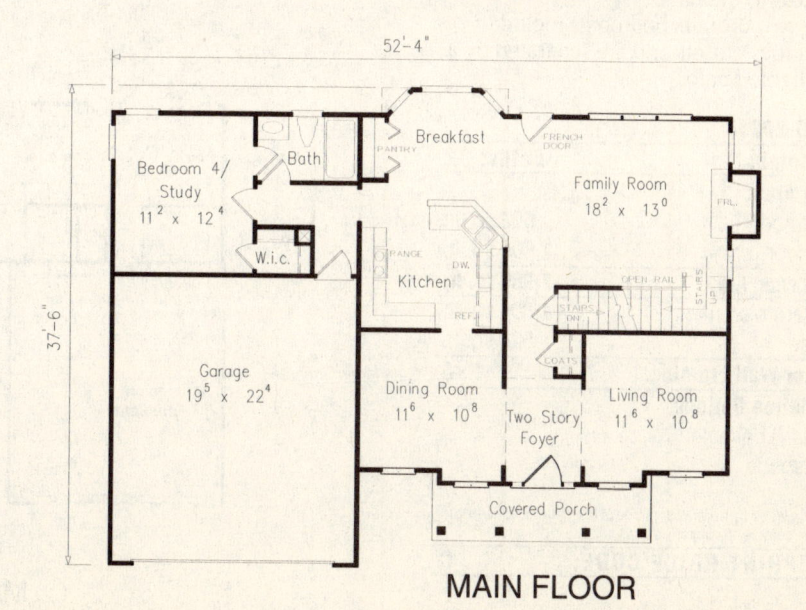

MAIN FLOOR

ORDER BLUEPRINTS ANYTIME!
CALL TOLL-FREE 1-888-626-2026

Plan FB-5579-BLAN

PRICES AND DETAILS
ON PAGES 12-15

133

FIRST LOOK! 64 STUNNING NEW DESIGNS

Rustic Touch

- A friendly gabled entrance, an elegant balustrade and attractive lap siding give the exterior of this home its irresistible and endearing aura of rusticity.
- Watch the world go by from the covered front porch, or relax in privacy on the rear patio.
- Inside, the 17-ft.-high foyer gives onto a dining room—the perfect setting for formal dinner parties.
- Through the galley kitchen, you'll find a cozy breakfast nook with a bay window and a unique, 10-ft. vaulted ceiling.
- The Great Room also enjoys a 10-ft. ceiling and shares an impressive two-way fireplace with the master suite.
- In addition to a full bath and huge walk-in closet, the master suite features a light-filled sitting room with private access to the patio.
- The two upstairs bedrooms include spacious closets and are separated by a skylighted bath.

Plan G-20214

Bedrooms: 3	Baths: 2½
Living Area:	
Upper floor	663 sq. ft.
Main floor	1,606 sq. ft.
Total Living Area:	**2,269 sq. ft.**
Standard basement	1,606 sq. ft.
Garage	528 sq. ft.
Exterior Wall Framing:	2x6
Foundation Options:	
Standard basement	
Crawlspace	
Slab	
(All plans can be built with your choice of foundation and framing. A generic conversion diagram is available. See order form.)	
BLUEPRINT PRICE CODE:	**C**

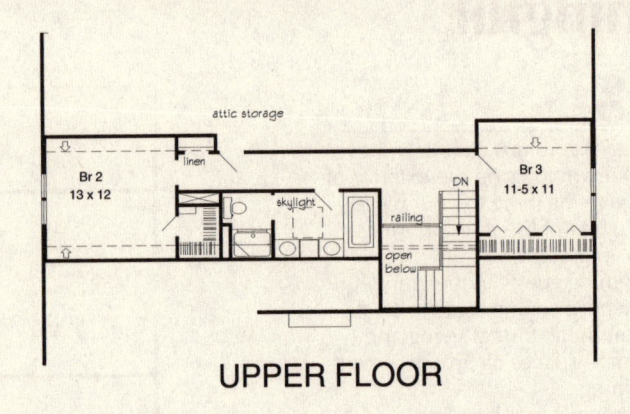

UPPER FLOOR

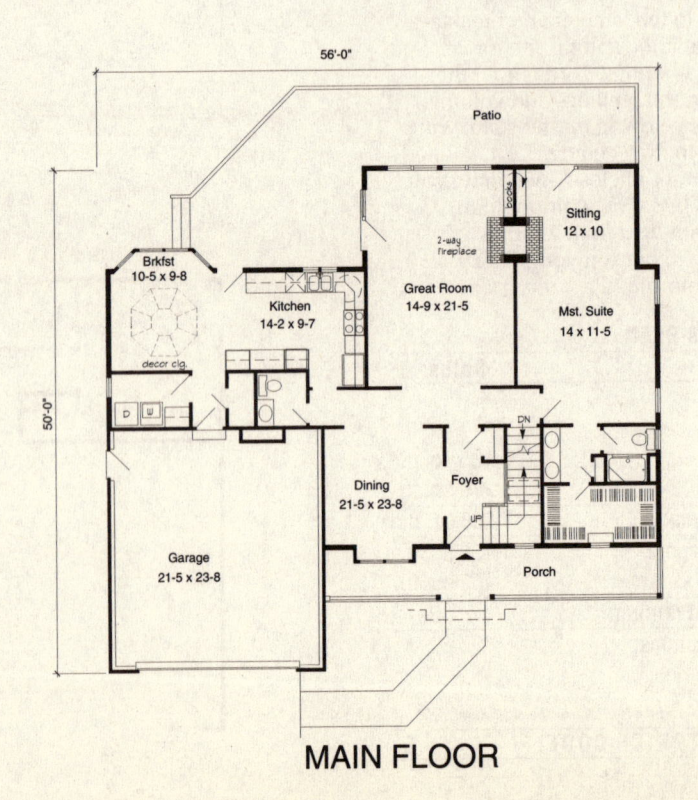

MAIN FLOOR

ORDER BLUEPRINTS ANYTIME!
CALL TOLL-FREE 1-888-626-2026

Plan G-20214

PRICES AND DETAILS
ON PAGES 12-15

134

FIRST LOOK! 64 STUNNING NEW DESIGNS

Completely Country

- Three charming dormers and a beautiful front porch give this two-story home a pure country style.
- The heart of the home is the huge Great Room, which features a fireplace, a media center and two sets of double doors that lead to a deck in back.
- Large enough to host the biggest barbecue parties, the deck is sure to see lots of outdoor fun.
- For formal affairs, use the elegant dining room; casual meals belong in the sunny dinette. The well-equipped kitchen serves both areas with ease.
- Soak your cares away in the master suite's bubbly whirlpool tub. The private bath also boasts a double vanity. A nice-sized walk-in closet gives you room to expand your wardrobe.
- Three additional bedrooms are on the upper floor. A compartmentalized bath is just a few steps from each.

Plan AHP-9740

Bedrooms: 4	Baths: 2½
Living Area:	
Upper floor	733 sq. ft.
Main floor	1,553 sq. ft.
Total Living Area:	**2,286 sq. ft.**
Standard basement	1,553 sq. ft.
Garage and storage	464 sq. ft.
Exterior Wall Framing:	2x4 or 2x6

Foundation Options:
Standard basement
Crawlspace
Slab

All plans can be built with your choice of foundation and framing. A generic conversion diagram is available. See order form.

BLUEPRINT PRICE CODE: C

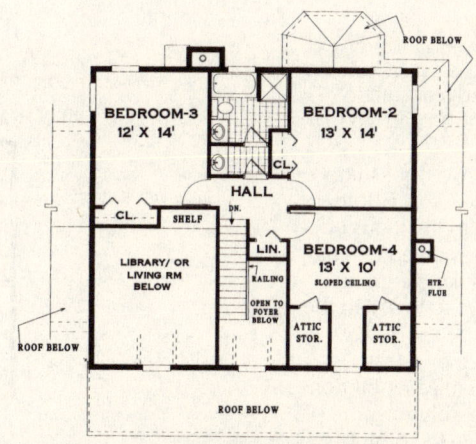

UPPER FLOOR

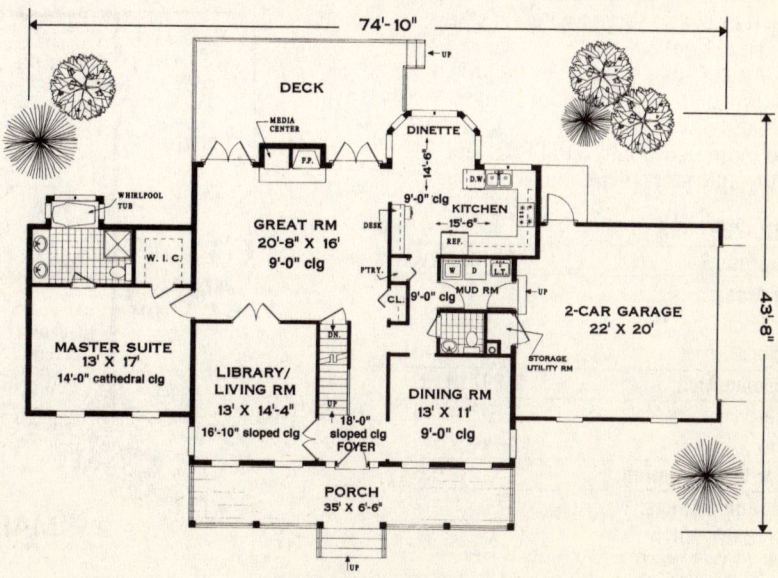

MAIN FLOOR

ORDER BLUEPRINTS ANYTIME!
CALL TOLL-FREE 1-888-626-2026

Plan AHP-9740

PRICES AND DETAILS ON PAGES 12-15

135

FIRST LOOK! 64 STUNNING NEW DESIGNS

Country Hideaway

- Classic exterior lines and a nostalgic front porch distinguish this charming country hideaway.
- An upper-floor balcony overlooks the 17-ft.-high foyer and the Great Room.
- The Great Room provides the focus of the home with a 15½-ft. vaulted ceiling, built-in bookshelves flanking a grand fireplace, and an elegant staircase to the upper floor.
- The dining room, topped by a 9-ft. stepped ceiling, is gracefully set off from the Great Room by four columns.
- A French door leads from the dining room onto the patio, the perfect spot for champagne brunches.
- A bay window complements the library, which may also serve as a quiet study or a cozy den.
- The master suite's amenities include a 9-ft. tray ceiling, a luxurious garden bath and a walk-in closet.
- Two more bedrooms, a full bath and handy attic storage are found upstairs.

Plan GL-2297-MA

Bedrooms: 3+	Baths: 2½
Living Area:	
Upper floor	530 sq. ft.
Main floor	1,767 sq. ft.
Total Living Area:	**2,297 sq. ft.**
Standard basement	1,762 sq. ft.
Garage	484 sq. ft.
Exterior Wall Framing:	2x6
Foundation Options:	
Standard basement	
(All plans can be built with your choice of foundation and framing. A generic conversion diagram is available. See order form.)	
BLUEPRINT PRICE CODE:	**C**

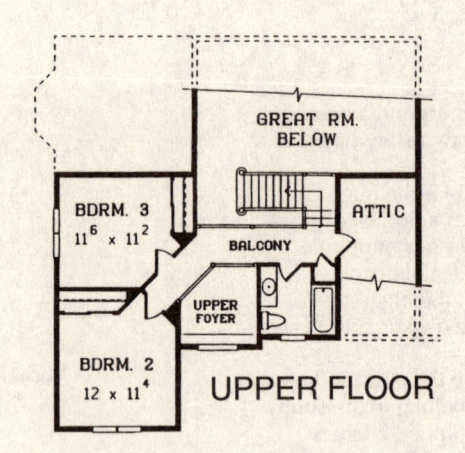

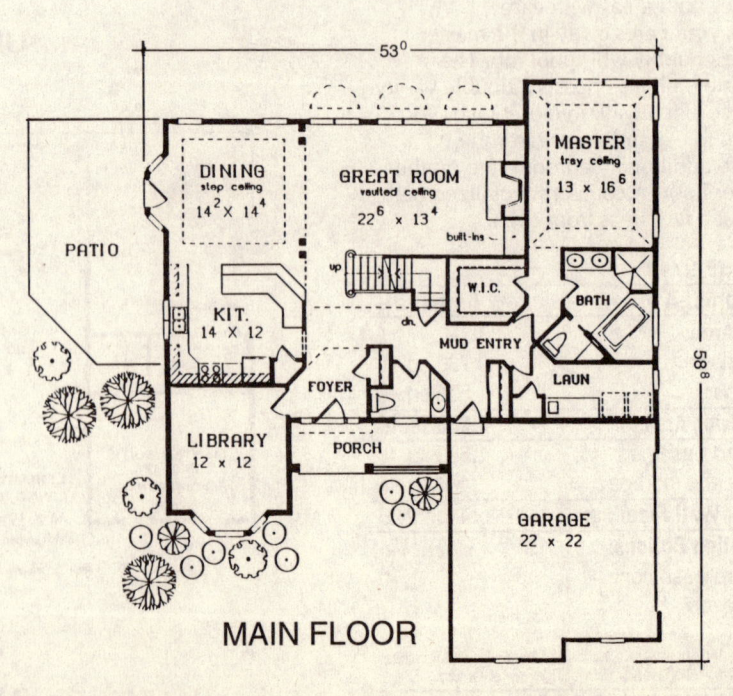

ORDER BLUEPRINTS ANYTIME! CALL TOLL-FREE 1-888-626-2026

Plan GL-2297-MA

PRICES AND DETAILS ON PAGES 12-15

FIRST LOOK! 64 STUNNING NEW DESIGNS

Country Estate

- Elegance, poise and a reserved charm make this country estate a home that's perfect for any family.
- Solid brick, lap siding, window boxes and oval windows add a pleasant dash of style to the exterior.
- The interior is ready for formal or casual events. Before serving dinner in the dining room, entertain your guests in the beautiful raised living room.
- Warmed by a classic brick fireplace, the huge family room is a natural spot for movie nights and holiday gatherings. When the events get too big, you can let folks spill out onto the lovely covered patio in back.
- Serving meals and hors d'oeuvres to any room in the house is easy from the centrally located kitchen. Nearby you'll find a sunny breakfast nook ideal for quick morning meals.
- All four bedrooms are on the upper floor, including an incredible master suite with an enormous walk-in closet. The secondary bedrooms are within easy reach of their own skylighted bath.

Plan CC-2306-M

Bedrooms: 4	Baths: 2½
Living Area:	
Upper floor	1,115 sq. ft.
Main floor	1,191 sq. ft.
Total Living Area:	**2,306 sq. ft.**
Standard basement	1,191 sq. ft.
Garage	591 sq. ft.
Exterior Wall Framing:	2x4

Foundation Options:
Standard basement
(All plans can be built with your choice of foundation and framing. A generic conversion diagram is available. See order form.)

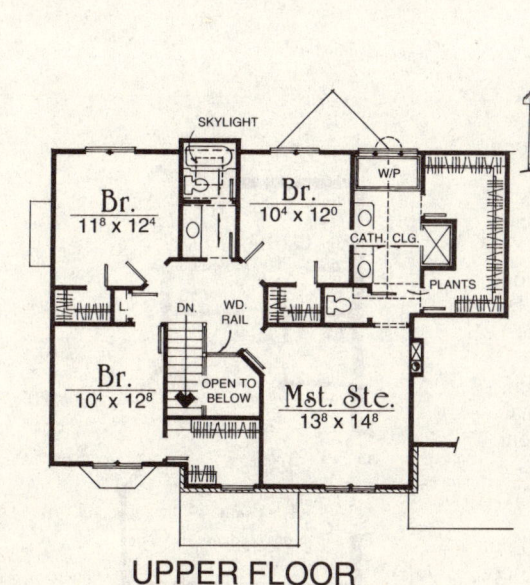

BLUEPRINT PRICE CODE: C

UPPER FLOOR

REAR VIEW

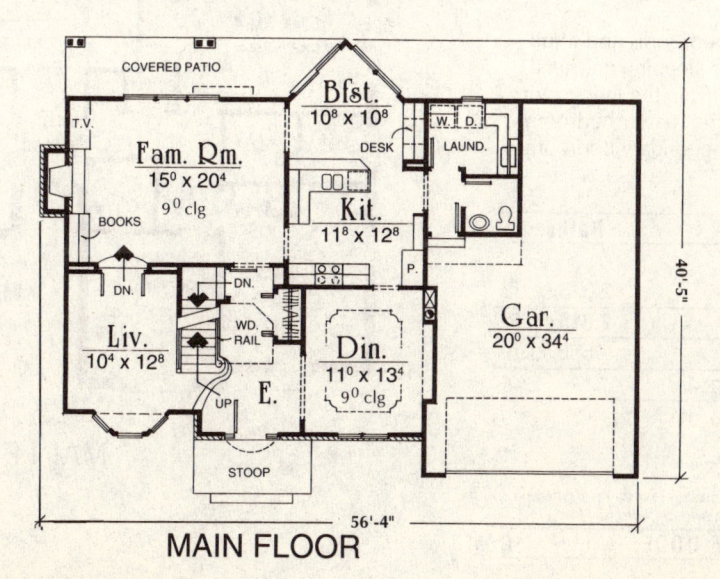

MAIN FLOOR

ORDER BLUEPRINTS ANYTIME!
CALL TOLL-FREE 1-888-626-2026

Plan CC-2306-M

PRICES AND DETAILS ON PAGES 12-15

137

FIRST LOOK! 64 STUNNING NEW DESIGNS

Peaks and Valleys

- A dynamic peaks-and-valleys roofline and elegant French styling set this home apart from the rest.
- Gorgeous arched windows present a cheery look inside and out. A 13-ft. ceiling in the foyer lends an aura of grandeur to greetings and introductions.
- In the living room, a neat bookshelf by the fireplace holds media equipment and family photos. A triple window arrangement overlooks the rear porch.
- A formal dining room and an informal breakfast nook provide serving options for every type of occasion.
- The kitchen features "acres" of counter space and a handy pantry.
- The master suite showcases a boxed-out window, as well as twin walk-in closets and a bath with a sunny garden tub and a dual-sink vanity.
- Three additional bedrooms and a full bath round out the sleeping quarters.
- Ceilings rise to 10 ft. in the living room, the dining room, the master bedroom and the foremost secondary bedroom.

Plan RD-2315

Bedrooms: 4	Baths: 2½
Living Area:	
Main floor	2,315 sq. ft.
Total Living Area:	**2,315 sq. ft.**
Garage and storage	552 sq. ft.
Exterior Wall Framing:	2x4
Foundation Options:	
Crawlspace	
Slab	
(All plans can be built with your choice of foundation and framing. A generic conversion diagram is available. See order form.)	
BLUEPRINT PRICE CODE:	**C**

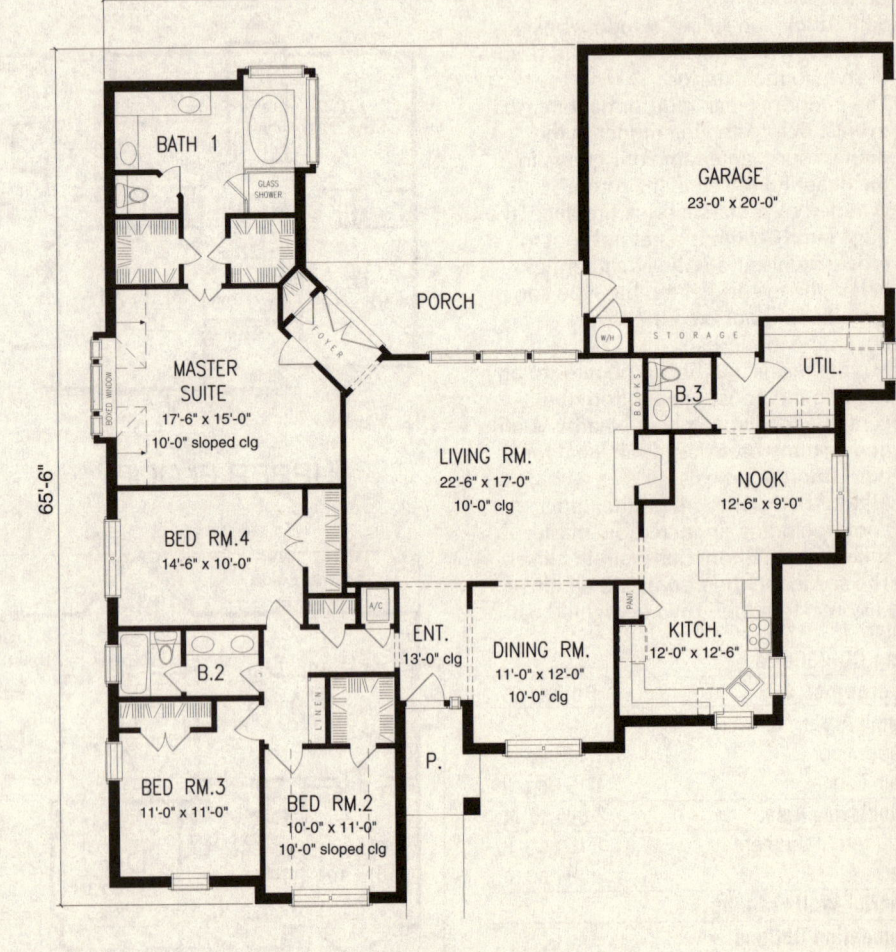

MAIN FLOOR

ORDER BLUEPRINTS ANYTIME!
CALL TOLL-FREE 1-888-626-2026

Plan RD-2315

PRICES AND DETAILS ON PAGES 12-15

138

FIRST LOOK! 64 STUNNING NEW DESIGNS

Zesty Saltbox

- This saltbox design adds a dash of good taste to any neighborhood!
- The vestibule features ample closet space and a flagstone floor, in keeping with the home's Early American facade.
- Formal spaces flank the foyer. The large living room is warmed by a fireplace with a tidy, attached wood box. Built-in bookshelves and cabinets line one wall of the adjoining den.
- On the other side of the foyer, the formal dining room is serviced by a handy butler's pantry. The kitchen includes a bayed dinette and a built-in desk for jotting down shopping lists.
- A skylighted keeping room boasts a corner fireplace, a 17-ft., 4-in. vaulted ceiling and sliding doors to a terrace.
- Upstairs, the master suite flaunts its own romantic fireplace and a walk-in closet. The private bath embraces a whirlpool tub and a separate shower.
- Expansion space above the garage may be used as a spare bedroom, a home office or studio space.

Plan AS-5196

Bedrooms: 3+	Baths: 2½
Living Area:	
Upper floor	994 sq. ft.
Main floor	1,326 sq. ft.
Total Living Area:	**2,320 sq. ft.**
Expansion loft	282 sq. ft.
Standard basement	1,326 sq. ft.
Garage	444 sq. ft.
Exterior Wall Framing:	2x6
Foundation Options:	
Standard basement	
(All plans can be built with your choice of foundation and framing. A generic conversion diagram is available. See order form.)	
BLUEPRINT PRICE CODE:	**C**

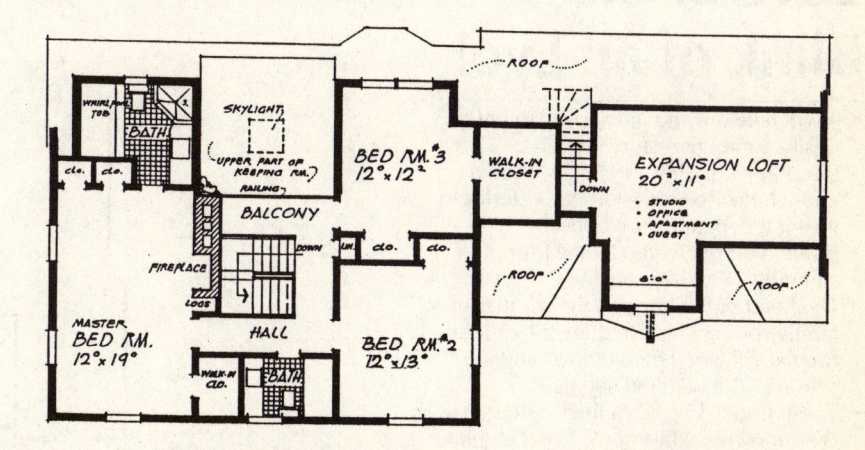

UPPER FLOOR

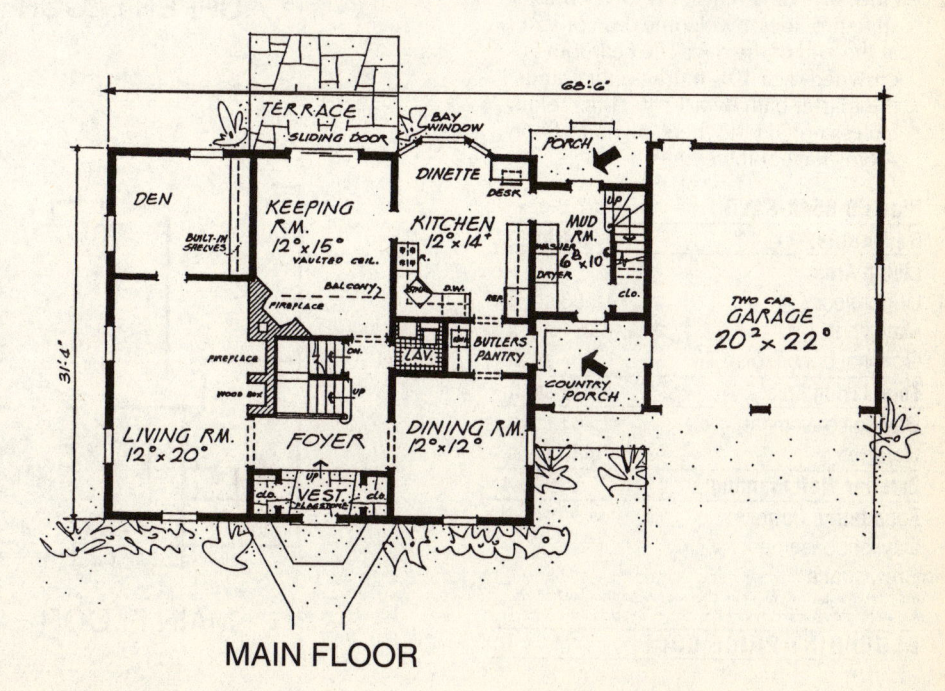

MAIN FLOOR

ORDER BLUEPRINTS ANYTIME!
CALL TOLL-FREE 1-888-626-2026

Plan AS-5196

PRICES AND DETAILS
ON PAGES 12-15

139

FIRST LOOK! 64 STUNNING NEW DESIGNS

Love in the Blink of an Eye!

- It will take only a nanosecond to fall for this beautiful two-story home!
- Decorative quoins, keystones, shutters and window boxes adorn the exterior to give it a dynamic curb appeal.
- Inside, you're greeted by the foyer's stunning 18-ft. high ceiling.
- The heart of the home is the wonderful family room, which features a beautiful fireplace flanked by windows and a soaring 18-ft. vaulted ceiling.
- You'll find a 13½-ft. vaulted ceiling in the sunny breakfast nook. What a great spot to enjoy your morning meal!
- Filled with amenities, the lovely master suite provides a welcome dose of luxury at the end of the day. The bedroom is crowned by a 10½-ft. tray ceiling and the master bath by a 13-ft., 9-in. ceiling.
- Unless noted elsewhere, all main-floor rooms have 9-ft. ceilings.

Plan FB-5542-SAVO

Bedrooms: 3+	Baths: 3
Living Area:	
Upper floor	588 sq. ft.
Main floor	1,761 sq. ft.
Optional bonus room	267 sq. ft.
Total Living Area:	**2,616 sq. ft.**
Daylight basement	1,761 sq. ft.
Garage	435 sq. ft.
Exterior Wall Framing:	2x4

Foundation Options:
Daylight basement
Crawlspace
(All plans can be built with your choice of foundation and framing. A generic conversion diagram is available. See order form.)

BLUEPRINT PRICE CODE: D

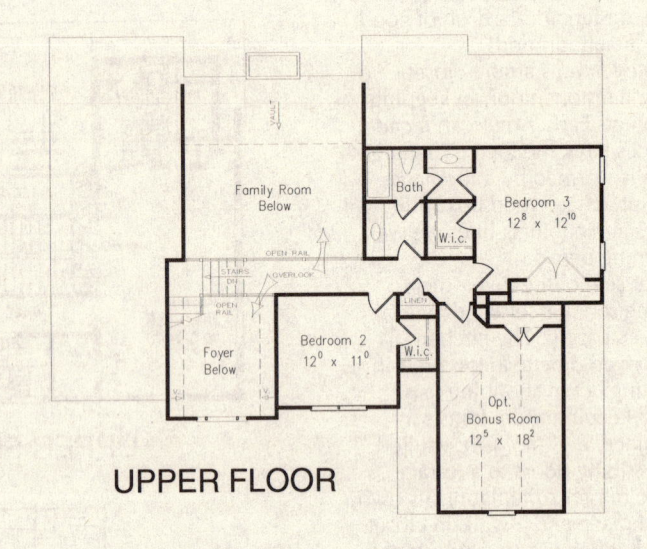

UPPER FLOOR
- Family Room Below
- Bath
- Bedroom 3 12⁸ x 12¹⁰
- W.i.c.
- Bedroom 2 12⁰ x 11⁰
- Foyer Below
- Opt. Bonus Room 12⁵ x 18²

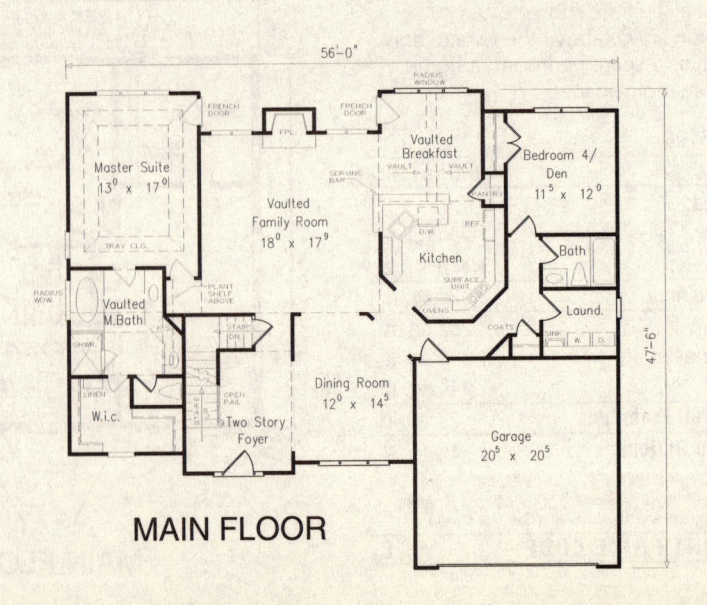

MAIN FLOOR 56'-0" × 47'-6"
- Master Suite 13⁰ x 17⁰
- Vaulted Breakfast
- Bedroom 4/Den 11⁵ x 12⁰
- Vaulted Family Room 18⁰ x 17⁹
- Kitchen
- Bath
- Laund.
- Vaulted M.Bath
- W.i.c.
- Two Story Foyer
- Dining Room 12⁰ x 14⁵
- Garage 20⁰ x 20⁵

ORDER BLUEPRINTS ANYTIME! CALL TOLL-FREE 1-888-626-2026
Plan FB-5542-SAVO
PRICES AND DETAILS ON PAGES 12-15

FIRST LOOK! 64 STUNNING NEW DESIGNS

Smart Spaces

- Angular gables and hips offset the solid brick facade of this comfortable family home. An inviting covered front entry greets visitors.
- Every square foot is used to the greatest advantage. A large central living room with a stepped ceiling nestles diagonally in the center of the house.
- Separated from the living room by a space-defining half-wall, the formal dining room is a lovely space, perfect for elegant gatherings.
- The convenient island kitchen connects to a sunny breakfast nook, which overlooks the backyard through a bay window. A French door gives access to a large covered porch.
- The master suite also opens onto the porch, and features a spa with a separate shower, a dual-sink vanity and a walk-in closet.
- Ample space to the rear of the garage is ideal for storing lawn furniture, badminton sets and other backyard items. The plan also features a future room above the garage.

Plan L-361-MB	
Bedrooms: 3+	**Baths:** 2-3
Living Area:	
Upper floor	377 sq. ft.
Main floor	2,349 sq. ft.
Total Living Area:	**2,726 sq. ft.**
Garage and storage	729 sq. ft.
Exterior Wall Framing:	2x4
Foundation Options:	

Slab
(All plans can be built with your choice of foundation and framing. A generic conversion diagram is available. See order form.)

BLUEPRINT PRICE CODE: D

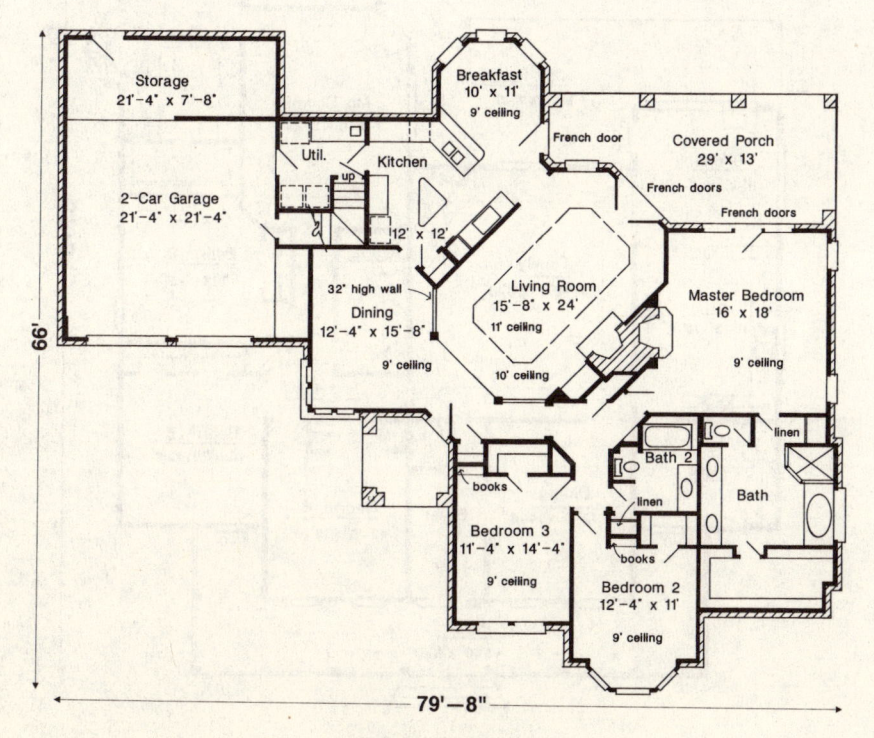

MAIN FLOOR

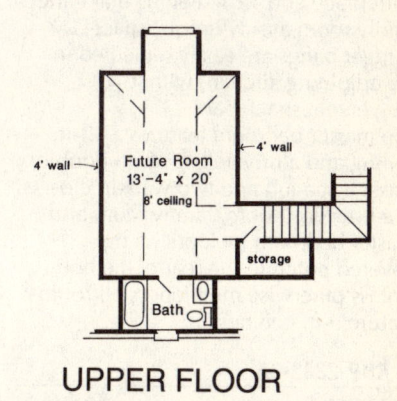

UPPER FLOOR

ORDER BLUEPRINTS ANYTIME!
CALL TOLL-FREE 1-888-626-2026

Plan L-361-MB

PRICES AND DETAILS ON PAGES 12-15

FIRST LOOK! 64 STUNNING NEW DESIGNS

Southern Hospitality

- Bring home the warm hospitality of the Deep South with this cozy yet spacious four-bedroom cottage.
- Imagine sipping lemonade on the inviting porch, enjoying the company of friends and neighbors, or simply spending quiet time watching the world go by.
- The foyer leads family and close friends to the family room or formal guests to the dining room.
- A fireplace and 12-ft. ceiling make the family room a truly unique space. Hunger pangs are easily remedied in the adjoining kitchen, with its convenient snack bar.
- The master bedroom features a 12-ft. ceiling and a private bath with double sinks, a spa tub and two walk-in closets.
- The breakfast room, family room and master bedroom look out on the covered porch to the rear of the home.
- Unless otherwise mentioned, all rooms feature 9-ft. ceilings.

Plan CHP-2342-3A

Bedrooms: 4	Baths: 2
Living Area:	
Main floor	2,355 sq. ft.
Total Living Area:	**2,355 sq. ft.**
Garage	553 sq. ft.
Exterior Wall Framing:	2x4

Foundation Options:
Crawlspace
Slab
(All plans can be built with your choice of foundation and framing. A generic conversion diagram is available. See order form.)

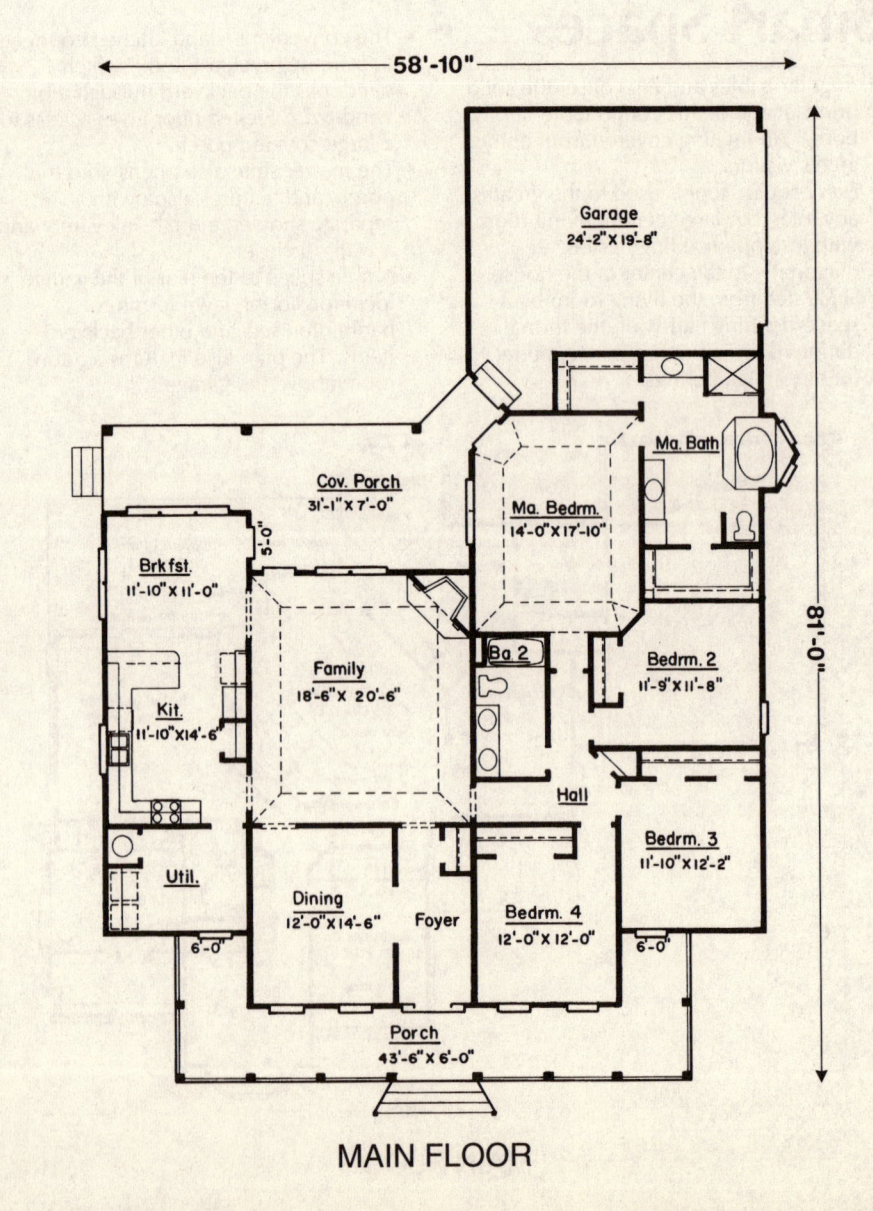

BLUEPRINT PRICE CODE: C

MAIN FLOOR

Plan CHP-2342-3A

ORDER BLUEPRINTS ANYTIME! CALL TOLL-FREE 1-888-626-2026

PRICES AND DETAILS ON PAGES 12-15

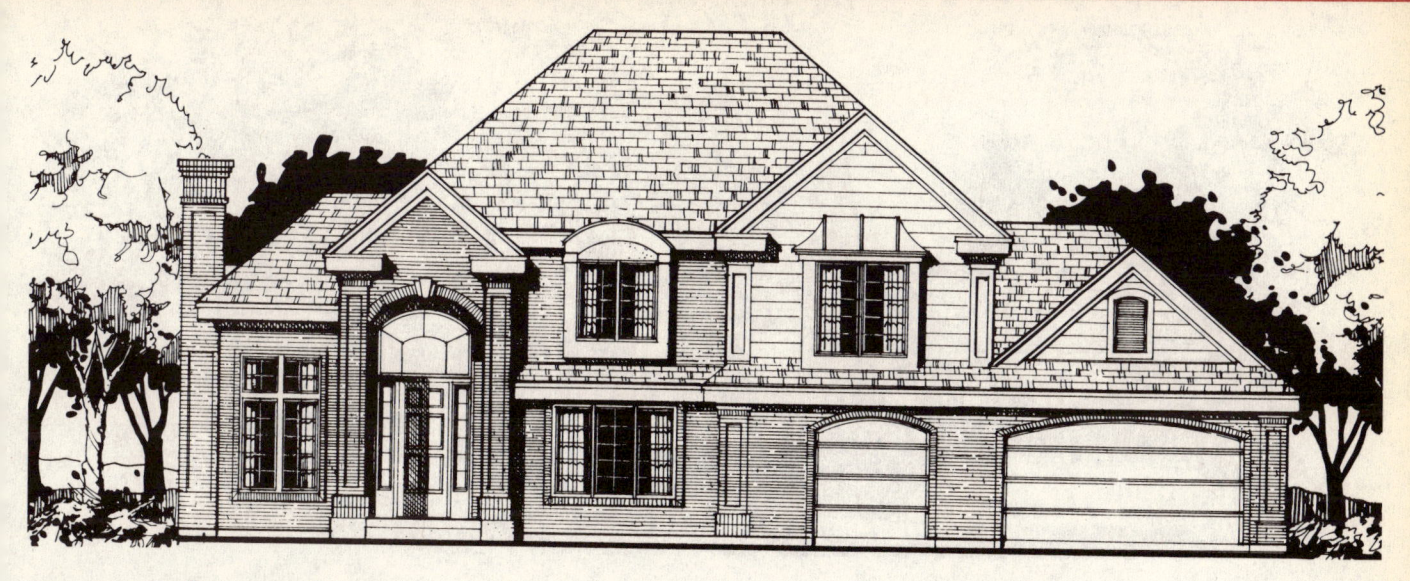

FIRST LOOK! 64 STUNNING NEW DESIGNS

Tour de Force

- This feat of design ingenuity wraps an open, flowing floor plan in a traditional brick and lap siding exterior.
- Dominating the 17-ft.-high entry is a fanned, open-railed stairway. A 17-ft. vaulted ceiling tops the adjacent living room and the formal dining room.
- A see-through fireplace warms the dining room and the adjoining family room. Space is provided in the family room for a built-in media center.
- The island kitchen is centrally located and features a walk-in pantry. An innovative forked staircase allows access to the upstairs.
- An angled snack counter services the family room, as well as the skylighted breakfast nook, where sliding glass doors lead out to a backyard patio.
- On the upper floor, double doors open to the master suite, which enjoys a sumptuous private bath with an oval soaking tub and a sit-down shower.
- Window seats adorn the two secondary bedrooms, providing a great spot for a bedtime story or heart-to-heart chats.

Plan AG-2302

Bedrooms: 3+	**Baths:** 2½
Living Area:	
Upper floor	988 sq. ft.
Main floor	1,407 sq. ft.
Total Living Area:	**2,395 sq. ft.**
Standard basement	1,390 sq. ft.
Garage	660 sq. ft.
Exterior Wall Framing:	2x4

Foundation Options:
Standard basement
(All plans can be built with your choice of foundation and framing. A generic conversion diagram is available. See order form.)

BLUEPRINT PRICE CODE: C

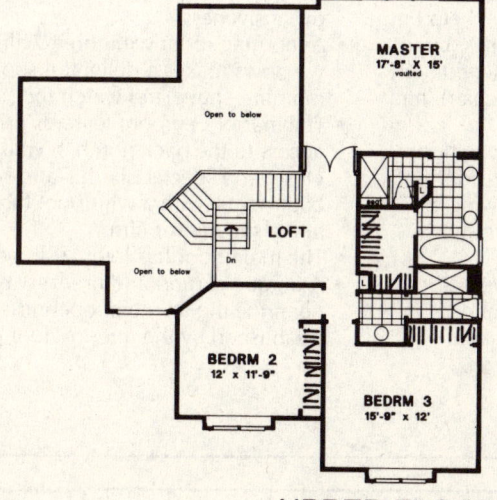

UPPER FLOOR

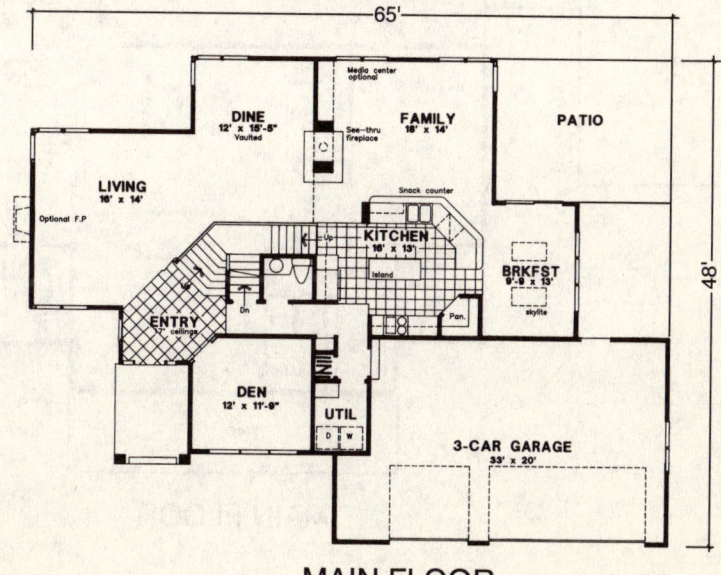

MAIN FLOOR

ORDER BLUEPRINTS ANYTIME!
CALL TOLL-FREE 1-888-626-2026

Plan AG-2302

PRICES AND DETAILS ON PAGES 12-15

FIRST LOOK! 64 STUNNING NEW DESIGNS

Great Gables!

- The exterior of this house can't help but entrance you with its clean lines, large porches in front and in back (crying out for a porch swing or rocking chair), and, of course, its glorious gables!
- The interior is unique in its open floor plan, allowing unsurpassed freedom of movement among the main living areas.
- Although individual rooms are subtly defined—the dining room by architectural columns, the Great Room by its 19½-ft. vaulted ceiling and fireplace, the kitchen by an island cooktop with an eating bar—the overwhelming impression is one of expansiveness.
- A morning room with three walls of windows makes a delightful spot to sip morning coffee and watch the sunrise.
- The master bedroom features private access to the back porch, a walk-in closet and spectacular his-and-hers bathrooms, with a whirlpool tub for her and a shower for him.
- The main floor has lofty 10-ft. ceilings.
- A unique carport and breezeway continue the theme of openness established by the interior floor plan.

Plan VL-2486

Bedrooms: 3	Baths: 2½

Living Area:
Upper floor	596 sq. ft.
Main floor	1,890 sq. ft.
Total Living Area:	**2,486 sq. ft.**
Carport	528 sq. ft.
Exterior Wall Framing:	2x4

Foundation Options:
Crawlspace
Slab
(All plans can be built with your choice of foundation and framing. A generic conversion diagram is available. See order form.)

BLUEPRINT PRICE CODE: C

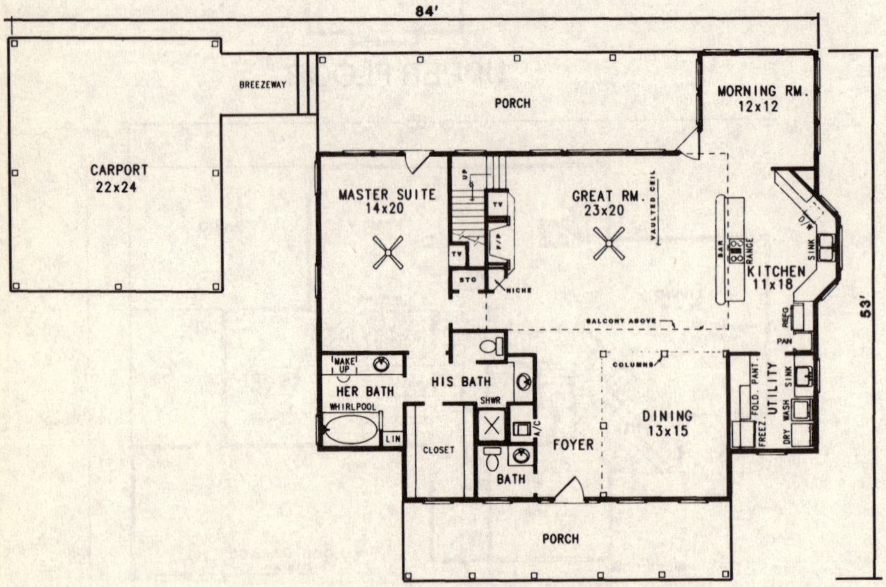

MAIN FLOOR

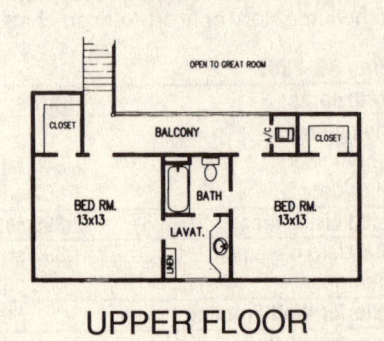

UPPER FLOOR

ORDER BLUEPRINTS ANYTIME! CALL TOLL-FREE 1-888-626-2026

Plan VL-2486

PRICES AND DETAILS ON PAGES 12-15

FIRST LOOK! 64 STUNNING NEW DESIGNS

Lofty Sentiment

- Traditional styling conceals an innovative, open interior.
- To the left of the foyer, the dining room is set off by elegant columns.
- Double doors on the right lead to a study, which can also serve as a fourth bedroom for guests or growing families.
- Quick meals can be served at the snack bar in the kitchen or, if you'd like a little sunshine, in the cheery breakfast nook.
- A fireplace and an entertainment center make the Great Room the natural focus of the house. A dramatic 18-ft.-high ceiling tops the room with style.
- Nine-foot ceilings throughout the rest of the main floor help to add a sense of spaciousness.
- On the upper floor, a loft looks down onto the Great Room.
- A bay-windowed sitting room off the master bedroom is the perfect spot for a reading chair, desk or exercise bike.
- The plans provide an option for an expanded master bath, featuring a large garden tub, separate shower and his-and-hers sinks.

Plan GL-2491	
Bedrooms: 3+	Baths: 2½
Living Area:	
Upper floor	1,096 sq. ft.
Main floor	1,395 sq. ft.
Total Living Area:	**2,491 sq. ft.**
Standard basement	1,376 sq. ft.
Garage	528 sq. ft.
Exterior Wall Framing:	2x4
Foundation Options:	
Standard basement	

(All plans can be built with your choice of foundation and framing. A generic conversion diagram is available. See order form.)

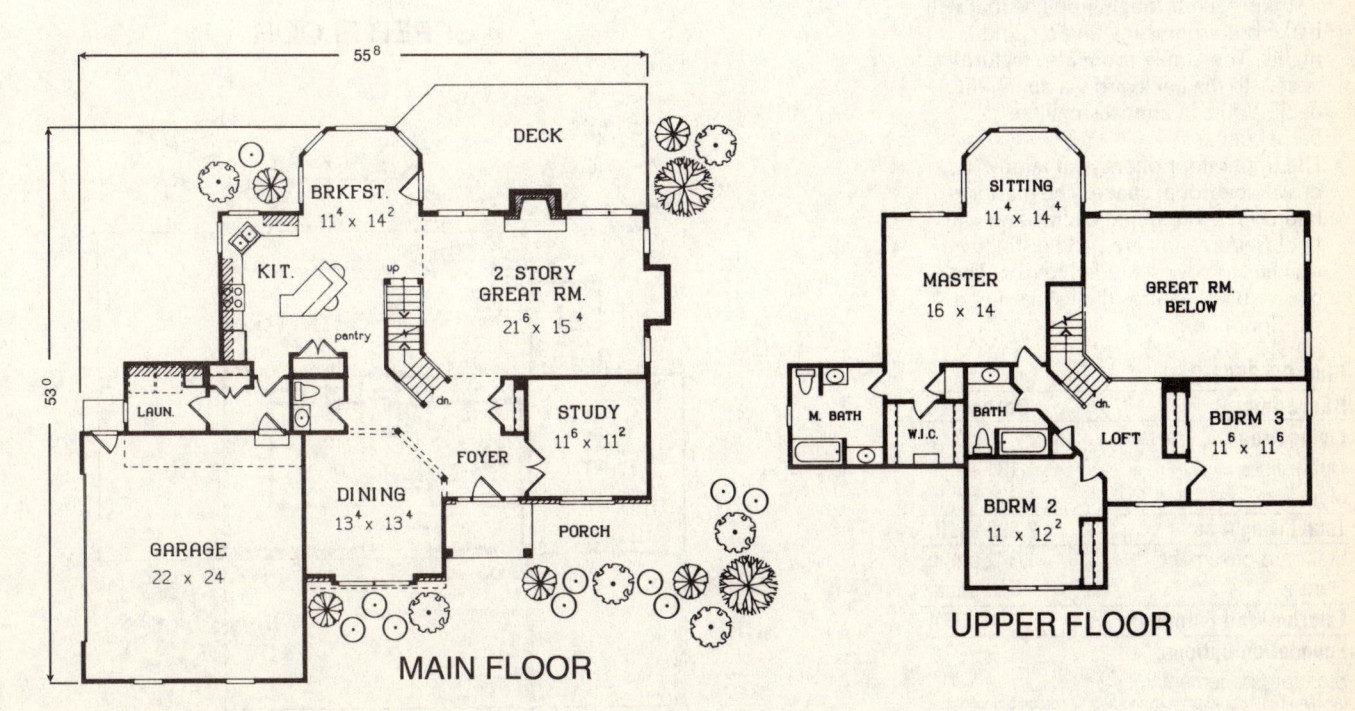

BLUEPRINT PRICE CODE: C

ORDER BLUEPRINTS ANYTIME!
CALL TOLL-FREE 1-888-626-2026

Plan GL-2491

Prices and details
ON PAGES 12-15

FIRST LOOK! 64 STUNNING NEW DESIGNS

Savor the Country Life

- Country living will be a dream come true in this four-bedroom home. The wraparound front porch invites you to sit back in a rocking chair and savor the country life.
- Formal occasions will be extra special in the impressive dining room, which features a 9-ft. ceiling. Informal meals can be taken at the kitchen snack counter or in the breakfast room.
- The family room and living room share a striking see-through fireplace that will make both rooms inviting on cold nights. The family room also features access to the backyard via an inviting deck. You can almost smell the barbecue!
- The upper floor offers your family private bedroom space. The master bedroom's 9-ft. tiered ceiling and walk-in closet/dressing area add distinctive touches to your secluded retreat. The master bath features dual sinks and a whirlpool tub.

Plan CC-2502-2

Bedrooms: 4	Baths: 2½
Living Area:	
Upper floor	1,131 sq. ft.
Main floor	1,371 sq. ft.
Total Living Area:	**2,502 sq. ft.**
Standard basement	1,371 sq. ft.
Garage	518 sq. ft.
Exterior Wall Framing:	2x4
Foundation Options:	
Standard basement	

(All plans can be built with your choice of foundation and framing. A generic conversion diagram is available. See order form.)

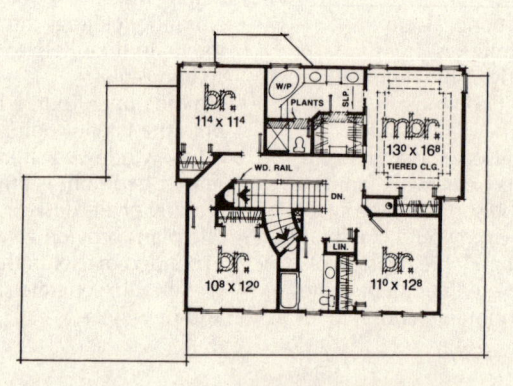

BLUEPRINT PRICE CODE:	**D**

UPPER FLOOR

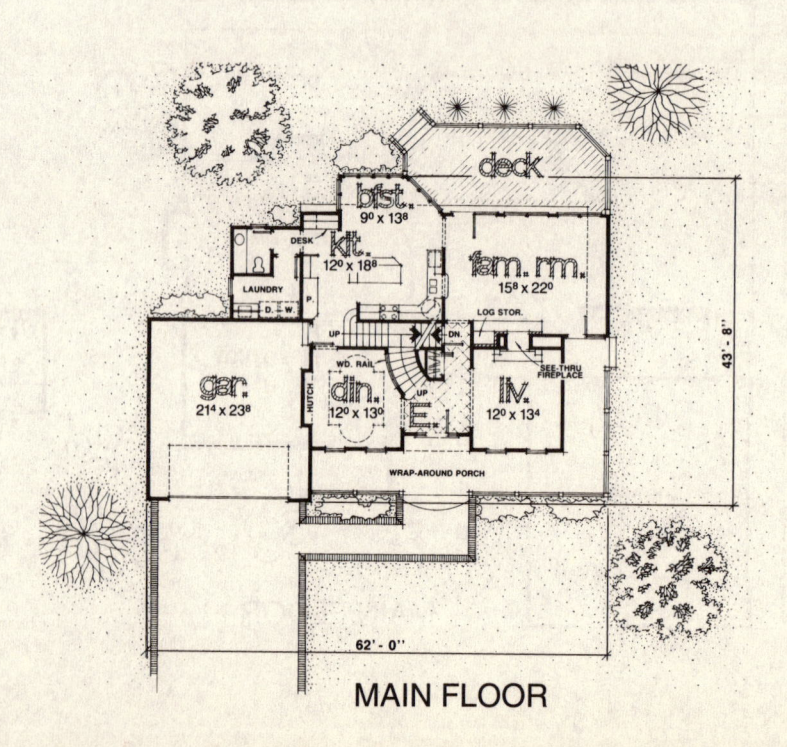

MAIN FLOOR

ORDER BLUEPRINTS ANYTIME!
CALL TOLL-FREE 1-888-626-2026

Plan CC-2502-2

PRICES AND DETAILS ON PAGES 12-15

FIRST LOOK! 64 STUNNING NEW DESIGNS

Memories of the Future

- One look at this Early American farmhouse, and you'll look forward to remembering your family growing and playing here.
- The wraparound porch extends almost completely around the home, and provides endless space for greeting guests, barbecuing or sitting back to enjoy the sunset.
- Inside, the foyer and the enormous Great Room are graced by a lofty 18½-ft. ceiling, for a refreshing sense of openness. A corner fireplace keeps the atmosphere cozy on chilly evenings.
- The convenient kitchen is flanked by the bayed formal dining room and the sunny breakfast nook, which provides access to a secluded morning porch.
- Located on the main floor for privacy, the master suite includes a walk-in closet, a garden tub, a seated shower and a dual-sink vanity.
- Unless otherwise noted, all main-floor rooms are topped by 9-ft. ceilings.
- Upstairs, two secondary bedrooms and a game room share a full bath. The front-facing bedroom, with a 10-ft., 7-in. vaulted ceiling, is sure to capture your teenager's fancy.

Plan VL-2558	
Bedrooms: 3+	**Baths:** 2½
Living Area:	
Upper floor	981 sq. ft.
Main floor	1,577 sq. ft.
Total Living Area:	**2,558 sq. ft.**
Carport	484 sq. ft.
Storage	132 sq. ft.
Exterior Wall Framing:	2x4

Foundation Options:
Crawlspace
Slab
(All plans can be built with your choice of foundation and framing. A generic conversion diagram is available. See order form.)

BLUEPRINT PRICE CODE: D

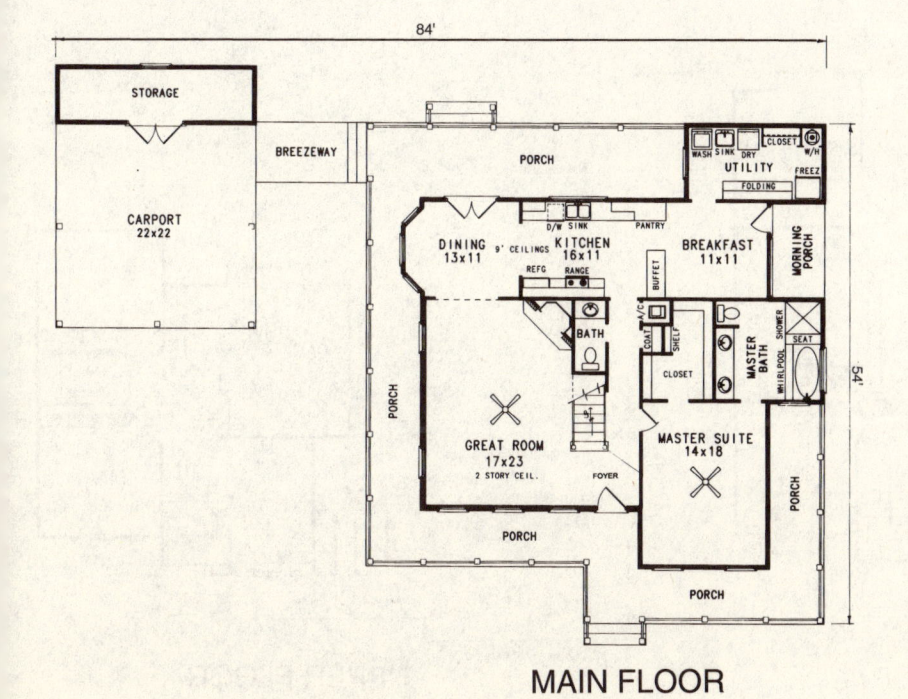

MAIN FLOOR

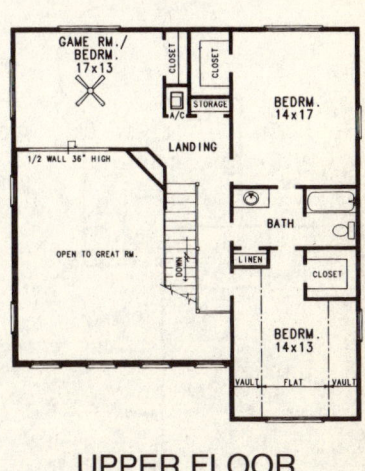

UPPER FLOOR

ORDER BLUEPRINTS ANYTIME!
CALL TOLL-FREE 1-888-626-2026

Plan VL-2558

PRICES AND DETAILS
ON PAGES 12-15

147

FIRST LOOK! 64 STUNNING NEW DESIGNS

Southern Hybrid

- This design's facade displays a gracious, and distinctly Southern, combination of country and European influences.
- Inside, the sidelighted foyer is anchored by an open-railed stairway. Elegant columns flank archways leading to the home's formal spaces.
- Generous in proportion, the central living room hosts a holiday open house as easily as it does afternoon coffee with neighbors. A see-through fireplace is shared with the nearby breakfast nook.
- A built-in desk and a walk-in pantry are among the kitchen's special amenities. A snack bar extends to the bayed breakfast nook, where a French door leads out to a covered rear porch.
- The master suite features a bright sitting area and a plush private bath with a walk-in closet, a private toilet chamber and separate shower and tub facilities. A dual-sink vanity provides room for both of you during the morning rush.
- Upstairs, two bedrooms with double closets share a full bath.
- A short flight of stairs leads up to an expansive game room that you can use for casual family times. Or perhaps a home office better suits your needs.

Plan BOD-25-22A

Bedrooms: 4+	Baths: 3

Living Area:

Upper floor	830 sq. ft.
Main floor	2,028 sq. ft.
Total Living Area:	**2,858 sq. ft.**
Garage and storage	551 sq. ft.
Exterior Wall Framing:	2x4

Foundation Options:

Crawlspace
Slab

(All plans can be built with your choice of foundation and framing. A generic conversion diagram is available. See order form.)

BLUEPRINT PRICE CODE: D

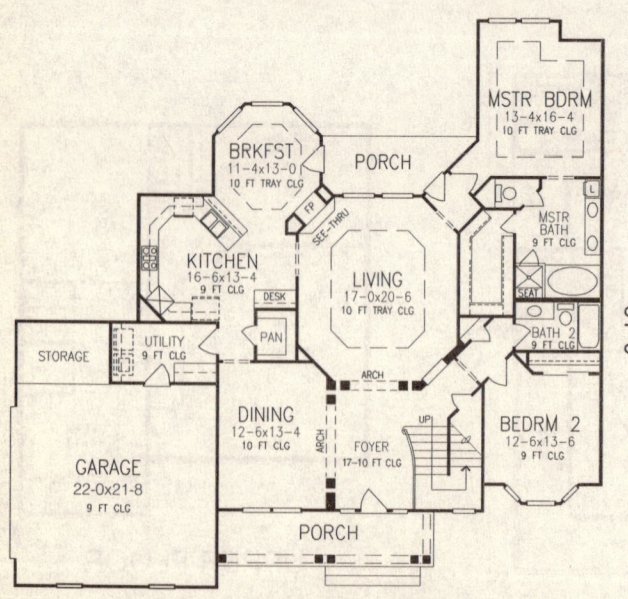

MAIN FLOOR

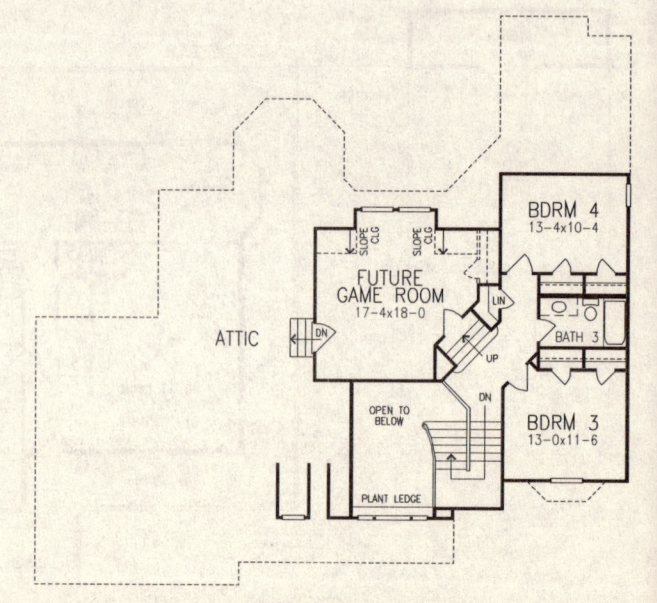

UPPER FLOOR

ORDER BLUEPRINTS ANYTIME! CALL TOLL-FREE 1-888-626-2026

Plan BOD-25-22A

PRICES AND DETAILS ON PAGES 12-15

FIRST LOOK! 64 STUNNING NEW DESIGNS

Second-Look Symmetry

- The balanced appearance of this fine Colonial design gives it a curb appeal that will turn more than a few heads.
- The easy traffic flow between the airy foyer and the flanking formal living room and dining room makes this area well-suited to entertaining on any scale.
- The two-story family room, with its warming fireplace and backyard view, is brightened by a sunny, stacked window arrangement.
- Meal preparation is made more enjoyable by the casual kitchen layout. Here, an island cooktop offers freedom of movement, and a butler's pantry off the formal dining room helps get your Thanksgiving feast to the table on time.
- The master suite is entered through double doors. The bedroom is topped by a cathedral ceiling, and the private bath boasts a soothing whirlpool tub.
- Upstairs, three secondary bedrooms are arranged around a balcony hallway that overlooks the family room below.

Plan OH-274

Bedrooms: 4	Baths: 2½
Living Area:	
Upper floor	880 sq. ft.
Main floor	1,744 sq. ft.
Total Living Area:	**2,624 sq. ft.**
Standard basement	1,744 sq. ft.
Garage	501 sq. ft.
Exterior Wall Framing:	2x4
Foundation Options:	
Standard basement	
(All plans can be built with your choice of foundation and framing. A generic conversion diagram is available. See order form.)	
BLUEPRINT PRICE CODE:	**D**

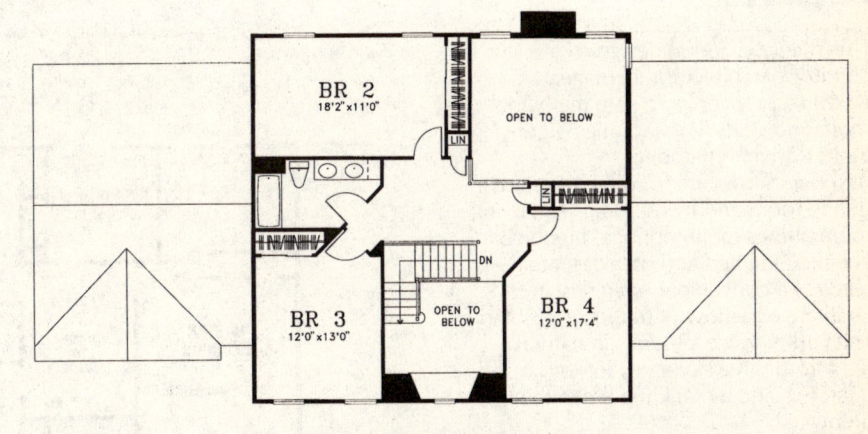

UPPER FLOOR

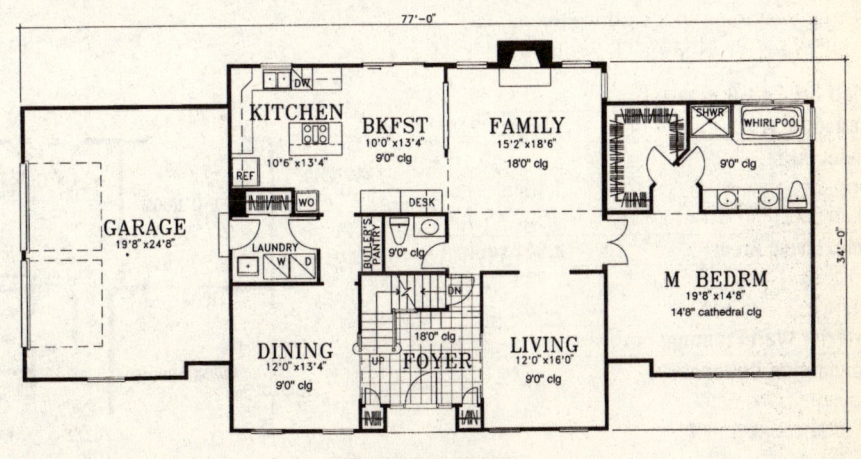

MAIN FLOOR

ORDER BLUEPRINTS ANYTIME!
CALL TOLL-FREE 1-888-626-2026

Plan OH-274

PRICES AND DETAILS ON PAGES 12-15

FIRST LOOK! 64 STUNNING NEW DESIGNS

American Beauty

- This stately Colonial design recalls our country's architectural heritage.
- A two-story foyer looks into the living room and study. A charming balcony looks down from above.
- Bayed windows are found in the study, dining room and living room. The living room allows for an optional fireplace.
- The tiled kitchen and breakfast area features a convenient open design to facilitate easy flow of traffic.
- The family room abounds in natural light from three skylights, lots of windows and a crackling fire in the fireplace.
- The master bedroom features a vaulted ceiling, dual sinks and luxurious spa tub to soak your cares away.
- Three additional upstairs bedrooms and a large storage space above the garage allow plenty of growing room.

Plan CH-243-A

Bedrooms: 4	Baths: 2½
Living Area:	
Upper floor	1,104 sq. ft.
Main floor	1,537 sq. ft.
Total Living Area:	**2,641 sq. ft.**
Basement	733 sq. ft.
Garage	462 sq. ft.
Exterior Wall Framing:	2x4
Foundation Options:	
Daylight basement	
Standard basement	
Crawlspace	
(All plans can be built with your choice of foundation and framing. A generic conversion diagram is available. See order form.)	
BLUEPRINT PRICE CODE:	D

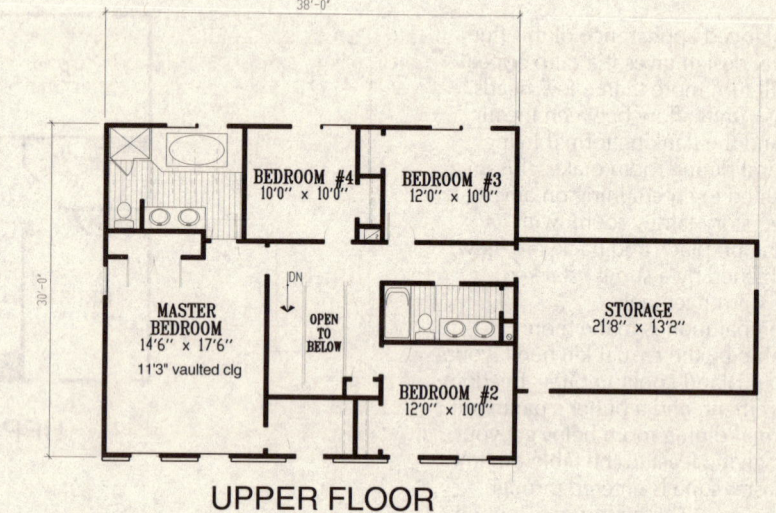

ORDER BLUEPRINTS ANYTIME!
CALL TOLL-FREE 1-888-626-2026

Plan CH-243-A

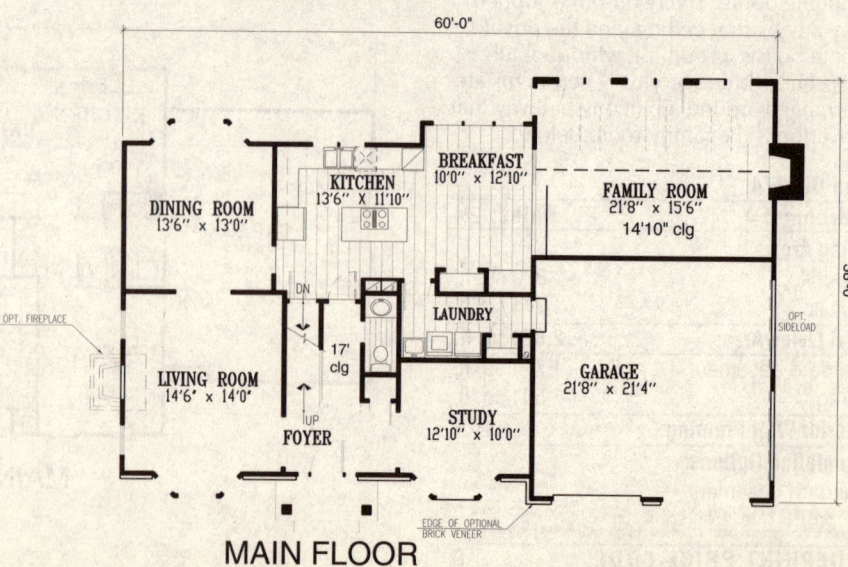

PRICES AND DETAILS ON PAGES 12-15

FIRST LOOK! 64 STUNNING NEW DESIGNS

Country Living

- A sweeping wraparound porch surrounds much of this house, lending it a nostalgic touch.
- The thoughtful floor plan creates a sense of continuity among the family spaces, yet tucks bedrooms away for privacy.
- A fireplace and media shelf stand at one end of the living room, which is surrounded on three sides by windows looking out onto the porch.
- The kitchen encourages family interaction with its open layout and a snack bar shared with the dining room.
- A large, screened porch off the kitchen is the perfect spot for a midsummer candlelight dinner.
- Nine-foot ceilings throughout the main floor add a spacious feel.
- The master bedroom enjoys a private bath and walk-in closet, as well as access to the screen porch.
- A second bedroom and a full bath are located on the lower floor. Stairs lead from the living room to two additional bedrooms on the upper floor.
- The huge third bedroom could also serve as a den or children's playroom.

Plan BRF-2685

Bedrooms: 4	Baths: 3
Living Area:	
Upper floor	942 sq. ft.
Main floor	1,743 sq. ft.
Total Living Area:	**2,685 sq. ft.**
Exterior Wall Framing:	2x4

Foundation Options:
Crawlspace
(All plans can be built with your choice of foundation and framing. A generic conversion diagram is available. See order form.)

BLUEPRINT PRICE CODE: D

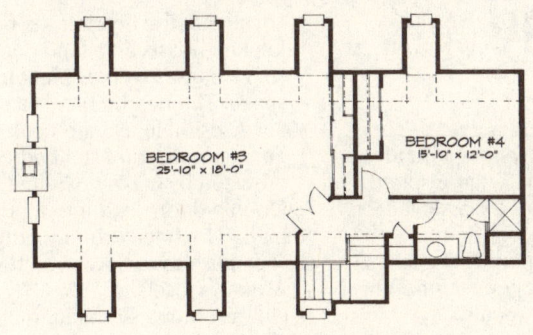

UPPER FLOOR

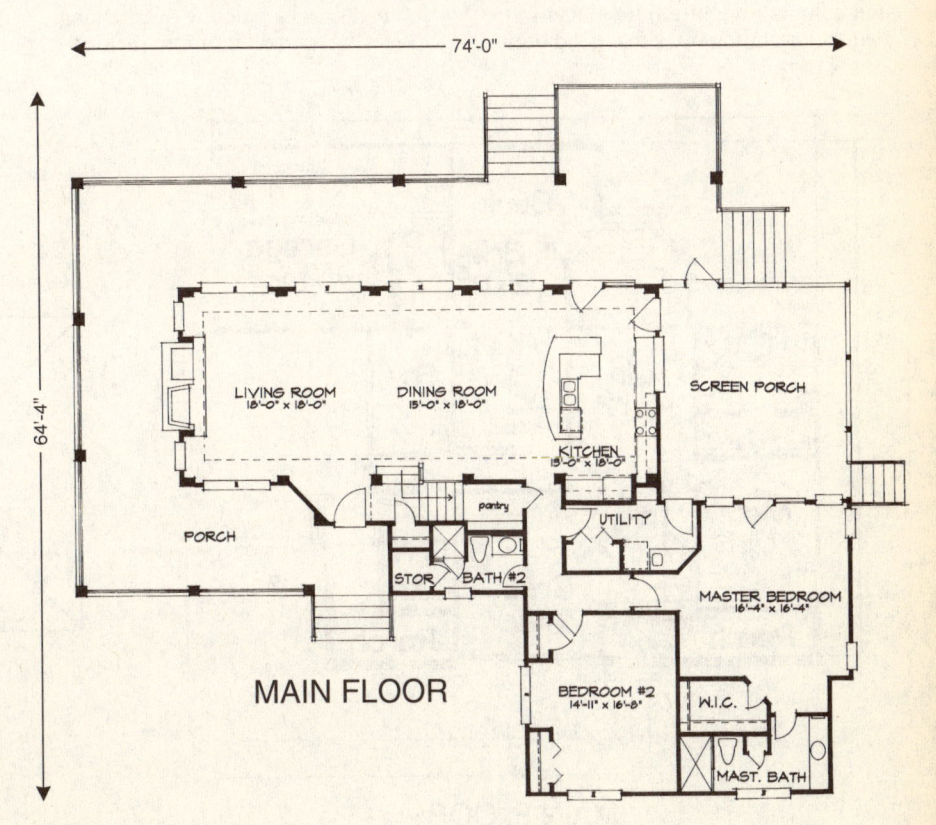

BEDROOM #3 25'-10" x 18'-0"
BEDROOM #4 15'-10" x 12'-0"

MAIN FLOOR

74'-0" / 64'-4"

LIVING ROOM 18'-0" x 18'-0"
DINING ROOM 15'-0" x 18'-0"
KITCHEN 15'-0" x 12'-0"
SCREEN PORCH
PORCH
PANTRY
STOR
BATH #2
UTILITY
MASTER BEDROOM 16'-4" x 16'-4"
BEDROOM #2 14'-11" x 16'-8"
W.I.C.
MAST. BATH

ORDER BLUEPRINTS ANYTIME! CALL TOLL-FREE 1-888-626-2026

Plan BRF-2685

PRICES AND DETAILS ON PAGES 12-15

FIRST LOOK! 64 STUNNING NEW DESIGNS

Nooks and Crannies

- You'll find interesting spaces around every corner of this Victorian-inspired home, which combines a classic facade with a thoroughly modern floor plan.
- An 18-ft.-high foyer opens to the formal dining room, which is perfect for dinner parties or quiet family meals.
- The foyer also opens to the Great Room, which is anchored by a cozy fireplace and adjoins a bright sun room that's perfect for curling up with a good book.
- Located at the heart of the home, the kitchen boasts an island cooktop and a snack bar, as well as plentiful counter space. The nearby breakfast nook accesses the backyard deck.
- The main-floor master bedroom is crowned by a 14-ft. vaulted ceiling. Double doors lead into a private master bath, which features a whirlpool tub, a separate shower, two vanities and twin walk-in closets.
- Unless otherwise noted, main-floor rooms are topped by 10-ft. ceilings.
- Upstairs are three more bedrooms, two full baths and a balcony overlooking the foyer—perfect for prom pictures!

Plan UDA-95125	
Bedrooms: 4+	**Baths:** 3½
Living Area:	
Upper floor	964 sq. ft.
Main floor	1,764 sq. ft.
Sun room	104 sq. ft.
Total Living Area:	**2,832 sq. ft.**
Garage	460 sq. ft.
Exterior Wall Framing:	2x4
Foundation Options:	
Crawlspace	
(All plans can be built with your choice of foundation and framing. A generic conversion diagram is available. See order form.)	
BLUEPRINT PRICE CODE:	**D**

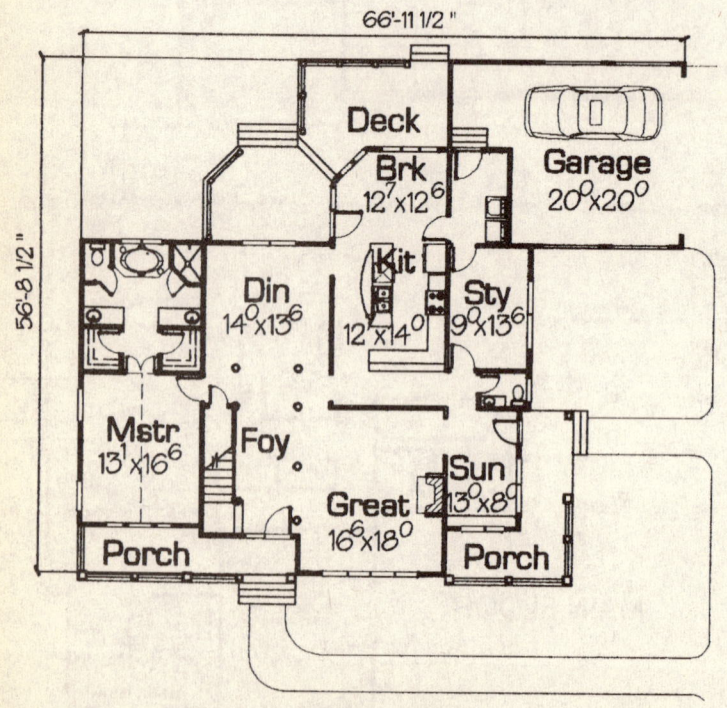

MAIN FLOOR

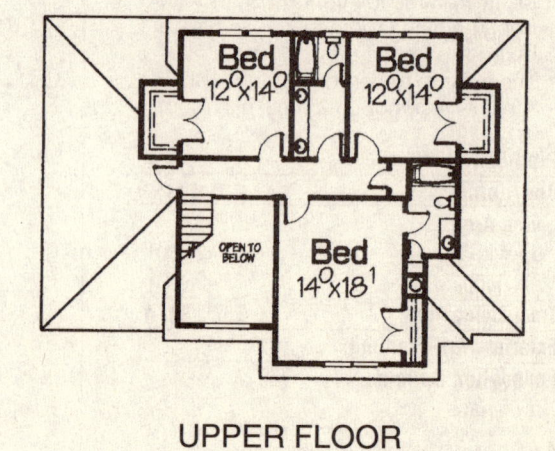

UPPER FLOOR

ORDER BLUEPRINTS ANYTIME! CALL TOLL-FREE 1-888-626-2026

Plan UDA-95125

PRICES AND DETAILS ON PAGES 12-15

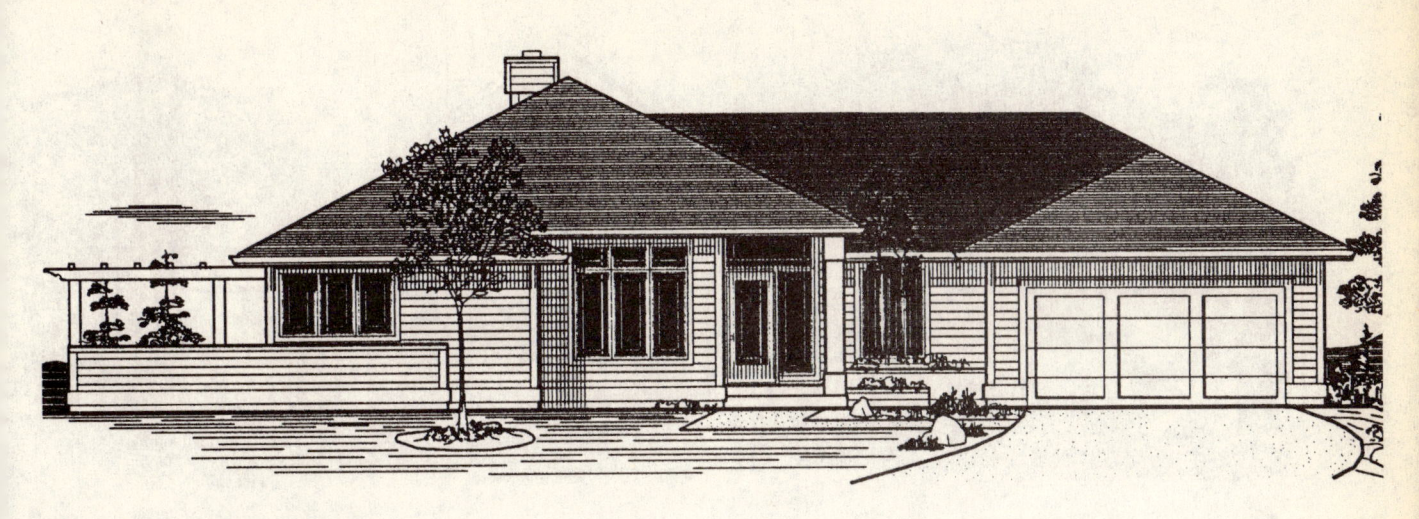

FIRST LOOK! 64 STUNNING NEW DESIGNS

Deck-adence

- Deck space abounds in this wonderful indoor/outdoor design.
- A 9½-ft. vaulted ceiling tops the roomy sidelighted foyer, where double doors lead to a cozy den with an elegant 9½-ft. coved ceiling.
- Ahead, the living room is brightened by a large picture window and is warmed by a fireplace. The living room and adjoining dining room are topped by 12½-ft. vaulted ceilings that lend this space its wide-open feel.
- Copious windows, a skylight and an island cooktop make the kitchen and adjoining nook as attractive as they are functional. A French door opens onto the main deck.
- The master bedroom features its own deck and a bay window that creates a sunny sitting area. A trellised courtyard is entered through the private bath and is the perfect spot for a hot tub.
- Downstairs, the family room provides space for casual relaxing. Two more bedrooms, a full bath and plenty of storage/expansion space are here, too.

Plan S-91995

Bedrooms: 3+	Baths: 2 full, 2 half
Living Area:	
Main floor	1,850 sq. ft.
Daylight basement	1,006 sq. ft.
Total Living Area:	**2,856 sq. ft.**
Daylight basement	453 sq. ft.
Garage and shop	441 sq. ft.
Exterior Wall Framing:	2x6
Foundation Options:	
Daylight basement	
(All plans can be built with your choice of foundation and framing. A generic conversion diagram is available. See order form.)	
BLUEPRINT PRICE CODE:	**D**

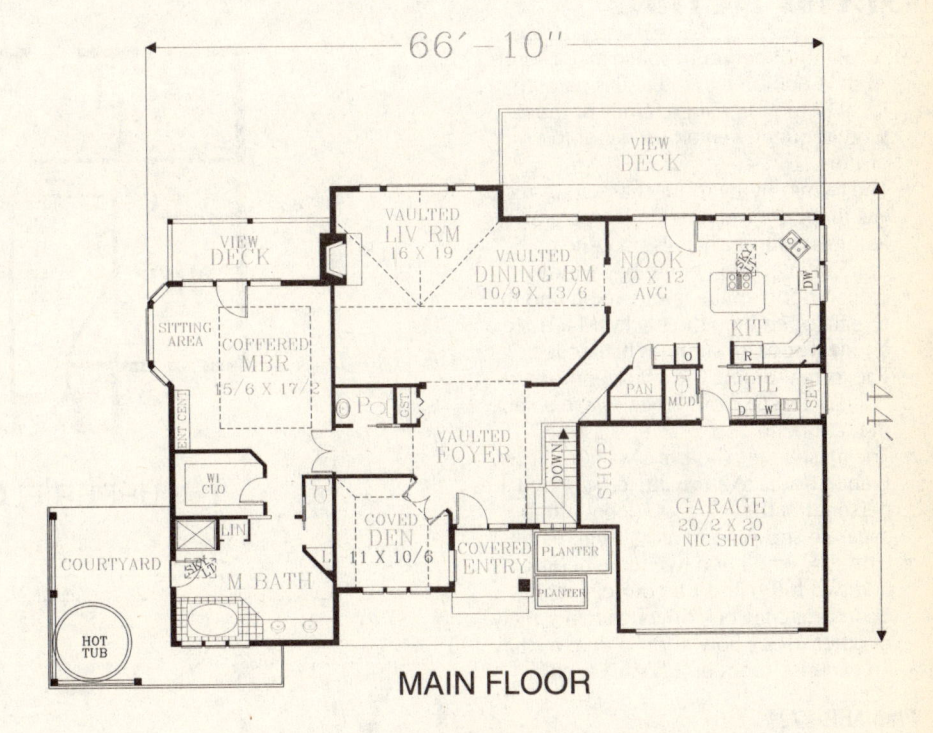

MAIN FLOOR

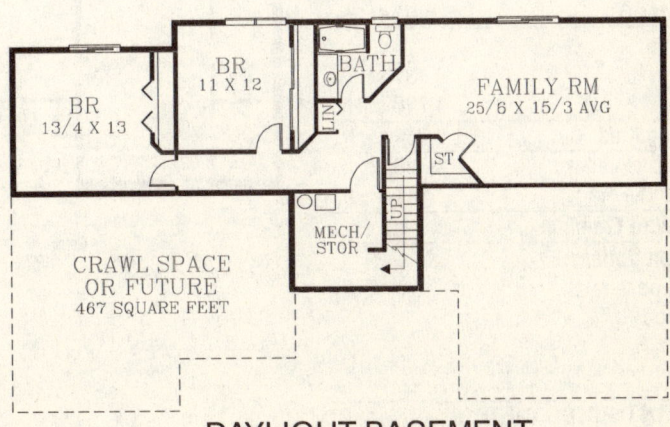

DAYLIGHT BASEMENT

ORDER BLUEPRINTS ANYTIME!
CALL TOLL-FREE 1-888-626-2026

Plan S-91995

PRICES AND DETAILS
ON PAGES 12-15

153

FIRST LOOK! 64 STUNNING NEW DESIGNS

Sixth Sense

- A wealth of bedroom space and a sense of style combine to make this plan an ideal home for a large family or those who frequently entertain out-of-town visitors.
- The formal living room shares a no-fuss, gas fireplace with the family room and features built-in shelves opposite a dramatic floor-to-ceiling bay window.
- French doors in the family room and the dinette open onto the backyard terrace, an ideal spot for summer barbecues.
- The formal dining room accommodates holiday feasts; casual meals have a spot in the dinette.
- The master suite boasts a walk-in closet, French doors to a private terrace, and a personal bath with a whirlpool tub, a separate shower and a dual-sink vanity.
- Upstairs, you'll find five more bedrooms and two full baths. Of course, vacant bedrooms may be converted to a variety of other uses—how about a den, a study an exercise room or a home office?

Plan AHP-9721

Bedrooms: 6	Baths: 3½
Living Area:	
Upper floor	1,136 sq. ft.
Main floor	1,728 sq. ft.
Total Living Area:	**2,864 sq. ft.**
Standard basement	1,728 sq. ft.
Garage and storage	511 sq. ft.
Exterior Wall Framing:	2x4 or 2x6

Foundation Options:
Standard basement
Crawlspace
Slab
(All plans can be built with your choice of foundation and framing. A generic conversion diagram is available. See order form.)

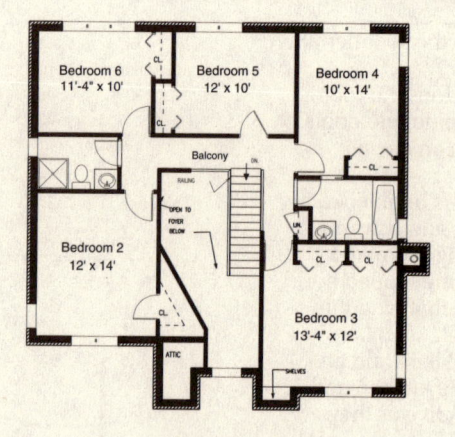

BLUEPRINT PRICE CODE: D

UPPER FLOOR

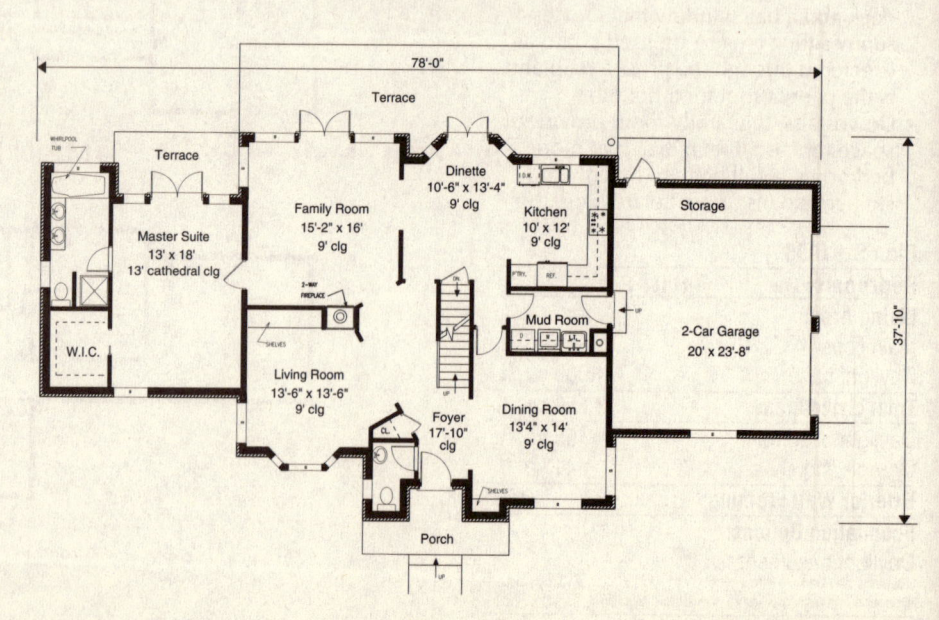

MAIN FLOOR

ORDER BLUEPRINTS ANYTIME!
CALL TOLL-FREE 1-888-626-2026

Plan AHP-9721

PRICES AND DETAILS ON PAGES 12-15

FIRST LOOK! 64 STUNNING NEW DESIGNS

Chic Chateau

- Large Palladian windows and a peaceful symmetrical facade enhance this design's distinguished image.
- To either side of the foyer, the formal living and dining rooms are graced by elegant columns.
- The majestic family room boasts a 20-ft. ceiling and a staircase leading up to a long balcony.
- A set of double doors on either side of the stately fireplace open onto a covered rear porch.
- The large kitchen centers around a convenient island, and adjoins both the sun-filled breakfast area and the elegant formal dining area.
- A cozy loft upstairs is an ideal spot for any leisurely pursuit.
- Tucked into a corner of the home, the luxurious master bedroom boasts a private bath complete with two walk-in closets and an oversized garden tub. Dual sinks come in handy on hectic mornings.
- Three additional bedrooms, two more full baths and a future space allow plenty of room for a growing family.
- The main floor is topped by airy 10-ft. ceilings, while the upper floor features 9-ft. ceilings.

Plan CHP-2843-13A

Bedrooms: 4	**Baths:** 3

Living Area:
Upper floor — 717 sq. ft.
Main floor — 2,152 sq. ft.
Total Living Area: 2,869 sq. ft.
Garage — 475 sq. ft.
Exterior Wall Framing: 2x4
Foundation Options:
Crawlspace
Slab
(All plans can be built with your choice of foundation and framing. A generic conversion diagram is available. See order form.)
BLUEPRINT PRICE CODE: D

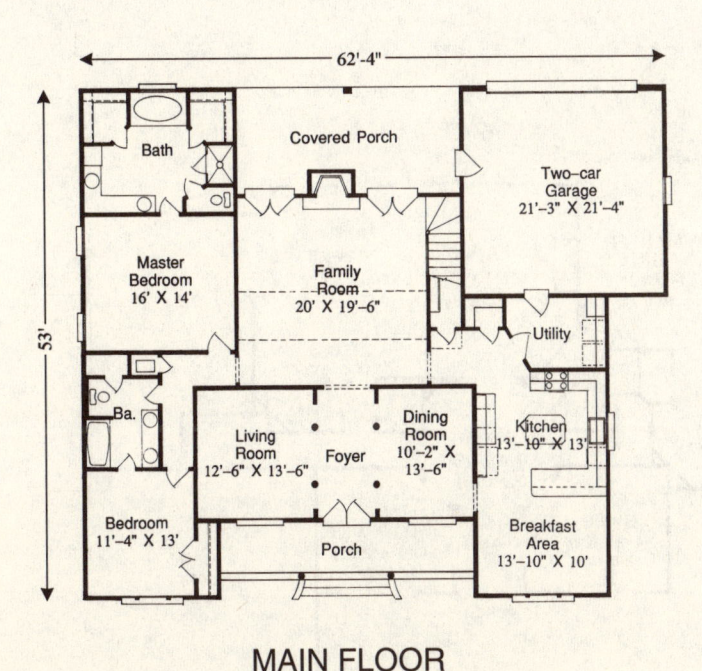

MAIN FLOOR

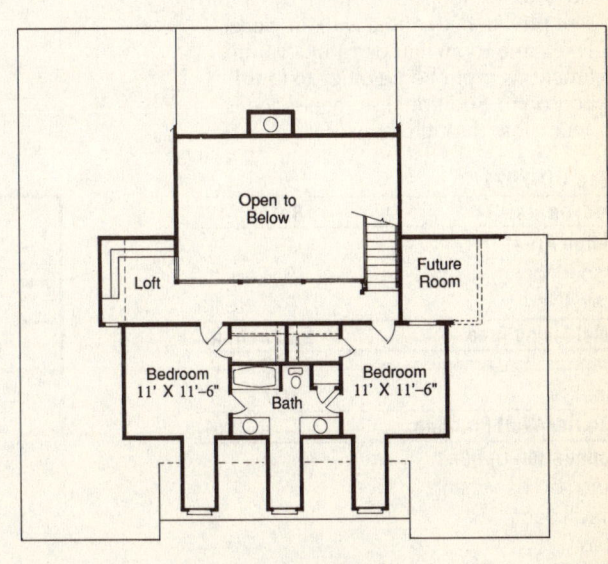

UPPER FLOOR

ORDER BLUEPRINTS ANYTIME!
CALL TOLL-FREE 1-888-626-2026

Plan CHP-2843-13A

PRICES AND DETAILS
ON PAGES 12-15

FIRST LOOK! 64 STUNNING NEW DESIGNS

Eight is Enough

- A stunning two-story octagonal foyer provides the centerpiece in this attractive home.
- From the foyer, you have a variety of destinations to choose from; the formal living and dining rooms, the master suite, the family room or the kitchen.
- The kitchen, which comes equipped with a walk-in pantry and snack bar, opens to a sunny morning room.
- Features in the family room include built-in bookshelves and a fireplace, as well as views to the patio.
- The master bedroom receives sunlight from a large bay window; a relaxing corner spa tub and a spacious walk-in closet provide additional luxury.
- Each upper-floor bedroom enjoys a full-size private bath and a walk-in closet.
- The game room can perform a variety of functions, from home office to fourth bedroom. Additional storage space is accessible through the closet.

Plan DD-2921

Bedrooms: 3+	Baths: 4½
Living Area:	
Upper floor	954 sq. ft.
Main floor	1,923 sq. ft.
Total Living Area:	**2,877 sq. ft.**
Standard basement	1,923 sq. ft.
Garage	427 sq. ft.
Exterior Wall Framing:	2x4

Foundation Options:
Standard basement
Crawlspace
Slab
(All plans can be built with your choice of foundation and framing. A generic conversion diagram is available. See order form.)

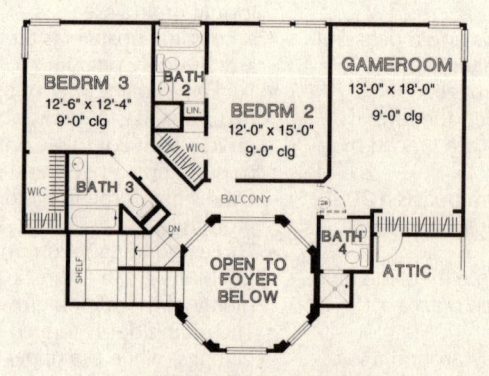

BLUEPRINT PRICE CODE: **D**

UPPER FLOOR

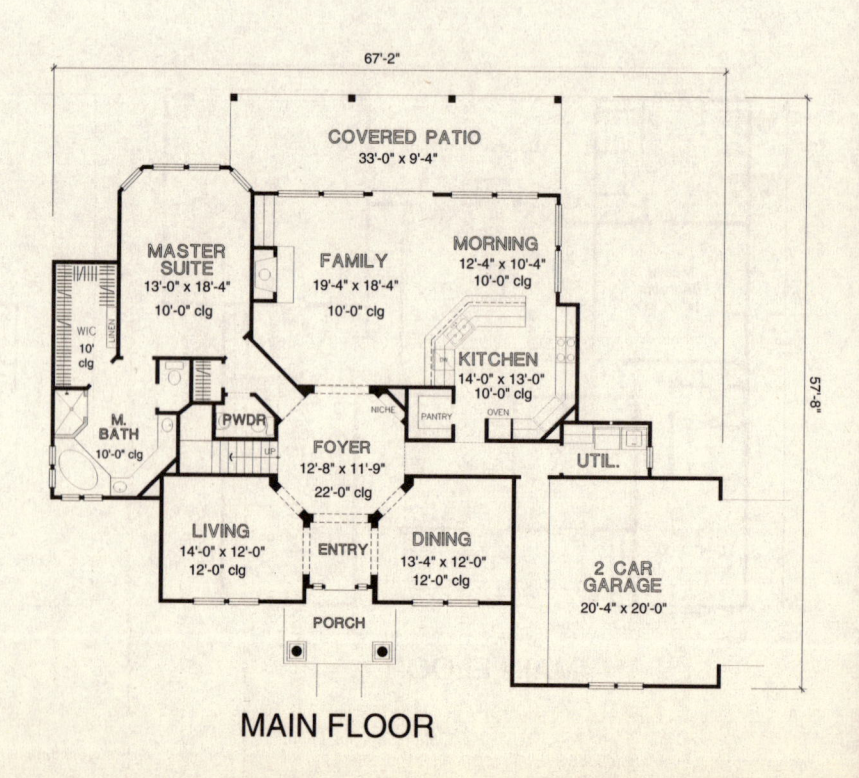

MAIN FLOOR

ORDER BLUEPRINTS ANYTIME!
CALL TOLL-FREE 1-888-626-2026

Plan DD-2921

PRICES AND DETAILS
ON PAGES 12-15

FIRST LOOK! 64 STUNNING NEW DESIGNS

Passionate Embrace

- Romantic outdoor spaces and cozy indoor areas give this two-story Victorian-style home an ambience that your family will embrace passionately.
- In front, the huge wraparound veranda gives you a place to stretch before your morning jog; better yet, stretch out on a hammock and relax while you watch the other joggers glide by.
- From the foyer, the formal living areas present themselves. To the right is the living room; to the left is the dining room. Both feature bay windows.
- The spacious family room is perfect for holiday get-togethers. It boasts a big, bold fireplace, a window seat, a media center and access to the covered porch in the backyard.
- Upstairs, you'll find a luxurious master suite complete with a bay window, a window seat, a walk-in closet and a lush, secluded bath.
- The two additional bedrooms each offer a pleasant walk-in closet and a full-sized private bath.
- An optional game room above the garage creates expansion possibilities.

Plan L-945-VSB	
Bedrooms: 3+	**Baths:** 4
Living Area:	
Upper floor	1,308 sq. ft.
Main floor	1,353 sq. ft.
Game room	311 sq. ft.
Total Living Area:	**2,972 sq. ft.**
Garage	494 sq. ft.
Exterior Wall Framing:	2x4

Foundation Options:
Slab
(All plans can be built with your choice of foundation and framing. A generic conversion diagram is available. See order form.)

BLUEPRINT PRICE CODE: D

REAR VIEW

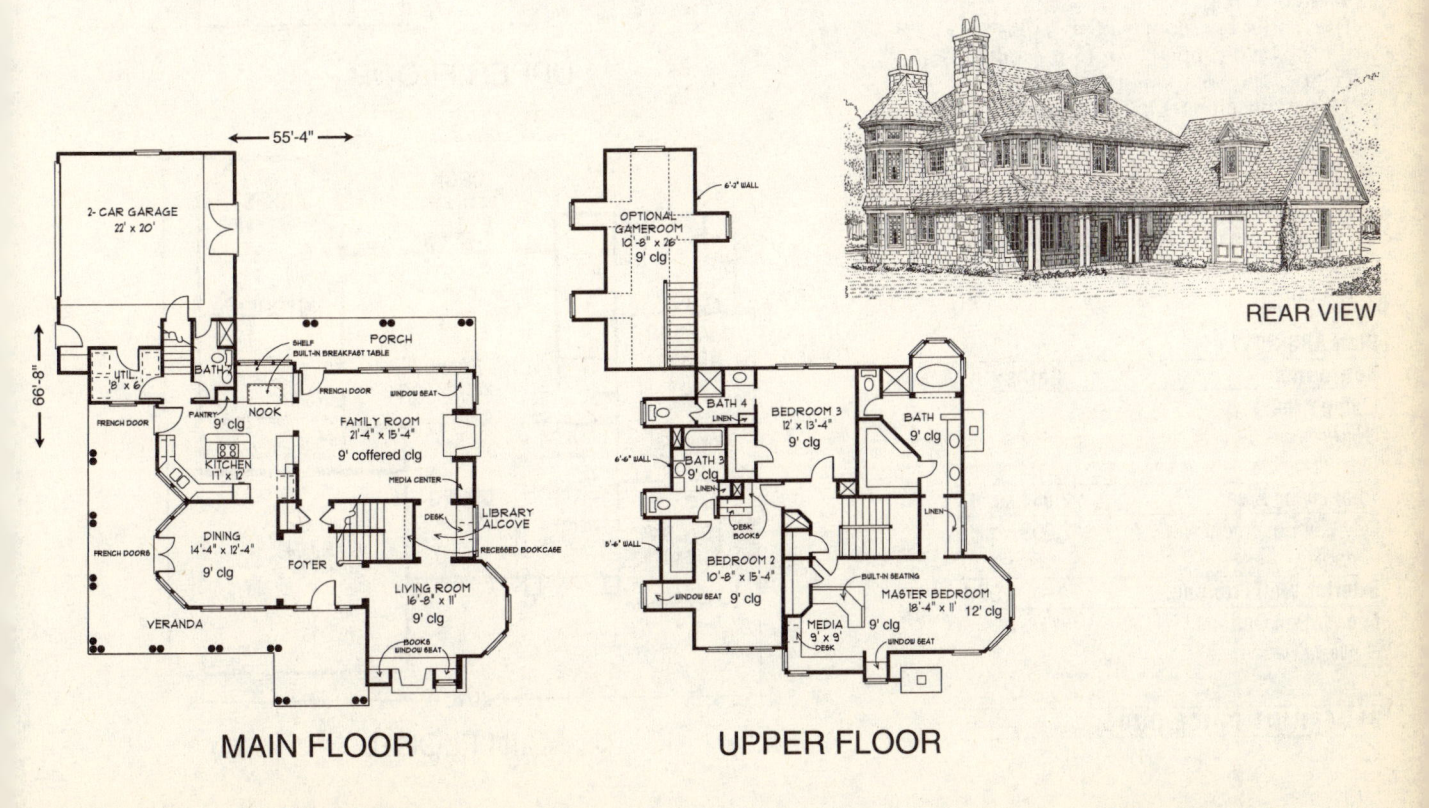

MAIN FLOOR

UPPER FLOOR

ORDER BLUEPRINTS ANYTIME!
CALL TOLL-FREE 1-888-626-2026

Plan L-945-VSB

PRICES AND DETAILS
ON PAGES 12-15

FIRST LOOK! 64 STUNNING NEW DESIGNS

So Nice

- This attractive home's brick exterior is accented by stucco-trimmed windows with decorative keystones.
- To the right of the 18-ft.-high foyer, a spacious dining room is set off by elegant columns.
- Ahead is the family room, where a fireplace is flanked by large windows looking out onto the patio. An 18-ft. ceiling crowns this gorgeous space.
- A snack bar in the kitchen allows for quick meals. The adjoining breakfast nook is an ideal spot to work through the Sunday paper. It's topped by a 14-ft. vaulted ceiling.
- The master bedroom features a plush private bath capped by a 15-ft. vaulted ceiling. The bedroom itself boasts an 11-ft. tray ceiling. Optional pocket doors lead to a study with a 15-ft. vaulted ceiling and a fireplace.
- The remaining main-floor rooms are graced by 9-ft. ceilings.
- Upstairs, a hall overlooking the family room connects three bedrooms and two full baths.

Plan APS-2911	
Bedrooms: 4	**Baths:** 3½
Living Area:	
Upper floor	861 sq. ft.
Main floor	2,093 sq. ft.
Total Living Area:	**2,954 sq. ft.**
Daylight basement	2,093 sq. ft.
Garage	480 sq. ft.
Exterior Wall Framing:	2x4
Foundation Options:	
Daylight basement	
(All plans can be built with your choice of foundation and framing. A generic conversion diagram is available. See order form.)	
BLUEPRINT PRICE CODE:	**D**

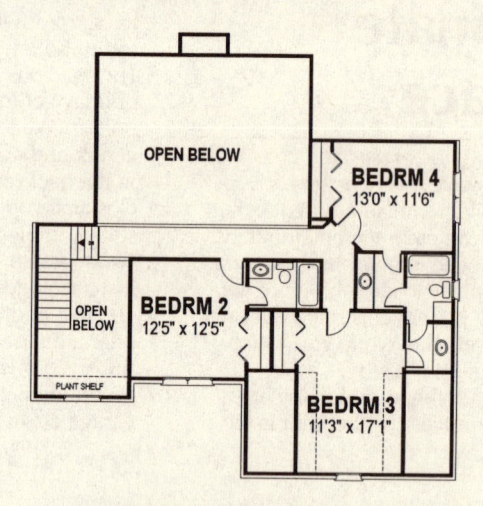

UPPER FLOOR
- OPEN BELOW
- BEDRM 4 — 13'0" x 11'6"
- OPEN BELOW
- BEDRM 2 — 12'5" x 12'5"
- BEDRM 3 — 11'3" x 17'1"
- PLANT SHELF

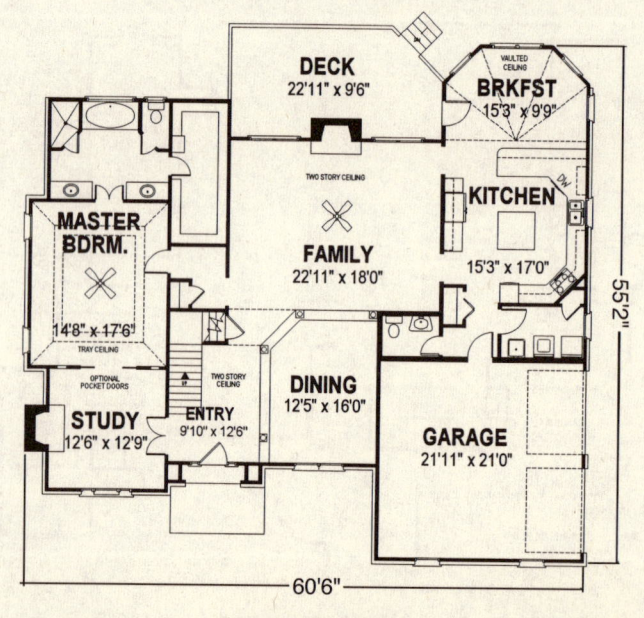

MAIN FLOOR
- DECK — 22'11" x 9'6"
- BRKFST (VAULTED CEILING) — 15'3" x 9'9"
- KITCHEN — 15'3" x 17'0"
- MASTER BDRM. — 14'8" x 17'6" (TRAY CEILING)
- FAMILY (TWO STORY CEILING) — 22'11" x 18'0"
- DINING — 12'5" x 16'0"
- STUDY — 12'6" x 12'9"
- ENTRY (TWO STORY CEILING) — 9'10" x 12'6"
- GARAGE — 21'11" x 21'0"
- OPTIONAL POCKET DOORS
- 60'6" x 55'2"

ORDER BLUEPRINTS ANYTIME! CALL TOLL-FREE 1-888-626-2026

Plan APS-2911

PRICES AND DETAILS ON PAGES 12-15

158

FIRST LOOK! 64 STUNNING NEW DESIGNS

Step into a Dream

- Extensive built-ins, elegant French styling and lofty ceilings make this dream home the picture of perfection.
- Upon entering to the foyer, you'll first notice the formal living room, an ideal setting for entertaining guests.
- An enormous Palladian window and a coffered ceiling give the dining room a palatial air.
- The kitchen's center island and walk-in pantry make fixing meals a breeze.
- Relaxing is easy in the spacious family room. A handsome fireplace and a built-in entertainment center provide homey touches.
- Built-in bookshelves and a bay window adorn the study, which can also serve as a fourth bedroom.
- A windowed sitting area, two walk-in closets and a sumptuous bath highlight the master suite.
- Unfinished space upstairs can serve any number of purposes: storage, recreation, hobbies or a children's playroom.

Plan KLF-9713

Bedrooms: 3+	Baths: 2½
Living Area:	
Main floor	2,959 sq. ft.
Total Living Area:	**2,959 sq. ft.**
Bonus room	531 sq. ft.
Garage	628 sq. ft.
Exterior Wall Framing:	2x4

Foundation Options:
Slab
(All plans can be built with your choice of foundation and framing. A generic conversion diagram is available. See order form.)

BLUEPRINT PRICE CODE: D

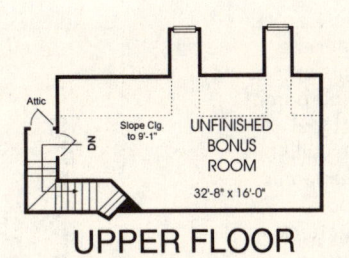

UPPER FLOOR

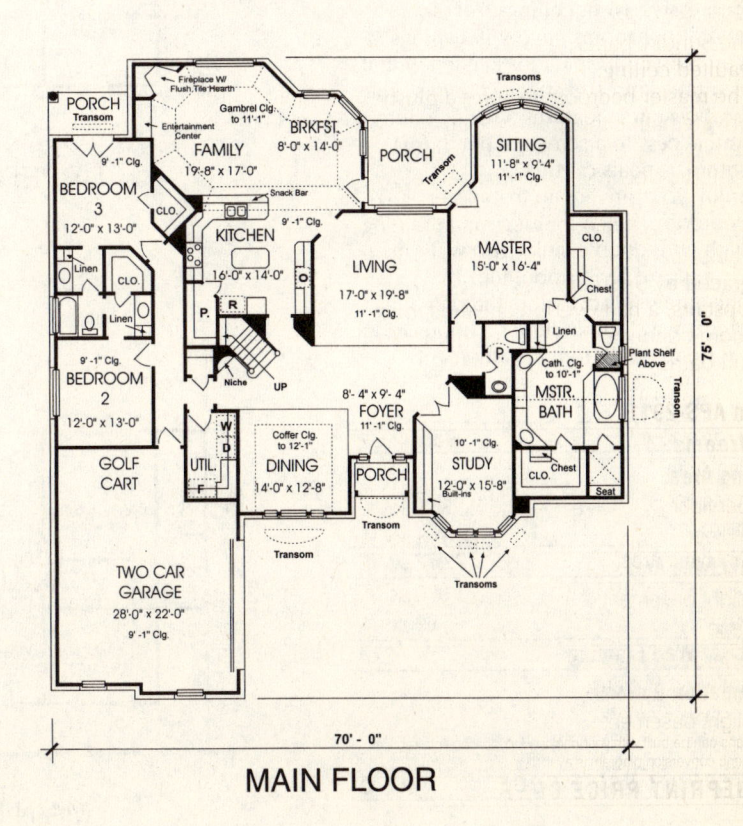

MAIN FLOOR

ORDER BLUEPRINTS ANYTIME!
CALL TOLL-FREE 1-888-626-2026

Plan KLF-9713

PRICES AND DETAILS ON PAGES 12-15

159

FIRST LOOK! 64 STUNNING NEW DESIGNS

Warm Family Memories

- This inviting four-bedroom farmhouse will provide your family with lots of room to breathe. The wraparound porch heightens the home's traditional feel.
- On cold winter nights, memories will be made around the fireplace in the family room. During warm weather you can move the events to the backyard deck.
- The foyer and family room feature impressive 18-ft. ceilings. All other main-floor rooms have 9-ft. ceilings.
- You'll love the spacious kitchen with its central island and snack counters. The breakfast area features a handy pantry and access to a screened porch for summer meals outside.
- Enjoy your privacy in the master bedroom, which includes an adjoining bath with double sinks, two walk-in closets and a whirlpool tub.
- The garage is accessible through a breezeway, and includes a bonus room for storage or future development.

Plan APS-2913

Bedrooms: 4	Baths: 3½
Living Area:	
Upper floor	986 sq. ft.
Main floor	1,986 sq. ft.
Total Living Area:	**2,972 sq. ft.**
Daylight basement	1,986 sq. ft.
Garage	799 sq. ft.
Exterior Wall Framing:	2x4

Foundation Options:
Daylight basement
(All plans can be built with your choice of foundation and framing. A generic conversion diagram is available. See order form.)

BLUEPRINT PRICE CODE: D

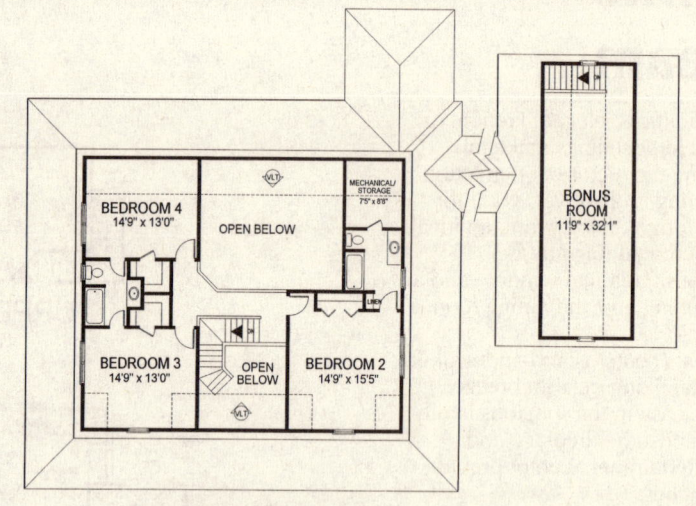

UPPER FLOOR

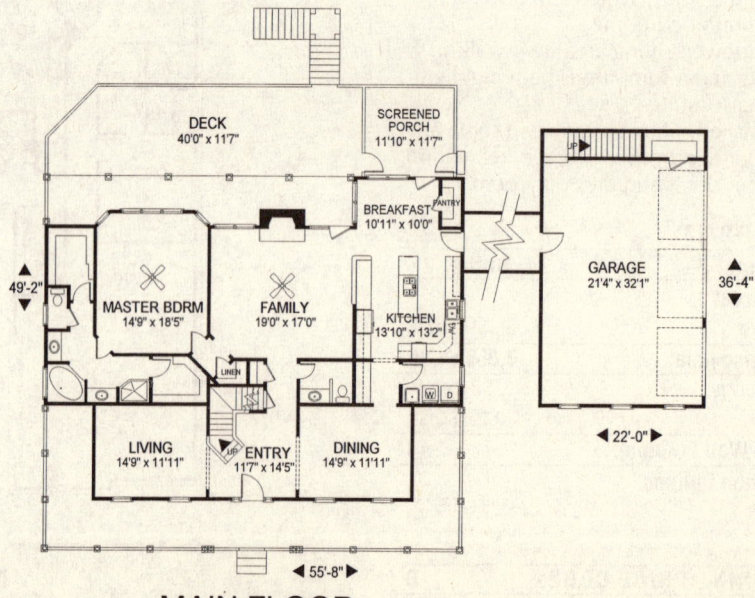

MAIN FLOOR

ORDER BLUEPRINTS ANYTIME!
CALL TOLL-FREE 1-888-626-2026

Plan APS-2913

PRICES AND DETAILS ON PAGES 12-15

FIRST LOOK! 64 STUNNING NEW DESIGNS

True Showcase

- A treasure both inside and out, this home features a grand two-story entry. Here, a display niche highlights the landing of a dramatic angled staircase.
- The majestic living room leads into an intimate dining area, which is set off gracefully by four columns.
- Cozy up in front of the family room fireplace, grill out on the patio, or lounge at the kitchen island with a late-night snack.
- A full-size closet enables the den/office to serve as an extra bedroom.
- Soak in sunshine and suds in the master bath's corner tub, which is framed by windows on two sides.
- The master suite also benefits from a vaulted ceiling in the bedroom, a walk-in closet and dual vanities.
- Three secondary bedrooms round out the upper floor. The foremost rooms, each with a private vanity, share a bath, while the rear bedroom enjoys its own full bath.
- A three-car garage delivers plenty of storage or hobby space.

Plan AG-3053	
Bedrooms: 4+	**Baths:** 3½
Living Area:	
Upper floor	1,417 sq. ft.
Main floor	1,636 sq. ft.
Total Living Area:	**3,053 sq. ft.**
Standard basement	1,590 sq. ft.
Garage and storage	695 sq. ft.
Exterior Wall Framing:	2x4
Foundation Options:	
Standard basement	
All plans can be built with your choice of foundation and framing. A generic conversion diagram is available. See order form.	
BLUEPRINT PRICE CODE:	E

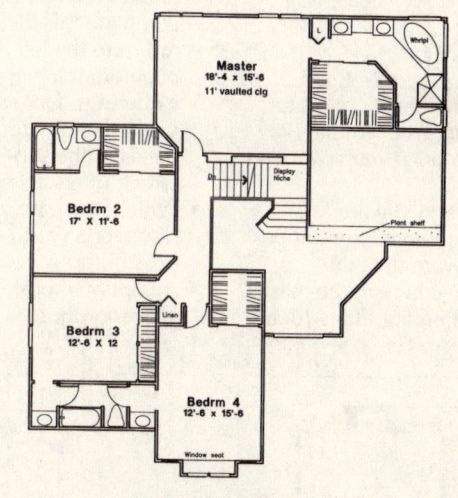

UPPER FLOOR

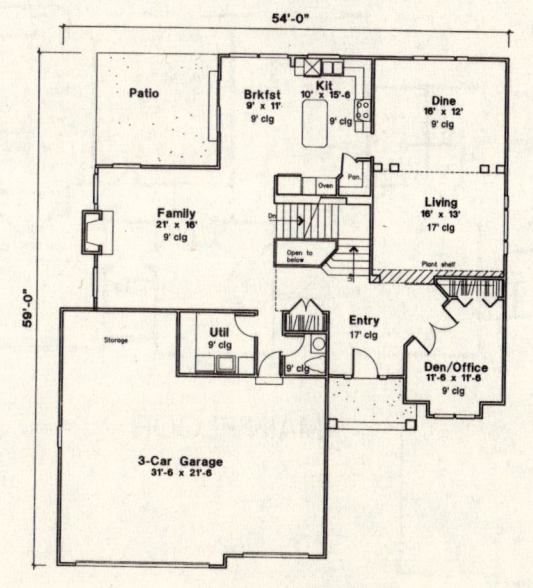

MAIN FLOOR

ORDER BLUEPRINTS ANYTIME!
CALL TOLL-FREE 1-888-626-2026

Plan AG-3053

PRICES AND DETAILS ON PAGES 12-15

FIRST LOOK! 64 STUNNING NEW DESIGNS

Delicious Dilemma

- To enter this breathtaking home is to succumb to a delicious dilemma: Which way to turn once you've arrived in the foyer?
- A turn to the right and you are enraptured by the intimate, sumptuous master suite. The warmth of the fireplace will draw you from the master bedroom to the adjoining sitting room. An enormous, vaulted bath, a walk-in closet and access to the outdoors complete this idyllic space.
- A turn to the left brings you to the site of entertaining and joyous family gatherings. Linger before the fire in the vaulted family room; enjoy casual meals in the sun-filled breakfast area, which offers access to a covered porch.
- Whichever path you choose, you will discover a world of luxury and possibility.
- An optional upstairs offers extra living space for those with larger families.

Plan FB-5580-FINL

Bedrooms: 3+	Baths: 2½-3½
Living Area:	
Main floor	2,491 sq. ft.
Total Living Area:	**2,491 sq. ft.**
Optional upper floor	588 sq. ft.
Garage and storage	522 sq. ft.
Exterior Wall Framing:	2x4

Foundation Options:
Crawlspace
(All plans can be built with your choice of foundation and framing. A generic conversion diagram is available. See order form.)

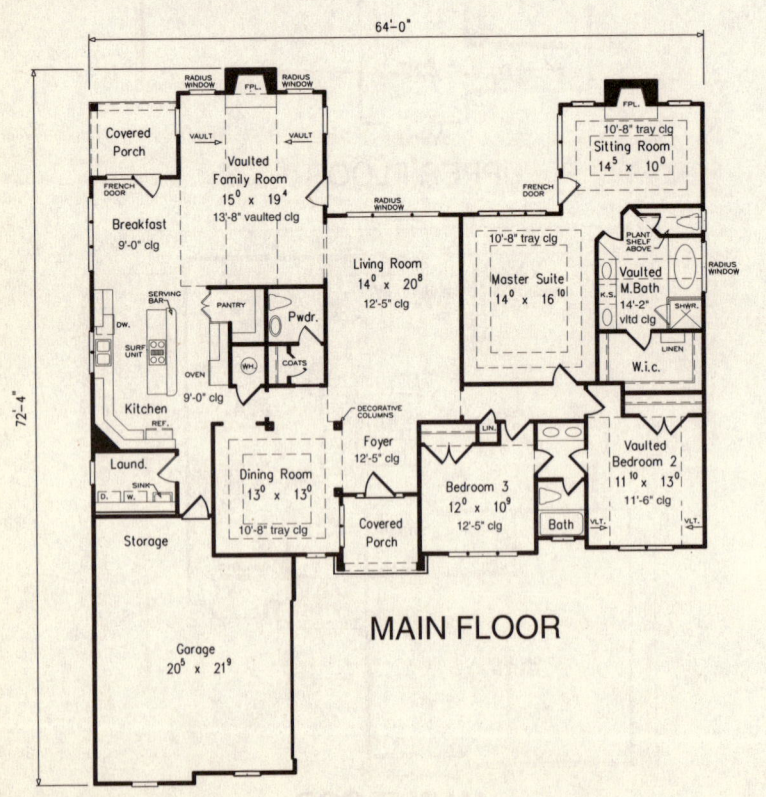

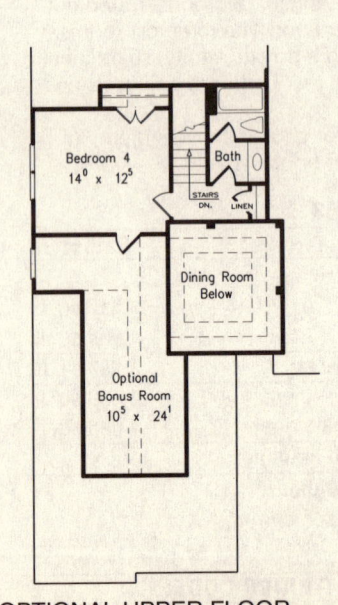

BLUEPRINT PRICE CODE: C

MAIN FLOOR

OPTIONAL UPPER FLOOR

Plan FB-5580-FINL

FIRST LOOK! 64 STUNNING NEW DESIGNS

Unique Conveniences

- This home is designed to combine unique modern conveniences with warmth and comfort.
- Casual evenings with friends and relatives will be spent in the family room, which boasts a fireplace and access to a covered porch.
- A fireplace is also one of the highlights of the cozy master suite. The adjoining bath has double sinks, a walk-in closet and a dressing area. A private porch offers an outdoor retreat.
- You'll love the kitchen's snack bar and its convenient access to the dining room, breakfast area and utility room.
- The exercise room allows you to work out without leaving home! A spiral staircase gets you to the upper-floor study in style!
- The whole family will enjoy the upper-floor game room, which features a wet bar. The computer room creates a space for homework and internet surfing.
- Plans for a detached, three-car garage are included in the blueprints.

Plan HDC-3105
Bedrooms: 3+	Baths: 2½
Living Area:	
Upper floor	1,112 sq. ft.
Main floor	1,993 sq. ft.
Total Living Area:	3,105 sq. ft.
Detached garage	894 sq. ft.
Exterior Wall Framing:	2x4
Foundation Options:	
Slab	

All plans can be built with your choice of foundation and framing. A generic conversion diagram is available. See order form.

BLUEPRINT PRICE CODE: E

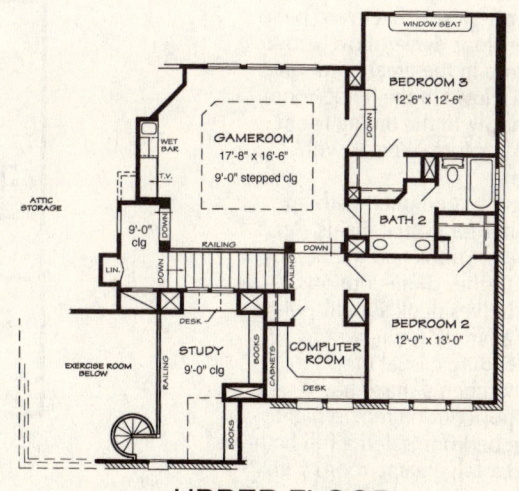

UPPER FLOOR

◄ 61'-4" ►

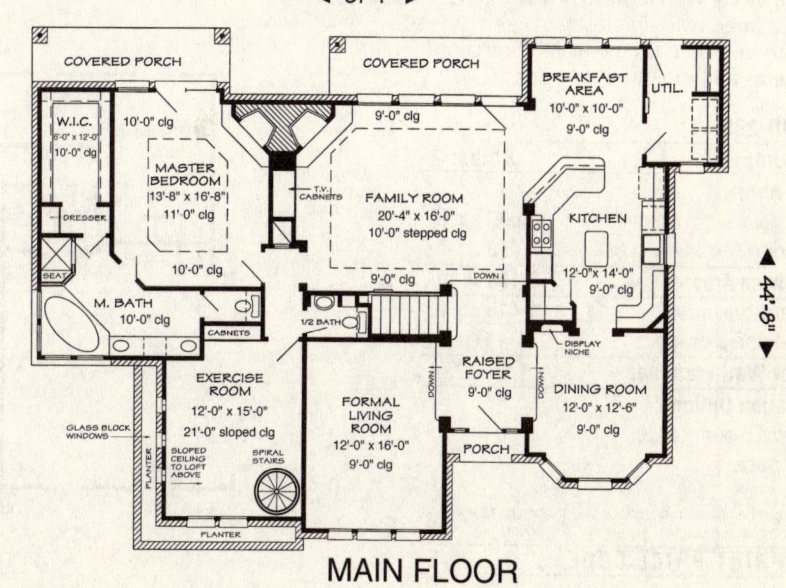

MAIN FLOOR

ORDER BLUEPRINTS ANYTIME!
CALL TOLL-FREE 1-888-626-2026

Plan HDC-3105

PRICES AND DETAILS
ON PAGES 12-15

FIRST LOOK! 64 STUNNING NEW DESIGNS

Alfresco Living

- This home's front porch, backyard patio and two upper-floor decks allow you to spend more time in the great outdoors.
- Tall arched windows in the living room and a bay window in the dining room flood the design's formal areas with natural sunlight.
- The kitchen comes equipped with an angled snack bar for casual meals. An adjacent breakfast nook and the nearby patio provide further dining options.
- Built-in bookshelves flank a focal-point fireplace in the family room, where you'll love spending casual time together. The kitchen's snack bar serves up pizza and popcorn on movie night.
- Upstairs, three bedrooms and a full bath cluster around a large game room with access to a covered rear deck.
- The master bedroom enjoys a deck of its own, along with a plush private bath and a large walk-in closet.
- A fifth bedroom on the main floor could serve as a home office or a den.

Plan DD-2952-1

Bedrooms: 5	Baths: 3
Living Area:	
Upper floor	1,690 sq. ft.
Main floor	1,418 sq. ft.
Total Living Area:	**3,108 sq. ft.**
Standard basement	1,418 sq. ft.
Garage and storage	441 sq. ft.
Exterior Wall Framing:	2x4

Foundation Options:
Standard basement
Crawlspace
Slab
(All plans can be built with your choice of foundation and framing. A generic conversion diagram is available. See order form.)

BLUEPRINT PRICE CODE: E

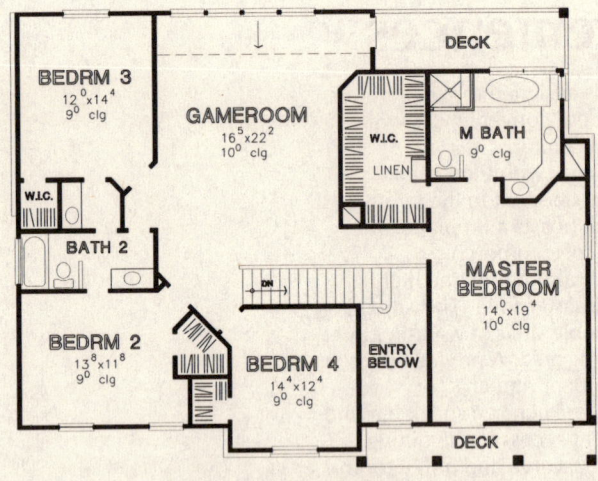

UPPER FLOOR

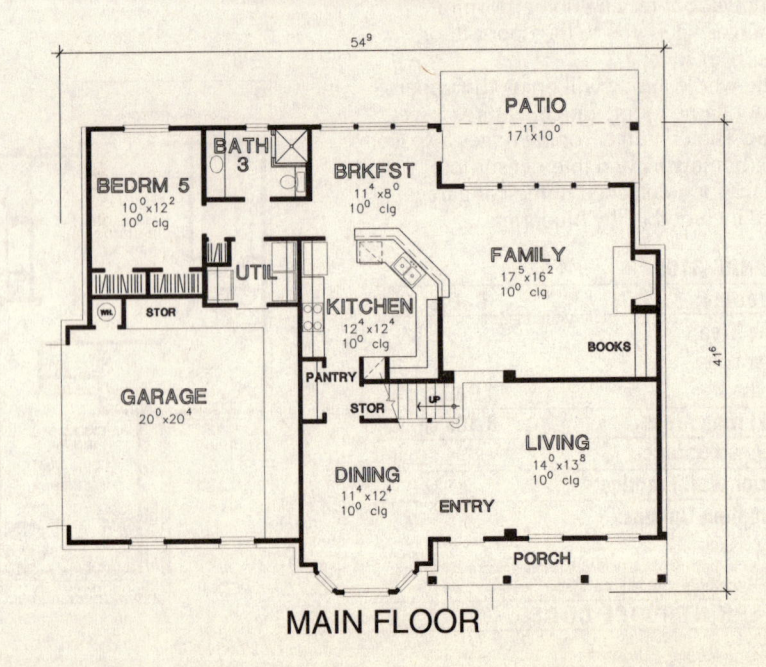

MAIN FLOOR

ORDER BLUEPRINTS ANYTIME!
CALL TOLL-FREE 1-888-626-2026

Plan DD-2952-1

PRICES AND DETAILS ON PAGES 12-15

FIRST LOOK! 64 STUNNING NEW DESIGNS

Contemporary Collector

- Display your collection and dazzle your guests in the splendor of this home's central hall. Comprised of the entry, the gallery and the Great Room, this striking expanse enjoys a lofty 12-ft. ceiling and light from the lanai.
- The high-ceilinged dining room and sun room offer additional milieux for prized artwork. The sun room features three large skylights, a fireplace and access to the lanai.
- A circular eating bar in the kitchen invites conversation and informal gatherings.
- Art niches lead the way to the master suite, where the elegant tray ceiling, enormous walk-in closet and private lanai access create a unique retreat. The oval tub receives maximum sunlight from two windows, while an exterior wall maintains privacy.
- Three roomy bedrooms are situated across the home from the master suite.
- An oversized garage with ample storage space completes this artful picture.

Plan KY-3111

Bedrooms: 3+	**Baths:** 3

Living Area:
Main floor	3,111 sq. ft.
Total Living Area	**3,111 sq. ft.**
Garage and storage	781 sq. ft.
Exterior Wall Framing	2x4

Foundation Options:
Slab
(All plans can be built with your choice of foundation and framing. A generic conversion diagram is available. See order form.)

BLUEPRINT PRICE CODE: E

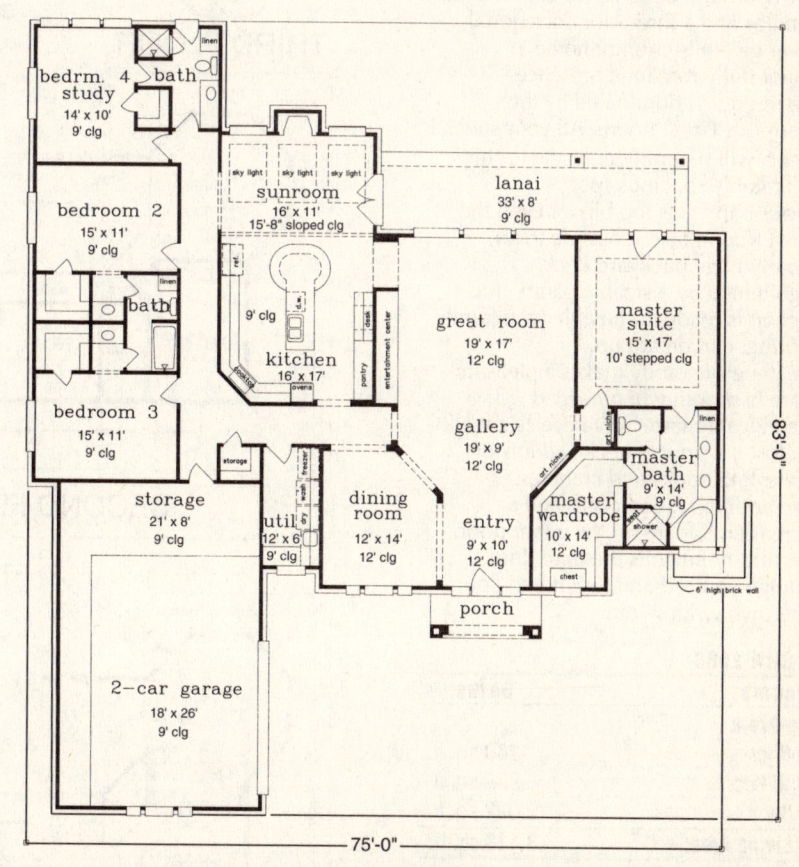

MAIN FLOOR

ORDER BLUEPRINTS ANYTIME! CALL TOLL-FREE 1-888-626-2026

Plan KY-3111

PRICES AND DETAILS ON PAGES 12-15

165

FIRST LOOK! 64 STUNNING NEW DESIGNS

Country Romance

- A wraparound covered porch, fishscale shingles and a three-story octagonal tower give this country home a wonderfully romantic presence.
- The interior is dominated by the enormous Great Room. All your special events will naturally gravitate to this remarkably spacious spot.
- If your party gets too big for even the Great Room, take it outside to an equally huge backyard deck.
- Highlighted by a sizable pantry, the kitchen is ready for anything the family gourmet can dream up.
- The generous study makes a pleasant spare bedroom when needed.
- The elegant master suite boasts a walk-in closet, a private deck and lots of interesting nooks and crannies.
- Two additional bedrooms and a recreation loft are on the upper floor.
- The library inhabits the third floor. Indulge yourself and turn it into your very own writing loft.

Plan SUN-2580

Bedrooms: 3+	Baths: 3
Living Area:	
Third floor	268 sq. ft.
Second floor	828 sq. ft.
Main floor	2,022 sq. ft.
Total Living Area:	**3,118 sq. ft.**
Exterior Wall Framing:	2x6

Foundation Options:
Crawlspace
Slab
(All plans can be built with your choice of foundation and framing. A generic conversion diagram is available. See order form.)

BLUEPRINT PRICE CODE: E

THIRD FLOOR

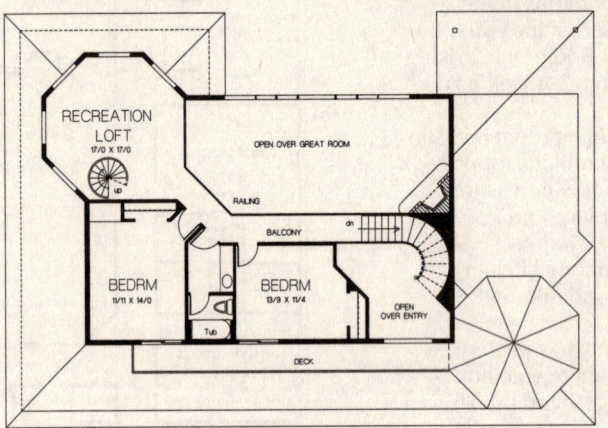

SECOND FLOOR

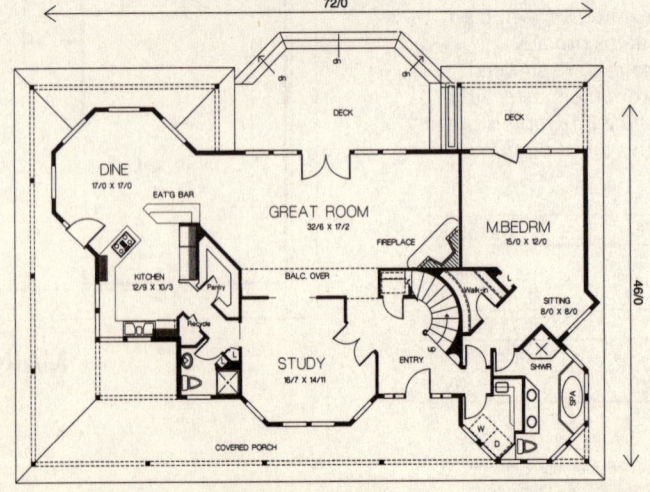

MAIN FLOOR

REAR VIEW

Plan SUN-2580

ORDER BLUEPRINTS ANYTIME!
CALL TOLL-FREE 1-888-626-2026

PRICES AND DETAILS ON PAGES 12-15

FIRST LOOK! 64 STUNNING NEW DESIGNS

Stately Manor

- The stately facade of this two-story home creates quite an impression.
- Enter the home through the 17-ft.-high vaulted entry, accented by a striking curved staircase.
- The living room features a fireplace and a bay window that overlooks the front lawn. Double doors access the nearby den with its classy tray ceiling.
- The dining room also has a tray ceiling, as well as access to the kitchen through a convenient butler's pantry. The kitchen itself has a central island and a breakfast nook that precedes the patio.
- The family room's 17-ft. ceiling and warm fireplace make it a unique and inviting gathering spot for you and your loved ones.
- Upstairs, curl up in the window seat in the master suite, which is topped by a 13-ft. vaulted ceiling. The adjoining private bath boasts his-and-hers walk-in closets, a whirlpool tub and a glass shower. An adjacent sitting area may be converted to a fourth bedroom or a nursery if desired.

Plan B-90038

Bedrooms: 3+	Baths: 2½
Living Area:	
Upper floor	1,437 sq. ft.
Main floor	1,758 sq. ft.
Total Living Area:	**3,195 sq. ft.**
Standard basement	1,758 sq. ft.
Garage	672 sq. ft.
Exterior Wall Framing:	2x6
Foundation Options:	
Standard basement	

(All plans can be built with your choice of foundation and framing. A generic conversion diagram is available. See order form.)

BLUEPRINT PRICE CODE: E

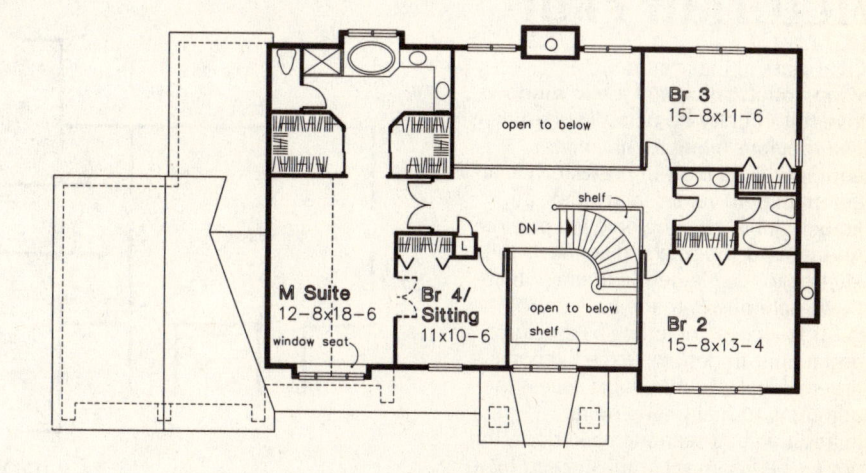

UPPER FLOOR

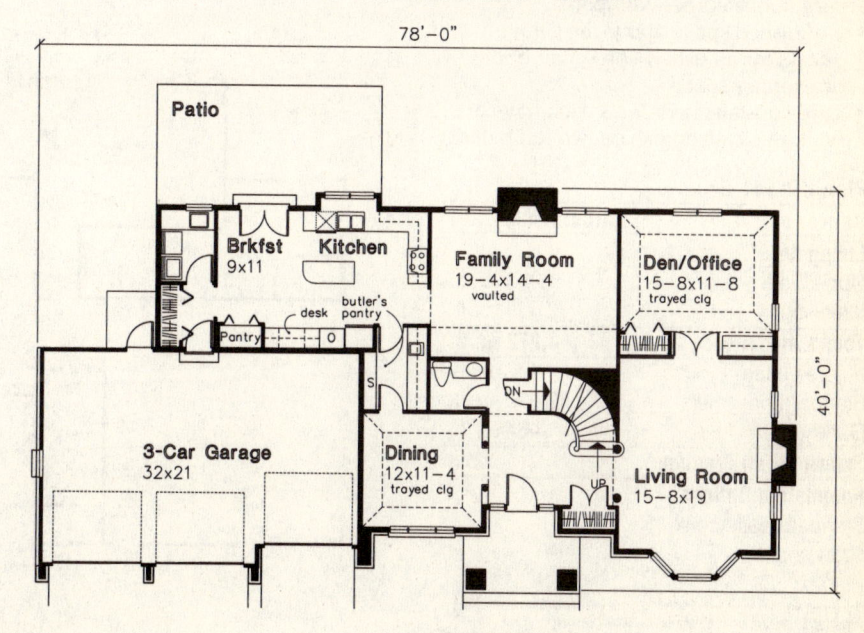

MAIN FLOOR

ORDER BLUEPRINTS ANYTIME!
CALL TOLL-FREE 1-888-626-2026

Plan B-90038

PRICES AND DETAILS ON PAGES 12-15

FIRST LOOK! 64 STUNNING NEW DESIGNS

Victorian Flair

- Oval glass in the front door, a wraparound porch and a bay window give this country home a Victorian flair.
- The spacious living room comes equipped with built-in bookshelves, an entertainment center, a fireplace and French doors opening onto the porch.
- An informal snack island connects the kitchen to the Gathering Room, which flows naturally onto the back patio.
- Subtle touches, including a lazy Susan and a built-in desk, give the kitchen a timeless feel. Double doors access the adjoining formal dining room.
- In addition to a separate patio door, the master bedroom is complemented by a private bath whose highlight is a sumptuous corner whirlpool.
- Unfinished space above the garage allows for an extra bedroom or hobby or exercise space.
- Three upstairs bedrooms each have a walk-in closet and share two full baths.

Plan UD-141-E	
Bedrooms: 4+	**Baths:** 3 full, 2 half
Living Area:	
Upper floor	1,233 sq. ft.
Main floor	2,039 sq. ft.
Total Living Area:	**3,272 sq. ft.**
Future space	477 sq. ft.
Standard basement	2,039 sq. ft.
Garage	484 sq. ft.
Exterior Wall Framing:	2x4

Foundation Options:
Standard basement
Crawlspace
Slab
(All plans can be built with your choice of foundation and framing. A generic conversion diagram is available. See order form.)

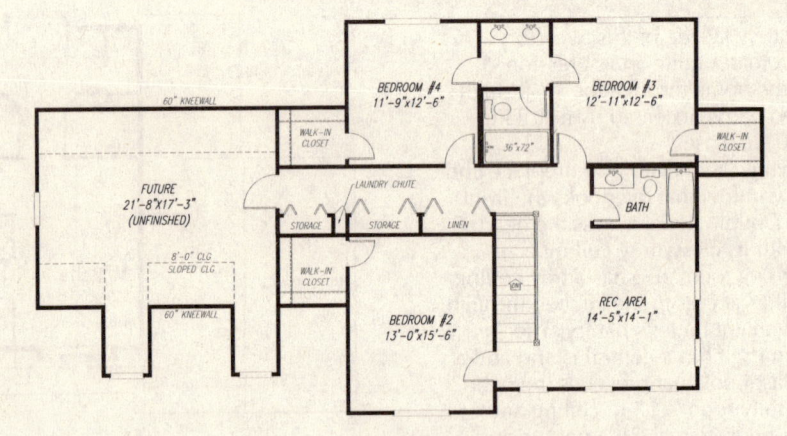

BLUEPRINT PRICE CODE: E

UPPER FLOOR

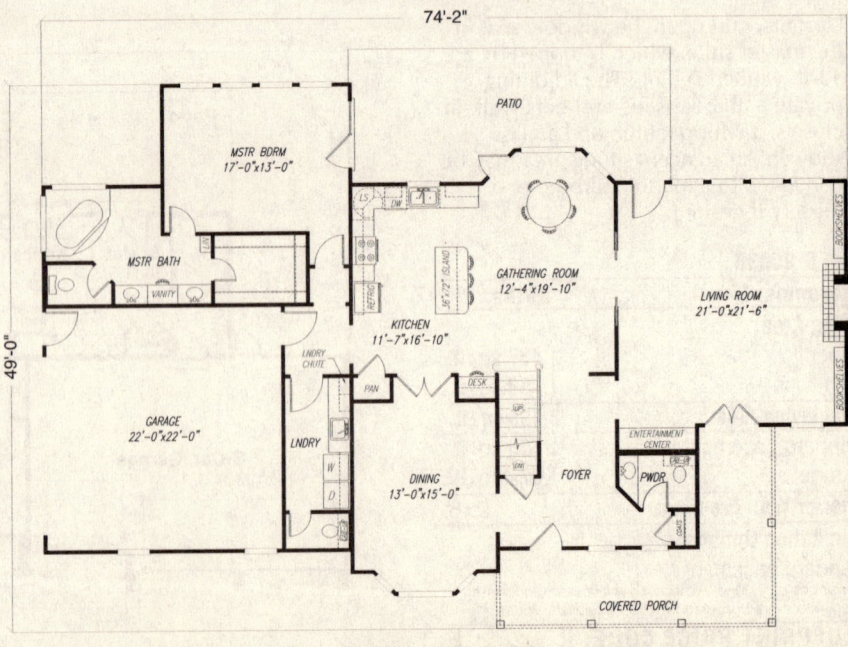

MAIN FLOOR

---

168   ORDER BLUEPRINTS ANYTIME! CALL TOLL-FREE 1-888-626-2026   Plan UD-141-E   PRICES AND DETAILS ON PAGES 12-15

FIRST LOOK! 64 STUNNING NEW DESIGNS

Details Make the Difference

- The details found in this design make all the difference, giving it the flair of a custom home—at a fraction of the cost.
- Inside, the 18-ft.-high, vaulted foyer ushers guests into the home's formal areas. In the dining room, a butler's pantry and a pass-through to the kitchen make parties enjoyable for you, too.
- Even the most complicated recipes will come off without a hitch in the gourmet kitchen. Here, an island cooktop frees up space for mixing, while a desk keeps family business close at hand.
- A wet bar nearby serves the family room, where a woodstove and a built-in media center provide fun focal points.
- Unless otherwise noted, all main-floor rooms include 9-ft. ceilings.
- Upstairs, a window seat in the master suite beckons you to curl up and reflect on the day. In the bath, a 10-ft. vaulted ceiling creates a look of elegance.
- The kids will love the other bedrooms, which each include a walk-in closet, a built-in desk or a built-in bookcase.

Plan CDG-2097	
Bedrooms: 4+	Baths: 2½
Living Area:	
Upper floor	1,456 sq. ft.
Main floor	1,541 sq. ft.
Bonus room	303 sq. ft.
Total Living Area:	**3,300 sq. ft.**
Garage	689 sq. ft.
Exterior Wall Framing:	2x6
Foundation Options:	
Crawlspace	
(All plans can be built with your choice of foundation and framing. A generic conversion diagram is available. See order form.)	
BLUEPRINT PRICE CODE:	**E**

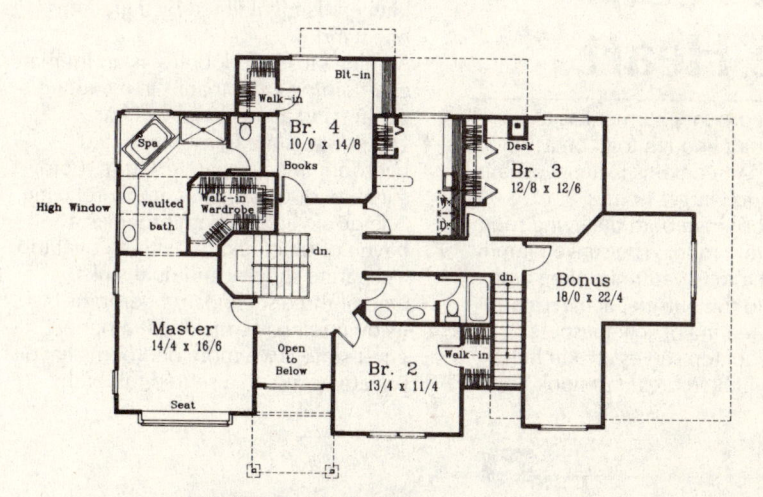

UPPER FLOOR

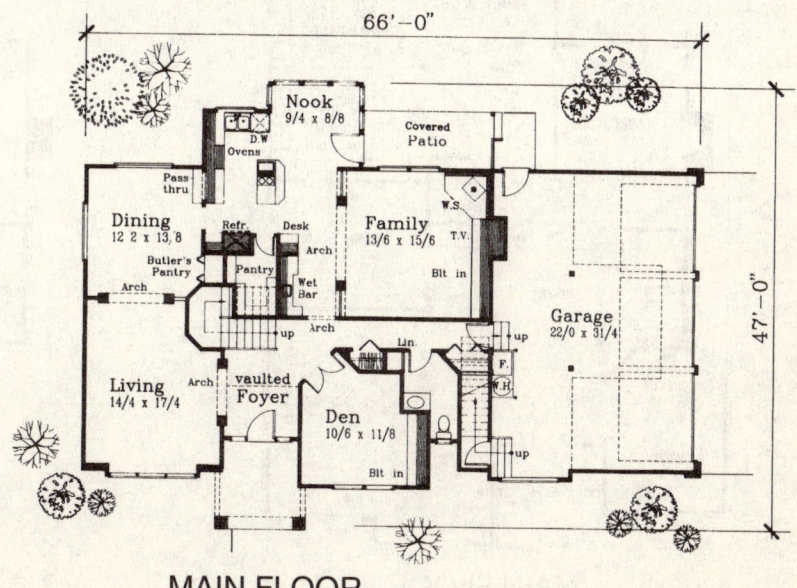

MAIN FLOOR

ORDER BLUEPRINTS ANYTIME!
CALL TOLL-FREE 1-888-626-2026

Plan CDG-2097

PRICES AND DETAILS ON PAGES 12-15

FIRST LOOK! 64 STUNNING NEW DESIGNS

Small Feet, Large Heart

- This four-bedroom charmer has a footprint small enough to fit on a narrow lot, yet contains features usually found in much larger homes.
- Fireplaces brighten both the living room and the family room. The sunken family room, with a lofty vaulted ceiling and two doors to the outside, achieves an impressive feeling of spaciousness.
- An island cooktop serves the kitchen and the skylighted breakfast nook.
- The formal dining room, just off the kitchen, is highlighted by a gracious bay window.
- An elegant study doubles as an intimate entertaining area, thanks to a vaulted ceiling and an optional wet bar.
- The master suite boasts a vaulted bedroom and a separate sitting room, suitable for dressing or simply relaxing. A large skylighted bath provides a haven of quiet luxury, with an oval tub, a separate shower and dual sinks.
- One of three secondary bedrooms has its own full bath, making it a perfect guest suite. Two more bedrooms have private access to a shared full bath.

Plan CH-720-A	
Bedrooms: 4+	**Baths:** 3½
Living Area:	
Upper floor	1,689 sq. ft.
Main floor	1,771 sq. ft.
Total Living Area:	**3,460 sq. ft.**
Basement	1,461 sq. ft.
Garage	440 sq. ft.
Exterior Wall Framing:	2x4

Foundation Options:

Daylight basement
Standard basement
Crawlspace

(All plans can be built with your choice of foundation and framing. A generic conversion diagram is available. See order form.)

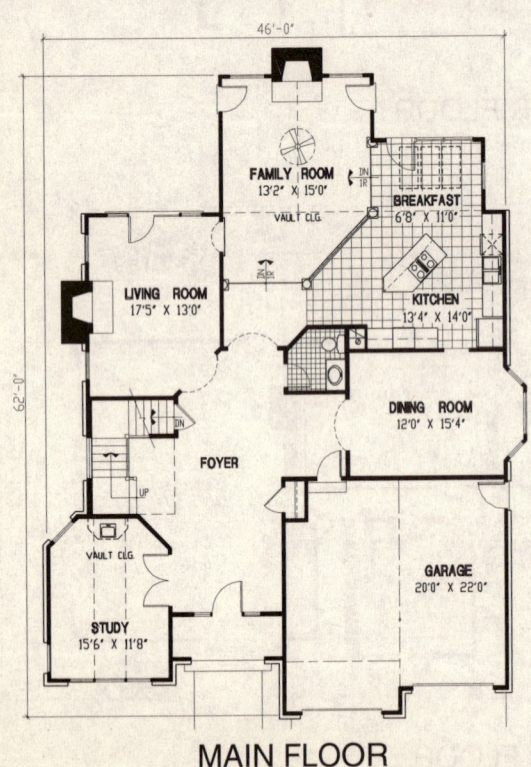

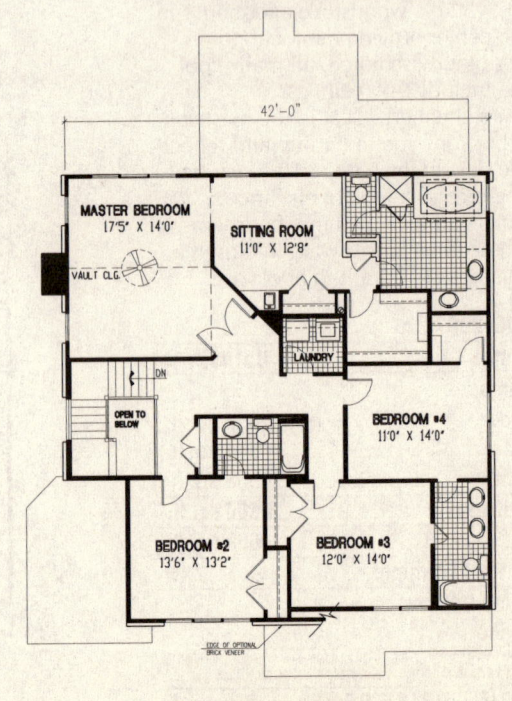

BLUEPRINT PRICE CODE: E

MAIN FLOOR

UPPER FLOOR

ORDER BLUEPRINTS ANYTIME!
CALL TOLL-FREE 1-888-626-2026

Plan CH-720-A

PRICES AND DETAILS ON PAGES 12-15

170

FIRST LOOK! 64 STUNNING NEW DESIGNS

Night in Tunisia

- An exotic blend of French and Mediterranean detailing, this home's exterior invites interest and exploration. From the intimate breakfast nook to the elegant architectural columns that set off the dining room, the interior promises pleasure and discovery.
- The master bedroom features an elegant tray ceiling, a walk-in closet and a spacious bath with a whirlpool tub and a dual-sink vanity. Private access to the deck is another of its virtues.
- Descend to the daylight basement to enjoy the excitements of an enormous recreation room, the perfect spot to let the kids play while the grown-ups socialize upstairs.
- A fourth bedroom—with private access to a full bath—awaits some lucky overnight guest.
- The words Ella Fitzgerald sings in *Night in Tunisia* will ring true indeed for the owner of this magical home: "The cares of the world seem to vanish; the end of the day brings relief." You'll relish every wonderful night.

Plan UDA-96163

Bedrooms: 4	Baths: 3½

Living Area:
Main floor .... 2,282 sq. ft.
Daylight basement .... 1,184 sq. ft.
Total Living Area: 3,466 sq. ft.
Tuck-under garage and storage ... 565 sq. ft.
Exterior Wall Framing: 2x4
Foundation Options:
Daylight basement
All plans can be built with your choice of foundation and framing. A generic conversion diagram is available. See order form.
BLUEPRINT PRICE CODE: .... E

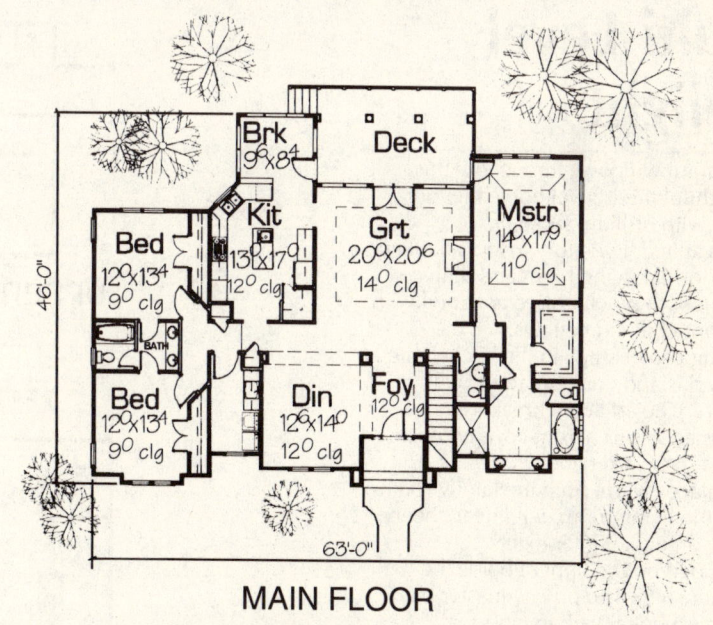

MAIN FLOOR

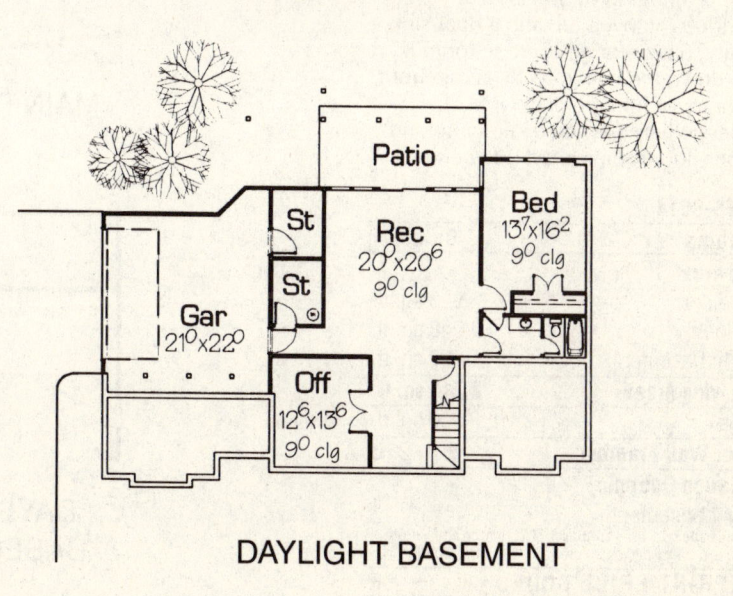

DAYLIGHT BASEMENT

ORDER BLUEPRINTS ANYTIME!
CALL TOLL-FREE 1-888-626-2026

Plan UDA-96163

PRICES AND DETAILS
ON PAGES 12-15

171

FIRST LOOK! 64 STUNNING NEW DESIGNS

Multi-Level Delight

- Bountiful windows throughout this delightful three-level home fill your days with brilliant sunlight.
- The vaulted, two-story foyer is flanked by a formal living room and dining room, both of which are crowned with elegant coffered ceilings.
- Taking center stage in the kitchen are an angled island cooktop and a walk-in pantry. The adjacent breakfast nook offers access to a front covered deck and a backyard patio.
- Fireplaces warm both the family room and the living room, lending a cheery glow on dark winter nights.
- Secluded on the upper floor is the master suite. The private master bath flaunts a huge walk-in closet, a luxurious alcoved tub and a dual-sink vanity. Space for an exercise room is just down the hall, directly across from a library or home office.
- Unless otherwise noted, all main- and upper-floor rooms boast 9-ft. ceilings.

Plan TS-9614

Bedrooms: 3+	Baths: 4
Living Area:	
Upper floor	928 sq. ft.
Main floor	2,048 sq. ft.
Daylight basement	537 sq. ft.
Total Living Area:	**3,513 sq. ft.**
Garage	900 sq. ft.
Exterior Wall Framing:	2x6

Foundation Options:
Daylight basement
(All plans can be built with your choice of foundation and framing. A generic conversion diagram is available. See order form.)

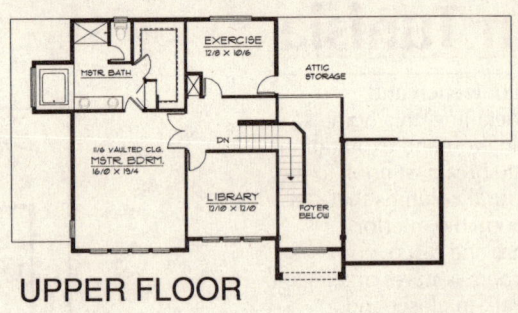

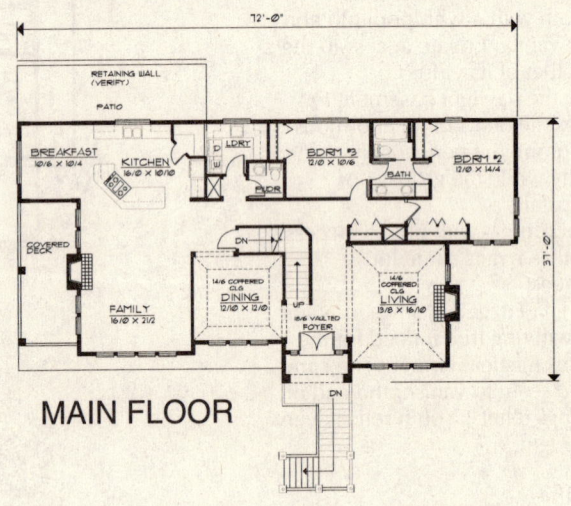

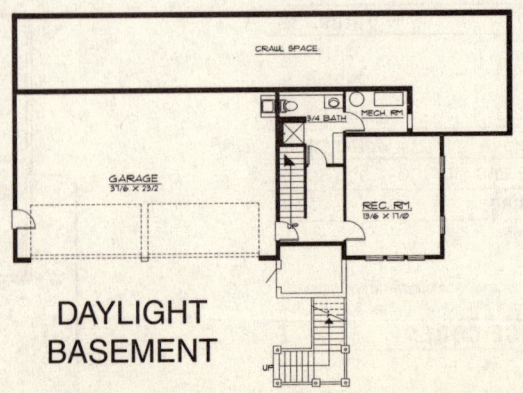

BLUEPRINT PRICE CODE: F

UPPER FLOOR

MAIN FLOOR

DAYLIGHT BASEMENT

172 ORDER BLUEPRINTS ANYTIME! CALL TOLL-FREE 1-888-626-2026

Plan TS-9614

PRICES AND DETAILS ON PAGES 12-15

FIRST LOOK! 64 STUNNING NEW DESIGNS

Hillside Secret

- The true size of this design, which is ideal for a lakefront or other graded lot, becomes apparent only from the inside of the home.
- A 13-ft. vaulted ceiling arches over the entry and the central Great Room, which is warmed by a handsome fireplace. An airy, skylighted breakfast nook off the island kitchen overlooks the backyard, contrasting with the elegant octagonal formal dining room.
- The master suite boasts a walk-in closet and a lush bath with a spa tub, a separate shower, a private toilet and a dual-sink vanity. A romantic gas fireplace warms one corner of the sleeping chamber. French doors open onto the deck, which lines the rear of the house, and connects to the Great Room and the breakfast nook.
- A finished daylight basement forms a congenial family and recreation area. The generous family room, complete with a fireplace, a built-in entertainment center and a wet bar, allows entry to a covered patio.
- A three-car garage accesses the house through a handy laundry room.

Plan SUN-3295

Bedrooms: 3+	**Baths:** 3

Living Area:
Main floor	2,112 sq. ft.
Daylight basement (finished)	1,506 sq. ft.
Total Living Area:	**3,618 sq. ft.**
Daylight basement (unfinished)	466 sq. ft.
Garage	840 sq. ft.
Exterior Wall Framing:	2x6

Foundation Options:
Daylight basement
(All plans can be built with your choice of foundation and framing. A generic conversion diagram is available. See order form.)

BLUEPRINT PRICE CODE: F

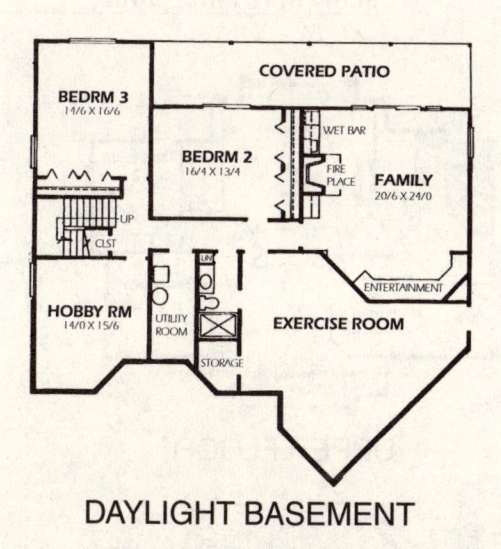

DAYLIGHT BASEMENT

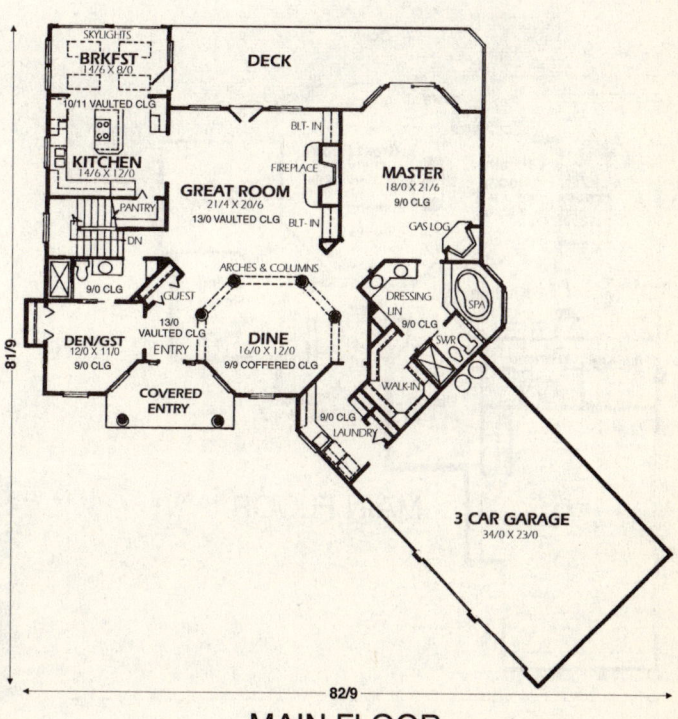

BEDRM 3 14/6 x 16/6
BEDRM 2 16/4 x 13/4
COVERED PATIO
WET BAR
FIRE PLACE
FAMILY 20/6 x 24/0
HOBBY RM 14/0 x 15/6
UTILITY ROOM
STORAGE
ENTERTAINMENT
EXERCISE ROOM

MAIN FLOOR

SKYLIGHTS
BRKFST 14/6 x 8/0
DECK
10/11 VAULTED CLG
KITCHEN 14/6 x 12/0
BLT-IN
FIREPLACE
GREAT ROOM 21/4 x 20/6
13/0 VAULTED CLG
BLT-IN
MASTER 18/0 x 21/6
9/0 CLG
GAS LOG
PANTRY
DN
9/0 CLG
ARCHES & COLUMNS
DRESSING 9/0 CLG
SPA
DEN/GST 12/0 x 11/0
13/0 VAULTED CLG ENTRY
DINE 16/0 x 12/0
9/9 COFFERED CLG
SWR
WALK-IN
9/0 CLG
COVERED ENTRY
9/0 CLG LAUNDRY
3 CAR GARAGE 34/0 x 23/0

81/9
82/9

ORDER BLUEPRINTS ANYTIME!
CALL TOLL-FREE 1-888-626-2026

Plan SUN-3295

PRICES AND DETAILS ON PAGES 12-15

FIRST LOOK! 64 STUNNING NEW DESIGNS

Natural Beauty

- From its cedar and river-rock exterior that harmonizes with the landscape to interior spaces featuring wood floors and a stunning stone fireplace, this home's natural beauty is irresistible.
- The foyer leads to a sunken Great Room showcasing a two-way fireplace, which is shared with the adjacent family room. A towering window wall affords views of the scenery beyond the wraparound rear deck. A screened porch is nearby.
- The open kitchen is fronted by an island cooktop and snack bar that extends to the family room. Granite countertops are an elegant touch. An adjoining sun room has a door leading to the deck.
- Upstairs, double doors usher you into the master suite. French windows open into the space above the Great Room. A cozy sitting area boasts access to a private balcony. The personal bath includes twin vanities, an oversized shower and a huge whirlpool tub set beneath greenhouse windows.
- Down the hall, two secondary bedrooms share a skylighted full bath.
- Floor-to-ceiling windows brighten a loft with a built-in bookcase.

Plan GA-9701

Bedrooms: 3+	**Baths:** 2 full, 2 half

Living Area:

Upper floor	1,393 sq. ft.
Main floor	2,148 sq. ft.
Sun room	79 sq. ft.
Total Living Area:	**3,620 sq. ft.**
Standard basement	2,227 sq. ft.
Garage and storage	762 sq. ft.
Screened porch	167 sq. ft.
Exterior Wall Framing:	2x6

Foundation Options:
Standard basement
(All plans can be built with your choice of foundation and framing. A generic conversion diagram is available. See order form.)

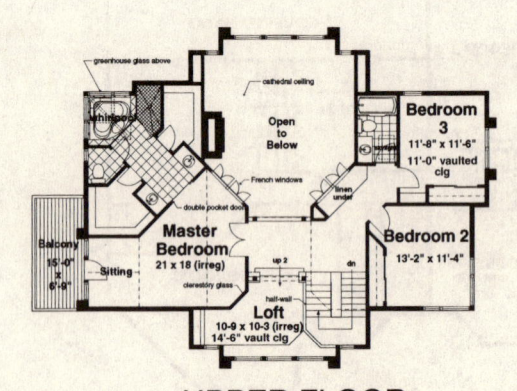

BLUEPRINT PRICE CODE: F

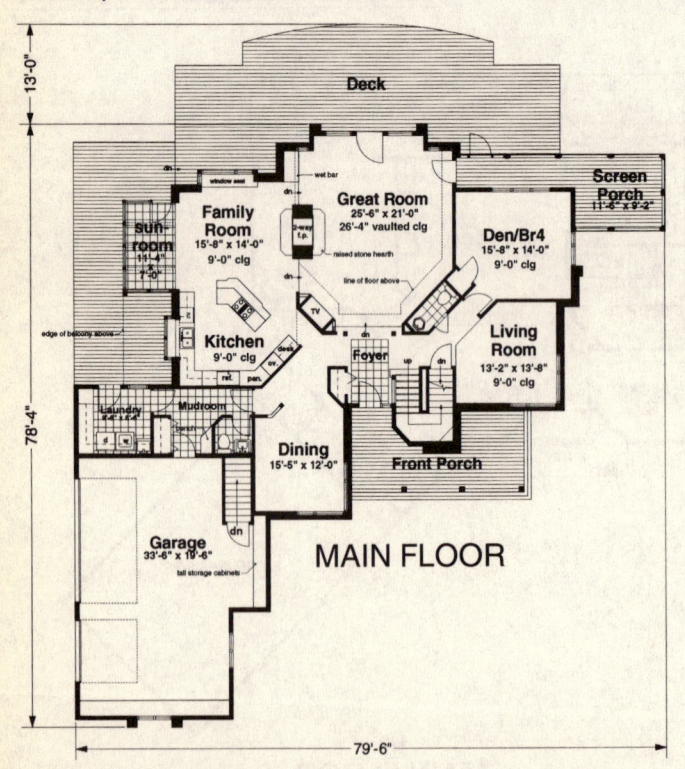

Plan GA-9701

ORDER BLUEPRINTS ANYTIME! CALL TOLL-FREE 1-888-626-2026

PRICES AND DETAILS ON PAGES 12-15

FIRST LOOK! 64 STUNNING NEW DESIGNS

Sublime Illumination

- Illuminated by sparkling window walls, this sublime Prairie-style home offers a perfect place for wonderful living.
- Divided into distinct sections, the main floor waits to greet guests. To the left lie the shared living areas, including a formal living and dining room and a spacious family room. The living room and family room each boast a handsome fireplace.
- Functional and attractive, the huge kitchen will be the source of all your gourmet meals. Its adjacent nook empties onto a beautiful back patio.
- The right side of the main floor is highlighted by an incredible master suite, where you'll find a large, L-shaped walk-in closet and a sizable private bath.
- The two additional bedrooms on the upper floor make room for your growing family. Each room is just a few steps from a full bath.
- A multipurpose recreation room on the lower level adds an extra option.

Plan R-4044-A	
Bedrooms: 3+	**Baths:** 2 full, 2 half
Living Area:	
Upper floor	589 sq. ft.
Main floor	2,296 sq. ft.
Partial daylight basement	742 sq. ft.
Total Living Area:	**3,627 sq. ft.**
Garage	957 sq. ft.
Exterior Wall Framing:	2x6
Foundation Options:	
Partial daylight basement	

(All plans can be built with your choice of foundation and framing. A generic conversion diagram is available. See order form.)

BLUEPRINT PRICE CODE: F

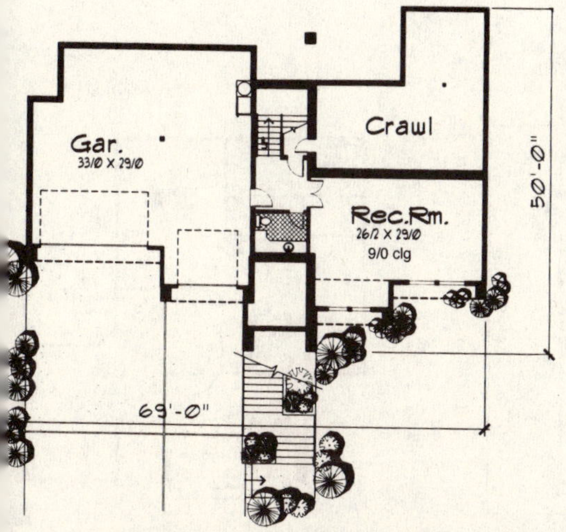

DAYLIGHT BASEMENT

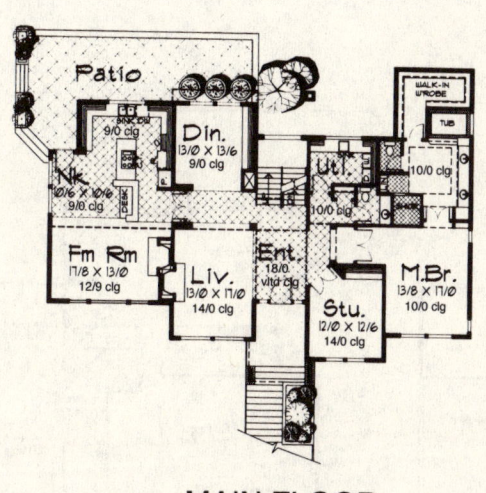

MAIN FLOOR

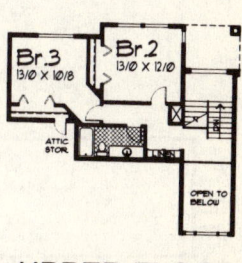

UPPER FLOOR

ORDER BLUEPRINTS ANYTIME!
CALL TOLL-FREE 1-888-626-2026

Plan R-4044-A

PRICES AND DETAILS ON PAGES 12-15

FIRST LOOK! 64 STUNNING NEW DESIGNS

Hillside Perch

- A tastefully striking exterior and spectacular interior views characterize this lovely hillside home.
- A balcony overlooks the foyer, which is graced by a 17-ft. vaulted ceiling and a skylight that brightens the stairway.
- The formal living room and dining room share an 11-ft., 8-in. vaulted ceiling. Elegant French doors in the dining room lead to the wraparound deck and are accented by a transom window above.
- An island cooktop links the kitchen to other casual living areas, including a sunny breakfast nook and a large family room with a fireplace.
- A large bay window fills the den with natural sunlight.
- Unless otherwise noted, all main-floor rooms are topped by 9-ft. ceilings.
- Upstairs, the master suite features a luxurious tub, an oversized shower, dual sinks and a walk-in closet.
- Two secondary bedrooms boast private vanities and walk-in closets; they share a skylighted bath.
- A fourth bedroom, a full bath and a large recreation room with a fireplace are found in the daylight basement.

Plan CDG-4020

Bedrooms: 4+	Baths: 3½
Living Area:	
Upper floor	1,248 sq. ft.
Main floor	1,457 sq. ft.
Daylight basement	1,136 sq. ft.
Total Living Area:	**3,841 sq. ft.**
Garage	647 sq. ft.
Exterior Wall Framing:	2x6 |//
Foundation Options:	

Daylight basement
(All plans can be built with your choice of foundation and framing. A generic conversion diagram is available. See order form.)

BLUEPRINT PRICE CODE: F

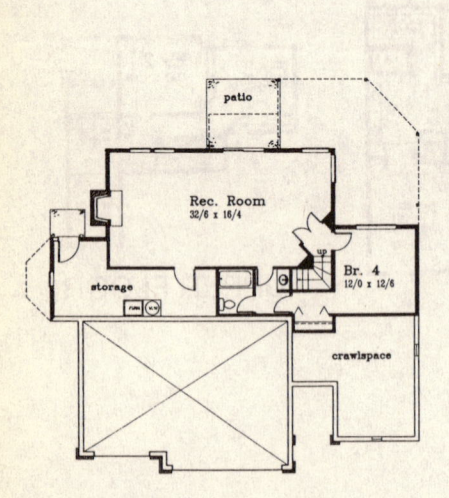

DAYLIGHT BASEMENT 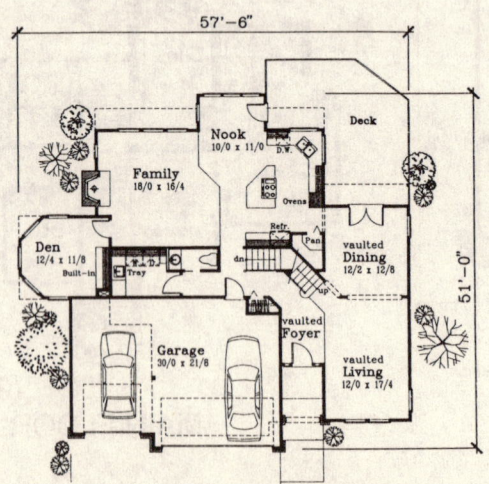   **MAIN FLOOR** 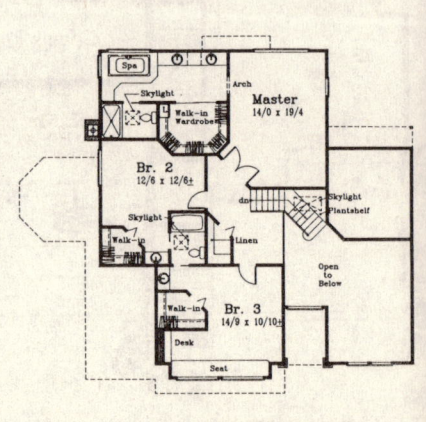   **UPPER FLOOR**

ORDER BLUEPRINTS ANYTIME! CALL TOLL-FREE 1-888-626-2026

Plan CDG-4020

PRICES AND DETAILS ON PAGES 12-15

FIRST LOOK! 64 STUNNING NEW DESIGNS

Upstairs, Downstairs

- This home's convenient, two-story floor plan creates a center of communal activity above, a haven for individual pursuits below.
- The main floor of this European-style retreat is anchored by a large family room with an inviting fireplace. Next to this locus of activity is a stunning kitchen—a gourmet's dream, complete with a work island and a roomy eating nook that accesses a covered deck.
- The master suite has its own private access to a sun deck. A whirlpool tub, a separate shower and a walk-in closet adorn the spacious master bath.
- The lower level of this home invites leisure and recreation. A large den with a fireplace suggests quiet evenings with a book or drinks with friends. The oversized garage with a workbench and a nearby storage room would make an ideal workshop. The recreation room offers endless possibilities.

Plan WH-9333	
Bedrooms: 4+	**Baths:** 3
Living Area:	
Main floor	2,187 sq. ft.
Daylight basement	1,505 sq. ft.
Total Living Area:	**3,692 sq. ft.**
Garage and work area	612 sq. ft.
Storage	203 sq. ft.
Exterior Wall Framing:	2x6
Foundation Options:	
Daylight basement	
(All plans can be built with your choice of foundation and framing. A generic conversion diagram is available. See order form.)	
BLUEPRINT PRICE CODE:	**F**

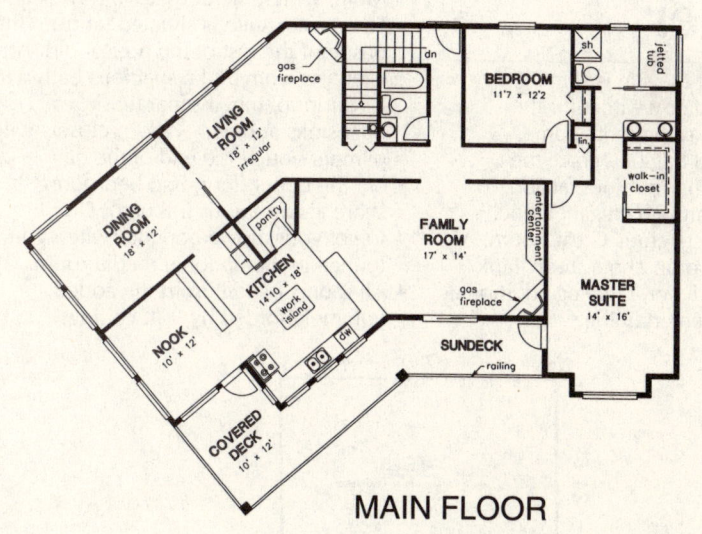

MAIN FLOOR

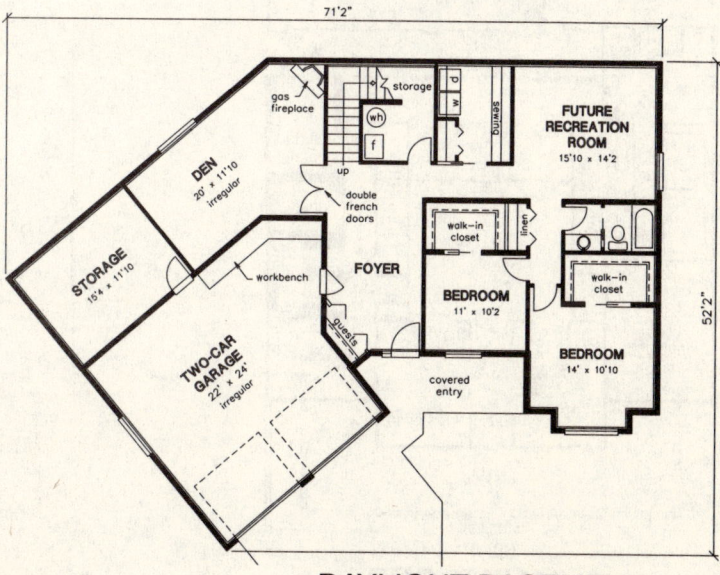

DAYLIGHT BASEMENT

ORDER BLUEPRINTS ANYTIME!
CALL TOLL-FREE 1-888-626-2026

Plan WH-9333

PRICES AND DETAILS
ON PAGES 12-15

FIRST LOOK! 64 STUNNING NEW DESIGNS

Always Fair Weather

- Whether or not the sun is shining, there's always fair weather for the owners of this exceptional home.
- Both porch and balcony grace the symmetry of a harmonious facade.
- Usher guests through elegant French doors into the spacious Great Room. A formal dining room and a study flank the 19-ft.-high foyer, creating additional backdrops for entertaining.
- A convenient eating bar separates the kitchen from the cheery breakfast room, which includes a window seat.
- The master suite is situated far from the bustle of the rest of the household. An exercise room and a spacious bath with a whirlpool tub, a separate shower, dual sinks and two walk-in closets will pamper you at the end of the day.
- On the upper floor, two bedrooms share a sumptuous full bath. Don't forget your movie popcorn when you lounge in the optional media room.
- All rooms benefit from the added volume afforded by 9-ft. ceilings.

Plan NBV-13496

Bedrooms: 3+	Baths: 2½
Living Area:	
Upper floor	1,233 sq. ft.
Main floor	2,473 sq. ft.
Total Living Area:	**3,706 sq. ft.**
Detached garage	912 sq. ft.
Exterior Wall Framing:	2x4

Foundation Options:

Crawlspace
Slab
(All plans can be built with your choice of foundation and framing. A generic conversion diagram is available. See order form.)

BLUEPRINT PRICE CODE: F

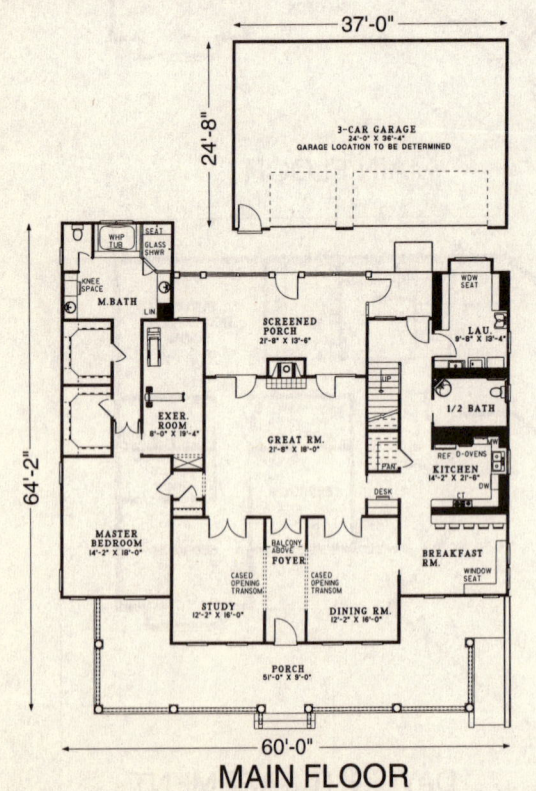

MAIN FLOOR

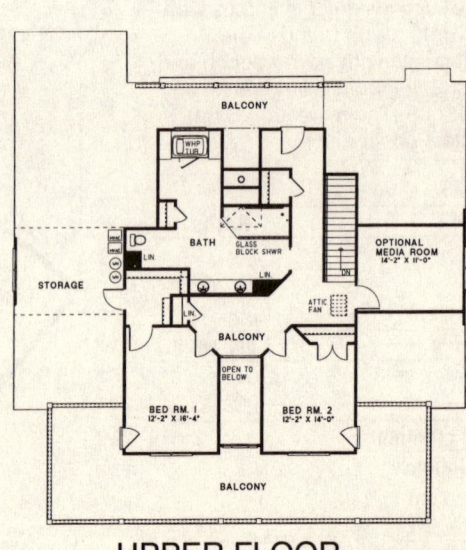

UPPER FLOOR

ORDER BLUEPRINTS ANYTIME!
CALL TOLL-FREE 1-888-626-2026

Plan NBV-13496

PRICES AND DETAILS ON PAGES 12-15

178

FIRST LOOK! 64 STUNNING NEW DESIGNS

Pastoral Pleasures

- From the front porch of this traditional southern country home, you can almost see bluegrass waving in the paddocks.
- The 16½-ft. vaulted foyer welcomes you. Stroll into the formal living room, which shares a see-through fireplace with the master suite, or find the dining room, an ideal setting for elegant meals.
- The kitchen is roomy and efficient, with a large center island, a snack bar and a built-in desk. This work space opens to the sun room and the hearth room.
- The master suite flows into the study or out to its own patio. The bath features an oversized walk-in closet, a whirlpool tub and a sit-down shower.
- Unless otherwise specified, all main-floor rooms include 9-ft. ceilings.
- Around the upstairs balcony, you'll find three bedrooms with charming window seats. They share two full baths. Roomy 10-ft. ceilings enhance the upper floor.

Plan NBV-14396

Bedrooms: 4+	Baths: 4½

Living Area:

Upper floor	1,089 sq. ft.
Main floor	2,465 sq. ft.
Sun room	186 sq. ft.
Total Living Area:	**3,740 sq. ft.**
Bonus room	497 sq. ft.
Garage	912 sq. ft.

Exterior Wall Framing: 2x4

Foundation Options:
Crawlspace
Slab

All plans can be built with your choice of foundation and framing. A generic conversion diagram is available. See order form.

BLUEPRINT PRICE CODE: F

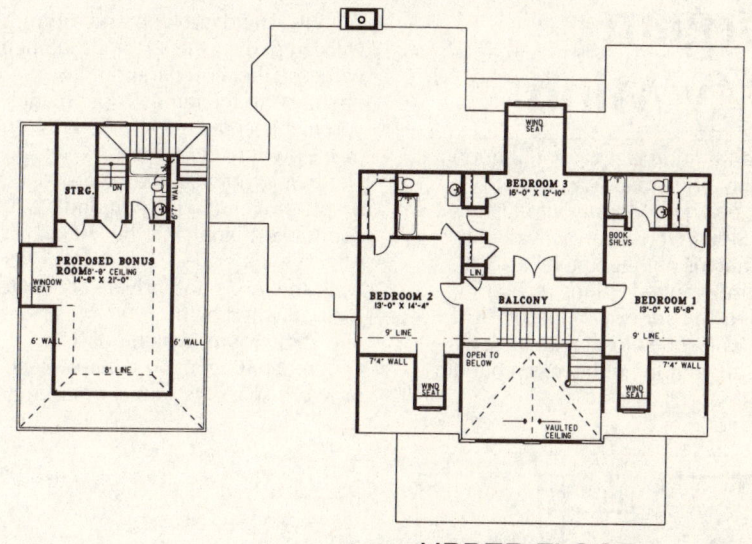

UPPER FLOOR

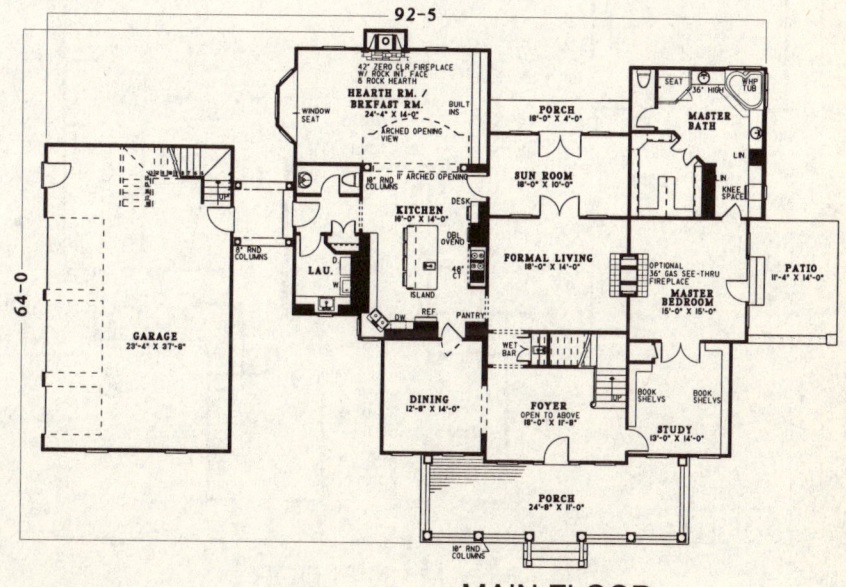

MAIN FLOOR

ORDER BLUEPRINTS ANYTIME!
CALL TOLL-FREE 1-888-626-2026

Plan NBV-14396

PRICES AND DETAILS ON PAGES 12-15

FIRST LOOK! 64 STUNNING NEW DESIGNS

Georgian on My Mind

- Updated tradition is what you'll find in this stately brick manor home.
- At day's end, cocoon in your master retreat. Slough those cares away in the bath, which is highlighted by a 13-ft., 9-in. barrel-vaulted ceiling. Linger in the seated shower or whirlpool. An elegant wardrobe closet with built-ins holds it all, and the utility room handles the chores.
- With its island cooktop and roomy walk-in pantry, the spacious kitchen will ease meal preparation. Its openness to the family room means you can keep an eye on the kids while they unwind after school.
- The living room shares a two-sided fireplace with the kitchen and overlooks a lanai and the backyard.
- All three upper-floor bedrooms offer walk-in closets and private access to their attached baths.
- The game room, which boasts a coffered ceiling and a window seat, provides space for family amusements.

Plan KY-3750	
Bedrooms: 4+	**Baths:** 3 full, 2 half
Living Area:	
Upper floor	1,284 sq. ft.
Main floor	2,466 sq. ft.
Total Living Area:	**3,750 sq. ft.**
Garage	549 sq. ft.
Exterior Wall Framing:	2x4
Foundation Options:	
Slab	

(All plans can be built with your choice of foundation and framing. A generic conversion diagram is available. See order form.)

BLUEPRINT PRICE CODE: F

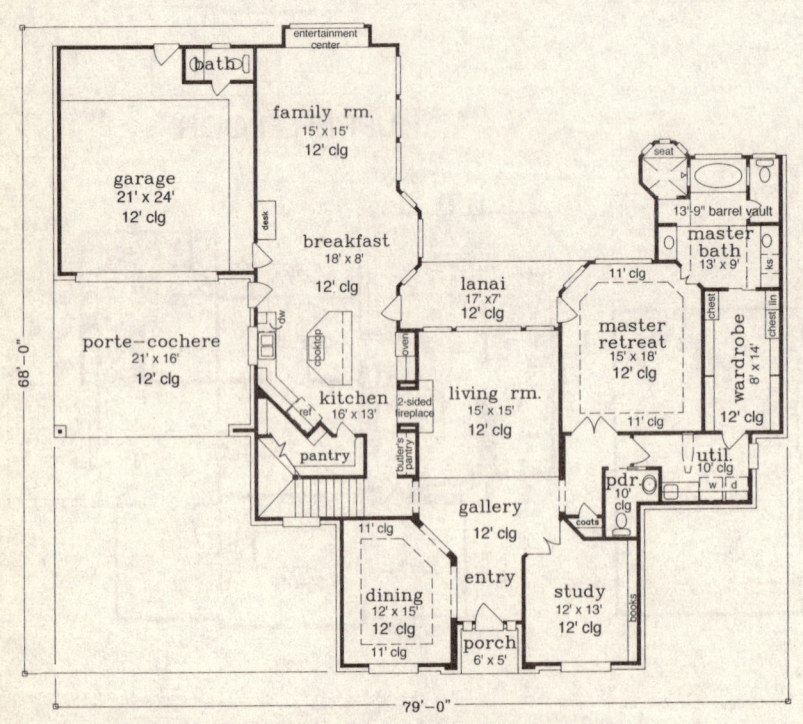

MAIN FLOOR

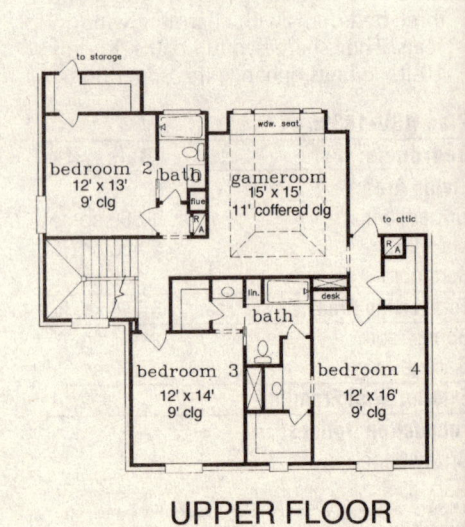

UPPER FLOOR

ORDER BLUEPRINTS ANYTIME! CALL TOLL-FREE 1-888-626-2026

Plan KY-3750

PRICES AND DETAILS ON PAGES 12-15

FIRST LOOK! 64 STUNNING NEW DESIGNS

Appealing Details

- Extra details give this home its winning appeal. A stucco and brick exterior and dramatic windows add a touch of Europe to your everyday life.
- Step from the foyer directly into the spacious living room, then continue out to a porch at the back of the home.
- An intimate space at the front of the design could be used as a home office, a den or a quiet study/computer room.
- The efficient kitchen features an island cooktop, a snack counter and easy access to the sun-filled dining nook.
- The family room at the rear of the home includes a fireplace and French doors leading to the porch.
- The master suite has its own fireplace, two walk-in closets and a roomy bath with dual sinks, a private toilet and a garden tub.
- Two bedrooms share two full baths on the upper floor, as well as a lovely balcony that overlooks the backyard. Growing families also have the option of expanding into the bonus room.

Plan HDS-99-348

Bedrooms: 3+	**Baths:** 3½
Living Area:	
Upper floor	842 sq. ft.
Main floor	2,517 sq. ft.
Bonus room	573 sq. ft.
Total Living Area:	**3,932 sq. ft.**
Garage	517 sq. ft.
Exterior Wall Framing:	8-in. concrete block

Foundation Options:
Slab
(All plans can be built with your choice of foundation and framing. A generic conversion diagram is available. See order form.)

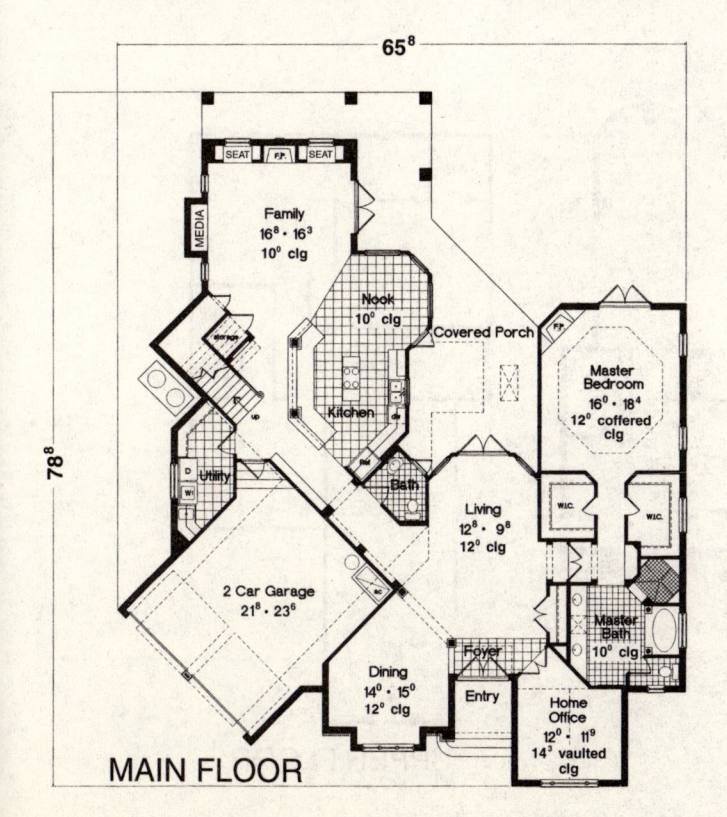

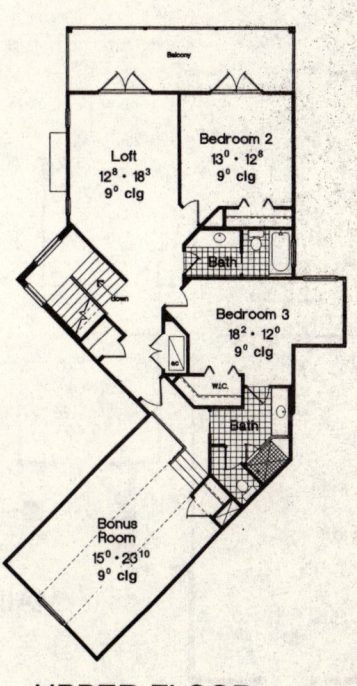

BLUEPRINT PRICE CODE: F

MAIN FLOOR

UPPER FLOOR

ORDER BLUEPRINTS ANYTIME!
CALL TOLL-FREE 1-888-626-2026

Plan HDS-99-348

PRICES AND DETAILS
ON PAGES 12-15

FIRST LOOK! 64 STUNNING NEW DESIGNS

It's All Here!

- A classic stone and stucco exterior, a dynamic multi-gable roofline and multiple columns give this dream home instant curbside appeal.
- Separate living, dining, study and family rooms provide a wealth of common space on the main floor.
- The spacious kitchen features a large island workspace, a walk-in pantry and an inviting breakfast area.
- The cozy family room adjoining the kitchen is ideal for fireside relaxation or intimate conversation, while the living room and dining room welcome more formal entertaining.
- The extravagant master bedroom features two walk-in closets and a dazzling whirlpool tub.
- The covered rear porch is accessible from the living room, master bedroom and breakfast nook, making it an integral part of the home during the warmer months.
- Upstairs, three additional bedrooms and a bonus room provide ample space for family and guests.
- An expansive three-car garage allows for extra storage and hobby space.

Plan HDS-99-299

Bedrooms: 4+	**Baths:** 4
Living Area:	
Upper floor	1,415 sq. ft.
Main floor	2,677 sq. ft.
Total Living Area:	**4,092 sq. ft.**
Garage	734 sq. ft.
Exterior Wall Framing:	8-in concrete block

Foundation Options:
Slab
(All plans can be built with your choice of foundation and framing. A generic conversion diagram is available. See order form.)

BLUEPRINT PRICE CODE: G

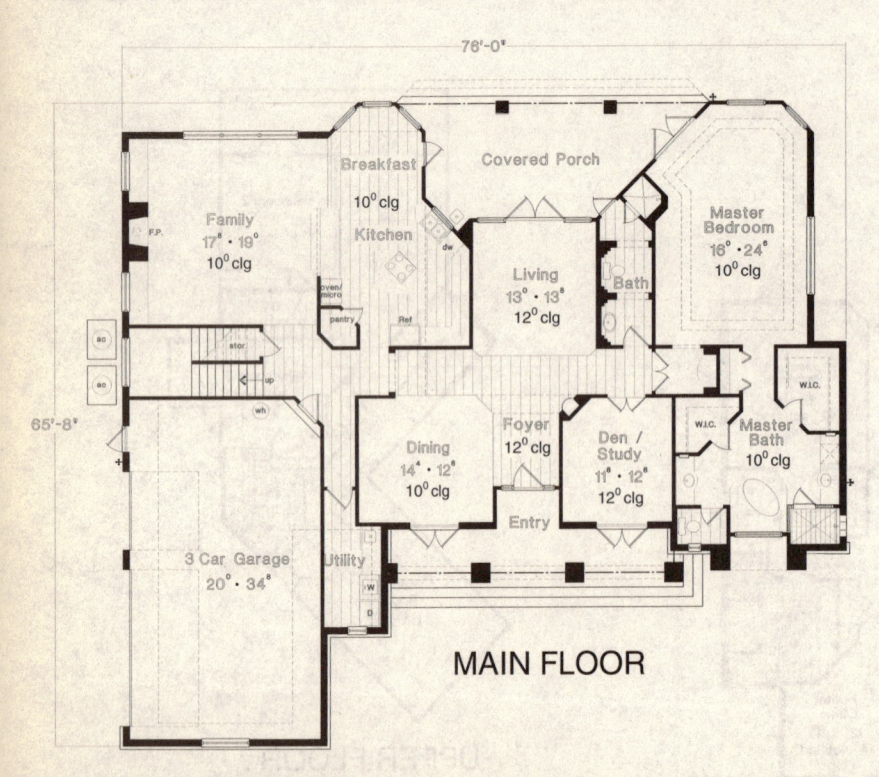

MAIN FLOOR

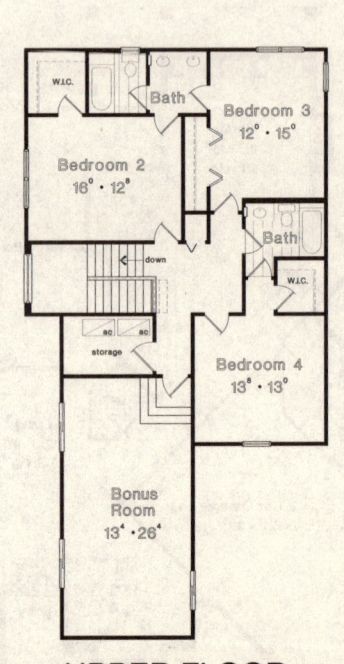

UPPER FLOOR

Plan HDS-99-299

FIRST LOOK! 64 STUNNING NEW DESIGNS

Old-World Sophistication

- Enjoy the finest of old-world style in this magnificent home's open and ornately detailed spaces.
- The impressive grand foyer is open to the second-floor gallery loft, creating an immediate impression of spaciousness.
- The central, two-story living room is anchored by a fireplace and features French doors out to the rear veranda.
- Spend private time with family in the leisure room. It includes its own cozy fireplace, veranda access and easy accessibility to the kitchen.
- The master suite's stepped ceiling makes your private haven especially distinctive. Two walk-in closets and an adjoining bath with a private toilet, a bidet, double sinks and a whirlpool tub provide the extra touches you desire.
- Your guests will be impressed by the upper-floor suite, which boasts a private bath and access to a covered deck.

Plan SG-6656

Bedrooms: 4+	**Baths:** 3½
Living Area:	
Upper floor	1,079 sq. ft.
Main floor	3,027 sq. ft.
Total Living Area:	**4,106 sq. ft.**
Standard basement	3,027 sq. ft.
Garage	802 sq. ft.
Exterior Wall Framing:	2x6
Foundation Options:	
Standard basement	
Slab	
(All plans can be built with your choice of foundation and framing. A generic conversion diagram is available. See order form.)	
BLUEPRINT PRICE CODE:	**G**

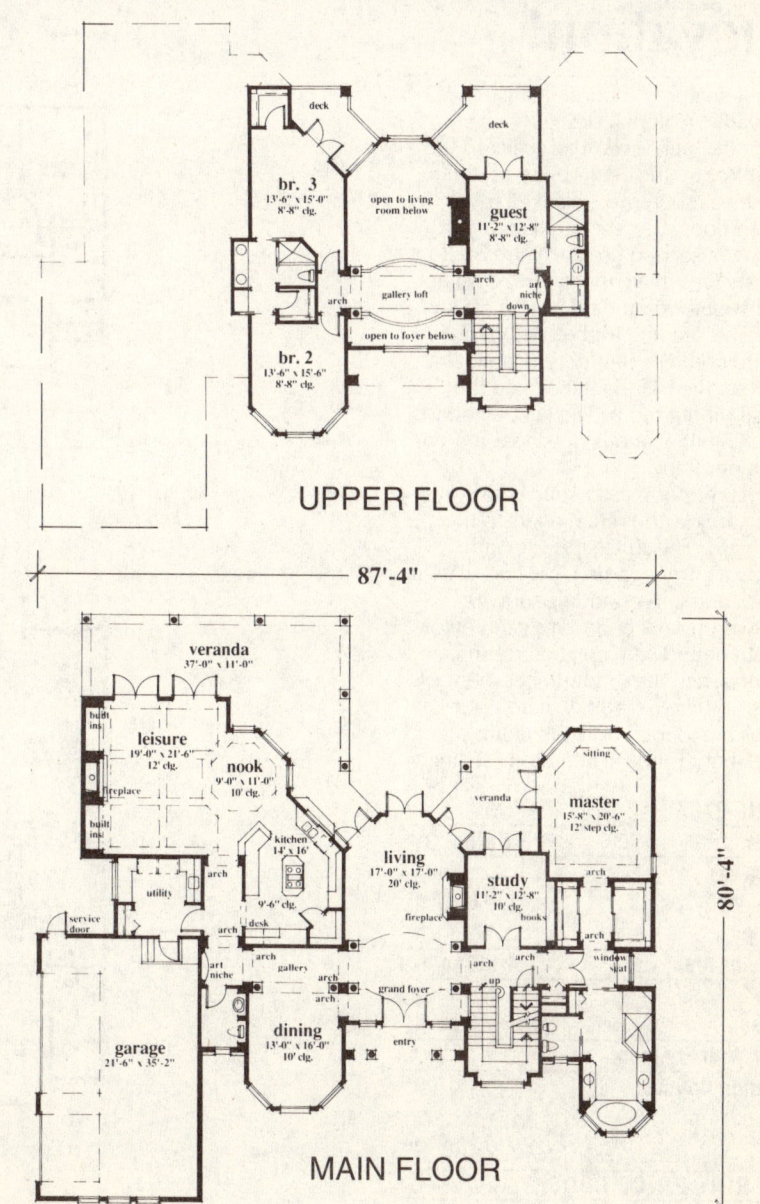

UPPER FLOOR

MAIN FLOOR

ORDER BLUEPRINTS ANYTIME!
CALL TOLL-FREE 1-888-626-2026

Plan SG-6656

Prices and details
ON PAGES 12-15

183

FIRST LOOK! 64 STUNNING NEW DESIGNS

Innovation!

- Unique features abound in this innovative Colonial design.
- The 20-ft.-high foyer leads back to the Great Room, the centerpiece of which is an elegant fireplace flanked by French doors to a sheltered courtyard.
- Nearby, a second fireplace and built-in bookshelves make the family room an ideal spot for casual relaxation. It, too, has doors leading to the courtyard.
- A handy butler's pantry is located between the island kitchen and the formal dining room. The kitchen boasts a 20-ft. ceiling and is open to a loft on the upper floor.
- The main-floor master suite boasts a sitting area with French doors to the courtyard. The suite's private bath flaunts a corner garden tub, two walk-in closets and a freestanding shower.
- The two upstairs bedrooms each enjoy a private bath. The recreation room can be converted into a fourth bedroom.
- Unless otherwise noted, main-floor rooms are topped by 10-ft. ceilings, and upper-floor rooms feature 9-ft. ceilings.

Plan SUL-2767

Bedrooms: 3+	Baths: 3½
Living Area:	
Upper floor	1,350 sq. ft.
Main floor	2,762 sq. ft.
Total Living Area:	**4,112 sq. ft.**
Garage	415 sq. ft.
Storage	approx. 56 sq. ft.
Exterior Wall Framing:	2x4

Foundation Options:
Slab
(All plans can be built with your choice of foundation and framing. A generic conversion diagram is available. See order form.)

BLUEPRINT PRICE CODE: G

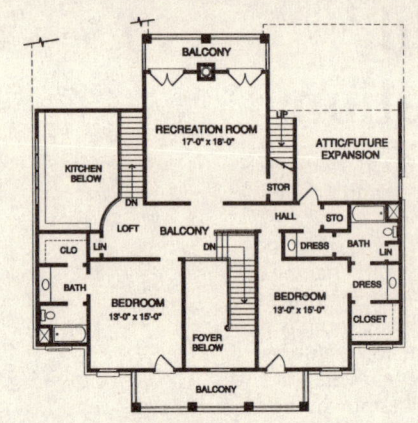

UPPER FLOOR

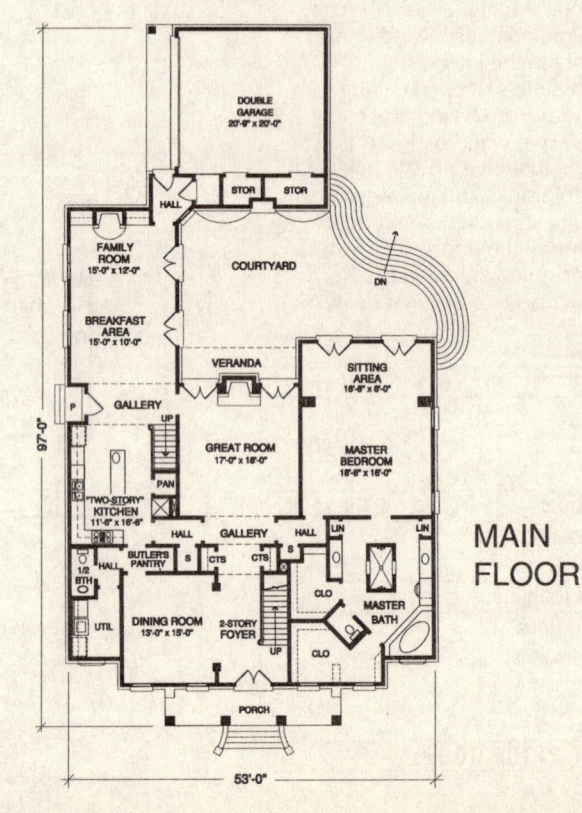

MAIN FLOOR

Plan SUL-2767

FIRST LOOK! 64 STUNNING NEW DESIGNS

Countryside Harmony

- Relax on the porch of this charming two-story design and revel in the natural harmony provided by the surrounding countryside.
- Stone and stucco give the home a classic appeal; keystones and lintels add a touch of elegance.
- Inside, guests are greeted by the dramatic 21½-ft.-high, tray-ceilinged foyer. Flanking the foyer are the formal dining and living rooms.
- The island kitchen features a sizable pantry and a computer center to store all your time-tested recipes. A serving bar holds snacks for the bay-windowed nook or the huge family room.
- Lit by flames from its cozy fireplace, the enchanting family room is the perfect spot for spending warm nights with loved ones. Its 19-ft.-high ceiling adds to the open feel.
- Upstairs, you'll find an 11-ft., 10-in. tray ceiling in the master bedroom, a 9-ft., 10-in. tray ceiling in the sitting room and a 12-ft., 2-in. vaulted ceiling in the master bath.
- The two bedrooms on the left side of the upper floor share a nice full bath. The remaining bedroom has its own bath, a walk-in closet, a built-in desk and an 11-ft. ceiling.
- Unless otherwise noted, all main- and upper-floor rooms feature 9-ft. ceilings.

Plan FB-5661-CLAI

Bedrooms: 4+	**Baths:** 4½

Living Area:
Upper floor	2,067 sq. ft.
Main floor	2,058 sq. ft.
Total Living Area:	**4,125 sq. ft.**
Daylight basement	2,058 sq. ft.
Garage	819 sq. ft.

Exterior Wall Framing: 2x4

Foundation Options:
Daylight basement
Crawlspace
(All plans can be built with your choice of foundation and framing. A generic conversion diagram is available. See order form.)

BLUEPRINT PRICE CODE: G

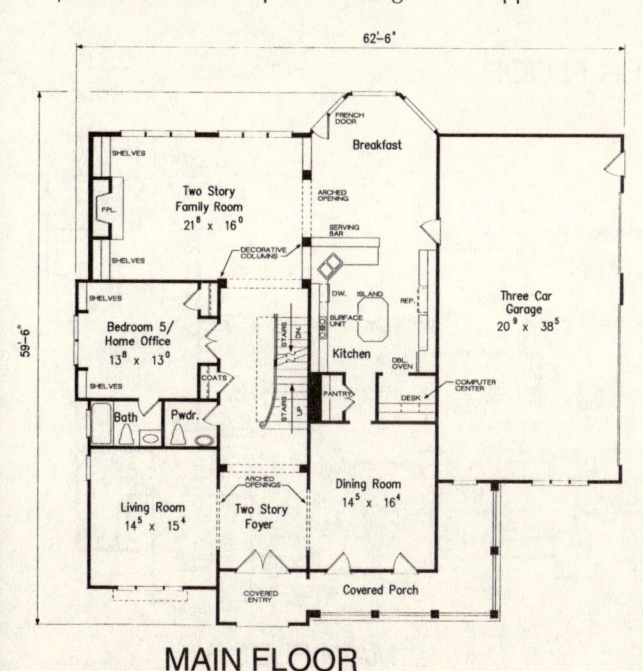

MAIN FLOOR

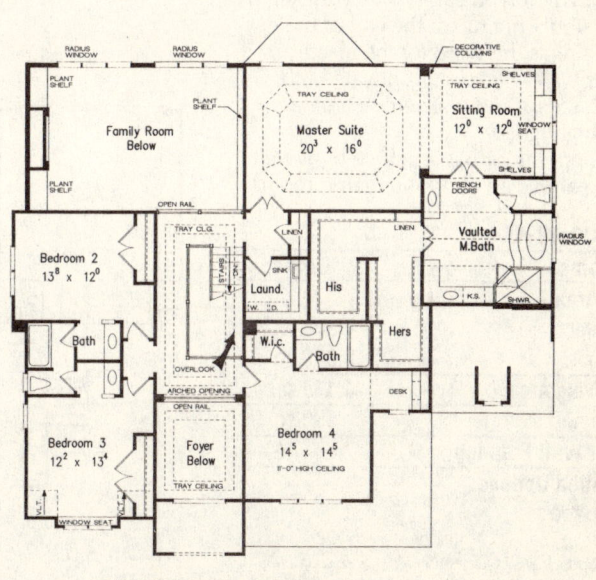

UPPER FLOOR

ORDER BLUEPRINTS ANYTIME!
CALL TOLL-FREE 1-888-626-2026

Plan FB-5661-CLAI

PRICES AND DETAILS ON PAGES 12-15

185

FIRST LOOK! 64 STUNNING NEW DESIGNS

Elegant Outdoor Fun!

- A trio of outdoor-oriented areas bring a sunny splendor to the back of this elegant home.
- Stucco and brick combine to create a clean, attractive exterior.
- Inside, interesting living spaces stretch throughout the home. From the foyer, the formal living room and dining room present themselves; each is entered through a grand arch.
- Waiting for all your holiday events is the spacious family room, which boasts a fireplace and access to a gorgeous screened room. From there, you can enter a stunning trellis-covered patio.
- The third outdoor area is the sizable deck, where you can soothe yourself in the bubbly hot tub at the end of the day.
- Amazing is the word for the master suite; walk-in closets, a private bath, deck access and an exercise area are key highlights.
- The upper floor has a unique light well rising above an enormous game room.

Plan BOD-41-1A

Bedrooms: 4+	Baths: 4
Living Area:	
Upper floor	868 sq. ft.
Main floor	3,328 sq. ft.
Total Living Area:	**4,196 sq. ft.**
Garage and storage	598 sq. ft.
Exterior Wall Framing:	2x4

Foundation Options:
Crawlspace
Slab
(All plans can be built with your choice of foundation and framing. A generic conversion diagram is available. See order form.)

BLUEPRINT PRICE CODE: G

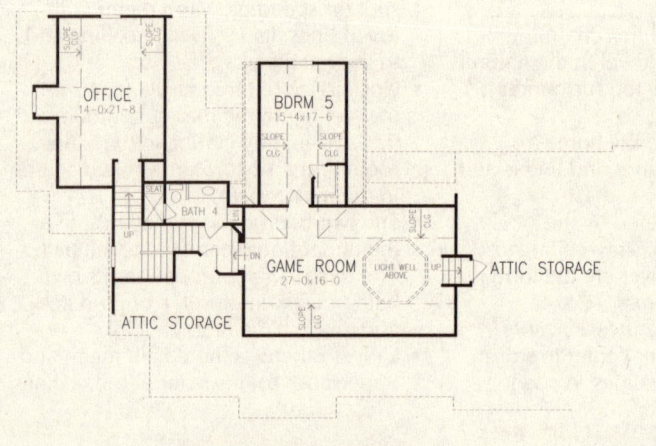

UPPER FLOOR

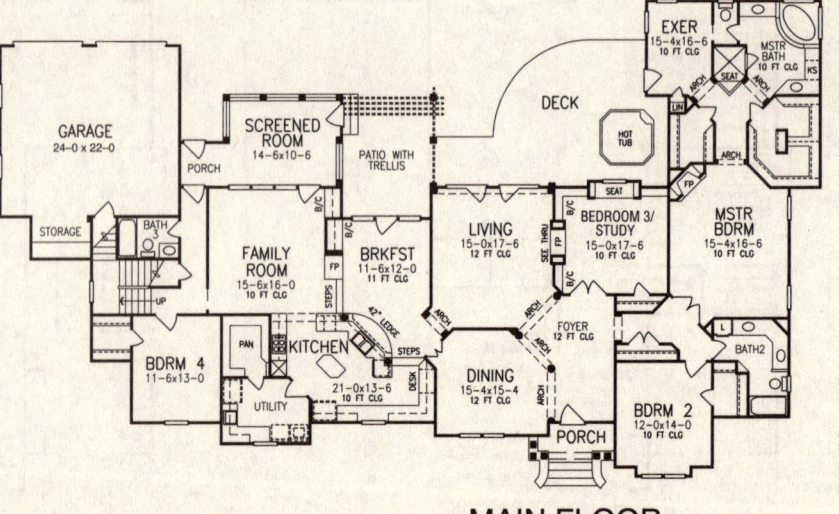

MAIN FLOOR

WIDTH 108'-2"
DEPTH 61'-6"

ORDER BLUEPRINTS ANYTIME!
CALL TOLL-FREE 1-888-626-2026

Plan BOD-41-1A

PRICES AND DETAILS ON PAGES 12-15

FIRST LOOK! 64 STUNNING NEW DESIGNS

Tradition and Comfort

- Tradition and comfort meet in this spacious home. An impressive facade prepares you and your guests for the breathtaking 18-ft.-high foyer.
- The kitchen features the convenience of an island/snack bar and a breakfast room for informal meals with your family. On special occasions, gather everyone around the table in the formal dining room.
- Visitors will love the first-floor guest suite so much, they may never want to leave!
- You'll enjoy basking in the glow of the fireplace in the family room. A 13-ft., 9-in. cathedral ceiling adds a nice openness. The adjoining study allows private time, while the living room offers a smaller, cozier common area.
- The master suite features a sitting room, a huge walk-in closet and a private bath with a whirlpool tub. Three more bedrooms and a sitting area provide comfort for your entire family.

Plan OH-302	
Bedrooms: 5+	**Baths:** 3½
Living Area:	
Upper floor	1,986 sq. ft.
Main floor	2,230 sq. ft.
Total Living Area:	**4,216 sq. ft.**
Standard basement	2,230 sq. ft.
Garage	660 sq. ft.
Exterior Wall Framing:	2x4
Foundation Options:	
Standard basement	
(All plans can be built with your choice of foundation and framing. A generic conversion diagram is available. See order form.)	
BLUEPRINT PRICE CODE:	**G**

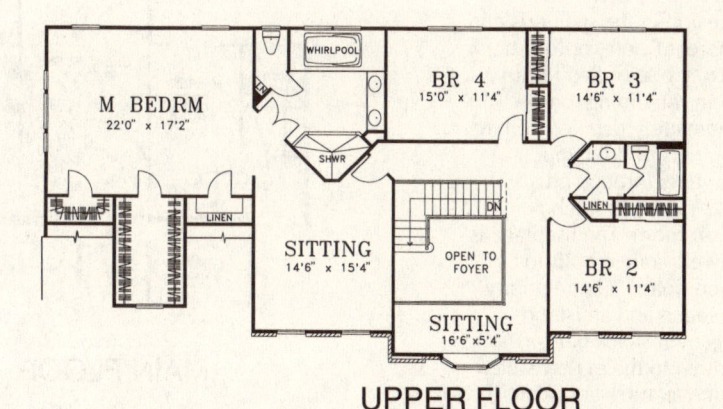

UPPER FLOOR

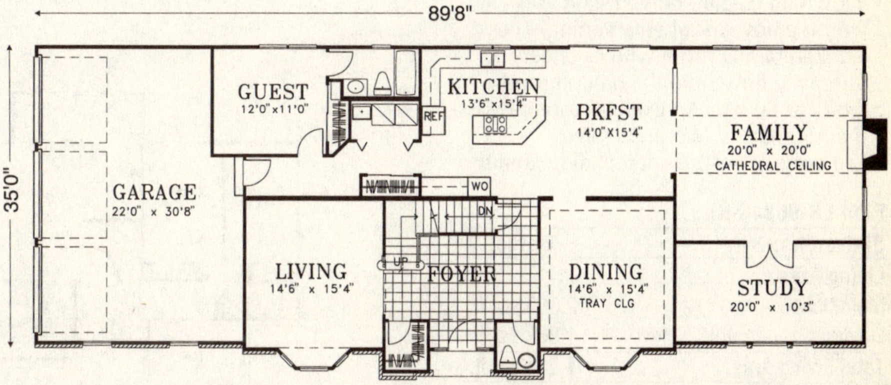

MAIN FLOOR

ORDER BLUEPRINTS ANYTIME!
CALL TOLL-FREE 1-888-626-2026

Plan OH-302

PRICES AND DETAILS
ON PAGES 12-15

FIRST LOOK! 64 STUNNING NEW DESIGNS

Savoir Faire

- Savor life's pleasures in this charming French chateau of your own.
- Spend hours fireside in the spacious and sun-drenched Great Room, or lose track of time in the cozy book-filled library.
- Just steps away in the dining room you'll note an elegantly detailed ceiling and built-in cabinets to hold your heirloom china. Pass through an attached butler's pantry to the bow-windowed hearth room. The fireplace is accented with well-crafted built-ins.
- The open kitchen boasts a large pantry, lots of counter space and an island cooktop with its own snack bar.
- Double doors open to the master suite. This superb space features abundant closets and a well-lighted whirlpool bath with dual sinks and a private toilet.
- Down an elegant curved staircase, you'll enjoy casual entertaining. The sunken family room with its cheery fireplace flows into the billiard room and casual bar. An exercise room, two bedrooms and two impressive storerooms ensure additional flexibility.

Plan LS-96846-KL

Bedrooms: 3+	Baths: 3
Living Area:	
Main floor	2,367 sq. ft.
Daylight basement	1,867 sq. ft.
Total Living Area:	**4,234 sq. ft.**
Three-season porch	255 sq. ft.
Garage and storage	782 sq. ft.
Exterior Wall Framing:	2x6
Foundation Options:	
Daylight basement	
(All plans can be built with your choice of foundation and framing. A generic conversion diagram is available. See order form.)	
BLUEPRINT PRICE CODE:	**G**

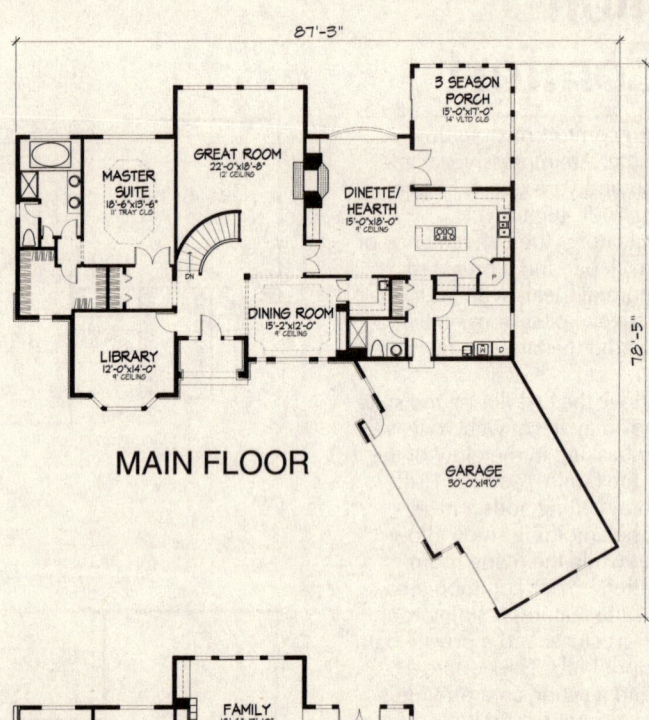

MAIN FLOOR

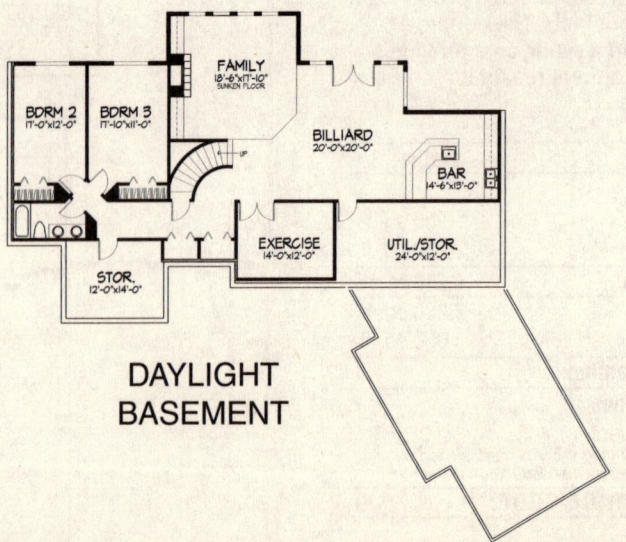

DAYLIGHT BASEMENT

ORDER BLUEPRINTS ANYTIME!
CALL TOLL-FREE 1-888-626-2026

Plan LS-96846-KL

PRICES AND DETAILS ON PAGES 12-15

FIRST LOOK! 64 STUNNING NEW DESIGNS

Classic Lines

- Four noble columns give this grand two-story home its classic appeal.
- The crisp stucco exterior is highlighted by a covered entry and a covered balcony. These twin outdoor areas are sure to add an extra dose of sunshine to your life.
- Inside, the foyer leads visitors straight into the central living room. A convenient wet bar serves guests before they sample the gourmet fare you've laid out in the formal dining room.
- Memorable movie nights have a home in the family room, where a corner fireplace adds a cozy glow to the impressive media wall.
- Opening to a huge covered patio in back is the expansive master suite, which also features two walk-in closets and a deluxe private bath.
- The patio's summer kitchen comes in handy during your neighborhood's annual barbecue contest.
- You'll find four nice-sized bedrooms and two full baths on the upper floor, as well as a spacious bonus room.

Plan HDS-99-329

Bedrooms: 5+	**Baths:** 3 full, 2 half

Living Area:

Upper floor	1,351 sq. ft.
Main floor	2,755 sq. ft.
Bonus room	569 sq. ft.
Total Living Area	**4,675 sq. ft.**
Garage	864 sq. ft.
Exterior Wall Framing:	2x6

Foundation Options:
Slab
(All plans can be built with your choice of foundation and framing. A generic conversion diagram is available. See order form.)

BLUEPRINT PRICE CODE: H

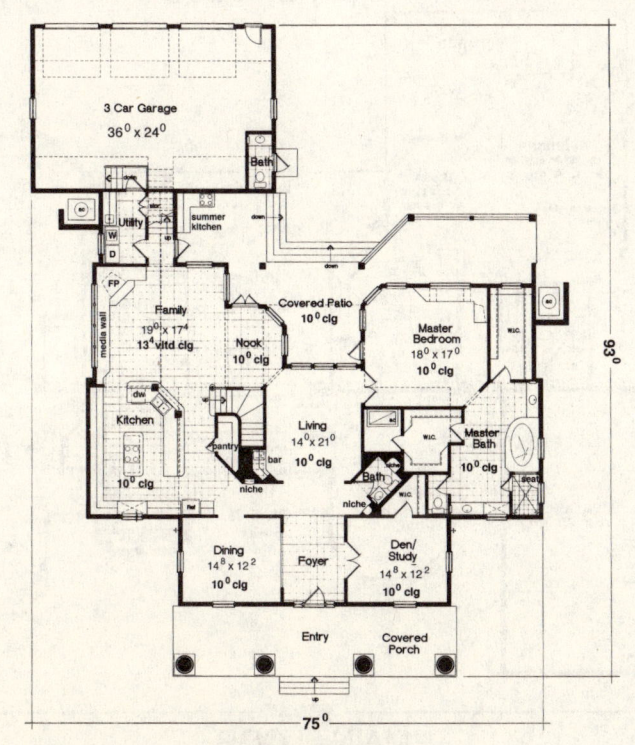

MAIN FLOOR

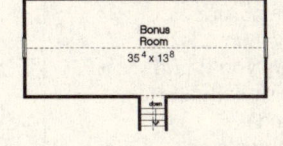

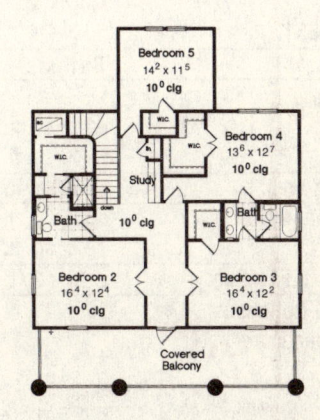

UPPER FLOOR

ORDER BLUEPRINTS ANYTIME!
CALL TOLL-FREE 1-888-626-2026

Plan HDS-99-329

PRICES AND DETAILS
ON PAGES 12-15

189

FIRST LOOK! 64 STUNNING NEW DESIGNS

Indulge Your Senses!

- This dramatic two-story home indulges all your senses with its long list of wonderful amenities!
- Brick, stucco and exquisite windows combine to create a beautiful exterior.
- In from the arched entry, guests step from the grand foyer into the two-story living room, which boasts a two-way fireplace that's shared with the adjacent study. Three sets of double doors access the rear covered veranda.
- A second great gathering spot is the leisure room, highlighted by a built-in entertainment center and three more sets of double doors to the outside.
- On the opposite end of the home is the elegant master suite, where you'll find two walk-in closets, a lavish bath and private access to the veranda.
- The upper floor contains three more bedrooms, two of which include French doors to their very own balconies.

Plan SG-6651

Bedrooms: 4+	**Baths:** 3½
Living Area:	
Upper floor	1,213 sq. ft.
Main floor	3,546 sq. ft.
Total Living Area:	**4,759 sq. ft.**
Standard basement	3,546 sq. ft.
Garage	822 sq. ft.
Exterior Wall Framing	2x6

Foundation Options:
Standard basement
Slab
(All plans can be built with your choice of foundation and framing. A generic conversion diagram is available. See order form.)

BLUEPRINT PRICE CODE: H

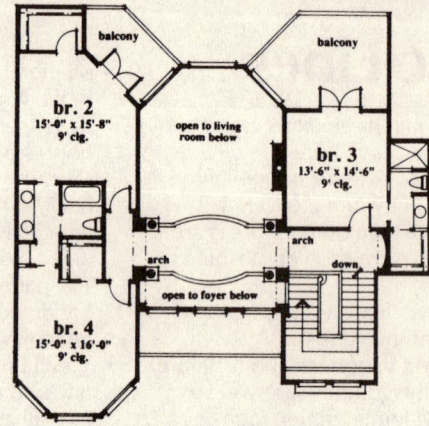

UPPER FLOOR

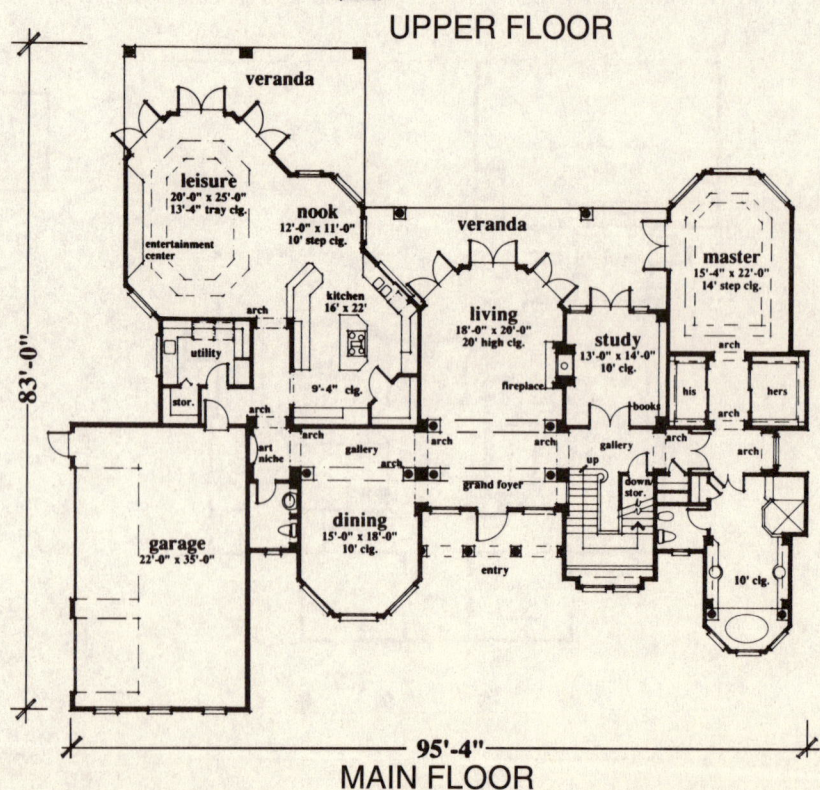

MAIN FLOOR

Plan SG-6651

FIRST LOOK! 64 STUNNING NEW DESIGNS

Work of Art

- Architecturally amazing and daringly dramatic, this breathtaking work of art will bring a world-class lifestyle to its lucky owners!
- Chateau styling abounds—including a steep hip roof, spire-topped towers, ornamental metal cresting and petite dormers.
- Inside, guests get a stunning welcome in the grand foyer. From here, the palatial floor plan unfolds before them.
- The reception hall teams with the dining hall to host all your black-tie affairs. Nearby, the island kitchen is aided by a unique herb garden and a butler's pantry. A charming secret door opens to the laundry room and a walk-in pantry.
- A pretty nature garden rests outside the grand suite, which offers his-and-hers closets and a sumptuous private bath.
- A family gathering hall, an outdoor grill, a relaxing veranda, a home office/workshop, a media room and a billiard room top a long list of the other great spaces to explore!

Plan HDS-99-283

Bedrooms: 3+ **Baths:** 5 full, 3 half

Living Area:

Upper floor	2,588 sq. ft.
Main floor	3,874 sq. ft.
Total Living Area:	**6,462 sq. ft.**
Garage	1,000 sq. ft.

Exterior Wall Framing:
2x6 and 8-in. concrete block

Foundation Options:
Slab
(All plans can be built with your choice of foundation and framing. A generic conversion diagram is available. See order form.)

BLUEPRINT PRICE CODE: I

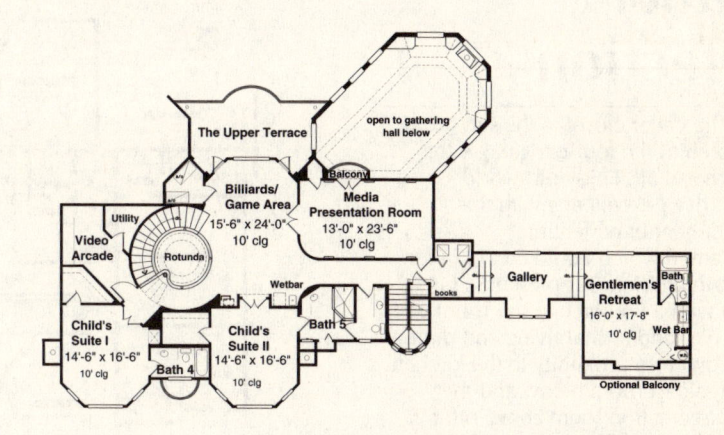

UPPER FLOOR

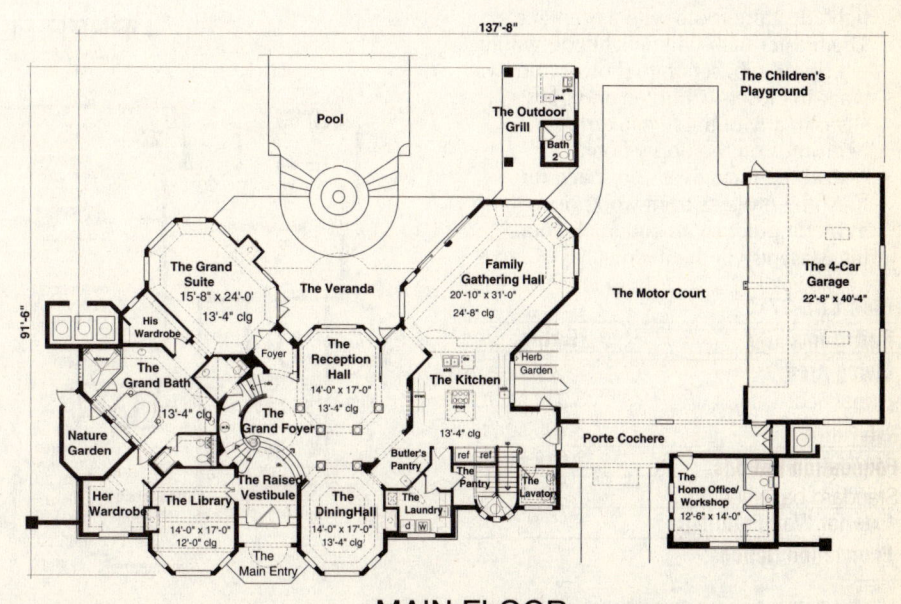

MAIN FLOOR

ORDER BLUEPRINTS ANYTIME!
CALL TOLL-FREE 1-888-626-2026

Plan HDS-99-283

PRICES AND DETAILS ON PAGES 12-15

191

FIRST LOOK! 64 STUNNING NEW DESIGNS

Palatial Perfection

- From the cedar closet to the sun room, the porch to the four-car garage, this home has it all. Enjoy old-world standards of excellence with this embodiment of perfection.
- Every amenity you could dream of for entertaining friends is present: a Great Room with a fireplace, a sun room with a wet bar, and formal living and dining rooms in close proximity to the kitchen.
- The breakfast room below and the roomy recreation room above offer ample space for family fun and intimate gatherings.
- The master bedroom features a well lighted sitting room with a fireplace. The master bath will delight you with its whirlpool tub, separate shower and two walk-in closets. Children and guests can sleep in any of the five luxurious bedrooms on the upper floor.
- A sizable office gives you space for finishing projects from work; or set it up as a computer room and track your investments via the internet.

Plan SUL-3710	
Bedrooms: 6+	**Baths:** 6½
Living Area:	
Upper floor	3,314 sq. ft.
Main floor	3,705 sq. ft.
Total Living Area:	**7,019 sq. ft.**
Garage	1,230 sq. ft.
Exterior Wall Framing:	2x4
Foundation Options:	
Slab	
(All plans can be built with your choice of foundation and framing. A generic conversion diagram is available. See order form.)	
BLUEPRINT PRICE CODE:	I

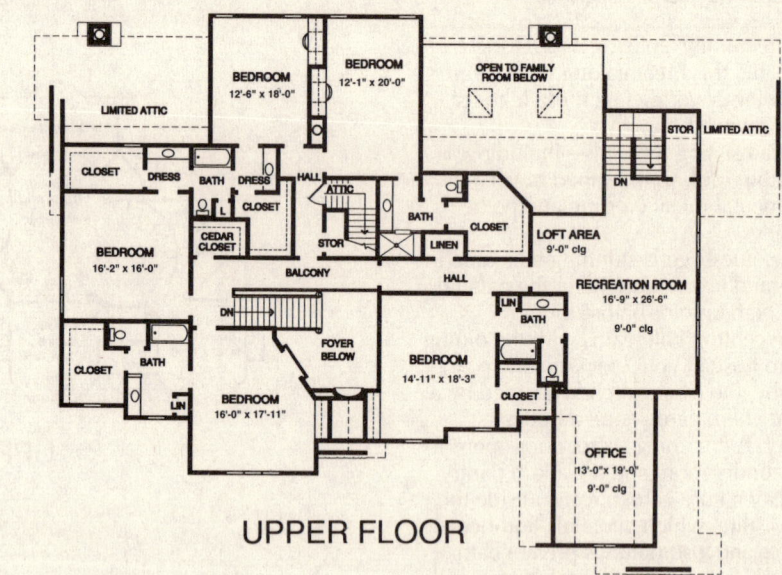

UPPER FLOOR

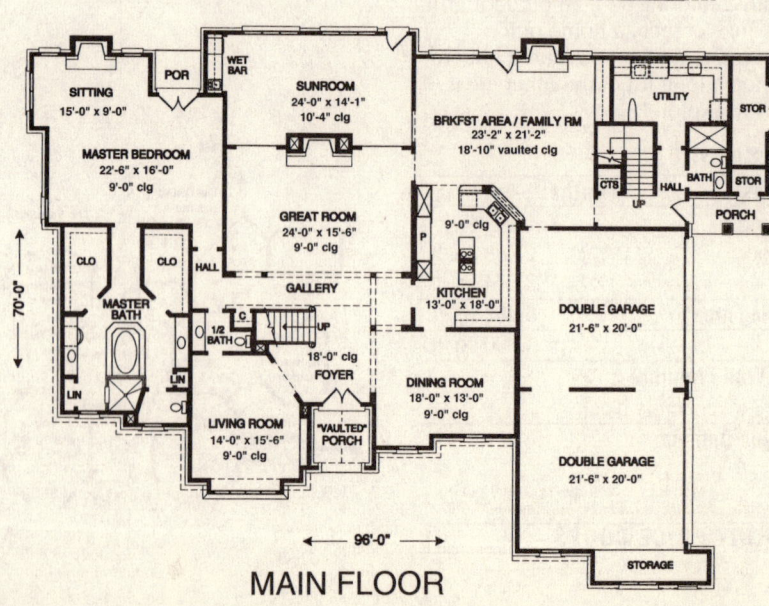

MAIN FLOOR

ORDER BLUEPRINTS ANYTIME!
CALL TOLL-FREE 1-888-626-2026

Plan SUL-3710

PRICES AND DETAILS ON PAGES 12-15

MORE WELL-APPOINTED HOMES

Stately Style

- Classic columns and half-round windows enhance the facade of this beautiful two-story home.
- The bright, sidelighted foyer offers views across a columned half-wall into the living room, which boasts a 17-ft. vaulted ceiling and a cozy fireplace.
- Decorative columns also flank the entrance to the formal dining room.
- Close by, the gourmet kitchen adjoins a charming breakfast nook. French doors set into a wall of windows open to a spacious backyard deck.
- The nearby sunken family room with a 17-ft. vaulted ceiling promises fun-filled evenings. Its amenities include a wet bar, a cheery fireplace and French doors to the deck.
- Adjacent to the family room, a swing suite with private bath access can be tailored to meet changing needs.
- Upstairs, the luxurious master bedroom features a 12-ft. vaulted ceiling and a quiet sitting room for private reflection in comfort. The master bath is enhanced by a walk-through closet, a platform tub and a dual-sink vanity.

Plan B-93019

Bedrooms: 4+	Baths: 3
Living Area:	
Upper floor	1,190 sq. ft.
Main floor	1,433 sq. ft.
Total Living Area:	**2,623 sq. ft.**
Standard basement	1,433 sq. ft.
Garage	450 sq. ft.
Exterior Wall Framing:	2x4
Foundation Options:	

Standard basement
(All plans can be built with your choice of foundation and framing. A generic conversion diagram is available. See order form.)

BLUEPRINT PRICE CODE: D

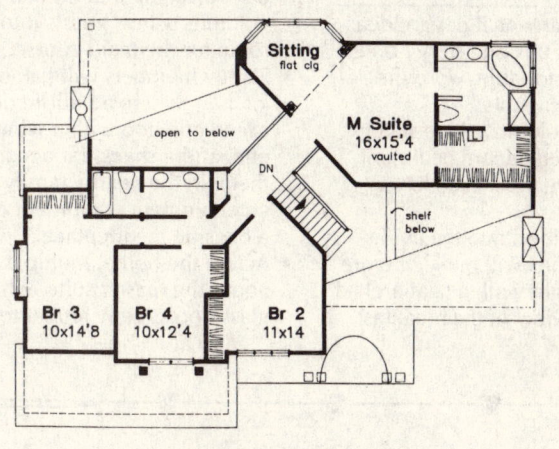

UPPER FLOOR

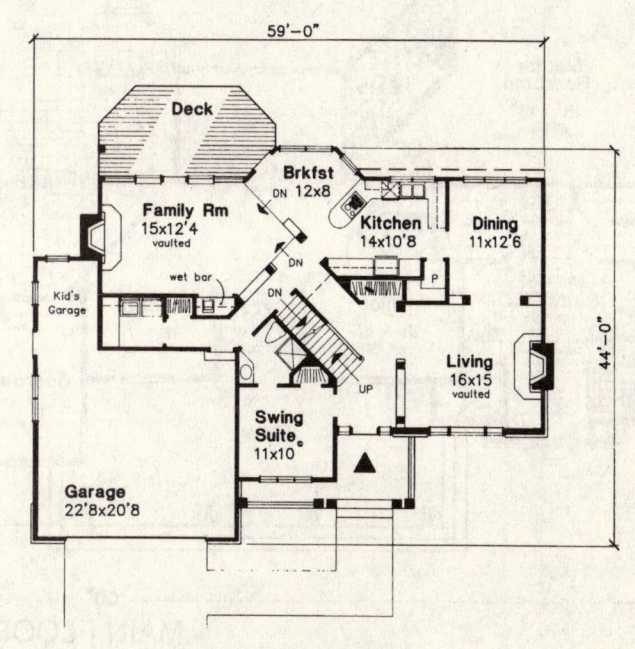

MAIN FLOOR

ORDER BLUEPRINTS ANYTIME!
CALL TOLL-FREE 1-888-626-2026

Plan B-93019

PRICES AND DETAILS
ON PAGES 12-15

Full of Ideas

- Because of the many neat design ideas found throughout this one-story home, it promises a comfortable, worry-free lifestyle for its occupants.
- Four handsome columns, three stately dormers and a pretty acorn pediment over the entry give the facade its distinguished air.
- Inside, the foyer flows into the living room, where friends will mingle before dinner. On the right wall, a neat arched cut-out allows a view of the breakfast nook and kitchen. After some pleasant discourse, an arch framed by two columns ushers guests into the dining room for the main course.
- Family members will gather often in the kitchen, where a built-in desk, an island cooktop with a wine rack on the end, and a snack bar accommodate them. In the nearby family room, entertainment equipment can be stored alongside the fireplace.
- Across the home, multiple plant shelves adorn the master suite, while sliding glass doors allow retreat to the porch.

Plan HDS-99-294

Bedrooms: 3+	**Baths:** 3
Living Area:	
Main floor	2,636 sq. ft.
Total Living Area:	**2,636 sq. ft.**
Garage	789 sq. ft.
Exterior Wall Framing:	2x4
Foundation Options:	
Slab	

(All plans can be built with your choice of foundation and framing. A generic conversion diagram is available. See order form.)

BLUEPRINT PRICE CODE: D

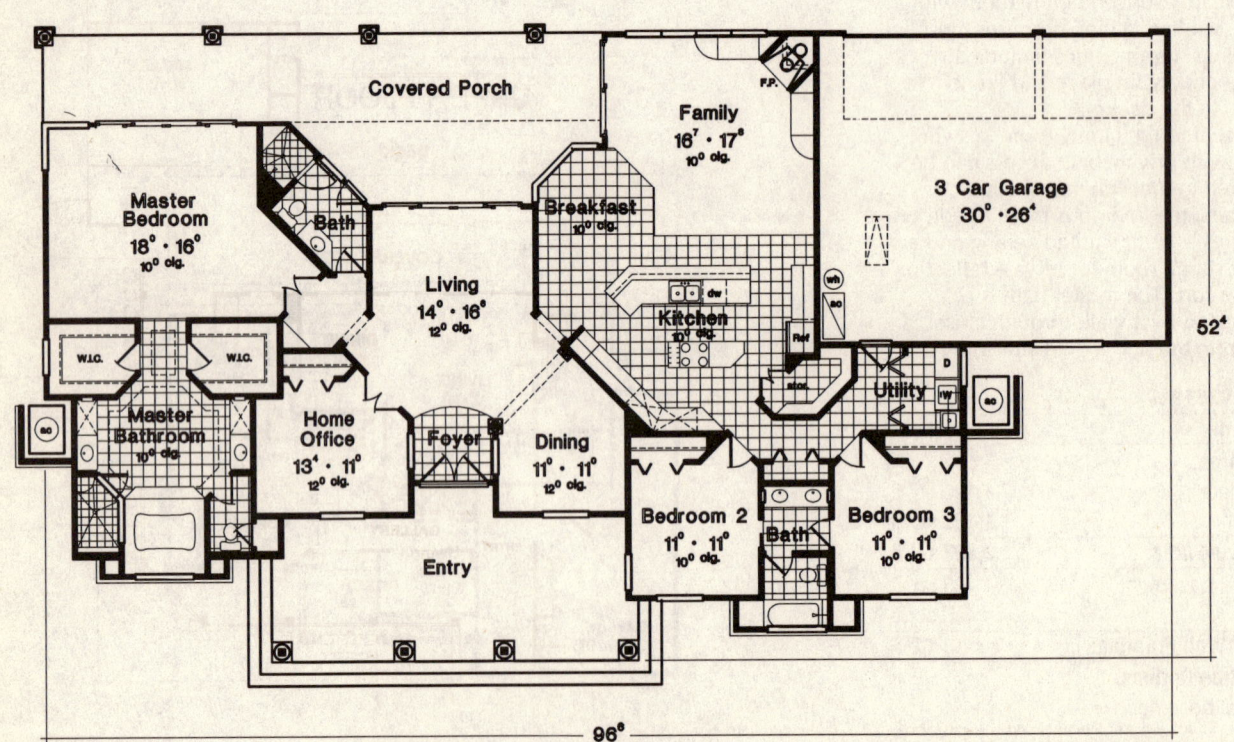

MAIN FLOOR

Plan HDS-99-294

Home at Last!

- Whether you're returning from a business trip or a personal vacation, you'll never get tired of coming home to this spectacular stucco delight.
- Breezy outdoor spaces parade around the home, starting with a nostalgic front porch and ending at a relaxing spa tub on a sprawling backyard deck.
- The spacious interior is bright and open. Past the entry, a gallery with French doors leads to the superb kitchen.
- The family can discuss the day's news over breakfast at the big snack bar or in the sunny bayed morning room.
- For activities of a larger scale, the living room offers an engaging fireplace, exciting views and enough space to house your entertainment equipment.
- A two-sided fireplace adds a romantic glow to the master bedroom and private sitting area. The elegant, skylighted master bath promises luxury for two!
- All main-floor rooms have 9-ft. ceilings.
- The upper-floor bedrooms are furnished with a shared bath and their own walk-in closets and sunny sitting spaces.

Plan DD-2617

Bedrooms: 4	Baths: 3
Living Area:	
Upper floor	609 sq. ft.
Main floor	2,034 sq. ft.
Total Living Area:	**2,643 sq. ft.**
Standard basement	2,034 sq. ft.
Garage and storage	544 sq. ft.
Exterior Wall Framing:	2x4

Foundation Options:
Standard basement
Crawlspace
Slab
(All plans can be built with your choice of foundation and framing. A generic conversion diagram is available. See order form.)

BLUEPRINT PRICE CODE: D

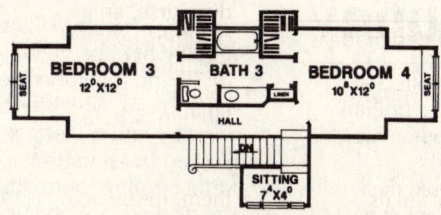

UPPER FLOOR

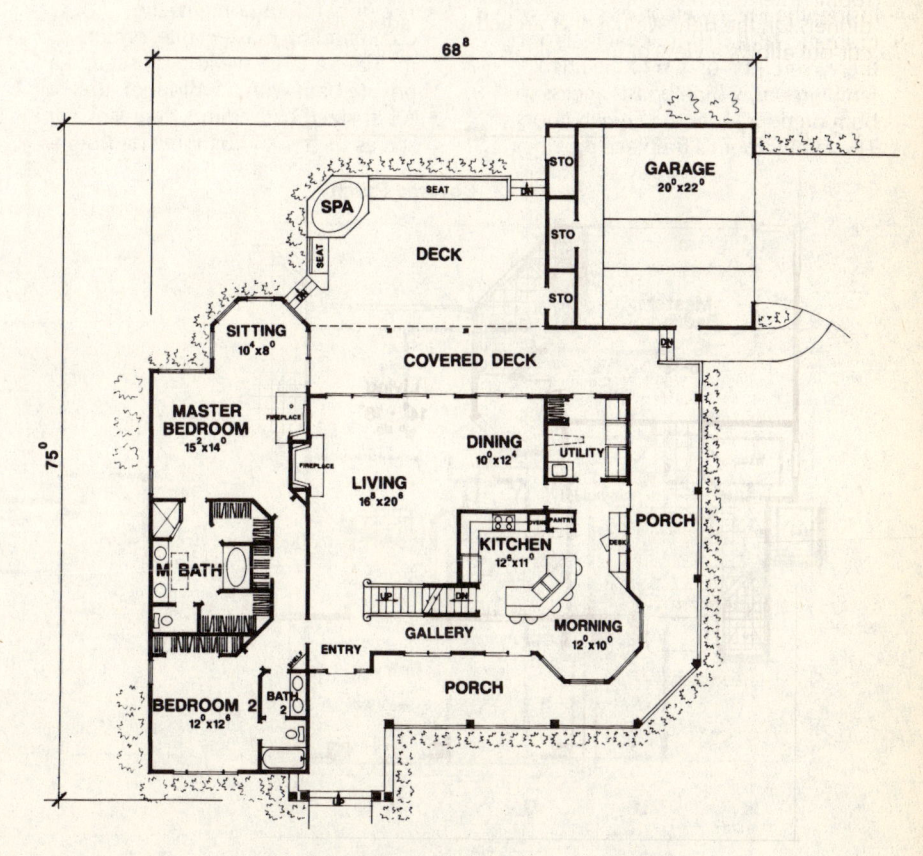

MAIN FLOOR

ORDER BLUEPRINTS ANYTIME!
CALL TOLL-FREE 1-888-626-2026

Plan DD-2617

PRICES AND DETAILS
ON PAGES 12-15

Bold and Sunny

- This bold two-story design offers an outstanding floor plan and a brilliant use of windows and outdoor areas to help bring in the sunshine!
- A large, wraparound covered deck in front and an equally spacious sun deck in back give you plenty of room to host a grand summertime barbecue.
- Inside, the foyer welcomes guests with a dramatic 16-ft., 10-in. ceiling. From there, you'll be drawn to the huge family room, which boasts access to both outdoor areas via French doors. The family room's fireplace provides warmth when the nights get chilly, and mood when the night is young.
- You'll find a second fireplace in the living room, which features a bay window and a 10-ft., 3-in. tray ceiling.
- Nestled between the nook and the formal dining room, the island kitchen stands ready for any occasion.
- A quiet study, which converts easily to a bedroom, completes the main floor.
- The upper floor contains the commanding master suite, which includes a large walk-in closet and a private bath with a whirlpool tub.
- A full-sized bath with a dual-sink vanity serves the remaining three bedrooms.

Plan IDG-2023	
Bedrooms: 4+	**Baths:** 2½
Living Area:	
Upper floor	1,179 sq. ft.
Main floor	1,464 sq. ft.
Total Living Area:	**2,643 sq. ft.**
Daylight basement	1,282 sq. ft.
Garage	506 sq. ft.
Exterior Wall Framing:	2x6

Foundation Options:
Daylight basement
(All plans can be built with your choice of foundation and framing. A generic conversion diagram is available. See order form.)

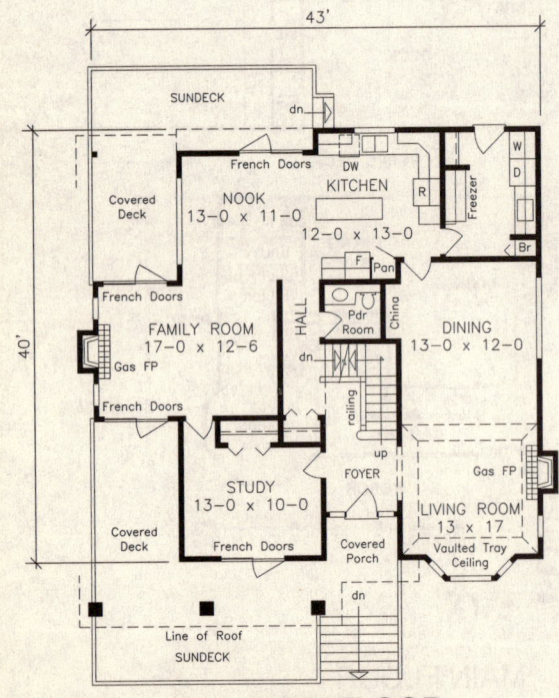

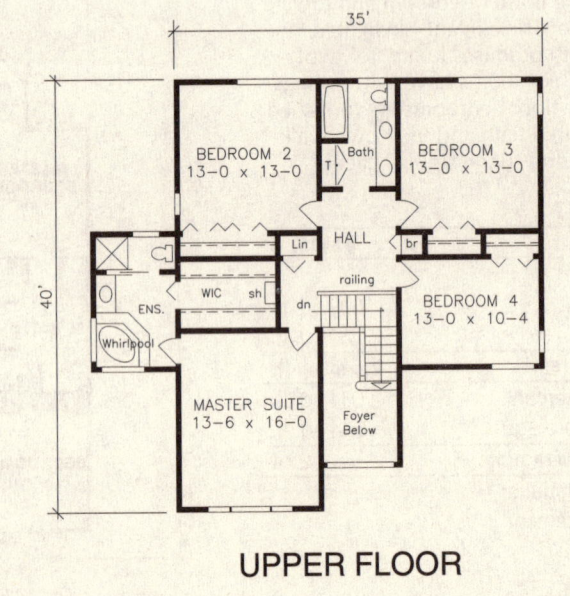

BLUEPRINT PRICE CODE: D

MAIN FLOOR

UPPER FLOOR

Plan IDG-2023

Balcony Bonus

- This home's stone facade and unique metal roof add appeal, while balconies at the front and rear are extra bonuses.
- Inside, the entry flows past a bookcase to the living room. A 20-ft. sloped ceiling soars over both rooms.
- In the living room, a warm fireplace and a neat media center topped by an attractive arch serve as fun diversions.
- The breakfast nook, which opens to a patio through a French door, shares a snack bar with the island kitchen. A pass-through between the kitchen and the dining room simplifies meals.
- Across the home, a bayed sitting area and an entertainment center make the master bedroom an exciting retreat. The master bath leads to a double walk-in closet, where shoe shelves and a bench make the most of the space.
- Unless otherwise mentioned, every main-floor room includes a 9-ft. ceiling.
- Upstairs, two bedrooms and a study, all with sloped 10-ft. ceilings, share a hall bath. The study has a private balcony, and the rear bedroom has its own deck.

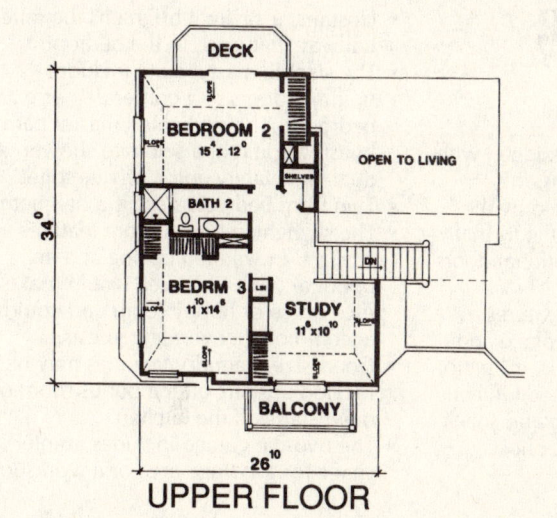

Plan DD-2703-1

Bedrooms: 3+	Baths: 2½

Living Area:

Upper floor	727 sq. ft.
Main floor	1,921 sq. ft.
Total Living Area:	**2,648 sq. ft.**
Standard basement	1,921 sq. ft.
Garage and storage	600 sq. ft.
Exterior Wall Framing:	2x4

Foundation Options:
Standard basement
Crawlspace
Slab

(All plans can be built with your choice of foundation and framing. A generic conversion diagram is available. See order form.)

BLUEPRINT PRICE CODE: D

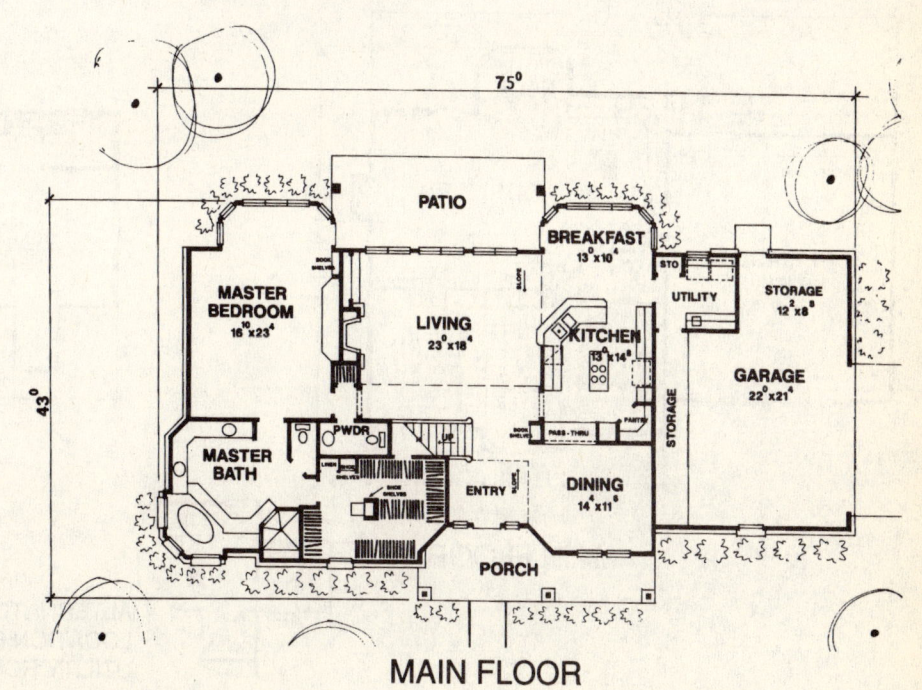

UPPER FLOOR

MAIN FLOOR

ORDER BLUEPRINTS ANYTIME!
CALL TOLL-FREE 1-888-626-2026

Plan DD-2703-1

PRICES AND DETAILS ON PAGES 12-15

Outstanding Options

- This terrific two-story was designed with oodles of outstanding options.
- The 17-ft.-high foyer is flanked by the columned dining room and the formal living room, which offers optional doors to the family room.
- The oversized family room features a built-in desk, an inviting fireplace and French-door access to a backyard patio.
- The focal point of the L-shaped kitchen is its versatile island cooktop and snack bar. The bay-windowed nook hosts casual meals.
- Upstairs, a skylight brightens the railed hallway that leads to the bedrooms.
- The sizable master suite includes optional doors to a corner den or extra bedroom. The skylighted master bath boasts a spa tub, a separate shower, a dual-sink vanity and a private toilet.
- Two front bedrooms share a hall bath.
- The skylighted bonus room features an 11-ft., 6-in. vaulted ceiling and an optional bath. This area would make a nice office or hobby room and could accommodate overnight guests.
- Good-sized laundry facilities may be located upstairs off the bonus room or downstairs off the kitchen.
- The two-car garage includes ample space for a storage area or a workshop.

Plan S-41693

Bedrooms: 3+	Baths: 2½-3½

Living Area:

Upper floor	1,087 sq. ft.
Main floor	1,164 sq. ft.
Bonus room	400 sq. ft.
Total Living Area:	**2,651 sq. ft.**
Basement	1,104 sq. ft.
Garage	644 sq. ft.
Exterior Wall Framing:	2x6

Foundation Options:

Daylight basement
Standard basement
Crawlspace
Slab

(All plans can be built with your choice of foundation and framing. A generic conversion diagram is available. See order form.)

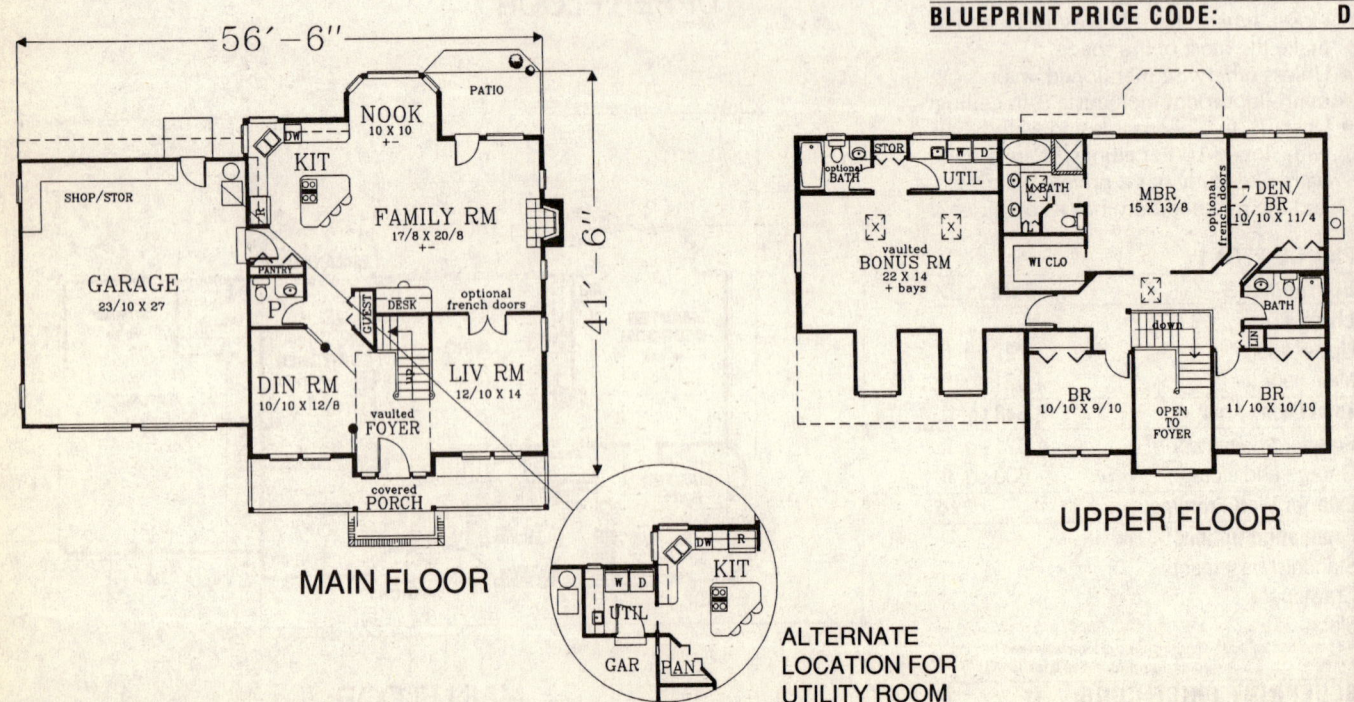

BLUEPRINT PRICE CODE: D

MAIN FLOOR

ALTERNATE LOCATION FOR UTILITY ROOM

UPPER FLOOR

Plan S-41693

Patio Living

- A well-executed floor plan sets this impeccable design apart from the ordinary. Rooms of various shapes are arranged to maintain openness and to take advantage of a wonderful patio.
- The granite-paved foyer is open to the large living room, which provides a terrific view of the covered patio.
- The octagonal dining room and den or study flank the foyer and also face the living room.
- The uniquely shaped family room, with a fireplace centered between a wall of built-ins, has a dynamic view of the outdoors and is open to the kitchen.
- The spacious kitchen has an island range, a pantry and an octagonal nook.
- All of the living areas are enhanced by 11-ft.-high volume ceilings.
- Two nicely placed bedrooms allow for privacy. They have 9-ft., 4-in. ceilings and share a full bath, which is also accessible from the patio.
- The master suite is a wing in itself. The bedroom boasts a fireplace, walls of glass and a 9-ft., 8-in. ceiling. The posh bath includes a whirlpool tub, a corner shower and separate dressing areas.

Plan HDS-99-137

Bedrooms: 3	Baths: 2½

Living Area:

Main floor	2,656 sq. ft.
Total Living Area:	**2,656 sq. ft.**
Garage	503 sq. ft.

Exterior Wall Framing:
2x4 and 8-in. concrete block

Foundation Options:
Slab
(All plans can be built with your choice of foundation and framing. A generic conversion diagram is available. See order form.)

BLUEPRINT PRICE CODE: D

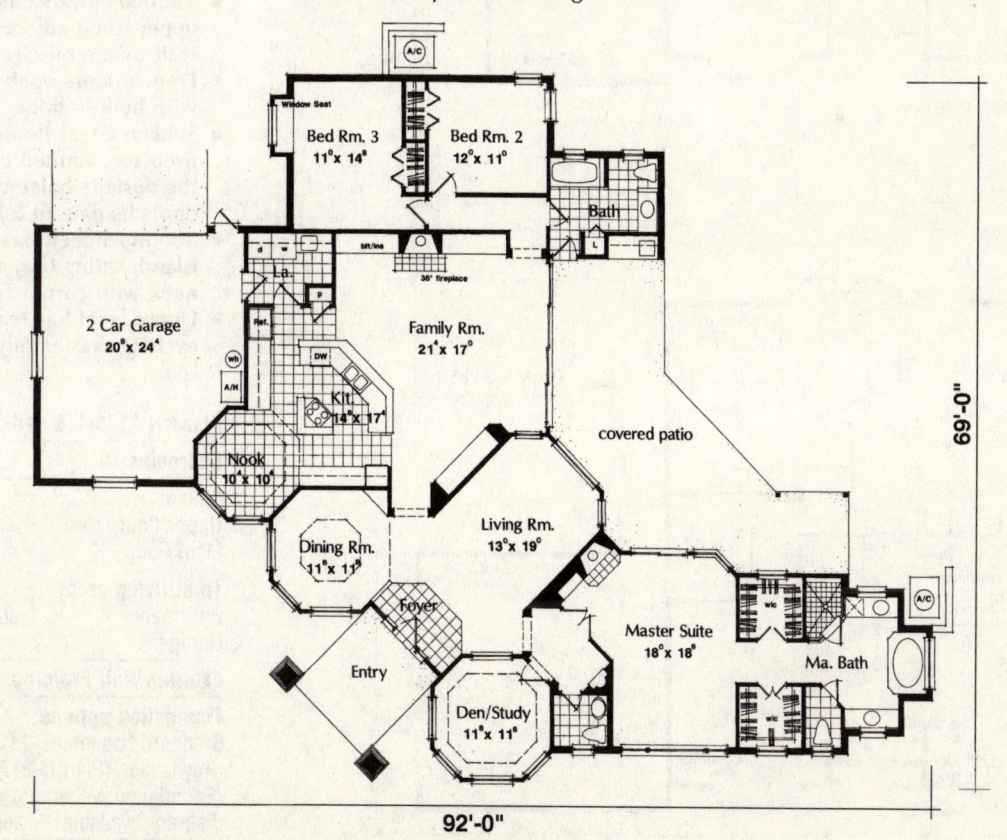

MAIN FLOOR

Plan HDS-99-137

ORDER BLUEPRINTS ANYTIME!
CALL TOLL-FREE 1-888-626-2026

PRICES AND DETAILS
ON PAGES 12-15

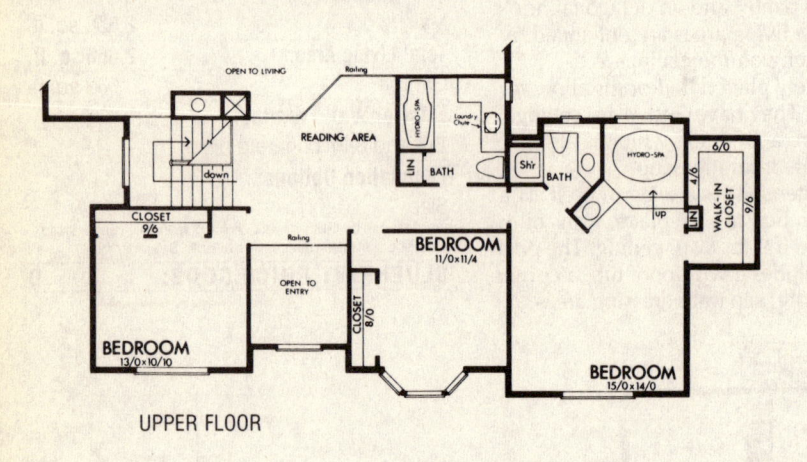

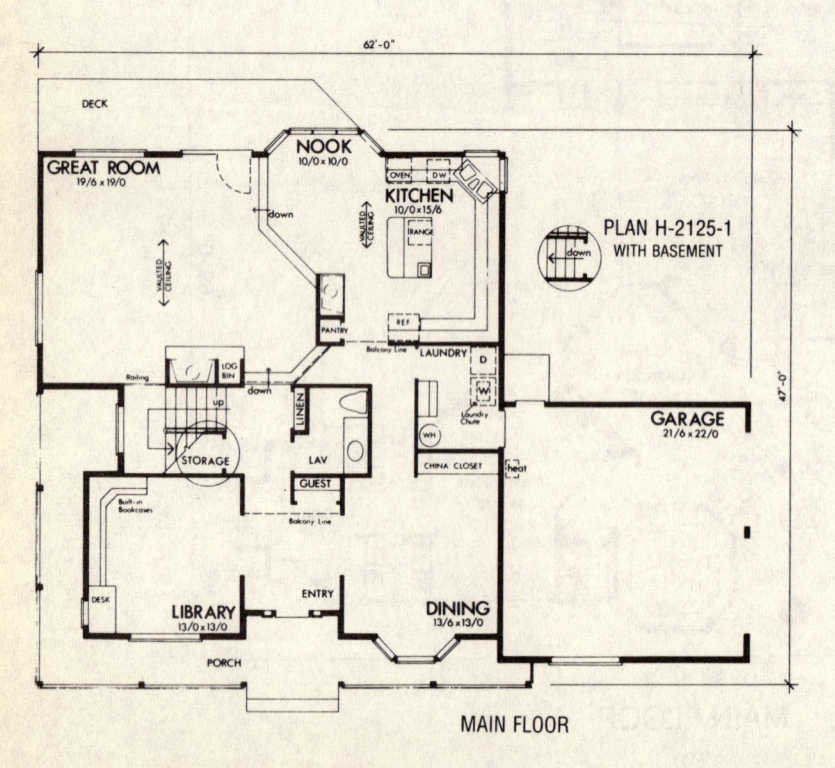

Delightful Blend of Old and New

- A contemporary floor plan is hidden in a traditional farmhouse exterior.
- Vaulted entrance is open to the upper level; adjacent open stairwell is lit by a semi-circular window.
- French doors open into a library with built-in bookcase and deck.
- Sunken Great Room features a fireplace, vaulted ceiling open to the upstairs balcony, and French doors leading to a backyard deck.
- Roomy kitchen has center cooking island, eating bar, and attached nook with corner fireplace.
- Upper level has reading area and exciting master suite with hydro-spa.

Plans H-2125-1 & -1A

Bedrooms: 3	Baths: 2½

Space:
Upper floor: 1,105 sq. ft.
Main floor: 1,554 sq. ft.

Total living area: 2,659 sq. ft.
Basement: approx. 1,554 sq. ft.
Garage: 475 sq. ft.

Exterior Wall Framing: 2x6

Foundation options:
Standard basement (Plan H-2125-1).
Crawlspace (Plan H-2125-1A).
(Foundation & framing conversion diagram available — see order form.)

Blueprint Price Code: D

ORDER BLUEPRINTS ANYTIME! CALL TOLL-FREE 1-888-626-2026

Plans H-2125-1 & -1A

PRICES AND DETAILS ON PAGES 12-15

Double Take

- Family entertainment is a priority in one corner of this stunning home, where you'll find a joined family room and media room.
- If you care for lively conversation, settle into a comfortable furniture ensemble in the family room. If the evening calls for homespun cinema, treat yourselves to a big-screen flick in the media room. Even your in-laws' home movies will look great!
- Under a blistering sky, a dip in the backyard spa will cool and refresh you. It's nestled into a partially covered deck so you can run for shelter and still enjoy a steamy summer storm.
- Inside, the island kitchen lends itself easily to formal entertainment and everyday routines.
- Escape to the master suite for a little pampering. You can slip out to the deck on cool spring mornings or curl up with a crossword puzzle by the bay window. The master bath offers two walk-in closets and a dual-sink vanity.

Plan DD-2665

Bedrooms: 3+	Baths: 2½
Living Area:	
Main floor	2,666 sq. ft.
Total Living Area:	**2,666 sq. ft.**
Standard basement	2,666 sq. ft.
Garage	411 sq. ft.
Exterior Wall Framing:	2x4

Foundation Options:
Standard basement
Crawlspace
Slab
(All plans can be built with your choice of foundation and framing. A generic conversion diagram is available. See order form.)

BLUEPRINT PRICE CODE:	D

MAIN FLOOR

ORDER BLUEPRINTS ANYTIME!
CALL TOLL-FREE 1-888-626-2026

Plan DD-2665

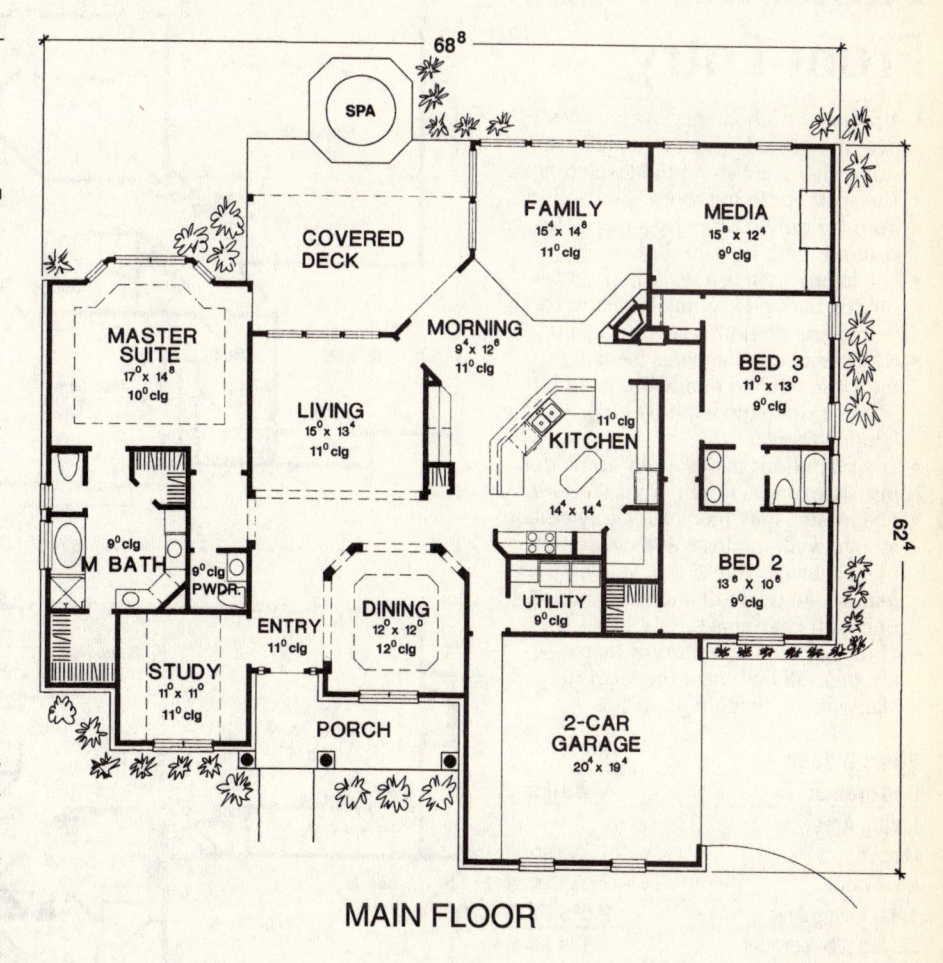

PRICES AND DETAILS
ON PAGES 12-15

Fantastic Front Entry

- A fantastic arched window presides over the 18-ft.-high entry of this two-story, giving guests a bright welcome.
- The spacious living room is separated from the dining room by a pair of boxed columns with built-in shelves.
- The kitchen offers a walk-in pantry, a serving bar and a sunny breakfast room with a French door to the backyard.
- A boxed column accents the entry to the 18-ft. vaulted family room, which boasts a dramatic window bank and an inviting fireplace.
- The main-floor den is easily converted into an extra bedroom or guest room.
- The master suite has a 10-ft. tray ceiling, a huge walk-in closet and decorative plant shelves. The 15½-ft. vaulted bath features an oval tub and two vanities, one with knee space.
- Three additional bedrooms share another full bath near the second stairway to the main floor.

Plan FB-2680

Bedrooms: 4+	Baths: 3
Living Area:	
Upper floor	1,256 sq. ft.
Main floor	1,424 sq. ft.
Total Living Area:	**2,680 sq. ft.**
Daylight basement	1,424 sq. ft.
Garage	496 sq. ft.
Exterior Wall Framing:	2x4

Foundation Options:
Daylight basement
Crawlspace
(All plans can be built with your choice of foundation and framing. A generic conversion diagram is available. See order form.)

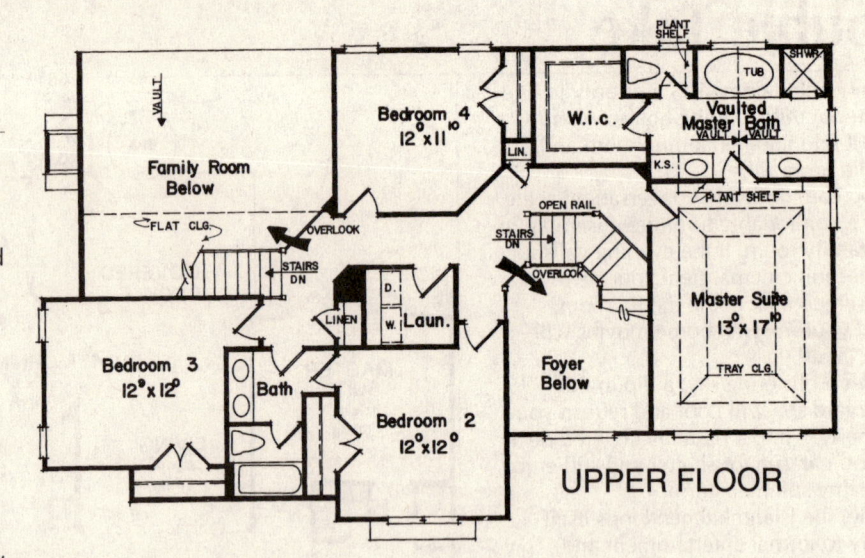

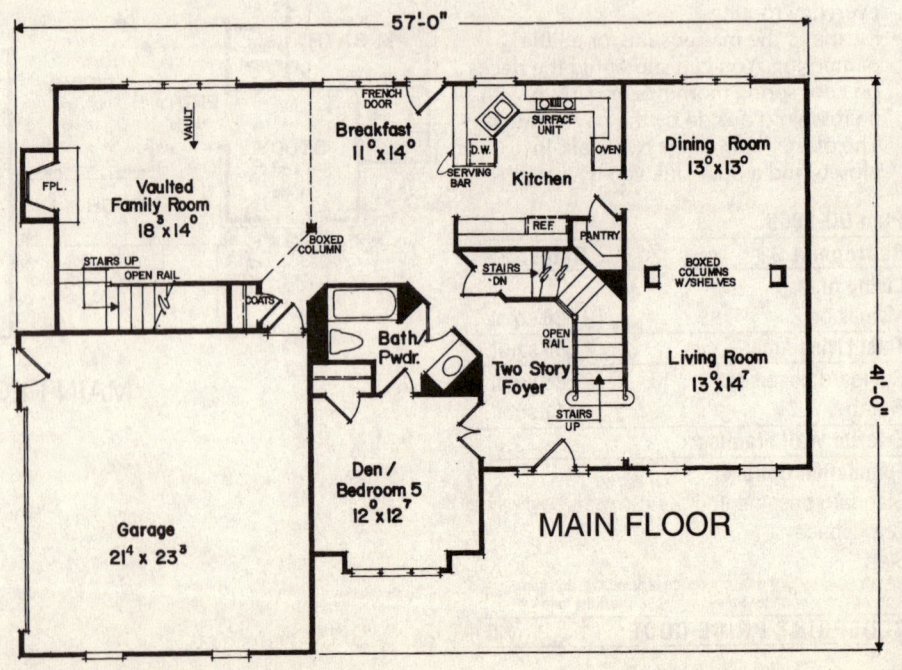

BLUEPRINT PRICE CODE: D

ORDER BLUEPRINTS ANYTIME! CALL TOLL-FREE 1-888-626-2026

Plan FB-2680

PRICES AND DETAILS ON PAGES 12-15

Two-Story Palace

- Decorative brick borders, a columned porch and dramatic arched windows give a classy look to this magnificent two-story palace.
- The open, sidelighted entry is flanked by the formal dining and living rooms, both of which feature elegant paned-glass windows. A coat closet and a powder room are just steps away.
- The spacious family room is warmed by a fireplace and brightened by a beautiful arched window set into a high-ceilinged area.
- The well-planned kitchen, highlighted by an island worktop and a windowed sink, is centrally located to provide easy service to both the dining room and the bayed morning room. The morning room offers access to a large, inviting backyard deck.
- A bright and heartwarming sun room also overlooks the deck, and is a perfect spot to read or just relax.
- A handy laundry/utility area is located at the entrance to the two-car garage.
- Windows surround the main-floor master suite, which boasts a luxurious bath with a garden tub, a separate shower and a dual-sink vanity. Three walk-in closets provide plenty of space for wardrobe storage.
- Ceilings in all main-floor rooms are 9 ft. high for added spaciousness.
- Upstairs, three good-sized bedrooms share a compartmentalized bath. A large and convenient attic area offers additional storage possibilities.

Plan DD-2689	
Bedrooms: 4	**Baths:** 2½
Living Area:	
Upper floor	755 sq. ft.
Main floor	1,934 sq. ft.
Total Living Area:	**2,689 sq. ft.**
Standard basement	1,934 sq. ft.
Garage	436 sq. ft.
Exterior Wall Framing:	2x4

Foundation Options:
Standard basement
Crawlspace
Slab
(All plans can be built with your choice of foundation and framing. A generic conversion diagram is available. See order form.)

BLUEPRINT PRICE CODE: D

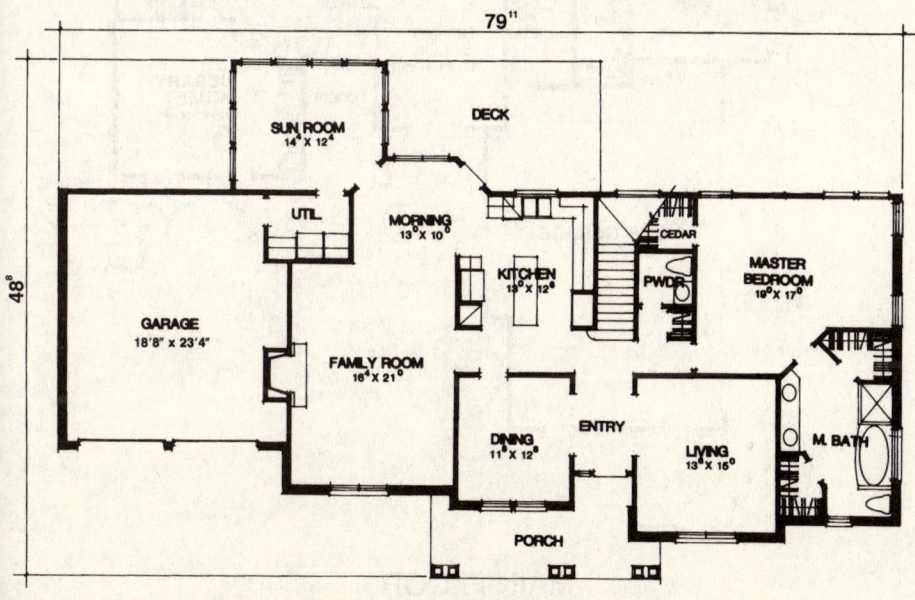

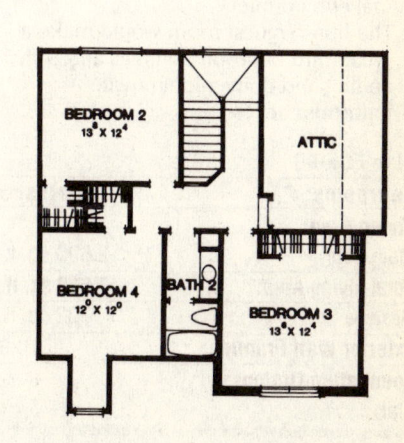

MAIN FLOOR

UPPER FLOOR

ORDER BLUEPRINTS ANYTIME! CALL TOLL-FREE 1-888-626-2026

Plan DD-2689

PRICES AND DETAILS ON PAGES 12-15

Twice as Nice

- Graced with two deluxe master suites, this beautiful Mediterranean-style home is comfortable and elegant.
- The impressive columned entrance opens into the bright and airy 12-ft.-high foyer, which is highlighted by an arched transom window. The adjacent formal dining room features a 12-ft. coffered ceiling and a stunning window wall.
- The gourmet kitchen includes a pantry, a snack counter and a bay-windowed morning room, which offers access to a covered back porch.
- Warmed by a fireplace, the spacious central parlour boasts a 12-ft. ceiling and French doors to the porch.
- Both master suites have 12-ft. ceilings. The first suite features a bay-windowed sitting area, his-and-hers walk-in closets and private porch access. The second suite offers a roomy walk-in closet and access to a private backyard patio. Both master baths include corner garden tubs, dual vanities and sit-down makeup counters.
- The library/guest room would make a great third bedroom, with its airy 9-ft. ceiling and convenient private bathroom access.

Plan EOF-68

Bedrooms: 2+	Baths: 3
Living Area:	
Main floor	2,690 sq. ft.
Total Living Area:	**2,690 sq. ft.**
Garage	732 sq. ft.
Exterior Wall Framing:	2x6

Foundation Options:
Slab
(All plans can be built with your choice of foundation and framing. A generic conversion diagram is available. See order form.)

BLUEPRINT PRICE CODE:	D

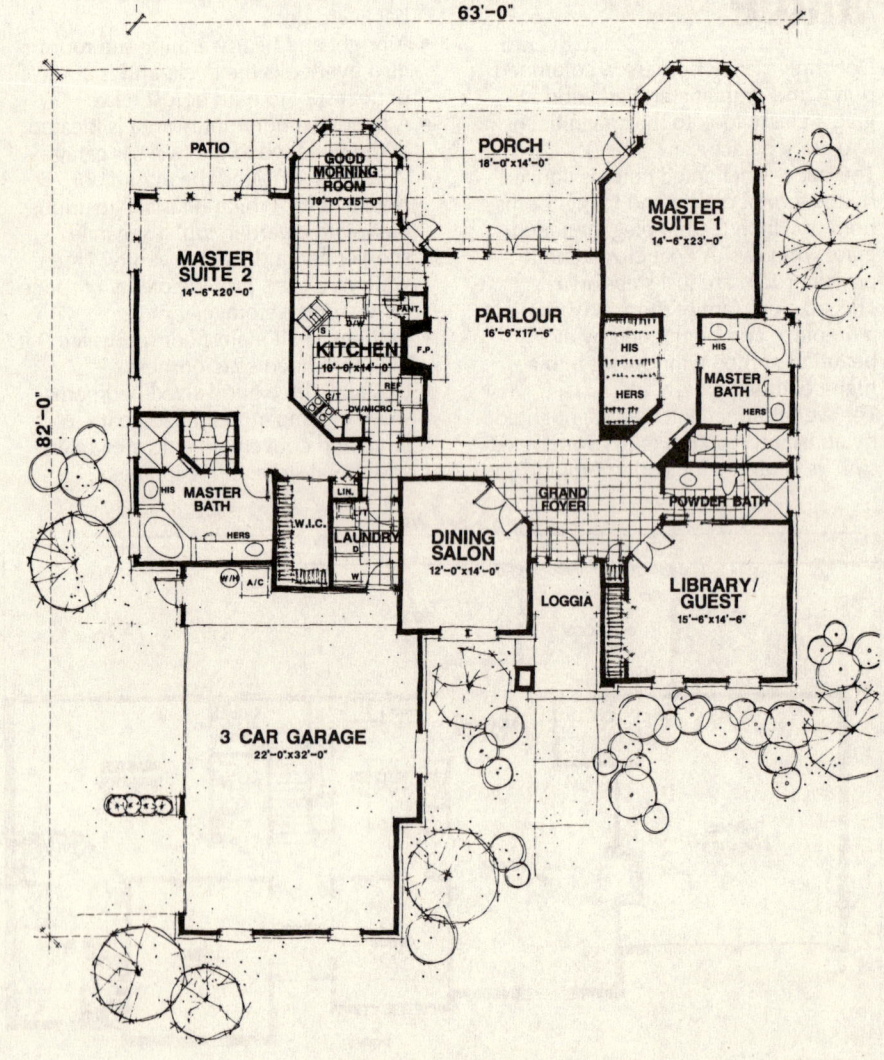

MAIN FLOOR

Plan EOF-68

Classic Cape Cod

- Six eye-catching dormer windows and a charming front porch create a stately, dignified look for this handsome home.
- An elegant open staircase is the focal point of the inviting foyer, which is set off from the formal dining room by decorative wood columns.
- A swinging door leads to the exciting kitchen, which includes an angled counter overlooking the breakfast room.
- The spectacular skylighted family room boasts a soaring 17-ft.-high ceiling. A cozy fireplace is flanked by tall windows and a set of French doors to the backyard.
- The deluxe master bedroom offers a vaulted ceiling and a charming bay window. The skylighted master bath has a spa tub, a separate shower, two walk-in closets and a dual sink vanity.
- Upstairs, a railed balcony overlooks the family room and foyer. Three bright bedrooms share a hallway bath.

Plan CH-445-A

Bedrooms: 4	Baths: 2½

Living Area:

Upper floor	988 sq. ft.
Main floor	1,707 sq. ft.
Total Living Area:	**2,695 sq. ft.**
Basement	1,118 sq. ft.
Garage	802 sq. ft.
Exterior Wall Framing:	2x4

Foundation Options:
Partial daylight basement
Partial basement
Crawlspace
(All plans can be built with your choice of foundation and framing. A generic conversion diagram is available. See order form.)

BLUEPRINT PRICE CODE: D

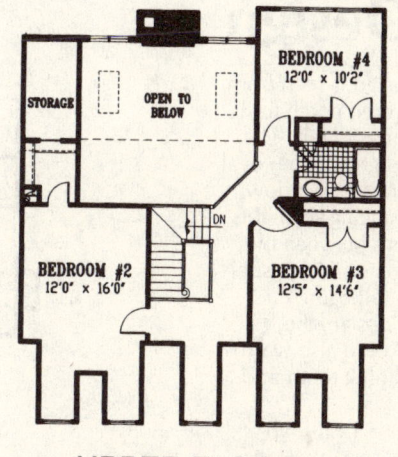

UPPER FLOOR

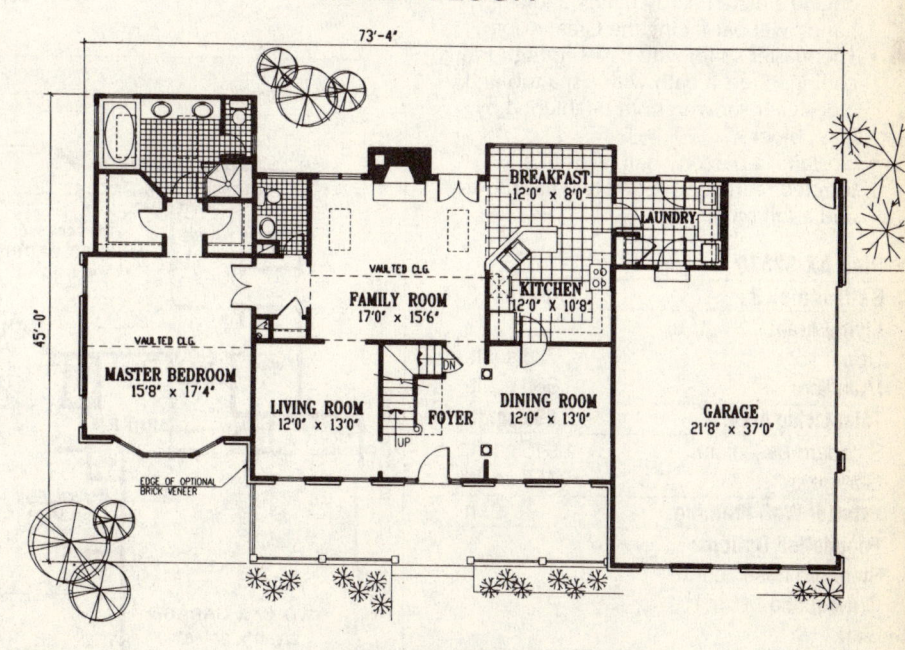

MAIN FLOOR

ORDER BLUEPRINTS ANYTIME!
CALL TOLL-FREE 1-888-626-2026

Plan CH-445-A

PRICES AND DETAILS ON PAGES 12-15

Distinct Design

- This home's distinct design is seen from the curvature of its covered porch to its decorative wrought-iron roof rail.
- The 17-ft.-high foyer is lighted in an oval theme, through the clerestory window, the front door and its flanking sidelights. The broad foyer stretches between the vaulted formal living areas and a casual TV room across from a full bath.
- With its unique corner design, the fireplace in the Great Room also warms the unusual rounded dining room and the breakfast area.
- The dining room boasts a 14-ft-high ceiling, while the kitchen features an angled sink, a nearby pantry and a handy wet bar facing the Great Room.
- The master suite, with its 13-ft.-high tray ceiling, offers a bath with a spa tub and a designer shower, both brightened by glass blocks.
- Upstairs, a balcony hall leads to a turreted recreation room, two bedrooms and a full bath.

Plan AX-92326

Bedrooms: 3+	Baths: 3

Living Area:
Upper floor	736 sq. ft.
Main floor	1,960 sq. ft.
Total Living Area:	**2,696 sq. ft.**
Standard basement	1,915 sq. ft.
Garage	455 sq. ft.

Exterior Wall Framing: 2x4

Foundation Options:
Standard basement
Crawlspace
Slab
(All plans can be built with your choice of foundation and framing. A generic conversion diagram is available. See order form.)

BLUEPRINT PRICE CODE: D

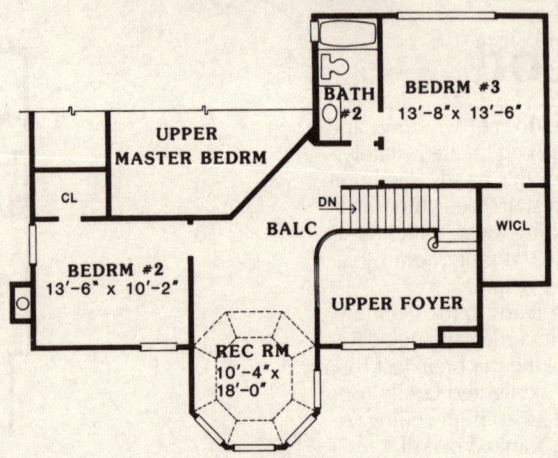

ORDER BLUEPRINTS ANYTIME!
CALL TOLL-FREE 1-888-626-2026

Plan AX-92326

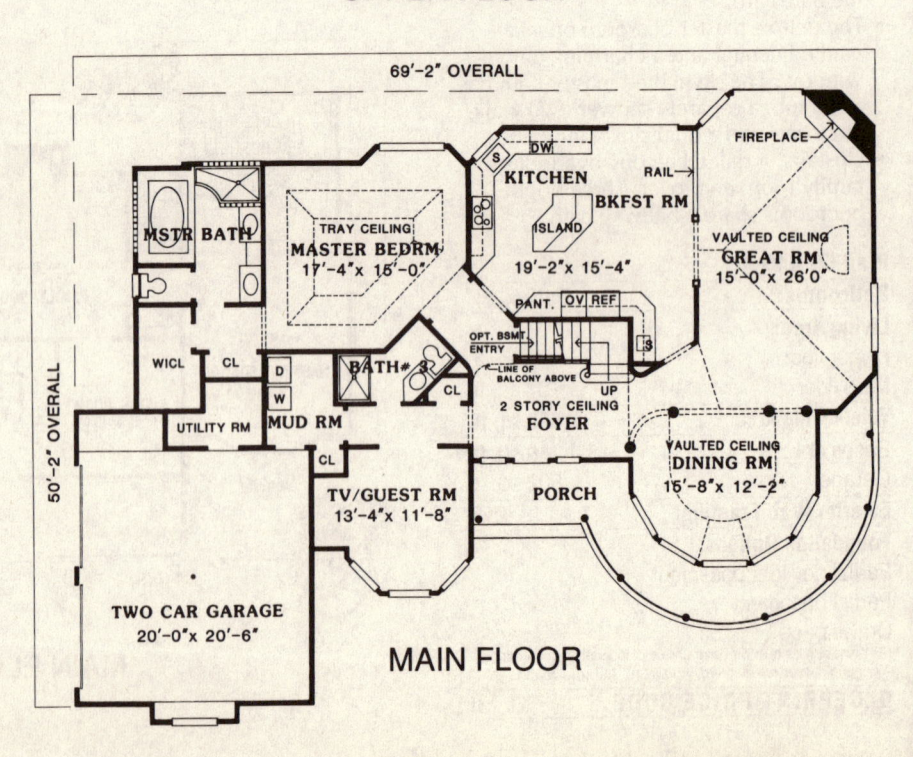

PRICES AND DETAILS ON PAGES 12-15

Striking Hillside Home Design

- This striking home is designed for a sloping site. The two-car garage and sideyard deck are nestled into the hillside, while cedar siding and a shake roof blend in nicely with the terrain.
- Clerestory windows brighten the entry and the living room, which unfold from the covered front porch. The huge living/dining area instantly catches the eye, with its corner fireplace, 17-ft. sloped ceiling and exciting window treatments. The living room also offers an inviting window seat, while the dining room has sliding glass doors to the large deck.
- The adjoining nook and kitchen also have access to the deck, along with lots of storage and work space.
- The isolated bedroom wing includes a master suite with his-and-hers closets and a private bath. The two smaller bedrooms share a hall bath.
- The daylight basement hosts a laundry room, a recreation room with a fireplace and a bedroom with two closets, plus a large general-use area.

Plan H-2045-5

Bedrooms: 4	Baths: 3
Living Area:	
Main floor	1,602 sq. ft.
Daylight basement	1,133 sq. ft.
Total Living Area:	**2,735 sq. ft.**
Tuck-under garage	508 sq. ft.
Exterior Wall Framing:	2x4
Foundation Options:	
Daylight basement	

(All plans can be built with your choice of foundation and framing. A generic conversion diagram is available. See order form.)

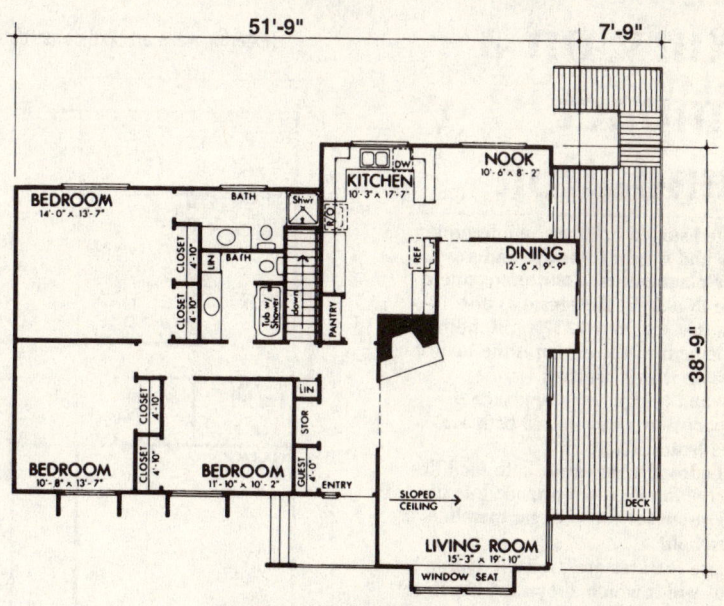

BLUEPRINT PRICE CODE: D

MAIN FLOOR

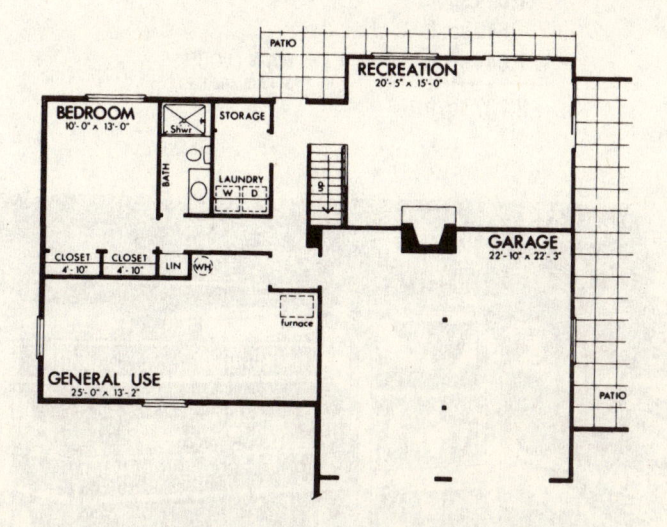

DAYLIGHT BASEMENT

ORDER BLUEPRINTS ANYTIME!
CALL TOLL-FREE 1-888-626-2026

Plan H-2045-5

PRICES AND DETAILS ON PAGES 12-15

FRONT VIEW

Luxury on a Compact Foundation

Sky-lighted sloped ceilings, an intriguing stairway and overhead bridge and a carefully planned first floor arrangement combine to delight the senses as one explores this spacious 2737 sq. ft. home. A major element of the design is the luxurious master suite that is reached via the stairway and bridge. An abundance of closet space and an oversized bath are welcome features here.

Two bedrooms, generous bath facilities and a large family room provide lots of growing room for the younger members of the household.

All these features are available within a mere 36' width which allows the house to be built on a 50' wide lot — a real bonus these days.

Main floor:	1,044 sq. ft.
Upper level:	649 sq. ft.
Lower level:	1,044 sq. ft.
Total living area:	2,737 sq. ft.
(Not counting garage)	

(Exterior walls are 2x6 construction)

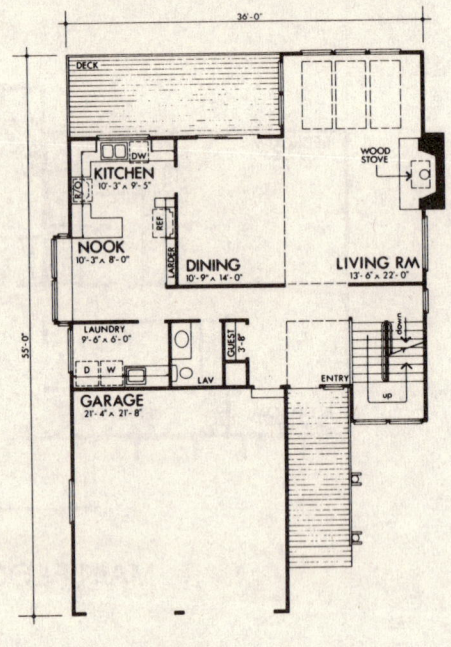

MAIN FLOOR
1044 SQUARE FEET

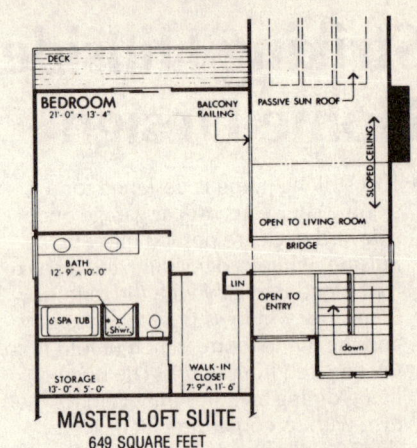

MASTER LOFT SUITE
649 SQUARE FEET

LOWER LEVEL
1044 SQUARE FEET

REAR VIEW

Blueprint Price Code D
Plan H-2110-1B

ORDER BLUEPRINTS ANYTIME!
CALL TOLL-FREE 1-888-626-2026

PRICES AND DETAILS ON PAGES 12-15

208

Family Treasure

- This warm, pleasant home will be a cherished place that your family will treasure for years to come.
- The front and back porches are long enough for the kids to fully extend that strip of race track for their miniature hot rods. They're also great spots for sitting with your budding angler and teaching her the nuances of tying her first homemade flies.
- Inside, the Great Room will attract the whole family. Stoke the fireplace, pop some popcorn and gather round to enjoy your weekly movie night.
- Use the casual breakfast nook for morning waffles or after-school snacks. Dressy meals have a home in the formal dining room.
- At day's end, Mom and Dad can unwind in the master suite. Dual walk-in closets and a spacious private bath add a welcome dose of luxury.
- Each of the three bedrooms upstairs features a charming window seat; two boast walk-in closets. If guests visit, or your family expands, convert the main-floor study into a fifth bedroom.

Plan NBV-11196

Bedrooms: 4+	Baths: 3
Living Area:	
Upper floor	885 sq. ft.
Main floor	1,854 sq. ft.
Total Living Area:	**2,739 sq. ft.**
Garage	430 sq. ft.
Storage	79 sq. ft.
Exterior Wall Framing:	2x4

Foundation Options:
Slab
(All plans can be built with your choice of foundation and framing. A generic conversion diagram is available. See order form.)

BLUEPRINT PRICE CODE: D

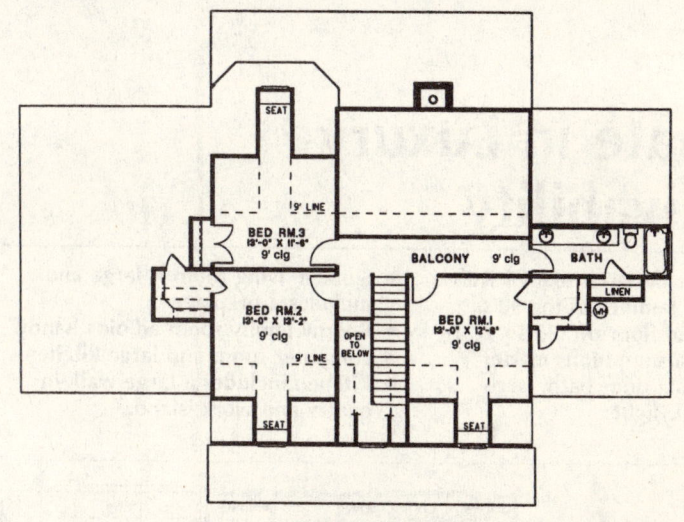

UPPER FLOOR

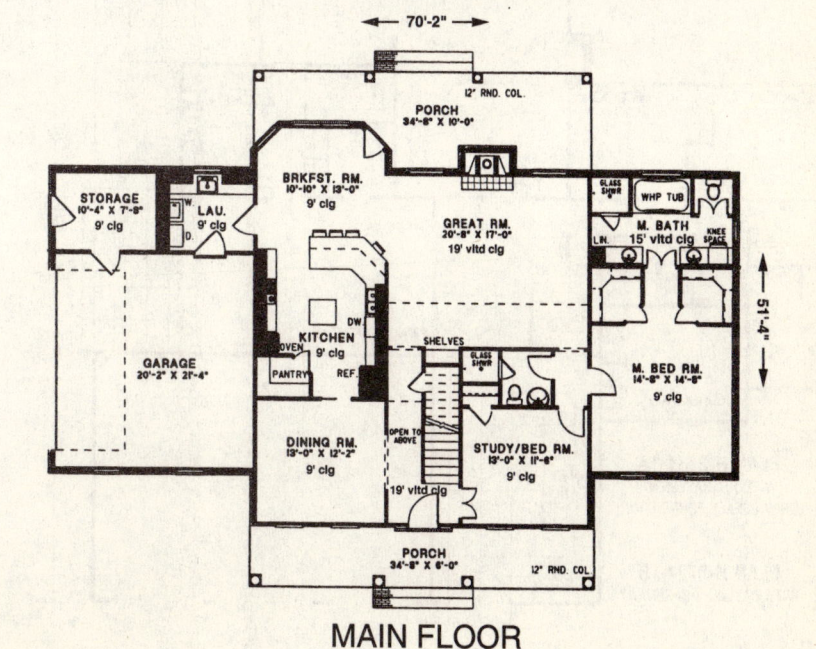

MAIN FLOOR

ORDER BLUEPRINTS ANYTIME!
CALL TOLL-FREE 1-888-626-2026

Plan NBV-11196

PRICES AND DETAILS ON PAGES 12-15

Ultimate in Luxury and Livability

- This popular design is loaded with features for families of the 90's.
- Entire second floor of 735 sq. ft. is devoted to a sumptuous master suite with luxurious bath, large closet and skylights.
- Sunken living room is large and includes a fireplace.
- Roomy family room adjoins handy computer room and large kitchen.
- Kitchen includes a large walk-in pantry and work island.

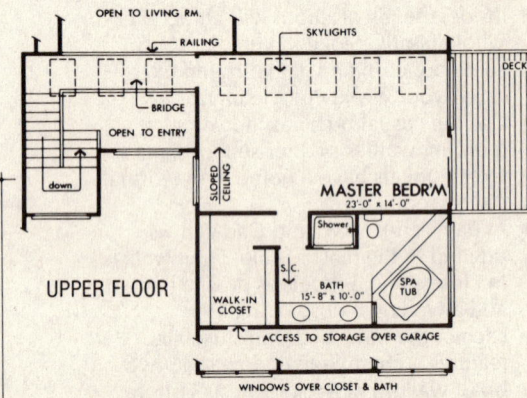

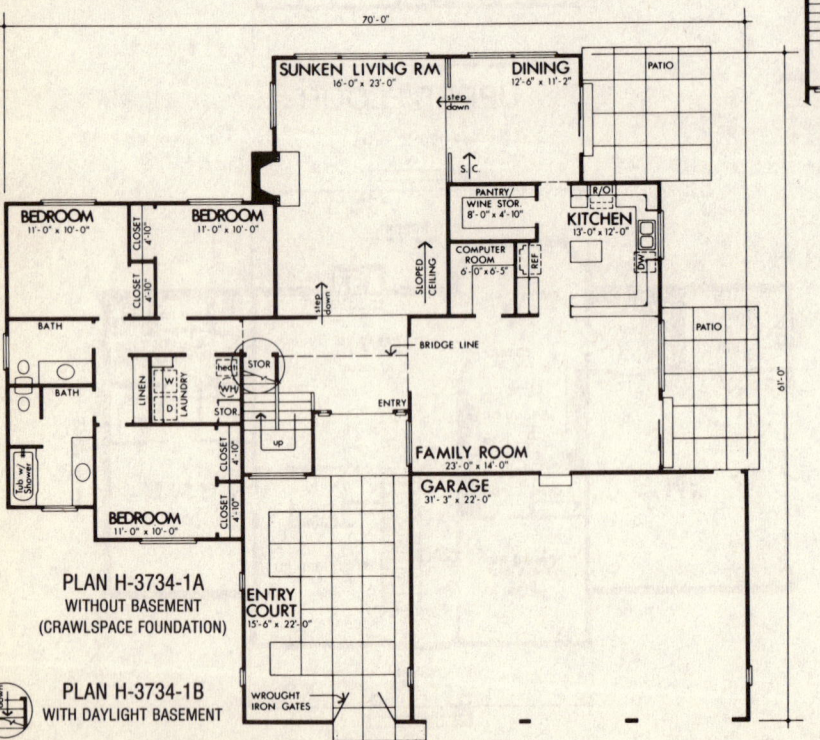

Plans H-3734-1A & -1B

Bedrooms: 4	Baths: 2½

Space:
Upper floor: 735 sq. ft.
Main floor: 2,024 sq. ft.

Total living area: 2,759 sq. ft.
Basement: 2,024 sq. ft.
Garage: 687 sq. ft.

Exterior Wall Framing: 2x6

Foundation options:
Daylight basement, Plan H-3734-1B.
Crawlspace, Plan H-3734-1A.
(Foundation & framing conversion diagram available — see order form.)

Blueprint Price Code: D

PLAN H-3734-1A
WITHOUT BASEMENT
(CRAWLSPACE FOUNDATION)

PLAN H-3734-1B
WITH DAYLIGHT BASEMENT

Plans H-3734-1A & -1B

Rites of Passage

- As your family's life passes from stage to stage, you'll appreciate how this warm country home remains flexible.
- When the kids are robust and rowdy, there's plenty of room to roam in the central Great Room. On warm days, if they're not content in their upper-floor bedrooms, you can shoo them to the home's huge front porch.
- Mornings will find you in the island kitchen, the smell of bacon wafting over the adjoining breakfast nook.
- Your circle of friends will change from time to time; entertaining them is easy in the formal living and dining rooms, which are open to each other, but defined by eye-catching columns.
- A fabulous oasis awaits you in the master bedroom, which basks in natural sunlight from its bayed window. The master bath includes a whirlpool tub beneath a 12-ft. ceiling.
- As your parents pass into the autumn of their lives, they can live with dignity in their secluded suite, which pampers them with private access to a porch, plus a walk-in closet and a full bath.

Plan AX-5372

Bedrooms: 4	Baths: 3½
Living Area:	
Upper floor	581 sq. ft.
Main floor	2,182 sq. ft.
Total Living Area:	**2,763 sq. ft.**
Future attic expansion	437 sq. ft.
Standard basement	2,180 sq. ft.
Garage and storage	594 sq. ft.
Exterior Wall Framing:	2x4

Foundation Options:
Standard basement
Crawlspace
Slab
(All plans can be built with your choice of foundation and framing. A generic conversion diagram is available. See order form.)

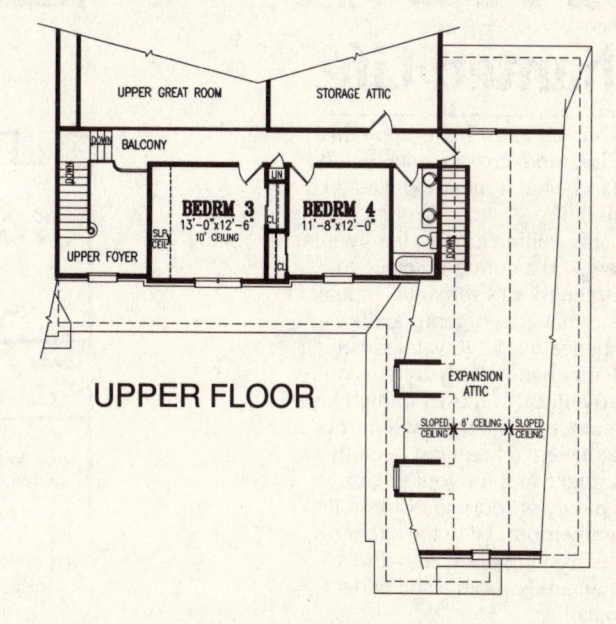

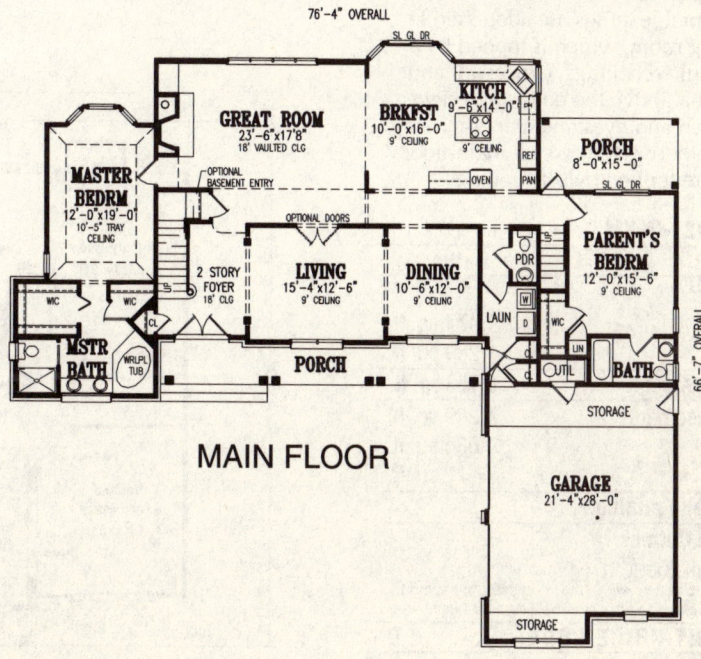

BLUEPRINT PRICE CODE: D

UPPER FLOOR

MAIN FLOOR

ORDER BLUEPRINTS ANYTIME!
CALL TOLL-FREE 1-888-626-2026

Plan AX-5372

PRICES AND DETAILS ON PAGES 12-15

Enchanted Life

- When your gaze first lights upon this home's luxurious master suite, you'll understand what it means to lead an enchanted life.
- A 10-ft. tray ceiling crowns the sleeping chamber. Add a corner fireplace to heighten the room's romantic appeal. In the master bath, a gorgeous garden tub resides beneath a 12-ft. vaulted ceiling.
- The balcony hall politely ushers you past an overlook of the 18-ft.-high foyer to the main floor. Here, you'll find your morning haven: a breakfast nook that offers a bright spot for your yogurt.
- There's plenty of room to move in the huge family room. With the kitchen's columned serving bar within arm's reach, the family room is the perfect party space!
- Your formal leanings are addressed in the living room, which is topped by an 18-ft. vaulted ceiling. A kneewall and plant shelf above the entry keep sight lines open and eyes entertained.
- Unless otherwise noted, all main-floor rooms are topped by 9-ft. ceilings.

Plan FB-5027-OLYM

Bedrooms: 4	Baths: 3½

Living Area:

Upper floor	1,474 sq. ft.
Main floor	1,289 sq. ft.
Total Living Area:	**2,763 sq. ft.**
Daylight basement	1,289 sq. ft.
Garage	534 sq. ft.
Storage	72 sq. ft.
Exterior Wall Framing:	2x4

Foundation Options:
Daylight basement
(All plans can be built with your choice of foundation and framing. A generic conversion diagram is available. See order form.)

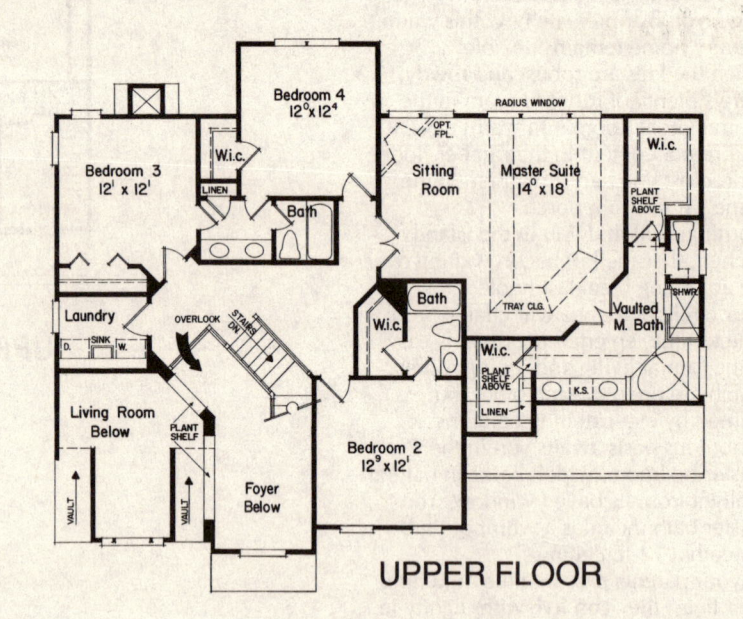

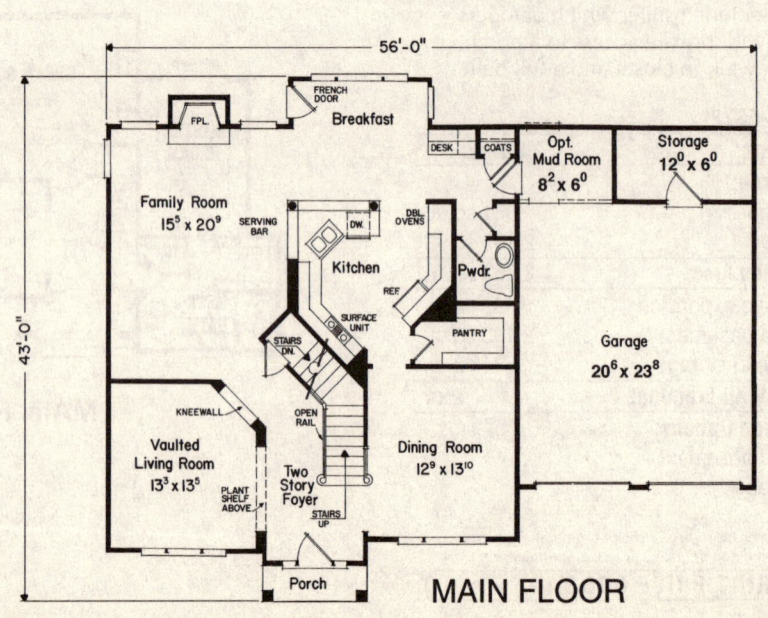

BLUEPRINT PRICE CODE: D

UPPER FLOOR

MAIN FLOOR

ORDER BLUEPRINTS ANYTIME! CALL TOLL-FREE 1-888-626-2026

Plan FB-5027-OLYM

PRICES AND DETAILS ON PAGES 12-15

Victorian Romance

- If the romance of Victorian-style living is in your blood, consider life in this charming two-story.
- Delightful exterior features, including diamond-cut cedar shingles, metal roof accents, decorative fretwork and a nifty arbor, lend character to any boulevard.
- Inside, large and comfortable living spaces radiate from a central stairway. Rich hardwood floors sweep across the foyer, living room, dining room and study, which is accessible through two sets of French doors.
- A room you'll always cherish, the study features 30-in.-high bookcases that create functional wraparound seating.
- The big kitchen offers a convenient serving counter to the family room.
- Upstairs, four generous-sized bedrooms are arranged for ultimate privacy; each includes a walk-in closet and direct access to one of three baths. The bayed master bath boasts two pedestal sinks.
- Note the bright alcove extending from the bedroom immediately off the stairs.

Plan L-774-VSB	
Bedrooms: 4+	**Baths:** 3½
Living Area:	
Upper floor	1,418 sq. ft.
Main floor	1,354 sq. ft.
Total Living Area	**2,772 sq. ft.**
Garage and storage	499 sq. ft.
Exterior Wall Framing:	2x4

Foundation Options:
Slab
(All plans can be built with your choice of foundation and framing. A generic conversion diagram is available. See order form.)

BLUEPRINT PRICE CODE: D

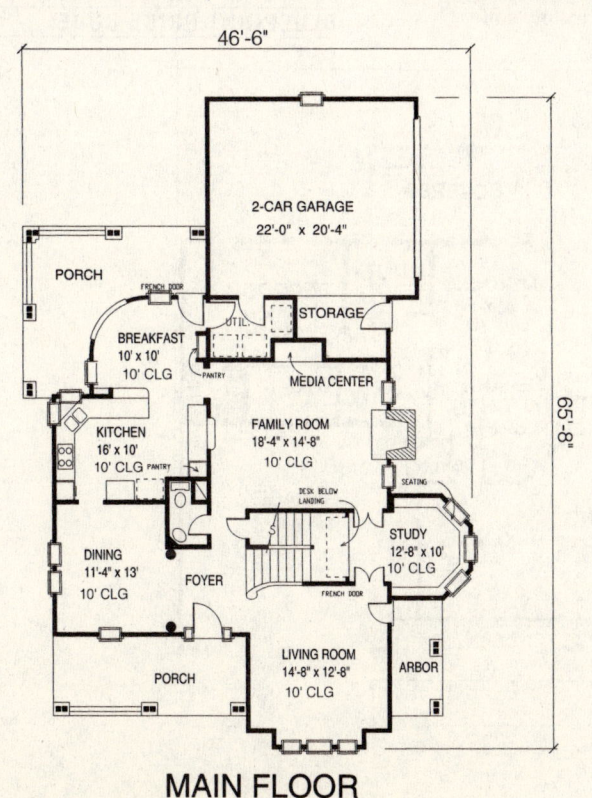

MAIN FLOOR

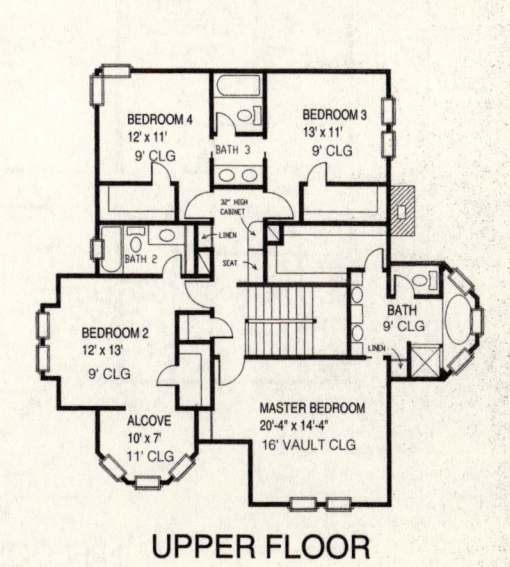

UPPER FLOOR

Plan L-774-VSB

Visual Feast

- Attention to exterior details such as keystones, quoins and beautiful arched windows transforms this radiant one-story home into a fabulous feast for the eyes.
- Combine an evening of engaging conversation with a sumptuous meal in the formal living and dining rooms. The area is distinguished from the elegant, skylighted entry by a set of stately columns.
- Spacious and bright, the family room presents numerous possibilities for entertaining both friends and relatives. Step out to a covered deck to catch a summer snooze.
- Perfectly placed to serve both the morning room and the dining room, the island kitchen offers several amenities, including an attractive skylight and a handy pantry.
- Natural light floods the tray-ceilinged master bedroom through a sparkling Palladian window. The lavish master bath flaunts a Jacuzzi tub, a dual-sink vanity and a huge walk-in closet.
- Two additional bedrooms and a full bath lie near the master bedroom. A fourth bedroom across the home could serve as a guest or in-law suite.

Plan DD-2811

Bedrooms: 4	Baths: 3

Living Area:
Main floor — 2,811 sq. ft.
Total Living Area: **2,811 sq. ft.**
Basement — 2,811 sq. ft.
Garage — 523 sq. ft.
Exterior Wall Framing: 2x4
Foundation Options:
Daylight basement
Standard basement
Slab
(All plans can be built with your choice of foundation and framing. A generic conversion diagram is available. See order form.)
BLUEPRINT PRICE CODE: D

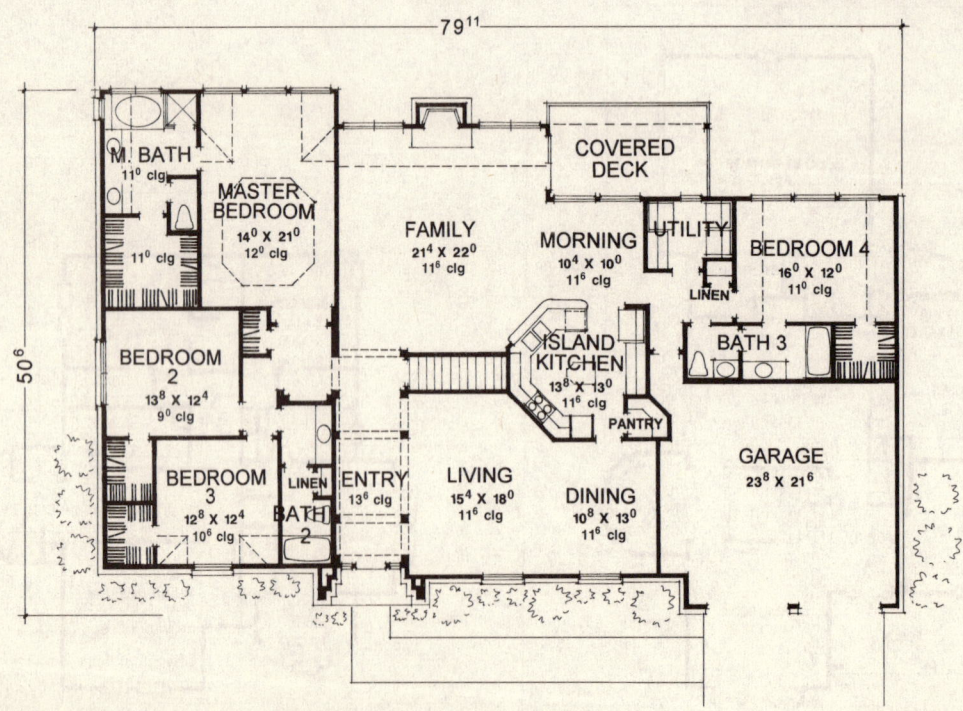

MAIN FLOOR

Plan DD-2811

Home with Sparkle

- This dynamite design simply sparkles, with the main living areas geared toward a gorgeous greenhouse at the back of the home.
- At the front of the home, a sunken foyer introduces the formal dining room, which is framed by a curved half-wall. The sunken living room boasts a 17-ft. vaulted ceiling and a nice fireplace.
- The spacious kitchen features a bright, two-story skywell above the island. The family room's ceiling rises to 17 feet. These rooms culminate at a solar greenhouse with an indulgent hot tub and a 12-ft. vaulted ceiling. The neighboring bath has a raised spa tub.
- Upstairs, the impressive master suite includes its own deck and a stairway to the greenhouse. A vaulted library with a woodstove augments the suite. Ceilings soar to 16 ft. in both areas.

Plan S-8217

Bedrooms: 3+	Baths: 2
Living Area:	
Upper floor	789 sq. ft.
Main floor	1,709 sq. ft.
Bonus room	336 sq. ft.
Total Living Area:	**2,834 sq. ft.**
Partial basement	1,242 sq. ft.
Garage	441 sq. ft.
Exterior Wall Framing:	2x6

Foundation Options:
Partial basement
Crawlspace
Slab
(All plans can be built with your choice of foundation and framing. A generic conversion diagram is available. See order form.)

BLUEPRINT PRICE CODE: D

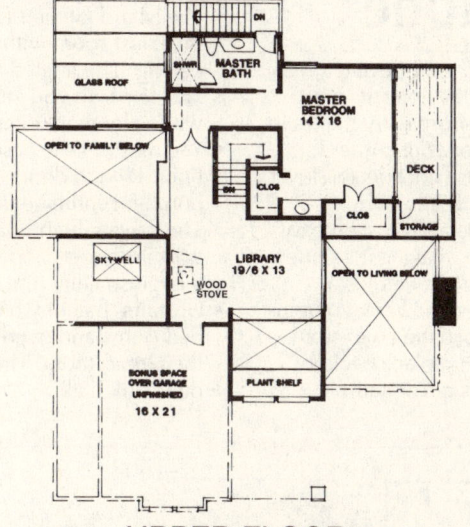

UPPER FLOOR

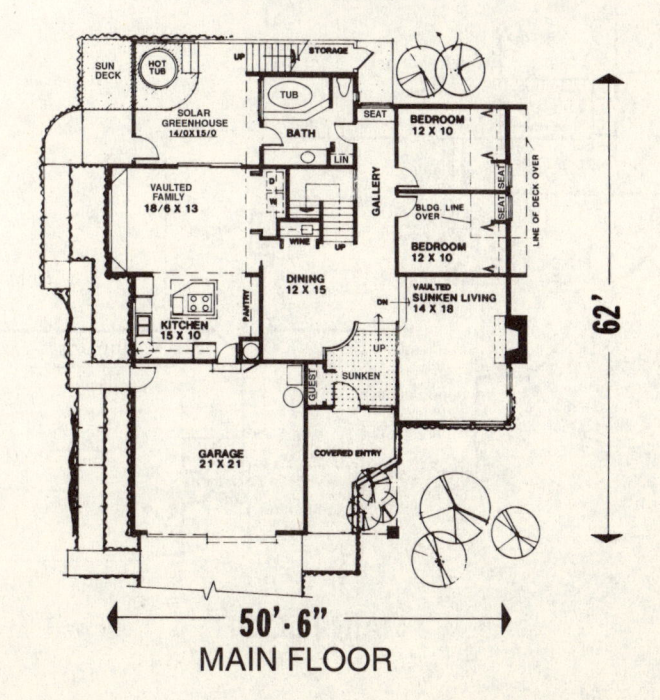

MAIN FLOOR

50'-6"
62'

ORDER BLUEPRINTS ANYTIME!
CALL TOLL-FREE 1-888-626-2026

Plan S-8217

PRICES AND DETAILS ON PAGES 12-15

Cornerstone

- A peaks-and-valleys roofline and a rich brick exterior give this home its curb appeal. The angled front entry makes it an elegant choice for your corner lot.
- A grand split staircase anchors the foyer; tucked away beneath it is a brick planter. To the left is a study with easy access to a full bath, making it a perfect guest room. To the right unfolds a formal dining room defined by columns.
- Beyond the foyer, a soaring two-story Great Room with a fireplace beckons. French doors access a rear patio.
- The island kitchen flows into a bayed breakfast room with an airy cathedral ceiling. The angled sink overlooks the backyard, so you can watch the kids while cleaning up after lunch.
- The master suite is secluded on the first floor. French doors open to a covered porch for intimate talks at day's end. The private bath boasts his-and-hers walk-in closets and vanities, as well as a large soaking tub.
- Upstairs, balcony hallways link three bedrooms and overlook the foyer and the Great Room. The bedrooms share a dual-sink bath.

Plan BOD-28-1A	
Bedrooms: 4+	**Baths:** 3
Living Area:	
Upper floor	872 sq. ft.
Main floor	1,966 sq. ft.
Total Living Area:	**2,838 sq. ft.**
Garage and storage	569 sq. ft.
Exterior Wall Framing:	2x4
Foundation Options:	
Crawlspace	
Slab	

(All plans can be built with your choice of foundation and framing. A generic conversion diagram is available. See order form.)

BLUEPRINT PRICE CODE: D

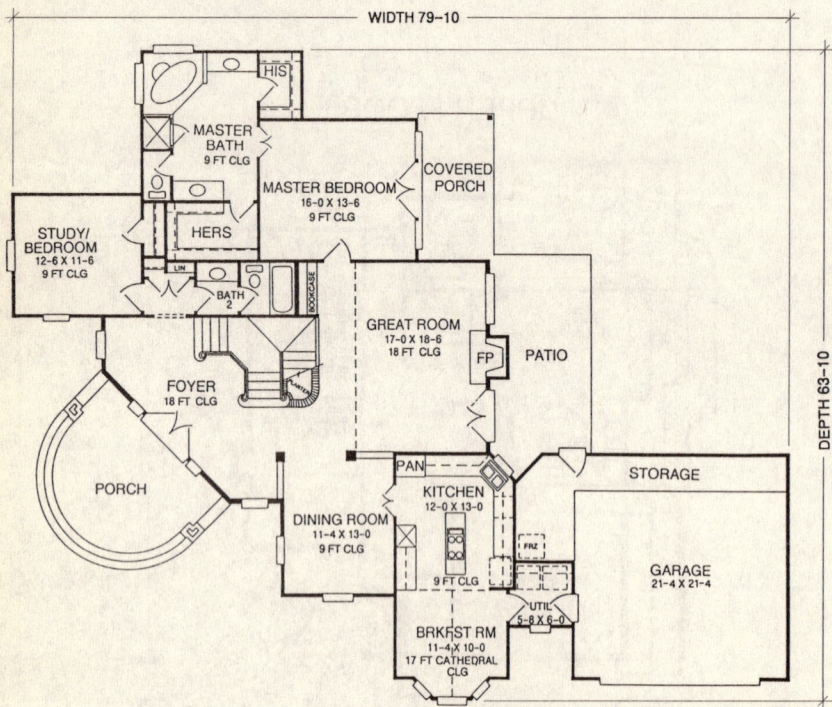

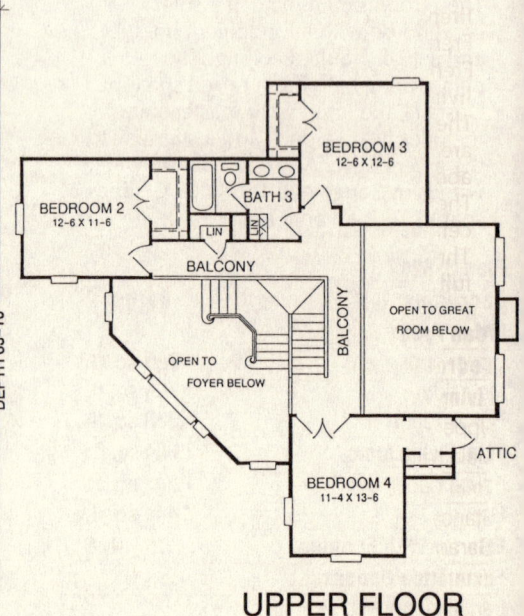

MAIN FLOOR

UPPER FLOOR

Plan BOD-28-1A

Meant to Impress

- From the exquisite exterior detailing, reminiscent of a stately English manor, to the elegant yet comfortable interior living spaces, this home is sure to impress.
- The kitchen is at the core of the design, featuring a breakfast bar that faces the bayed dinette and an island work center that provides extra space while directing traffic flow. A built-in desk, a deluxe walk-in pantry and a lazy Susan are other features.
- The sunken family room boasts a fireplace, a 12-ft. tray ceiling and French doors to the backyard.
- French doors also open to the charming living room and the cozy study.
- The stairway and the 17-ft. vaulted foyer are illuminated by a clerestory window above the front door.
- The master bedroom offers a 12-ft. tray ceiling, and a sumptuous spa bath. Three more bedrooms share another full bath.

Plan A-2210-DS

Bedrooms: 4+	Baths: 2½
Living Area:	
Upper floor	1,208 sq. ft.
Main floor	1,634 sq. ft.
Total Living Area:	**2,842 sq. ft.**
Standard basement	1,634 sq. ft.
Garage	484 sq. ft.
Exterior Wall Framing:	2x6

Foundation Options:
Standard basement
(All plans can be built with your choice of foundation and framing. A generic conversion diagram is available. See order form.)

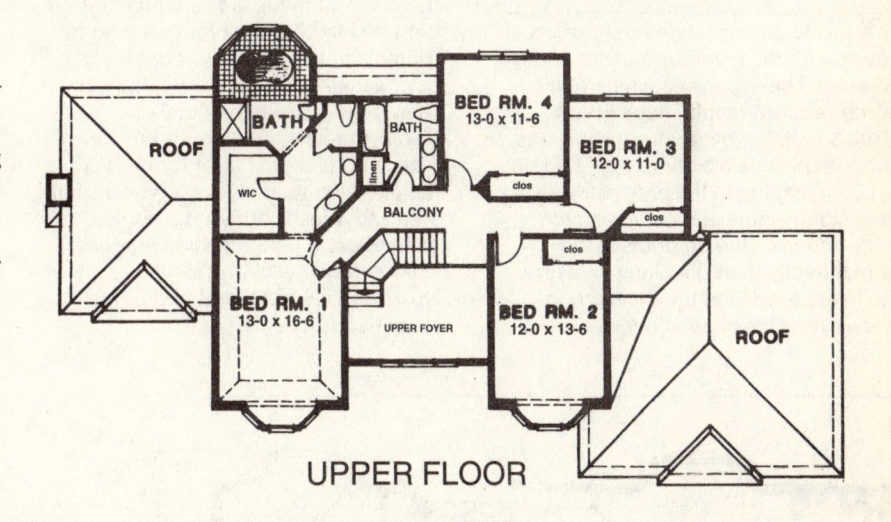

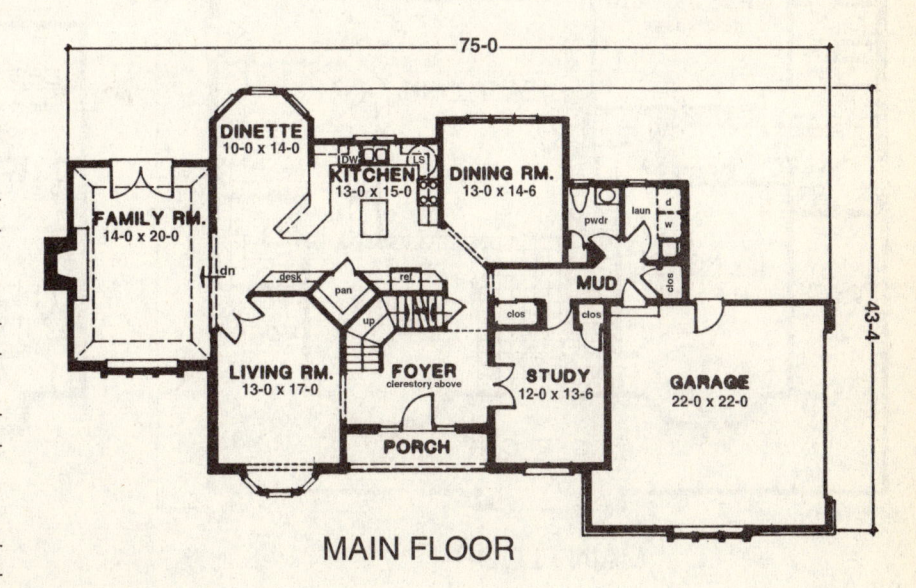

BLUEPRINT PRICE CODE: D

ORDER BLUEPRINTS ANYTIME!
CALL TOLL-FREE 1-888-626-2026

Plan A-2210-DS

PRICES AND DETAILS ON PAGES 12-15

Good Manners

- This lovely country-style home greets guests with the gracious manner of days gone by. The expansive wraparound porch beckons family members and visitors to linger over refreshments and comfortable conversation.
- A 17½-ft. ceiling in the entry adds an open atmosphere and creates a nice transition from the outdoors to the formal living areas. Flanking the entry, the living room and the dining room feature matching bay windows.
- Ease of communication is paramount in the informal living areas, which are clustered toward the rear of the home.
- A fireplace in the family room invites cozy gatherings, while a serving bar shared with the kitchen makes displaying hors d'oeuvres a breeze.
- Situated on the first floor for privacy, the master suite includes a bayed sitting area and a lush bath with a corner garden tub, a separate shower, dual sinks and two walk-in closets.
- Upstairs, four additional bedrooms share two full baths.

Plan RD-2843

Bedrooms: 5	**Baths:** 3½
Living Area:	
Upper floor	1,033 sq. ft.
Main floor	1,810 sq. ft.
Total Living Area:	**2,843 sq. ft.**
Exterior Wall Framing:	2x4

Foundation Options:
Crawlspace
Slab
(All plans can be built with your choice of foundation and framing. A generic conversion diagram is available. See order form.)

BLUEPRINT PRICE CODE: D

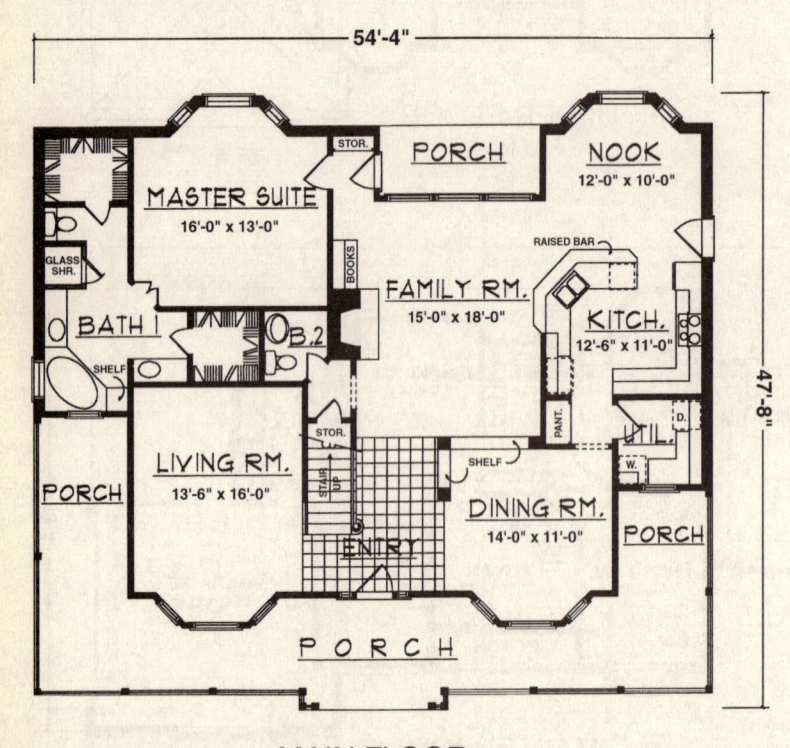

MAIN FLOOR

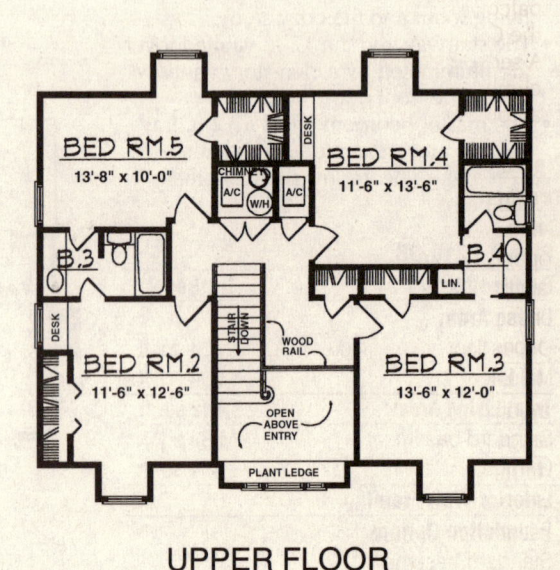

UPPER FLOOR

ORDER BLUEPRINTS ANYTIME!
CALL TOLL-FREE 1-888-626-2026

Plan RD-2843

PRICES AND DETAILS
ON PAGES 12-15

Symmetrical Bay Windows

- This home's ornate facade proudly displays a pair of symmetrical copper-topped bay windows.
- A bright, two-story-high foyer stretches to the vaulted Great Room, with its fireplace and backyard deck access.
- The island kitchen offers a snack bar and a breakfast nook that opens to the deck and the garage.
- The main-floor master suite features private deck access, dual walk-in closets and a personal bath with a corner garden tub. A laundry room and a bayed study are nearby.
- Upstairs, three secondary bedrooms and another full bath are located off the balcony bridge, which overlooks both the Great Room and the foyer.
- A second stairway off the breakfast nook climbs to a bonus room, which adjoins an optional full bath and closet.

Plan C-9010

Bedrooms: 4+	Baths: 2½-3½

Living Area:

Upper floor	761 sq. ft.
Main floor	1,637 sq. ft.
Bonus room	347 sq. ft.
Optional bath and closet	106 sq. ft.
Total Living Area:	**2,851 sq. ft.**
Daylight basement	1,637 sq. ft.
Garage	572 sq. ft.

Exterior Wall Framing:	2x4

Foundation Options:
Daylight basement
Crawlspace
(All plans can be built with your choice of foundation and framing. A generic conversion diagram is available. See order form.)

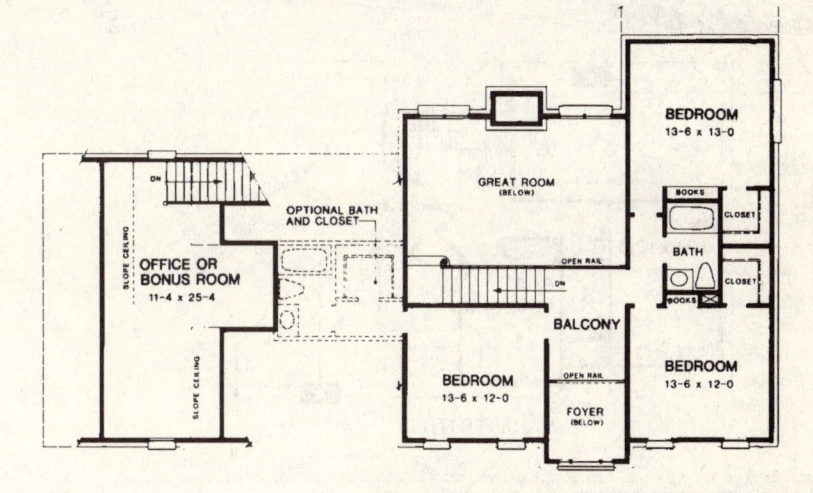

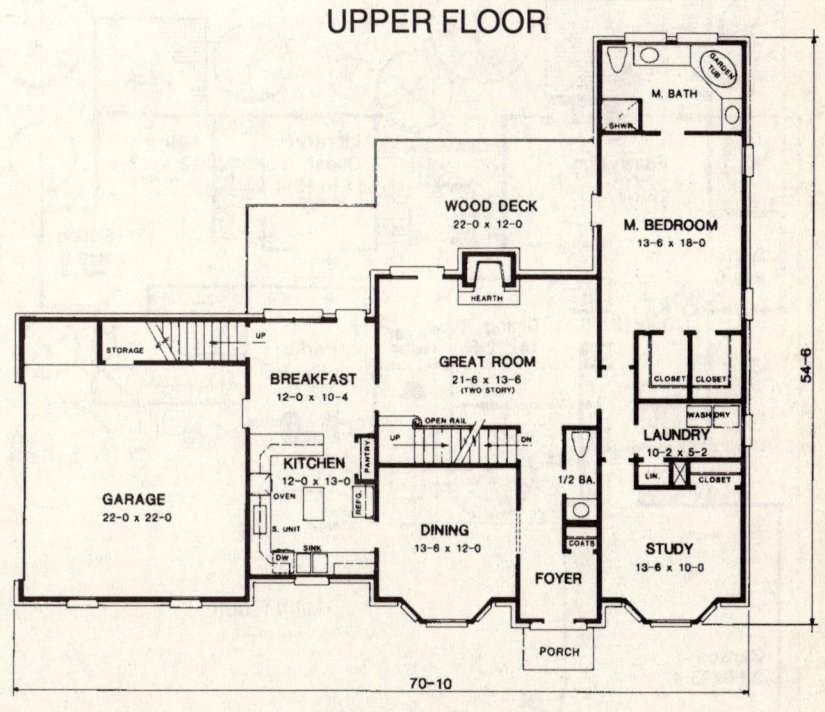

BLUEPRINT PRICE CODE:	**D**

ORDER BLUEPRINTS ANYTIME!
CALL TOLL-FREE 1-888-626-2026

Plan C-9010

PRICES AND DETAILS
ON PAGES 12-15

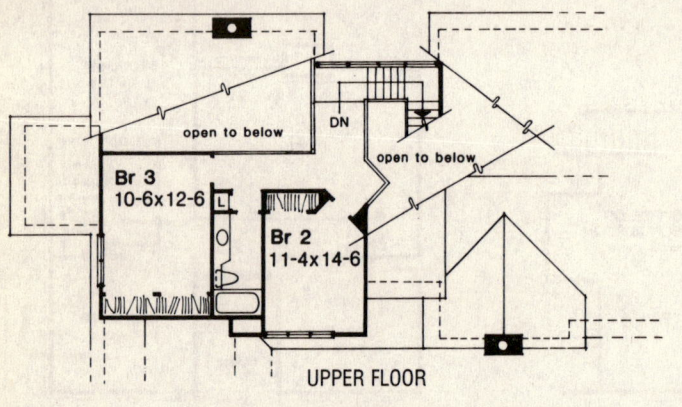

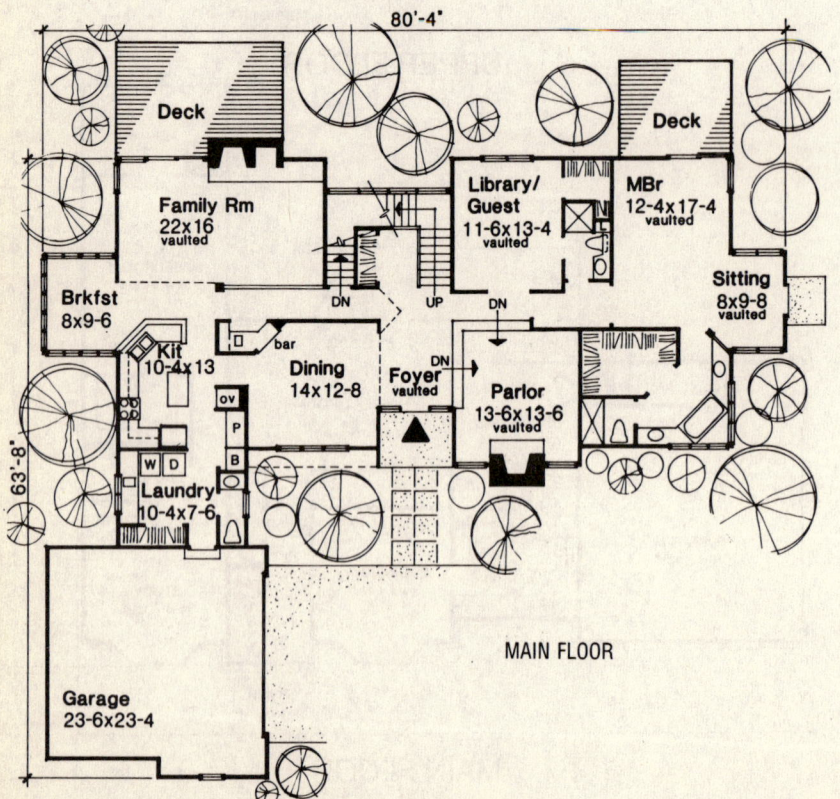

Special Touches In Luxury Home

- Projections and gables in the facade make this an impressive home when viewed from the street.
- The interior, loaded with special design touches, is equally impressive.
- A delightfully bright breakfast area is perfect for everyday meals.
- The plan also includes an impressive foyer, parlor, formal dining room and library/guest bedroom.
- The superb master bedroom includes a sunny sitting area, vaulted ceiling, and deluxe private bath with separate tub and shower and double vanities.

Plan B-127-8509

Bedrooms: 3-4	Baths: 3½

Space:
Upper floor: 635 sq. ft.
Main floor: 2,230 sq. ft.

Total living area: 2,865 sq. ft.
Basement: approx. 1,200 sq. ft.
Garage: 548 sq. ft.

Exterior Wall Framing: 2x4

Foundation options:
Partial basement only.
(Foundation & framing conversion diagram available — see order form.)

Blueprint Price Code: D

ORDER BLUEPRINTS ANYTIME! CALL TOLL-FREE 1-888-626-2026

Plan B-127-8509

PRICES AND DETAILS ON PAGES 12-15

Ever Exquisite!

- The rich brick facade of this exquisite home is embellished by more brick in its decorative columns and arches.
- Past the stately covered stoop, the dramatic entry boasts a 17-ft., 10-in. ceiling and a high plant ledge.
- A wood column sets off the formal dining room; built-in hutch space and a bayed window seat add extra flair.
- The enormous Great Room commands attention with its spectacular half-round window wall. A tile-faced fireplace and a railed opening to the stairway are other highlights.
- A beautiful arch announces the adjacent hearth room, where an exciting media center and corner fireplace await! Patio doors offer an invitation to the backyard.
- A smart hardwood floor extends into the adjoining breakfast area and kitchen, which are divided by a raised snack bar. High transom windows along the breakfast bay add light and ambience.
- French doors open to the secluded master suite, complete with a romantic sitting area and a private garden bath.
- Stairways from the foyer and kitchen climb to a landing before reaching the three upper-floor bedrooms.

Plan CC-2865-M

Bedrooms: 4	Baths: 2½
Living Area:	
Upper floor	745 sq. ft.
Main floor	2,120 sq. ft.
Total Living Area	**2,865 sq. ft.**
Standard basement	2,120 sq. ft.
Garage	700 sq. ft.
Exterior Wall Framing:	2x4

Foundation Options:
Standard basement
(All plans can be built with your choice of foundation and framing. A generic conversion diagram is available. See order form.)

BLUEPRINT PRICE CODE: D

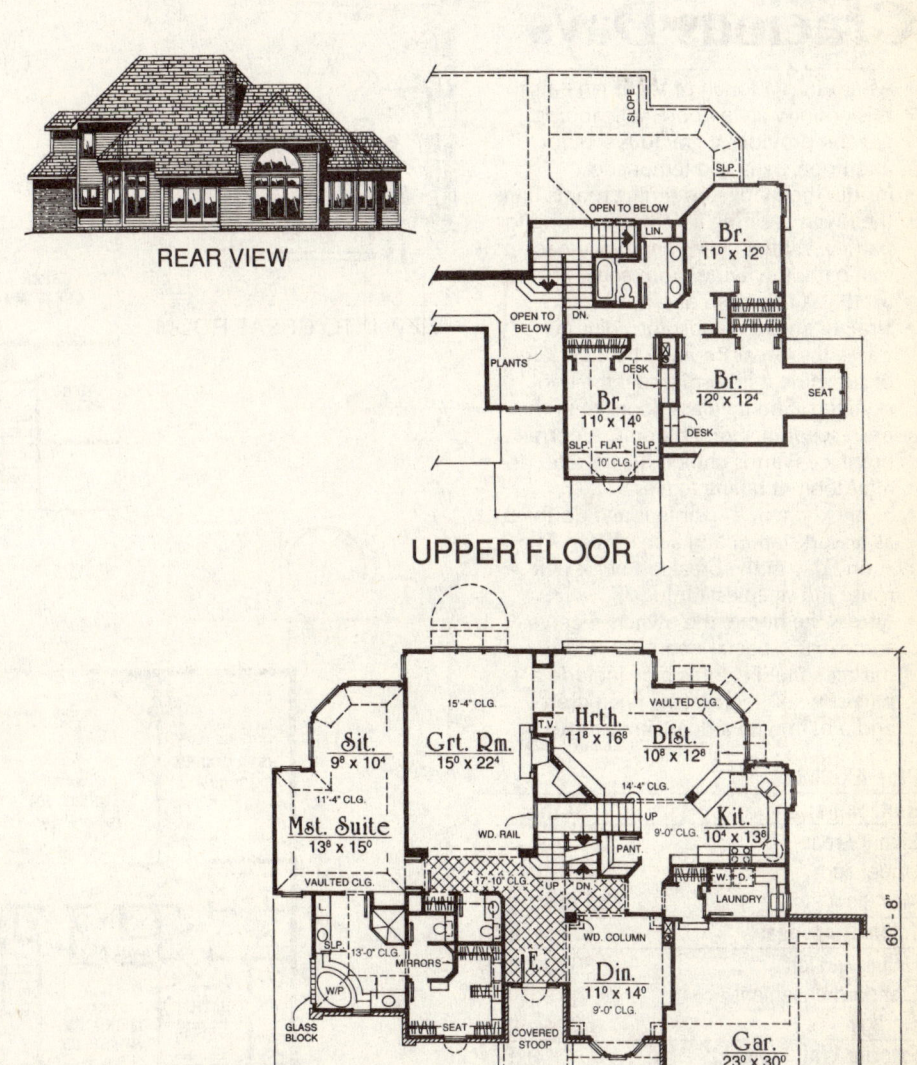

REAR VIEW

UPPER FLOOR

MAIN FLOOR

ORDER BLUEPRINTS ANYTIME!
CALL TOLL-FREE 1-888-626-2026

Plan CC-2865-M

PRICES AND DETAILS ON PAGES 12-15

221

Gracious Days

- As it brings a touch of Victorian flair to this country-style home, a charming gazebo provides a gracious spot for afternoon visits and lemonade.
- Inside, the living and dining rooms flank the foyer, creating an elegant setting for parties. With a closet and private access to a bath, the living room could also be used as a bedroom or a home office.
- Straight ahead, handsome columns frame the Great Room, where puddles of sunshine will form under the two skylights. Sliding glass doors let in the fresh scent of spring blooms. A corner fireplace warms chilled fingers after an afternoon of raking leaves.
- In the kitchen, a sizable island doubles as a workstation and a snack bar. The sunny bay in the breakfast nook will rouse the sleepiest child.
- Across the home, the owners receive some extra special treatment in the master suite. Features here include a pair of walk-in closets, a linen closet and a bath with a dual-sink vanity.

VIEW INTO GREAT ROOM

Plan AX-95349

Bedrooms: 3+	Baths: 3
Living Area:	
Upper floor	728 sq. ft.
Main floor	2,146 sq. ft.
Total Living Area:	**2,874 sq. ft.**
Unfinished loft	300 sq. ft.
Standard basement	2,146 sq. ft.
Garage	624 sq. ft.
Exterior Wall Framing:	2x6

Foundation Options:
Standard basement
Crawlspace
Slab
(All plans can be built with your choice of foundation and framing. A generic conversion diagram is available. See order form.)

BLUEPRINT PRICE CODE: D

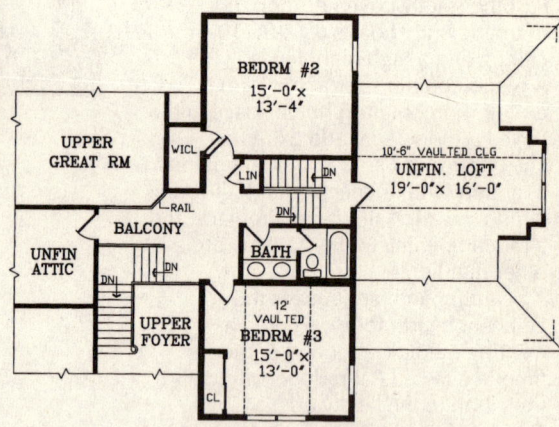

UPPER FLOOR

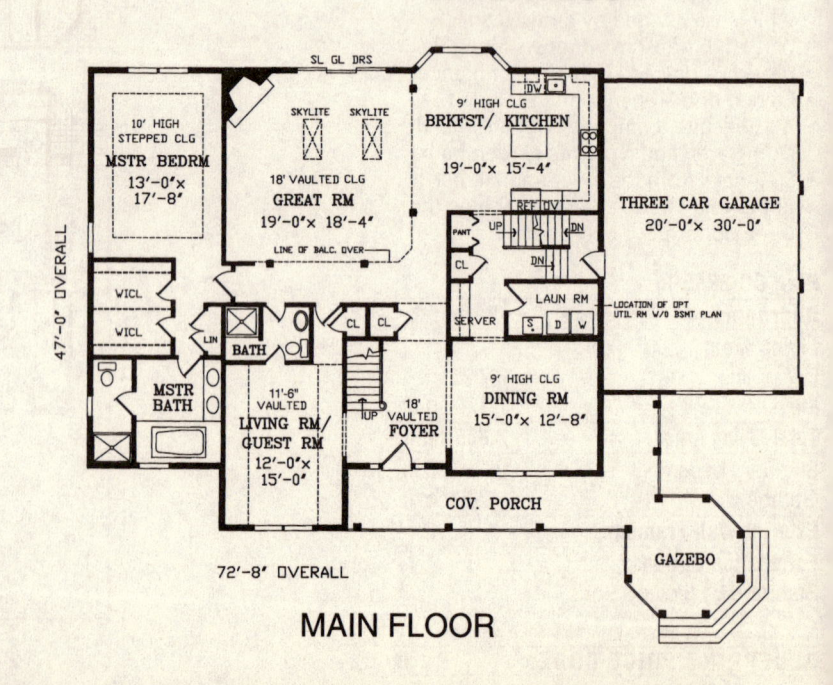

MAIN FLOOR

ORDER BLUEPRINTS ANYTIME!
CALL TOLL-FREE 1-888-626-2026

Plan AX-95349

PRICES AND DETAILS ON PAGES 12-15

Sweet Tooth

- Sparkling paned windows and a sweet, many-leveled roofline make this a delectable home for those with taste.
- Guests will smile as they enter the raised foyer, which flows gracefully into the formal entertaining spaces.
- Conversation is easy around the cozy fireplace in the living room, and lively in the adjoining dining room. Open the French doors to the outside and add a touch of starry ambience to your meal.
- The expansive island kitchen features a windowed sink, plenty of counter space and a lovely octagonal morning room surrounded by windows.
- A window seat highlights the airy living room. A wet bar, with a plant shelf above it, keeps occasions festive.
- Three secondary bedrooms are tucked into a private sleeping area at the front of the home; two share a full bath, while another accesses a hall bath.
- Dominating the right wing of the home, the luscious master suite dishes up a variety of treats, including a sitting area with a gazebo ceiling, a massive walk-in closet and a skylighted bath with a luxurious spa tub.

Plan L-2885

Bedrooms: 4	Baths: 3
Living Area:	
Main floor	2,885 sq. ft.
Total Living Area:	2,885 sq. ft.
Exterior Wall Framing:	2x4

Foundation Options:
Slab
(All plans can be built with your choice of foundation and framing. A generic conversion diagram is available. See order form.)

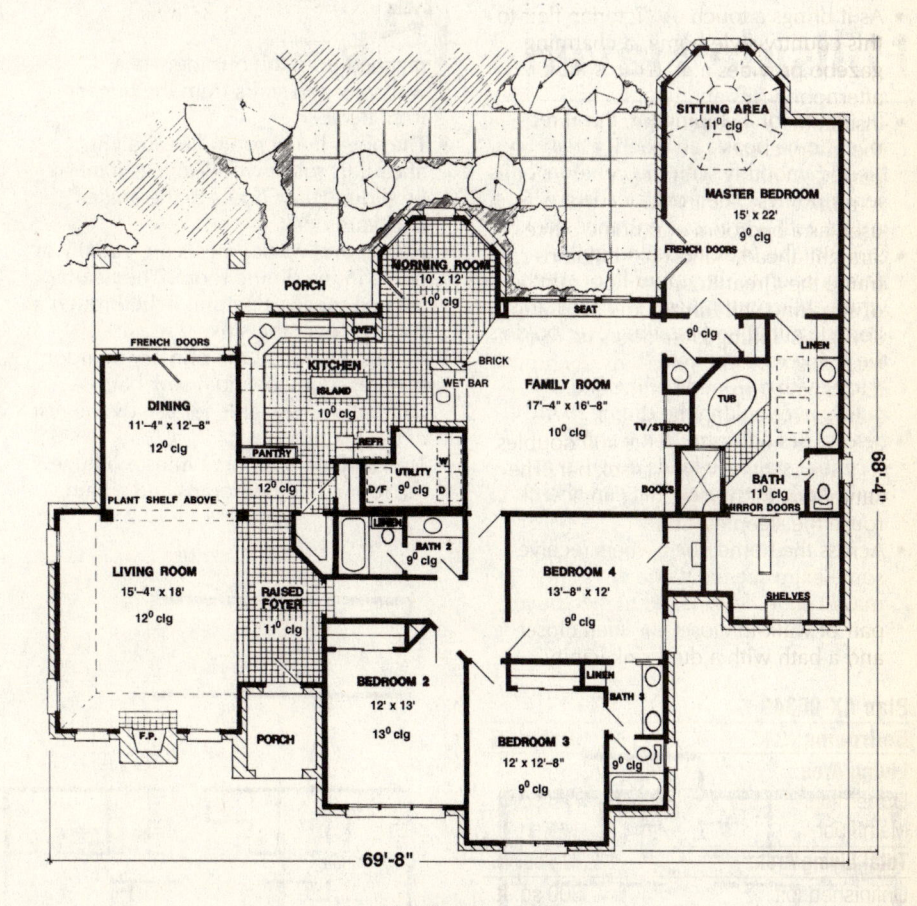

BLUEPRINT PRICE CODE: D

MAIN FLOOR

Plan L-2885

REAR VIEW

Hillside Haven

- Designed for a sloping lot, this three-level home boasts an exterior that blends smoothly with the contours of its surroundings. The front facade greets guests with a gracious entrance deck.
- Doors at the front deck and in the garage open to the upper-floor entry, which welcomes guests with skylights, a sloped ceiling and a railing overlooking the living room below.
- A loft, with a sloped ceiling and a railing overlooking the dining room below, lies adjacent to the entry.
- A central staircase leads down to a main-floor entry area that can also be reached from the outside, via a walkway and stairs from the upper front deck.
- The open living room lies straight ahead. Its rustic woodstove is flanked by sliding glass doors to the angled backyard deck.
- Formal and casual meals are equally at home in the dining room. The nearby kitchen receives natural light through a window over the sink.
- Across the home, the primary bedroom features a private, dual-sink bath. A half-bath is available for use by the rest of the main floor.
- The daylight basement houses a huge rec room, two bedrooms and a bath.

Plan H-966-1B	
Bedrooms: 3+	**Baths:** 2½
Living Area:	
Upper floor	378 sq. ft.
Main floor	1,256 sq. ft.
Daylight basement	1,256 sq. ft.
Total Living Area:	**2,890 sq. ft.**
Garage	528 sq. ft.
Exterior Wall Framing:	2x6

Foundation Options:
Daylight basement
(All plans can be built with your choice of foundation and framing. A generic conversion diagram is available. See order form.)

BLUEPRINT PRICE CODE: D

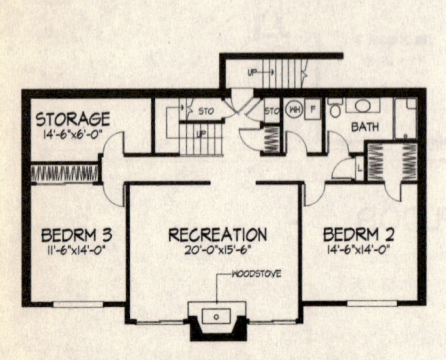

DAYLIGHT BASEMENT

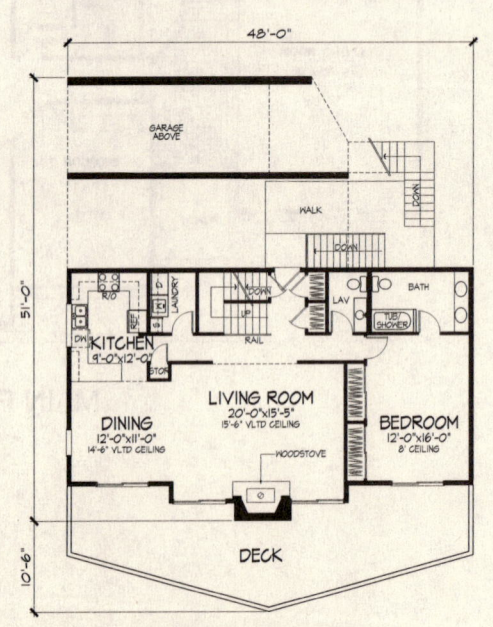

MAIN FLOOR

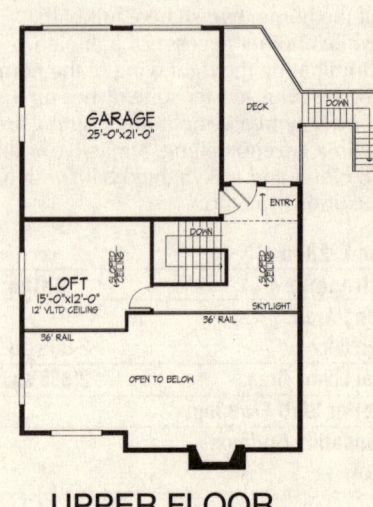

UPPER FLOOR

Plan H-966-1B

Angled Interior

- This plan gives new dimension to one-story living. The exterior has graceful arched windows and a sweeping roofline. The interior is marked by unusual angles and stately columns.
- The living areas are clustered around a large lanai, or covered porch. French doors provide lanai access from the family room, the living room and the master bedroom.
- The central living room also offers arched windows and shares a two-sided fireplace with the family room.
- The island kitchen and the bayed morning room are open to the family room, which features a wet bar next to the striking fireplace.
- The master bedroom features an irresistible bath with a spa tub, a separate shower, dual vanities and two walk-in closets. Two more good-sized bedrooms share another full bath.
- A 12-ft. cathedral ceiling enhances the third bedroom. Standard 8-ft. ceilings are found in the second bedroom and the hall bath. All other rooms boast terrific 10-ft. ceilings.

Plan DD-2802

Bedrooms: 3+	Baths: 2½

Living Area:

Main floor	2,899 sq. ft.
Total Living Area:	**2,899 sq. ft.**
Standard basement	2,899 sq. ft.
Garage	568 sq. ft.
Exterior Wall Framing:	**2x4**

Foundation Options:
Standard basement
Crawlspace
Slab
(All plans can be built with your choice of foundation and framing. A generic conversion diagram is available. See order form.)

BLUEPRINT PRICE CODE: D

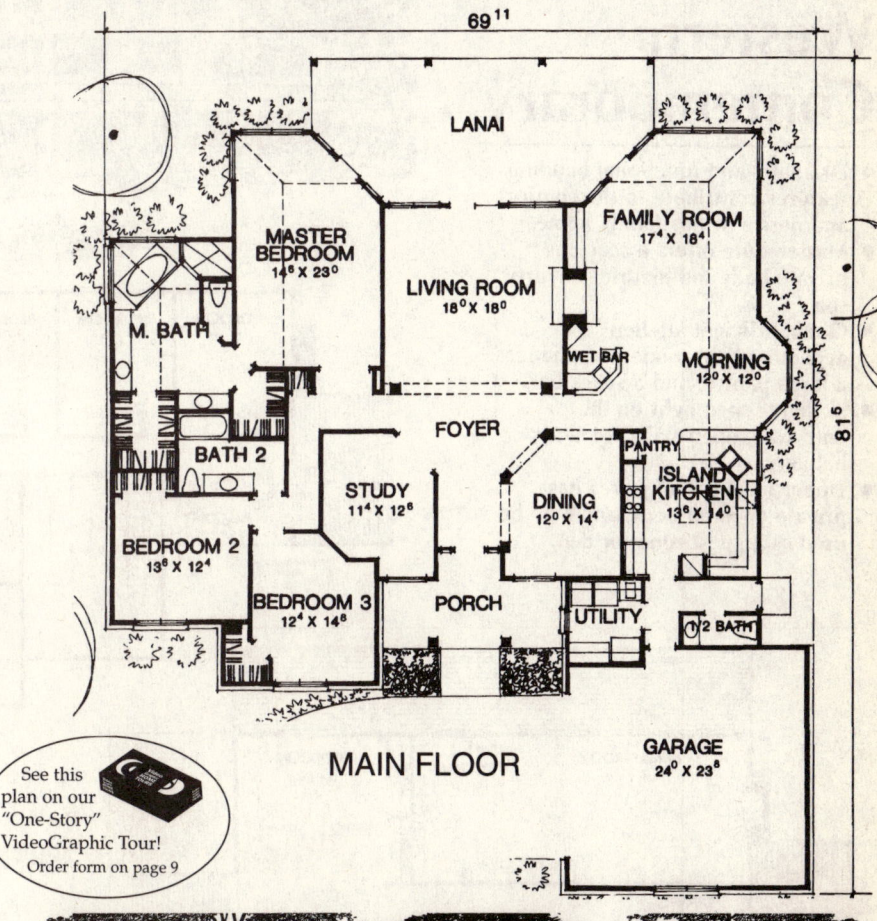

MAIN FLOOR

REAR VIEW

ORDER BLUEPRINTS ANYTIME!
CALL TOLL-FREE 1-888-626-2026

Plan DD-2802

PRICES AND DETAILS
ON PAGES 12-15

225

FRONT VIEW

Dramatic Western Contemporary

- Dramatic and functional building features contribute to the comfort and desire of this family home.
- Master suite offers a spacious private bath and luxurious hydro spa.
- Open, efficient kitchen accommodates modern appliances, a large pantry, and a snack bar.
- Skylights shed light on the entryway, open staircase, and balcony.
- Upper level balcony area has private covered deck, and may be used as a guest room or den.

REAR VIEW

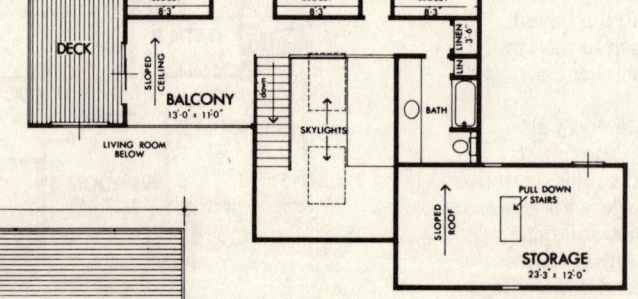

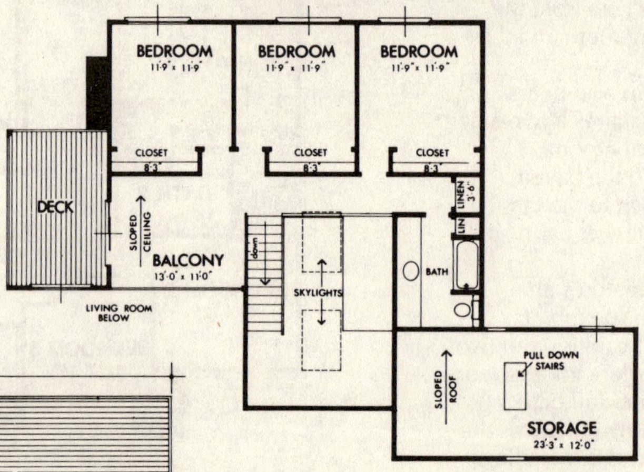

UPPER FLOOR

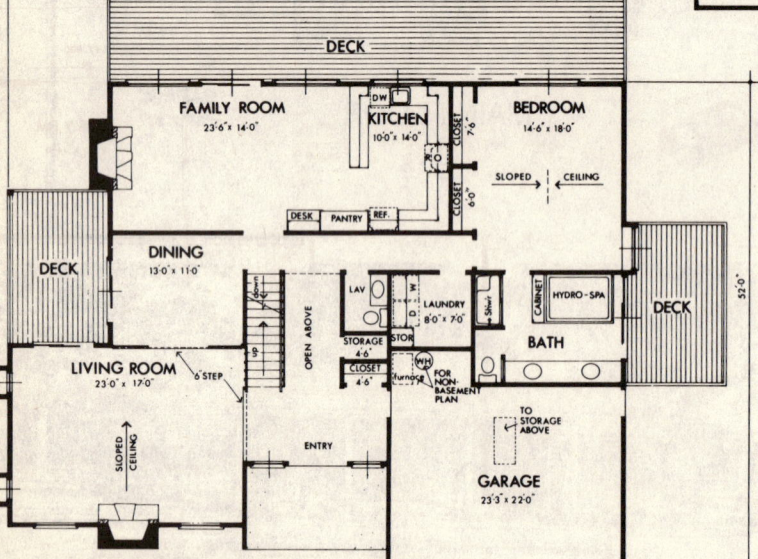

MAIN FLOOR

Plans H-3708-1 & -1A

Bedrooms: 4	Baths: 2½

Space:	
Upper floor:	893 sq. ft.
Main floor:	2,006 sq. ft.
Total living area:	**2,899 sq. ft.**
Basement:	approx. 2,006 sq. ft.
Garage:	512 sq. ft.

Exterior Wall Framing:	2x6

Foundation options:
Daylight basement (Plan H-3708-1).
Crawlspace (Plan H-3708-1A).
(Foundation & framing conversion diagram available — see order form.)

Blueprint Price Code:	D

ORDER BLUEPRINTS ANYTIME!
CALL TOLL-FREE 1-888-626-2026

Plans H-3708-1 & -1A

PRICES AND DETAILS
ON PAGES 12-15

A Family Tradition

- This traditional design has clean, sharp styling, with family-sized areas for formal and casual gatherings.
- The sidelighted foyer is graced with a beautiful open staircase and a wide coat closet. Flanking the foyer are the spacious formal living areas.
- The everyday living areas include an island kitchen, a bayed dinette and a large family room with a fireplace.
- Just off the entrance from the garage, double doors open to the quiet study, which boasts built-in bookshelves.
- A powder room and a deluxe laundry room with cabinets are convenient to the active areas of the home.
- Upstairs, the master suite features a roomy split bath and a large walk-in closet. Three more bedrooms share another split bath.

Plan A-118-DS

Bedrooms: 4+	Baths: 2½
Living Area:	
Upper floor	1,344 sq. ft.
Main floor	1,556 sq. ft.
Total Living Area:	**2,900 sq. ft.**
Standard basement	1,556 sq. ft.
Garage	576 sq. ft.
Exterior Wall Framing:	2x4

Foundation Options:
Standard basement
(All plans can be built with your choice of foundation and framing. A generic conversion diagram is available. See order form.)

BLUEPRINT PRICE CODE: D

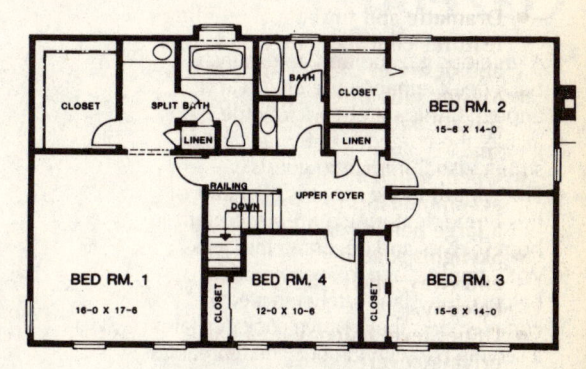

UPPER FLOOR

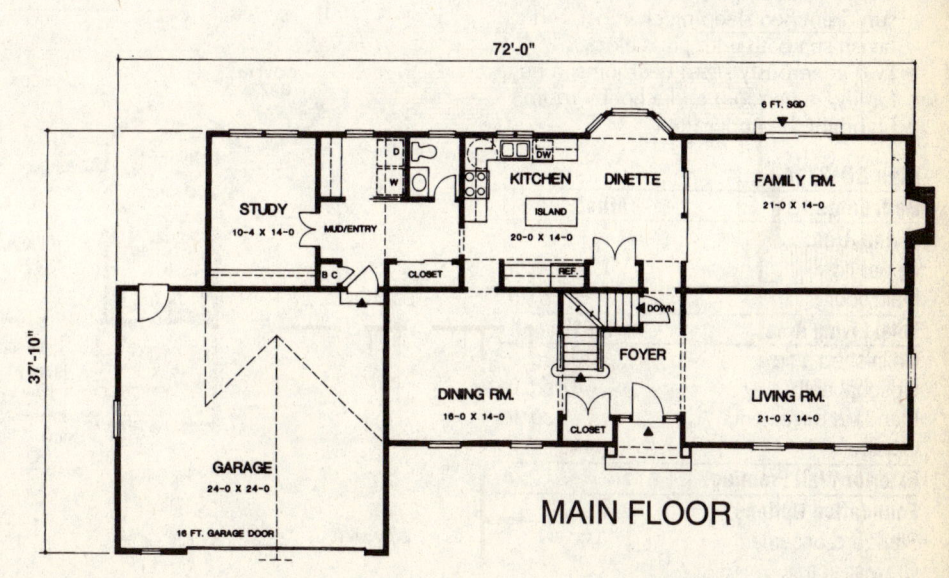

MAIN FLOOR

ORDER BLUEPRINTS ANYTIME!
CALL TOLL-FREE 1-888-626-2026

Plan A-118-DS

PRICES AND DETAILS ON PAGES 12-15

Gracious Gazebo

- A gracious gazebo and an expansive back deck enhance the charm and appeal of this stately brick home.
- Inside, the gorgeous entry delivers a strong visual impact to guests.
- The central living room is the heart of this home, featuring a fireplace, built-in bookshelves and access to the deck.
- With ample space to accommodate helpers, the island kitchen perfectly complements the creative cook. It shares a serving bar with the octagonal breakfast room, which steps out to the gazebo.
- Secluded for privacy and quiet, the elegant master suite boasts a sun-drenched sleeping chamber and a lavish spa bath with glass block.
- Two generously sized bedrooms, a huge family/game room and a hobby room highlight the upper floor.

Plan DD-2714

Bedrooms: 3+	Baths: 2½-3½
Living Area:	
Upper floor	1,144 sq. ft.
Main floor	1,775 sq. ft.
Total Living Area:	**2,919 sq. ft.**
Unfinished attic	206 sq. ft.
Optional bath	47 sq. ft.
Standard basement	1,775 sq. ft.
Garage	440 sq. ft.
Exterior Wall Framing:	2x4

Foundation Options:
Standard basement
Crawlspace
Slab
(All plans can be built with your choice of foundation and framing. A generic conversion diagram is available. See order form.)

BLUEPRINT PRICE CODE: D

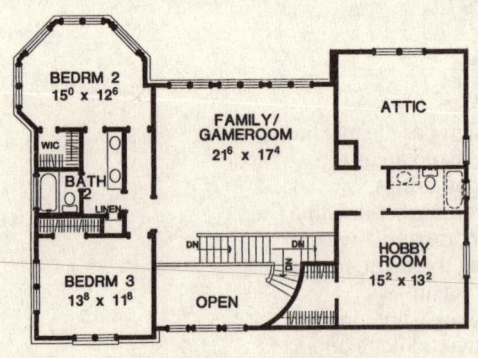

UPPER FLOOR

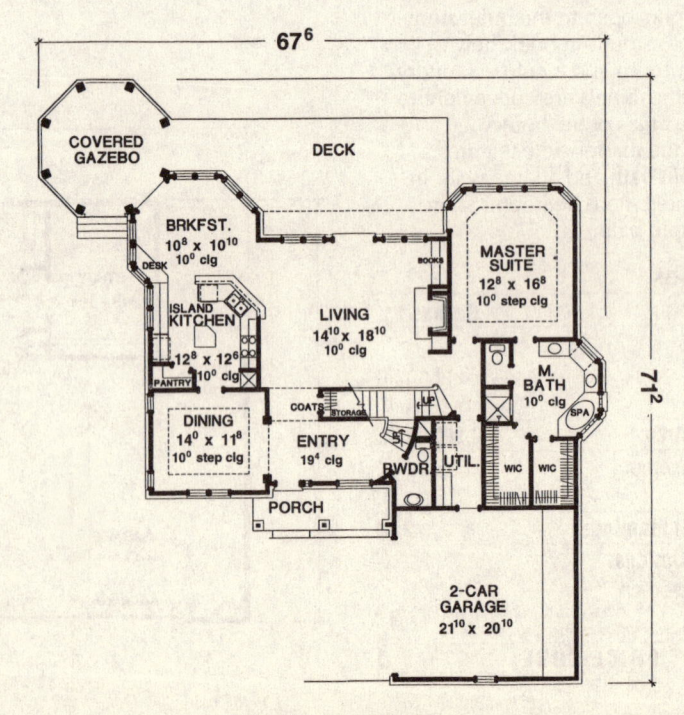

MAIN FLOOR

ORDER BLUEPRINTS ANYTIME! CALL TOLL-FREE 1-888-626-2026

Plan DD-2714

PRICES AND DETAILS ON PAGES 12-15

228

Sprawling French Country

- A hip roof and gable accents give this sprawling home a country, French look.
- To the left of the entry, the formal dining room is illuminated with a tall arched window arrangement.
- The spectacular living room stretches from the entry of the home to the rear. A vaulted ceiling in this expansive space rises to 19 ft., and windows at both ends offer light and a nice breeze.
- Angled walls add interest to the roomy informal areas, which overlook the covered lanai. The island kitchen opens to the adjoining morning room and the sunny family room.
- The spacious main-floor master suite is highlighted by a 13-ft. vaulted ceiling and a bayed sitting area. The master bath features dual walk-in closets, a large spa tub and a separate shower.
- Three extra bedrooms and two more baths share the upper level.

Plan DD-2889

Bedrooms: 4	**Baths:** 3½

Living Area:
Upper floor	819 sq. ft.
Main floor	2,111 sq. ft.
Total Living Area:	**2,930 sq. ft.**
Standard basement	2,111 sq. ft.
Garage	622 sq. ft.
Exterior Wall Framing:	2x4

Foundation Options:
Standard basement
Crawlspace
Slab

All plans can be built with your choice of foundation and framing. A generic conversion diagram is available. See order form.

BLUEPRINT PRICE CODE: D

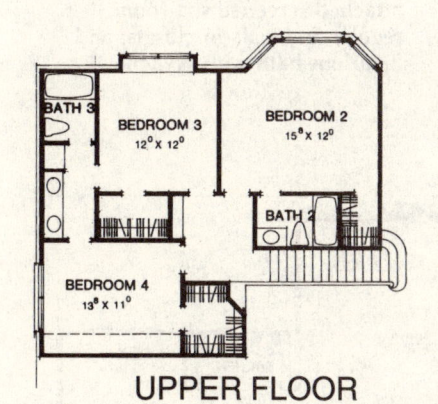

UPPER FLOOR

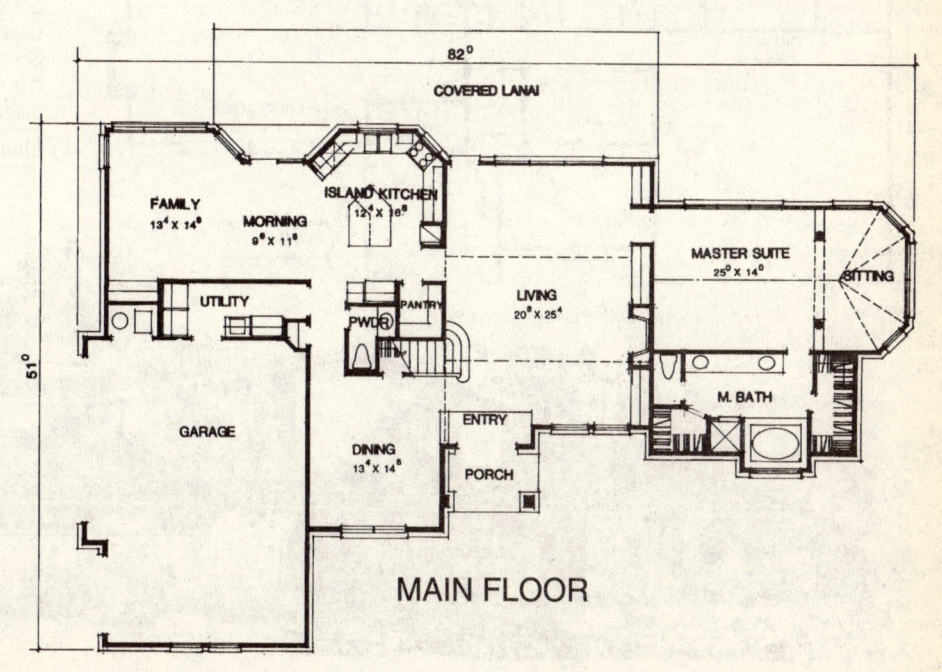

- BATH 3
- BEDROOM 3 — 12⁰ x 12⁰
- BEDROOM 2 — 15⁶ x 12⁰
- BATH 2
- BEDROOM 4 — 13⁶ x 11⁰

MAIN FLOOR

- 82⁰
- 51⁰
- COVERED LANAI
- FAMILY — 13⁴ x 14⁶
- MORNING — 9⁶ x 11⁶
- ISLAND KITCHEN — 12⁶ x 9⁶
- MASTER SUITE — 25⁶ x 14⁶
- SITTING
- UTILITY
- PANTRY
- LIVING — 20⁶ x 25⁴
- PWD
- M. BATH
- GARAGE
- DINING — 13⁴ x 14⁶
- ENTRY
- PORCH

ORDER BLUEPRINTS ANYTIME!
CALL TOLL-FREE 1-888-626-2026

Plan DD-2889

PRICES AND DETAILS ON PAGES 12-15

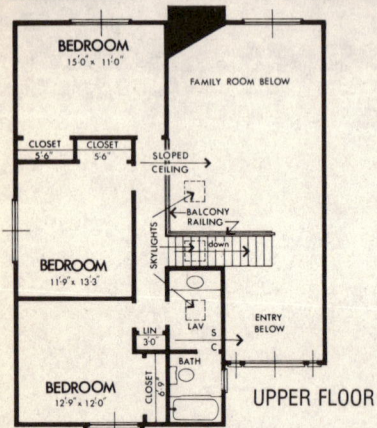

Pure Luxury in a Choice of Styles

- Southwestern colonial or Western contemporary exteriors are available when deciding if this spacious design is for you.
- Elaborate master suite features attached screened spa room, regular and walk-in closets, and luxurious bath with skylight.
- Study, large family and living room with sloped ceilings and rear patio are other points of interest.
- Three additional bedrooms make up the second level.
- The Spanish version (M2A) offers a stucco exterior and slab foundation.

Plans H-3714-1/1A/1B/M2A

Bedrooms: 4	Baths: 3

Space:
Upper floor:	740 sq. ft.
Main floor:	2,190 sq. ft.
Total living area:	**2,930 sq. ft.**
Basement:	1,153 sq. ft.
Garage:	576 sq. ft.

Exterior Wall Framing: 2x6

Foundation options:
Daylight basement (Plan H-3714-1B).
Standard basement (Plan H-3714-1).
Crawlspace (Plan H-3714-1A).
Slab (Plan H-3714-M2A).
(Foundation & framing conversion diagram available — see order form.)

Blueprint Price Code: D

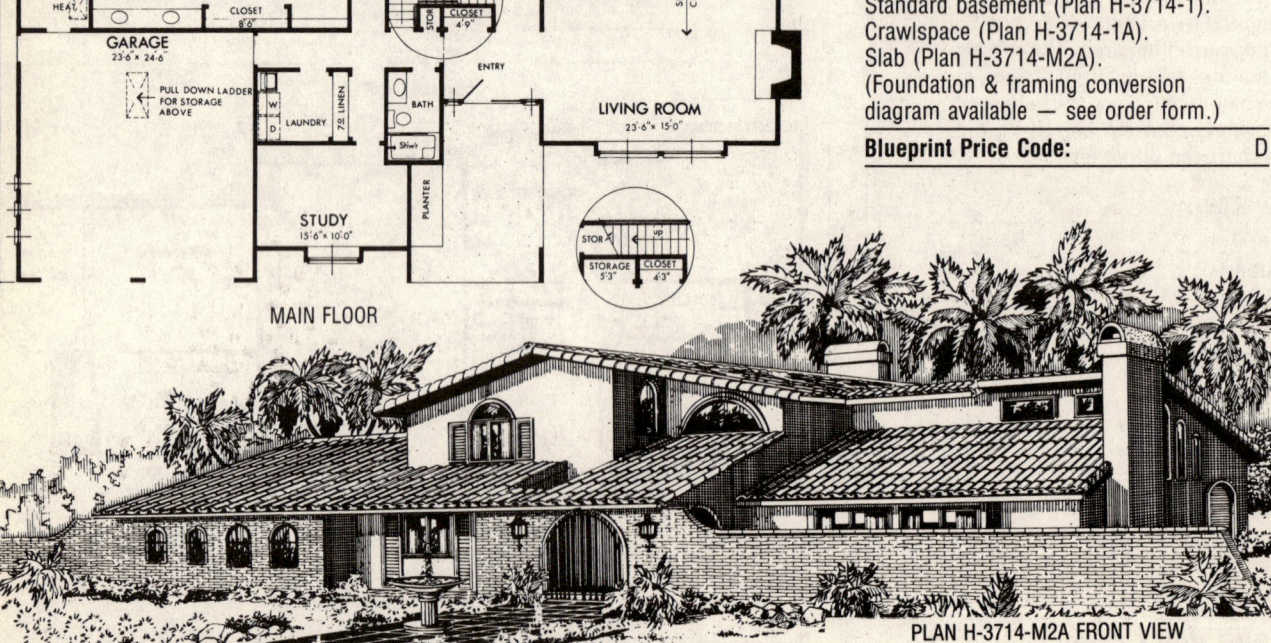

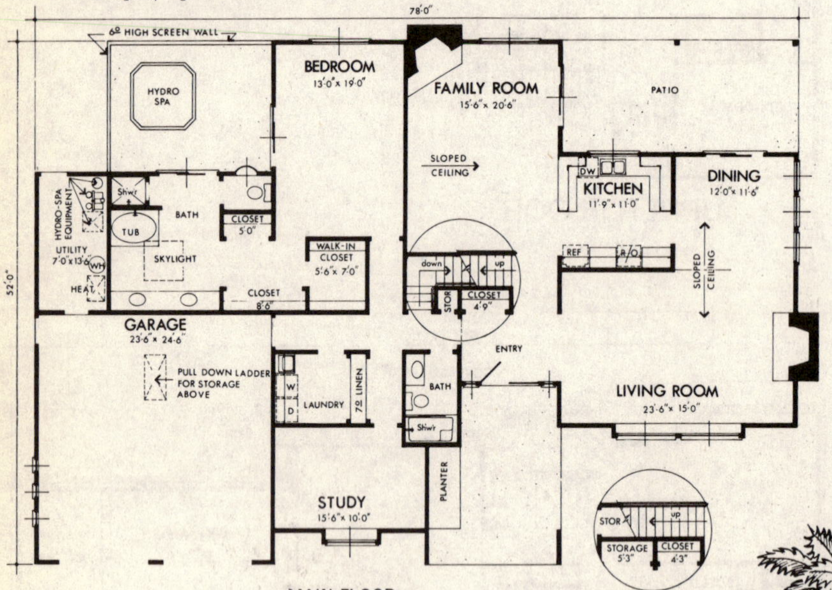

PLAN H-3714-M2A FRONT VIEW

ORDER BLUEPRINTS ANYTIME!
CALL TOLL-FREE 1-888-626-2026
Plans H-3714-1/1A/1B/M2A
PRICES AND DETAILS ON PAGES 12-15

Warm Country

- Three beautiful fireplaces exude wonderful warmth and ambience throughout this stately country home.
- A wide wraparound porch encloses the facade and frames the sidelighted entry. The 23-ft.-high foyer shows off a sweeping stairway as it flows into the formal dining room.
- On the opposite side of the foyer, a roomy study is accessed by French doors and features a handsome fireplace accented by built-in bookshelves.
- A gallery unfolds to the family room, where a French door opens to a porch.
- This porch can also be accessed from the master bedroom. The master bath boasts a large walk-in closet, a Jacuzzi tub and a separate shower.
- The kitchen has a long snack/serving bar that is also great for meal preparation. The adjacent nook sports a built-in breakfast booth and a French door to another porch.
- Along the 14-ft.-high balcony hall are three more bedrooms. One bedroom flaunts its own private bath; another has a built-in desk.
- Unless otherwise specified, all rooms are topped by 9-ft. ceilings.

Plan L-934-VSB

Bedrooms: 4+	Baths: 3½

Living Area:

Upper floor	933 sq. ft.
Main floor	1,999 sq. ft.
Total Living Area:	**2,932 sq. ft.**
Garage	530 sq. ft.
Exterior Wall Framing:	2x4

Foundation Options:
Slab
(All plans can be built with your choice of foundation and framing. A generic conversion diagram is available. See order form.)

BLUEPRINT PRICE CODE: D

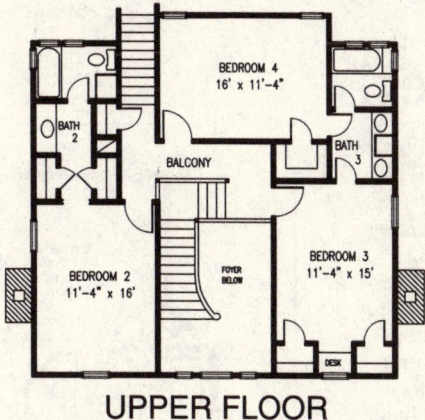

TOUR THIS HOME BEFORE YOU BUILD!
See page 9 for details on Interactive Floor Plans.

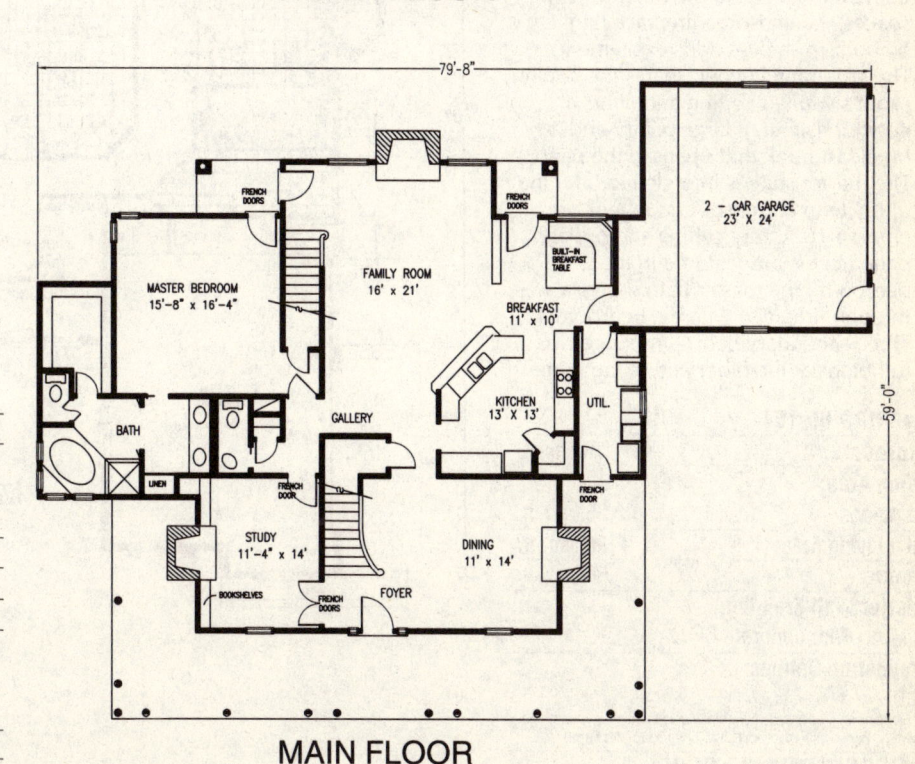

UPPER FLOOR

MAIN FLOOR

ORDER BLUEPRINTS ANYTIME!
CALL TOLL-FREE 1-888-626-2026

Plan L-934-VSB

PRICES AND DETAILS ON PAGES 12-15

Super Features!

- Super indoor/outdoor living features are the main ingredients of this sprawling one-story home.
- Beyond the columned entry, the foyer features a 16-ft.-high ceiling and is brightened by a fantail transom. The dining room and the living room enjoy ceilings that vault to nearly 11 feet.
- The family room, with a 15-ft. vaulted ceiling, sits at the center of the floor plan and extends to the outdoor living spaces. A handsome fireplace flanked by built-in shelves adds excitement.
- The adjoining kitchen shares the family room's vaulted ceiling and offers a cooktop island, a large pantry and a breakfast nook that opens to the patio.
- The master suite is intended to offer the ultimate in comfort. A double-door entry, a 10-ft. tray ceiling and private patio access are featured in the bedroom. The master bath shares a see-through fireplace with the bedroom.
- Three secondary bedrooms share two full baths at the other end of the home.

Plan HDS-99-164

Bedrooms: 4	Baths: 3
Living Area:	
Main floor	2,962 sq. ft.
Total Living Area:	**2,962 sq. ft.**
Garage	567 sq. ft.

Exterior Wall Framing:
2x4 and 8-in. concrete block

Foundation Options:
Slab
(All plans can be built with your choice of foundation and framing. A generic conversion diagram is available. See order form.)

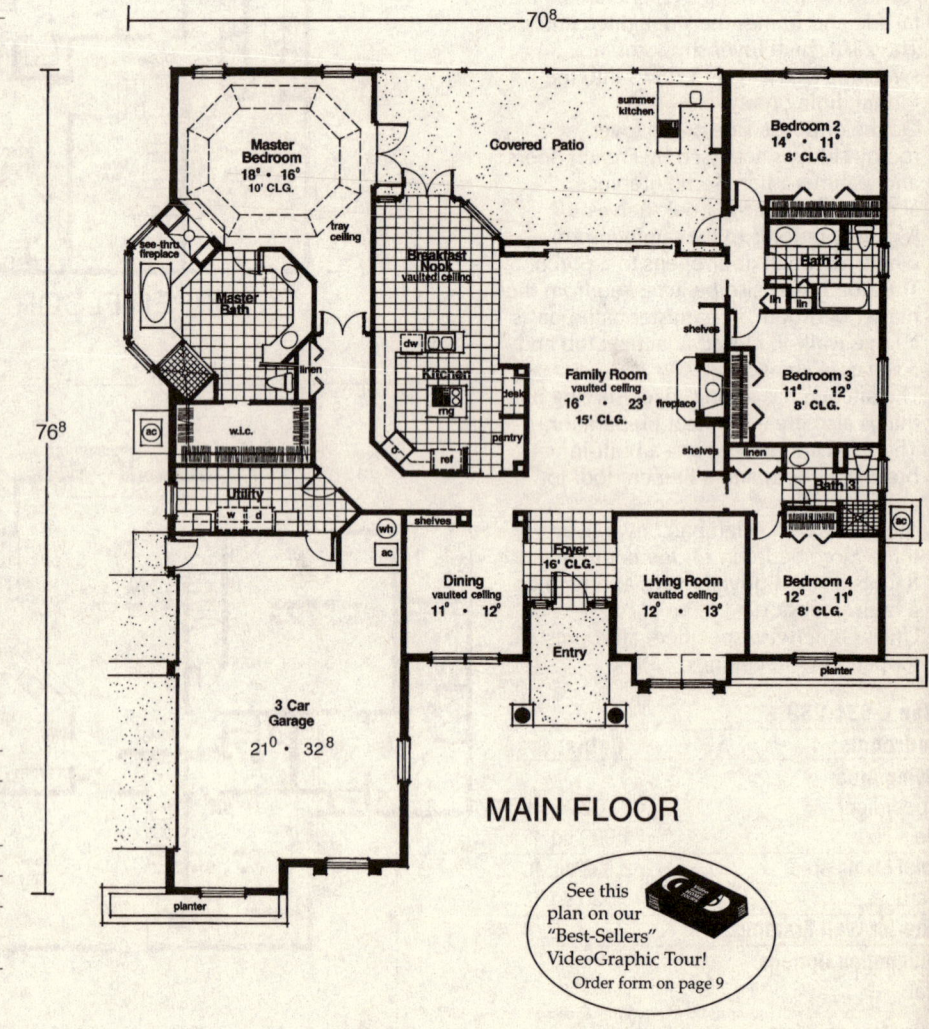

BLUEPRINT PRICE CODE: D

MAIN FLOOR

See this plan on our "Best-Sellers" VideoGraphic Tour! Order form on page 9

ORDER BLUEPRINTS ANYTIME! CALL TOLL-FREE 1-888-626-2026

Plan HDS-99-164

PRICES AND DETAILS ON PAGES 12-15

Stately Elegance

- The elegant interior of this home is introduced by the barrel vault and stately columns at the front entry.
- Double doors open from the entry to the two-story-high foyer, where a half-round transom window brightens the central open-railed stairway.
- Off the foyer, the living room is separated from the sunny dining room by impressive columns.
- The island kitchen offers a bright corner sink, a walk-in pantry and a bayed breakfast area that merges with the spacious family room.
- A door opens from the family room to the backyard patio, plus a wet bar and a fireplace enhance the whole area.
- Upstairs, the master suite boasts a wall of windows and a private bath with two walk-in closets, a corner garden tub and a separate shower. Three additional bedrooms have private access to one of two more full baths.

Plan DD-2968-A

Bedrooms: 4+	Baths: 3½

Living Area:

Upper floor	1,382 sq. ft.
Main floor	1,586 sq. ft.
Total Living Area:	**2,968 sq. ft.**
Standard basement	1,586 sq. ft.
Garage	521 sq. ft.
Exterior Wall Framing:	2x4

Foundation Options:
Standard basement
Crawlspace
Slab
(All plans can be built with your choice of foundation and framing. A generic conversion diagram is available. See order form.)

BLUEPRINT PRICE CODE: D

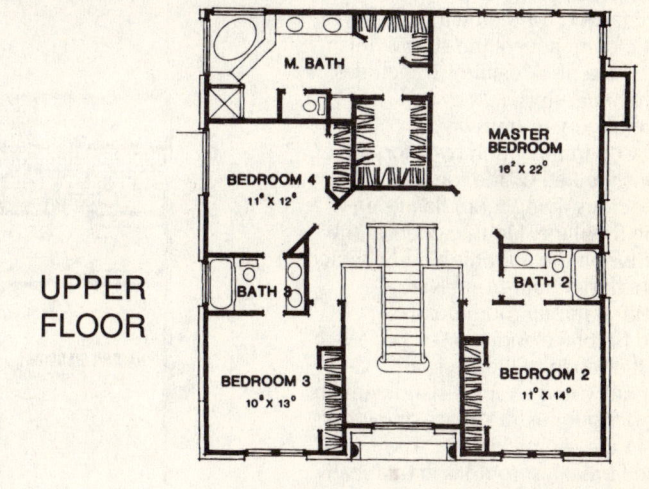

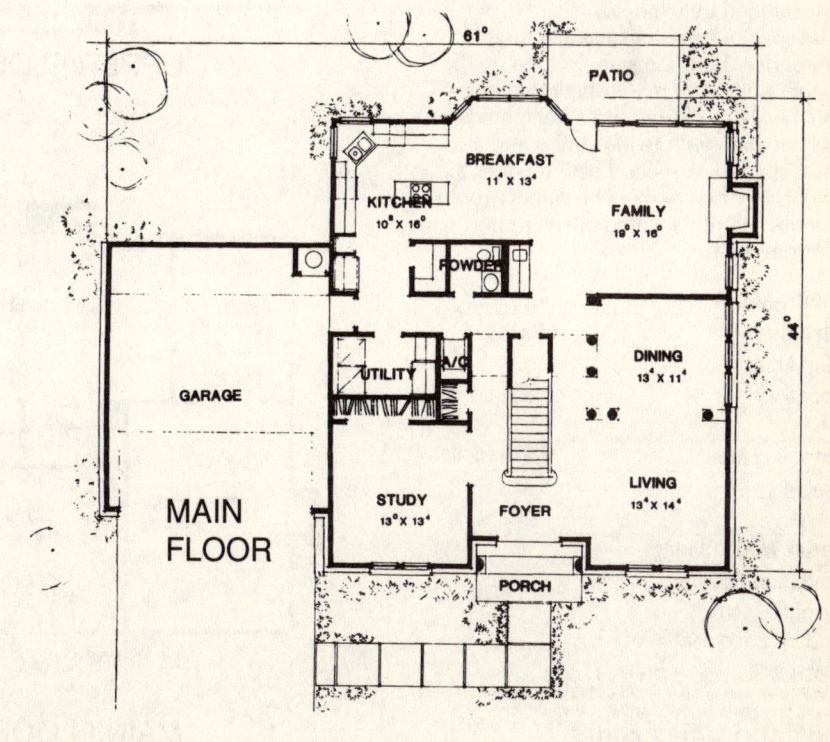

ORDER BLUEPRINTS ANYTIME!
CALL TOLL-FREE 1-888-626-2026

Plan DD-2968-A

PRICES AND DETAILS
ON PAGES 12-15

233

Live in Luxury

- This luxurious home is introduced by a striking facade. Arched windows and a majestic entry accent the stucco finish. An alternate brick exterior is included with the blueprints.
- A graceful curved stairway is showcased in the grand two-story foyer, which is flanked by the formal rooms. The spacious living room flaunts an inviting fireplace. Double doors at the rear close off the adjoining study, which has functional built-in shelves.
- The central family room boasts a second fireplace and two sets of French doors that open to the backyard.
- A full pantry and a range island with an eating bar offer extra storage and work space in the roomy kitchen. The attached breakfast room is dramatically surrounded by windows.
- The spacious master suite and three secondary bedrooms are located on the upper floor. The master bedroom offers dual walk-in closets and a skylighted private bath with twin vanities and an oval spa tub. A second bath services the secondary bedrooms. The laundry room is conveniently located on the upper floor as well.

Plan CH-360-A	
Bedrooms: 4	Baths: 2½
Living Area:	
Upper floor	1,354 sq. ft.
Main floor	1,616 sq. ft.
Total Living Area:	**2,970 sq. ft.**
Basement	1,616 sq. ft.
Garage	462 sq. ft.
Exterior Wall Framing:	2x4

Foundation Options:
Daylight basement
Standard basement
Crawlspace
(All plans can be built with your choice of foundation and framing. A generic conversion diagram is available. See order form.)

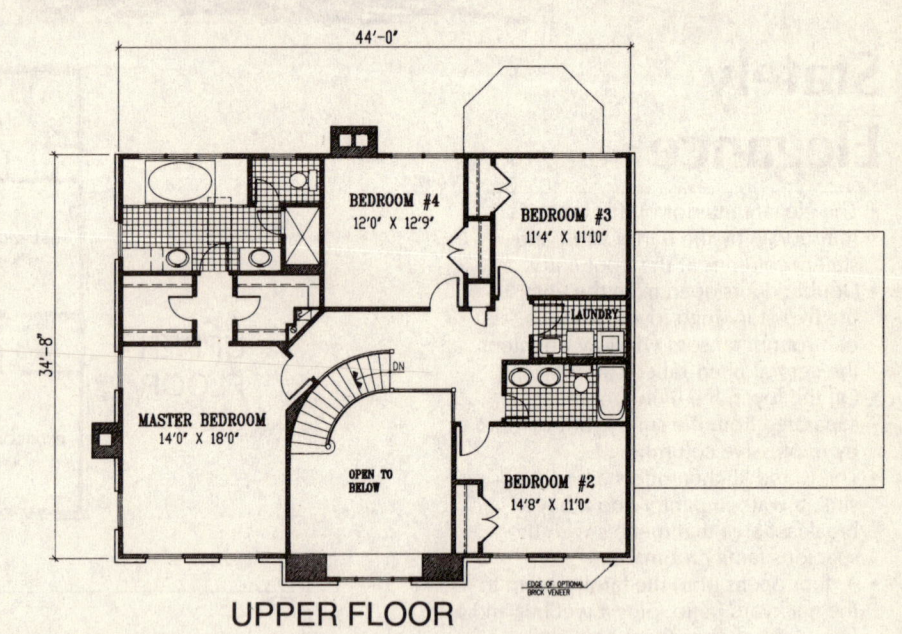

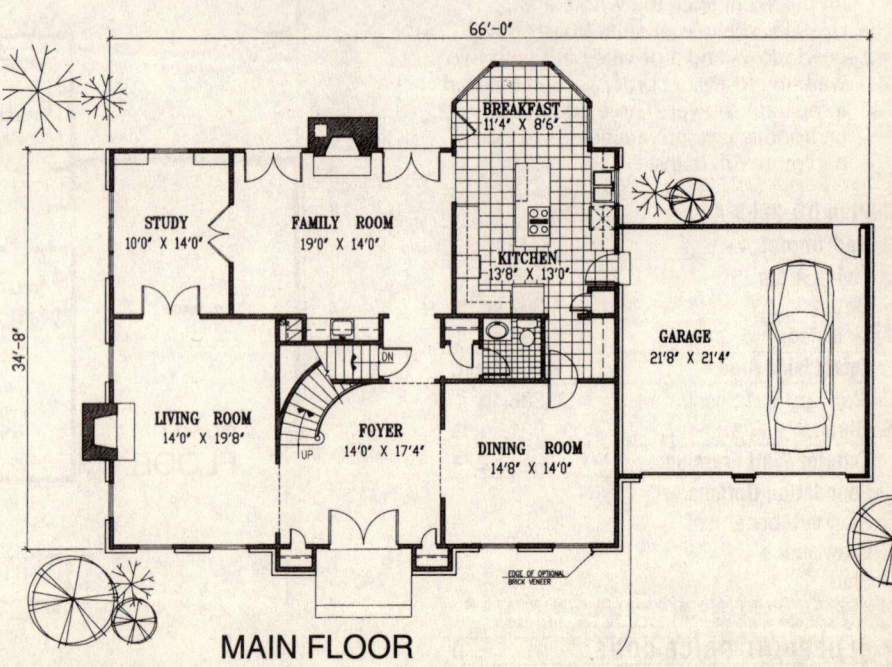

BLUEPRINT PRICE CODE: D

UPPER FLOOR

MAIN FLOOR

ORDER BLUEPRINTS ANYTIME!
CALL TOLL-FREE 1-888-626-2026

Plan CH-360-A

PRICES AND DETAILS ON PAGES 12-15

For Today's Lifestyles

- The facade of this traditional design is elegantly decorated with arched, shuttered windows, a columned, double-doored entrance and an exterior finish of brick or stucco.
- The two-story foyer features a curved stairway and is flanked by the formal living spaces. An optional fireplace would dress up the living room, which could open to the family room through double doors.
- The family room features its own fireplace and access to the outdoors.
- A spacious activity center stretches along the rear of the home, with the merging of the family room, kitchen and breakfast area. The kitchen boasts a functional island range with a snack counter, and an oversized pantry and serving station near the dining room.
- The upper level contains four bedrooms, including a vaulted master suite with a luxurious private bath and large walk-in closets.

Plan CH-180-A

Bedrooms: 4	Baths: 2½
Living Area:	
Upper floor	1,393 sq. ft.
Main floor	1,578 sq. ft.
Total Living Area:	**2,971 sq. ft.**
Basement	1,564 sq. ft.
Garage	462 sq. ft.
Exterior Wall Framing:	2x4

Foundation Options:
Daylight basement
Standard basement
Crawlspace
(Typical foundation & framing conversion diagram available—see order form.)

BLUEPRINT PRICE CODE: D

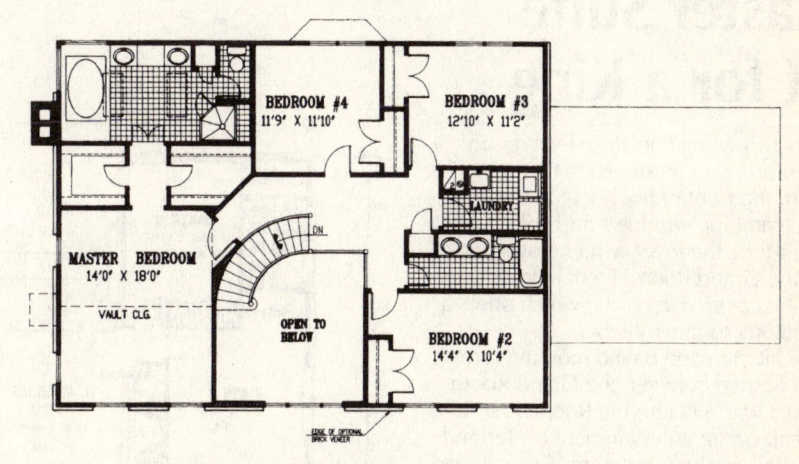

UPPER FLOOR

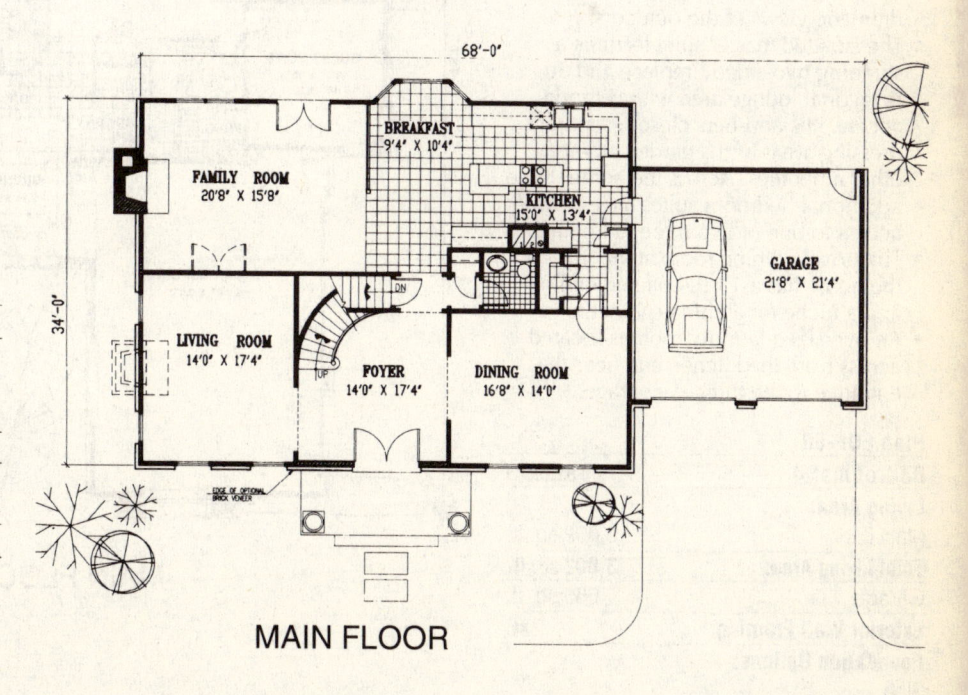

MAIN FLOOR

ORDER BLUEPRINTS ANYTIME!
CALL TOLL-FREE 1-888-626-2026

Plan CH-180-A

PRICES AND DETAILS ON PAGES 12-15

235

Master Suite Fit for a King

- This sprawling one-story features an extraordinary master suite that stretches from the front of the home to the back.
- Eye-catching windows and columns introduce the foyer, which flows back to the Grand Room. French doors open to the covered veranda, which offers a fabulous summer kitchen.
- The kitchen and bayed morning room are nestled between the Grand Room and a warm Gathering Room. A striking fireplace, an entertainment center and an ale bar are found here. This exciting core of living spaces also offers dramatic views of the outdoors.
- The isolated master suite features a stunning two-sided fireplace and an octagonal lounge area with veranda access. His-and-hers closets, separate dressing areas and a garden tub are other amenities. Across the home, three additional bedroom suites have private access to one of two more full baths.
- The private dining room at the front of the home has a 13-ft. coffered ceiling and a niche for a china cabinet.
- An oversized laundry room is located across from the kitchen and near the entrance to the three-car garage.

Plan EOF-60

Bedrooms: 4	Baths: 3
Living Area:	
Main floor	3,002 sq. ft.
Total Living Area:	**3,002 sq. ft.**
Garage	660 sq. ft.
Exterior Wall Framing:	2x6

Foundation Options:
Slab
(All plans can be built with your choice of foundation and framing. A generic conversion diagram is available. See order form.)

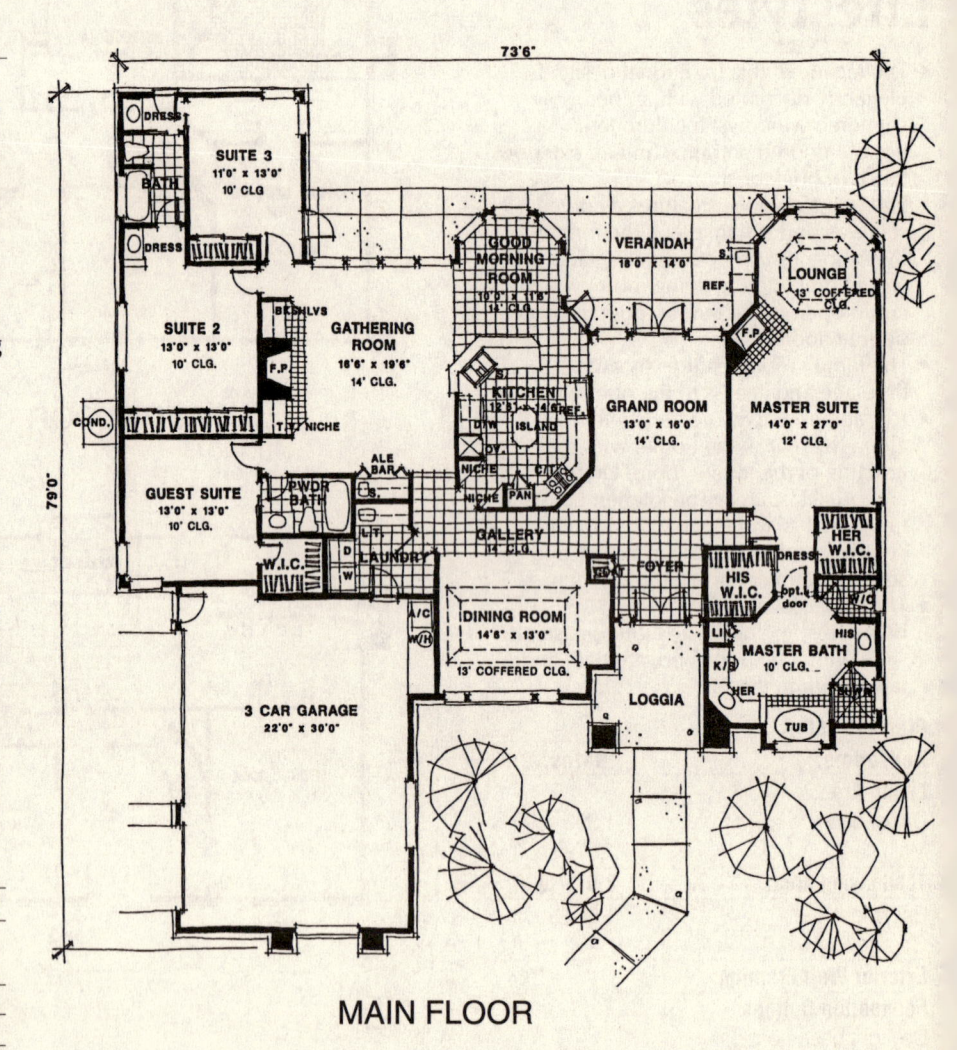

BLUEPRINT PRICE CODE: E

MAIN FLOOR

ORDER BLUEPRINTS ANYTIME!
CALL TOLL-FREE 1-888-626-2026

Plan EOF-60

PRICES AND DETAILS ON PAGES 12-15

Doubled Up

- Double porches, stately columns and stunning half-round windows highlight this home's facade.
- Located near the foyer and next to a full bath, the quiet study would serve nicely as a guest room.
- A wide, arched entrance to the right of the foyer showcases the formal dining room. A rear door closes off the kitchen.
- Beautiful columns dress up the kitchen and breakfast nook, where views to the backyard make morning meals fun and relaxing. Dramatic windows escalate to the nook's 17-ft., 3-in.-high ceiling.
- French doors open to a covered backyard porch from the Great Room, where a fireplace exudes warmth.
- The master bedroom boasts a 12-ft., 9-in. vaulted ceiling and a sumptuous bath that includes a vast walk-in closet, a whirlpool tub and a separate shower.
- Unless otherwise noted, all main-floor rooms have 9-ft. ceilings.
- Upstairs, classy French doors open to balconies at the front and rear. A spacious playroom with a view of the nook below gives kids a space of their own to explore and enjoy.
- One of the three secondary bedrooms flaunts an efficient built-in desk.

Plan J-9420	
Bedrooms: 4+	**Baths:** 4
Living Area:	
Upper floor	1,145 sq. ft.
Main floor	1,863 sq. ft.
Total Living Area:	**3,008 sq. ft.**
Standard basement	1,863 sq. ft.
Garage and storage	570 sq. ft.
Exterior Wall Framing:	2x4
Foundation Options:	
Standard basement	
Crawlspace	
Slab	

(All plans can be built with your choice of foundation and framing. A generic conversion diagram is available. See order form.)

BLUEPRINT PRICE CODE: E

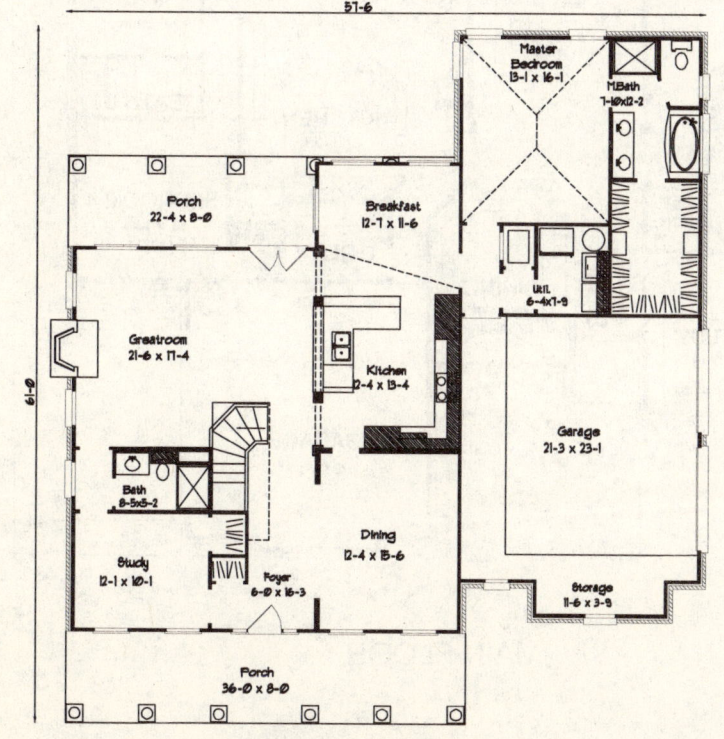

MAIN FLOOR

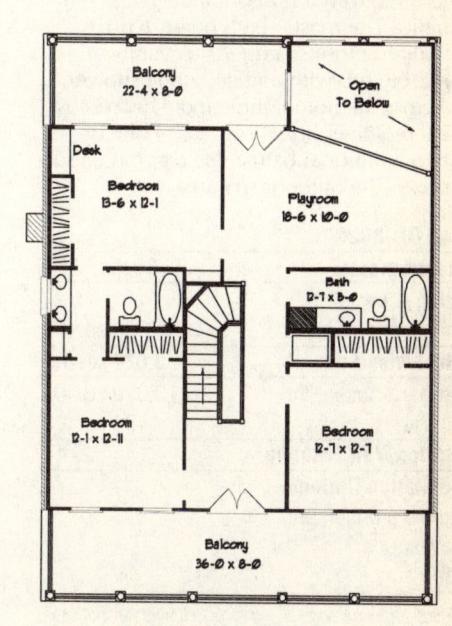

UPPER FLOOR

ORDER BLUEPRINTS ANYTIME!
CALL TOLL-FREE 1-888-626-2026

Plan J-9420

PRICES AND DETAILS
ON PAGES 12-15

Manor Defined

- This grand manor is defined from the outset, with stylish gables, artistic masonry and tall, arched windows.
- Inside the home, raised ceilings add to the elegance throughout. At the front, a grand entry flows between a study and the formal dining room.
- A wall of windows in the tray-ceilinged living room brightens any occasion.
- Around the corner, the gourmet kitchen offers plenty of space for meal planning and preparation. Not without style though, the kitchen's breakfast area shares a see-through fireplace with the family room.
- A corner window in the family room directs the focus out of doors, where an inviting patio offers a built-in spa tub.
- The master bedroom has its own door to the covered portion of the back patio. The master bath boasts twin walk-in closets, a dual-sink vanity and a marble tub with a neighboring shower.
- Across the home, three more bedrooms each deliver private access to one of two additional baths. The rear bath also serves the outdoor spa area.

Plan DD-3029

Bedrooms: 4+	Baths: 3½

Living Area:

Main floor	3,029 sq. ft.
Total Living Area:	**3,029 sq. ft.**
Standard basement	3,029 sq. ft.
Garage	484 sq. ft.
Exterior Wall Framing	2x4

Foundation Options:
Standard basement
Crawlspace
Slab

(All plans can be built with your choice of foundation and framing. A generic conversion diagram is available. See order form.)

BLUEPRINT PRICE CODE: E

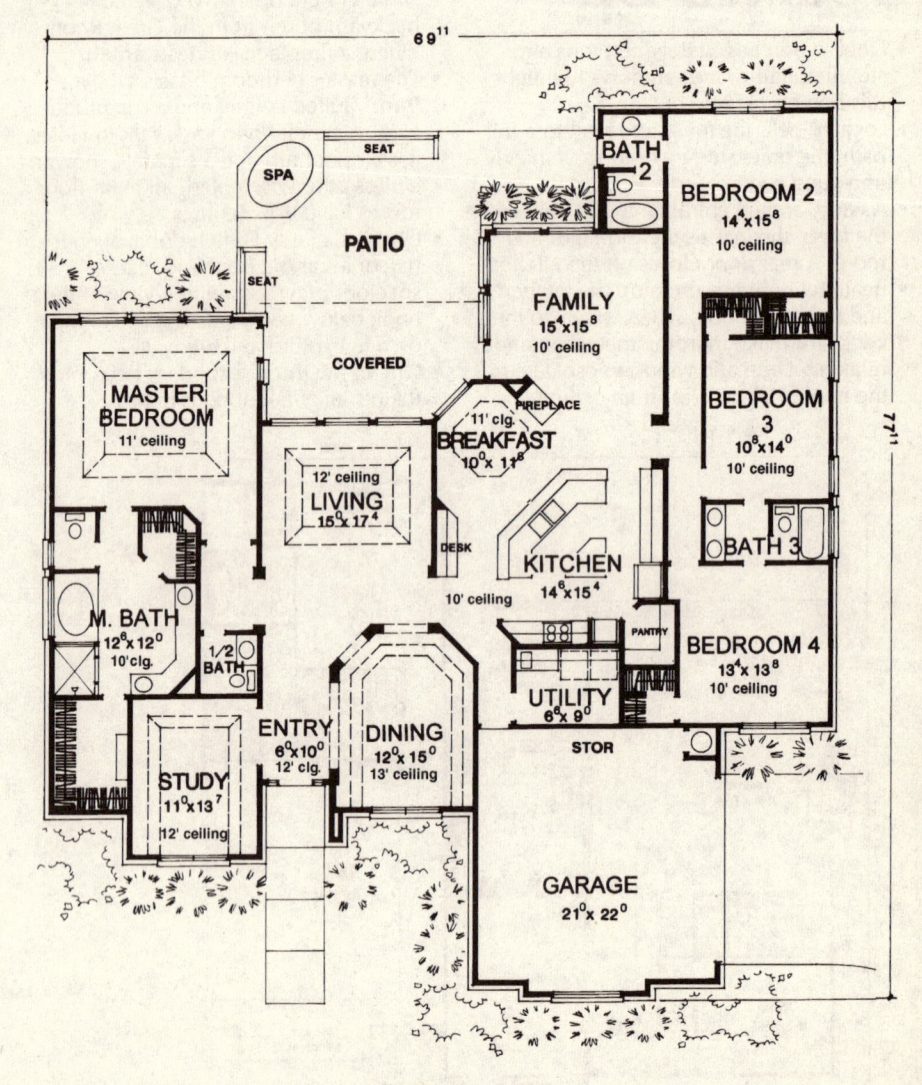

MAIN FLOOR

Plan DD-3029

ORDER BLUEPRINTS ANYTIME!
CALL TOLL-FREE 1-888-626-2026

PRICES AND DETAILS ON PAGES 12-15

High Comfort

- Metal roof overhangs, paneled shutters and an ornate arched entry are appropriate adornments for this exquisite luxury home.
- From the three-car garage to the sprawling master suite, this home is designed for maximum comfort.
- All four of the bedrooms have generous closet space and private access to a bath. The master bedroom suite includes a private garden bath and also enjoys a plush octagonal sitting room.
- Another bonus? Dirty clothes can be piled up in the central laundry room without climbing any stairs!
- The kitchen below has so much cabinet space, you may be pressed to fill it. With the work desk, extra oven space, massive pantry and oversized island, being organized was never this easy!
- Relaxation is possible for everyone in the huge two-story family room, complete with a blazing fireplace and a convenient pass-through to the kitchen.
- When entertaining, guests can mingle between the dining and living rooms.

Plan FB-5545-HUNT

Bedrooms: 4	Baths: 3½
Living Area:	
Upper floor	1,632 sq. ft.
Main floor	1,415 sq. ft.
Total Living Area:	**3,047 sq. ft.**
Daylight basement	1,415 sq. ft.
Garage	766 sq. ft.
Exterior Wall Framing:	2x4

Foundation Options:
Daylight basement
(All plans can be built with your choice of foundation and framing. A generic conversion diagram is available. See order form.)

BLUEPRINT PRICE CODE: E

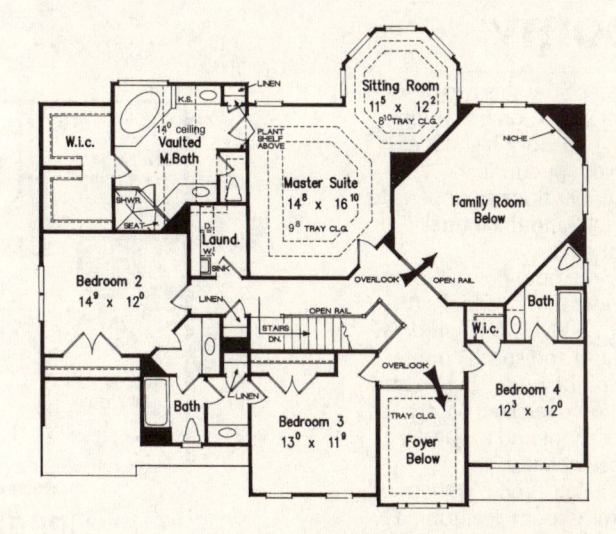

UPPER FLOOR

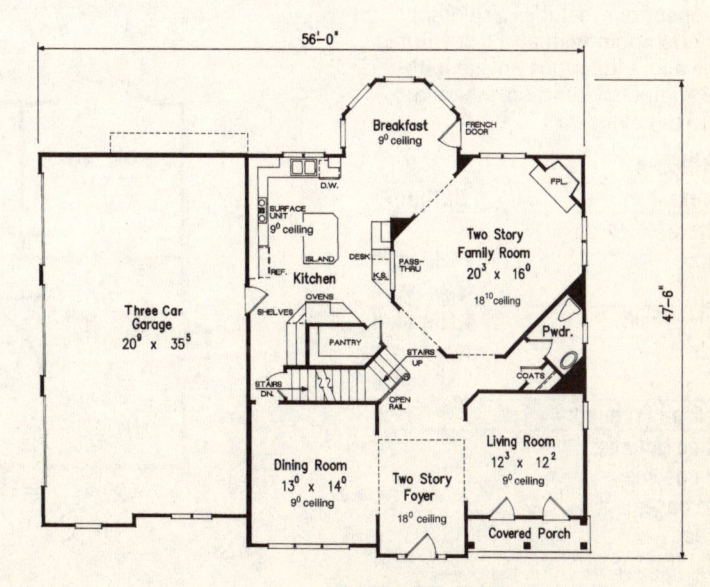

MAIN FLOOR

ORDER BLUEPRINTS ANYTIME!
CALL TOLL-FREE 1-888-626-2026

Plan FB-5545-HUNT

PRICES AND DETAILS
ON PAGES 12-15

Stately and Roomy

- The exquisite exterior of this two-story home opens to a very roomy interior.
- The magnificent two-story-high foyer shows off a curved, open-railed stairway to the upper floor and opens to a study on the right and the formal living areas on the left.
- The spacious living room flows into a formal dining room that overlooks the outdoors through a lovely bay window.
- A large work island and snack counter sit at the center of the open kitchen and breakfast room. An oversized pantry closet, a powder room and a laundry room are all close at hand.
- Adjoining the breakfast room is the large sunken family room, featuring a 12-ft.-high vaulted ceiling, a cozy fireplace and outdoor access.
- The upper floor includes a stunning master bedroom with an 11-ft. vaulted ceiling and a luxurious private bath.
- Three additional bedrooms share a second full bath.

Plan CH-280-A

Bedrooms: 4+	Baths: 2½
Living Area:	
Upper floor	1,262 sq. ft.
Main floor	1,797 sq. ft.
Total Living Area:	**3,059 sq. ft.**
Basement	1,797 sq. ft.
Garage	462 sq. ft.
Exterior Wall Framing:	2x4

Foundation Options:
Daylight basement
Standard basement
Crawlspace
(All plans can be built with your choice of foundation and framing. A generic conversion diagram is available. See order form.)

BLUEPRINT PRICE CODE: E

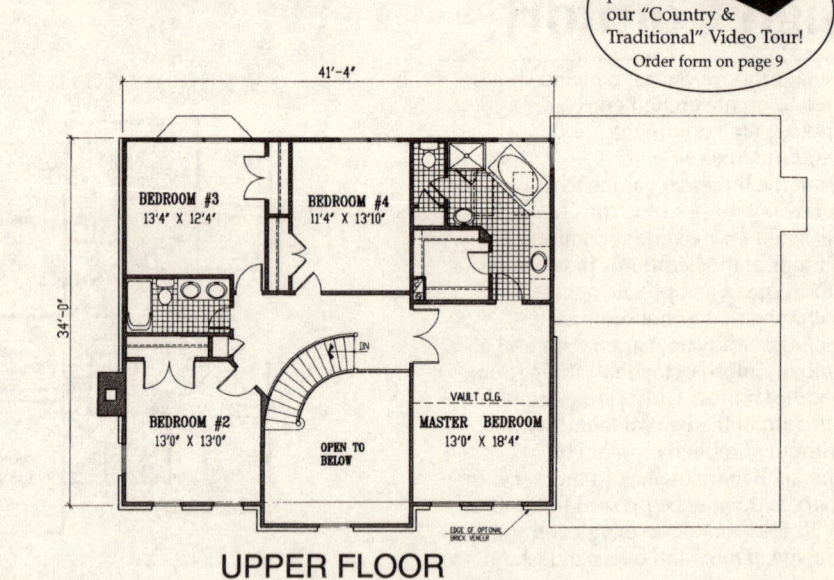

See this plan on our "Country & Traditional" Video Tour! Order form on page 9

UPPER FLOOR

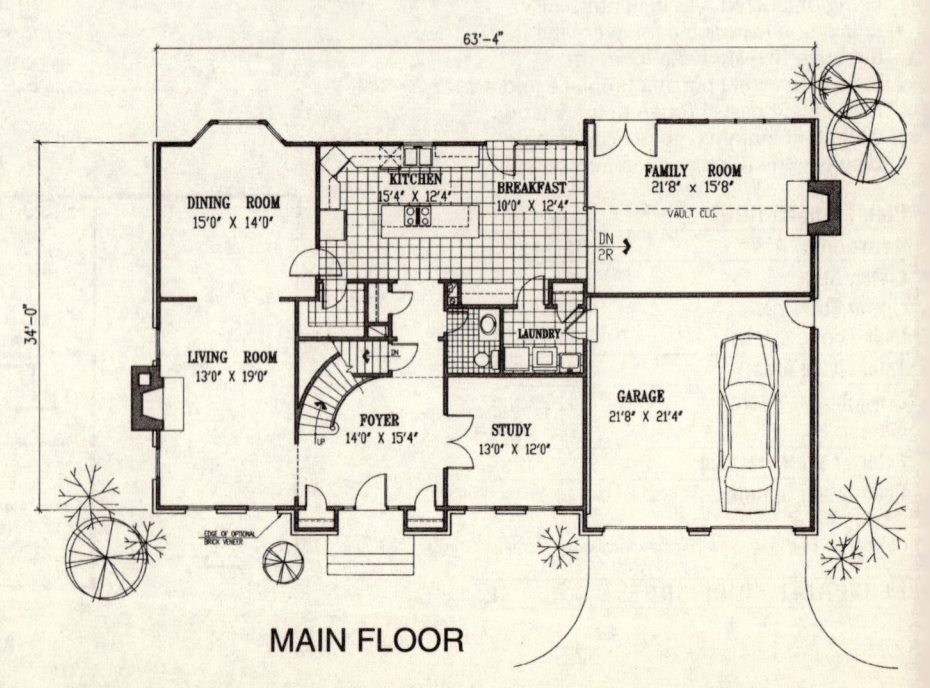

MAIN FLOOR

ORDER BLUEPRINTS ANYTIME!
CALL TOLL-FREE 1-888-626-2026

Plan CH-280-A

PRICES AND DETAILS ON PAGES 12-15

Formal, Casual Entertainment

- This charming home has plenty of space for both formal and casual entertaining.
- On the main floor, the huge central living room will pamper your guests with an impressive fireplace, a wet bar and two sets of French doors that expand the room to a backyard porch.
- The large formal dining room hosts those special, sit-down dinners.
- There's still more space in the roomy island kitchen and breakfast nook to gather for snacks and conversation.
- For quiet evenings alone, the plush master suite offers pure relaxation! A romantic two-way fireplace between the bedroom and the bath serves as the focal point, yet the whirlpool garden tub is just as inviting.
- The main-floor rooms are enhanced by 10-ft. ceilings; the upper-floor rooms have 9-ft. ceilings.
- The kids' recreation time can be spent in the enormous game room on the upper floor. Private baths service each of the vaulted upper-floor bedrooms.

Plan L-105-VC

Bedrooms: 4+	Baths: 4
Living Area:	
Upper floor	1,077 sq. ft.
Main floor	1,995 sq. ft.
Total Living Area:	**3,072 sq. ft.**
Garage	529 sq. ft.
Storage	184 sq. ft.
Exterior Wall Framing:	2x4

Foundation Options:
Slab
(All plans can be built with your choice of foundation and framing. A generic conversion diagram is available. See order form.)

BLUEPRINT PRICE CODE: E

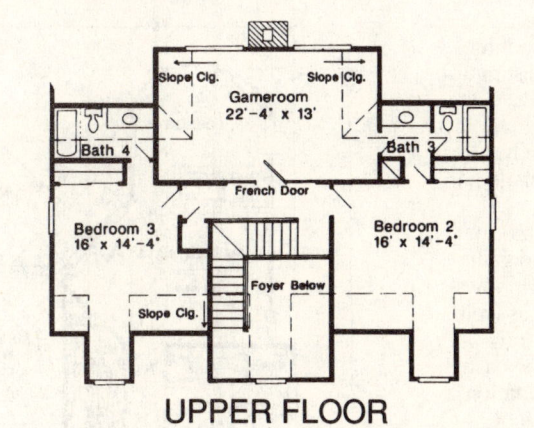

TOUR THIS HOME BEFORE YOU BUILD!

See page 9 for details on Interactive Floor Plans.

UPPER FLOOR

MAIN FLOOR

ORDER BLUEPRINTS ANYTIME!
CALL TOLL-FREE 1-888-626-2026

Plan L-105-VC

PRICES AND DETAILS ON PAGES 12-15

Distinguished Living

- Beautiful arches, sweeping rooflines and a dramatic entry court distinguish this one-story from all the rest.
- Elegant columns outline the main foyer. To the right, the dining room has a 13-ft. coffered ceiling and an ale bar with a wine rack.
- The centrally located Grand Room can be viewed from the foyer and gallery. French doors and flanking windows allow a view of the veranda as well.
- A large island kitchen and sunny morning room merge with the casual Gathering Room. The combination offers a big fireplace, a TV niche, bookshelves and a handy snack bar.
- The extraordinary master suite flaunts a 12-ft. ceiling, an exciting three-sided fireplace and a TV niche shared with the private bayed lounge. A luxurious bath, a private library and access to the veranda are also featured.
- The two smaller bedroom suites have private baths and generous closets.

Plan EOF-62

Bedrooms: 3+	Baths: 3½

Living Area:

Main floor	3,090 sq. ft.
Total Living Area:	**3,090 sq. ft.**
Garage	660 sq. ft.
Exterior Wall Framing:	2x6

Foundation Options:
Slab
(All plans can be built with your choice of foundation and framing. A generic conversion diagram is available. See order form.)

BLUEPRINT PRICE CODE: E

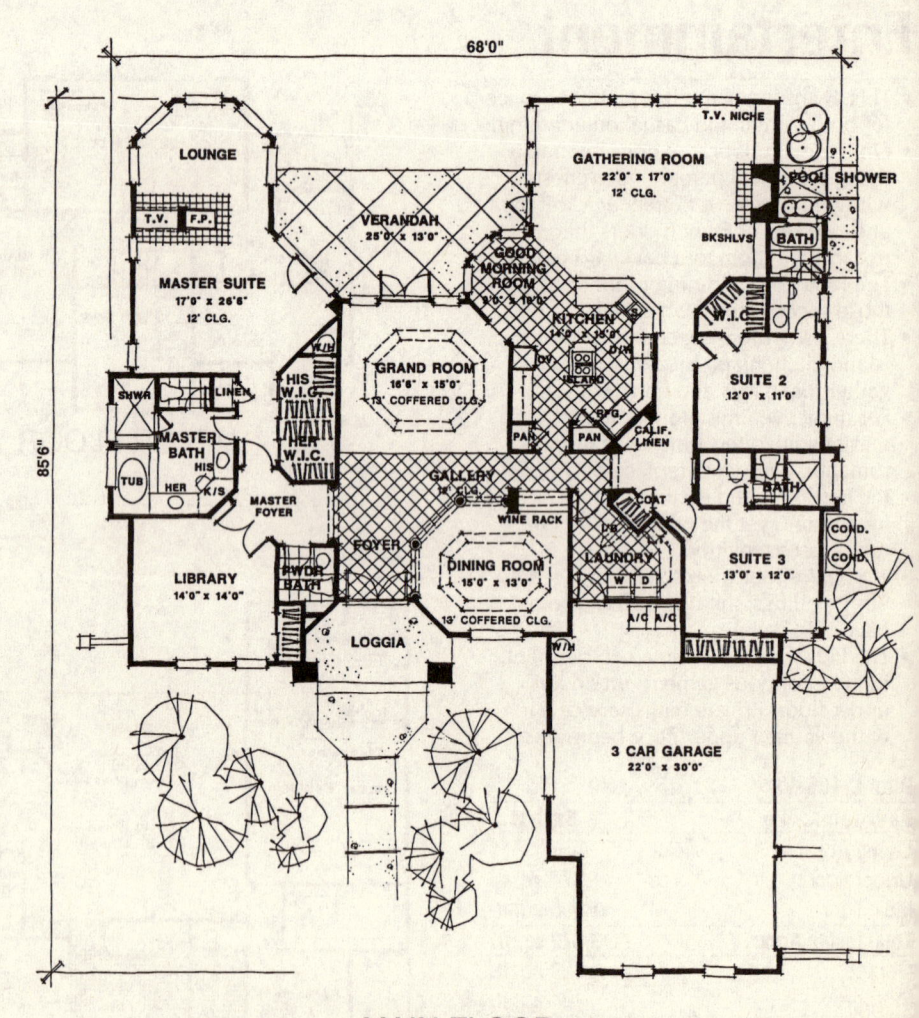

MAIN FLOOR

See this plan on our "One-Story" VideoGraphic Tour! Order form on page 9

Plan EOF-62

Creative Curves

- A creative floor plan adds excitement to this elegant European-inspired estate.
- Brightened by high windows, the two-story-high foyer features a curved staircase. Visible from the foyer past a columned half-wall, the formal dining room is serviced by a uniquely shaped wet bar in the island kitchen.
- The designer kitchen, enhanced by a 12-ft. domed ceiling, has wraparound windows over the corner sink, a panoramic breakfast area and a built-in media center with a computer desk.
- The family room, which has an 18-ft. ceiling and sliding glass doors to a rear deck, is separated from the two-story-high living room by a warming see-through fireplace.
- The master suite has a 9-ft. tray ceiling and a stylish bow window. The master bath boasts a spa tub, a separate shower, dual vanities and a walk-in closet.
- Upstairs, a railed balcony overlooks the foyer and the living room. Ideal for use as guest quarters, one of the three upstairs bedrooms has a private bath.

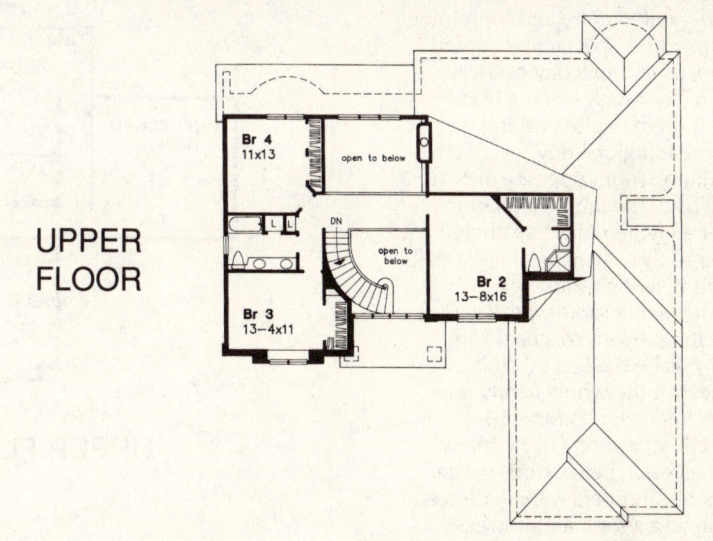

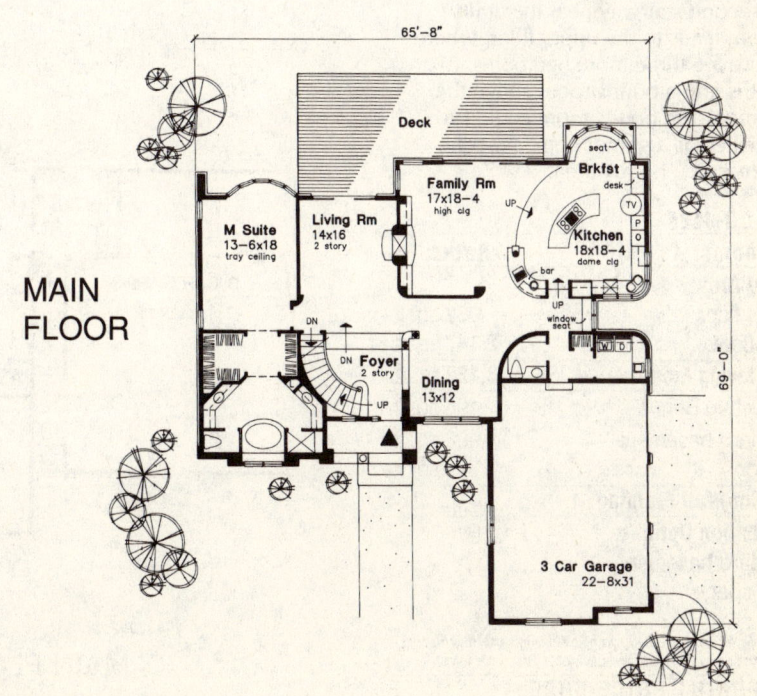

Plan B-91029	
Bedrooms: 4	**Baths:** 3½
Living Area:	
Upper floor	909 sq. ft.
Main floor	2,194 sq. ft.
Total Living Area:	**3,103 sq. ft.**
Standard basement	2,194 sq. ft.
Garage	692 sq. ft.
Exterior Wall Framing:	2x6
Foundation Options:	
Standard basement	
All plans can be built with your choice of foundation and framing. A generic conversion diagram is available. See order form.	
BLUEPRINT PRICE CODE:	**E**

UPPER FLOOR

MAIN FLOOR

ORDER BLUEPRINTS ANYTIME!
CALL TOLL-FREE 1-888-626-2026

Plan B-91029

PRICES AND DETAILS ON PAGES 12-15

Tall Two-Story

- This gorgeous two-story is introduced by a barrel-vaulted entry and supporting columns. Inside, a spectacular curved staircase leads to a balcony overlook.
- Off the two-story-high foyer, a library with a 16-ft.-high vaulted ceiling is perfect for reading or study.
- A formal dining room opposite the library opens to the fabulous island kitchen. The kitchen offers an angled serving bar to the bayed breakfast area and adjoining living room.
- The spacious living room, with an 18-ft. vaulted ceiling, opens to a backyard patio. A fireplace flanked by built-in shelving warms the whole family area.
- The master bedroom boasts a 10-ft. gambrel ceiling, a sunny bay window and patio access. The spacious master bath offers his-and-hers walk-in closets, an oval tub and a separate shower.
- A second stairway near the utility room leads to the upper floor, where there are three more bedrooms, two baths and a bonus room above the garage. The bonus room could be finished as a game room, a media center or a hobby area.

Plan DD-3125

Bedrooms: 4+	Baths: 3½

Living Area:

Upper floor	982 sq. ft.
Main floor	2,147 sq. ft.
Total Living Area:	**3,129 sq. ft.**
Unfinished Bonus	196 sq. ft.
Standard basement	1,996 sq. ft.
Garage	771 sq. ft.
Exterior Wall Framing:	2x4

Foundation Options:
Standard basement
Crawlspace
Slab
(All plans can be built with your choice of foundation and framing. A generic conversion diagram is available. See order form.)

BLUEPRINT PRICE CODE: E

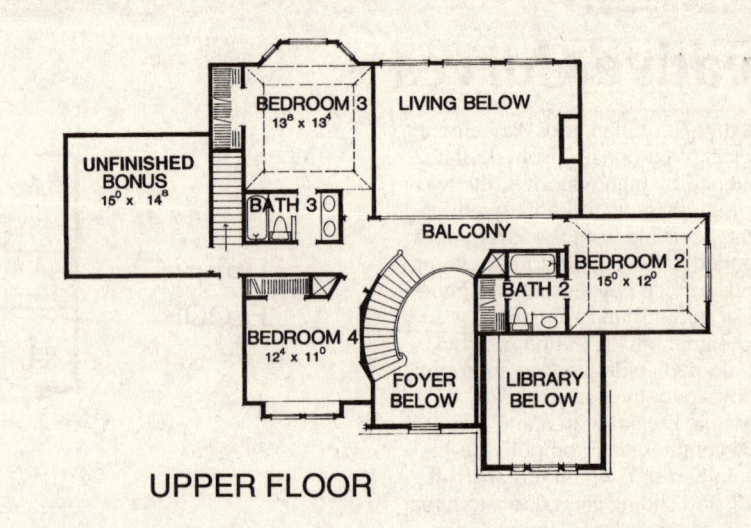

UPPER FLOOR

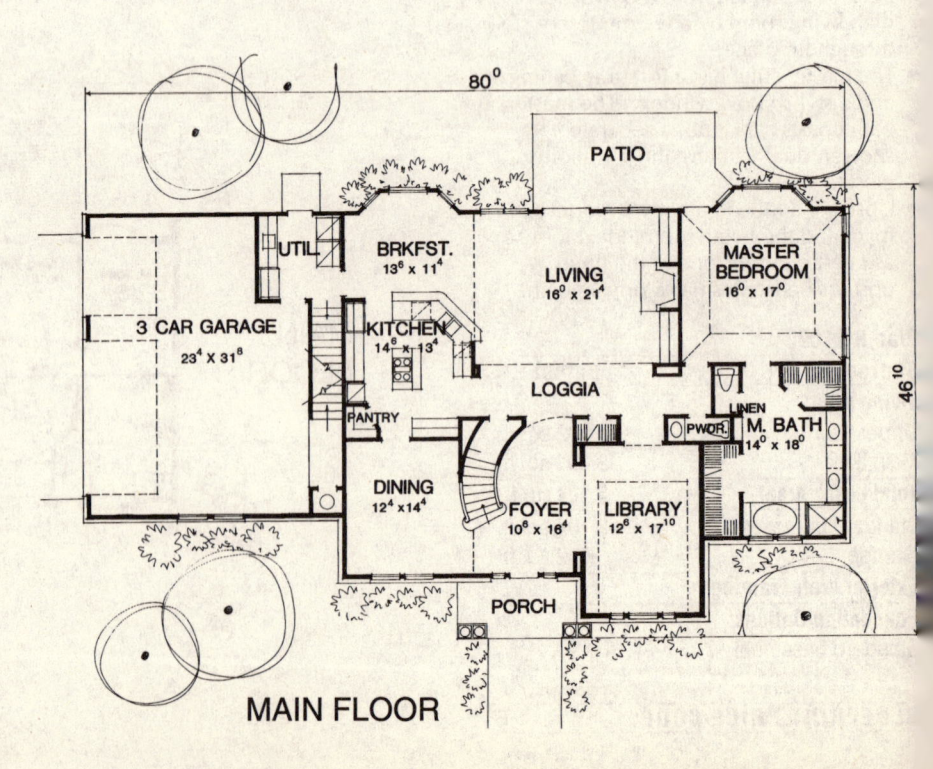

MAIN FLOOR

Plan DD-3125

ORDER BLUEPRINTS ANYTIME!
CALL TOLL-FREE 1-888-626-2026

PRICES AND DETAILS ON PAGES 12-15

One-Floor Gracious Living

- An impressive roofscape, stately brick with soldier coursing and an impressive columned entry grace the exterior of this exciting single-story home.
- The entry opens to the the free-flowing interior, where the formal areas merge near the den, or guest room.
- The living room offers a window wall to a wide backyard deck, and the dining room is convenient to the kitchen.
- The octagonal island kitchen area offers a sunny breakfast nook with a large corner pantry.
- The spacious family room adjoins the kitchen and features a handsome fireplace and deck access. Laundry facilities and garage access are nearby.
- The lavish master suite with a fireplace and a state-of-the-art bath is privately situated in the left wing.
- Three secondary bedrooms have abundant closet space and share two baths on the right side of the home.
- The entire home features expansive 9-ft. ceilings.

Plan DD-3076

Bedrooms: 4+	**Baths:** 3

Living Area:
Main floor — 3,076 sq. ft.
Total Living Area: **3,076 sq. ft.**
Standard basement — 3,076 sq. ft.
Garage — 648 sq. ft.
Exterior Wall Framing: 2x4
Foundation Options:
Standard basement
Crawlspace
Slab
(All plans can be built with your choice of foundation and framing. A generic conversion diagram is available. See order form.)
BLUEPRINT PRICE CODE: E

MAIN FLOOR

ORDER BLUEPRINTS ANYTIME!
CALL TOLL-FREE 1-888-626-2026

Plan DD-3076

PRICES AND DETAILS ON PAGES 12-15

245

High on Luxury

- With an exterior of stucco and stone and an interior enhanced by arched openings and climbing ceilings, this two-story home is high on luxury.
- Beyond the towering entry, the foyer reveals a 19-ft., 8-in. tray ceiling and an elegant stairway to an overlook above.
- Alongside the foyer, the living room boasts a 12-ft., 8-in. tray ceiling; the formal dining room offers French doors to a covered front porch.
- The casual areas converge at the family room, where bold columns, a warm fireplace and a lofty 18-ft.-high ceiling equal pure excitement. A handy serving bar and a sunny breakfast bay extend from the adjoining kitchen.
- You'll enjoy the extra space in the sprawling master suite, which includes a romantic sitting area and a lavish 15½-ft. vaulted garden bath. A 10½-ft. tray ceiling hovers above your bed.
- Unless otherwise mentioned, the main-floor rooms have 9-ft. ceilings.
- Three more bedrooms and a versatile bonus room occupy the upper floor.

Plan FB-5551-SHEL

Bedrooms: 4+	**Baths:** 3½
Living Area:	
Upper floor	896 sq. ft.
Main floor	2,044 sq. ft.
Bonus room	197 sq. ft.
Total Living Area:	**3,137 sq. ft.**
Daylight basement	2,044 sq. ft.
Garage and storage	682 sq. ft.
Exterior Wall Framing:	2x4

Foundation Options:
Daylight basement
Crawlspace
(All plans can be built with your choice of foundation and framing. A generic conversion diagram is available. See order form.)

BLUEPRINT PRICE CODE: E

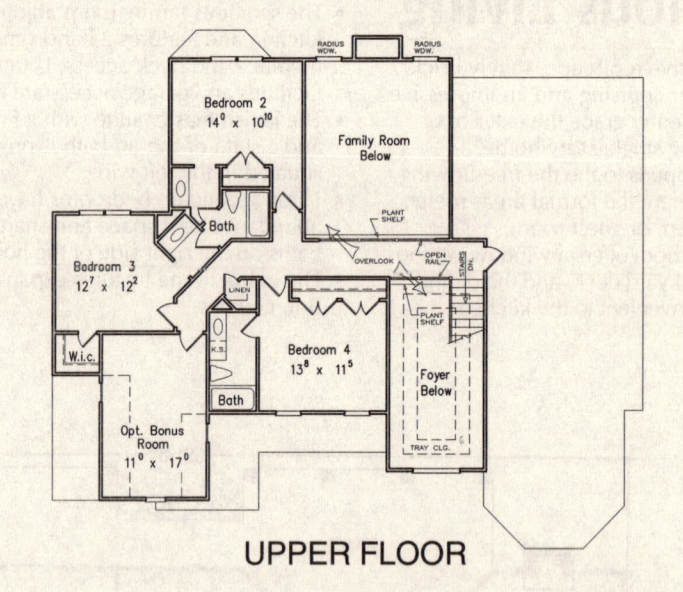

UPPER FLOOR

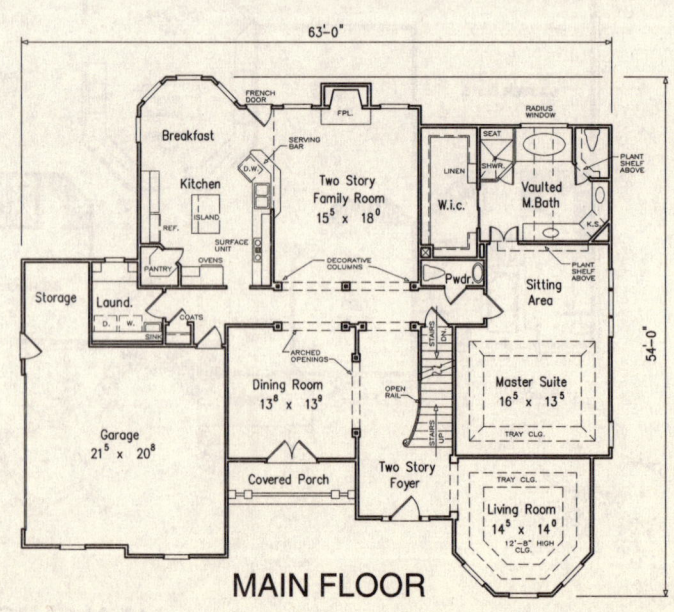

- Bedroom 2: 14⁰ x 10¹⁰
- Family Room Below
- Bedroom 3: 12⁷ x 12²
- Bedroom 4: 13⁸ x 11⁵
- Opt. Bonus Room: 11⁰ x 17⁰
- Foyer Below

MAIN FLOOR

63'-0" x 54'-0"

- Breakfast
- Kitchen
- Two Story Family Room: 15⁵ x 18⁰
- Vaulted M.Bath
- Storage
- Laund.
- Pantry
- Sitting Area
- Dining Room: 13⁸ x 13⁹
- Master Suite: 16⁵ x 13⁵
- Garage: 21⁵ x 20⁸
- Covered Porch
- Two Story Foyer
- Living Room: 14⁵ x 14⁰

Plan FB-5551-SHEL

Stunning Country-Style

- A lovely front porch that encases bay windows provides a friendly welcome to this stunning country-style home.
- Inside, the main living areas revolve around the large country kitchen and dinette, complete with an island worktop, a roomy built-in desk and access to a backyard deck.
- A raised-hearth fireplace, French doors and a 12-ft., 4-in. cathedral ceiling highlight the casual family room.
- The formal dining room is open to the living room and features an inviting window seat and a tray ceiling. A French door in the bay-windowed living room opens to the relaxing porch.
- A quiet den and a large laundry area/mudroom complete the main floor.
- The upper floor showcases a super master suite with a bay window, an 11-ft., 8-in. tray ceiling, two walk-in closets and a private bath with a garden tub and its own dramatic ceiling.
- Three additional bedrooms share a full bath designed for multiple users.

Plan A-538-R

Bedrooms: 4+	**Baths:** 2½

Living Area:
Upper floor	1,384 sq. ft.
Main floor	1,755 sq. ft.
Total Living Area:	**3,139 sq. ft.**
Standard basement	1,728 sq. ft.
Garage	576 sq. ft.
Exterior Wall Framing:	2x4

Foundation Options:
Standard basement
(All plans can be built with your choice of foundation and framing. A generic conversion diagram is available. See order form.)

BLUEPRINT PRICE CODE: E

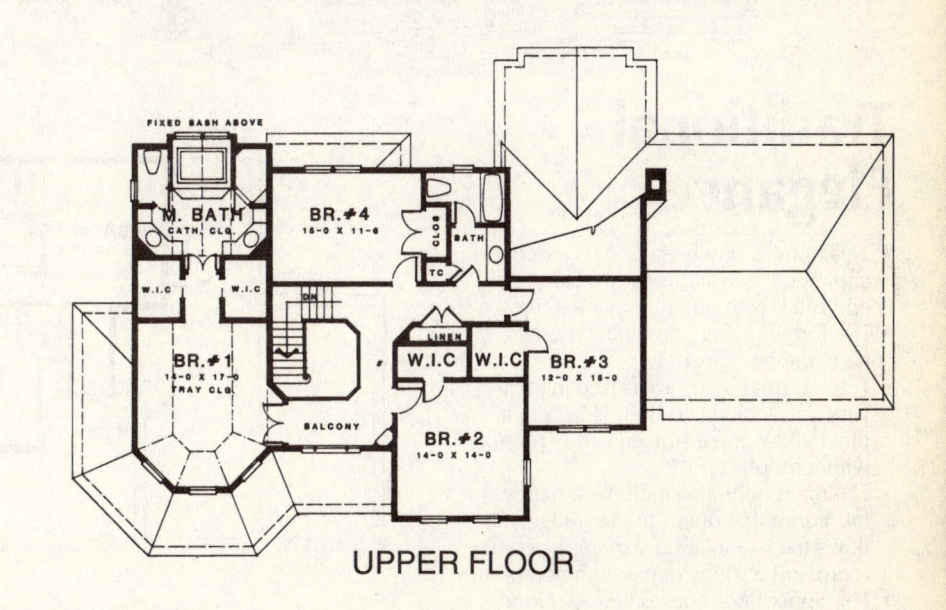

UPPER FLOOR

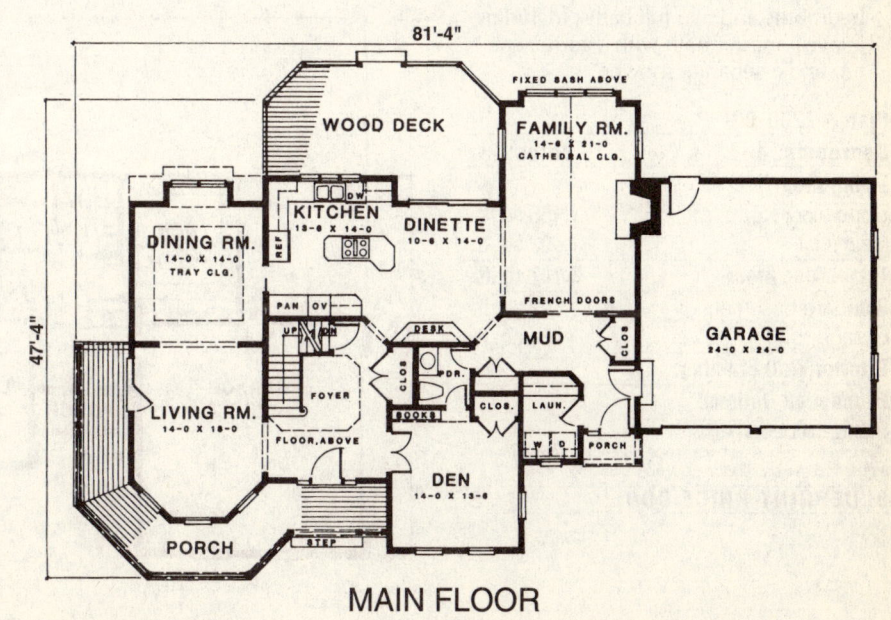

MAIN FLOOR

ORDER BLUEPRINTS ANYTIME!
CALL TOLL-FREE 1-888-626-2026

Plan A-538-R

PRICES AND DETAILS
ON PAGES 12-15

247

Traditional Elegance

- This home's stately traditional exterior is enhanced by a stunning two-story entry and brick with quoin corner details.
- The formal living and dining rooms flank the entry foyer.
- The informal living areas face the rear yard and include an island kitchen, a dinette bay and a sunken family room with a fireplace.
- The main floor also includes a handy mudroom that opens to the garage and flows back to a laundry room, a powder room and a sunny den or fifth bedroom.
- The upper floor houses four spacious bedrooms and two full baths, including a lavish master bath with a corner spa tub and a separate shower.

Plan A-2230-DS

Bedrooms: 4+	Baths: 2½

Living Area:
Upper floor	1,455 sq. ft.
Main floor	1,692 sq. ft.
Total Living Area:	**3,147 sq. ft.**
Standard basement	1,692 sq. ft.
Garage	484 sq. ft.

Exterior Wall Framing: 2x6

Foundation Options:
Standard basement
(All plans can be built with your choice of foundation and framing. A generic conversion diagram is available. See order form.)

BLUEPRINT PRICE CODE: E

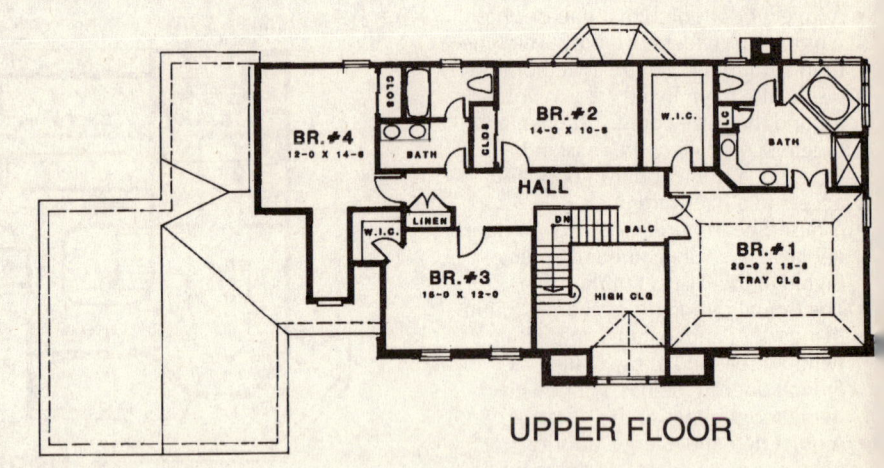

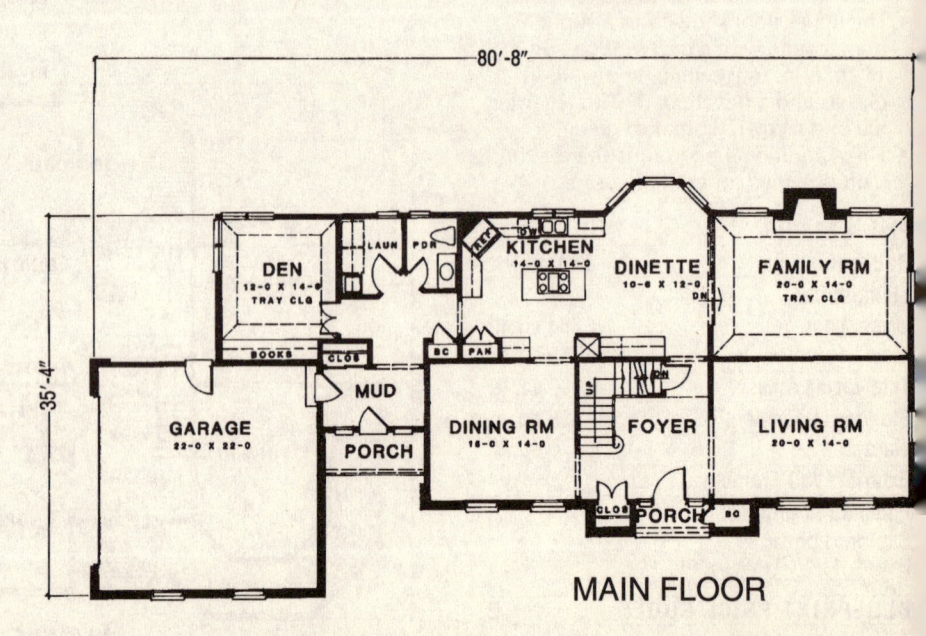

Plan A-2230-DS

All Good Things

- This stone-sturdy home pleases the eye with a rustic, country facade and a multitude of interior luxuries.
- Designed with your loved ones in mind, the family room, island kitchen and bayed breakfast nook flow into each other for a feeling of togetherness. From the nook, a huge backyard deck is quickly accessible.
- For formal gatherings, the living and dining rooms serve effortlessly.
- The master suite epitomizes comfort, with its private deck and adjoining office space. Opulence is apparent in the master bath, which features a spa tub and two walk-in closets.
- A stunning guest suite delivers a private deck and a kitchen area. With its full bath, it's the perfect spot for relatives who are enjoying their golden years.

Plan DD-3152	
Bedrooms: 3+	**Baths:** 3½
Living Area:	
Main floor	3,152 sq. ft.
Total Living Area:	**3,152 sq. ft.**
Standard basement	3,152 sq. ft.
Garage	610 sq. ft.
Exterior Wall Framing:	2x4

Foundation Options:
Standard basement
Crawlspace
Slab
(All plans can be built with your choice of foundation and framing. A generic conversion diagram is available. See order form.)

BLUEPRINT PRICE CODE: E

MAIN FLOOR

Plan DD-3152

Extravagant Arches

- The extravagant porch and window arches, an elegant upper balcony and a tiled roof give this home a striking Mediterranean look.
- Inside, formal living areas flank the long foyer, each adorned with entry columns and arched window treatments.
- The central family room offers a warm fireplace and a spectacular view of the patio and the optional pool.
- A large island kitchen is equipped with a walk-in pantry and generous counter space. A snack counter separates the kitchen from the bayed morning room, which also overlooks the patio.
- At the opposite end of the home is the spacious master suite, which features a bayed sitting area, a private bath, two walk-in closets and an exercise room.
- Upstairs are three more bedrooms, each with a private dressing area or bath. An exciting game room is also included!

Plan DD-3045

Bedrooms: 4	Baths: 3½
Living Area:	
Upper floor	1,202 sq. ft.
Main floor	1,952 sq. ft.
Total Living Area:	**3,154 sq. ft.**
Standard basement	1,728 sq. ft.
Garage	480 sq. ft.
Exterior Wall Framing:	2x4

Foundation Options:
Standard basement
Crawlspace
Slab
(Typical foundation & framing conversion diagram available—see order form.)

BLUEPRINT PRICE CODE: E

FRONT VIEW

UPPER FLOOR

MAIN FLOOR

REAR VIEW

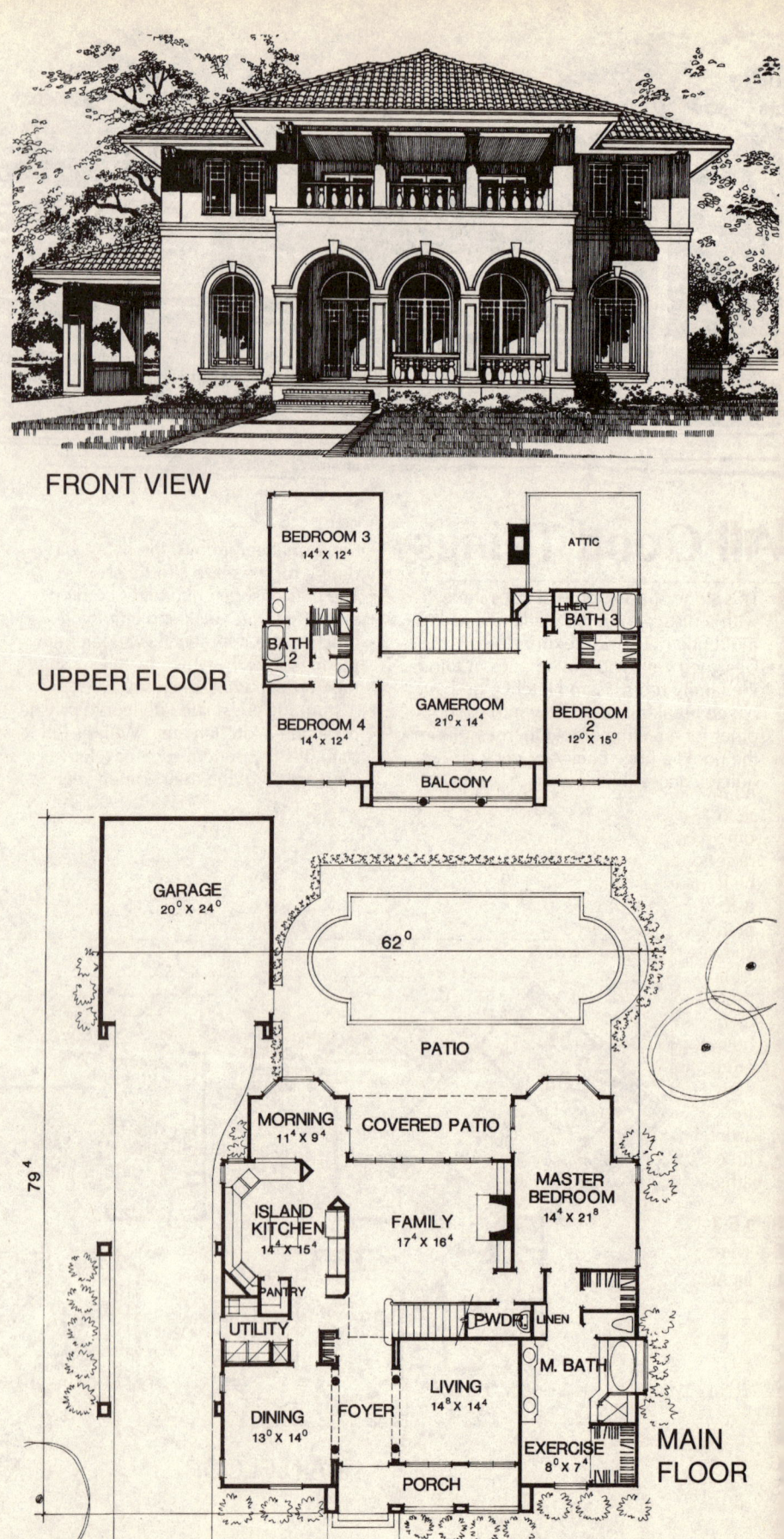

ORDER BLUEPRINTS ANYTIME! CALL TOLL-FREE 1-888-626-2026

Plan DD-3045

PRICES AND DETAILS ON PAGES 12-15

250

Intriguing Combination

- This intriguing home is finished with a combination of wood siding and brick, giving it a warm, rustic look.
- Geared for formal entertaining as well as family living, the home offers distinct activity zones. A built-in china hutch and a fireplace add style and function to the formal spaces at the front of the home. Both the living and dining rooms are set off by decorative columns.
- The large-scale family room features a 13-ft. ceiling, a fireplace and a built-in entertainment center. The skylighted sun room and the breakfast area include sloped ceilings and French doors opening to the patio. Typical ceiling heights elsewhere are 9 feet.
- The master suite has a 14-ft. sloped ceiling, private access to the patio and its own fireplace. The adjoining bath offers abundant storage space and a garden tub with glass-block walls.
- Three additional bedrooms and two baths are on the other side of the home.

Plan E-3102	
Bedrooms: 4	Baths: 3
Living Area:	
Main floor	3,158 sq. ft.
Total Living Area:	**3,158 sq. ft.**
Garage	559 sq. ft.
Storage	64 sq. ft.
Exterior Wall Framing:	2x6

Foundation Options:
Crawlspace
Slab
(All plans can be built with your choice of foundation and framing. A generic conversion diagram is available. See order form.)

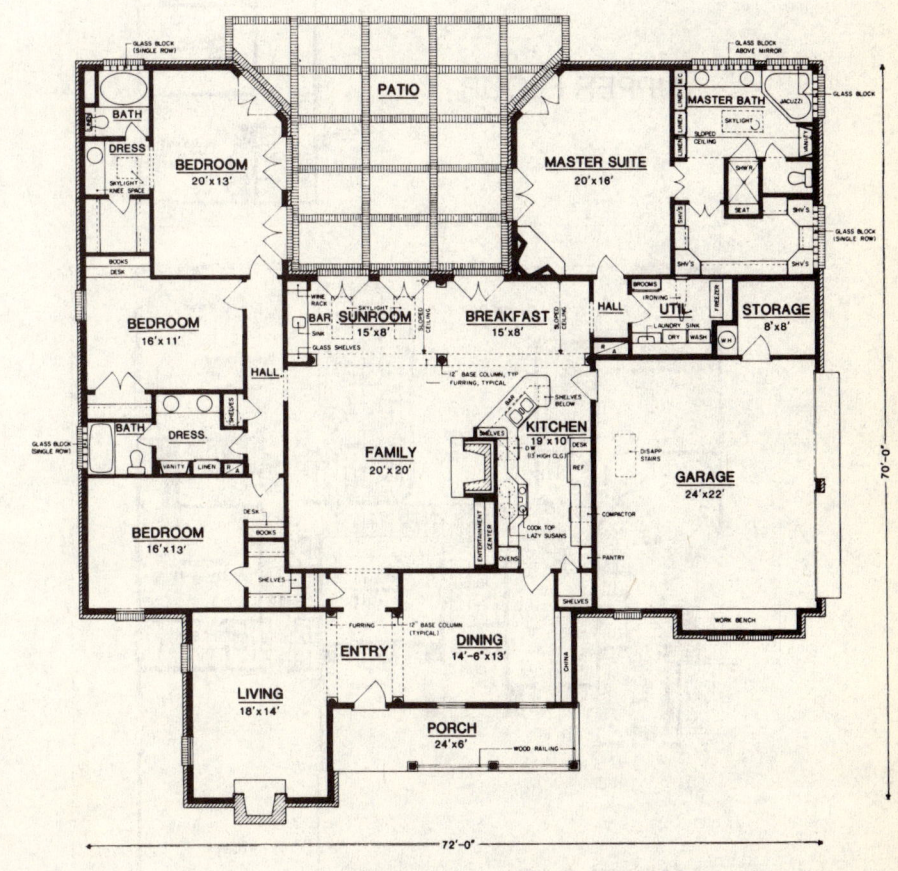

BLUEPRINT PRICE CODE: E

MAIN FLOOR

ORDER BLUEPRINTS ANYTIME!
CALL TOLL-FREE 1-888-626-2026

Plan E-3102

PRICES AND DETAILS
ON PAGES 12-15

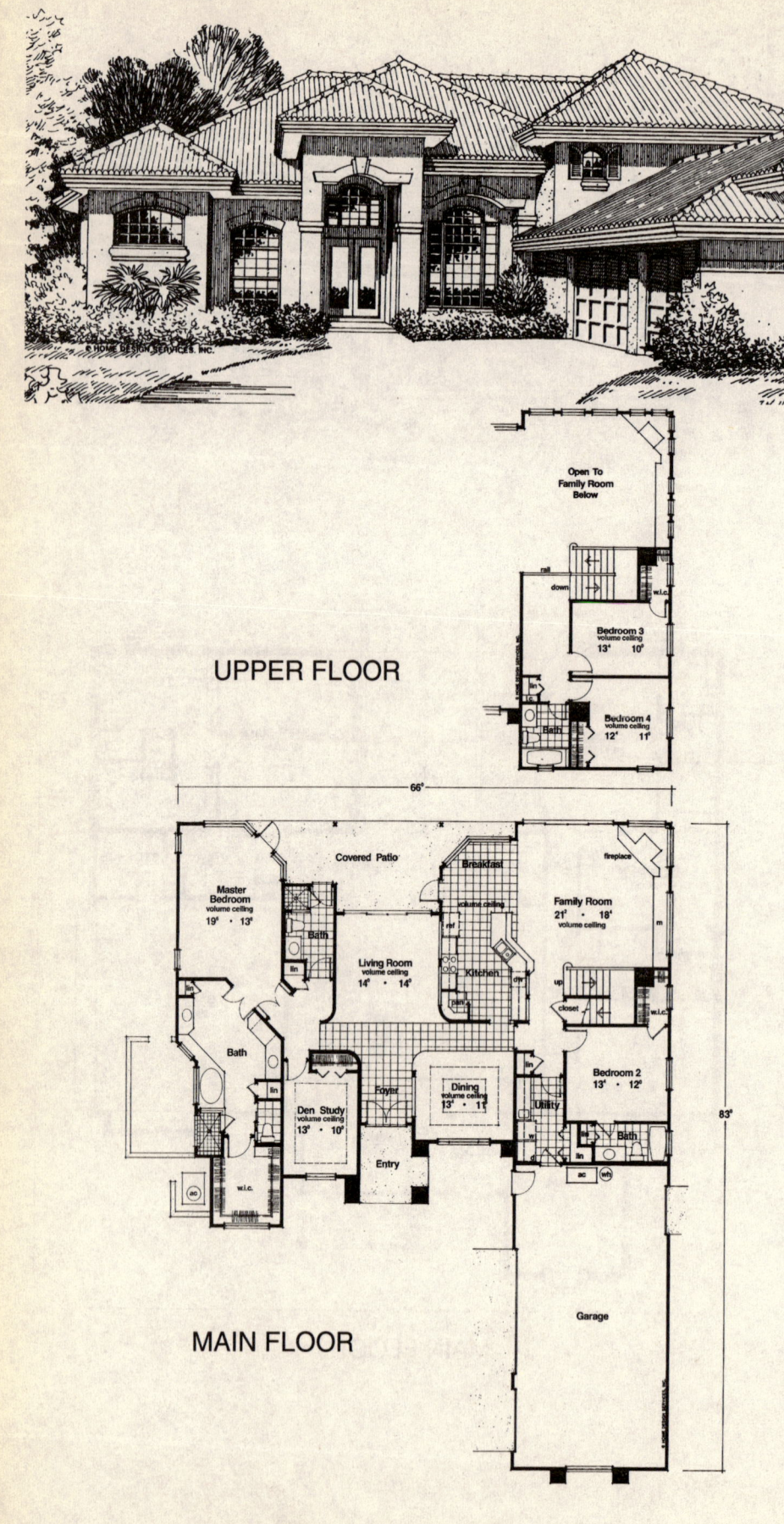

Innovative Use of Space

- This fascinating design is recognized for its innovative use of space.
- The central formal spaces separate the master suite and the den or study from the informal spaces. The rear window wall in the living room allows a view of the outdoors from the oversized foyer.
- The unique arrangement of the master suite lets traffic flow easily from the bedroom to the dressing areas, to the garden tub and to a walk-in closet that you could get lost in.
- The spacious two-story family room, kitchen and breakfast room open to one another, forming a large family activity area with corner fireplace, snack counter and surrounding windows.
- A second main-floor bedroom, two upper-floor bedrooms and three extra baths complete the floor plan.

Plan HDS-99-166

Bedrooms: 4-5	Baths: 4

Living Area:

Upper floor	540 sq. ft.
Main floor	2,624 sq. ft.
Total Living Area:	**3,164 sq. ft.**
Garage	770 sq. ft.
Exterior Wall Framing:	2x4

Foundation Options:
Slab
(Typical foundation & framing conversion diagram available—see order form.)

BLUEPRINT PRICE CODE: E

ORDER BLUEPRINTS ANYTIME!
CALL TOLL-FREE 1-888-626-2026

Plan HDS-99-166

PRICES AND DETAILS ON PAGES 12-15

Striking Octagonal Solarium

- The center of attraction in this dramatic design is the sunsoaking passive sun room. This 20' diameter solarium reaches above the roofline to capture the most possible solar energy from any direction.
- For passive cooling, several of the vertical windows in the dome can be opened. The room also includes a "splash pool" to provide humidity in the winter.
- Then rooms surrounding the solarium are equally striking, as well as spacious and convenient, providing plenty of space for casual family living as well as more formal entertaining.
- The master suite includes a bath fit for royalty and a huge walk-in closet. Two secondary bedrooms share a large second bath with separate tub and shower and double sinks.

Plans H-3719-1 & -1A

Bedrooms: 3	Baths: 2½

Space:
Total living area: 3,166 sq. ft.
(Includes 324 sq. ft. sun room)
Basement (under bedrooms & family room): approx. 1,400 sq. ft.
Garage: 850 sq. ft.
Storage: 132 sq. ft.

Exterior Wall Framing: 2x6

Foundation options:
Partial basement (H-3719-1).
Crawlspace (H-3719-1A)
(Foundation & framing conversion diagram available — see order form.)

Blueprint Price Code: E

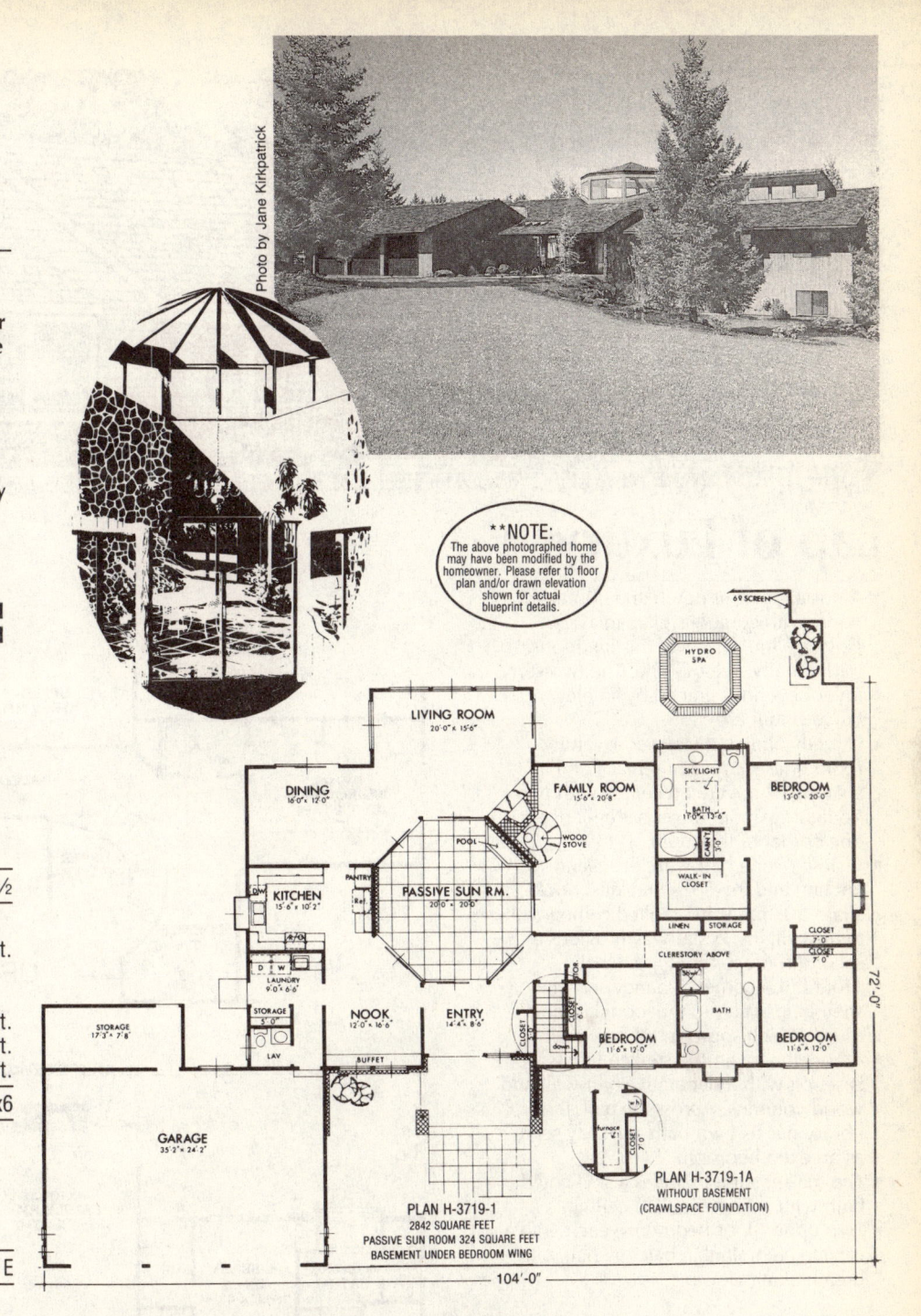

Photo by Jane Kirkpatrick

NOTE: The above photographed home may have been modified by the homeowner. Please refer to floor plan and/or drawn elevation shown for actual blueprint details.

PLAN H-3719-1
2842 SQUARE FEET
PASSIVE SUN ROOM 324 SQUARE FEET
BASEMENT UNDER BEDROOM WING

PLAN H-3719-1A
WITHOUT BASEMENT
(CRAWLSPACE FOUNDATION)

ORDER BLUEPRINTS ANYTIME!
CALL TOLL-FREE 1-888-626-2026

Plans H-3719-1 & -1A

PRICES AND DETAILS ON PAGES 12-15

Lap of Luxury

- A nostalgic front porch and double doors with gorgeous glass inlays decorate the facade of this luxurious traditionally styled home. The two-story foyer beyond is graced by an elegant curved staircase.
- Directly ahead, the spacious family room boasts a rustic fireplace and a soaring 19-ft. vaulted ceiling with two skylights. An open wet bar enhances one corner of the room.
- Visible over a half-wall, the island kitchen and the cozy breakfast nook share a 16-ft., 9-in. vaulted ceiling with twin skylights. A stairway provides a second route to the upper level.
- Around the corner, a handy serving shelf helps cater to the formal dining room, which sports a 9-ft. tray ceiling.
- Across the foyer, the sunken living room is set off with a decorative half-wall and wood columns. Across the hall, the library has its own bath and may serve as an extra bedroom.
- The master suite includes a skylighted bath with a 13-ft. vaulted ceiling.
- Two upper-floor bedrooms, each with a private bath, flank a balcony hall with breathtaking views.

Plan AX-92027

Bedrooms: 3+	Baths: 4½
Living Area:	
Upper floor	984 sq. ft.
Main floor	2,195 sq. ft.
Total Living Area:	**3,179 sq. ft.**
Standard basement	2,195 sq. ft.
Garage	630 sq. ft.
Exterior Wall Framing:	2x4
Foundation Options:	
Standard basement	
Crawlspace	

(All plans can be built with your choice of foundation and framing. A generic conversion diagram is available. See order form.)

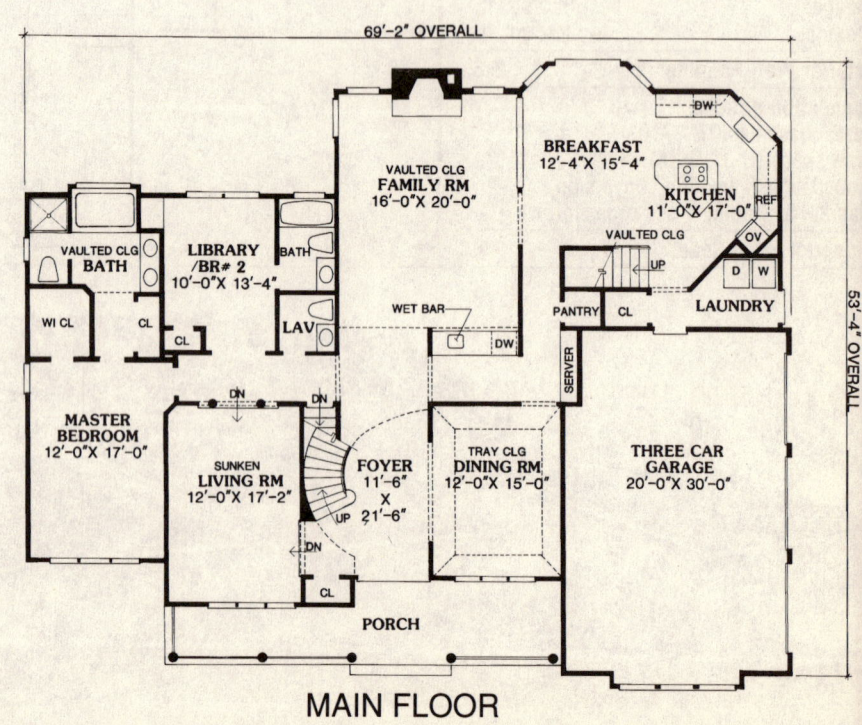

BLUEPRINT PRICE CODE: E

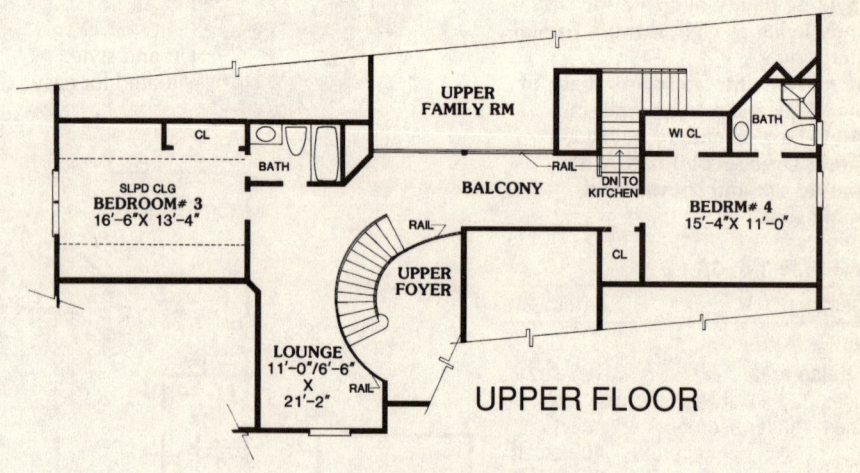

ORDER BLUEPRINTS ANYTIME!
CALL TOLL-FREE 1-888-626-2026

Plan AX-92027

PRICES AND DETAILS ON PAGES 12-15

Façade fantastique!

- Your mind will think French as you view the *magnifique* facade of this European-inspired masterpiece!
- The four arched windows may remind you of Parisian architecture.
- The theme of refinement is carried into the floor plan, where columns define the formal dining room.
- A quiet front-facing library could serve as a study or an elegant parlor.
- The large family room, warmed by a focal-point fireplace, can host events and holidays in comfort and style.
- The island kitchen is situated for easy service to the morning room. Imagine soufflé and café au lait on the patio!
- The secluded bedroom and bath by the garage are ideal for overnight guests.
- The home's pièce de résistance, the lovely master suite, boasts two walk-in closets and a fabulous, refreshing bath.
- At the top of the stairs, the den would make a nice game room.
- Three more spacious bedrooms and two full baths complete the plan.

Plan DD-3169

Bedrooms: 5+	Baths: 4
Living Area:	
Upper floor	1,172 sq. ft.
Main floor	2,018 sq. ft.
Total Living Area:	**3,190 sq. ft.**
Standard basement	2,018 sq. ft.
Garage	563 sq. ft.
Exterior Wall Framing:	2x4 and 2x6

Foundation Options:
Standard basement
Crawlspace
Slab

(All plans can be built with your choice of foundation and framing. A generic conversion diagram is available. See order form.)

BLUEPRINT PRICE CODE: E

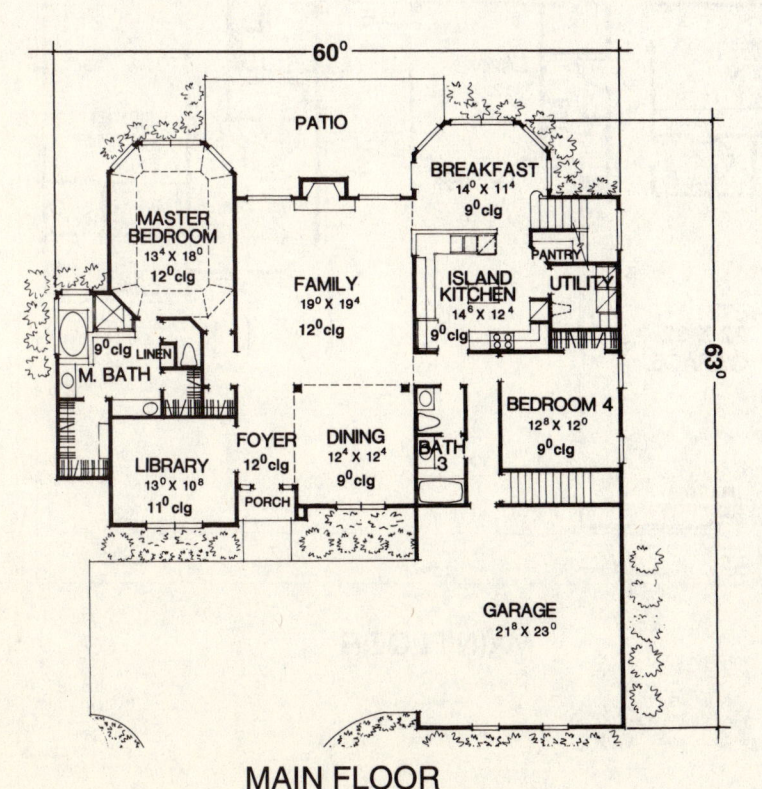

MAIN FLOOR

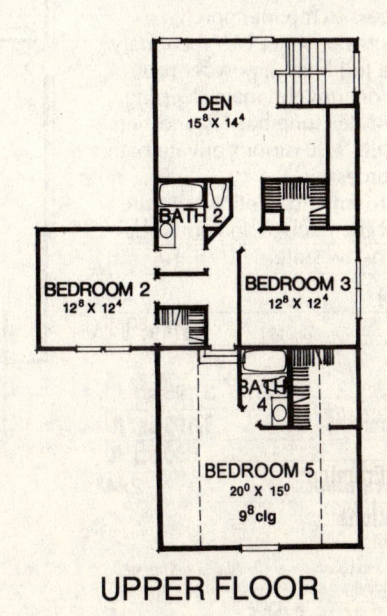

UPPER FLOOR

ORDER BLUEPRINTS ANYTIME!
CALL TOLL-FREE 1-888-626-2026

Plan DD-3169

PRICES AND DETAILS ON PAGES 12-15

Dramatically Different

- Dramatic angles distinguish this stunning home, allowing it to take full advantage of surrounding views.
- The impressive entry welcomes guests to the formal areas of the home. The delightful bayed dining room leads to the spacious living room with its soaring cathedral ceiling and French doors to a covered rear porch. An inviting fireplace is centered between built-in shelves on one wall.
- The exceptional dual island kitchen provides a unique and functional cooking experience. A cathedral ceiling tops the sun-filled breakfast area.
- An angled family room adjoins the kitchen and features a coffered ceiling, a dramatic fireplace set in a windowed bay and access to the rear porch.
- The angled master suite, two secondary bedrooms, a full bath, a powder room and a study occupy the main sleeping wing. The master suite has his-and-hers walk in closets, a luxurious private bath and porch access.
- A guest bedroom and another bath are located near the kitchen and could be used as an in-law suite.

Plan KLF-9229

Bedrooms: 4	Baths: 3½
Living Area:	
Main floor	3,195 sq. ft.
Total Living Area:	**3,195 sq. ft.**
Garage	650 sq. ft.
Exterior Wall Framing:	2x4

Foundation Options:
Slab
(All plans can be built with your choice of foundation and framing. A generic conversion diagram is available. See order form.)

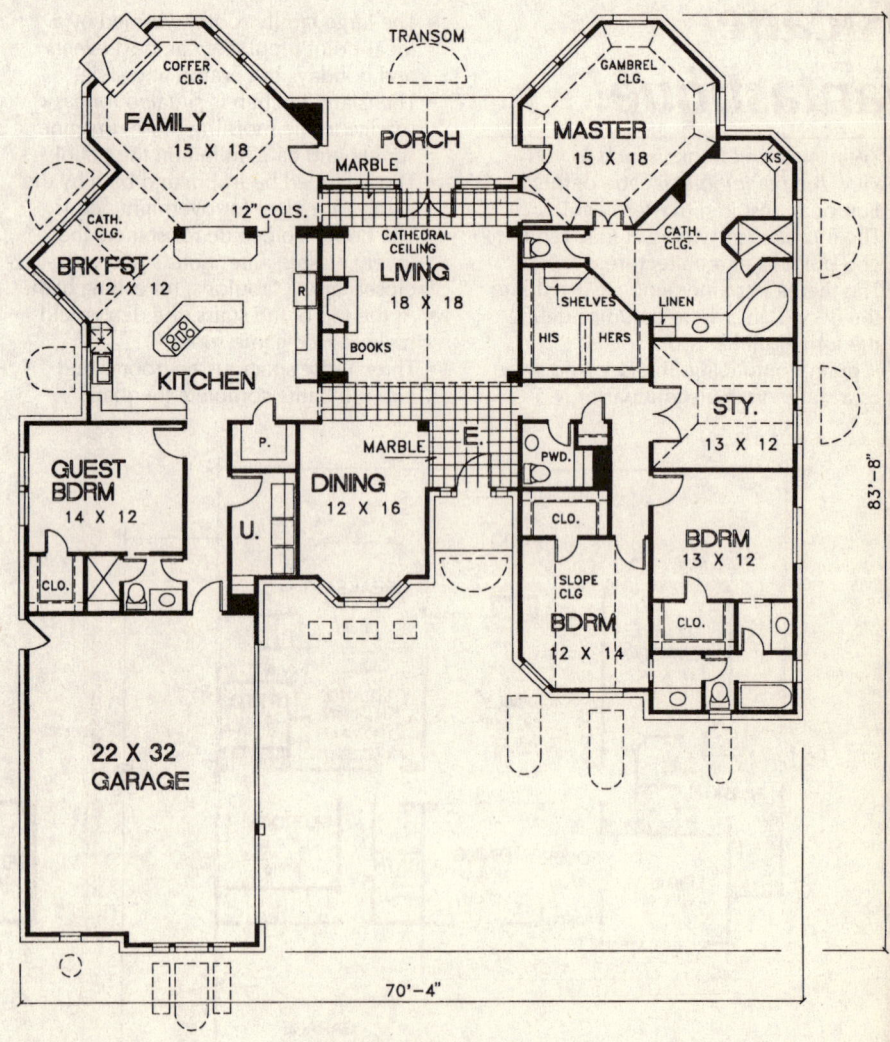

BLUEPRINT PRICE CODE: E

MAIN FLOOR

ORDER BLUEPRINTS ANYTIME!
CALL TOLL-FREE 1-888-626-2026

Plan KLF-9229

PRICES AND DETAILS ON PAGES 12-15

A Taste of Perfection

- Dignified and distinctive, this executive home's paned glass windows, steeply pitched roof and arched entrance create a sweet taste of perfection.
- The raised foyer offers a commanding view of the dining room and living room. The living room's all-glass wall and 11-ft. sloped ceiling add to the interesting sensation.
- Ten-foot ceilings are featured throughout the rest of the first floor, with the exception of the kitchen, which vaults up to a story-and-a-half.
- French doors open to a rear porch from the master bedroom, which also boasts a double-sided fireplace.
- The upper floor features three additional bedrooms and a large game room.
- Plans for an optional attached three-car garage, a bonus room and a sun room between the garage and the morning room are included with the blueprints.

Plan L-232-TCC

Bedrooms: 4+	Baths: 3½

Living Area:	
Upper floor	1,116 sq. ft.
Main floor	2,114 sq. ft.
Total Living Area:	**3,230 sq. ft.**
Optional sun room	270 sq. ft.
Optional bonus room	728 sq. ft.
Optional attached garage	865 sq. ft.
Exterior Wall Framing:	2x4

Foundation Options:
Slab
(All plans can be built with your choice of foundation and framing. A generic conversion diagram is available. See order form.)

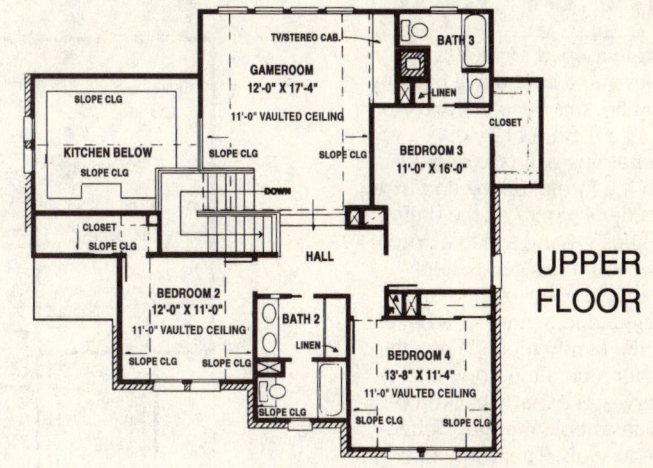

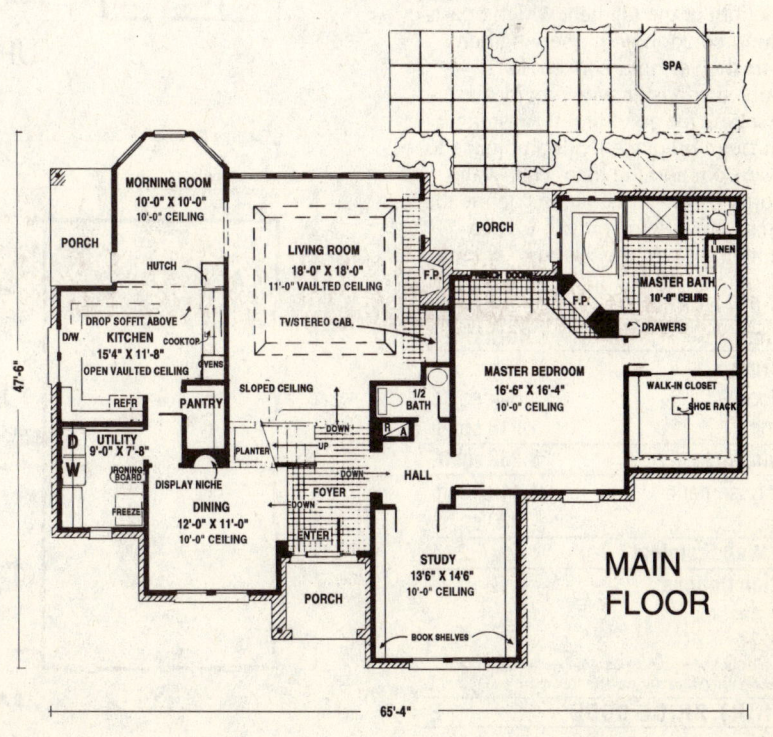

BLUEPRINT PRICE CODE: E

ORDER BLUEPRINTS ANYTIME!
CALL TOLL-FREE 1-888-626-2026

Plan L-232-TCC

PRICES AND DETAILS ON PAGES 12-15

Picture of Style

- With keystone-topped arches, front-facing gables and a decorative balcony above the entry, this beautiful two-story home is truly a picture of style.
- Inside, entertaining will take on added elegance in the formal dining and living rooms. A butler's pantry off the dining room simplifies serving, while a porch off the living room lets guests step outside to enjoy a view of the stars.
- Built-in shelves and a graceful arch lead the way to the family room. When the kids gather for a bedtime story, the fireplace serves as a toasty backdrop.
- In the breakfast nook, morning coffee revives sleepy souls. The family chef will delight in the kitchen, which boasts an island cooktop with a serving bar. Built-in shelves hold cookbooks.
- Upstairs, the master suite provides a great setting for quiet times. A romantic see-through fireplace lends ambience to the bedroom and the bath. Half-walls anchored by elegant columns define the sitting room, where you will love to settle in and savor the Sunday *Times*.

Plan FB-5477-CARM

Bedrooms: 4	Baths: 3½
Living Area:	
Upper floor	1,844 sq. ft.
Main floor	1,418 sq. ft.
Total Living Area:	**3,262 sq. ft.**
Daylight basement	1,418 sq. ft.
Garage	820 sq. ft.
Exterior Wall Framing:	2x4

Foundation Options:
Daylight basement
Crawlspace
(All plans can be built with your choice of foundation and framing. A generic conversion diagram is available. See order form.)

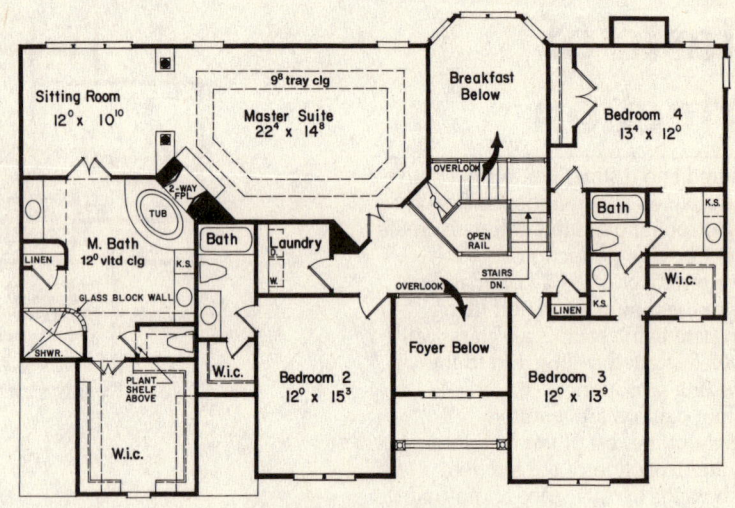

BLUEPRINT PRICE CODE: E

UPPER FLOOR

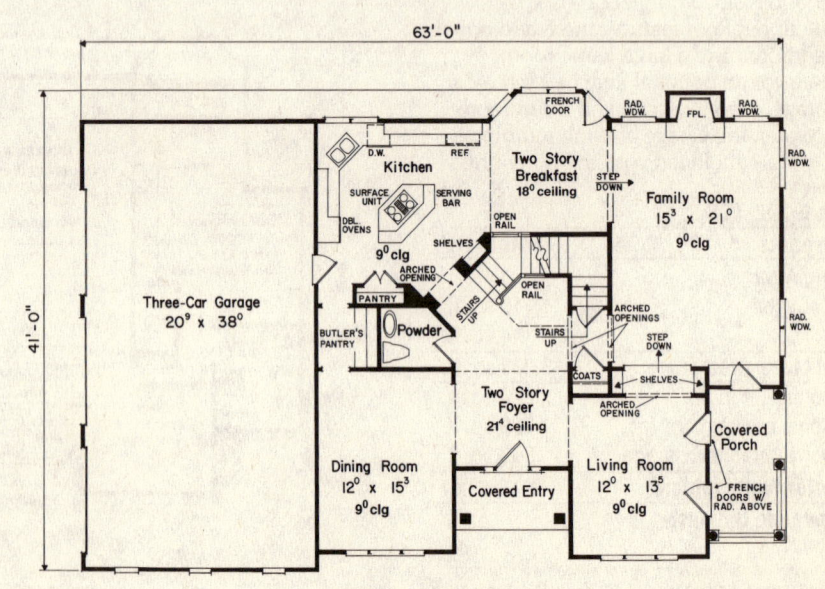

MAIN FLOOR

ORDER BLUEPRINTS ANYTIME!
CALL TOLL-FREE 1-888-626-2026

Plan FB-5477-CARM

PRICES AND DETAILS ON PAGES 12-15

Truly Nostalgic

- Designed after "Monteigne," an Italianate home near Natchez, Mississippi, this reproduction utilizes modern stucco finishes for the exterior.
- Columns and arched windows give way to a two-story-high foyer, which is accented by a striking, curved stairwell.
- The foyer connects the living room and the study, each boasting a 14-ft. ceiling and a cozy fireplace or woodstove.
- Adjacent to the formal dining room, the kitchen offers a snack bar and a bayed eating room. A unique entertainment center is centrally located to serve the main activity rooms of the home.
- A gorgeous sun room stretches across the rear of the main floor and overlooks a grand terrace.
- The plush master suite and bath boast his-and-hers vanities, large walk-in closets and a glassed-in garden tub.
- A main-floor guest bedroom features a walk-in closet and private access to another full main-floor bath.
- Two more bedrooms with private baths are located on the upper level. They share a sitting area and a veranda.

Plan E-3200

Bedrooms: 4	Baths: 4

Living Area:
Upper floor	629 sq. ft.
Main floor	2,655 sq. ft.
Total Living Area	**3,284 sq. ft.**
Standard basement	2,655 sq. ft.
Garage	667 sq. ft.
Exterior Wall Framing	2x6

Foundation Options:
Standard basement
Crawlspace
Slab
(All plans can be built with your choice of foundation and framing. A generic conversion diagram is available. See order form.)

BLUEPRINT PRICE CODE: E

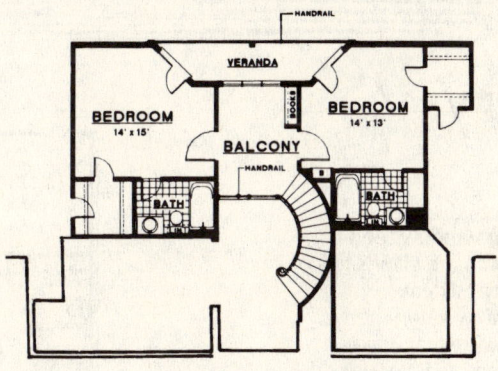

ORDER BLUEPRINTS ANYTIME!
CALL TOLL-FREE 1-888-626-2026

Plan E-3200

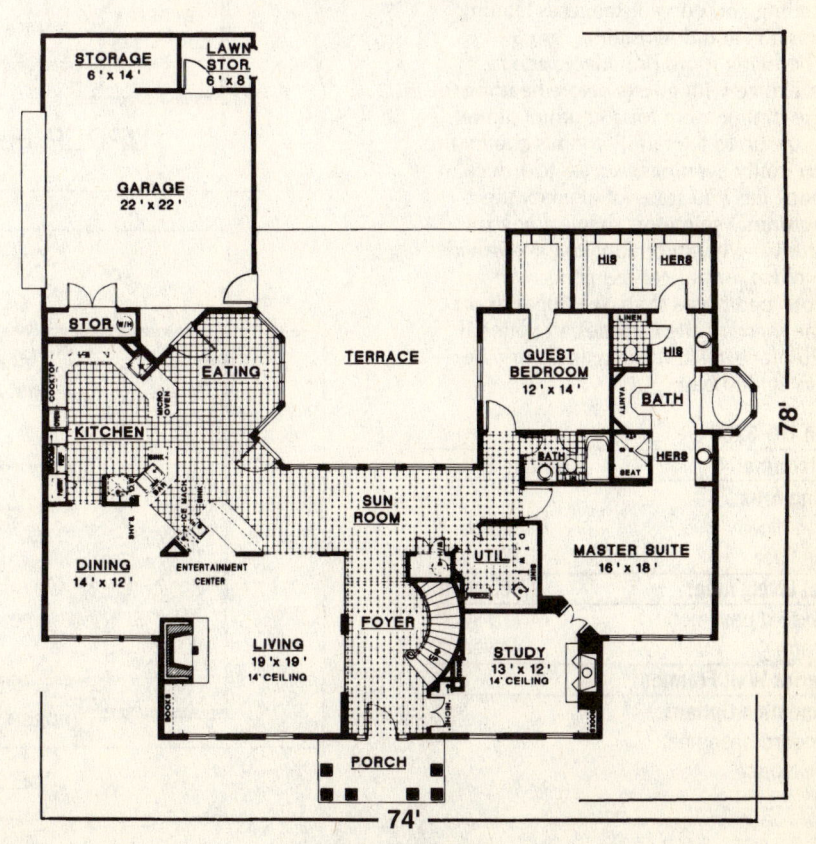

PRICES AND DETAILS ON PAGES 12-15

Legendary Quality

- Incredible round-top windows and a grand columned porch are clear signs of the legendary quality evident throughout this great two-story home.
- Looking for an entryway that makes a statement? The incredible foyer does just that, with a skylighted, two-story ceiling and curved staircases leading upstairs and downstairs.
- The living room provides space to socialize with guests before heading to the dining room for a gourmet dinner.
- Cozy up to the family room's cheery fire on chilly evenings. Access to a deck in back lets you step out to enjoy the autumnal splendors, while a nearby study—with an optional bath—provides a place for quieter moments.
- Four bedrooms share the upper floor; the master suite includes an optional fireplace, a sitting area and a private, skylighted bath.

Plan DD-3260

Bedrooms: 4+	Baths: 3½-4½

Living Area:
Upper floor	1,532 sq. ft.
Main floor	1,773 sq. ft.
Total Living Area:	**3,305 sq. ft.**
Standard basement	1,773 sq. ft.
Garage	445 sq. ft.
Exterior Wall Framing:	2x4

Foundation Options:
Standard basement
Crawlspace
Slab
(All plans can be built with your choice of foundation and framing. A generic conversion diagram is available. See order form.)

BLUEPRINT PRICE CODE: E

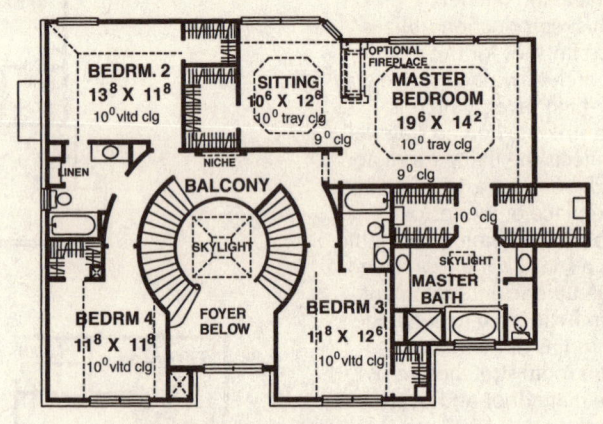

UPPER FLOOR

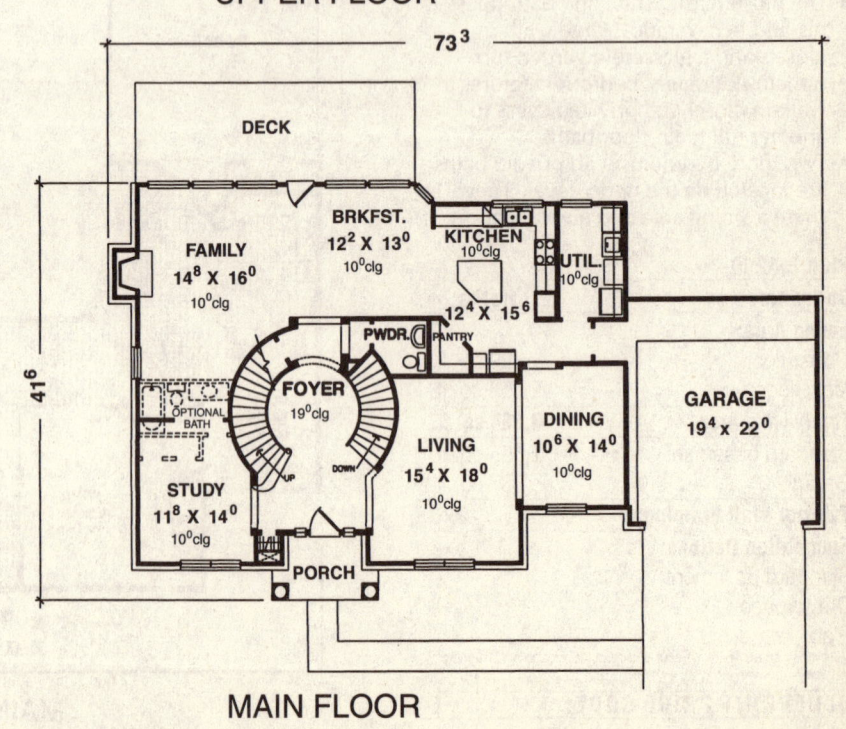

MAIN FLOOR

ORDER BLUEPRINTS ANYTIME!
CALL TOLL-FREE 1-888-626-2026

Plan DD-3260

PRICES AND DETAILS ON PAGES 12-15

European Look

- The beautiful stucco exterior of this European-style home features corner quoins and attractive arched windows.
- Inside, an 18-ft. tray ceiling and a plant ledge soar over the inviting foyer.
- A quiet study includes private access to a full bath, and would be an ideal guest room or extra bedroom.
- Columns neatly divide the combined living and dining rooms to the left. The bayed dining room opens to the deck.
- Double doors separate the formal areas from the island kitchen and the breakfast nook, where a menu desk, a walk-in pantry and a good-sized freezer room are much-appreciated features.
- An 18-ft. vaulted ceiling and a fireplace flanked by windows and bookcases highlight the family room. Elegant French doors provide deck access.
- Unless otherwise noted, every main-floor room includes a 9-ft. ceiling.
- Stairways in the foyer and the family room lead to the upper floor.
- A 14-ft. vaulted ceiling adds flair to the master suite, which boasts a private bath with a luxurious whirlpool tub.
- Two additional bedrooms and a vast bonus room are serviced by two full baths and a bright laundry room.

Plan APS-3302	
Bedrooms: 3+	**Baths:** 4
Living Area:	
Upper floor	1,276 sq. ft.
Main floor	1,716 sq. ft.
Bonus room/4th bedroom	382 sq. ft.
Total Living Area:	**3,374 sq. ft.**
Standard basement	1,716 sq. ft.
Garage	693 sq. ft.
Exterior Wall Framing:	2x4
Foundation Options:	
Standard basement	

(All plans can be built with your choice of foundation and framing. A generic conversion diagram is available. See order form.)

BLUEPRINT PRICE CODE: E

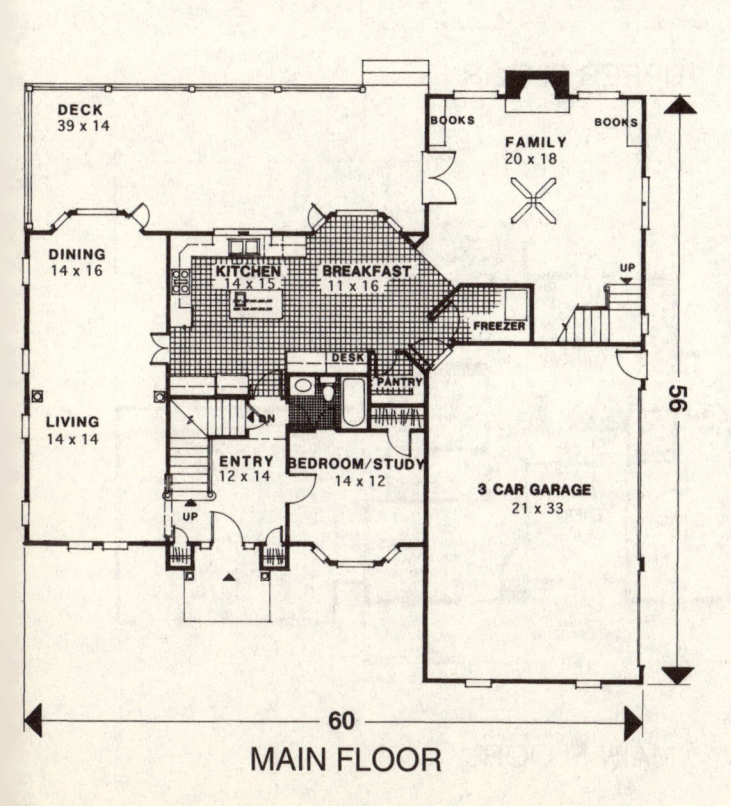

MAIN FLOOR

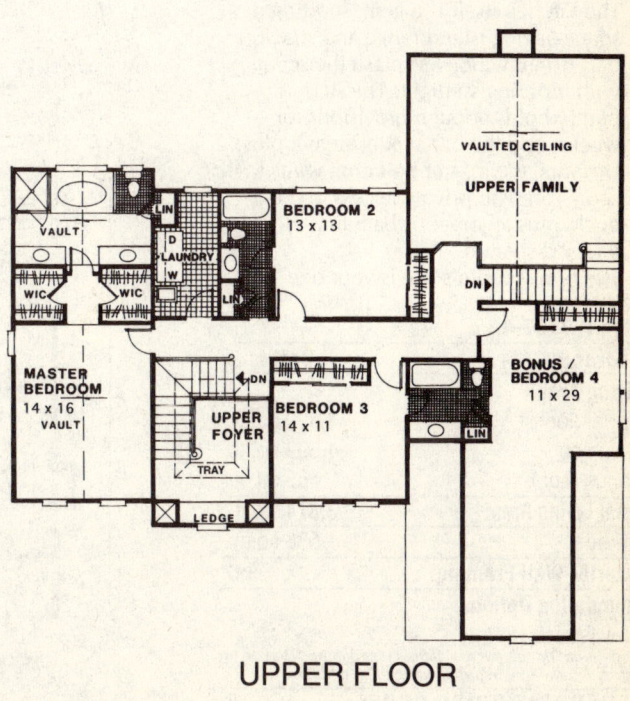

UPPER FLOOR

ORDER BLUEPRINTS ANYTIME!
CALL TOLL-FREE 1-888-626-2026

Plan APS-3302

PRICES AND DETAILS
ON PAGES 12-15

261

Extend Yourself

- Choose this design and marvel at how it allows your living environment to embrace both the warm sheltered spaces and the great outdoors.
- The home is fronted by a porch at ground level and a covered deck above. At the rear, two patios wait to fill your warm-weather days with sun and fun!
- Inside, joined formal rooms receive a healthy dose of dancing light from cheery windows and a fireplace.
- At the back of the home, a sprawling family room boasts its own fireplace and opens to the kitchen and adjoining breakfast nook.
- The kitchen itself is a gem, sporting a space-saving island range and snack bar. Bright windows splash the scene with morning sunlight. The step-in pantry holds enough provisions for weeks, and the bar sink is quite a plus!
- Upstairs, the master bedroom waits to spoil you with private access to the deck, plus a gorgeous bath that includes a raised spa tub.
- The bonus room's use is your decision!

Plan P-7767-4A

Bedrooms: 4+	Baths: 3
Living Area:	
Upper floor	1,320 sq. ft.
Main floor	1,599 sq. ft.
Bonus room	455 sq. ft.
Total Living Area:	**3,374 sq. ft.**
Garage	588 sq. ft.
Exterior Wall Framing:	2x6

Foundation Options:
Crawlspace
(All plans can be built with your choice of foundation and framing. A generic conversion diagram is available. See order form.)

BLUEPRINT PRICE CODE: E

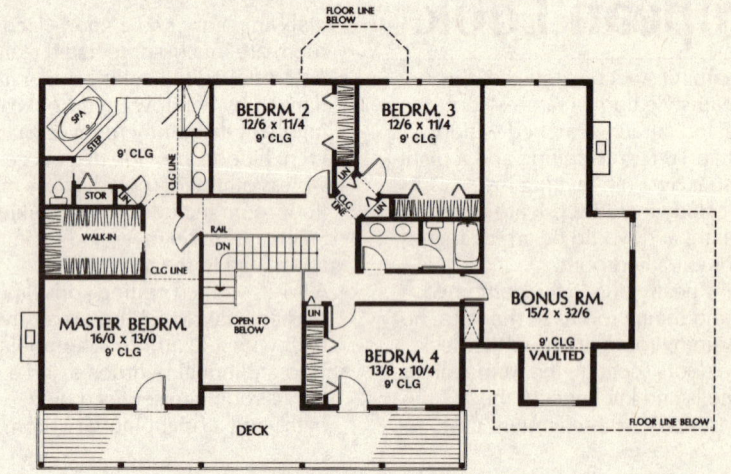

UPPER FLOOR

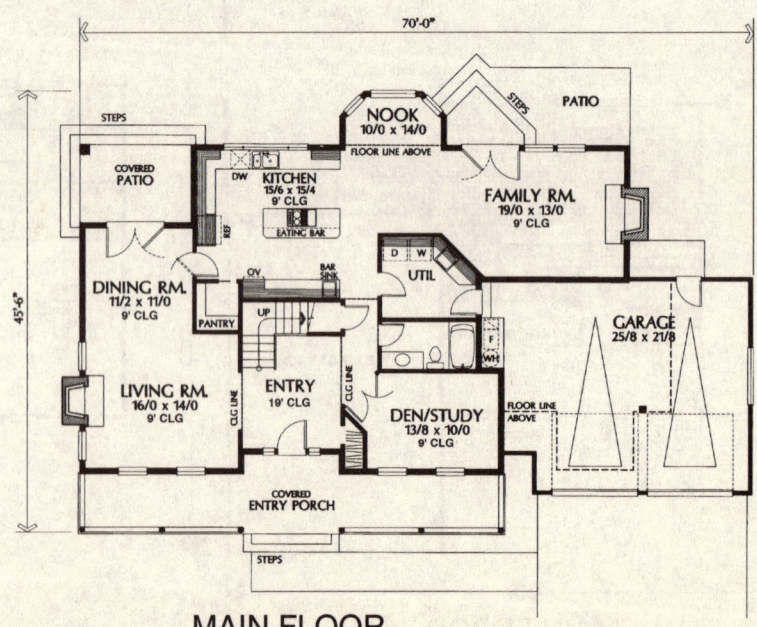

- BEDRM. 2 — 12/6 x 11/4 — 9' CLG
- BEDRM. 3 — 12/6 x 11/4 — 9' CLG
- MASTER BEDRM. — 16/0 x 13/0 — 9' CLG
- BEDRM. 4 — 13/8 x 10/4 — 9' CLG
- BONUS RM. — 15/2 x 32/6 — 9' CLG VAULTED

MAIN FLOOR

70'-0" x 45'-6"

- NOOK — 10/0 x 14/0
- KITCHEN — 15/6 x 15/4 — 9' CLG
- FAMILY RM. — 19/0 x 13/0 — 9' CLG
- DINING RM. — 11/2 x 11/0 — 9' CLG
- LIVING RM. — 16/0 x 14/0 — 9' CLG
- ENTRY — 19' CLG
- DEN/STUDY — 13/8 x 10/0 — 9' CLG
- GARAGE — 25/8 x 21/8

Plan P-7767-4A

ORDER BLUEPRINTS ANYTIME! CALL TOLL-FREE 1-888-626-2026

PRICES AND DETAILS ON PAGES 12-15

Executive Class

- Step up to classic comfort in this gorgeous European-tailored home.
- Soaring ceilings dominate the main floor; namely, the foyer, living room and family room. All three vault upward to an impressive 18 feet.
- In the master suite, an elegant wall of windows bathes the sleeping chamber in soft, early morning light. An 11-ft., 10-in. tray ceiling crowns the space. The private bath boasts a cavernous walk-in closet and a raised tub paired with a radiant window. A 14-ft. vaulted ceiling rises above the scene.
- Weekends were made for the island kitchen, which offers open access to the breakfast room. Turn to the cozy built-in desk to plan your week. Or step out to the rear porch with a pad and pencil.
- Unless otherwise noted, all main-floor rooms boast 9-ft. ceilings.
- Upstairs are two more bedrooms, along with a large bonus room. The foremost bedroom has an 11-ft. vaulted ceiling.

Plan FB-5404-OGLE

Bedrooms: 3+	Baths: 3½
Living Area:	
Upper floor	773 sq. ft.
Main floor	2,297 sq. ft.
Bonus room	333 sq. ft.
Total Living Area:	**3,403 sq. ft.**
Daylight basement	2,297 sq. ft.
Garage	510 sq. ft.
Exterior Wall Framing:	2x4

Foundation Options:
Daylight basement
Crawlspace
(All plans can be built with your choice of foundation and framing. A generic conversion diagram is available. See order form.)

BLUEPRINT PRICE CODE: E

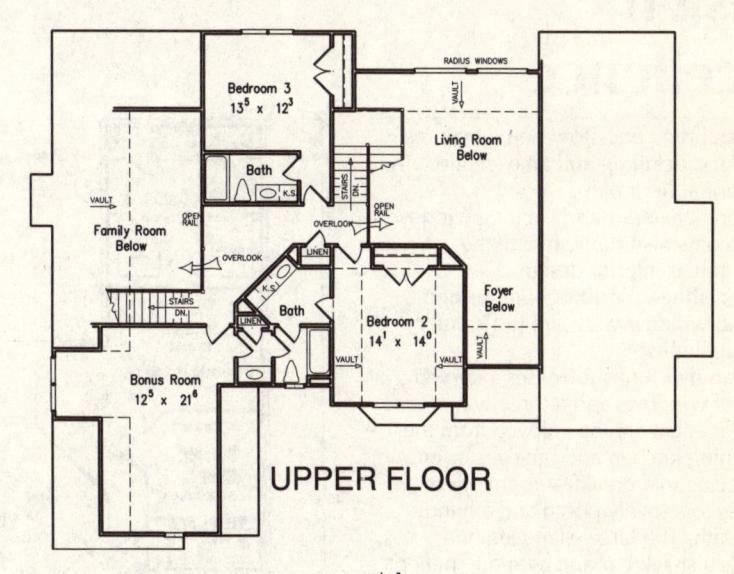

UPPER FLOOR

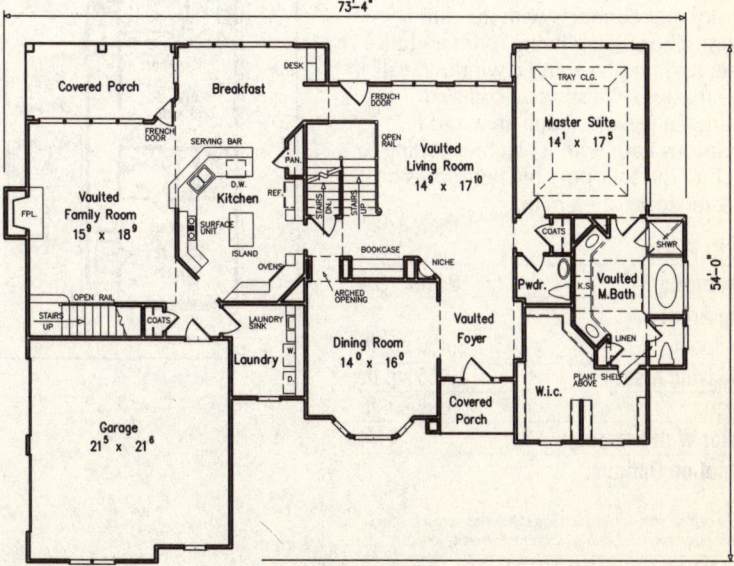

MAIN FLOOR

ORDER BLUEPRINTS ANYTIME!
CALL TOLL-FREE 1-888-626-2026

Plan FB-5404-OGLE

PRICES AND DETAILS ON PAGES 12-15

Design Excellence

- This stunning one-story home features dramatic detailing and an exceptionally functional floor plan.
- The brick exterior and exciting window treatments beautifully hint at the spectacular interior design.
- High ceilings, a host of built-ins and angled window walls are just some of the highlights.
- The family room showcases a curved wall of windows and a three-way fireplace that can be enjoyed from the adjoining kitchen and breakfast room.
- The octagonal breakfast room offers access to a lovely porch and a handy half-bath. The large island kitchen boasts a snack bar and a unique butler's pantry that connects with the dining room. The sunken living room includes a second fireplace and a window wall.
- The master suite sports a coffered ceiling, a private sitting area and a luxurious bath with a gambrel ceiling.
- Each of the four possible bedrooms has private access to a bath.

Plan KLF-922

Bedrooms: 3+	Baths: 3½

Living Area:

Main floor	3,450 sq. ft.
Total Living Area	**3,450 sq. ft.**
Garage	698 sq. ft.

Exterior Wall Framing: 2x4

Foundation Options:
Slab
(All plans can be built with your choice of foundation and framing. A generic conversion diagram is available. See order form.)

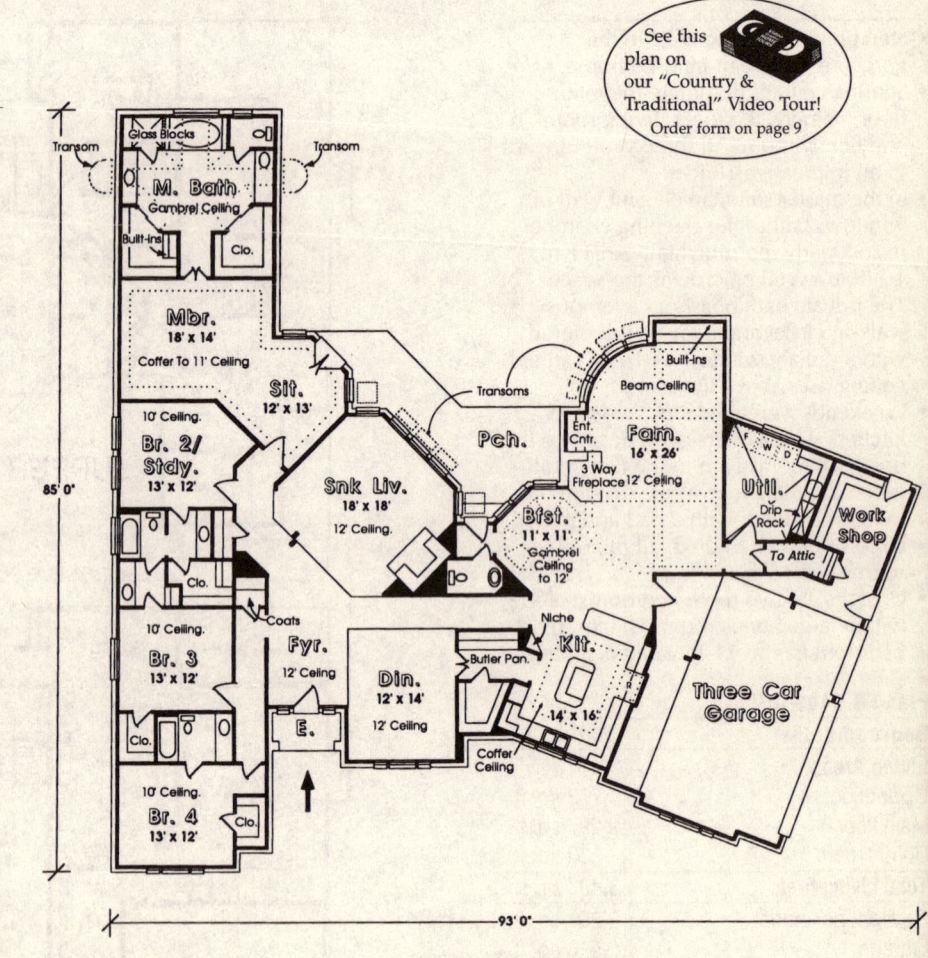

BLUEPRINT PRICE CODE: E

MAIN FLOOR

See this plan on our "Country & Traditional" Video Tour! Order form on page 9

Plan KLF-922

Room to Grow

- Arched windows, cedar siding and brick veneer accents highlight the facade of this beautiful home.
- Inside, the foyer shows off an 18-ft. vaulted ceiling. All other main-floor areas have 9-ft. ceilings. The quiet den boasts double doors and functional built-in storage shelves.
- An arched opening sets off the expansive bayed living room. The adjacent formal dining room is enhanced by a tray ceiling and French-door access to a private deck.
- The gourmet kitchen includes an island cooktop and a sunny breakfast nook that extends to a second deck.
- The huge family room features a fireplace, a wet bar and a dramatic window wall with deck access. A half-bath and a utility room with a sewing counter round out this level.
- Upstairs, the master suite is entered through elegant double doors and has a private access to the fourth bedroom, ideal for a nursery. The skylighted master bath flaunts a spa tub and his-and-hers vanities and walk-in closets.
- The blueprints suggest a layout for future expansion in the basement.

Plan CDG-2054

Bedrooms: 4+	**Baths:** 2½
Living Area:	
Upper floor	1,584 sq. ft.
Main floor	1,876 sq. ft.
Total Living Area:	**3,460 sq. ft.**
Partial daylight basement	1,297 sq. ft.
Garage	657 sq. ft.
Exterior Wall Framing:	2x6

Foundation Options:
Partial daylight basement
(All plans can be built with your choice of foundation and framing. A generic conversion diagram is available. See order form.)

BLUEPRINT PRICE CODE: E

UPPER FLOOR

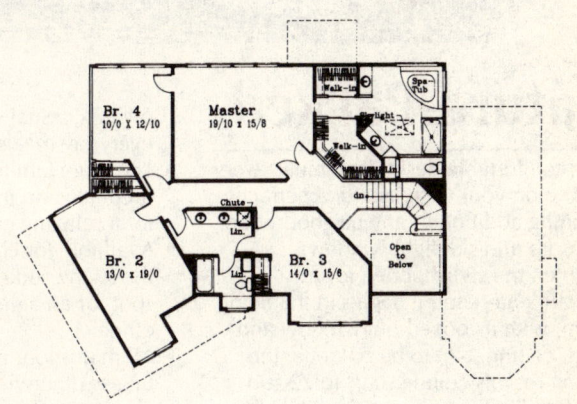

MAIN FLOOR

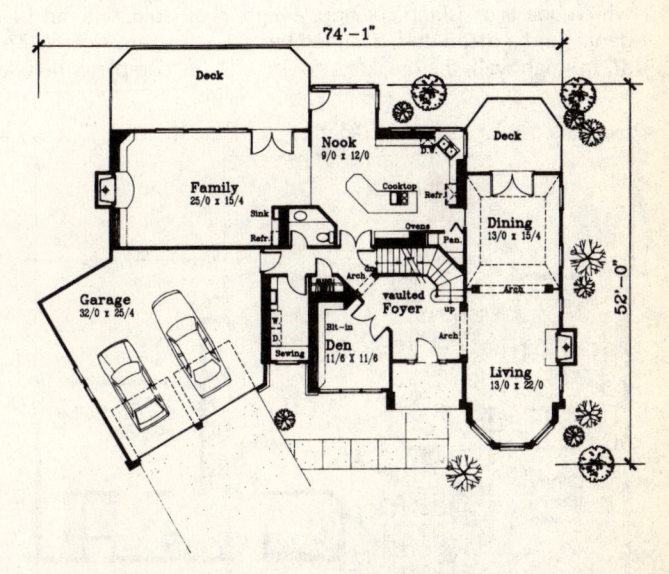

DAYLIGHT BASEMENT

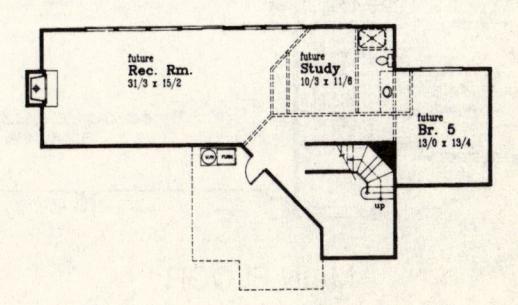

ORDER BLUEPRINTS ANYTIME!
CALL TOLL-FREE 1-888-626-2026

Plan CDG-2054

PRICES AND DETAILS ON PAGES 12-15

Feature-Packed

- This comfortable design combines every feature on your wish list, for a perfectly stunning addition to any neighborhood.
- Transom and sidelight windows brighten the stylish, open foyer.
- Tasteful entertaining begins in the living room, with its boxed-out window and 18-ft. ceiling. Not to be outdone, the dining room's ceiling soars to 22 feet.
- The family chef will love the kitchen, which boasts an island cooktop, a big pantry and a menu desk. Defined by a 36-in.-high wall, the breakfast nook offers a casual spot for enjoying everyday meals.
- The large family room's wet bar, fireplace and media niche set you up for a relaxing evening at home.
- Available for changing family needs, the swing suite would make a perfect spot for an aging parent or a home office.
- All main-floor rooms offer 9-ft. ceilings, unless otherwise noted.
- The upper floor hosts a fabulous master suite with an 11-ft. ceiling and a great exercise area. Three more bedrooms complete the plan.

Plan B-93020	
Bedrooms: 4+	**Baths:** 4
Living Area:	
Upper floor	1,590 sq. ft.
Main floor	1,890 sq. ft.
Total Living Area:	**3,480 sq. ft.**
Standard basement	1,890 sq. ft.
Garage and storage	629 sq. ft.
Exterior Wall Framing:	2x6
Foundation Options:	

Standard basement
(All plans can be built with your choice of foundation and framing. A generic conversion diagram is available. See order form.)

BLUEPRINT PRICE CODE: E

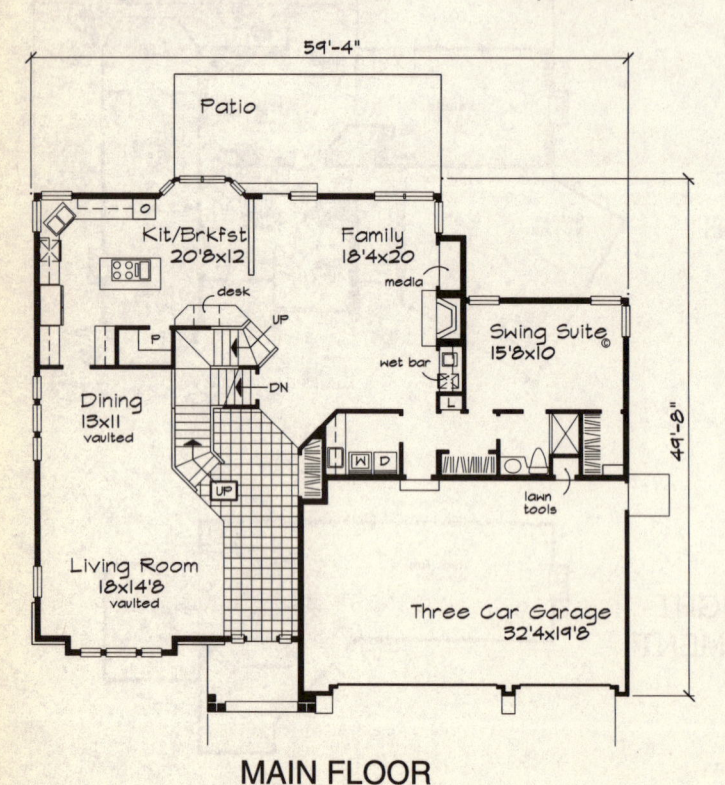

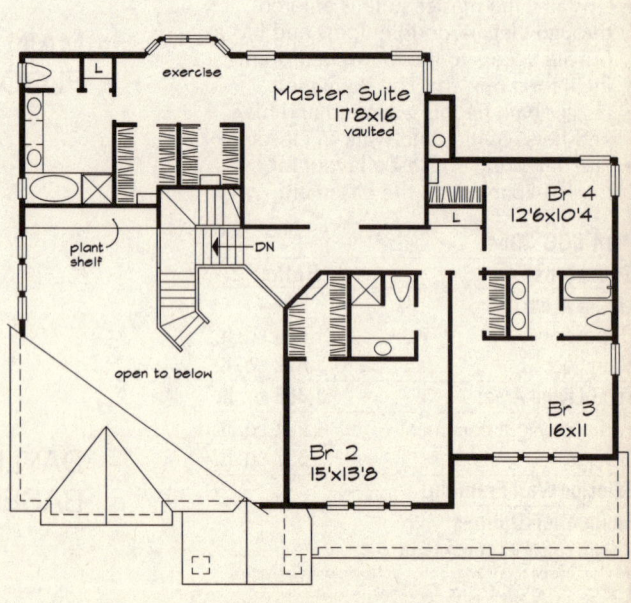

MAIN FLOOR

UPPER FLOOR

ORDER BLUEPRINTS ANYTIME!
CALL TOLL-FREE 1-888-626-2026

Plan B-93020

PRICES AND DETAILS ON PAGES 12-15

Break the Rules

- Who says comfort comes only in ponderous proportions? This traditional-style home delivers it all with a square footage you can live with—and in!
- Ease of living is paramount in this roomy charmer. A wraparound porch blesses the home's countenance. At the rear, an exciting deck provides an excellent spot for Sunday picnics.
- The home's interior is a marvel of free-flowing design. The family room, island kitchen and breakfast nook are joined by nothing but air. French doors lead from the nook to a radiant sun porch.
- For your formal affairs, nothing beats the dining and living rooms, which flank the airy foyer.
- Tucked into a quiet corner and sporting an exposed-beam ceiling, the study gives your family's budding novelist an appropriate space to pursue the muse.
- Upstairs, gorgeous views await you on the master suite's private balcony. Each night, you'll glory in the bath, which hosts a soothing garden tub.

Plan LS-95958-MC

Bedrooms: 4+	**Baths:** 2½

Living Area:
Upper floor	1,705 sq. ft.
Main floor	1,580 sq. ft.
Sun porch	200 sq. ft.
Total Living Area:	**3,485 sq. ft.**
Daylight basement	1,580 sq. ft.
Garage	892 sq. ft.
Exterior Wall Framing:	2x6

Foundation Options:
Daylight basement

All plans can be built with your choice of foundation and framing. A generic conversion diagram is available. See order form.

BLUEPRINT PRICE CODE: E

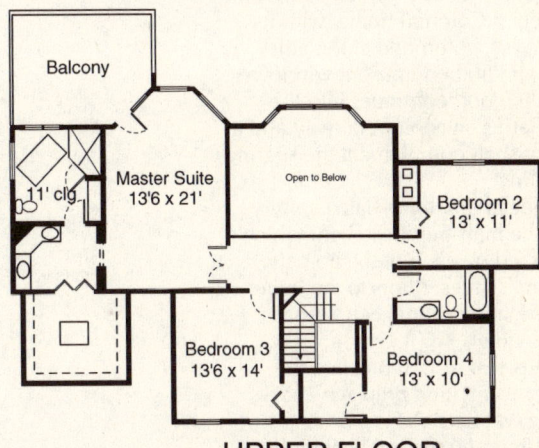

UPPER FLOOR
- Balcony
- Master Suite 13'6 x 21' — 11' clg
- Open to Below
- Bedroom 2 13' x 11'
- Bedroom 3 13'6 x 14'
- Bedroom 4 13' x 10'

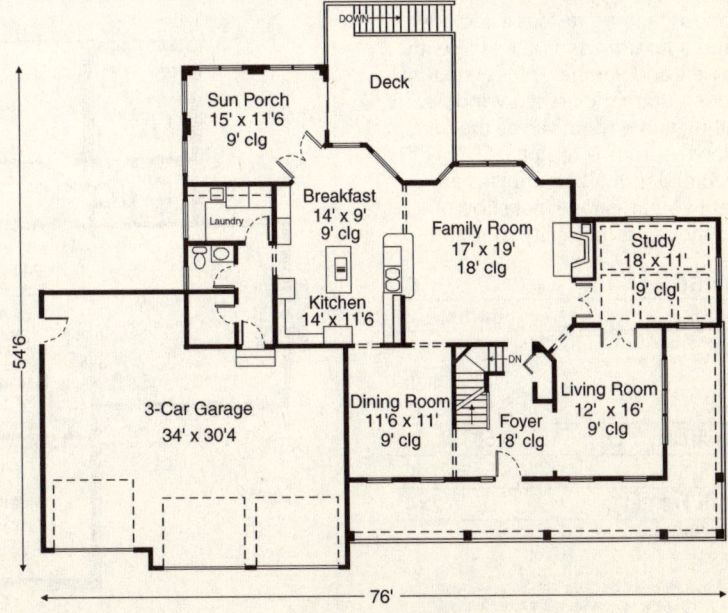

MAIN FLOOR (76' x 54'6)
- Sun Porch 15' x 11'6 — 9' clg
- Deck
- Breakfast 14' x 9' — 9' clg
- Laundry
- Family Room 17' x 19' — 18' clg
- Study 18' x 11' — 9' clg
- Kitchen 14' x 11'6
- 3-Car Garage 34' x 30'4
- Dining Room 11'6 x 11' — 9' clg
- Foyer 18' clg
- Living Room 12' x 16' — 9' clg

ORDER BLUEPRINTS ANYTIME!
CALL TOLL-FREE 1-888-626-2026

Plan LS-95958-MC

PRICES AND DETAILS ON PAGES 12-15

Colonial Spirit

- This elegant two-story captures the spirit of the French Colonial home, with its brick exterior, columned entry, attic dormers and arched transom windows.
- The stately mood continues into the foyer, where a sweeping stairway and a high plant shelf complement the soaring 18-ft. ceiling.
- Straight ahead, an abbreviated gallery leads to the high-traffic kitchen, which is intersected by each of the home's main living spaces; doors to the living room and dining room keep formal occasions quiet.
- Your guests will also appreciate the living room's inviting fireplace and refreshing wet bar.
- High half-round transoms beautifully frame the home's second fireplace in the relaxing family room.
- In the opposite wing resides a secluded study and a luxurious master suite with dual closets and vanities, plus a step-up tub under a dramatic arched window.
- An exciting game room serves the four secondary bedrooms upstairs.
- Also included in the blueprints is an optional two-car garage (not shown), which attaches at the utility room.

Plan L-505-GC

Bedrooms: 5+	Baths: 3½
Living Area:	
Upper floor	1,346 sq. ft.
Main floor	2,157 sq. ft.
Total Living Area:	**3,503 sq. ft.**
Garage	592 sq. ft.
Exterior Wall Framing:	2x4

Foundation Options:
Slab
(All plans can be built with your choice of foundation and framing. A generic conversion diagram is available. See order form.)

BLUEPRINT PRICE CODE: F

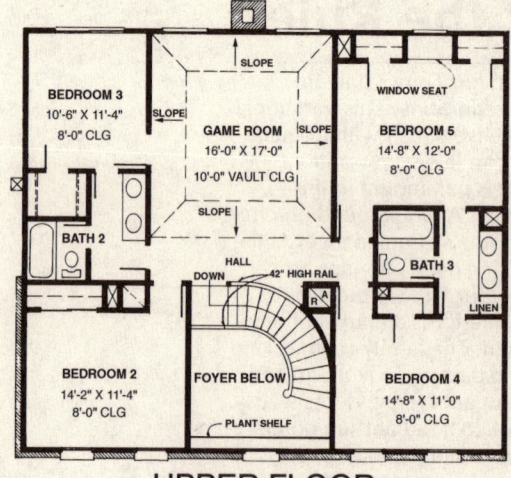

ORDER BLUEPRINTS ANYTIME!
CALL TOLL-FREE 1-888-626-2026

Plan L-505-GC

PRICES AND DETAILS ON PAGES 12-15

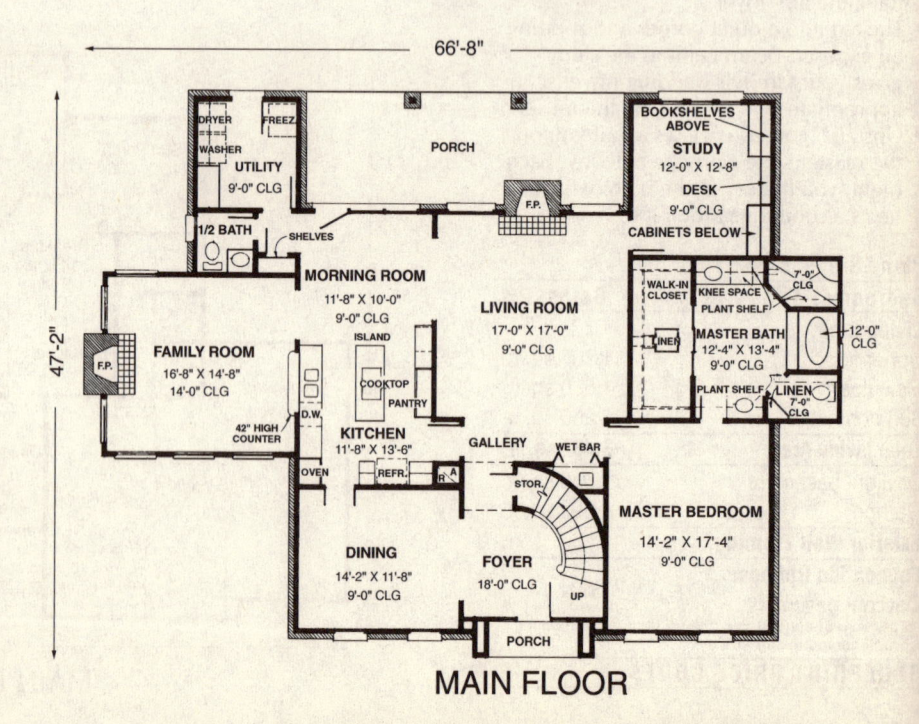

268

Soaring Gables

- Majestic arched windows and soaring gables adorn the exterior of this incredible brick home.
- Inside, the two-story entry provides breathtaking views into the open Great Room, which showcases a wet bar and a handsome fireplace flanked by picture windows and high arched transoms.
- Lovely columns define the sun-drenched dining room, which includes hutch space and a lovely bay window.
- The spacious kitchen features access to the upper floor, plus a columned island that serves the breakfast nook and adjoining hearth room.
- French doors open to the luxurious master suite. Amenities here include two huge walk-in closets and a glamorous whirlpool bath.
- A curved stairway climbs gracefully to the upper floor, which overlooks the entry below.
- Three bedrooms are housed on this level, one of which boasts a private balcony and bi-fold doors that look out over the breakfast nook.

Plan CC-3505-M	
Bedrooms: 4+	**Baths:** 3½
Living Area:	
Upper floor	1,013 sq. ft.
Main floor	2,492 sq. ft.
Total Living Area:	**3,505 sq. ft.**
Standard basement	2,492 sq. ft.
Garage	769 sq. ft.
Exterior Wall Framing:	2x4
Foundation Options:	
Standard basement	
(All plans can be built with your choice of foundation and framing. A generic conversion diagram is available. See order form.)	
BLUEPRINT PRICE CODE:	**F**

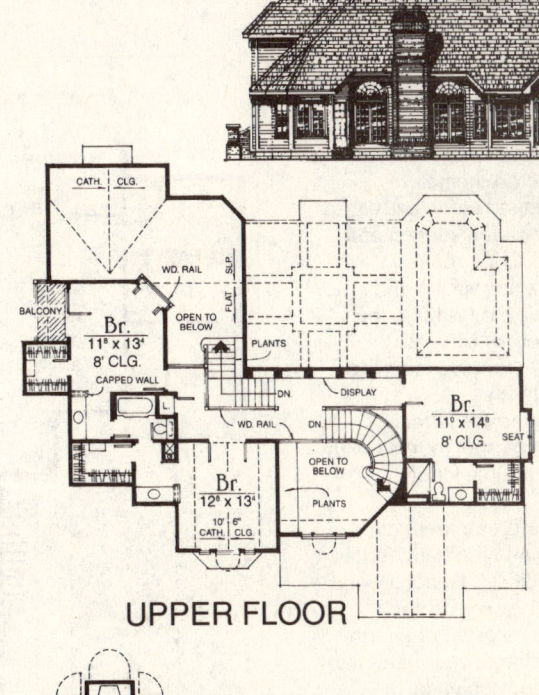

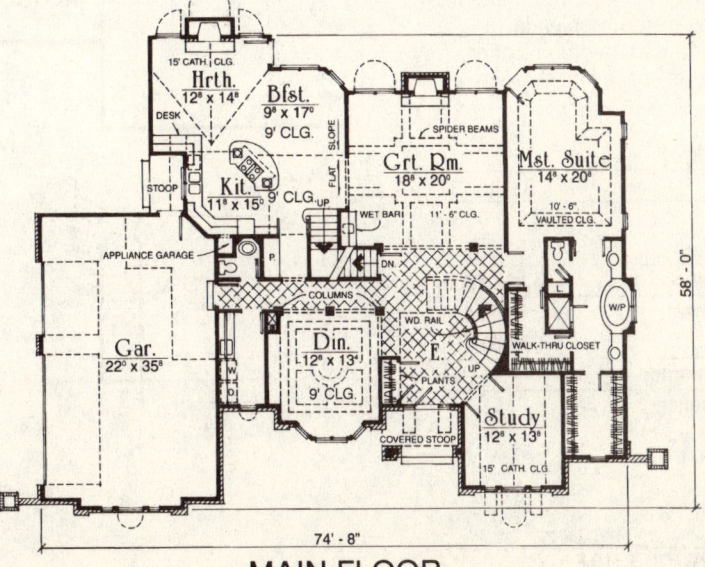

REAR VIEW

UPPER FLOOR

MAIN FLOOR

ORDER BLUEPRINTS ANYTIME!
CALL TOLL-FREE 1-888-626-2026

Plan CC-3505-M

PRICES AND DETAILS ON PAGES 12-15

Lap of Luxury

- A high, sweeping roofline with dormers, half-round window details and a rich-looking arched entry with support columns give a formal, estate look to this luxurious one-story home.
- The cathedral-ceilinged entry leads guests between the island kitchen and library to the grand living room.
- With 10-ft. ceilings, a fireplace and glass-wall views to a rear terrace, the living and dining rooms can easily accommodate large, formal gatherings or day-to-day family life.
- French doors unfold to the terrace, which provides a nice spot to relax with a novel or to entertain the family's budding florist.
- The master suite features a fireplace with shelving, plus a lavish bath and an enormous walk-in closet. French doors open to the terrace. A bayed sitting room adds an extra measure of charm, allowing you to recharge your batteries while basking in sunny splendor!
- The three secondary bedrooms offer abundant closet space and share two more baths.

Plan DD-3512-A

Bedrooms: 4+	Baths: 3½
Living Area:	
Main floor	3,512 sq. ft.
Total Living Area:	**3,512 sq. ft.**
Standard basement	3,512 sq. ft.
Garage	810 sq. ft.
Exterior Wall Framing:	2x6

Foundation Options:
Standard basement
Crawlspace
Slab
(All plans can be built with your choice of foundation and framing. A generic conversion diagram is available. See order form.)

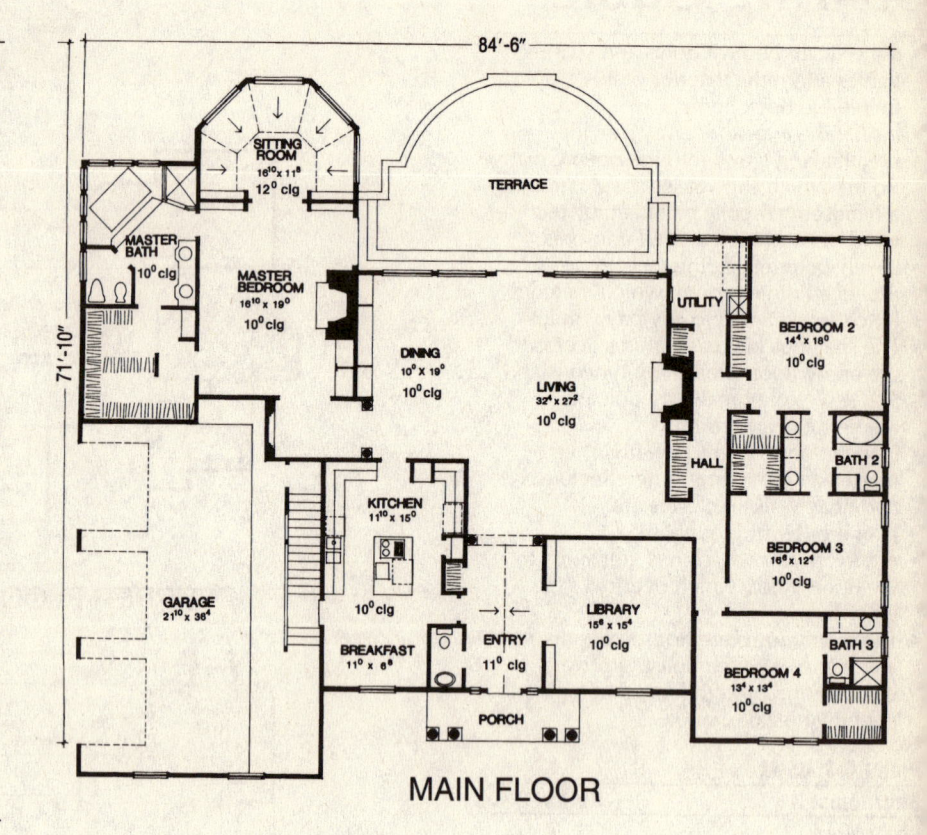

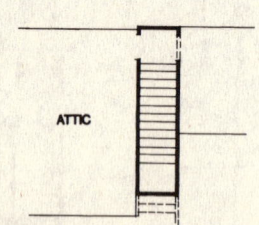

BLUEPRINT PRICE CODE:	F

MAIN FLOOR

Plan DD-3512-A

Splashy Design

- This French design features a charming bathhouse that would be the perfect complement to a splashy pool.
- Beyond the home's brick entry, the 10-ft.-high foyer unfolds to the dining room, which boasts a 12-ft. ceiling. French doors introduce a study, which boasts a nice fireplace, an 11-ft. ceiling and built-in shelves.
- A posh gallery embraces the family room, where a second fireplace flanked by a media center adds a warm glow. A 12-ft. ceiling further increases appeal.
- The sunny breakfast room opens to a peaceful covered porch through a French door, and the efficient kitchen features a convenient snack bar.
- Eye-catching hardwood floors enhance all of the rooms mentioned above.
- Two bedrooms share a bath that offers a private vanity for each room.
- Across the home, an 11-ft. tray ceiling rises above the master bedroom. The lush bath is highlighted by a garden tub.
- The main-floor ceiling heights not mentioned above are all 9 feet.
- A vast bonus area above the garage includes a full bath.

Plan L-2908-FC

Bedrooms: 3+	Baths: 3½-4½
Living Area:	
Main floor	2,908 sq. ft.
Bonus area	479 sq. ft.
Bathhouse	131 sq. ft.
Total Living Area:	**3,518 sq. ft.**
Garage	748 sq. ft.
Exterior Wall Framing:	2x4
Foundation Options:	
Slab	
All plans can be built with your choice of foundation and framing. A generic conversion diagram is available. See order form.	
BLUEPRINT PRICE CODE:	**F**

REAR VIEW

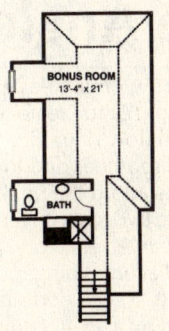

BONUS AREA

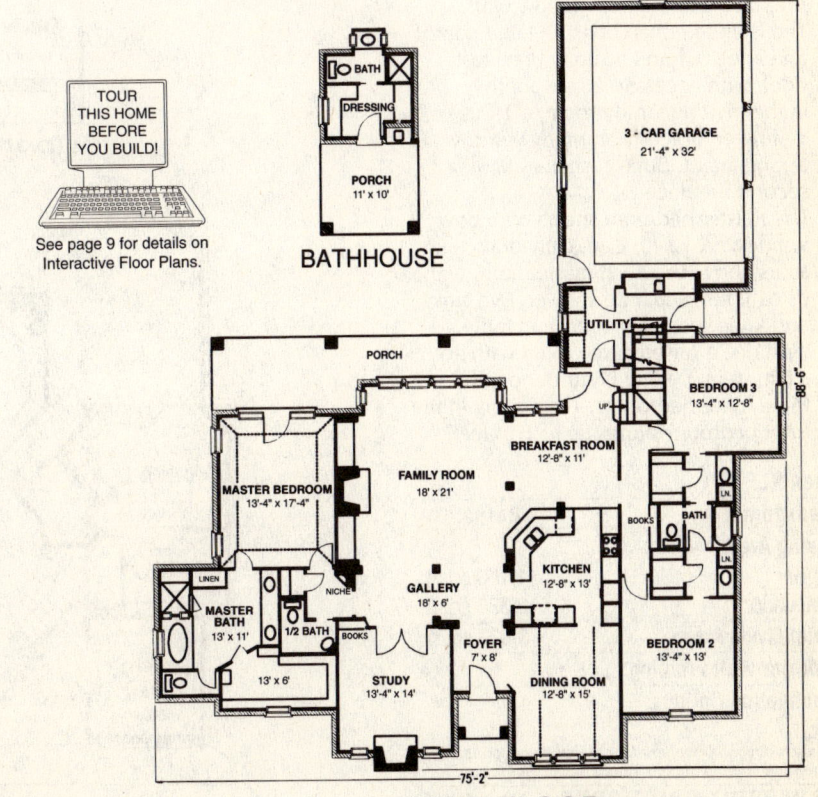

TOUR THIS HOME BEFORE YOU BUILD!
See page 9 for details on Interactive Floor Plans.

BATHHOUSE

MAIN FLOOR

ORDER BLUEPRINTS ANYTIME!
CALL TOLL-FREE 1-888-626-2026

Plan L-2908-FC

PRICES AND DETAILS ON PAGES 12-15

Nice Angles

- This award-winning design utilizes angular spaces to create a logical and functional flow of traffic.
- Dramatic rooflines and lovely window treatments adorn the brick exterior.
- Inside, the two-story foyer reveals a graceful curved stairway. Columns set off the adjacent dining room.
- On the left, a secluded study is enhanced by a 12-ft. ceiling.
- An 11-ft. coffered ceiling presides over the central living room, with its corner fireplace and angled window wall.
- The island kitchen boasts a large pantry, an eating bar and a sunny breakfast nook with access to a rear porch.
- In the inviting family room, a 14-ft. ceiling embraces a stunning window arrangement. Built-in shelves flank a second fireplace.
- The master bedroom shows off a bow window. A 12-ft., 3-in. cathedral ceiling soars above the posh master bath, with its oval tub, separate shower, two sinks and knee space for a makeup table.
- Upstairs, a raised game room with an 11-ft., 8-in. ceiling is surrounded by three more bedrooms. The ceiling in the front bedroom slopes up to 10½ feet.

Plan KLF-921

Bedrooms: 4+	Baths: 3½
Living Area:	
Upper floor	1,150 sq. ft.
Main floor	2,383 sq. ft.
Total Living Area:	**3,533 sq. ft.**
Exterior Wall Framing:	2x4

Foundation Options:
Slab
(All plans can be built with your choice of foundation and framing. A generic conversion diagram is available. See order form.)

BLUEPRINT PRICE CODE: F

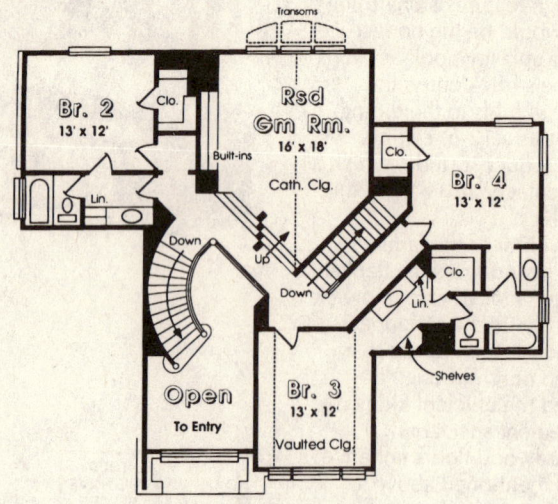

UPPER FLOOR

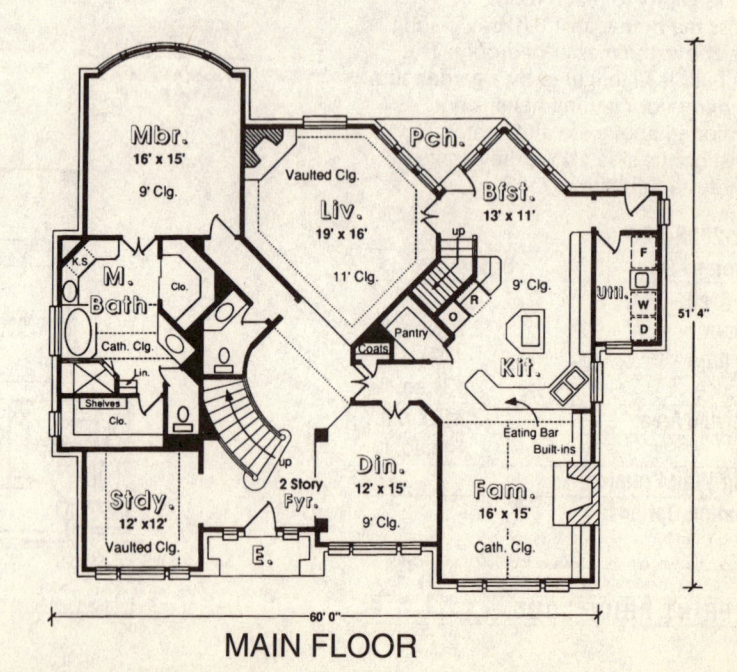

MAIN FLOOR

Plan KLF-921

Prominent Portico

- A prominent portico accented by dramatic windows and a Spanish tile roof draws attention to this home. Grand double doors open into a foyer with an airy 14-ft. ceiling.
- Straight ahead, an elegant curved gallery frames the living room, which opens to a skylighted patio. Arched openings along one wall add high style.
- The quiet den and the formal dining room feature striking 12-ft. ceilings.
- The island kitchen boasts a big pantry and a neat pass-through to the patio, which offers a summer kitchen with a bar sink. A powder room is nearby.
- A 14-ft. vaulted ceiling, plus a fireplace set into a media wall make the family room a fun indoor gathering place.
- Two secondary bedrooms share a split bath with a dual-sink vanity.
- Across the home, a three-way fireplace and an entertainment center separate the master bedroom from its bayed sitting room. An exercise area, a wet bar and a posh bath are other pleasures!
- Unless otherwise mentioned, every room features a 10-ft. ceiling.

Plan HDS-99-242

Bedrooms: 3+	Baths: 3½
Living Area:	
Main floor	3,556 sq. ft.
Total Living Area:	**3,556 sq. ft.**
Garage	809 sq. ft.
Exterior Wall Framing:	8-in. concrete block

Foundation Options:
Slab
(All plans can be built with your choice of foundation and framing. A generic conversion diagram is available. See order form.)

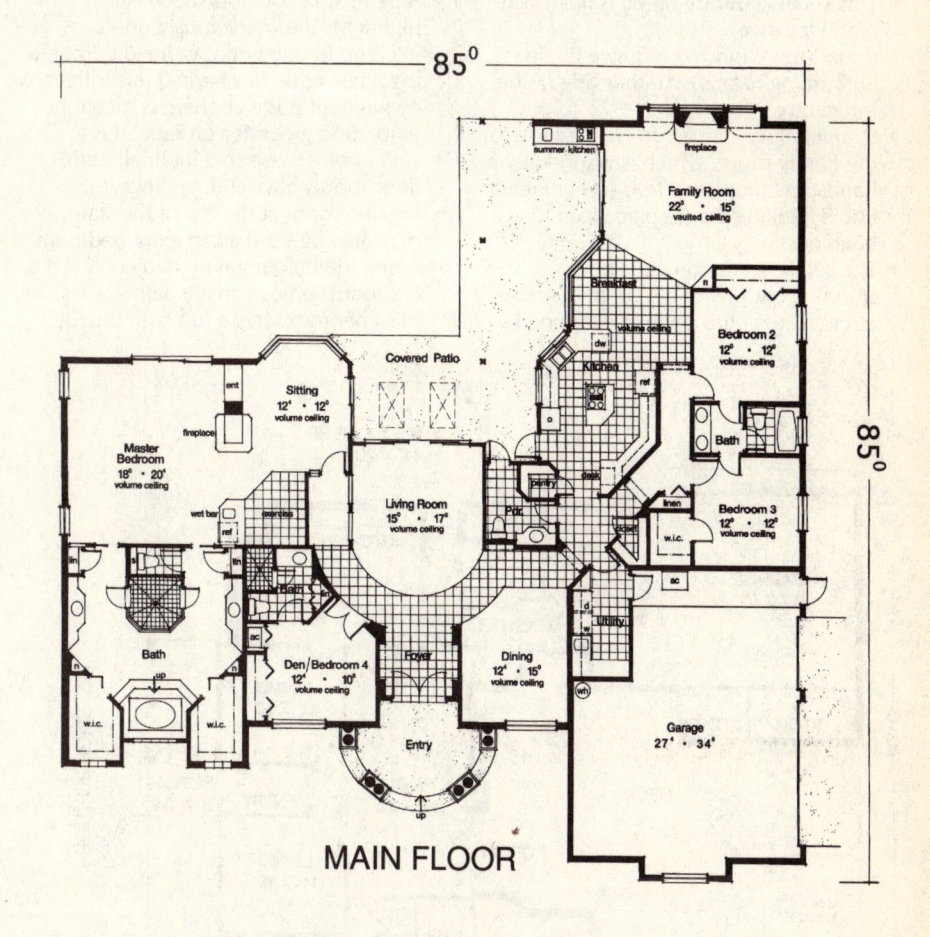

BLUEPRINT PRICE CODE: F

MAIN FLOOR

ORDER BLUEPRINTS ANYTIME!
CALL TOLL-FREE 1-888-626-2026

Plan HDS-99-242

PRICES AND DETAILS ON PAGES 12-15

Elegant Country

- This stately country home is filled with high elegance.
- Round-top windows brighten the living and dining rooms on either side of the long entry.
- Straight ahead, an 18-ft. ceiling crowns the family room, which is warmed by a handsome fireplace. Two sets of French doors flanking the fireplace lead to a huge deck.
- The secluded master suite boasts a stunning bath, with a step-up quarter-circle Jacuzzi tub under a columned pergola, an arched window and a 12-ft. sloped ceiling!
- A peninsula cooktop/snack bar highlights the marvelously open kitchen. In one window-lined corner, a breakfast nook lies bathed in sunlight. A convenient porte cochere is nice for unloading groceries on rainy days.
- Unless otherwise specified, all main-floor rooms have 9-ft. ceilings.
- A game room at the top of the stairs may also be used as an extra bedroom.
- Along the balcony hall, two good-sized bedrooms enjoy private bath access. A third bedroom has a full bath nearby.

Plan E-3501	
Bedrooms: 4+	**Baths:** 3½
Living Area:	
Upper floor	1,238 sq. ft.
Main floor	2,330 sq. ft.
Total Living Area:	**3,568 sq. ft.**
Standard basement	2,348 sq. ft.
Garage and storage	848 sq. ft.
Exterior Wall Framing:	2x6
Foundation Options:	
Standard basement	
Crawlspace	
Slab	

(All plans can be built with your choice of foundation and framing. A generic conversion diagram is available. See order form.)

BLUEPRINT PRICE CODE: F

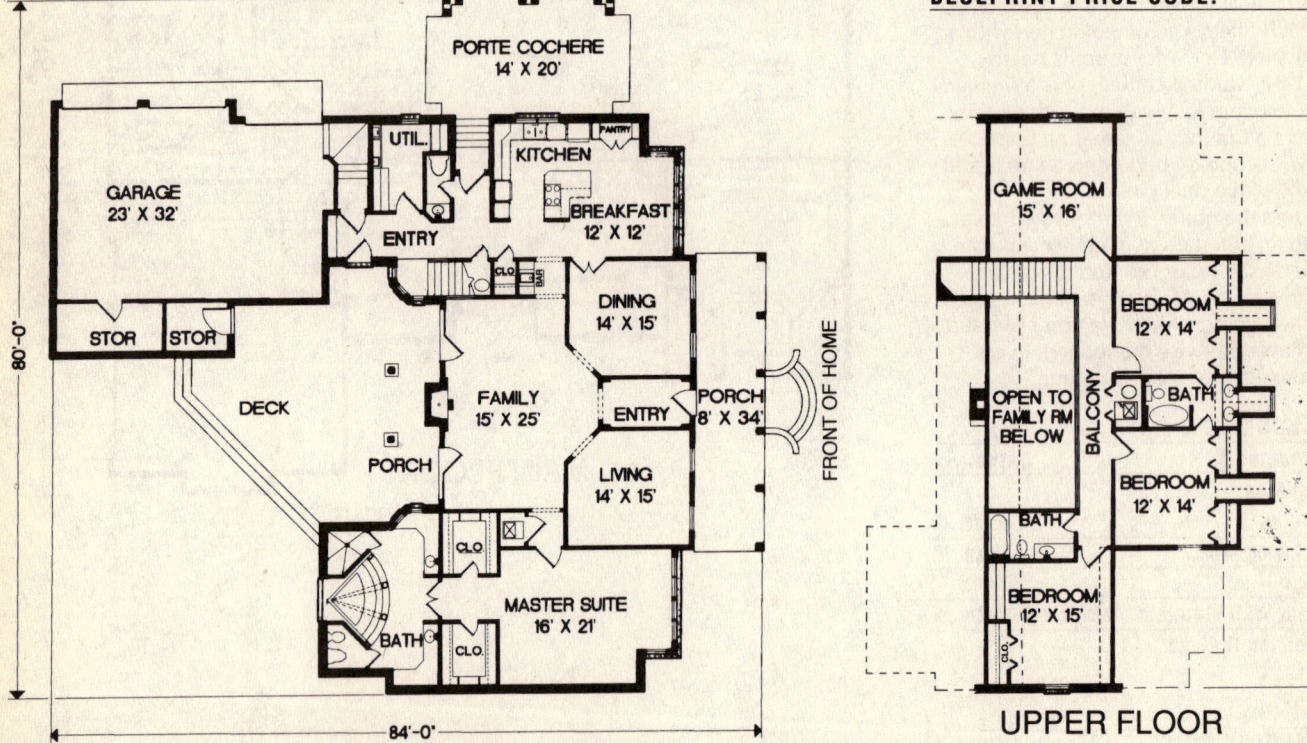

MAIN FLOOR

UPPER FLOOR

Plan E-3501

Stately Flair

- Stately columns, an arched entry and dramatic rooflines give this home its distinguished flair.
- Inside, the two-story foyer is flanked by the formal dining room and a quiet library with a 19-ft. cathedral ceiling and a tall arched window.
- The spacious central living room offers an 18-ft., 4-in. ceiling, a nice fireplace and access to a backyard patio.
- The modern island kitchen and bayed breakfast area merge with the living room, creating a flowing, open feel.
- The large main-floor master suite boasts a 10½-ft. ceiling, a sunny bay window, private patio access and an elegant bath with a spa tub, a separate shower and a dual-sink vanity with knee space.
- Unless otherwise specified, all main-floor rooms have 9-ft. ceilings.
- On the upper floor, a versatile media room and a computer room provide plenty of space for work and play. Two of the three bedrooms are enhanced by 10-ft. gambrel ceilings.
- The large workshop off the garage is great for do-it-yourselfers and hobbyists.

Plan DD-3583

Bedrooms: 4+	Baths: 3½
Living Area:	
Upper floor	1,436 sq. ft.
Main floor	2,147 sq. ft.
Total Living Area:	**3,583 sq. ft.**
Standard basement	2,147 sq. ft.
Garage and workshop	594 sq. ft.
Exterior Wall Framing:	2x4

Foundation Options:
Standard basement
Crawlspace
Slab
(All plans can be built with your choice of foundation and framing. A generic conversion diagram is available. See order form.)

BLUEPRINT PRICE CODE: F

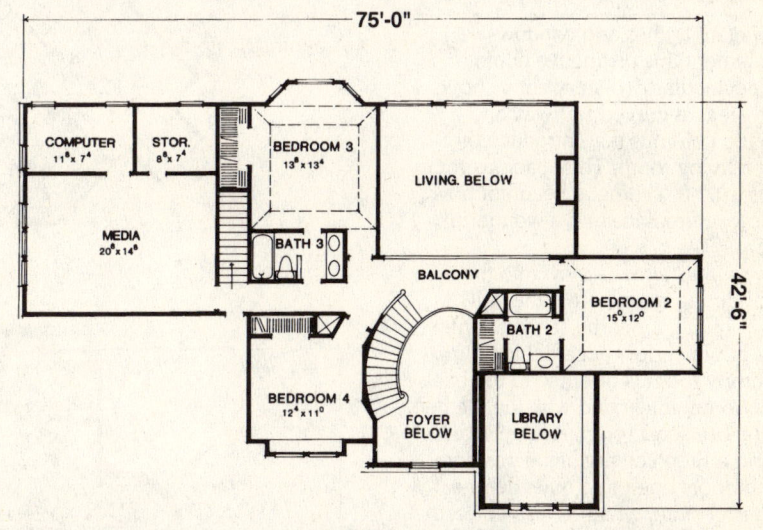

UPPER FLOOR

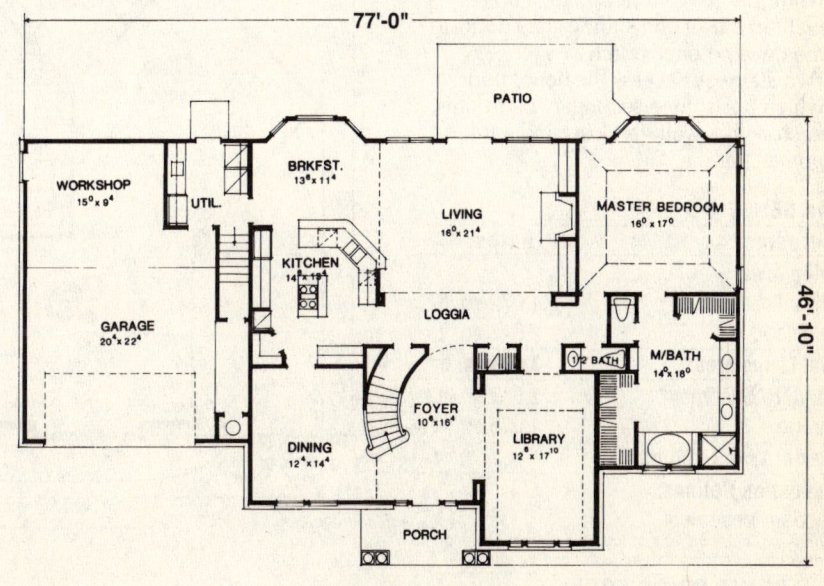

MAIN FLOOR

ORDER BLUEPRINTS ANYTIME!
CALL TOLL-FREE 1-888-626-2026

Plan DD-3583

PRICES AND DETAILS
ON PAGES 12-15

Four Fabulous Bedroom Suites

- Extravagant arches and windows complement this distinctive home.
- The spectacular two-story entry shows off an elegant curved stairway and dramatic columns that introduce the sunken living room. This spacious room boasts a 10-ft. ceiling, a beautiful bow window, a fireplace and a wonderful wet bar.
- Open railings allow a view into the formal dining room across the hall. A built-in hutch, a nearby serving center and a bow window accent this room.
- The family room is oriented to the back of the home, integrated with the kitchen and the breakfast room. A large snack bar and a fireplace are highlights here.
- French doors open to a quiet den near the master suite, which is also entered through double doors. The plush suite offers a private bath with an oval whirlpool tub, a toilet room, a huge walk-in closet and sliding glass doors to the covered back porch.
- Two stairways access the upper floor, which hosts three secondary bedrooms, each with a walk-in closet and a full private bath.

Plan DBI-2218

Bedrooms: 4+	Baths: 4½
Living Area:	
Upper floor	1,072 sq. ft.
Main floor	2,617 sq. ft.
Total Living Area:	**3,689 sq. ft.**
Standard basement	2,617 sq. ft.
Garage	1,035 sq. ft.
Exterior Wall Framing:	2x4
Foundation Options:	
Standard basement	
(All plans can be built with your choice of foundation and framing. A generic conversion diagram is available. See order form.)	
BLUEPRINT PRICE CODE:	**F**

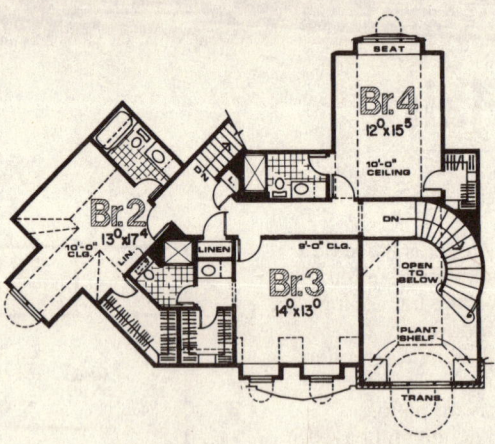

UPPER FLOOR

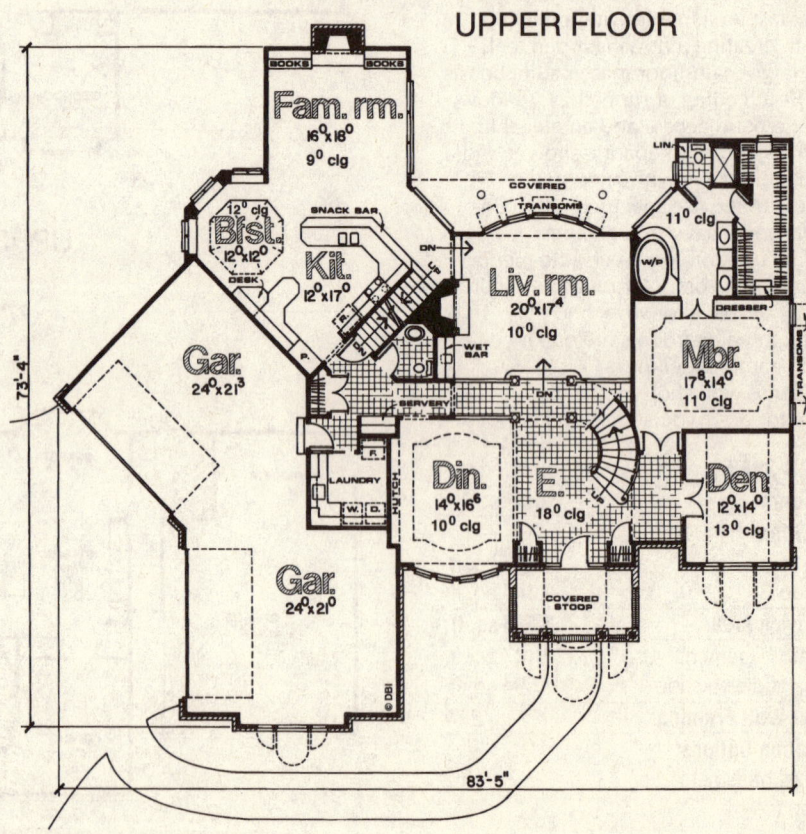

MAIN FLOOR

ORDER BLUEPRINTS ANYTIME! CALL TOLL-FREE 1-888-626-2026

Plan DBI-2218

PRICES AND DETAILS ON PAGES 12-15

FRONT VIEW

Spacious Western Ranch

REAR VIEW

- A three-bedroom sleeping wing is separated from the balance of the home, with the master suite featuring a raised tub below skylights and a walk-in dressing room.
- Sunken living room is enhanced by a vaulted ceiling and fireplace with raised hearth.
- Family room is entered from the central hall through double doors; a wet bar and a second fireplace grace this gathering spot.
- Kitchen has functional L-shaped arrangement, attached nook, and pantry.

Plan H-3701-1A	
Bedrooms: 4	**Baths:** 3½
Total living area:	3,735 sq. ft.
Garage:	830 sq. ft.
Exterior Wall Framing:	2x4
Foundation options: Crawlspace only. (Foundation & framing conversion diagram available — see order form.)	
Blueprint Price Code:	F

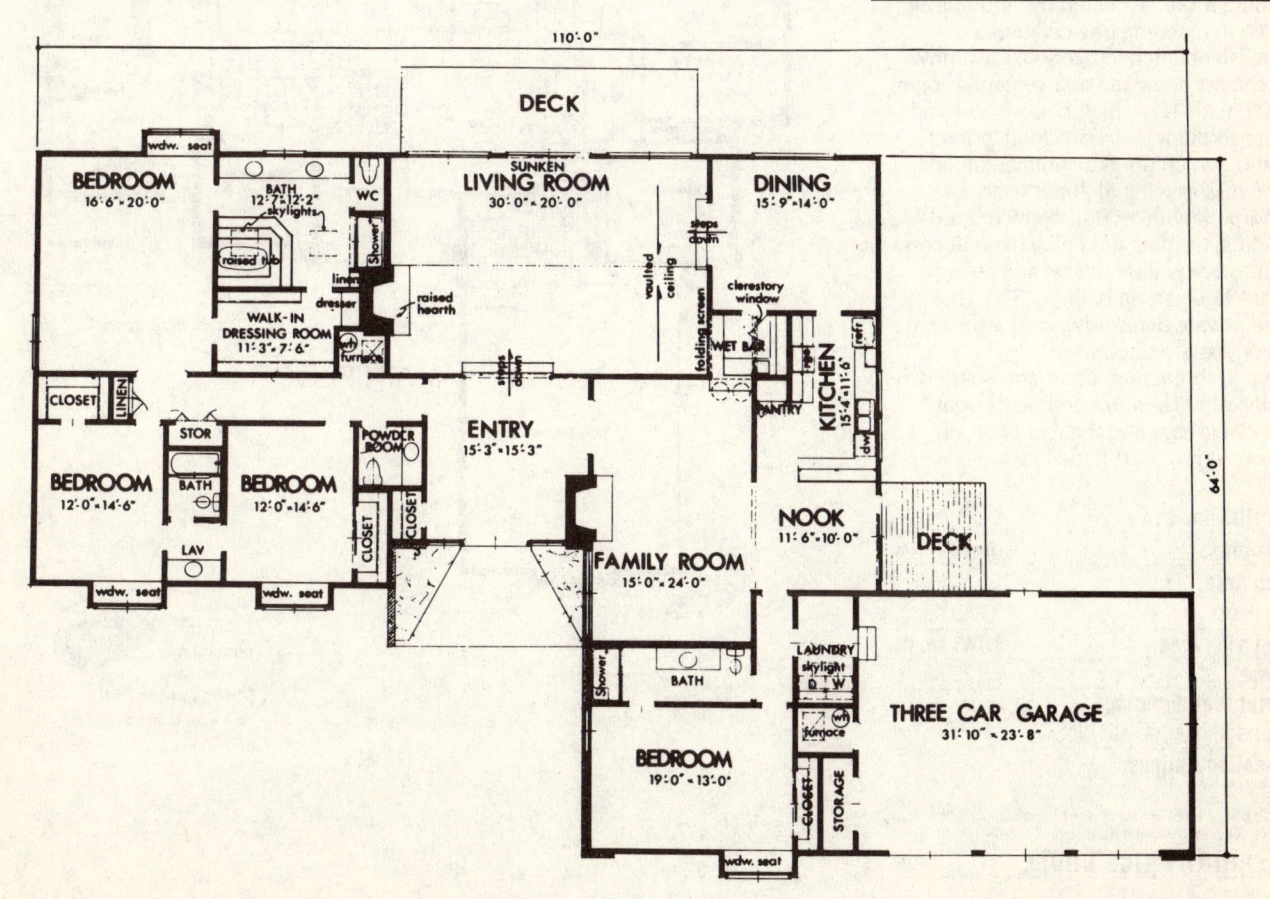

ORDER BLUEPRINTS ANYTIME!
CALL TOLL-FREE 1-888-626-2026

Plan H-3701-1A

PRICES AND DETAILS ON PAGES 12-15

277

Bright Design

- Sweeping rooflines, arched transom windows and a stucco exterior give this exciting design a special flair.
- Inside the high, dramatic entry, guests are greeted with a stunning view of the living room, which is expanded by a 12-ft. volume ceiling. This formal expanse is augmented by an oversized bay that looks out onto a covered patio and possible pool area.
- To the left of the foyer is the formal dining room, accented by columns and a 14-ft. receding tray ceiling.
- The island kitchen overlooks a sunny breakfast nook and a large family room, each with 12-ft.-high ceilings. A handy pass-through transports food to the patio, which offers a summer kitchen.
- The master wing includes a large bedroom with a 10-ft.-high coffered ceiling, a sitting area with patio access, a massive walk-in closet and a sun-drenched garden bath.
- The private den/study could also serve as an extra bedroom.
- Two to three more bedrooms share two full baths. The front bedrooms boast 12-ft. ceilings and the rear bedroom is accented by a 10-ft. ceiling.

Plan HDS-90-814

Bedrooms: 3+	Baths: 3½

Living Area:

Main floor	3,743 sq. ft.
Total Living Area:	**3,743 sq. ft.**
Garage	725 sq. ft.

Exterior Wall Framing:
2x4 and 8-in. concrete block

Foundation Options:
Slab
(All plans can be built with your choice of foundation and framing. A generic conversion diagram is available. See order form.)

BLUEPRINT PRICE CODE: F

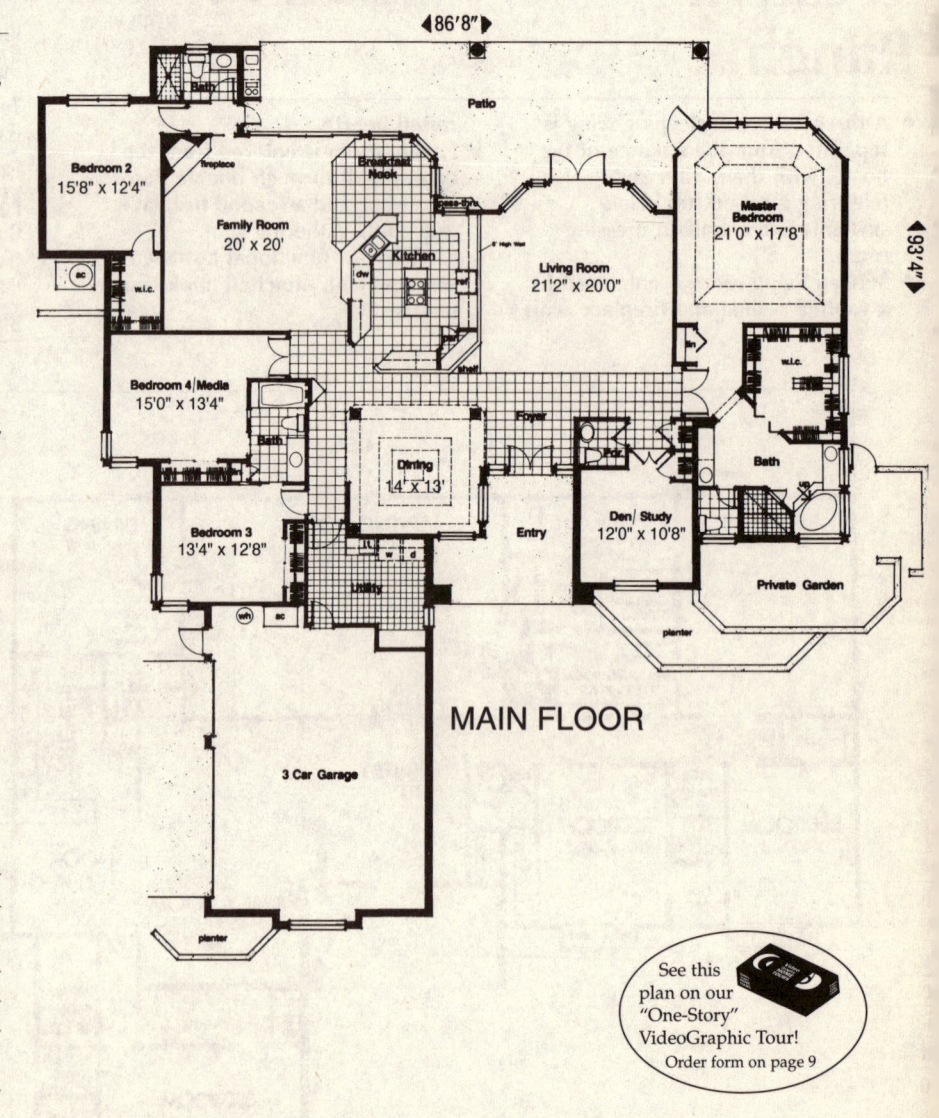

MAIN FLOOR

See this plan on our "One-Story" VideoGraphic Tour!
Order form on page 9

278 ORDER BLUEPRINTS ANYTIME! CALL TOLL-FREE 1-888-626-2026

Plan HDS-90-814

PRICES AND DETAILS ON PAGES 12-15

Bold and Beautiful

- Bold styling and luxurious spaces define this two-level French beauty.
A fashionable see-through fireplace and a wall of windows welcome guests to the family room. A bayed study, which shares the fireplace, opens to a deck. Spoil yourself in the master suite. Double doors open into the room, which is brightened by a dramatic arched window and boasts a deluxe master bath, complete with a whirlpool tub, a dual-sink vanity and an enormous walk-in closet.
Enjoy the daily paper while you sip your morning coffee in the kitchen/breakfast area. A large eating bar and a pair of lazy Susans are unique to the space. Downstairs, the huge recreation room, with a beautiful fireplace framed by built-in shelves, joins the game room and a wet bar to create the ultimate entertainment area. Two large bedrooms share a dual-sink bath to round out the floor.

Plan CC-2260-M

Bedrooms: 3+	**Baths:** 2 Full, 2 Half

Living Area:
Main floor	2,260 sq. ft.
Partial daylight basement	1,530 sq. ft.
Total Living Area:	**3,790 sq. ft.**
Garage	736 sq. ft.
Exterior Wall Framing:	2x4

Foundation Options:
Partial daylight basement
(All plans can be built with your choice of foundation and framing. A generic conversion diagram is available. See order form.)

BLUEPRINT PRICE CODE: F

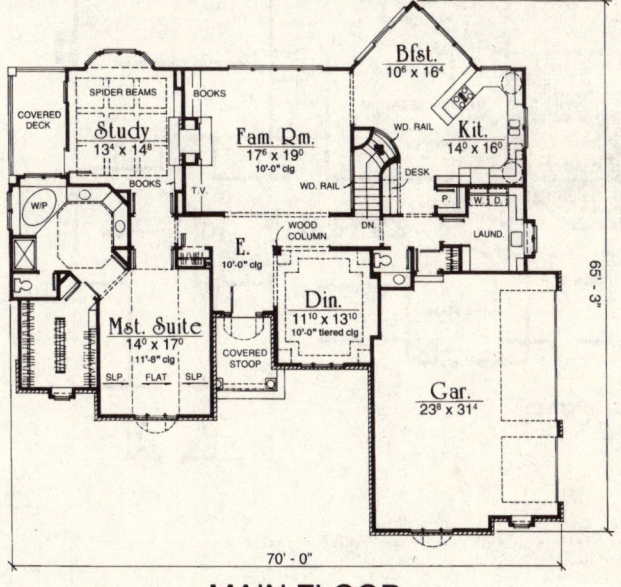

MAIN FLOOR

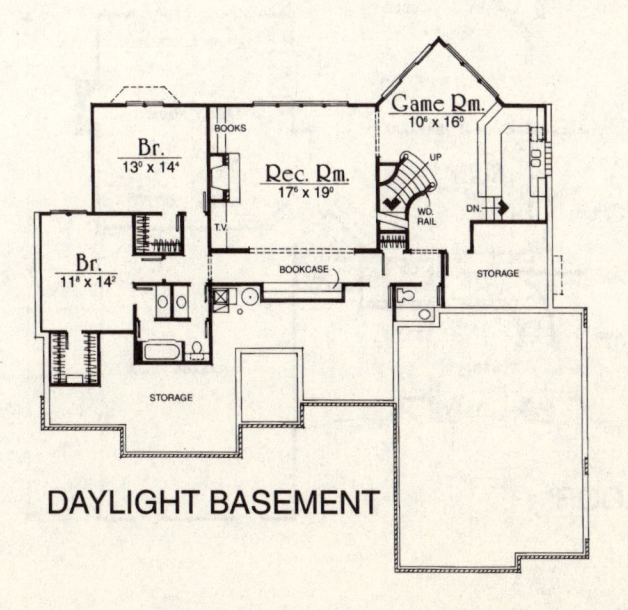

DAYLIGHT BASEMENT

ORDER BLUEPRINTS ANYTIME!
CALL TOLL-FREE 1-888-626-2026

Plan CC-2260-M

PRICES AND DETAILS
ON PAGES 12-15

Timeless Traditional

- Bay windows, stylish quoins and a commanding Palladian window lend a timeless elegance to this brick home.
- A dramatic, two-story foyer ushers visitors into the bayed living room with fireplace. The large dining room offers splendid views through triple windows.
- An island kitchen features a bayed breakfast area, an oversized pantry and access to a fabulous wraparound deck.
- The vaulted family room has a wet bar, a second fireplace and French doors opening to the deck. A railed staircase provides a second access to the upstairs.
- The master suite is awesome, with its tray ceiling, French doors, private deck, bayed sitting area, garden tub, separate shower and walk-in closet.
- The adjacent bedroom has its own bath. The third bedroom shares a bath with the bonus room, which could be used as a bedroom, hobby room or studio.
- The bayed main-floor study can serve as a fifth bedroom if needed.

Plan APS-3404

Bedrooms: 3-5	Baths: 3½

Living Area:	
Upper floor	1,426 sq. ft.
Main floor	2,005 sq. ft.
Bonus room	374 sq. ft.
Total Living Area:	**3,805 sq. ft.**
Standard basement	1,760 sq. ft.
Garage	672 sq. ft.

Exterior Wall Framing: 2x4

Foundation Options:
Standard basement
(Typical foundation & framing conversion diagram available—see order form.)

BLUEPRINT PRICE CODE: F

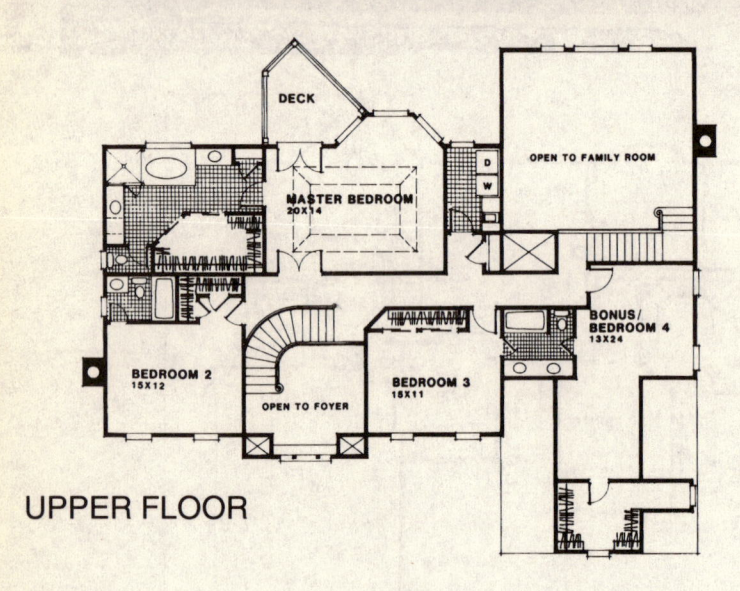

UPPER FLOOR

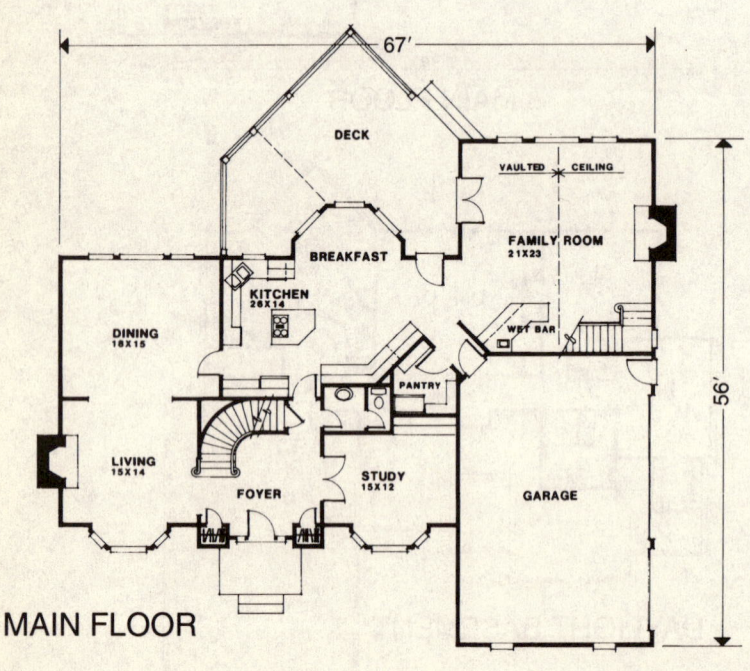

MAIN FLOOR

Plan APS-3404

Rambling Comfort

- Comfort rambles throughout this big, beautiful traditional home.
- Beyond a wraparound veranda and an ornate entrance, sprawling living spaces parade along the main floor.
- At the center, an expansive living room welcomes guests with its handsome fireplace, built-in entertainment center and sweeping views of the outdoors.
- With abundant counter space, a built-in desk and a walk-in pantry, the kitchen accommodates all of your storage needs—and then some.
- A hobby room and a study add function and versatility to the home.
- The master suite is enveloped in luxury with its romantic sitting area, fireplace, private garden bath and sauna!
- Three large upstairs bedrooms, each with a walk-in closet and a personal dressing area, offer privacy and room for growth. Exciting recreational spaces fulfill your leisure time.
- Plans for a two-car detached garage are included with the blueprints.

Plan L-4053-VC

Bedrooms: 4+	Baths: 3½
Living Area:	
Upper floor	1,529 sq. ft.
Main floor	2,524 sq. ft.
Total Living Area:	**4,053 sq. ft.**
Exterior Wall Framing:	2x4

Foundation Options:
Slab
(All plans can be built with your choice of foundation and framing. A generic conversion diagram is available. See order form.)

BLUEPRINT PRICE CODE: G

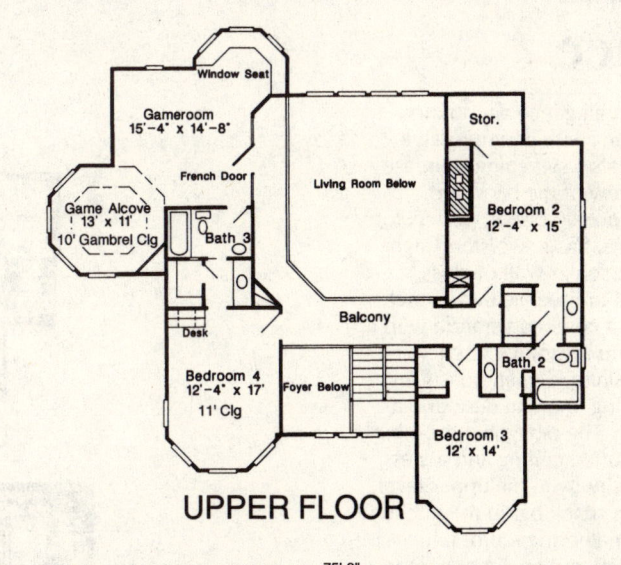

UPPER FLOOR

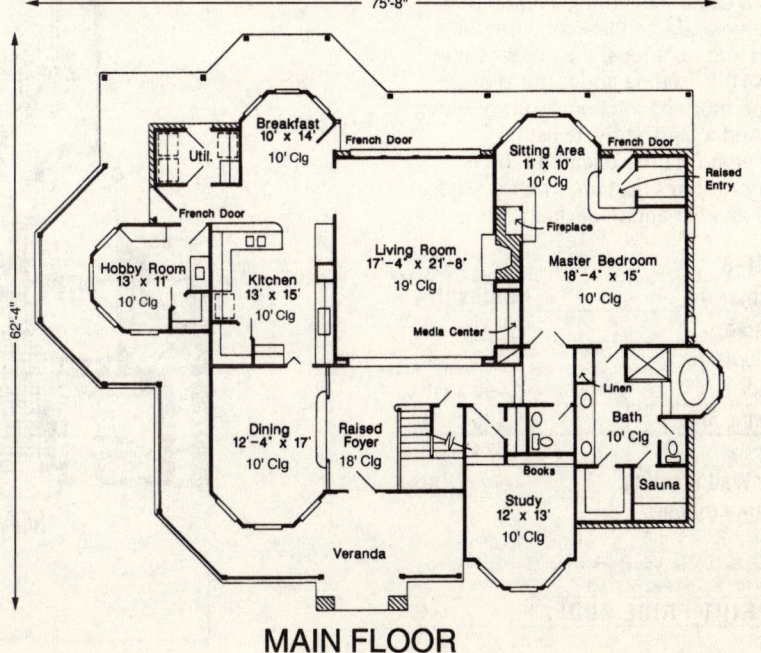

MAIN FLOOR

ORDER BLUEPRINTS ANYTIME!
CALL TOLL-FREE 1-888-626-2026

Plan L-4053-VC

PRICES AND DETAILS ON PAGES 12-15

Ultimate Elegance

- The ultimate in elegance and luxury, this home begins with an impressive foyer that reveals a sweeping staircase and a direct view of the backyard.
- The centrally located parlor, perfect for receiving guests, has a two-story-high ceiling, a spectacular wall of glass, a fireplace and a unique ale bar. French doors open to a covered veranda with a relaxing spa and a summer kitchen.
- The gourmet island kitchen boasts an airy 10-ft. ceiling, a menu desk and a walk-in pantry. The octagonal morning room has a vaulted ceiling and access to a second stairway to the upper level.
- A pass-through snack bar in the kitchen overlooks the gathering room, which hosts a cathedral ceiling, French doors to the veranda and a second fireplace.
- Bright and luxurious, the master suite has a 10-ft. ceiling and features a unique morning kitchen, a sunny sitting area and a lavish private bath.
- The curved staircase leads to three bedroom suites upstairs. The rear suites share an enchanting deck.

Plan EOF-3

Bedrooms: 4+	**Baths:** 5½
Living Area:	
Upper floor	1,150 sq. ft.
Main floor	3,045 sq. ft.
Total Living Area:	**4,195 sq. ft.**
Garage	814 sq. ft.
Exterior Wall Framing:	2x6

Foundation Options:
Slab
(All plans can be built with your choice of foundation and framing. A generic conversion diagram is available. See order form.)

BLUEPRINT PRICE CODE: G

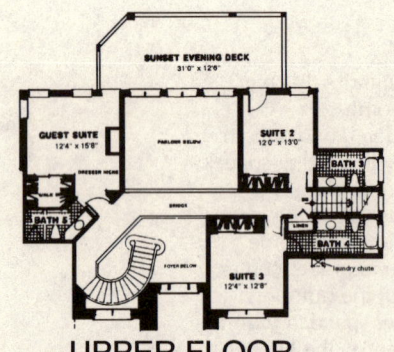

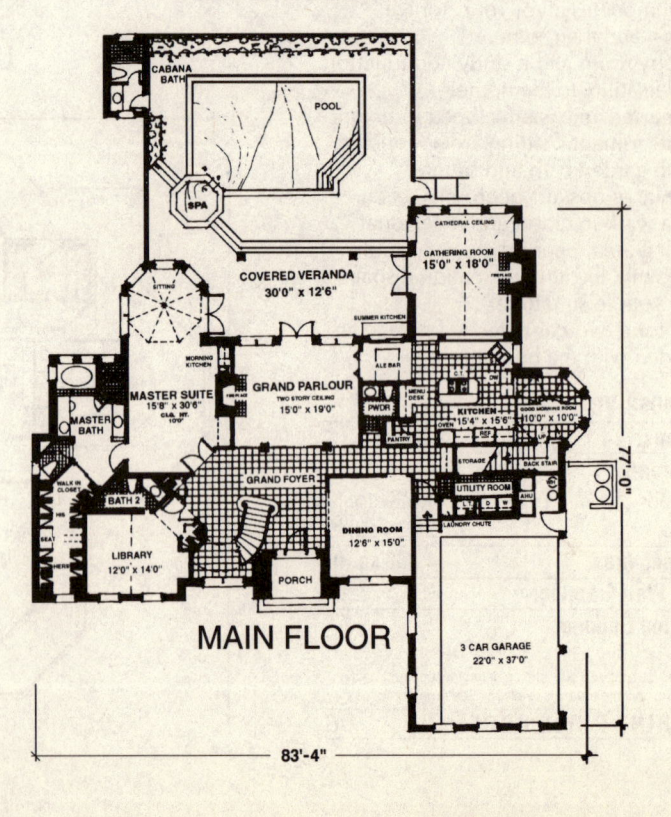

Design Leaves Out Nothing

- This design has it all, from the elegant detailing of the exterior to the exciting, luxurious spaces of the interior.
- High ceilings, large, open rooms and lots of glass are found throughout the home. Nearly all of the main living areas, as well as the master suite, overlook the veranda.
- Unusual features include an ale bar in the formal dining room, an art niche in the Grand Room and a TV niche in the Gathering Room. The Gathering Room also features a fireplace framed by window seats, a wall of windows facing the backyard and a half-wall open to the sunny morning room.
- The centrally located cooktop-island kitchen is conveniently accessible from all of the living areas.
- The delicious master suite includes a raised lounge, a three-sided fireplace and French doors that open to the veranda. The spiral stairs nearby lead to the "evening deck" above. The master bath boasts two walk-in closets, a sunken shower and a Roman tub.
- The upper floor hosts two complete suites and a loft, plus a vaulted bonus room reached via a separate stairway.

See this plan on our "Two-Story" VideoGraphic Tour! Order form on page 9

Plan EOF-61

Bedrooms: 3+	Baths: 4½

Living Area:

Upper floor	877 sq. ft.
Main floor	3,094 sq. ft.
Bonus room	280 sq. ft.
Total Living Area:	**4,251 sq. ft.**
Garage	774 sq. ft.
Exterior Wall Framing:	2x6

Foundation Options:
Slab
(All plans can be built with your choice of foundation and framing. A generic conversion diagram is available. See order form.)

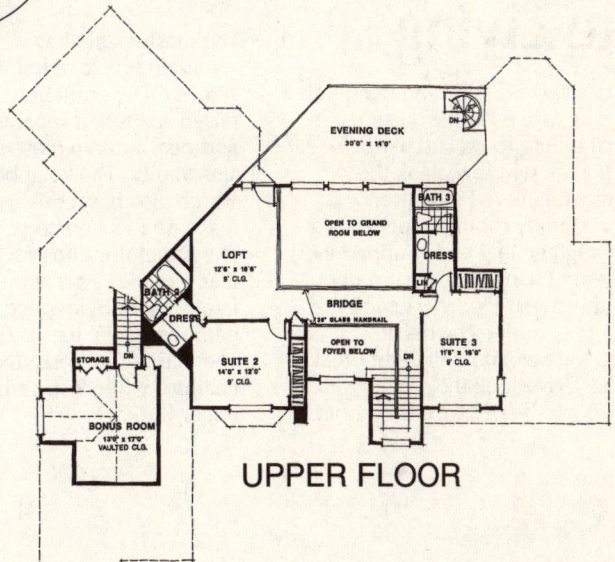

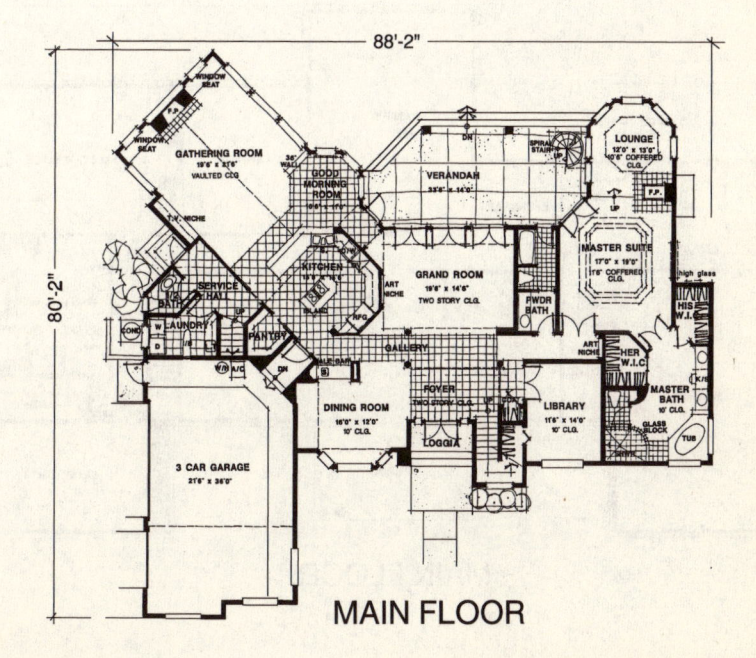

BLUEPRINT PRICE CODE: G

ORDER BLUEPRINTS ANYTIME!
CALL TOLL-FREE 1-888-626-2026

Plan EOF-61

PRICES AND DETAILS ON PAGES 12-15

Estate Living

- This grand estate is as big and beautiful on the inside as it is on the outside.
- The formal dining room and parlor, each with a tall window, flank the entry's graceful curved staircase.
- The sunken family room is topped by a two-story-high ceiling and wrapped in floor-to-ceiling windows. A patio door opens to the covered porch, which features a nifty built-in barbecue.
- The island kitchen and the bright breakfast area also overlook the porch, with access through the deluxe utility room.
- The master suite has it all, including a romantic fireplace framed by bookshelves. The opulent bath offers a raised spa tub, a separate shower, his-and-hers walk-in closets and a dual-sink vanity. The neighboring bedroom, which also has a private bath, would make an ideal nursery.
- The upper floor hosts a balcony hall that provides a breathtaking view of the family room below. Each of the two bedrooms here has its own bath.
- The main floor is expanded by 10-ft. ceilings, while 9-ft. ceilings grace the upper floor.

Plan DD-4300-B

Bedrooms: 4	Baths: 4½
Living Area:	
Upper floor	868 sq. ft.
Main floor	3,416 sq. ft.
Total Living Area:	**4,284 sq. ft.**
Standard basement	3,416 sq. ft.
Garage and storage	633 sq. ft.
Exterior Wall Framing:	2x4 or 2x6

Foundation Options:
Standard basement
Crawlspace
Slab
(All plans can be built with your choice of foundation and framing. A generic conversion diagram is available. See order form.)

BLUEPRINT PRICE CODE: G

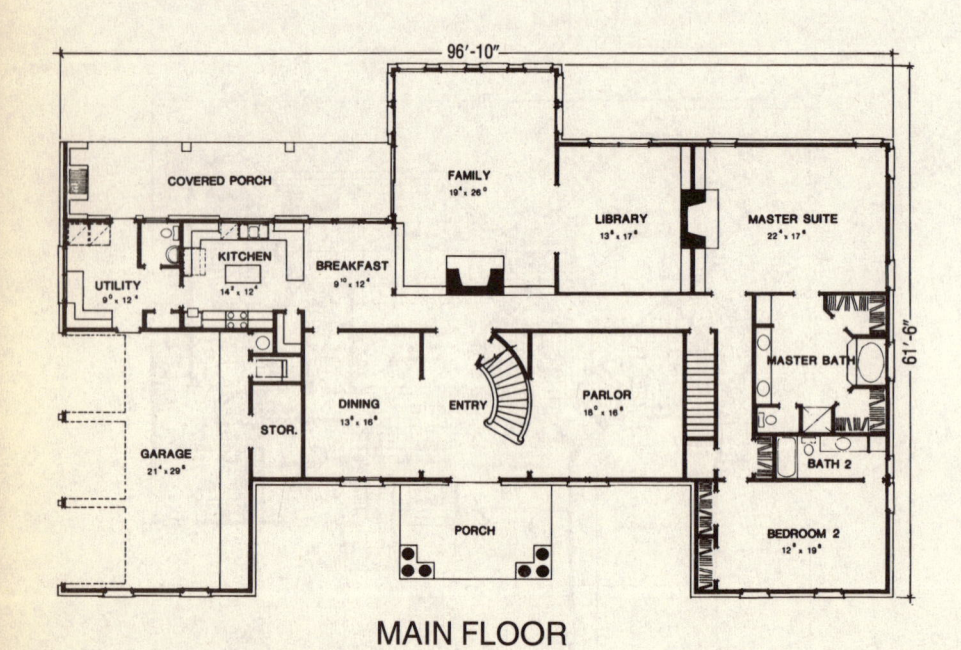

MAIN FLOOR

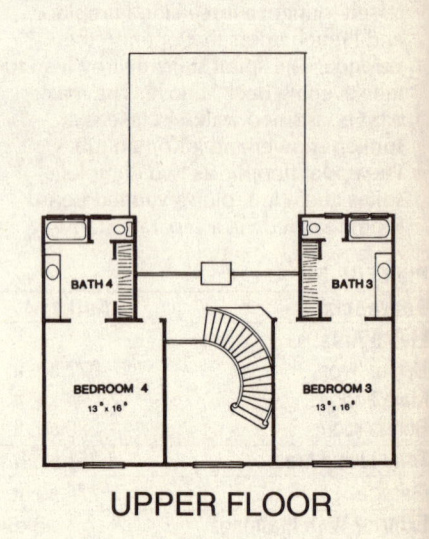

UPPER FLOOR

Plan DD-4300-B

ORDER BLUEPRINTS ANYTIME! CALL TOLL-FREE 1-888-626-2026

PRICES AND DETAILS ON PAGES 12-15

Elegance Perfected

The grand style of this luxurious home brings elegance and grace to perfection. The contemporary architecture exudes an aura of grandeur, drawing the eye to its stately 2½-story entry portico. The interior is equally stunning with open, flowing spaces, high ceilings and decorative, room-defining columns. The formal zone is impressive, with a vast foyer and a sunken living room highlighted by dramatic window walls and a 20½-ft. ceiling. Round columns set off a stunning octagonal dining room with a 19-ft., 4-in. ceiling. A curved wet bar completes the effect! The informal areas consist of an island kitchen, a breakfast nook, a large family room and an octagonal media room. Activities can be extended to the covered back patio through doors in the breakfast nook and the family room. The fabulous master suite shows off a romantic fireplace, a 12-ft. ceiling, an enormous walk-in closet and a garden bath with a circular shower! Two more main-floor bedrooms, an upper-floor bedroom and loft area, plus two more baths complete the plan.

Plan HDS-90-819

Bedrooms: 4+	Baths: 3½
Living Area:	
Upper floor	765 sq. ft.
Main floor	3,770 sq. ft.
Total Living Area:	**4,535 sq. ft.**
Garage	750 sq. ft.
Exterior Wall Framing:	2x4
Foundation Options:	
Slab	

All plans can be built with your choice of foundation and framing. A generic conversion diagram is available. See order form.

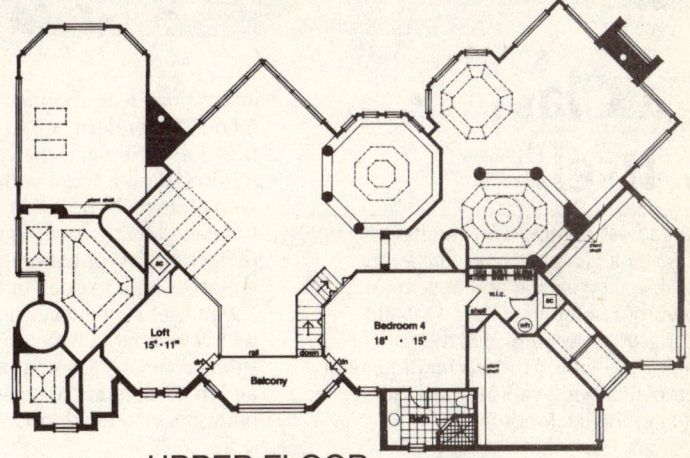

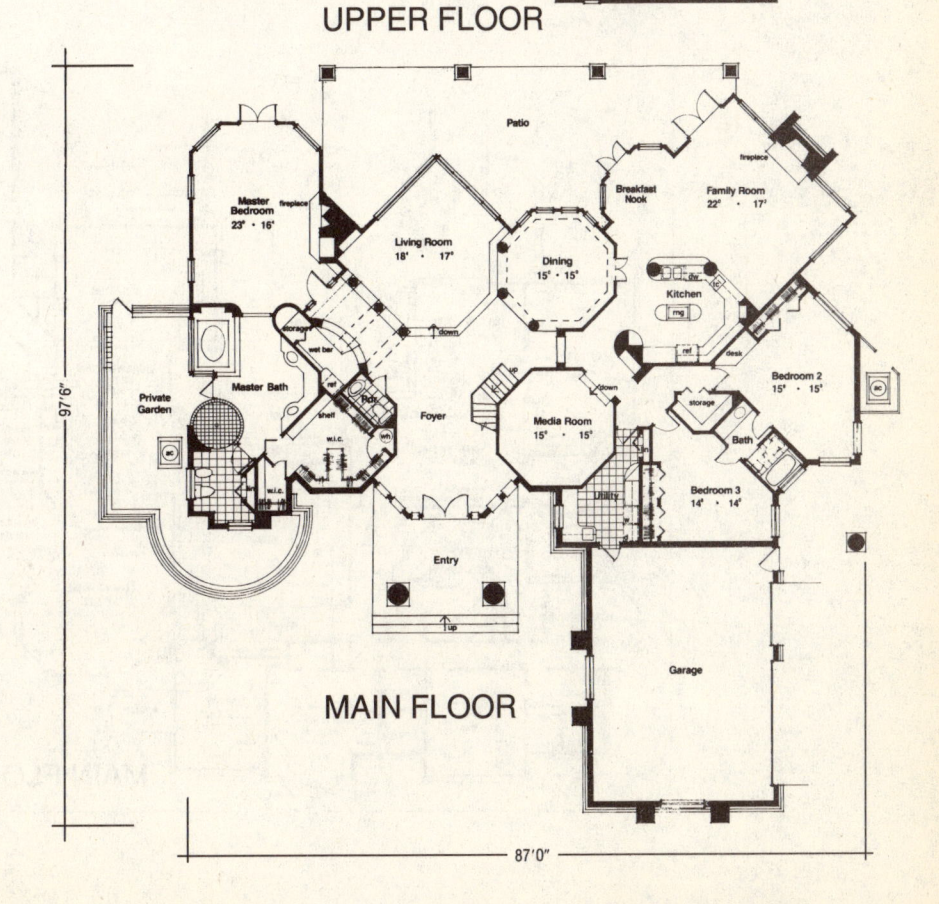

BLUEPRINT PRICE CODE: H

UPPER FLOOR

MAIN FLOOR

ORDER BLUEPRINTS ANYTIME!
CALL TOLL-FREE 1-888-626-2026

Plan HDS-90-819

PRICES AND DETAILS
ON PAGES 12-15

285

In a Class by Itself

- The endless number and variety of exquisite features ensures that every possible urge is met, and puts this wonderful home in a class by itself!
- The raised foyer steps into the remarkable family room, complete with a fireplace, book cabinets and French doors to the back porch.
- Interesting areas abound, including a media center designed to make movie nights as thrilling as the local multiplex.
- A raised dining room with its own china hutch sits next to a gorgeous fireplaced living room to provide the perfect places for entertaining. Lots of windows help to coax in the sun.
- The master suite leaves nothing out, with a wet bar, a two-way fireplace, a sitting room, a stunning private bath and three different accesses to the outdoors via French doors.

Plan L-062-EME

Bedrooms: 4+	Baths: 3½
Living Area:	
Main floor	4,958 sq. ft.
Total Living Area:	**4,958 sq. ft.**
Optional loft	1072 sq. ft.
Optional maid's quarters	608 sq. ft.
Garage and storage	866 sq. ft.
Exterior Wall Framing:	2x4

Foundation Options:
Slab
(All plans can be built with your choice of foundation and framing. A generic conversion diagram is available. See order form.)

BLUEPRINT PRICE CODE: H

MAIN FLOOR

Plan L-062-EME

ORDER BLUEPRINTS ANYTIME! CALL TOLL-FREE 1-888-626-2026

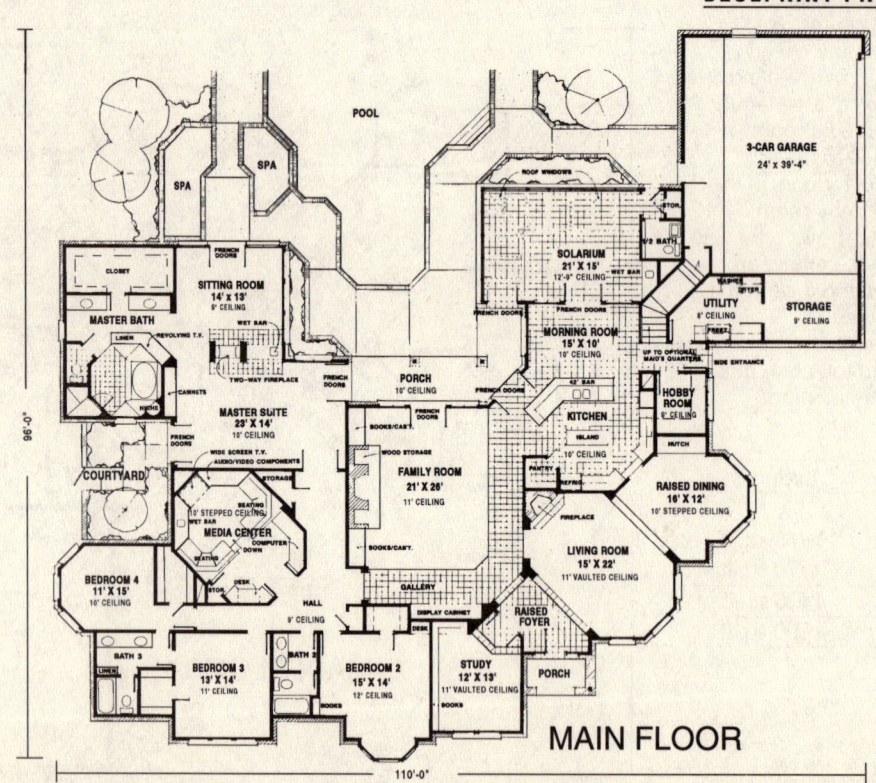

PRICES AND DETAILS ON PAGES 12-15

Superbly Done!

- A tile roof and extravagant glass are a just a prelude to the many amenities found in this superb home.
- The raised foyer offers a breathtaking view through French doors to a lanai and a potential pool area beyond.
- The grand living room has a curved wall of glass, plus a 22-ft. sloped ceiling with exposed rafters under a metal deck roof.
- High 12-ft. vaulted ceilings enhance both the nearby den and the sitting room in the posh master suite.
- The master suite offers a three-way fireplace and a raised exercise room with a 9½-ft. ceiling and a private deck. An 11-ft. ceiling tops the sleeping area and the bath, which boasts a whirlpool tub and a sit-down shower, each defined by a glass-block wall.
- The formal dining room is enhanced by tall glass and a 14½-ft. vaulted ceiling.
- High 14-ft. ceilings augment the bright morning room, the island kitchen and the family room, where a fireplace, a TV niche and deck access are featured.
- A nice ale bar has a pass-through for easy service to the pool area. A summer kitchen on the deck hosts barbecues.
- Three secondary bedrooms and two full baths complete this wing of the home.

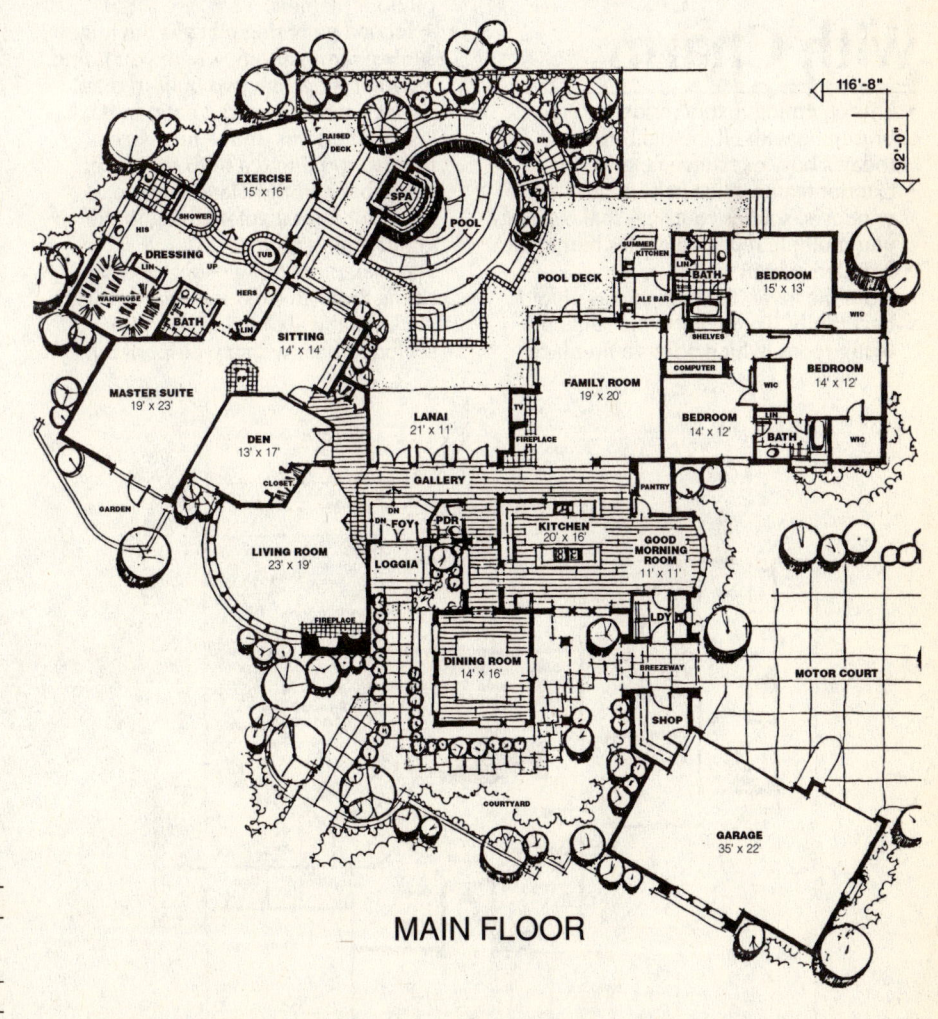

Plan EOF-70

Bedrooms: 4+	Baths: 3½

Living Area:

Main floor	5,013 sq. ft.
Total Living Area:	**5,013 sq. ft.**
Garage and shop	902 sq. ft.

Exterior Wall Framing: 8-in. concrete block

Foundation Options:
Slab

All plans can be built with your choice of foundation and framing. A generic conversion diagram is available. See order form.

BLUEPRINT PRICE CODE: I

MAIN FLOOR

ORDER BLUEPRINTS ANYTIME!
CALL TOLL-FREE 1-888-626-2026

Plan EOF-70

PRICES AND DETAILS
ON PAGES 12-15

Brimming with Charm

- This charming luxury residence is brimming with all the right stuff for today's busy executive family!
- Exterior features like half-round windows, soldier coursing, shake siding and multiple repeated gables hint at the wonders within.
- From the foyer, the living areas unfold beautifully. To the left is the sunken living room, which boasts a fireplace and overlooks one of several lovely outdoor planters.
- A second gathering place is the huge sunken family room, where you'll find a corner fireplace, two built-in plant shelves and access to a patio in back.
- Just up the stairs, in the nice-sized library, you'll find a third fireplace.
- A wet bar and the island kitchen are ready for formal entertaining in the grand dining room.
- The incredible master suite offers a sitting area, an exercise area, a private deck, dual walk-in closets and a secluded bath with a whirlpool tub.

Plan B-87137

Bedrooms: 4	**Baths:** 3 full, 2 half

Living Area:
Upper floor	1,244 sq. ft.
Main floor	3,798 sq. ft.
Total Living Area:	**5,042 sq. ft.**
Standard basement	3,600 sq. ft.
Garage	590 sq. ft.

Exterior Wall Framing: 2x4

Foundation Options:
Standard basement
(All plans can be built with your choice of foundation and framing. A generic conversion diagram is available. See order form.)

BLUEPRINT PRICE CODE:

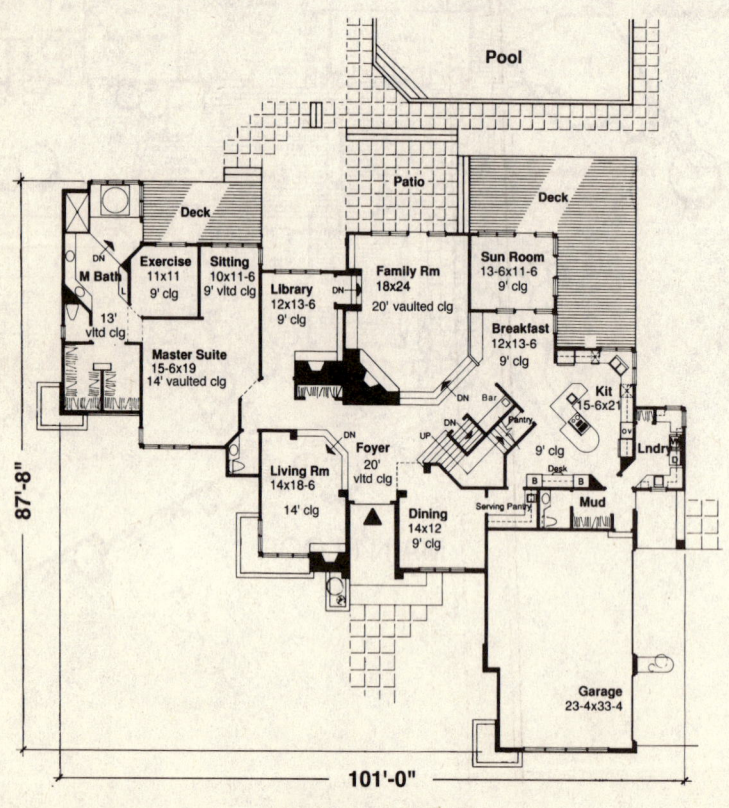

MAIN FLOOR

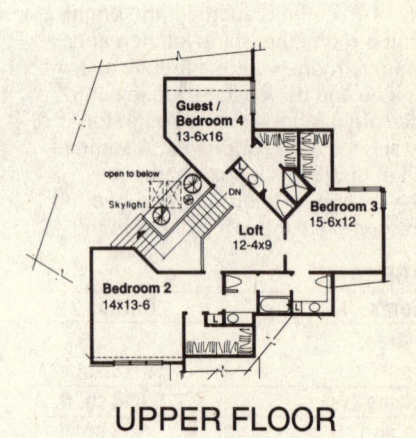

UPPER FLOOR

ORDER BLUEPRINTS ANYTIME! CALL TOLL-FREE 1-888-626-2026

Plan B-87137

PRICES AND DETAILS ON PAGES 12-15